The United States and West Africa

Rochester Studies in
African History and the Diaspora

Toyin Falola, Senior Editor
The Frances Higginbotham Nalle Centennial Professor in History
University of Texas at Austin
(ISSN: 1092–5228)

A complete list of titles in the Rochester Studies in African History and the Diaspora, in order of publication, may be found at the end of this book.

The United States and West Africa

Interactions and Relations

Edited by
ALUSINE JALLOH AND TOYIN FALOLA

UNIVERSITY OF ROCHESTER PRESS

First published 2008

University of Rochester Press
668 Mt. Hope Avenue, Rochester, NY 14620, USA
www.urpress.com
and Boydell & Brewer Limited
PO Box 9, Woodbridge, Suffolk IP12 3DF, UK
www.boydellandbrewer.com

Cloth ISBN-13: 978–1–58046–277–8
Paperback ISBN-13: 978–1–58046–308–9

ISSN: 1092–5228

Library of Congress Cataloging-in-Publication Data

The United States and West Africa : interactions and relations / edited by Alusine Jalloh and Toyin Falola.
    p. cm. — (Rochester studies in African history and the diaspora, ISSN 1092–5228 ; v. 34)
  Papers based on an international conference held Apr. 28–30, 2005, convened by the Africa Program, University of Texas at Arlington.
  Includes bibliographical references and index.
  ISBN-13: 978–1–58046–277–8 (hardcover : alk. paper)
  ISBN-10: 1–58046–277–4 (hardcover : alk. paper)
  1.   Africa, West—Relations—United States—Congresses.   2.   United States—Relations—Africa, West—Congresses.   I. Jalloh, Alusine, 1963–
II. Falola, Toyin.
  DT509.63.U6U55 2008
  303.48′273066—dc22
                                    2008021659

A catalogue record for this title is available from the British Library.

This publication is printed on acid-free paper.
Printed in the United States of America.

To the scholar-activist, Dr. Leon H. Sullivan

Contents

Preface

This edited collection is the result of an international conference on the United States and West Africa convened by the Africa Program, University of Texas at Arlington (UTA), which was held April 28–30, 2005. Established in 1994, the Africa Program seeks to promote business, educational, and technological relations between the state of Texas and Africa.

The conference was organized in recognition of the growing public and scholarly interest in relations between the United States and West Africa. Scholars from Africa, Europe, and the United States offered multidisciplinary perspectives on the history and complex relationships between the United States and West Africa. In particular, the conference recognized the West African heritage of African Americans. The ancestral homeland of most African Americans is West Africa. Knowing the history of West Africa is, therefore, important in achieving an understanding of the people who became the first African Americans. West Africa was also the place where the first and the majority of African American returnees to Africa settled in the eighteenth through the twentieth centuries.

Furthermore, the conference recognized the increasing importance of West Africa to the United States from an energy, security, and counterterrorism perspective. For a long time, the United States has been interested in African oil resources as an alternative to those of the Middle East, and the United States now defines African oil as a strategic national interest. The United States' preoccupation with energy security makes West African countries that have oil relevant to the United States. The U.S. National Intelligence Council projects that the United States' oil supplies from West Africa will increase to 25 percent by 2015. This would surpass the oil imports from the entire Persian Gulf. Studies indicate that the greatest increase in oil production globally in the next decade is likely to come from West Africa, and the United States is following this trend closely.

We would like to express our gratitude to Dana Dunn, provost and vice president for academic affairs, for delivering the welcome address at the conference. We would also like to thank the following UTA faculty for serving as panel chairs: Stephen E. Maizlish, associate professor of history; Sonya Y. Ramsey, assistant professor of history; Robert L. Bing, associate professor of criminal justice; David Buisseret, professor of history and the Jenkins and Virginia Garrett Endowed Chair in Southwestern Studies and the History of Cartography; Steven G. Reinhardt, associate professor of history; Dennis P. Reinhartz, professor of history; and Roberto Trevino, assistant professor of history. In addition, we would like to recognize the late Mark A. Baxter, former director of the Maguire Energy Institute at Southern Methodist University, who chaired the panel on oil in West Africa. We also thank the following discussants: Nemata Blyden, George Washington University; Wumi Iledare, Louisiana State University; Abdul K. Bangura, American University; Hakeem I. Tijani, Morgan State University; Ibrahim Sundiata, Brandeis University; Andrew I. E. Ewoh, Prairie View A&M University; Bessie House, Kent State University; Okechukwu Iheduru, Arizona State University; and Sylvia O. Macauley, Truman State University. In the preparation of the manuscript for press, we owe a debt of gratitude to Steven Huff and Amanda Warnock. Finally, we would like to thank all the participants from Africa, Europe, and the United States for helping to make the conference a success and also for their contributions to this volume.

Alusine Jalloh
University of Texas at Arlington

Toyin Falola
University of Texas at Austin

Introduction

Amanda Warnock, Toyin Falola, and Alusine Jalloh

Today, communities of Nigerians flourish in major American cities such as Houston and Dallas. Sierra Leoneans attend college in the United States working part time jobs in order to send remittances back to their families in West Africa. This year hundreds of African American tourists will visit Gorée Island, drawn by the weight of history and memory to uncover their African pasts. These scenarios speak to the larger narrative of modern U.S.–West African relations; the social, cultural, political, and economic bonds that date back for centuries and that have, in recent years, drawn these two world regions into increasingly closer contact. It is this complex, often contradictory, relationship that is the subject of this volume.

A Brief History of U.S.–West African Relations

U.S.–West African relations can be traced back to the era of the transatlantic slave trade, which saw between nine and thirteen million Africans transported to the American continent. Although the majority went to Brazil and the Caribbean, an estimated 400,000 slaves, or roughly 4 percent of the total, were carried to British North America. This group of Africans and their African American descendents established the basis for the relationship between the United States and West Africa.

While these early contacts brought enslaved laborers from West African shores to American plantations and left the enduring legacy of the African diaspora in the American continent, modern relations can be traced to the early-nineteenth-century development of the so-called "legitimate trade" on the West African coast and the establishment of the colony of Liberia in 1822. In the early nineteenth century, the American Colonization Society (ACS) formulated a political project that sought to repatriate Africans and African Americans to West Africa. Debates exist as to the motivations of the ACS, with scholars arguing over the extent to which the project was in favor of or against slavery. Nevertheless, the emigrationist movement represented a singular moment in the history of U.S.–West African relations, and one that reverberates to the present day.

The late nineteenth and early twentieth centuries witnessed the expansion of trade between the United States and West Africa, with the deployment of consular officials aiding the expansion of relations between these two localities. An active commerce in strategic commodities such as kerosene and petroleum developed between the United States and Nigeria, in spite of the disapproval of colonizing power Great Britain.

From the late nineteenth century through the 1940s, the colonial presence in West Africa provided a backdrop to contacts with the United States. While economic exchange was relatively limited during this period, the revival of emigrationist sentiment provided the basis for African Americans to forge sociocultural contacts with the continent. The Garveyist and Pan-Africanist movements of the early twentieth century brought African Americans in touch, literally and figuratively, with Africa. Although the movements failed to generate a mass migration to West Africa, they did serve to raise awareness of the joint histories of African Americans and West Africans.

The coming of World War II drastically altered the political and economic relations between the United States and West Africa. With the Pacific effectively blockaded, the United States increased its imports of strategic minerals, such as tin and manganese, from West Africa. In the case of Liberia, a historic ally, the United States established a substantial military presence, constructing an airfield and a port and even convincing the Liberian government to declare war on Germany.[1]

But it was not exclusively in the political and economic realms that contacts between West Africa and the United States increased. African students educated in the United States became some of the earliest proponents of African independence. Prominent personalities such as Kwame Nkrumah of Ghana and Nnamdi Azikiwe of Nigeria spent their formative years living and studying in the United States. The Pan-Africanist writings of W. E. B. DuBois, among others, influenced the development of their political ideology.

With the coming of the Cold War, African decolonization served to increase ties between West Africa and the United States. The departure of the colonial powers provided an opportunity for the United States to step in and exert its power in the region. In the battle over political and economic doctrines that occupied the East and the West, the United States and the USSR viewed the nascent African republics as pawns to be won over to one or the other camp. From the 1950s to the 1980s, the United States provided economic aid to the nations of West Africa while promoting its sociocultural agenda through organizations such as the Peace Corps and the U.S. Information Service.

While some of these programs, such as the Peace Corps, have continued to maintain a presence in West Africa, the 1980s and 1990s saw a significant shift in policy toward the region. During the political-military conflicts that raged in Liberia and Sierra Leone in the 1990s, the United States assumed a stance of nonintervention. Largely inspired by the failed military mission in Somalia in 1992 and 1993, the government has been extremely reluctant to intervene in conflicts where its interests are not directly at stake. U.S. policy, particularly since the attacks of September 11, 2001, has been aimed at identifying potential terrorist threats and securing energy resources (especially in Nigeria) rather than at averting humanitarian disasters.

More recently, the United States has received criticism for downplaying the conflict and genocide in the Sudan and failing to come to the aid of its victims. Despite a denunciation of the belligerents and the imposition of sanctions against the Sudanese government, the United States has granted little in the way of material aid to alleviate the crisis plaguing the region of Darfur.

Organization and Structure of the Book

Over the last several decades, historians have conducted extensive research into U.S.–West African contacts during the era of the transatlantic trade. Yet we still understand relatively little about the more recent relations between the United States and West Africa. The reasons for this are at least threefold. First, scholars frequently employ nation states as their primary units of analysis. Thus, much of the research on U.S. relations with or policies toward Africa focuses on relationships between the United States and specific countries. While this constitutes an important effort in its own right, it fails to provide a broader picture of the U.S. role in the region. Second, studies of contemporary U.S.–West African relations that treat particular African national or ethnic groups in the United States often neglect to explore the broader context for African migrants as a whole. Many see the African migration to the United States as a discrete historical phenomenon, ignoring the linkages that Africans in the diaspora have forged with continental Africans and vice versa. The third reason speaks to the way most Americans conceptualize the African continent. As Curtis Keim has pointed out in his book, *Mistaking Africa: Curiosities and Inventions of the American Mind,* the media and the educational system in the United States have socialized Americans to view Africa as a homogenous entity, lacking in ethnic diversity and individual political units.[2] Even news commentators will frequently refer to U.S. policies in Africa without the caveat that policy toward Egypt, for example, will differ drastically from policy toward Botswana.

The essays contained in this work represent the first effort to provide a comprehensive treatment of U.S.–West African relations. We have divided them into four parts, each treating one facet of the U.S.–West African relationship.

Part 1, "Trade and Politics in the Nineteenth and Twentieth Centuries," examines the linkages that brought the United States and West Africa together during the era of European colonial rule of Africa. Six chapters treat the political and economic relations between the United States and West Africa, arguing that, despite the structures of colonialism, a relationship had begun to develop that would lay the groundwork for closer ties as the twentieth century progressed.

Adebayo Oyebade and Toyin Falola begin part 1 with a review of U.S.–West African relations from the West African voyages of Columbus until the present. They open with a discussion of the transatlantic slave trade, which brought to the Americas millions of Africans, who, through their labor and their culture, contributed significantly to the formation of the United States. While early contacts were largely unidirectional, bringing Africans to the Americas, the African colonization project, in establishing the colony of Liberia in 1822, represented the first effort to repatriate large numbers of Africans and African Americans to West Africa. Oyebade and Falola then compare the African colonization attempts of the nineteenth century with the Garveyism of the 1920s and 1930s, arguing that, in spite of their limited successes in promoting cooperation between African Americans and West Africans, these movements failed to win widespread support in either the United States or West Africa. The chapter continues by providing a review of the social, political, and economic linkages that have developed over the course of the twentieth century, demonstrating how, even in light of the profound historical bonds that they share, Africa has never featured high on the U.S. foreign policy agenda. The chapter closes with a summary of contemporary U.S. policy with regard to the region.

In chapter 2, Ibrahim Kargbo looks at the complex nexus of trading arrangements in Sierra Leone during the late nineteenth century. Following the lead of the European powers, which established consular posts in Sierra Leone during the 1840s, in 1858 the United States sent a representative to Freetown with the express mission of promoting U.S. commercial interests. The establishment of a consulate in Freetown altered the trade arrangements between U.S. traders and African middlemen as the former gained leverage in their negotiations with the latter. The 1860s and 1870s saw the United States extend its commercial activities in Sierra Leone, frustrating British attempts to control the region's foreign trade and leaving the consular officials and the U.S. Department of State to navigate this contested terrain.

Turning to the Liberian settlement project of the American Colonization Society (ACS), chapter 3, by John Wess Grant, discusses the obstacles to emigration faced by black families in Richmond, Virginia. Attempting to shift the discussion of the ACS's activities away from debate over whether the organization was proslavery or antislavery, Grant opts to look at the social and economic challenges faced by potential émigrés. He highlights the part played by the process of manumission in the decision to emigrate to Liberia. For, as the frequency of manumissions declined in the early nineteenth century, the number of families who counted both free coloreds and slaves among their members rose. Not wanting to leave enslaved relatives behind, free coloreds invested their limited resources in the purchase of family members rather than in the passage back to Africa.

Like Grant, Ibrahim Sundiata explores the possibilities and challenges facing African American emigration movements. In chapter 4, Sundiata situates Marcus Garvey's United Negro Improvement Association (UNIA) within the broader tradition of Pan-Africanism. Although many works have focused on the rise and fall of Garveyism, this chapter argues that one must understand the social and political conditions in post–World War I Liberia in order to fully understand the defeat of the Garveyist program. For Garvey's plan to promote the mass migration of African Americans to Liberia was met with trepidation, and at times open hostility, by the Liberian political elite. As a conservative, ingrown caste composed of the descendants of nineteenth-century émigrés, Liberian leaders overwhelmingly rejected Garvey's overtures. Ultimately, Sundiata explains, Liberia was a state divided between a small elite and the largely disenfranchised masses. This division, based on class rather than color, prevented the Garveyist project from achieving its aims.

While Sundiata explores the powerful legacies of the American Colonization Society in Liberia, Ayodeji Olukoju in chapter 5 exposes the fractured nature of British colonialism in West Africa. Olukoju discusses the increasing trade between the United States and Nigeria from 1900 to 1950. He contextualizes Nigerian–U.S. trade within the framework of the United States' post–World War I emergence as a global political and economic superpower. The chapter argues that, although the volume of trade was low, the strategic importance of U.S. imports to Nigeria, particularly kerosene and petroleum, made the relationship crucial for Nigerian development. In Nigeria, U.S. firms frequently found themselves at odds with British colonial policy. Yet, even amidst this conflict, the development of trade between the United States and Nigeria accelerated through the early twentieth century, propelling Nigeria's integration into the global economy even as it remained a British colony.

While the authors discussed above treat individual countries, in chapter 6 Hakeem Ibikunle Tijani takes a regional view, treating U.S. political and economic activities in West Africa during the late colonial period. Tijani identifies anti-Communism and mineral exploitation as the two motives driving American interests in the region. As early as 1950, the United States recognized West Africa's strategic position and sought to develop further ties to the region. Throughout the 1950s, U.S. policy furthered the joint aims of

containing leftist political expression and securing cobalt, tin, industrial diamonds and palm oil, among other products. Tijani contends that West Africa
was not, in fact, a foreign policy "backwater," as other scholars have suggested, but rather a region of importance to the United States.

The second and third parts of this volume discuss the cultural linkages
that have drawn America into Africa and Africa into America since the mid-
twentieth century. Part 2, "Forging Cultural Connections: America in
Africa," provides an in-depth exploration of the "American" presence in
West Africa. Each of the chapters speak to a different facet of U.S. involvement in the region, focusing on the contributions of individuals and institutions from the United States in shaping West African cultures. From the
political posturing of the United States Information Agency (USIA) during
the Cold War to the growth of the African American community in Ghana,
the chapters in part 2 are a diverse representation of the most recent scholarship on U.S.–West African cultural exchanges.

In chapter 7, Karen B. Bell explores the political and cultural linkages that
bound the United States and West Africa together during the Cold War. By
examining the cultural agenda of the United States in Africa, an important
but previously neglected topic, Bell demonstrates how policymakers sought
to generate mutual goodwill, thus limiting the influence of the Soviet Union
and the People's Republic of China. The programs of the USIA, the main
conduit of U.S. "cultural diplomacy" in Africa, used educational exchanges
and various forms of media to present the USIA's vision of American culture
to the African continent. USIA programs downplayed the civil rights struggles of the era in an effort to promote racial harmony. To this end, they
deployed "cultural ambassadors" such as musicians, actors, academics, and
sports figures in the hope that their presence would generate positive associations with American culture, thus advancing U.S. political goals in the
region.

Chapters 8 and 9 look at the social, political, cultural, and economic relationships that have developed between Ghanaians and African Americans
over the past several decades. Kwame Essien illuminates the complexities of
the ties between the two groups. Using the work of W. E. B. DuBois as a starting point, Essien emphasizes the "double consciousness" of African
Americans as a means to understand why they would want to return to their
motherland. Essien traces the history of African American migration to
Ghana, explaining that three separate groups of migrants have had significant influence on Ghanaian development. Beginning in 1950, the first wave
of African Americans arrived to aid President Kwame Nkrumah in implementing postindependence reforms. The second period of migration, from
approximately 1970 until 1995, saw the arrival of only a small number of
African Americans, as the political and economic hardships of the era, particularly during the military rule of Jerry Rawlings, discouraged potential

returnees. Since the 1990s, however, the number of African Americans returning to live in Ghana has increased substantially. Essien argues that, while tensions have certainly strained relations between black American returnees and native Ghanaians, contacts have been characterized far more by positive interactions than by negative interactions. In support of his point, Essien cites nongovernmental organizations established by African Americans, such as One Africa, that have benefited Ghanaian citizens and advanced the socioeconomic development of the country.

Using first-hand interviews, Harold R. Harris further explores the intricacies of ties between Ghanaians and African Americans, presenting a viewpoint different from that of Essien. Like Essien, Harris uses W. E. B. DuBois' concept of "double consciousness," but he uses it to argue that African Americans possess the trait of individualism, acquired as a result of their life in the United States, while at the same time they maintain a tendency toward communalism, a remnant of their African heritage. According to Harris, Ghanaians tend toward a more strongly communal outlook, often criticizing African American returnees for becoming mired in problems of their own creation. Harris's analysis is grounded in a discussion of the history and culture of Ghanaians. He provides an overview of religion, social rituals, family life, gender, education, politics, and economics in Ghana. From there he moves on to the question, how do Ghanaians view African Americans? Based on his first-hand research Harris concludes that, due to the economic and cultural distance that separates the two groups, the relationship has been historically tense. In recent years, however, Ghanaians have adopted some African American religious traditions and cultural institutions. In conclusion, Harris suggests some potential solutions to the problems that have kept Ghanaians apart from African Americans.

Part 3, "Forging Cultural Connections: Africa in America," moves across the Atlantic to the United States. The three chapters in this section explore aspects of the interconnectedness of people and cultures in America and the ongoing linkages to West Africa. Each author elaborates the diaspora paradigm, both historically and at the present day, demonstrating the ongoing relevance of relationships between Africans and African Americans.

In chapter 10, Fred Johnson challenges the reader to reexamine the historical relationship between Africans and African Americans by highlighting the intricacies of the legacy of slavery and the slave trade with regard to present-day identity formation. Johnson argues that the weight of history imposes itself on today's struggles. For example, while African Americans have worked to achieve equality in a racist society, West Africans have been plagued by tribalism. Also, while African Americans have pressed the U.S. government to correct the injustices they have faced, West Africans have often sought relief *from* the repression of their governments. Returnees have frequently encountered an environment that appears to be divided by ethnicity, region, and religion rather than united by race. Within this context, misunderstandings abound. Johnson points out the resentment that many West Africans feel toward their American sisters and brothers, accusing them of complaining about past injustices as excuses for their lack of success in a land of immense material wealth. In turn, African Americans often fail to comprehend the African environment, asking insulting questions such as whether people have indoor plumbing and wear shoes, to cite but two examples. Johnson concludes that only by attempting to understand the historical roots of today's problems can we hope to alleviate the tension that continues to exist between West Africans and Americans of African descent.

Bayo Lawal, in chapter 11, also probes the relationship between African Americans and West Africans. As with Essien and Harris before him, Lawal situates his analysis within the paradigm of W. E. B. DuBois' concept of "double consciousness." The longing for one's homeland, he argues, is not unique to African Americans but common to all diasporic groups. Lawal's chapter begins with a discussion of the phenomenon of "double consciousness," and the way it relates to African Americans. The author then recounts the history of the Pan-Africanist movements aimed at bringing African Americans into contact with African culture, explaining how contemporary linkages are part of a longer-lived trend that shows no signs of abating. Since the establishment of Liberia in 1822, African Americans have actively participated, and they continue to participate, in the cultural life of West Africa. Similarly, recent West African immigrants have forged cultural contacts with African Americans in the United States. Ultimately, explains Lawal, the bonds of culture that have developed between African Americans and West Africans represent one expression of a Pan-African identity that has enriched both groups.

While Johnson and Lawal treat the region of West Africa as a whole, Alusine Jalloh moves the discussion of diaspora to the specific case of Sierra Leone. Jalloh examines the Sierra Leonean diaspora in the United States from the 1960s through the 1980s. Migrants came for a number of reasons. First, many came to pursue higher education during the 1960s and 1970s, most planning to return to Sierra Leone to begin their professional careers. This changed during the 1980s when an increasing number of migrants opted to stay and work in the United States, establishing the basis of the Sierra Leonean diaspora. Second, in the 1970s, political repression under President Siaka Stevens prompted many to migrate to the United States. Third, the marked economic decline since the 1970s, exacerbated by structural adjustment programs imposed by the International Monetary Fund (IMF), led to a further substantial migration, augmenting the Sierra Leonean diaspora in the United States. With the arrival of larger numbers of migrants, communities became fragmented, often dividing along ethnic and regional lines. However, from the 1970s onward, the convergence of political corruption, violence, and economic crisis inspired many Sierra Leoneans to remain engaged with the politics of their homeland, organizing protests, coordinating transnational action and at times returning to Sierra Leone to work for change from the inside.

Part 4 of this book, "U.S. Political and Economic Interests in West Africa," discusses U.S. foreign policy with regard to West Africa from the Cold War through the end of the twentieth century. The chapters in part 4 treat different areas of U.S. policy, ranging from economic assistance through the United States Agency for International Development (USAID), to funding for trade networks, to the Cold War political calculations surrounding the potential spread of Communism.

In chapter 13, Peter A. Dumbuya chronicles the development of political and economic relations between the United States and Africa, providing a historical overview of the period between European colonization and the early 1960s. Dumbuya explains that in the nineteenth century the United States acceded to the European conquest of Africa, particularly after the Berlin Conference of 1884–85. Then, following World War II, the United States, fueled by the joint goals of limiting the spread of Communism and furthering its own economic agenda, stepped in to replace the outgoing colonial powers. Throughout the Cold War era, the United States voiced support for the nascent African states while frequently propping up corrupt regimes such as South Africa and Zaire under Joseph Mobutu. With the fall of the Soviet bloc, U.S. interest in Africa waned, and thereafter the minimal development aid pledged to African states reflects the ongoing marginalization of the continent in the formulation of U.S. foreign policy.

In chapter 14, Andrew I. E. Ewoh also looks at U.S. foreign policy toward Africa at the present day. He focuses on the interrelated, though often contradictory goals of furthering geopolitical and economic objectives while promoting political stability and economic development. Ewoh opens his chapter with an explanation of how foreign policy is constructed in the United States, employing the political subsystems approach, which stresses the interconnectedness of interests among institutions and actors involved in crafting policy. He then reviews the foreign policy records of each presidential administration since the 1950s in order to establish the historical background against which present-day policy is being constructed. As other authors point out, the exigencies of forestalling Communist infiltration in Africa shaped U.S. foreign policy toward the continent from the Eisenhower through the Reagan administrations. Ewoh explains that, from the 1940s until 1976 the U.S. maintained little involvement in African affairs. Under Jimmy Carter, the primary policy goal remained the prevention of Communist expansion in West Africa but also included the implementation of trade embargoes aimed at castigating the government of South Africa for its apartheid policies. This newfound focus on human rights in Africa did not last long. Reagan was more concerned with fighting the Cold War than he was with engaging constructively with African governments. The George H. W. Bush administration shifted to the development of a more hands-on policy with regard to mediating African conflicts. The most radical change in policy, however, occurred under Bill Clinton, with the promotion of a humanitarianist agenda in Africa. George W. Bush has maintained some of his predecessor's objectives with humanitarian programs such as his AIDS initiative. Yet the majority of the administration's stated objectives focus on expanding democracy, trade, and security in West Africa. In his final assessment, Ewoh concludes that the U.S. government must take a regional approach in order to achieve its goals, crafting policy based on the potential shown by particular clusters of African countries in areas such as security, democracy, and free trade.

Abdul Karim Bangura also explores U.S. foreign policy and the concomitant financial assistance to West Africa. He provides a detailed examination of the factors that have shaped U.S. development aid to Africa, delving into the reasons behind and purpose of American aid and explaining the process by which the U.S. government makes foreign policy. U.S. policymakers, explains Bangura, are influenced by "American" values such as individuality, liberalism, and democracy but differ with regard to the goals of economic assistance. At the heart of U.S. policy toward Africa are the same strategic interests that shape foreign policy in many world regions: the need to maintain regional security and protect economic investments. But in comparison to other locations, Africa has not been a high priority for the U.S. government. Because of this limited commitment to West African development and the inconsistent nature of the dispensing of funds, individual nations have found it difficult to invest in long-term projects, stymied by the possibility that the aid pledged will not continue over time. Bangura asserts that the only true path to African development would be the implementation of a policy akin to the Marshall Plan, which helped to rebuild Europe following World War II. The chapter closes with a call for a policy that promotes regional integration while strengthening West African democracies.

Anita Spring's work complements that of Bangura by providing a specific example of how U.S. economic assistance *has* supported regional cooperation in West Africa. Spring highlights the role of USAID—one of a coalition of international donors—in offering support to the West African Enterprise Network (WAEN). She explains that in the early 1990s, U.S. policy shifted with regard to the promotion of international development. Recognizing the failures of West African governments to strengthen the private sector, USAID sought to deal directly with entrepreneurs in an attempt to facilitate the growth of business networks. Between 1993 and 2003, USAID helped to organize and implement the program. The goals of the project were to increase the volume of trade, both interregional and international, minimize government rent seeking, promote financial transparency, and support the growth of West African private enterprise. Having analyzed data collected during this period, Spring determines that, despite the constraints of poor infrastructure, inadequate capital, minimal security of investments, and low production capacity, WAEN was largely successful in accomplishing its goals.

While Spring provides an account of the success of one development program, Stephen Kandeh discusses the weaknesses of another. Kandeh illustrates the failures of development programs in alleviating poverty in Sierra Leone, examining the role of institutions in preventing positive reforms. As one of the world's poorest nations, Sierra Leone has, since independence, been plagued by illiteracy, high infant mortality, low life expectancy, and poor economic performance. Kandeh's overview of Sierra Leone's history reveals that the roots of many contemporary problems extend back to the precolonial era, when "multiple and disparate institutional structures and values" coexisted. With British colonization came indirect rule, which distorted traditional power structures. After the end of colonial rule Sierra Leone sank deeper into economic crisis. The civil war of 1992 to 2002 exacerbated the problems of underdevelopment. Despite receiving a substantial amount of foreign aid from the United States (and Great Britain), Sierra Leone continues to experience grinding poverty. Every development strategy attempted, from export-led growth to import-substitution industrialization, to structural adjustment, served to increase reliance on foreign aid while failing to alleviate conditions of poverty. Although scholars and policymakers have suggested that a large capital infusion, such as is recommended by the "poverty trap" model of development, would aid Sierra Leone, Kandeh argues that only a fundamental shift in social and cultural values would generate any serious progress. He suggests that we can use the "institutional trap model" to explain the failure of capital infusion to spur economic growth. In contrast to the supposition that foreign capital investment will spur economic growth, the "institutional trap model" presents an alternative analysis, arguing for radical social and cultural changes as a means to reshape the institutional structures of Sierra Leone.

Osman Gbla's chapter also examines the difficulties experienced by Sierra Leone in the post–Cold War era, comparing U.S. policies toward Sierra Leone with U.S. policies toward Liberia. Gbla's work challenges the previously held assumption that following the Cold War the United States would increase its involvement in West African states to ensure peace, democracy, and stability. Gbla argues that the West African nations of Liberia and Sierra Leone have remained on the back burner in terms of U.S. strategic calculations, despite the United States' historical connections to both states. Liberia has historical ties to the United States and was, from its establishment in 1822 through the 1980s, considered a close ally of the U.S. Sierra Leone also shares elements of a common heritage with the United States. The Gullahs of South Carolina, for example, are direct descendents of slaves taken from the "rice coast" of Sierra Leone. With the end of British colonial rule in the 1960s, the U.S. sought closer relations with Sierra Leone, gradually augmenting its political and economic presence over the next three decades. Civil war began in Liberia in 1989 and Sierra Leone in 1991, causing massive human casualties, destruction of infrastructure, and economic crisis. The United States, although in a position to intervene, opted to pursue a policy of limited engagement. In addition to providing an overview of U.S. policy with regard to the civil wars in Liberia and Sierra Leone, Gbla offers recommendations for building stable, democratic West African states, advocating a U.S. commitment to the promotion of poverty alleviation programs and peace-building efforts.

Part 5, "Looking toward the Future: U.S.–West African Linkages in the Twenty-first Century," treats areas of particular salience in contemporary U.S.–West African relations. For the attacks of September 11 have altered the United States' strategic priorities, reshaping foreign policy. The authors of the chapters in part 5 show how these policy shifts have shaped the political and economic milieus of West Africa.

Ismail Olawale opens the section with the analysis of the involvement of the United States in the Liberian conflict in 2003. Like the relationships between West African states and the former colonial powers, the United States has long played a role in Liberian affairs. The author offers the examples of the British in Sierra Leone and the French in Côte d'Ivoire as models for the potential of U.S. intervention in Liberia. In addition to direct military action the U.S. commitments were expected to strengthen democratic institutions, promote diplomacy, build security, and prevent or alleviate humanitarian disasters. The author argues that shifting geopolitical priorities, particularly West Africa's strategic importance in the War on Terror and the increased reliance on the region for meeting U.S. energy needs, warrants an increase in resources devoted to conflict management.

Stephan A. Harmon's "Radical Islam in the Sahel: Implications for U.S. Policy and Regional Stability" also addresses U.S. policy within the West African region. In chapter 20, Harmon discusses the currently relevant issue of the growth of radical Islam in the West African Sahel. Due to the purported influence of Algerian rebels, the presence of foreign Islamic preachers, and the expansion of indigenous Islamic communities, the United States currently ranks the Sahel as number two on its list of African fronts in the War on Terror. Consequently, several U.S. agencies—including USAID and the State Department—have been active in the region, in an effort to limit the influence of foreign Islamist extremists. Harmon suggests that radical Islamist groups have indeed seen an increase in membership in the Sahel in recent years. However, he explains that it is chronic poverty that has generated ethnic rivalries and authoritarianism and that the growth of radical Islam is merely a symptom of the economic dislocations experienced by West African states.

Ken Vincent's chapter examines the recent development of oil infrastructure in the West African state of Chad. The Chad-Cameroon pipeline, at $3.7 billion dollars, represents the single largest foreign investment in African history. Heavily financed and overseen by the World Bank, the pipeline, it is estimated, will increase Chadian revenues by 45 to 50 percent. This contrasts with the considerably bleaker potential for growth in Cameroon, despite the fact that 85 percent of the pipeline lies in that nation. Estimates suggest that Cameroon would experience only a 2 percent increase in revenues. Vincent's chapter outlines the scope of the project, comparing it to the hydrocarbon-development failures of Angola and Nigeria. In spite of the possibilities of failure, however, the extent of poverty in Chad makes the pipeline project a viable option. Overall, Vincent's assessment is optimistic, as both domestic and international actors have worked to address issues of transparency, environmental impact, and respect for indigenous people who live and work in the region.

Chapter 22, by Christopher Ruane, closes the volume with a discussion of U.S. foreign policy toward Africa today and in the near future. Ruane's chapter asks the crucial question, why does West Africa barely feature on the U.S. foreign policy agenda for 2005 through 2009? The author explains that the United States devotes minimal attention to West Africa based on a conceptualization of the region as primarily (a) a resource supplier, (b) a terrorist base, and (c) a region of widespread human rights abuses. The proliferation of human rights abuses does not figure heavily in the calculus of U.S. policymakers, whose priorities are largely focused on combating the threat of terrorism. Within this framework, only those regions, such as the Middle East, that have experienced a substantial growth of radical Islam warrant U.S. attention. While the United States considers the West African Sahel to be a potential terrorist breeding ground, Ruane characterizes terrorist threats in West Africa as more rumor than fact. In closing, he identifies two cases in which the region could merit increased attention in the next few years. First, any threats of terrorism could prompt U.S. intervention. And second, the emergence of one or more strong democracies could lead the United States to lend more support as such democracies could serve as good examples or "model nations." In the end, though, Ruane remains pessimistic about the possibility of West Africa's rising to prominence on the United States' priority list in the coming five years. Minimal threats of terrorism combined with a scarcity of desirable resources (other than oil) make it unlikely that U.S. policy will shift its focus to West Africa.

Taken together, the chapters in this volume constitute a major work devoted to interrogating the complex relationship—both historical and contemporary—between the United States and West Africa. It is our hope that these essays will inspire controversy, debate, and ultimately, more research on the subject of U.S.–West Africa relations.

Notes

1. See chapter 1 in this volume.
2. Curtis Keim, *Mistaking Africa: Curiosities and Inventions of the American Mind* (Boulder, CO: Westview Press, 1999).

Part One

Trade and Politics in the Nineteenth and Twentieth Centuries

1

West Africa and the United States in Historical Perspective

Adebayo Oyebade and Toyin Falola

During World War II, the exigencies of America's national security caused the forging of new and more enduring relations between the African continent and the United States. What had hitherto been a "dark continent" to many Americans became something of significance to the United States during the war. Yet the history of interactions between the two entities dates back several centuries before the global war of 1939–45. The possibility of pre-Columbian American interaction with the region, particularly with West Africa, has been suggested in the literature, even if it has not been firmly established as fact. But the Atlantic slave trade and the establishment of an American colony, Liberia, on the West African coast, represented more significant epochs in the history of relations between the United States and West Africa. This chapter will situate in historical perspective the centuries of interactions between America and West Africa.

West Africa and Pre-Columbian America

The famed Christopher Columbus, the "discoverer" of America, first sailed to the New World in 1492 under the sponsorship of Queen Isabella and King Ferdinand, who had just established the Spanish nation-state through the union of their two independent kingdoms. The age of exploration in Europe was unfolding in the fifteenth century and enterprising adventurers embarked on voyages of discovery. One of the noted architects of European exploration was Prince Henry the Navigator, son of King John I of Portugal. Between 1444 and 1446, Henry, who was never an explorer himself, organized and sponsored a series of voyages along the coast of West Africa that ultimately led to the circumnavigation of Africa and the charting of an oceanic route to the Indies.

Less well known was a voyage by Columbus to the Gold Coast in West Africa in 1481, sponsored by King John II of Portugal. In contrast to the Eurocentric myth of disorder and barbarism prevalent in Africa, during this voyage Columbus encountered civilized communities and well-established states with very complex social, political, and economic structures. At the time of Columbus's visit, the most impressive medieval West African empire, Songhay, was still in existence. Its noted center of scholarship, Timbuktu, the home of the world-renowned higher educational institution, the Sankoré University, still possessed a great deal of its splendor. Columbus, who visited the Portuguese fortress of Elmina on the Gold Coast, was impressed by the riches of the land, especially its gold. But as an explorer, Columbus learned valuable lessons in geography and oceanography. This undoubtedly sparked his interest in a voyage westward across the Atlantic, which he erroneously believed would take him to India and establish direct access to the coveted riches of the Orient. More importantly, Columbus's voyage to West Africa may have laid the groundwork for the first contact between that part of Africa and the Americas. A few West Africans were said to have returned with him to Europe and eventually accompanied him on his voyages to the New World between 1492 and 1504.

Some scholars, however, have suggested the possibility of an African presence in the Americas before the arrival of Columbus. The argument is that some West African people, probably from the Senegambia area, were known to Native Americans prior to the arrival of Columbus. The most forceful argument along these lines has been provided by Rutgers linguist and anthropologist Ivan Van Sertima, who marshaled an array of archaeological, historical, and botanical evidence to argue his case.[1]

The Era of the European Slave Trade in West Africa

Systematic transportation of Africans to the Americas as slaves began in the early sixteenth century and lasted till the early nineteenth century. The trade represented the most significant series of events in the history of interaction between West Africa and the United States. Not only did it bring about a direct and long-lasting connection between the two regions, but one of its most important repercussions was the planting of an African diaspora in America.[2]

The Atlantic trade established a durable commercial collaboration between European or American and African merchants. In this collaborative venture, the primary role of African traders was to procure slaves, which were then sold to European dealers stationed at the coastal forts for onward transportation to the Americas. In the New World they were promptly put to work as slaves on the various plantations.

The expansion of the American plantation system, particularly in the eighteenth century, increased the volume of the Atlantic trade. More and more

Africans, primarily from West Africa, were shipped annually to the New World. Apart from the Central African region of Angola and Kongo, the entire west coast of Africa, from Senegal to the Bight of Biafra, constituted the major source of slaves for the Americas. At least three distinct regions of West Africa constituted significant catchment areas for the Atlantic trade. Perhaps most prominent was the "Slave Coast," the region around the Bight of Benin extending from Grand Popo in the present-day Republic of Benin to Benin in Nigeria. The second major region was the Gold Coast, encompassing the region around present-day Côte d'Ivoire and Ghana. The third was the Bight of Biafra, a region extending from the Niger Delta to the riverine area of southwestern Nigeria, all the way to the Cross River. Also important was the Senegambia valley, a region of the upper Guinea forest on the far western coast of West Africa.[3] Thus, members of West African ethnic groups such as the Wolof, Serer, Mandingo, Asante, Yoruba, Igbo, and many others constituted a large proportion of the Africans exported to the Americas. A number of ports along the coast, such as Gorée, Elmina, Cape Coast, Grand Popo, Porto Novo, Badagry, Lagos, Bonny, and Elem Kalabari (New Calabar), served at various times during the trade as important outlets for slave exportation. A number of major West African states such as the kingdoms of Dahomey, Oyo, Benin, and Asante were involved in the slave trade with the Europeans at the coastal forts.

The African Diaspora

The shipment of several million Africans, mostly from West Africa, across the Atlantic to the New World represented the largest forced migration in human history, one that would establish a permanent African presence in America. By the seventeenth century, enslaved Africans constituted a prominent part of the population in the American colonies that eventually became the United States; and by the eighteenth, they outnumbered whites in some counties in the South.

Slavery was, of course, fundamental to the success of European capitalist ventures in the New World. In the United States, the agrarian economy of the South was wholly sustained by the labor of enslaved Africans. Despite the hardships of life in servitude, enslaved Africans attempted as far as they could construct communities in an oppressive system that sought to rid them of any cultural heritage. The literature has shown that elements of West African culture survived, particularly in the U.S. South.[4] The forced migration of Africans to the New World was accompanied by the introduction of aspects of West African culture into the United States. While the slaves, having no choice, adopted the culture of their new environment, they equally imparted their own culture to the white community, to an extent that has not always been appreciated. Indeed, from the beginning, the enslaved population of Africans impacted their new American environment as much as their new environment impacted them. West African languages, music, dance, and art forms contributed to the formation of American culture.

The Back-to-Africa Experiments

Historical racial oppression in America persuaded many free American blacks that assimilation into white society with equal rights was unattainable, and consequently, persuaded them that colonization was the solution. But there were two main perspectives on colonization. First, there was the notion that colonization could be achieved within the United States, where African Americans would be given territories of their own to settle. In the hope of realizing this dream, many free blacks seeking to escape racial oppression in the South moved west and established their own communities in Kansas and Oklahoma.

The other perspective on colonization was that African Americans would be expatriated to Africa and settled in a colony of their own. In America before the Civil War, many free blacks, particularly in the South, saw moving away from the United States as the only way they could truly experience freedom. Attempts at colonization were made in various locations in the Americas, including Canada and Mexico, with varying degrees of success. But more vigorously pursued was the establishment of a colony in Africa. Attempts were made to resettle American blacks in various parts of West Africa such as Yorubaland, in Nigeria.[5]

The Foundation of Liberia

The most successful attempt to repatriate and resettle freed blacks in Africa took place when the colony of Liberia was established in 1822 on the west coast of the continent. This back-to-Africa experiment was the culmination of the antislavery and abolitionist campaign that had gained ground in America by the early nineteenth century. While various African Americans and leaders of the abolitionist movement campaigned for colonization, the establishment of Liberia was sponsored by the American Colonization Society (ACS).

The Liberian project was the product of emancipation and the idea of colonization. The abolition of slavery was tied to the question of what would become of freed slaves after emancipation. Many abolitionists held the view that free blacks would never be given equal rights in America, and so true freedom could best be achieved if they were repatriated and settled in a colony of their own in Africa. For others, particularly whites who supported colonization, repatriation to a colony in Africa would rid the United States of the growing population of unwanted free blacks. The idea of repatriation was thus quite popular among whites.

The ACS established the first Liberian settlement, Monrovia, on Cape Mesurado, in January 1822. Following its expansion as a result of the establishment of other settlements, the colony of Liberia was later incorporated as the Commonwealth of Liberia. Monrovia, named for the U.S. president, James Monroe, became its capital.

Liberia grew steadily as increased emigration swelled its population. After the slave trade had been abolished in the United States, African captives rescued by American naval patrols aboard slave ships on the Atlantic still trafficking illegally in humans were resettled in Liberia. In 1847, the ACS relinquished its authority over the commonwealth, which declared its independence, ending its ambiguous status in the international community as neither a sovereign nation nor an American colony. By 1866, more than 13,000 American blacks had been settled in Liberia.[6]

The young African nation faced a number of problems in its formative years. The settlers were constantly harassed by local African groups such as the Kru and the Grebo, who feared the colonists' encroachment on their lands. Also, Liberia was a victim of European imperialist ambitions of territorial aggrandizement. Surrounded by British and French possessions, Liberia was threatened by recurring incidents of encroachment on its territory. The United States responded to both of these problems and saved Liberia from oblivion. Washington provided military assistance to quell local uprisings and intervened to preserve Liberia's territorial integrity in the many border disputes that plagued its relations with its neighbors, the French territory of the Ivory Coast and the English colony of Sierra Leone.[7]

Yet, for most of its early history, Liberia did not enjoy close or special relations with the United States as expected by many settlers. Inherent racial prejudice in America colored its relations with Liberia and attitudes toward the young nation. This prevented deeper American political engagement with its de facto informal colony, beyond missionary activities and some trading interests. The United States' less than profound interest in Liberia could be seen in its failure to recognize the country's sovereignty for fifteen years after the republic had declared its independence with a constitution and political institutions fashioned out of the American system.[8]

Despite the success of Liberia, the African colonization project did not win broad approval in the African American community. Many notable black leaders, including the Harvard-trained scholar W. E. B. DuBois and the great abolitionist Frederick Douglass, opposed the idea. Douglass once stated that blacks in America must be "counted upon as a permanent element of the population of the United States." Among his reasons for opposition to colonization were "the expense of removal to a foreign land, [and] the difficulty of finding a country where the conditions of existence are more favorable than here."[9] Many African Americans correctly interpreted repatriation to

Africa as a ploy by racist whites and many white supporters of abolitionism to rid America of black people. As attested by ACS records, some slave masters desired to free their bondsmen on the condition that they would be repatriated to Liberia.[10] Thus, among the vast majority of African Americans to whom Africa was already an alien land, repatriation to Liberia was not a viable proposition. Indeed, following the pioneering efforts of the ACS, subsequent attempts at repatriation to Liberia, such as that of Henry McNeal Turner, a notable black leader, in 1894 through his International Migration Society, were hardly successful.

Garveyism

The "Back-to-Africa" movement can be more readily associated with the Jamaican nationalist, Marcus Garvey, who championed the idea in the 1920s and 1930s. In the interwar years, Marcus Garvey led a mass organization called the Universal Negro Improvement Association (UNIA), which, among other things, called for the repatriation of American blacks to Africa. With its headquarters in Harlem, New York, Garveyism, a radical philosophy that has been variously termed "messianic," "pseudo-fascist," and "Black Zionist,"[11] became a powerful movement among working-class African Americans, who were mesmerized by Garvey's charisma and his message of black separatism and solidarity, racial pride, and race redemption.

Garvey's purpose in espousing repatriation and colonization seemed to be to promote business cooperation between American blacks and Africans. The Black Star Line, Garvey's steamship company created in 1919 to operate a shipping line between the United States and Africa, was partly designed to promote inter-Atlantic economic intercourse. In principle, the business class in black America and in West Africa, particularly in Liberia, was receptive to this. However, such enterprises rarely made significant headway.[12]

While Garveyism made some waves in Liberia, in other parts of West Africa it did not have a significant impact, either in its economic component or in its anti-imperialist political message. which called for the liberation of African colonies. Although UNIA branches existed in some West African cities like Freetown in Sierra Leone and Lagos in Nigeria, as Judith Stein has remarked, "Garveyism in West Africa was [only] an occasional inspiration for Africans."[13]

World War II and West Africa

World War II marked a new phase in the United States' perception of Africa. Prior to the war, except for episodic intervention in Liberia, the African continent hardly featured in America's foreign policy. However, the war brought the continent, particularly West Africa, into the United States' strategic planning in both military and economic terms.

West Africa entered America's war effort in August 1941 when President Franklin D. Roosevelt decided that the United States would assume the operation of an air ferry service across West Africa to North Africa and the Middle East. The possibility that the hard-pressed British desert forces might capitulate to the German military machine in the North African theatre was unthinkable in Washington. It could lead to an Axis advance into West Africa, and consequently a threat to the security of the Western hemisphere. Thus it was urgent and imperative for the United States to aid the British North African forces with supplies of military hardware, and this was the primary consideration in America's decision to take over the air ferry service across Africa. Through the ferry service, military supplies, particularly much-needed combat aircraft, were flown from Florida via Parnamirim air base in Natal, Brazil, to North Africa. West African ports such as Dakar in Senegal, Bathurst in the Gambia, Takoradi in the Gold Coast, and Lagos and Maiduguri in Nigeria served as transit points on the ferry route. Apart from ferrying bombers, this route eventually served to transport American troops to North Africa. The ferry service was a major military operation undertaken by the United States, although it was achieved under the auspices of a civil aviation company, Pan-American Airways (PANAM). This was necessary since at the commencement of the operation the United States was technically not yet a belligerent nation. The ferry service put the entire west coast of Africa within the framework of America's strategic planning in the southern Atlantic.[14]

America's wartime economic needs also helped to define a strategic interest in West Africa. Before World War II the United States' trade and investment in the whole of Africa were paltry. In West Africa, aside from the activities of the American rubber company, Firestone, in Liberia, the United States' economic interest was insignificant. This drastically changed during World War II when the United States was forced to turn to the region as a source of strategic raw materials, agricultural and mineral, needed to fuel the war effort. This situation had been created by the Japanese occupation of Southeast Asia, which deprived the United States of its traditional source of vital resources. A replacement for critical strategic commodities was found in mineral-rich and agriculturally productive West Africa. America's wartime supply of much-needed mineral products came principally from various parts of West Africa: tin from Nigeria, manganese form the Gold Coast, and diamonds from Sierra Leone and the Gold Coast. In terms of agricultural products, the United States obtained natural rubber from Liberia; palm oil and palm products from the Gold Coast, Nigeria, and Sierra Leone; cocoa from Nigeria; and ginger from Sierra Leone. The increased demand for West African products during the war significantly raised the volume of the United States' trade in the region.[15]

America's military and economic wartime presence in West Africa was particularly profound in Liberia. During the war, Liberia emerged as an ally of the US, and even declared war on Germany at the prodding of Washington. In 1942, the United States signed a defense pact with Liberia, militarizing the country by permitting America's use of its territory for military purposes. The United States developed military bases in Liberia, constructing the country's first port, the Free Port of Monrovia, and the air base, Roberts Field, using American financial assistance and expertise. Roberts Field and other American bases in Liberia were used as storage depots for the United States' military supplies and as transit points for onward dispatch to North Africa. A 5,000-strong all-black regiment from the 41st Engineers and Defense Detachment served in Liberia, manning military depots and maintaining inventories.

The strategic importance of Liberia to the United States during the war produced a special relationship between the two nations. Liberia's newfound status in America's foreign relations was underscored by President Roosevelt's visit to the country on January 26–27, 1943, on his way back from the Casablanca Conference in Morocco. During this visit, Roosevelt conferred with the Liberian president, Edwin Barclay, on war issues and other issues concerning bilateral relations.

America's wartime special relations with Liberia brought important benefits to the West African nation. Liberia's transportation system was modernized through airport and harbor development and road construction. The Liberian economy saw tremendous growth, significantly raising government revenue. The impact of American influence on the Liberian economy could be seen in Monrovia's replacement of the British West African currency with the American dollar as legal tender. The American-owned rubber company, Firestone, continued to play a major role in the political economy of Liberia in the postwar period.

Decolonization and Independence

West African nationalism greatly benefited from black nationalist thought in America during the interwar years. The writings and activism of W. E. B. DuBois, Marcus Garvey, and Booker T. Washington, to mention just a few prominent black leaders, inspired many West African nationalists. Although the three above-mentioned leaders differed considerably in approach and method, they all wanted an end to European colonial rule in Africa. DuBois was one of the earliest African Americans who through prolific writing sought to emphasize the importance of racial pride. As a scholar, indeed, the first African American to hold a PhD in history, he upheld black history as an integral part of the history of human civilization. Many of his books dealt with the history and culture of Africa including its diaspora.[16] Also, DuBois wrote profusely about the need for black people to come together and fight for the advancement of the black race. "If the

Negro were to be a factor in the world history, it would be through a Pan-Negro movement," he once wrote.[17] As the editor of *The Crisis*, the official organ of the National Association for the Advancement of Colored People (NAACP) between 1910 and 1934, DuBois used the paper to attack European imperialism in Africa.[18] Beyond using writing as a weapon to advance the interests of the African world, DuBois was also an activist and a Pan-Africanist. In the interwar years he was instrumental in the organization of four Pan-African congresses. The first one, held in Paris in 1919, was attended by the Senegalese Blaise Diagne, a deputy in the French Parliament. With DuBois' help, more delegates from Nigeria, the Gold Coast, Sierra Leone, and Liberia, attended subsequent congresses, particularly the last one, held in 1927.

Marcus Garvey's Pan-African activism in the United States influenced many nationalists. Garveyism preached at one point or another intense racial consciousness and pride, ultra-nationalism, militant anticolonialism, and economic self-reliance. Garvey's fiery speeches ignited the hope and expectations of many a black man. Elected the "Provisional President of Africa" at a 1920 convention organized by the UNIA, he was seen by many as the liberator of Africa. Garveyism as a political philosophy was influential in some urban centers in West Africa. Although local branches of the UNIA were not particularly strong in West African cities like Monrovia, Lagos, and Freetown, nevertheless, many West African nationalists were influenced by Garveyism. Azikiwe, for instance, was inspired by Garvey's radical Pan-Africanism.[19]

Earlier, Booker T. Washington had been the dominant figure in African American intellectual circles and had also been involved in Pan-Africanism, although he eschewed the militancy of Garvey or the radicalism of DuBois. His approach to the question of colonial subjugation of Africa was through gradualism and caution. He convened the International Conference on the Negro at Tuskegee Institute in April 1912. The conference drew African delegates including one of the earliest West African nationalists, J. E. Casely Hayford of the National Congress of British West Africa (NCBWA).

During World War II, West African nationalism, particularly in British West Africa, gathered steam. One of the main reasons for this was the wartime American anticolonial policy demanding an end to colonial empires. This policy was directed particularly at Britain, the most formidable colonial power in Africa. Indeed, Washington was more than willing to irritate London, its major ally, over the question of the retention of British colonial possessions after the war.[20] The president and other high-ranking Washington officials consistently warned that America was not fighting to preserve the British Empire. The anticolonial mood in the United States was expressed in *Life* magazine in late 1942. In an "Open Letter to the people of England," the magazine warned London that "[O]ne thing we are sure we are not fighting for is to hold the British Empire together."[21]

West African students in the United States, mostly from the British colonies, contributed their quota to the burgeoning anticolonial movement at home during World War II. Goaded by American anti-imperialism, these students, whose numbers had begun to increase significantly in American institutions from the 1930s, mobilized and organized. Many of them had been radicalized by the racism prevailing in American society and the practice of racial segregation. At the same time, however, the political thought of these students was greatly influenced by American democratic ideals with their profession of the values of freedom, liberty, and justice. Some of them, including Nnamdi Azikiwe, Nwafor Orizu, and Kingsley Mbadiwe from Nigeria, and Kwame Nkrumah from the Gold Coast (later Ghana), wrote during the war expressing strong nationalistic fervor and condemning in no uncertain terms European imperialism in Africa.[22] These budding nationalists became political giants in their respective countries after independence. In postcolonial Nigeria, Azikiwe emerged as the first president; Mbadiwe served as minister in various departments, and Orizu was at one time senate president. Kwame Nkrumah led the Gold Coast to independence and became the first prime minister of independent Ghana.

Particularly in West Africa, American wartime anticolonialism served as a catalyst for the escalation of nationalist activities. Nationalists were impressed and encouraged by American anticolonial rhetoric. When the British prime minister, Winston Churchill, declared that the Atlantic Charter, a joint British-American statement that called for national self-determination after the war, did not apply to African dependencies, he was roundly condemned and denounced in West Africa. The vibrant and politically conscious West African press wrote stinging editorials and articles to denounce Churchill's interpretation of the document.[23] West African nationalists spared no effort in condemning the prevailing British perspective as well. Indeed, London was bombarded with delegations from British West Africa with demands for constitutional reform including a postwar order based on a system of representative government.[24] In their condemnation of Churchill's view of the Atlantic Charter, West African nationalists were emboldened by Roosevelt's broad interpretation of the charter. The American president had on a number of occasions indicated that the principles enunciated in the charter were applicable to all dependent peoples of the world. For example, on February 23, 1942, Roosevelt stated categorically that the "Atlantic Charter applies not only to the parts of the world that border the Atlantic, but to the whole world."[25]

The United States, however, was not prepared to back up its anticolonial rhetoric with concrete action. America's disapproval of European colonial rule in Africa in the final analysis went no farther than rhetoric. The Atlantic Charter raised the hopes of many in the colonial world for greater progress toward self-determination. But it proved to be nothing more than a scrap of paper. It was not a formally signed document, but only a vague press release designed to sway the public, especially anti-interventionists. As the world entered the postwar Cold War era, the dynamics of postwar East-West relations forced America, finally, to abandon the path of anticolonialism it had vainly pursued during the war.

Decolonization in Africa moved at a rapid pace in the 1950s and early 1960s. In 1960 alone, seventeen African nations achieved political independence, a great many of them former colonies in West Africa. In the Cold War atmosphere in which decolonization was taking shape, the Soviet Union sought to exploit the moment to further its ideological interest in the continent by fully supporting the African independence movement. As African states rapidly achieved independence, the question that faced Washington was how to preserve these states' loyalty to the West and insulate them from the Soviet bloc.

The Cold War

Consistent with America's postwar foreign policy, Washington's overriding interest in Africa during the Cold War was to prevent the burgeoning Soviet influence in the continent, an interest that had begun to manifest itself in the late 1950s. Apart from obvious Soviet satellite states in southern and eastern Africa, some states in West Africa provided ground in which Soviet interests could flourish. While in West Africa there were no pro-Soviet Marxist-Leninist regimes as were found in Ethiopia, Angola, and Mozambique, Ghana under Kwame Nkrumah and Ahmed Sékou Touré's Guinea flirted with Communism in the 1960s and became recipients of limited economic aid from Warsaw Pact countries.

Soviet influence in West Africa in the 1960s was not, however, perceived in Washington as dangerous to Western interests. First, West African recipients of Soviet aid were not wholly committed to the Kremlin. Indeed, at the same time, these countries also received military and economic assistance from Western countries. With the fall from power in Ghana of the socialist-oriented Nkrumah and his ruling Convention People's Party (CPP) in 1966 and the emergence of a pro-West military junta, the chances of Soviet infiltration in West Africa were considerably lessened. Also, although the Nigerian Civil War of 1967–70 offered the Soviet Union an opportunity to make inroads into the country through its military assistance to the federal government, the Kremlin was never able to capitalize on this. While professing a policy of nonalignment, Nigeria after its civil war was staunchly pro-West.[26]

The U.S. response to the possible advancement of Soviet interests in Africa in the early years of African independence was to rely on the erstwhile colonial masters to ensure a neocolonial relationship with their former colonies. Thus in West Africa, the United States could count on Britain and France to promote Western influence in their former colonies.

The Post–Cold War Era

A dominant feature of post–Cold War West Africa is the preponderance of major conflicts. Indeed, from the late 1980s to the end of the century, West Africa was a zone of intense conflicts that threatened to destabilize the region. In addition to low-level internal and cross-border conflicts in many parts of West Africa, major civil wars broke out in Liberia and Sierra Leone. America's response to these conflicts constitutes an integral part of post–Cold War U.S. policy toward West Africa and the continent as a whole.

The United States and Conflicts in Liberia and Sierra Leone

The Liberian Civil War broke out in December 1989 when a rebel group, the National Patriotic Front of Liberia (NPFL), led by Charles Taylor invaded the country from Côte d'Ivoire, initially to unseat the government of President Samuel Doe, who himself had usurped power in a violent military coup in 1980. In the following years the war assumed a more complex dimension, with at least seven warring factions involved. The war initially ended in 1996 with a peace accord and the emergence of Taylor as president the following year. However, peace and political stability did not immediately return to Liberia. In 2002, renewed violence, often referred to as the second civil war, broke out; this ultimately forced President Taylor to resign from office in August 2003 and move to exile in Nigeria. After nearly fourteen years of brutal civil war, Liberia had been utterly devastated; hundreds of thousands of people had died and thousands more had been displaced; the economy had been destroyed, creating enormous hardship for the vast majority of the people. At the end of the war, Liberia emerged as one of the poorest countries in the world.[27]

The Liberian war affected practically every nation in the vicinity. In March 1991, the war spilled over into Sierra Leone when a renegade insurgent group, the Revolutionary United Front (RUF), led by Foday Sankoh and reportedly sponsored by Charles Taylor, launched an attack on the eastern part of the country from Liberia.[28] The RUF war proved to be another protracted conflict in West Africa, which successive governments in Sierra Leone were unable to end. What further characterized this war was its sheer brutality, especially against the civilian population. The RUF rebels committed grievous atrocities such as sexual violence against women and young girls, massive looting, abduction and murder of defenseless villagers, indiscriminate amputation of limbs, and the use of child soldiers on a large scale. On May 27, 1997, a military coup that overthrew the elected government of

President Ahmed Tejan Kabbah further escalated the war. When the war ended in mid-2000, nine years after it had begun, Sierra Leone, like Liberia, had been reduced to one of the world's poorest nations, with enormous postwar challenges such as the reintegration of child combatants into civil society.[29]

The United States' attitude toward the civil wars in Liberia and Sierra Leone reveals Washington's post–Cold War policy of distancing itself from conflicts in which American national interests were not directly at stake. The disastrous U.S. intervention in the crisis in Somalia in 1992–93, code-named "Operation Restore Hope," had altered America's perception of its role in intractable African conflicts.[30] A new American policy on multinational peace operations involving U.S. forces, Presidential Decision Directive 25 (PDD-25) of May 6, 1994, was a direct outcome of the failed American intervention in Somalia. This policy established new and stringent guidelines for the participation of American troops in future peacekeeping efforts around the world.[31]

Liberians, by virtue of historical connection with the United States, expected direct American intervention in the bloody civil war that was wrecking their nation. Rather than direct military intervention in the conflicts in Liberia and Sierra Leone, however, the administrations of Presidents Bill Clinton and George W. Bush emphasized that the role of the United States would be to support the efforts of the West African regional organization, the Economic Community of West African States (ECOWAS), to resolve the conflicts. Throughout the period of the crises in Liberia and Sierra Leone, the United States limited itself to providing financial and logistical support for the subregional peacekeeping force, the ECOWAS Monitoring Group (ECOMOG), in its efforts to deal effectively with the conflicts.[32] With American troops spread thin as a result of the wars in Afghanistan and then Iraq, in the renewed war in Liberia in 2002–3, President Bush adamantly refused the American military intervention that was demanded by most Liberians. The United States saw Charles Taylor's continued presence in Liberia as president as the main impediment to peace. Thus, instead of engaging in military intervention, Washington pressurized Taylor to resign. Following Taylor's forced resignation and exile in Nigeria, in August 2003, disappointingly to Liberians, the United States sent to Monrovia not a peacekeeping force but a "military assessment team . . . to begin gauging humanitarian needs and possibly to lay the groundwork for a deployment of U.S. peacekeeping troops."[33] No American peacekeeping force was ever deployed to Liberia.

To avoid sending American troops to deal with intractable African conflicts, the Clinton administration attempted in the 1990s to assist Africa to establish an all-African rapid-response peacekeeping force that could be deployed to conflict zones around the continent. A project called the

African Crisis Response Initiative (ACRI), sponsored by the United States, was inaugurated in the mid 1990s as contingents of troops from a number of African states were trained to constitute the nucleus of the force. Washington emphasized the role of American troops in this project as "to train and equip peacekeeping troops from a number of African nations, stationed but ready in their nation of origin, for rapid deployment to areas of crises in Africa."[34] Among the volunteers for the American-provided training were West African states such as Ghana, Mali, and Senegal. While troops from these countries participated in the project, Nigeria, the regional power with long-standing experience in regional and international peacekeeping, was opposed to the American initiative. The military administration of General Sani Abacha argued that rather than a new peacekeeping apparatus, what Africa needed was "financial and logistics support to enable the existing peacekeeping mechanisms [to] function effectively."[35]

The United States and a Regional Power, Nigeria

Nigeria understandably occupies an important place in America's foreign policy in Africa. Despite its economic woes, Nigeria is still a regional power; it is the most populous black nation in the world with the potential to be the largest black democracy. Besides this, Nigeria is indispensable to the United States because a fifth of U.S. oil comes from the West African nation.

America's oil interest in Nigeria demanded the creation of a stable democratic government in that country. After the end of the Cold War, Washington began to encourage democratic reforms in Nigeria and the country's return to constitutional, elected government. During Abacha's military's dictatorship, the United States played a leading part in the international isolation of the regime as a result of its poor human rights record, extensive violations of basic civil rights, and failure to move the country toward genuine democracy. Not only did American criticism of the Abacha regime increase considerably after the execution of writer and environmentalist Ken Saro-Wiwa and his Ogoni colleagues on November 10, 1995, but Washington also imposed limited sanctions on Nigeria. Also, the United States persuaded its allies to treat Nigeria as a pariah state. Thus, Western nations placed visa restrictions on Nigerian government officials wanting to visit the West.

However, while still opposed to the Nigerian dictatorship, the Clinton administration in the later years of Abacha's regime refrained from pursuing a hard-line policy toward Abuja. This was in spite of persistent calls for a tougher stand against Nigeria, both within the United States, especially from African American constituencies, and from the prodemocracy elements in Nigeria.[36] Thus, the United States resisted the pressure to impose comprehensive oil sanctions on Nigeria; a step that many believed would easily have forced the Abacha dictatorship to concede to the demand for popular democracy. Rather, the policy of the Clinton administration was akin to "constructive engagement" with Abuja. Perhaps the clearest demonstration of this policy was Clinton's tacit approval of Abacha's candidacy in the presidential election scheduled for August 1998. During his African tour, Clinton had indicated that an Abacha candidacy would be acceptable to the United States.[37]

In 1999, Nigeria returned to democracy with the election of President Olusegun Obasanjo. Even though Obasanjo was reelected in 2003, Nigeria's democratic experiment has been very fragile amidst incessant ethnic and religious conflicts and massive political corruption, which have threatened the very survival of the state. The United States continues to be concerned with the survival of democracy and a stable polity in Nigeria partly because of its oil interests. Already, ethnic violence against foreign oil interests and the Nigerian government in the oil-producing southeastern part of the country has had some adverse effects on the global oil market and thus the energy industry in America.[38]

Aside from the issues of oil and democratic governance, the United States has also been concerned with drug trafficking from Nigeria to America. In May 1994, the U.S. State Department classified Nigeria as a major drug-trafficking country and called for concrete action by the Nigerian authorities. But Washington remained unsatisfied with Nigeria's apparently poor drug-control measures, which did not succeed in curtailing the country's drug-trafficking problem. In 1988, the State Department described Nigeria as "the hub of African narcotics trafficking," and blamed Nigerian traffickers for being "responsible for a significant portion of the heroin that is abused in the United States."[39]

The War on Terrorism

Since the terrorist attacks on America on September 11, 2001, the global war on terrorism has been the central element of the Bush administration's foreign policy. West Africa was linked to terrorism when, in May 2005, the administration of former President Charles Taylor of Liberia was accused of harboring al-Qaeda militants who were sought as a result of alleged connections with the bombing of the American embassies in Kenya and Tanzania.[40]

Generally, in Africa as in other parts of the world, Islamic fundamentalism is seen in Washington as detrimental to the defeat of terrorism. In Nigeria, in particular, constant religious violence fomented by Islamic militancy has been a major problem that has so far defied solution. Indeed, one of the most violent riots in early 2006 in the Islamic world against the Danish newspaper's caricature of the Prophet Mohammed occurred in Nigeria. Yet, the United States sees Nigeria as a major partner in the antiterrorist war in Africa.[41]

West African Cultural Influences on America

In contemporary times, particularly since the era of the Black Power movement in the late 1960s, African Americans have consciously and increasingly
sought to promote an African identity and incorporate African values into
their daily lives. An impressive example of the carryover of West African culture is the planting of a Yoruba community, the Oyotunji African Village, in
Sheldon, South Carolina. This community, which describes itself as "the
sacred village of Oyo-Tunji,"[42] was established in 1970. Deriving its name
from the famous ancient northern Yoruba town, Oyo, the community is modeled after traditional Yoruba towns and practices the culture and customs of
the Yoruba people of West Africa, predominantly found in western Nigeria
but also in parts of Togo and the Republic of Benin. The community's
founder and first *oba* (king, in the Yoruba language) was an African American
cultural nationalist, Walter Eugene King, who, on his coronation as the *oba*,
became known as Efuntola Oseijeman Adelabu Adefunmi I. It is noteworthy
that the coronation in 1981, and the bestowing of the royal title on Adefunmi
I, was performed by the paramount Yoruba king, Oba Okunade Sijuwade,
Olubuse II, the *ooni* of Ife, the sacred Yoruba town in Nigeria believed to be
the cradle of the Yoruba people. Oba Sijuwade himself is generally accepted
as the representative of the Yoruba progenitor, Oduduwa.[43]

Displaying of Yoruba culture is, indeed, quite popular in many African
American communities. Cultural and social values have been widely dis-
played, whether in terms of ceremonies (for example, marriage or child
naming) or in mode of dress (for example, wearing *danshiki* and *agbada*).
The practice of different forms of Yoruba traditional religion by many
American blacks is also known across the country. The Odunde festival held
annually in Philadelphia since 1975 is intended as a replica of the famous
Osun festival in Osogbo, western Nigeria: a celebration and worship of the
Yoruba deity, Osun, the sea goddess.

African open-air street markets are becoming common in the black community throughout the United States. The market at the Odunde festival is
the oldest and perhaps the most successful of these markets, which are popular in America's major cities. Odunde features the vending of a wide variety of wares including clothing, jewelry, craft products, CDs of African music,
and food by merchants from other parts of the United States, Latin America,
and West Africa.

Elements of other West African cultures have also been incorporated into
African American communities. The *kente* cloth of the Asante of Ghana is
very popular in contemporary black America, and often represents African
American cultural identity. One of its most popular uses is as decorative neck
and shoulder ties worn by African American college students during their
graduation ceremonies.[44]

On personal level, many African Americans have adopted West African names as a symbol of their heritage and historical connection with the region. One of the earliest noted blacks in America to do this was the Trinidadian-born American, Stokely Carmichael, the creator of "Black Power," the popular slogan and movement in black America in the 1960s. A frontline civil rights activist who was once the leader of the Student Nonviolent Coordinating Committee (SNCC) and a member of the Black Panther Party, Carmichael relocated to Guinea in 1969 and changed his name to Kwame Toure, combining the first name of the first prime minister of Ghana, Kwame Nkrumah, with the last name of the first president of Guinea, Sékou Touré. In recent times other prominent African Americans have also changed their names. The Temple University scholar, versatile author, and most famous proponent of the Afrocentric theory, Molefi Kete Asante, formerly known as Arthur Lee Smith, derived his African name from the Akan ethnic group of Ghana. An intellectual cultural nationalist, in 1995, Asante was installed as the Kyldomhene of Tafo, Akyem, Ghana, with the traditional title of Nana Okru Asante Peasah.

Conclusion

America's connections and intercourse with West Africa have been long and enduring, dating back to the period before the transatlantic slave trade. In historical perspective, despite the antiquity of this interaction, U.S. relations with Africa have never been of a level comparable to U.S. relations with Latin America and Asia. For the greater part of the period of connections, apart from periods of sporadic American presence in Africa, the continent remained insignificant in U.S. foreign relations. In his study of the Kennedy administration, renowned, Pulitzer Prize–winning historian and author Arthur M. Schlesinger stated this succinctly:

> Of all the continents this one had stayed longest on the outer fringes of the American consciousness. As late as 1960, our direct interests in Africa, political or economic, military or intellectual, were meager. No traditional doctrines guided our African policies. No alliances committed our troops, our foreign aid programs made only token contributions to African development. Of $30 billion overseas investment, less than 3% was in Africa. Our very sense of the continent below the Mediterranean rim was vague and dim.[45]

In contemporary times, the dynamics of global politics compel continued American interest in Africa, and, therefore, some sort of presence in the continent. As the basis of its presence in Africa and in pursuit of its interests, the United States has continued to emphasize partnership with the continent. America's major post–Cold War interests in Africa are the consolidation of democracy, economic reform, conflict resolution, and the prevention of the continent from becoming a haven for terrorists. As in the other parts of the continent, in West Africa, the United States continues to encourage democratic governance and economic growth, to support ECOWAS's efforts in conflict areas, and to court governments' support in the global war on terrorism.

Notes

1. See Ivan Van Sertima, *They Came before Columbus: The African Presence in Ancient America* (New York: Random House Trade Paperback, 2003).

2 . See, for instance, Mary Frances Berry and John W. Blassingame, *Long Memory: The Black Experience in America* (New York: Oxford University Press, 1982); Philip D. Morgan, *Slave Counterpoint: Black Culture in the Eighteenth-Century Chesapeake and Lowcountry* (Williamsburg, VA: University of North Carolina Press, 1998); and Herbert S. Klein, *The Atlantic Slave Trade* (New York: Cambridge University Press, 1999).

3. For more on the source regions for slaves, see Paul E. Lovejoy, *Transformations in Slavery: A History of Slavery in Africa* (Cambridge: Cambridge University Press, 2000), 49–61.

4. See, for instance, Berry and Blassingame, *Long Memory*; Mechal Sobel, *The World They Made Together: Black and White Values in Eighteenth-Century Virginia* (Princeton, NJ: Princeton University Press, 1987); Morgan, *Slave Counterpoint*; and Joseph Holloway, ed., *Africanism in American Culture* (Bloomington: Indiana University Press, 2005).

5. For example, the Jamaican-born journalist, teacher, and businessman, Robert Campbell, endeavored to establish a colony of African Americans in western Nigeria. See R. J. M. Blackett, "Return to the Motherland: Robert Campbell, a Jamaican in Early Colonial Lagos," *Phylon* 40, no. 4 (1979): 375–86. See also Richard Blackett, "Martin R. Delany and Robert Campbell: Black Americans in Search of an African Colony," *Journal of Negro History* 62, no. 1 (1977): 1–25; and Martin R. Delany and Robert Campbell, *Search for a Place: Black Separatism and Africa, 1860* (Ann Arbor: University of Michigan Press, 1969).

6. See "Table of Emigrants Settled in Liberia by the American Colonization Society," in *The African Repository and Colonial Journal* 43, no. 4 (April 1867), 117, General Collections (24), American Colonization Society Papers (ACSP), Library of Congress, Washington, DC.

7. There is an abundant literature on the early history of Liberia. See the following, for instance: Claude Andrew Clegg, *The Price of Liberty: African Americans and the Making of Liberia* (Chapel Hill: University of North Carolina Press, 2004); Catherine Reef, *This Our Dark Country: The American Settlers of Liberia* (New York: Clarion Books, 2002); and Yekutiel Gershoni, *Black Colonialism: The Americo-Liberian Scramble for the Hinterland* (Boulder, CO: Westview Press, 1985).

8. On the subject of the United States' Liberian policy, see, for instance, Lester S. Hyman, *United States Policy towards Liberia, 1822 to 2003: Unintended Consequences?* (Cherry Hill, NJ: Africana Homestead Legacy Publishers, 2003).

9. Frederick Douglass, "The Future of Blacks in the United States," in Michael Meyer, ed., *Frederick Douglass: The Narrative and Selected Writings* (New York: Random House, 1984), 389–90.

10. In one instance, twelve slaves owned by one Timothy Rogers of Bedford County, Virginia, were to be freed in his will provided they accepted repatriation to Liberia. See "Applicants for Passage to Liberia," ca. 1852, Manuscript Division (21), ACSP.

11. See Immanuel Geiss, *The Pan-African Movement: The History of Pan-Africanism in America, Europe and Africa* (New York: Africana Publishing Company, 1974), 263.

12. A good source on this subject is Judith Stein, *The World of Marcus Garvey: Race and Class in Modern Society* (New Orleans: Louisiana State University Press, 1986).

13. Ibid., 219.

14. For more on this subject, see Adebayo Oyebade, "Securing American Interest in Africa: West Africa in the United States Foreign Policy, 1939–1945" (PhD diss., Department of History, Temple University, May 1995), 119–68; and Deborah W. Ray, "Pan American Airways and the Trans-African Air Base Program of World War II" (PhD dissertation, New York University, June 1973).

15. For further analysis of West Africa's economic importance to the United States during the war, see Adebayo Oyebade, "Feeding America's War Machine: The United States Economic Expansion in West Africa during World War II," in *African Economic History* 26, no. 1 (1998): 119–40.

16. Some of DuBois' important works include *The Negro* (New York: H. Holt, 1915); *Black Folk Then and Now* (Millwood, NY: Kraus-Thomson Organization, 1975); *The World and Africa: An Inquiry into the Part Which Africa Has Played in World History* (New York: Kraus-Thomson Organization, 1976); *Black Reconstruction* (New York: Kraus-Thomson Organization, 1976); and *Color and Democracy: Colonies and Peace* (New York: Harcourt, Brace and Co., 1945).

17. W. E. B. DuBois, *The Conservation of Race* (Washington, DC: American Negro Academy, Occasional Papers, no. 2, 1987), 10.

18. For DuBois' role in the Pan-African movement, see Geiss, *The Pan-African Movement*, 229–62.

19. See "Nnamdi Azikiwe: Citation Accompanying the Honorary Degree of Doctor of Humane Letters, Conferred on May 19, 1980," U.P.G. 7.1., citations for honorary degrees, 1980, Archives of the University of Pennsylvania, Philadelphia. Garvey's Pan-African ideas are presented in Stein, *The World of Marcus Garvey*, and Geiss, *The Pan-African Movement*, 263–82.

20. On this subject, see Adebayo Oyebade, "'The Age of Imperialism is Ended': The Anglo-American Conflict over the British Empire during World War II," in *Journal of History and Diplomatic Studies* 2 (2005): 1–20.

21. *Life*, October 12, 1942, 34.

22. See for instance, Orizu, *Without Bitterness: Western Nations in Post-War Africa* (New York: Creative Age Press, 1944); and Kingsley Ozumba Mbadiwe, *British and Axis Aims in Africa* (New York: Wendell Malliet Company, 1942).

23. See, for instance, the Gold Coast newspaper, the *Spectator Daily*, June 22, 1943.

24. This was among the demands of a West African press delegation to London in August 1943. For details of their memorandum, titled, "The Atlantic Charter and British West Africa," which was presented to the British, see its installmental publication in the *Nigerian spokesman*, October 22–30, 1943.

25. From Roosevelt's Fireside Chat, February 23, 1942, reported in *New York Times*, February 24, 1942.

26. For an overview of superpower Cold War competition in Africa, see Adebayo Oyebade, "Africa's International Relations," in Toyin Falola, *Africa*, vol. 5, *Contemporary Africa* (Durham, NC: Carolina Academic Press, 2003), 363–88. Perspectives on Cold War superpower policies in Africa are also provided in George W. Breslauer, ed., *Soviet Policy in Africa* (Berkeley: University of California Press, 1992); Henry Jackson, *From the Congo to Soweto: U.S. Foreign Policy toward Africa since 1960* (New York: W. Morrow, 1982); and Craig R. Nation and Mark V. Kauppi, *The Soviet Impact in Africa* (Lexington, MA: Lexington Books, 1984).

27. There is an abundant literature on the Liberian conflict. See, for example, M. Weller, *Regional Peace-keeping and International Enforcement: The Liberian Crisis* (New York: Grotius Publications, 1994); Abiodun Alao, *The Burden of Collective Goodwill: The International Involvement in the Liberian Civil War* (Brookfield, VT: Ashgate, 1998); and Mark Huband, *The Liberian Civil War* (London: Frank Cass, 1998).

28. Taylor was indicted for war crimes by a UN special tribunal in June 1993 for his role in the Sierra Leone Civil War, especially his support for the RUF, which enabled the rebel organization to carry out an enormous number of atrocities.

29. The civil war in Sierra Leone has been extensively studied. See the following, for instance: Paul Richards, *Fighting for the Rain Forest: War, Youth and Resources in Sierra Leone* (Portsmouth, NH: Heinemann, 1996); Alfred B. Zack-Williams, "Sierra Leone: The Political Economy of Civil War, 1991–1998," *Third World Quarterly* 20, no. 1 (1999); Karl P. Magyar and Earl Conteh-Morgan, eds., *Peacekeeping in Africa: ECO-MOG in Liberia* (New York: St. Martin's Press, 1998); Abass Bundu, *Democracy by Force? A Study of International Military Intervention in the Civil War in Sierra Leone from 1991–2000* (Parkland, FL: Universal Publishers, 2001); Lansana Gberie, *A Dirty War in West Africa: The RUF and the Destruction of Sierra Leone* (London: C. Hurst & Co. 2005); and John-Peter Pham, *Child Soldiers, Adult Interests: Global Dimensions of the Sierra Leonean Tragedy* (New York: Nova Science Publishers, 2005).

30. This subject is further discussed in Adebayo Oyebade, "The Ghost of Somalia: The United States and African Crises in the Post–Cold War Period," *Journal of the Georgia Association of Historians* 25 (2004): 65–90.

31. For details of this policy, see "Clinton Administration Policy on Reforming Multilateral Peace Operations" (PDD25), Bureau of International Organizational Affairs, U.S. Department of State, February 22, 1996, http:www.fas.org/irp/offdocs/pdd25.htm.

32. See, for further analyses of ECOWAS's roles in the crises in Liberia and Sierra Leone, Antonia T. Okoosi, *Global versus Regional Peace-keeping: A Survey of Nigeria's Involvement in the ECOWAS ECOMOG Operation in Liberia* (Ibadan: Nigerian Institute of Social and Economic Research, 1997); Rafiu Adeshina, *The Reversed Victory: The Story of Nigerian Military Intervention in Sierra Leone* (Ibadan: Heinemann Educational Books [Nigeria], 2002); and Adebayo Oyebade, "Restoring Democracy in Sierra Leone: Nigeria's Hegemonic Foreign Policy in West Africa, 1993–1998," in *Nigeria in Global Politics: Twentieth Century and Beyond*, ed. Olayiwola Abegunrin and Olusoji Akomolafe (New York: Nova Science Publishers, 2006), 96–106.

33. CNN.com./World, Monday, July 7, 2003, http://www.cnn.com/2003/WORLD/africa/07/07/liberia/.

34. See "African Crisis Response Initiative (ACRI): A Peacekeeping Alliance in Africa," www.clw.org/pub/clw/un/acri.html; and press statement, U.S. Department of State, Office of the Spokesman, July 17, 1996. For some details on ACRI, see Marshall F. McCallie, "The African Crisis Response Initiative: America's Engagement for Peace in Africa," *Special Warfare* 11, no. 3 (Summer 1998).

35. Tom Ikimi, Nigeria's foreign minister, "Nigeria Opposes U.S. Crisis Response Initiative," Nigeria.Com News, http://london.nigeria.

36. See the letter to the White House by prominent African American leaders in *Post Express* (Lagos, Nigeria), May 23, 1998.

37. *Christian Science Monitor*, April 8, 1988, 20.

38. There have been reports of the kidnapping and detention of oil workers in Nigeria. See Liz George, "Is Oil Drawing Bush to Nigeria?" CNN.com./World, July 8, 2003, http://www.cnn.com/2003/WORLD/africa/07/07/nigeria.oil/index.html.

39. See Bureau for International Narcotics and Law Enforcement Affairs, *International Narcotics Control Strategy Report, 1997* (Washington, DC: U.S. Department of State, March 1988). See also "U.S. Descends on Nigeria over Drugs," *Prime Sunset* (Lagos, Nigeria), March 10, 1998, 1–2.

40. See Susannah Price, "UN pressed over Liberia's Taylor," BBC News, New York, May 24, 2005, http://news.bbc.co.uk/2/hi/africa/4577547.stm.

41. For more on this subject, see Olusoji Akomolafe, "Nigeria, the United States and the War on Terrorism: The Stakes and the Stance," in *Nigeria in Global Politics*, ed. Abegunrin and Akomolafe, 225–43.

42. The words are included in the inscription on the notice at the entrance to the village. Cited in Harry G. Lefever, "Leaving the United States: The Black Nationalist Themes of Orisha-Vodu," *Journal of Black Studies* 31, no. 2 (November 2000): 174.

43. For more studies of the Oyotunji village, see Oba Efuntola Oseijeman Adelabu Adefunmi I, *Olorisha: A Guidebook into Yoruba Religion* (Sheldon, SC: Great Benin, 1982); C. Hunt, *Oyotunji Village* (Washington, DC: University Press of America, 1979); and Mikelle Smith Omari, "Completing the Circle: Notes on African Art, Society, and Religion in Oyotunji, South Carolina," *African Arts* 24, no. 3 (July 1991): 66–75, 96.

44. On this subject, see Doran H. Ross, *Wrapped in Pride: Ghanaian Kente and African American Identity* (Los Angeles: UCLA Fowler Museum of Cultural History, 1998). See also Steven J. Salm and Toyin Falola, *Culture and Customs of Ghana* (Westport, CT: Greenwood Press, 2002).

45. Arthur M. Schlesinger, Jr., *A Thousand Days: John F. Kennedy in the White House* (Cambridge, MA: The Riverside Press, 1985), 551.

2

The U.S. Consulate and the Promotion of Trade in Sierra Leone, 1850–80

Ibrahim Kargbo

The establishment of a U.S. consulate in Freetown in 1858 and the official recognition of American commercial interests by the Department of State clearly underlined the commercial and strategic importance of Sierra Leone along the West African coast by the mid-nineteenth century. The U.S. government, cognizant of that viable and potential market and at the insistence of several prominent New England merchants, officially appointed John E. Taylor to serve as the first American commercial agent to Sierra Leone, a post in which he served from 1858 to 1866.[1]

As commercial agent, John Taylor was primarily responsible for promoting and protecting U.S. commercial interests in Sierra Leone. The American naval vessels that were present in the area were under orders to use force if necessary to expand American commercial interests in West Africa. The secretary of the navy made this objective clearly known to the president of the United States:

> The lack of such a force has enabled the English to exclude us from the most valuable part of the trade of the Gambia and Sierra Leone, and the French to exclude us entirely from Senegal.[2]

The American consulate, which was based in Freetown from 1858 to 1915 and later moved to Dakar, Senegal (where it was based from 1915 to 1931), played a vital role in the expansion of American commercial interests in Sierra Leone and along the West African coast.[3] The general function of the consulate was to promote trade and protect American citizens. Thus, all consular representatives to Sierra Leone were responsible for informing the Department of State, the Department of the Treasury, the Bureau of Foreign and Domestic Commerce, and the Department of the Navy of potential markets for American goods and any internal developments such as uprisings that would affect American commercial interests. They were responsible also for maintaining records of American vessels traveling to and from Sierra Leone, including their cargoes.[4]

The consulate in Freetown was periodically inundated with letters and catalogs from American companies inquiring about trade opportunities in Sierra Leone. Such inquiries included questions about the population of Sierra Leone, British trade restrictions, customs regulations, other countries that had commercial interests in Sierra Leone, the degree or extent of demand for certain goods, and the matter of establishing trade with existing companies already based in Sierra Leone. The regular consular correspondence between Freetown and Washington from 1858 to 1915 was with the Department of State, the Department of the Treasury, the Department of the Navy, and the Bureau of Foreign and Domestic Commerce.[5] These agencies provided American commercial interests with the necessary information on how to develop and maintain trade with Sierra Leone.[6]

American traders, companies, and individual firms relied heavily on the reports of the consular representatives on issues such as market conditions, the means of distributing goods, and information about reliable agents who could handle all commercial transactions in Sierra Leone and other areas along the West African coast.[7] Thus, one of the primary functions of the American consulate in Freetown was the expansion of American commercial interests, and by the end of the nineteenth century Sierra Leone was the only market along the West African coast that attracted considerable American commercial interests.[8]

The recognition of American commercial interests and the establishment of a U.S. consular post in 1858 occurred at a time when the commercial and strategic position of Sierra Leone attracted international attention, particularly among European nations such as Spain, Portugal, France, and the Netherlands, all of which had established consular posts there between 1840 and 1850, and were very much involved in the export and import trade between Freetown and their respective capitals. The total value of trade between Sierra Leone and these nations by 1855 is estimated at £404,862 or 45 percent of the entire trade of Sierra Leone.[9] The establishment of an American consular post and the decision by the Department of State to recognize officially U.S. commercial interests in Sierra Leone were, therefore, a direct result of the lucrative and prosperous commercial relations between European nations and Sierra Leone.[10]

Prior to the establishment of the consulate, American traders had engaged in commerce on a credit basis using resident middlemen and promissory notes. This pattern of trade provided no legal or diplomatic means for American traders to collect payment in the event that these middlemen disappeared because of death or change of residence.[11] With a consulate in

Sierra Leone, however, the practice of deception could be minimized; moreover, the consular representative provided background information on any potential agent or middleman. The following letter from an American company is typical of the requests that the consulate received:

> Dear Sir:
> We have recently had some correspondence referred to us concerning Mr. E.M.P. McCormack, of Freetown. We have been advised that Mr. McCormack is one of the principal merchants in that city but we have not been able to verify this as yet. We will appreciate a letter from you suggesting this gentleman's reliability. We cannot take any steps without knowing that he is a trustworthy man.[12]

The establishment of the consulate was a significant breakthrough for the expansion of commercial relations between the United States and Sierra Leone. Beginning in 1860, an increasing number of American commercial vessels, particularly from Boston, Salem, Baltimore, New York, New Orleans, and Charleston, traveled directly to Sierra Leone with their cargoes or to Liverpool, Bristol, and London for transshipment of their cargoes to British and other foreign vessels bound for Sierra Leone.[13] The numbers of vessels that arrived in Freetown in 1860 were thirty-five from the United States and twenty from other places such as France, Spain, the Netherlands, and Portugal.[14] In noting the rapid increase in the foreign trade of Sierra Leone, the governor of Sierra Leone reported in 1869 that

> The trade of this settlement and the produce exported from the Sierra Leone River is considerably in excess of what it has ever been, resulting mainly from the establishment of trade relations with the United States. The rapid increase of trade is evidenced by the number of steamers now running between England, France, and the United States and this settlement.[15]

Thus, the establishment of the consulate occurred at a time when the foreign trade of Sierra Leone was expanding significantly. The summary of trade returns for the period 1860 to 1865 reflects a tremendous increase in both the value and percentages of foreign trade. The imports into Sierra Leone for this period are estimated at a value of £1,110,900, while for the same period exports reached an estimated value of £1,521,314.[16] In fact, of the four British settlements in West Africa (Sierra Leone, Gold Coast, Gambia, and Lagos), Sierra Leone ranked first in foreign trade not only with the European nations but more particularly with the United States.[17]

The governor's report in 1868 emphasized that there was not only an increase in foreign trade between Sierra Leone and Britain and other European nations but also an increase of considerable importance in trade with the United States, and that the number of American merchants and companies involved in foreign trade with Sierra Leone had increased after

1860.[18] By 1865, there were several American companies and merchants with substantial and expanding commercial interests in Sierra Leone. Among these were Enoch Richard Ware and Company with its headquarters in New York; the Pingree Brothers Company, owned by Thomas and David Pingree, based in Salem; G. Amsinck and Company of New York; Douglas Company of New York; and the joint company of H. Roberts and Justin Rideout, based in Boston.[19]

However, despite the expansion of trade between the United States and Sierra Leone from 1860 to 1865, the American merchants and companies did not establish retail stores in Freetown or anywhere else within Sierra Leone to sell their goods; this was because of market constraints and lack of familiarity with the indigenous inland pattern of trade. Instead, the bulk of American goods was handled and sold either by Sierra Leonean merchants or by European commercial agents, usually recommended by the American consulate as reliable. For instance, an American pharmaceutical company, Harter Medicine Company, established in 1855, requested the consulate to provide information about a prominent Creole merchant in Freetown and his suitability to serve as commercial agent, asking specifically for "some information on J. F. McCarthy of Freetown, regarding his financial standing, business ability, and whether he would meet the business obligations."[20]

As a newly established company, the Harter Medicine Company of Dayton, Ohio, depended on the American consulate in Freetown to furnish all the necessary information on the possibility of expanding its commercial interests, not only in Sierra Leone but throughout West Africa, with Freetown as its center of distribution. This company continued its business operations in Sierra Leone until 1902.[21] The company's aggregate exports to Sierra Leone between 1860 and 1865 reached a total value of about $47,000, or 20 percent of its entire world trade for the same period.[22]

One of the important features of foreign trade with Sierra Leone between 1860 and 1865 was the position of the United States as a viable competitor to Britain as well as other European countries. The total value of American foreign trade with Sierra Leone for this period is estimated at £512,000, or 25 percent of the entire foreign trade of Sierra Leone.[23] The first five years of the American consulate's existence in Freetown were primarily devoted to maintaining and increasing U.S. commercial interests in Sierra Leone, and in his first series of reports Consul John Taylor emphasized the commercial importance of Sierra Leone for American foreign trade:

> Sierra Leone is the natural and most effective inlet for American foreign trade, possessing a more extensive coast line and a larger area of interior country. The leading merchants of Sierra Leone are obliged to keep constantly on hand a large supply of American goods, because of high demand.[24]

The expansion of American commercial interests between 1860 and 1865 coincided with a significant development within Sierra Leone, which had an enormous impact on the increasing demand for imported goods. Between 1850 and 1865, the population of Freetown and the surrounding villages increased from 46,000 to 57,000.[25] According to census returns for the period, the European and American residents in Freetown and other areas, mostly missionaries, merchants, or members of the British navy based in Freetown, accounted for more than 5 percent of the entire population. However, the records fail to provide specific numbers.[26]

In essence, with an increase in population, the market for imported goods significantly expanded. In his annual report of 1861, the governor of Sierra Leone noted this development when he reported that

> The recent population figures for this colony show encouraging signs. The foreign trade for the fiscal year increased tremendously, and no longer can British merchants and trading houses meet the increasing demands for imported goods. Because of their inexpensiveness and durability, American goods are imported in large quantities.[27]

The items mainly responsible for the increase in American trade between 1860 and 1865 were flour, kerosene oil, lumber, and rum. There was a significant decline in the import of cotton and tobacco because of the American Civil War. At the same time the United States imported large quantities of hides, palm oil, ginger, peanuts, and camwood. Indeed, the position of the United States in foreign trade with Sierra Leone since the establishment of the consulate improved so much that British merchants who had long since dominated the market in Freetown began to protest as early as 1860, asking the British government to control American commercial interests along the entire West African coast.[28]

The protest was initiated by the London based British Mercantile Association, of which British merchants and trading houses with extensive commercial interests in West Africa were members. It was opposed to the increasing share of the United States in foreign trade with Sierra Leone and other British areas on the West African coast. In a petition to the foreign secretary in 1861, the association stressed that unless action was taken to curtail American commercial interests in West Africa, the British mercantile trade was about to lose a vital market.[29] It observed that

> The trade of West Africa had recently been dominated by American merchants, because of their cheap and inexpensive goods. The British merchants can no longer compete with them, and even our governor in the colony of Sierra Leone recently reported on the growth of American trade with merchants of that settlement. Please we request that you pass some laws to protect British merchants.[30]

However, the Sierra Leone Mercantile Association, which was based in Freetown and was composed of indigenous and British merchants who were advocates of American trade with Sierra Leone, opposed any attempt by the foreign secretary to interfere with that flourishing trade.[31] Since most of these merchants were hired as commercial agents for individual American merchants as well as companies, any law to prohibit the importation of goods from the United States was seen as protectionism and in violation of the principle of free trade enunciated by the British Parliament in 1849. In fact, one of the early Creole newspapers in Freetown, the *New Era*, in an article published in 1859, strongly opposed trade restrictions.[32]

The official policy of the British government on trade was based on the principle of free trade for all nations. However, with regard to American commercial interests in Sierra Leone between 1860 and 1865, the principle of free trade was not implemented by the governor. In fact, between 1862 and 1865, several ordinances were enacted primarily to protect British commercial interests in Sierra Leone against the rapidly expanding economic interests of Americans. Thus, in February 1862 an ordinance for the further regulation of the Freetown harbor was passed to control the activities of American commercial vessels.[33]

The U.S. Department of State was bitterly opposed to this ordinance, and in a letter of protest to the British foreign secretary, the American secretary of state expressed the feelings of merchants who had been involved in foreign trade along the West African coast since the early nineteenth century:

> We deeply resent any attempt by your government to interfere in the smooth conduct of commerce and trade along the West African region. We have been informed by our consulate in Freetown that the ordinance of February 17, 1862, will restrict American commercial vessels and prevent the free flow of trade. This ordinance is in violation of the idea of free trade.[34]

However, the British Foreign Office maintained that the purpose of the ordinance was not to restrict American commercial vessels but primarily to regulate the flow of certain goods into Freetown, particularly weapons that entered the harbor undeclared. In March 1862, another ordinance was passed to authorize the governor of Sierra Leone to prohibit arms and ammunition from being imported into or carried coastwise beyond Freetown. This ordinance was an amendment to that of February 1862.[35]

The attempt to regulate American commercial interests in Sierra Leone did not cease with the amended ordinance of March 1862, because the British Mercantile Association continued to advocate trade restrictions and the protection of British merchants against American competition. In July 1862, for example, still another ordinance amended "all the laws in force respecting the delivery of all goods for home consumption from the bonded warehouses in Freetown."[36] The purpose of this ordinance was to allow the controller of customs in Freetown to deliver more British goods to the market to diminish the demand for American goods, which had wide market appeal. This measure had significant adverse economic consequences for the foreign trade of Sierra Leone in the second half of 1862.

The trade from July 1862 to December 1862 was exceptionally bad, and this was due specifically to the ordinance of July 1862.[37] The foreign trade of the United States with Sierra Leone showed a substantial decline for the period July to December 1862, and the American consul in Freetown recognized this in his annual report:

> The trade of the United States with Sierra Leone for the period July to December 1862 declined significantly. The recent ordinance has drastically cut down the demand for American goods among the people. I am afraid if the State Department allows this policy to continue American commercial interest in West Africa will disappear.[38]

The move to control American commercial interests continued in 1863 with the enactment of a series of ordinances designed to impose taxes and duty on all imported goods, but more specifically on goods from the United States. In March 1863, an ordinance to increase customs duties on all spirituous liquor and wine was passed in England and implemented by the Legislative Council in Sierra Leone.[39] This ordinance raised all customs fees on any form of alcoholic beverage imported into Freetown, a commodity mainly imported from the United States. Furthermore, this ordinance increased the duty paid on certain products exported from Sierra Leone, particularly animal skins, hides, and palm oil, for which there was a considerable demand in the United States.[40]

The role of the American consulate became extremely important between 1860 and 1865. Even the governor remarked in one of his annual reports that since the establishment of the American consulate in Freetown, the position of the United States in the foreign trade of Sierra Leone had become stronger and that, through the consulate, the Department of State was well informed of any major legislation that interfered with American commercial interests along the West African coast.[41] Moreover, the report continued, Consul John Taylor, within a short span of time, had gained the confidence of the Freetown business community, where a large number of trading agents was hired to handle goods for American companies and merchants.[42] Despite all the stringent trade restrictions, U.S. foreign trade with Sierra Leone between 1860 and 1865 was substantial and encouraging. It accounted for 25 percent of the entire foreign trade of Sierra Leone for the same period.[43]

The opportunity for the United States to expand its foreign trade with Sierra Leone became more intensive between 1865 and 1870. With the end of the American Civil War, U.S. commodities such as cotton cloth, raw cotton, and tobacco, which had declined drastically in both volume and value between 1860 and 1865, were exported in large quantities, and the trade figures for this period indicate that of all American goods exported to Sierra Leone, those products accounted for about 55 percent.[44] The decline in import of these commodities into Sierra Leone during the years 1860 to 1865 created a scarcity that resulted in higher purchase prices, but despite the higher prices a larger domestic demand developed in Sierra Leone, as declared in the consular report of 1865:

> The most important American exports to Sierra Leone and West Africa generally are cotton cloth, raw cotton, and tobacco. These goods are in high demand, particularly our cotton goods which are in much request among the natives because of their thickness and similitude to their own fabric. Lately, some goods were imported from Portugal, but they are not of high quality.[45]

The years between 1865 and 1870 were crucial in the history of American foreign trade with Sierra Leone. During those years the United States increased its imports from Sierra Leone, particularly palm oil and animal skins. The total American foreign trade with Sierra Leone for this period reached an estimated value of £700,500, an increase of 10 percent over the trade figures for the years 1860 to 1865.[46] The increase in the import of palm oil and animal skins was a result of a boom in the leather, shoe, soap, and lubrication industries in the United States. The large import of animal skins, for example, was to meet the increasing demand for leather goods, while palm oil was primarily imported in large quantities for use in manufacturing soap and lubricating greases.[47]

The Exporters' Association of America, an organization of American manufacturers, bankers, and carriers, which was primarily devoted to the expansion of American trade abroad, became directly involved in the promotion of American trade with Sierra Leone.[48] This association had as its affiliates several new companies, as well as private merchants with considerable interests in trade with Sierra Leone. Among the companies were H. Becker and Company of New York, Bonn and Spencer Company of New York, William Broadhurst and Company of New York, and Jacob H. Bloom and Company of New York.[49]

These companies imported palm oil, cocoa, animal skins, ginger, peanuts, and coconut oil from Sierra Leone and West Africa generally, while among their exports were shoes, soap, cotton goods, grain, rock salt, lumber, and other general merchandise.[50] The association, through the consulate in Freetown, informed these companies of market conditions and the general pattern of trade in Sierra Leone and along the West African coast. The following letter from the association to the American consulate in Freetown illustrates this point:

In recent searches we have been making for localities which produce large quantities of palm oil, nuts, and seeds, we have learned of the fact that palm oil and cocoa are produced in large quantities in Sierra Leone. On behalf of some large manufacturers of machines and presses for making oil, we are venturing to apply to you for a full and detailed report in this connection. We are endeavoring to find and develop new markets for them.[51]

In 1866, the association recommended to the Department of State the appointment of Henry Rider as consul to Sierra Leone to further enhance the expansion of American commercial interests. The department accepted the recommendation, and in May 1866 Rider became the new U.S. consul.[52] As a prominent merchant who had been involved in foreign trade, Rider was expected by the Exporters' Association of America to strengthen American commercial interests in Sierra Leone, and during his tenure, 1861 to 1866,[53] the role of the consulate in the expansion of trade increased.

In September 1866, the consulate requested and received from the Department of State a periodic listing of all companies and private merchants interested in the establishment of commercial relations with Sierra Leone.[54] This list enabled the consulate to determine the kind of commodities produced by some of the companies and the level of demand for such goods in Sierra Leone. This was the first time the consulate attempted to develop a base for a steady trade in Sierra Leone.

By 1867, several companies had officially registered with the Departments of State, Commerce, and the Treasury to begin direct trade with Sierra Leone. Among these companies were Fidanque Brothers and Sons of Baltimore, a company established in 1865; and H. S. Henry and Son of Boston, a company established in 1848.[55] These companies exported shoes, kerosene oil, and lamps, while they imported from Sierra Leone palm oil, animal skins, palm kernels, and peanuts.

Consul Rider made several recommendations to the Departments of State and Commerce and American companies on how to strengthen and expand commercial relations with Sierra Leone.[56] His previous experience on the East African coast made him sensitive to the concerns of both private merchants and large companies trading in Sierra Leone.[57] He recommended the transfer of the consulate from its original location to a larger building on Water Street, which was then the main commercial hub of Freetown. To underscore the commercial significance of the move, Rider gave this explanation in a letter to the Department of State in 1867:

The commerce of Sierra Leone has been expanding rapidly, and it is very much important for the United States to get a good share of this trade. Several other consulates in this colony have extended their commercial activities beyond Freetown. Also, they have increased their staff and recently Portugal, France, and the Netherlands moved their consulates to Water Street. If we are to continue our good commercial relations with this colony, we must follow the example of these countries.[58]

In June 1867, the Department of State approved the recommendation to increase the consulate staff and move to Water Street.[59] After 1867, the nature of American trade with Sierra Leone began to change in response to the pressure on the colonial government in Freetown to tighten trade sanctions on American goods. The British Mercantile Association and its affiliate members were extremely concerned about the Department of State's decision to increase the staff and relocate the consulate. The association perceived these developments as heralding an increasing commitment to American commercial interests and their further expansion. In fact, the representative of the association expressed serious concern in a letter of protest to the governor in 1867:

> The British Mercantile Association and its members are very much concerned about the continued expansion of American trade in this settlement. The decision to move the United States consulate to Water Street will create serious competition for the control of trade. The new Consul, Mr. Rider had increased the staff of the consulate five of whom are Creole merchants.[60]

Meanwhile, the influence of the association had declined, not only among indigenous merchants in Sierra Leone but also in England, particularly among merchants in Liverpool, Manchester, Glasgow, and Birmingham. For a long time, merchants in these areas had been discriminated against by the association, which was dominated by London merchants. In 1865, the disgruntled merchants formed a new trade organization, the British Export and Import Association, based in Liverpool.[61]

This new group extended its commercial ties in Liverpool, Manchester, Birmingham, and Glasgow. The Exporters' Association of America was the first to recognize the new group.[62] Even the American consulate in Freetown expressed satisfaction over the formation of this new organization. The British Export and Import Association gave a significant boost to American commercial interests in Sierra Leone, and this changed the pattern of U.S. trade after 1867.

Unlike the British Mercantile Association, which had long advocated severe trade restrictions on American trade, the British Export and Import Association advocated free trade for all nations.[63] As a newly established association with limited capital to invest in foreign trade, the Export and Import Association expressed an interest in becoming a commercial agent for American companies and transshipping their goods from ports in Liverpool, Bristol, London, or Lancashire to several parts of Africa, particularly Sierra Leone. The American consulate in Freetown increasingly received letters, bulletins, and advertisements from interested merchants in Glasgow, Liverpool, Manchester, and Birmingham. This was a major breakthrough for

American commercial interests because after 1867, goods were shipped to all these ports and transshipped to Sierra Leone by merchants who were members of the British Export and Import Association. In an 1868 report, for example, the consul explained to the Department of State the change in the pattern of U.S. trade with Sierra Leone and the role played by merchants in Glasgow, Liverpool, London, and Bristol:

> The foreign trade of the United States with Sierra Leone since the formation of the British Export and Import Association is very encouraging. This consulate received several letters from merchants in Bristol, London, Liverpool, and Glasgow, who are interested to represent American companies all over Africa.[64]

The formation of the British Export and Import Association had a significant impact in shaping the direction of American trade between 1868 and 1872, which was a matter of major concern to the colonial government. In fact, by 1868 there was a drastic decline in the total revenue collected from customs fees and taxes imposed on imports because, after 1867, American goods entered Sierra Leone as imports from the United Kingdom and were subjected to lower customs duties and taxes.[65] The gross revenue collected by the Customs Department between 1865 and 1867 amounted to £75,000. However, the total customs revenue for fiscal years 1867 to 1869 was only £40,000.[66]

The Legislative Council in Freetown enacted a series of laws between 1868 and 1870 to deal with this problem.[67] These laws were intended to obtain accurate information from exporters and importers on the origins of cargoes and their ultimate destination. Although some commercial representatives of American companies in Liverpool, Glasgow, Manchester, and Birmingham were willing to cooperate with the colonial government, the condition of trade generally on the West African coast made accurate information on commerce difficult to secure. Thus, these laws were circumvented and American goods continued to enter Sierra Leone registered as imports from the United Kingdom.

The foreign trade of Sierra Leone continued to show signs of expansion, despite the decline in revenue collected by the Customs Department. Between 1870 and 1875, total foreign trade reached a value of £2,556,845.[68] The number of vessels that entered the port of Freetown, as well as other ports, for that year was 344, of which 247 were registered as colonial vessels from the United Kingdom, 29 registered as from the United States, and 16 registered as French, while the rest had German, Portuguese, Italian, Austrian, Norwegian, Greek, Scandinavian, and Liberian registry. The colonial-registered vessels, according to their cargo manifests, carried various American goods registered as goods from the United Kingdom.[69]

This expansion of Sierra Leone's trade attracted considerable American interest between 1870 and 1875. The consulate continued to be instrumental in the expansion of trade and, at the same time, kept the Department of State and the Department of Commerce informed of any major developments such as trade legislation. Prior to his 1872 recall,[70] Consul Rider, in a confidential letter to the Department of State in 1871, emphasized the commercial importance of Sierra Leone and the fact that the U.S. government must maintain a highly visible presence:

> The commerce of the colony is too important for the United States to ignore. The number of American companies trading here since 1860 had increased year after year. We must keep this consular post open, if not our traders and vessels will be excluded from the commerce of this region. I recommend that in the future, we appoint one consul and one chief commercial agent for this consulate.[71]

The recommendation to keep the consulate in Freetown open was primarily a result of the temporary closing of the American consulate at Bathurst, Gambia, from 1867 to 1872.[72] During that time the consulate in Freetown became the only American consular post in a British colony along the West African coast. In 1872, the Department of State appointed a new consul to replace Consul Henry Rider at the Freetown post and, at the same time, the consulate at Bathurst was reopened. The new consul appointed to Sierra Leone, William Hogan, arrived in Freetown in June 1872,[73] at a time when American commercial interests were expanding.

The position of the United States in the foreign trade of Sierra Leone was further strengthened between 1870 and 1875. The total American trade for this period reached a value of £885,000, an increase of about 5 percent over the trade for the period 1865 to 1870.[74] However, this estimate does not include American goods that entered Sierra Leone as imports from the United Kingdom, particularly from Liverpool, Birmingham, Manchester, and Glasgow.

The favorable position of the United States resulted from two major developments between 1870 and 1875. The first was the severe economic depression in Europe in the 1870s[75] and the second was the general revision of tariffs in Sierra Leone in 1872.[76] Both of these developments contributed to the expansion of American commercial interests in West Africa and heightened the role of the consulate in Freetown.

Britain's share of world trade and world industrial production declined in the early 1870s, while that of the United States substantially increased. With the progress in industrial techniques and their diffusion in other countries, the advantages long enjoyed by British industrialists were lessened and Britain was confronted by severe competition, especially from the United States and Germany.[77] Thus, by 1875 Britain's preeminent industrial production had eroded perceptibly, while the United States and Germany developed their industrial production and exported manufactures in competition with Britain.

The second major development was the general revision of tariffs by the colonial government in 1872.[78] In 1872, the Legislative Council passed an ordinance to amend all existing customs regulations and introduced a new tariff system, which abolished the general and ad valorem duty and repealed all specific duties established in Sierra Leone since the 1820s.[79] Moreover, the new law made the following articles free to enter the port of Freetown without customs duty: bread, bacon, beef, biscuits, candles, clocks, flour, soap, tea, sugar, timber, and cheese.[80]

This tariff system also abolished the wharf fees and reduced the tonnage fees on all vessels that entered the port of Freetown.[81] These aspects of the new tariff directly benefited shipping interests, as shown by the large number of vessels that entered the port of Freetown after 1872.[82] Among these were American vessels loaded with large consignments of goods declared duty-free by the new tariff. However, the tariff of 1872 increased customs duties on alcoholic beverages, tobacco, and gunpowder, of which the United States was the largest exporter, but the increased duties on these commodities did not diminish the level of demand and importation, as the governor reported in 1873:

> The recent increase of customs duties on rum, tobacco, and gunpowder did not alter the importation of these commodities in large volumes. The consequence is that after meeting the large remissions of direct taxation, and providing for the reforms made in the other parts of the new tariff, the additional increase obtained from the new duties on spirits, tobacco, and gunpowder, has left a considerable surplus and high demand.[83]

The tariff of 1872 increased the demand for more American goods and attracted considerable attention in the United States, particularly among exporters of commodities such as flour, soap, candles, salted pork and beef, biscuits, clocks, tea, timber, sugar, and tobacco.[84] Between 1870 and 1890, several companies registered with the consulate in Freetown to establish commercial relations with leading firms or merchants interested in handling American goods.[85]

Among the companies that registered with the consulate during this period were Yates and Porterfield Company of New York, Getz Brothers and Company of San Francisco, Jas Goody and Company of Baltimore, Sawyer Crystal Blue Company of Boston, Pillsbury Flour Mills of Minneapolis, and Walter Baker and Company of Boston.[86]

One of these companies, Getz Brothers and Company, which was established in 1871, expressed interest in the expansion of the foreign trade of Sierra Leone in a letter to the American consul in 1872. This company had exclusive agency rights over several of the largest manufacturers of soap, candles, biscuits, and cotton fabrics, for which there was an expanding market in Sierra Leone and West Africa generally.

American Consul Henry Rider, in his annual report of 1871 to the Department of State, emphasized the growing importance of Sierra Leone as a lucrative and potential market for American companies:

> Sierra Leone is the major commercial center along the west coast of Africa. The opportunity for American trade in this colony is abundant. There is an increasing demand for our products not only in this colony but all over the coast. The trade for the past year was good, and this consulate will seek more markets for our merchants.[87]

As American trade with Sierra Leone expanded in the 1870s, changes were made within the consulate in Freetown to handle the proliferation of American commercial interests. These changes were in response to a growing concern among several American companies and private merchants over the conduct of trade along the West African coast, particularly the conduct of trade by some companies that were not registered with the consulate in Freetown as required by the Department of State and Department of Commerce.[88]

Some of these unregistered companies and merchants had fraudulently used the names of prominent companies so as to indicate that the lower-quality goods sold by the unregistered companies were actually products from prominent registered companies. One of the major markets for such goods was Sierra Leone, where, according to a Department of State report in 1871, several unregistered companies had been involved in such illegal trade practices, and as a result the sale of genuine goods by prominent American companies had been made impossible. Such practices, the report maintained, deprived the genuine manufacturers and companies of their profits and also damaged their international reputations as producers of high-quality goods.[89]

The Departments of State and Commerce became increasingly concerned about the broader implications of such illegal trade and its impact on American trade with Sierra Leone, especially since Freetown was the only port along the coast of West Africa where there were significant American commercial interests in the 1870s.[90] Moreover, there was a growing resentment among British commercial interests because of the expanding U.S. commercial relations with Sierra Leone. The British Foreign Office received several petitions of protest from companies in London, Manchester, and Birmingham demanding that severe restrictions should be imposed on American trade.[91]

It was against this background that the newly appointed American consul, William Hogan, was instructed by the Department of State to formulate and implement specific guidelines to prevent illegal trade practices by American commercial interests.[92] The consul, in his annual report, emphasized the importance of continuing to improve trade relations with Sierra Leone:

The growth of foreign trade in this colony for the past year has been rapid and remarkable. The market for the sale of American goods is a good one. There is a demand constantly for tobacco, cotton cloth, kerosene, pots, pans, flour, guns, and gunpowder. We are implementing new guidelines to protect our trade.[93]

One of the major changes in the trade guidelines formulated by Consul Hogan in 1873 involved the shipping and handling of tobacco, cotton fabrics, guns, gunpowder, and kerosene oil, commodities for which there was a significant demand all over West Africa. According to a report by the U.S. Treasury Department, these goods accounted for about 65 percent of the total American trade with Sierra Leone, and the increased demand for these goods was of major concern to British commercial interests, which constantly petitioned the Foreign Office to ban the importation of these goods from the United States into Freetown.[94]

The Foreign Office, in consultation with the governor in Freetown, recommended the introduction of a new tariff in 1874 primarily designed to reduce the level of American exports to Sierra Leone by increasing taxes on goods on which American commercial interests had a virtual monopoly.[95]

This tariff, however, like others in previous years, did not diminish the level of American exports to Sierra Leone. In fact, at the recommendation of the consulate in Freetown, more American companies established commercial relations in the country. In a commercial report, the consul issued the following statement to American merchants:

In order to enjoy the benefits which might result in the import of trade into Freetown, it would be almost necessary that American merchants establish branches here or appoint others as their representatives to conduct direct trade between Sierra Leone and the United States.[96]

The effort to increase foreign trade was well illustrated in the U.S. Congress when, in 1868, a joint select committee pointed out that it was necessary for all American consulates to publish commercial reports. Such reports, the committee maintained, had to be issued under the auspices of the State Department and made accessible to all merchants and manufacturers involved in foreign trade.[97]

Prior to the 1870s, the role of the consuls in the promotion and protection of American commercial interests was limited and unorganized. There was no official order from the Department of State on how to conduct and report on trade. However, as the need to expand foreign trade increased in the 1870s, the Department of State became increasingly involved in utilizing consular offices for the promotion and protection of trade.

As American domestic trade continued to decline, the State Department issued the following instruction to all the consular representatives abroad:

The present stagnation of prices in the United States favors foreign trade. It is the desire of the department that diplomatic and consular officers should devote attention to the question of methods by which trade with the United States can be most judiciously fostered. Consuls should inform the department on the kinds of manufactured articles now used in their districts, their nature and prices, and whether the United States can supply them.[98]

The consuls who served in Sierra Leone after the 1870s were appointed by the Department of State because of their long involvement in and knowledge of the patterns of trade along the West African coast. Some of these consular representatives had served as commercial agents for private merchants or large American trading companies in West Africa. Thus, they were familiar with market conditions as well as European policies of trade protectionism and were vigorously involved in the promotion and protection of American commercial interests.

In 1874, William Henry Randall was appointed consul, replacing William Hogan.[99] Prior to his appointment, Randall had served as a commercial agent in Freetown for the Boston company of Roberts and Mansfield. During his tenure as consul, there was an increase in the trade between the United States and Sierra Leone. The total trade between 1874 and 1878, for example, reached a value of £297,274.[100] However, the value of some commodities such as palm oil, hides, guns, copal, and peanuts declined because of an increase in export duties imposed in 1874.[101]

The colonial government had expected substantial increases in revenues and the restriction of American commercial interests after the tariff of 1874 was imposed. However, because foreign vessels traveled directly into the interior to trade and thus avoided payment of duties, there was a significant decline in revenues collected from export duties. The governor had to request an increase in appropriation from the Colonial Office in London to offset the loss of these revenues.[102]

The pattern of American trade changed between 1878 and 1880 because of the failure of the tariff of 1874 to prevent foreign commercial interests from trading directly in the interior regions of the country. Vessels from the United States and Europe carried cargoes beyond the port of Freetown into the Melakori and Scarcies Rivers, areas outside the colonial jurisdiction where all trade restriction laws were inapplicable.[103] Thus, several American vessels avoided the port of Freetown and enjoyed the lucrative trade in the interior.

Meanwhile, the British government attempted to put an end to this problem by authorizing the governor in 1879 to annex the Melakori and Scarcies Rivers and proclaim them under colonial jurisdiction.[104] Since American and French traders avoided the port of Freetown because of customs duties, the governor extended all customs duty laws into these newly annexed areas.

The French traders supported by French troops refused to recognize the British colonial claims and occupied the disputed territory until the British and French governments settled the dispute. The settlement allowed the French to annex the Melakori River, Rio Nunez, and Rio Pongo; while the British annexed the Scarcies River, Metacong, and territories along the northern rivers of Sierra Leone.[105]

Since the United States had no colonial claims in the disputed territory, the overall commercial interests of American traders were jeopardized by the settlement. The annexation of such lucrative commercial areas gave the colonial government in Freetown the ultimate power to impose all trade restriction laws on American and other foreign vessels that bypassed the port of Freetown. Moreover, the annexation of the northern rivers meant that the colonial government could proclaim any major commercial areas as part of its sphere of interests.[106]

The United States made its position clear in a letter that Consul Judson Lewis[107] wrote to the governor and the Legislative Council:

> The government of the United States remains opposed to any law or proclamation which obstruct trade between its citizens and people of this colony. The trade of this colony must remain open to American and other merchants who are not protected by your flag.[108]

These developments occurred on the eve of the Berlin Conference and were crucial for the expansion of American commercial interests in Sierra Leone and Africa generally. The commerce of Africa had been lucrative and had attracted American traders for several decades.[109] Moreover, the U.S. government was determined to see that the policy of open trade was adhered to by all European nations in any partitioning of Africa into spheres of interest. Thus, the active participation of the American delegates to the Berlin Conference was primarily intended to seek assurances from the European powers on the issue of open trade for American merchants.[110]

Notes

1. "American Merchants and the Trade of Sierra Leone," Document no. 86, Records of the Department of State, Record Group (RG) 59, National Archives and Records Administration, Washington, DC (NARA). Among these merchants were David and Thomas Pingree, Justin Rideout, N. B. Mansfield, H. O. Roberts, and Enoch Richard Ware, all of whom had traded extensively with Sierra Leone since the 1840s. See also George E. Brooks, *Yankee Traders, Old Coasters and African Middlemen: A History of American Legitimate Trade with West Africa in the Nineteenth Century* (Brookline, MA: Boston University Press, 1970), 217–19; U.S. Department of State and Consular Officers, August 1868, Records of the Department of State, RG 59, NARA.

2. Letter from Navy Secretary Isaac Toucey to President James Buchanan, November 1860, Document no. 886.1934, Records of the Department of State, RG 59, NARA.

3. The Register of the Department of State: American Consular Officers, 1880–1940, Records of the Department of State, RG 59, NARA.

4. Chester L. Jones, *The Consular Service of the United States: Its History and Activities* (Philadelphia: University of Pennsylvania Publications, 1906), 59–86. See E. J. Alagoa, "Preliminary Inventory of the Records of the United States Diplomatic and Consular Posts in West Africa, 1856–1935," *Journal of the Historical Society of Nigeria* 1 (1960): 78–104.

5. Outgoing and Incoming Correspondence, 1789–1944, Sierra Leone File, Records of the Department of State, RG 59, NARA.

6. Annual Publications on American Trade with Sierra Leone; Miscellaneous Correspondence, Numerical File 1789–1906 and Decimal File 1906–1944, Sierra Leone File, Records of the Department of State, RG 59, NARA.

7. E. J. Alagoa, "Preliminary Inventory of the Records of the United States Diplomatic and Consular Posts in West Africa, 1856–1935," *Journal of the Historical Society of Nigeria* 2 (December 1963): 78–104.

8. Brooks, *Yankee Traders, Old Coasters and African Middlemen*, 218.

9. Colonial Office (CO) 272/36, Blue Books of Trade and Statistics, Sierra Leone, 1845–60, Public Record Office London (PRO). Also see Foreign Consuls, *Sierra Leone Gazette*, 1840–50, PRO.

10. American Consuls in Sierra Leone, 1858–1915, Document no. 194, Records of the Department of State, RG 59, NARA.

11. George E. Brooks, "Enoch Richard Ware, African Trader, 1839–1850, Years of Apprenticeship," *The American Neptune, Journal of Maritime History* 30 (July 1970): 174–86.

12. Letter from the Philadelphia Commercial Museum to Hon. John T. Williams, United States Consul, Freetown, Sierra Leone, October 17, 1902, Records of the Department of State, RG 59, NARA.

13. CO 272/34/385, Trade and Port Privileges, Sierra Leone Customs Report on Vessel Clearances, PRO.

14. CO 272/34/479, Customs Record no. 29, Blue Books of Statistics, Sierra Leone, PRO.

15. CO 272/46, Dispatch no. 19 from Governor Arthur Kennedy to the British Foreign Office, June 1870, PRO.

16. CO 272/43, Group no. 2, Blue Books of Trade and Statistics, Sierra Leone, 1860–85, PRO.

17. CO 271/35, Reports on the Foreign Trade of Sierra Leone, Annual Reports nos. 16–70, Blue Books of Trade and Statistics, Sierra Leone, 1860–75, PRO.

18. CO 272/49, Government Publications Relating to Sierra Leone, 1808–1961, Document no. 96978/3, PRO. See also the Governor's Annual Report; *Sierra Leone Gazette*, 1870, PRO.

19. American Merchants and Companies in Sierra Leone, Document no. 880/17604B, Annual Consular Reports from Sierra Leone, 1850–70, Records of the Department of State, RG 59, NARA. See also Brooks, *Yankee Traders, Old Coasters and African Middlemen*, 216–19.

20. Letter from Dr. Harter, Harter Medicine Company, Dayton, Ohio, to the U.S. Consulate, Freetown, Sierra Leone, May 6, 1860, Document B/82, Collection Department, Records of the Department of State, RG 59, NARA.

21. *American Trade Index* (New York: National Association of Manufacturers, 1906), 85–102.

22. Ibid., 85–102.

23. CO 272/37–272/42, Document nos. 96354/45–97892/35, Blue Books of Trade and Statistics, Sierra Leone, 1860–65, PRO.

24. American Consular Reports, 1840–90, African Consular Department File, Records of the Department of State, RG 59, NARA.

25. CO 272/27–CO 272/42, "Annual Population Figures," Blue Books 1850–65, PRO. Also see Robert R. Kuczynski, *Demographic Survey of the British Colonial Empire* (Fairfield, NJ: A. M. Kelley, 1977), 1:154–60.

26. CO 272/44; Foreign Residents in Sierra Leone, *Sierra Leone Gazette*, 1850–65, PRO.

27. CO 267/38, Annual Report of the Governor of Sierra Leone, Document no. 951176/86, *Sierra Leone Gazette*, 1862, PRO.

28. British Merchants and American Trade in West Africa, Document no. 882/1163B, Reports from the United States Consul, Freetown, Sierra Leone, 1862, Records of the Department of State; RG 59, NARA. See also CO 271/28, American Trade in Sierra Leone, *Sierra Leone Gazette*, 1866, PRO.

29. CO 806/451, Petition to the Foreign Secretary for Trade Restrictions in West Africa, Report in the British Foreign Office Papers, 1825–70, PRO; Document no. 84639/113, British Library, London.

30. CO 272/38, Petition to the British Foreign Secretary from the British Mercantile Association; Document no. 96978/5, *Sierra Leone Gazette*, 1862, PRO.

31. CO 272/39, Appeal from the Sierra Leone Mercantile Association on Trade with the United States, Document no. 97543/6, *Sierra Leone Gazette*, 1862; PRO.

32. The *New Era*, which was founded in 1855, was the first Sierra Leone newspaper owned by a private individual: this was William Drape, who emigrated to Sierra Leone from Jamaica. The newspaper, which was short-lived, criticized the colonial government's position on trade. See CO 267/279 for bound volumes, PRO.

33. CO 272/39, An Ordinance for the Further Regulation of the Harbor in Freetown, February 17, 1862, Ordinances, PRO.

34. CO 272/36, American Protest to the Foreign Office, Document no. 76359/18–25B, U.S. Department of State, General and Confidential Correspondence, 1840–75, PRO.

35. CO 272/39, An Ordinance to Authorize the Governor of the Colony of Sierra Leone to Prohibit Arms and Ammunition, March 1, 1862 (Proclaimed in England), Document no. 96978/7, Ordinances, PRO.

36. CO 272/39, An Ordinance to Amend the Laws in Force Respecting the Delivery of Goods for Home Consumption from the Bonded Warehouse Established in the Colony, July 20, 1862 (Proclaimed in England), Document no. 98975/11, Ordinances, PRO.

37. CO 272/39, Decline in Trade, July–December 1862, Books of Trade and Statistics, Sierra Leone, Document Ser. no. 8463B/9341, PRO.

38. Report from the United States Consul, Hon. John E. Taylor, Freetown, Sierra Leone, Document no. 882/1561C, Records of the Department of State, RG 59, NARA.

39. CO. 272/41, An Ordinance for Altering the Duties on Spirituous Liquor and Wine, March 20, 1863 (Proclaimed in London), Document no. 101562/893F, Ordinances, PRO.

40. CO 272/41, An Ordinance to Raise Custom Dues on Duty upon Certain Articles on the Exportation Thereof from Sierra Leone, March 20, 1863 (Proclaimed in London), Document no. 102563/895F, Ordinances, PRO.

41. CO 272/44, Annual Report of the Governor in the Colony of Sierra Leone, 1863, 50–56, PRO.

42. Ibid., 60–67.

43. CO 272/496, "American Trade Increase," Annual Colonial Report on Trade, #90651, PRO.

44. Report on American Trade with West Africa Submitted by the Chief Officer Department of Commerce, Document no. 882/00/1076, Records of the Department of State, RG 59, NARA.

45. Reports from the United States Consul, Hon. John E. Taylor, Freetown, Sierra Leone, 1865, Records of the Department of State, RG 59, NARA.

46. CO 272/42–47, Blue Books of Trade and Statistics, Sierra Leone, 1865–70, PRO.

47. Report on Imports for Industrial Manufacturing, Document no. 95634/1143G, Bureau of Statistics, Records of the Department of Treasury, RG 56, NARA.

48. *Export Trade Directory* (New York: The Johnson Export Publishing Co., 1915), 20–25.

49. Ibid., 20–25.

50. Report on Exports to West Africa, Document no. 95637/1145H, Bureau of Statistics, Records of the Department of Treasury, RG 56, NARA. See Reports of the Secretary of the Treasury, Commerce, and Navigation of the United States, 1869, RG 56, NARA.

51. The Exporters' Association of America and the Expansion of Trade with Sierra Leone; Letter to the Hon. John E. Taylor, United States Consul, Freetown, February 10, 1866, Document no. 10104/63A, Records of the Department of State, RG 59, NARA.

52. The bulk of the letters sent to the American consulate came from merchants in New York, Boston, Salem, New Orleans, and Baltimore. Several of these merchants were attracted by the appointment of Consul Henry Rider.

53. Register of American Consular Officers, 1850–75, Records of the Department of State, RG 59, NARA.

54. Report from Consul Rider on How to Improve Trade with the Colony of Sierra Leone, Document no. 880.11674B, Dispatch from Freetown, Sierra Leone, September 6, 1866, Records of the Department of State, RG 59, NARA.

55. CO 272/44, Governor's Annual Report on the Trade of Sierra Leone, 1867, *Sierra Leone Gazette*, 1868, PRO. See section on American companies, 63–70.

56. Recommendations to Increase American Trade in Sierra Leone, Document no. 880.37263/B, Daily Consular Reports, Records of the Department of State, RG 59, NARA.

57. Consul Henry Rider was a New England trader from Boston and was among several merchants who traded extensively along the East African coast.

58. Letters from the American Consul, Henry Rider, Freetown, Sierra Leone, 1866–72, Records of the Department of State, RG 59, NARA.

59. CO 267/33, Letter to the Governor of Sierra Leone from the United States Department of State with Reference to the Relocation of the American Consulate and Staff Increase, June 24, 1867, PRO.

60. CO 267/33, British Mercantile Association Enclosure to the Governor of the Colony of Sierra Leone, American Trade with Sierra Leone, Confidential Dispatch, September 26, 1867, PRO.

61. CO 267/943, Document no. 11934, Governor's Report on the British Export and Import Association's Interest on Trade in Sierra Leone, PRO.

62. This report also identified the Exporters' Association of America as the first non-British association to recognize the new group.

63. CO 267/45, PRO. In a petition to the Foreign Office in August 1865, the members of the British Export and Import Association called for free trade and argued that if foreign merchants found a market for certain of their goods in Britain, mostly higher quality goods and also inexpensive goods in regard to which they had a comparative cost advantage, they must be allowed to trade with British citizens.

64. Report from Consul Henry Rider, Freetown, Sierra Leone, February 1868, Document no. 848.6395/74G, Records of the Department of State, RG 59, NARA.

65. Some manufactured goods and American products listed as exports from the United Kingdom were for transshipment to Sierra Leone, from where they were distributed to other areas along the West African coast.

66. CO 272/0481 no. 9318, Document no. 438691, Blue Books of Trade and Statistics, Sierra Leone, 1867–1369, PRO.

67. CO 271/1–3, Schedule of All the Laws, Proclamations, Orders-in-Council Promulgated in the Colony of Sierra Leone for the Years 1869–70, *Sierra Leone Gazette*, PRO.

68. CO 272/19234/A34, Document no. 8623, Blue Books of Trade and Statistics, PRO.

69. CO 272/47, Number, Tonnage, and Crews of Vessels of Each National Entered at Ports in the Colony of Sierra Leone in the Year 1870, PRO.

70. Consul Rider was recalled in 1872 due to serious ill health. When he returned to Boston, he continued to be involved with trade in Sierra Leone and generally along the West African coast, but he never went to West Africa after 1872.

71. Confidential Letter from Consul Henry Rider, Freetown, Sierra Leone, July 1871, Miscellaneous Correspondence from United States Consular Posts, 1789–1906, Records of the Department of State, RG 59, NARA.

72. The records of the United States Consulate at Bathurst, Gambia, have no explanation for the closing of that post, 1867–72.

73. The names of United States commercial agents and consuls to Sierra Leone was compiled from the General Records of the Department of State, RG 59, NARA. In line with Consul Rider's recommendation, another top ranking official, J. B. Upton, was appointed in February 1871 as assistant commercial agent to Sierra Leone and served simultaneously with Consul Hogan until 1874.

74. CO 272/034/691 and CO 272/196, Document no. 116/N48, Blue Books of Trade and Statistics, Sierra Leone, PRO.

75. Witt Bowden, Michael Karpovich, and Abbott P. Usher, *An Economic History of Europe since 1750* (New York: Fertig, 1970), 495–566.

76. CO 272/49, Laws Enacted in the Colony of Sierra Leone, Blue Books of Trade and Statistics, Sierra Leone, 1870–80, PRO.

77. Bowden, Karpovich, and Usher, *An Economic History of Europe*, 495–566.

78. CO 272/54, An Ordinance to Amend All Duties of Customs, Sierra Leone no. 13, 1872, PRO.

79. The general and ad valorem duty was levied on all imports that entered the port of Freetown.

80. CO 272/54, An Ordinance to Amend All Duties of Customs, Sierra Leone no. 13, 1872, PRO.

81. Tonnage fees were reduced from 1 shilling 9 pence to 1 shilling per ton.

82. CO 272/49, Number, Tonnage, and Crews of Vessels entered at the Ports in the Colony of Sierra Leone, 1872, PRO. A total of 400 vessels with cargoes entered the port of Freetown between October 1872 and April 1873.

83. CO 267/49, Annual Report of the Governor of Sierra Leone, 1873, General Dispatch to the British Secretary to State, Document Ser. no. 985367/N9, PRO.

84. CO 272/49, American Goods Entering the Port of Freetown, Blue Books of Trade and Statistics, December 1872, PRO.

85. CO 271/6, Registry of Foreign and British Companies, Firms and Merchants, *Sierra Leone Gazette*, May 1873, PRO.

86. CO 271/6, Registry of Foreign and British Companies, Firms, and Merchants; *Sierra Leone Gazette*, 1873, PRO. See also list of American companies in Sierra Leone, 1850–1930, also in CO 271/6.

87. CO 271/5, Reports of Foreign Consul Residing in the Colony of Sierra Leone, *Sierra Leone Gazette*, April 1872, PRO.

88. For names of American companies that were registered with the consulate, see the General Records of the Department of State, RG 59, NARA.

89. Report on American Foreign Commerce in West Africa, December 1871, Records of the Department of State, RG 59, NARA.

90. Brooks, *Yankee Traders, Old Coasters and African Middlemen*, 218–20.

91. CO 271/3, Requests for Trade Restriction Laws in the Colony of Sierra Leone, *Sierra Leone Gazette*, March 1870, PRO.

92. William Hogan was appointed as Consul to Sierra Leone on June 10, 1872, and served until 1874. Also see Guidelines in CO 271/43, 1873, Activities of Foreign Consuls, *Sierra Leone Gazette*, PRO.

93. Annual Consular Reports 1850–75, Records of the Department of State, RG 59, NARA. See section on commercial relations with Africa.

94. U. S. Treasury Department, Bureau of Statistics, *Exports of Products of Domestic Manufacture from the United States* (Washington, DC: Government Printing Office, 1899). Also see CO 271/6, Trade Petitions to the Foreign Office and Governor of the Colony of Sierra Leone, Supplementary Document no. HB 6593/L, *Sierra Leone Gazette*, 1873, PRO.

95. CO 272/51, Legislation no. 1: An Ordinance for Increasing the Duties of Customs and Revenue, 1874, PRO.

96. Consular Report on the Conduct of Trade in Sierra Leone, Miscellaneous Correspondence on the Sierra Leone File 1856–1910, Records of the Department of State, RG 59, NARA.

97. U.S., Congress, Senate, Senate Joint Committee Report, S. Doc. 154, 40th Cong., 2nd sess., 1868.

98. Circulars and Instructions to Consuls of the United States, 1830–80; Office of the Consular Bureau, Records of the Department of State, RG 59, NARA.

99. Consul William Hogan returned to the United States in January 1874 due to poor health.

100. CO 272/52–55, Blue Books of Trade and Statistics, Sierra Leone, 1874–78, PRO.

101. Brooks, *Yankee Traders, Old Coasters African Middlemen*, 219–21.

102. CO 271/7, Annual Budget and Expenditure for the Colony of Sierra Leone, *Sierra Leone Gazette*, 1874–78, PRO.

103. Christopher Fyfe, *A History of Sierra Leone* (London: Longman, 1962), 414–19.

104. CO 272/56, Government Publications Relating to Sierra Leone, *Sierra Leone Gazette* (1879), PRO.

105. Fyfe, *History of Sierra Leone*, 413–22.

106. CO 271/10, Supplementary Ordinance passed by the Legislative Council to Annex and Expand Colonial Jurisdiction, 1880, Document no. 6493/M6, PRO.

107. Judson A. Lewis was appointed in 1879 and served as consul until 1890. Prior to his appointment, he served as commercial agent in Sierra Leone for the New York–based company of Yates and Porterfield.

108. CO 271/7, Dispatches and Correspondence to and from the Governor and Legislative Council for the Colony of Sierra Leone 1860–90, Document no. 86953/J145, PRO.

109. Edward H. McKinley, *The Lure of Africa: American Interests in Tropical Africa. 1919–1939* (New York: Bobbs-Merrill, 1974), 90–92.

110. Peter Duignan and L. H. Gann, *The United States and Africa: A History* (Cambridge: Cambridge University Press, 1984), 266–70.

3

Stranded Families

Free Colored Responses to Liberian Colonization and the Formation of Black Families in Nineteenth-Century Richmond, Virginia

John Wess Grant

Richmond, Virginia, was a social minefield for many free coloreds and slaves before the American Civil War. There they spent a large portion of their productive energies negotiating the obstacles of Virginia's slave society. Most black Richmonders were therefore unable to exercise the option of emigrating to Liberia. The way black Richmonders interacted with the Virginia slave system had an enormous impact on this. As Virginia legislators began imposing stricter limits on manumission in the early nineteenth century, the number of black families consisting of slave and free colored members increased. These stranded families undermined American Colonization Society (ACS) efforts to enlarge the size of the settler population in Liberia. Fundamentally, Richmond free colored members of stranded families lived in a social and legal context where white political authorities altered the actual meaning of manumission and emigration from liberation to separation. In response to this change, free coloreds filed petitions with the Virginia legislature to redefine the meaning of manumission, making it a form of liberation, which would allow them to preserve the integrity of their families. As long as members of their families remained enslaved, these free coloreds continued to reject emigration as a practical liberation solution. Even fewer options for liberation existed for Richmond free coloreds who found themselves demoted in status by the Virginian legal system. For example, it was not unusual for poorer free coloreds to be drawn into an unofficial system of indentured servitude in instances where they could not afford to pay jail charges. There were also free coloreds involved in the risky business of purchasing themselves and/or close relatives out of slavery. Because these transactions took several years to complete, the free coloreds engaged in the purchasing process inadvertently removed themselves from the pool of eligible emigrants. A broader study of how these kinds of local inhibitors influenced black responses to Liberian colonization in the Upper South would explain why advocates of Liberian emigration failed to attract enough settlers to achieve Liberia's economic, diplomatic, and cultural goals. This chapter attempts to move the literature on Liberian colonization[1] in this direction, by using the case of black Richmond to show how the vicissitudes of life in a slave society could operate as a major roadblock to Liberian emigration.

As early as 1830, 27 percent of the free colored families in Richmond consisted of both enslaved and free colored members.[2] The most common families of this kind included a free colored husband, slave wife, and no children; a free colored husband, a slave wife, and slave children; a free colored wife, a slave husband, and no children; a free colored wife, a slave husband, and slave children; a free colored wife, a free colored husband, and slave children; and a free colored woman and slave children. Rarely was the composition of these stranded families ever fixed; rather, they fluctuated as slaves purchased themselves, family members purchased enslaved relatives, and slaves were manumitted by an owner's last will and testament. The main reason why free colored members of these stranded families were less likely to emigrate to Liberia than those in families composed solely of free coloreds was as follows. If free colored members of stranded families emigrated to Liberia, they always faced the prospect of having to leave enslaved relatives behind. In addition, the fact that many stranded families were entangled in the process of raising money to purchase enslaved kin discouraged emigration as well. Finally, there were slaves who wished to climb into the ranks of free coloreds and emigrate to Liberia, but the cost of manumission was often far too high for them to afford.

The manner in which most emigrants traveled to Liberia also explains why free colored members of stranded families did not take advantage of emigration. Most emigrants traveled in family units,[3] which meant Liberian emigration was essentially a family affair. In light of this trend, the enslaved kin of stranded families had to be released before the free colored members of these families would take Liberian emigration seriously. Emigration by such families was rare in the Richmond wing of the Liberian emigration movement, because white slaveholders were unwilling to release the slaves in these families. Most capital-poor free coloreds in these families thus chose to stay in Richmond near their enslaved kin.

The stories of Bureell Mann and Lott Cary highlight the sociopolitical borders of enslavement, manumission, and emigration that most black Richmonders negotiated or traversed. For example, Mann drove himself to secure his own manumission and emigrate to Liberia, although he ultimately remained trapped behind the political border of enslavement. Cary too lived a large portion of his adult life under the yoke of slavery, but he did find a way to buy his way out of slavery and play an important role in the founding of Liberia. Most free coloreds in Cary's peer group were not, however, able to use manumission as a gateway to emigration or as a platform to enhance their socioeconomic mobility. Instead they struggled to carve out lives for themselves between the porous borders of enslavement and manumission. This was especially true in Virginia, where white slaveholders possessed more power to regulate the lives of free coloreds than slaveholders in Caribbean and Brazilian slave societies. Three important variables contributed to the unfavorable situation in which most Virginia free coloreds were compelled to live. First, Virginia had always employed a relatively small number of slaves to produce the state's most profitable cash crop—tobacco. Therefore, Virginian slaveholders were not confronted with the problem of frequent slave rebellions that plagued the slave societies in the Caribbean and Brazil. Second, whites and slaves in Virginia consistently surpassed free coloreds in terms of natural population growth. This meant that Virginian free coloreds as a group never achieved the kind of numerical parity with the white population that proved beneficial to other free colored communities in the slaveholding Atlantic World. Third, the numerical superiority that whites managed to achieve over free coloreds allowed them to exclude free coloreds from participating in the law enforcement organizations that were designed to guard the commonwealth against slave rebellions and foreign invasions.[4] In light of these factors, over the course of two and a half centuries, Virginia slaveholders were able to build a slave society that did not have to make any major socioeconomic concessions to its free colored inhabitants. Free coloreds thus came to occupy a marginal place in the commonwealth's social and economic order. The utter force of this reality was nowhere more apparent than in the "Slave City" of Richmond.[5]

The manufacture of tobacco was the largest industry in nineteenth-century Richmond, which was supplied by an expanding network of plantations located in Virginia's Piedmont region.[6] Indeed, slaves represented the dominant labor force in Virginia's rural and urban tobacco-producing sectors. It was in the urban setting of Richmond that Bureell Mann's story took shape. Proprietor John Cosby bought and hired him out to work in a tobacco factory "attached to the Methodist Church, on union hill" in 1830. After seventeen years of service, Mann began to openly express his desire to "get" his "freedom" and work as a missionary in Liberia. As a missionary he planned to "preach the Gospel to the heathens" in Africa "all for the Sake of Christ and the Glory of his people in that continant [*sic*]." Otherwise, these "heathens" would be left in the wilderness without a friend to tell them "what they must do in order to go to heaven when they died."[7] Mann thus worked earnestly between the spring of 1847 and summer of 1849 to realize his dream, which entailed coordinating the logistics of his manumission with his owner's frequent trips out of town, and the schedules of ships that frequently departed Virginia for Liberia. He began by appealing to the local Methodist church, where he served as a lay preacher, the Methodist Missionary Society, the American Colonization Society in Washington, DC, and several northern pastors for the money to buy his way out of slavery. When these direct approaches failed, he made increasingly desperate proposals to raise the money. For example, he promised to be the slave of ACS officials if they purchased him from his current owner; he promised to be the slave of anyone who bought him and allowed him to pay off the debt with the money he earned as a slave hire; he promised to enliven support for the ACS in Richmond by selling copies of the *African Repository* to its residents,[8] and he promised that many black Richmonders would go to Liberia if he were purchased and allowed to go with them. Gracy Ann Clark (a manumitted slave and mother of two), the Brown family, Sterling Ruffin, the slaves of Francis G. Taylor in Hanover, the Cold family, and William Joiner (Joyner) were just a few of the persons he promised to deliver to Liberia.[9] When these proposals failed, he turned to the black community for support. Although he could not get anyone in the black community to grant him funds sufficient to purchase himself, he did receive a promise from the First African Baptist Church that they would repay anyone who would advance him the money for manumission. He also wrote to the Liberian government for financial assistance, but received no reply.

Mann's case illustrates just how "hard" it was "to Raise money for Such a purpose"[10] especially in a city where slave hires were highly valued for the rent revenues and status they brought to their owners. Details related to Mann's specific situation shed important light on this reality. First, he was a married man with a slave wife and slave children compelled to surrender to his owner all of his earnings, which were, at most, $80 a year. This was in addition to the $39 per year Mann was given to rent a room located on "Cary Street number 14 Street, leading to Mayos Bridge, at Mr. Hiram, B. Dickinsons Tobacco, Factory."[11] Second, Mann's owner raised the asking price for his manumission from the $300 he had paid for him in 1830 to $450 in 1847, after telling Mann he would be charged only "half" of his market "value."[12] Cosby was also careful not to promise to fix the purchase price at $450, meaning it was subject to increase. This explains why Mann's numerous letters to the ACS treasurer, Ralph R. Gurley, bore an increasingly urgent tone. Third, Mann provided no evidence of having any free colored family members or white allies that were willing to aid his cause, aside from Robert Ryland, who was the white pastor of First African Baptist Church and the president of Richmond College, Robert Ryland. Rather than making a large donation of his own, Ryland had agreed to broker the sale once the manumission money was raised. Fourth, Mann opposed the idea of picking up extra work to finance his own purchase because he feared this might prompt his owner to sell him to one of the local slave traders in a city that harbored the largest slave-trading industry in the Upper South.[13] The fact that his wife and children were eventually sold into this market demonstrates that his fears were well founded. All of these complications forced Mann to delay his plans to travel to Liberia from January 1848 to the summer of that year, and again to August 1848, when he stopped listing probable dates altogether. During this time, Mann's owner continued to "Call for his money."[14]

Mann became so despondent about his circumstances that at one point he confessed, "I must say that I never knew the value of being free before; for had I been a freeman I would have been in Africa long ago & would not be troubling the Good citizens of America as I now do."[15] His level of frustration rose steadily over the course of 1848, to the point where he began entertaining thoughts of running away. It was for this reason that he asked Gurley, "will the American Colonization Society take a person who goes from a Slave State, to a free One, and Colonize, That person, or persons in Liberia? Secondly Will they treat emigrants of this discription [*sic*] as well as they do others?" Due to the challenges of having to prepare his wife and children to escape with him, he decided against this course of action. He instead hoped Boston and Richmond Methodists would devise a plan to get the money for his manumission; even as the "Selling of" his "beloved Wife" and the "scattering" of his "children to the four winds of heaven" introduced a new set of "Heart Breaking Circumstances" into his life.[16] In spite of the fact that he had just lost his family, he refused to "Weep to stay in any part of America. But to go home to my forefathers Land? The Triumph of God, I trust will bring my Wife and children together at the day of judgment at which time Sinful parting will be done away."[17] Based on this strong conviction, Mann believed it was only a matter of time before his prayers about manumission and emigration would be answered. His response to news about his owner's decision to lower his purchase price to $400 reflected these feelings. There was, however, no evidence that the ACS authorities or Methodist churchmen to whom Mann wrote ever intervened on his behalf. Whether he eventually decided to run away or obtained manumission by some other means is unknown. Mann's absence on Liberian emigration rolls after 1849 suggests that he never realized his dream of working in the "mission fields of Africa."

Lott Cary's experience represents the opposite end of the enslavement-manumission-emigration continuum. Unlike Mann, Cary used his job as a shipper in one of Richmond's premier tobacco factories to traverse the borders of enslavement and manumission before he became one of the most influential settlers in Liberia's early colonial history. This progression did not occur overnight, however; rather, it unfolded over the course of seventeen years. Cary was born a slave on the Charles County plantation of

William Christian, located approximately thirty miles south of Richmond, Virginia. When he was an adolescent, his owner hired him out to work in Richmond's Shockoe tobacco factory (1804). While in Richmond, he married a slave woman who bore him two children. He initially turned to drink to cope with the harsh realities of enslavement, until a Christian conversion experience coupled with his decision to join Richmond's First Baptist Church convinced him that there were other solutions to the problems of earning a living, raising a slave family, and saving the money needed to buy himself and his family out of bondage. His religious experiences had other telling effects on him as well, such as encouraging him to learn to read, develop his own written interpretations of biblical scripture, and exceed the labor expectations of his white supervisors at the Shockoe factory. Indeed, his improved work performance also captured the attention of some of the city's most affluent tobacco merchants. One of these men was the president of the Richmond branch of the Bank of the United States, who later recommended that Cary serve as a middleman in what was anticipated to be a potentially lucrative tobacco trade with Liberia.[18] The next few years in Richmond were bittersweet for Cary, in that by 1815, he had finally saved enough money to secure manumission for himself and his children. His wife, however, had died two years earlier, and so she did not enjoy the same reward. Following her death, Cary married for a second time and was appointed to the position of lay preacher at the First Baptist Church, where black congregation members greatly outnumbered whites. In this new role Cary established a reputation for being a hands-on minister, known to concentrate his efforts on trying to resolve the everyday problems confronted by free colored and enslaved parishioners. He also amassed considerable influence at First Baptist. This was in spite of the fact that the church was officially led by a group of white ministers who conducted their everyday affairs in compliance with the laws governing Virginia's slave labor system.[19]

Cary's life underwent many changes between the time he entered the Richmond city limits and the time he left for West Africa with his family in 1821. After his second marriage he fathered two children, purchased his freedom, purchased his children's freedom, and became a preacher. Yet he conceived a broader destiny for free persons of color in the United States, a vision shared by a few other black men at First Baptist. This group formed an organization designed to send missionaries to Africa, with the assistance of one of First Baptist's white Sunday school teachers. The African Missionary Society (AMS) was the product of their efforts. Thus, when the ACS was founded two years later, members of the AMS and Cary were already prepared to make the trip to West Africa. In his farewell address to the black members of the First Baptist Church, he summarized the mission's motives:

I am about to leave you; and expect to see your faces no more. I long to preach to the poor Africans the way of life of salvation. I don't know what may befall me wether [*sic*] I may find a grave in the ocean, or among the *savage men*, or more savage wild beasts, on the Coast of Africa; nor am I anxious what may become of me. I feel it my duty to go; and I very much fear that many of those who preach the gospel in this country, will blush when the Saviour [*sic*] calls them to give an account of their labors in this cause, and tells them, "I commanded you to go into the world and preach the gospel to every creature (and with the most forcible emphasis he exclaimed) The Saviour [*sic*] may ask—Where have you been? What have you been doing? Have you endeavored to the utmost of your ability to fulfill the commands I gave you—or have you sought your own gratification and your own ease, regardless of my commands."[20]

The pro-colonizationist argument expressed in the above passage was similar to that of Southern white evangelicals of Cary's period. He clearly shared the view that colonization was a Christian crusade. However, he did not imply that Richmond free coloreds were a threat to the city's white population. He avoided an accommodationist tone, emphasizing that his primary objective was to win souls for Christianity among peoples he perceived to be lost in the "savage" climes of Africa. One observer of Cary's life observed that he would probably "never be able to divest himself of a kind of suspicious reserve, toward White people—especially his superiors—which universally attaches itself to those reared in slavery."[21] When one combines this assessment of Cary's outlook on race with his deep sense of responsibility toward missionary work, a complex cosmology emerges. This cosmology blended an American Protestant Christian sensibility with a wariness about white institutional leadership. More specifically, this cosmology laid the groundwork for what could be called black manifest destiny, an ideology that combined the notions of black self-determination, the proliferation of Protestant Christianity, territorial expansion, and Western commercial development.

Many blacks were, like Cary, familiar with laboring in the tobacco factories of Richmond, but very few had the means at their disposal to negotiate the borders of enslavement and manumission as he did. As a result, they carved out lives for themselves between the borders of enslavement and manumission. Stranded families were among the most common types of black family in Richmond symbolizing this kind of in-between living.

These families were an outgrowth of the major changes made in Virginia's manumission policy in the early nineteenth century. As the American Revolution drew to a close in the early 1780s, Virginian policymakers agreed not to interfere in cases where individual slaveholders wished to manumit their slaves. This policy was soon changed as the Haitian revolution (1791–1804) unfolded, and as Gabriel's slave revolt (1900) occurred in Richmond. In response to these major challenges to slavery, the Virginia Assembly passed a law that required all slaves manumitted after May 1, 1806, to leave the state within one year or suffer the consequence of reenslavement.[22] Though the effectiveness of this law remains a subject of debate,[23] it did influence the choices made by black Richmonders trying to prevent their families from being torn apart by manumission. The law also bred a new crop of stranded families, which resisted Liberian colonization for the sake of holding mixed-status family units together. The stories of Jacob Prosser, John Winston, Nellie Holmes, and Oscar Taliaferro shed important light on these developments.

The experience of Jacob Prosser was both similar to and different from those of Bureell Mann and Lott Cary. Like Cary, Prosser was permitted to keep a percentage of his wages, and that he used this to buy his way out of slavery. Although Cary had been a tobacco shipper and Prosser was a drayman, neither of them would have been able to raise the money for manumission if they had not been allowed to keep a portion of the money they earned through their work. Mann's unsuccessful attempt to raise the money accentuates this reality. After Prosser achieved his manumission, he submitted a petition to the Virginia Legislature requesting permission to remain in the state with his enslaved wife. The state granted his request. Emigration was, however, taken off the table as a feasible liberation option for the Prossers, because Prosser's wife remained enslaved. So, like Bureell Mann, the Prossers continued to live in Richmond.[24]

John Winston was not as fortunate as Prosser. Winston, who had been the slave of Izard Bacon in nearby Henrico County, was released from slavery by his owner's last will and testament. Unlike Prosser, Winston had neither the property nor the white allies most petitioners relied on to strengthen their bid to remain in the state. Winston was thus compelled to leave the state and "sacrifice his domestic happiness, by quitting his Wife and two children whom he most ardently and tenderly loves—without whom society, he finds it impossible for him to be happy." Instead of giving up, he lived in Pennsylvania for one year before asking the Virginia Legislature to permit him to be reunited with his enslaved family in Richmond. The Delegates of Virginia, however, rejected his request in January 1821.[25] So Winston and his family remained in the United States as the first Liberian settlement was being established at Monrovia.

Nellie Holmes' story bore many similarities to those of Prosser and Winston, with the exception that she was a woman, with an enslaved husband, and had three free colored children. Holmes was a slave who saved the money to purchase herself before giving birth to her children. Her former status had, however, influenced her to begin having children rather late in her adult life. By the time she had given birth to her last child, she had reached the age of fifty. Finding work and raising three children at a late age were only two of her many problems. She also had to confront the problem that her children's deeds of emancipation were not issued until 1832 and the fact that her husband remained enslaved. To solve these multiple problems that threatened to tear her family apart, she requested that she and her children be allowed to remain in Richmond for nine years with her husband until her children grew to an age when they could begin to support themselves. She also believed this would provide a sufficient amount of time for her husband to buy his own freedom. When this nine-year grace period ended, she believed her family would be in a better position to "remove to Liberia with every prospect of happiness and comfort." If permission was denied they would be "separated" from all that was important to them and forced to live among "strangers" who might not have this family's best interests in mind. Although Holmes' first petition was rejected in 1833, the Virginia Assembly submitted her second petition to the Courts of Justice in 1836.[26] Whether she was granted permission to stay is unknown.

Like Jacob Prosser and Nellie Holmes, Oscar Taliaferro was a self-purchaser who paid $400 to extract himself from bondage. He accomplished this by making a series of short-term loans to his owner, James Blakely. The aging Blakely used the money to pay for his own health care bills but claimed that he had lost it. When Taliaferro finally applied for his deed of emancipation he received the astonishing news that he was to be "sold to the south," where he would be "separated from his wife a slave in Richmond." Taliaferro responded to this potential disaster by arranging for a man named George Taylor to purchase him. This arrangement did not, however, come without strings. Part of the deal Taliaferro made with Taylor was that he would pay off the balance of his own purchase price. This meant Taliaferro was pushed into the unenviable position of having to pay for his freedom twice. One of the consequences of this situation was that Taliferro grew too old to finish raising the money he needed to buy his wife. The irony of this story is that the goal of purchasing his own and his wife's freedom had

> stimulated him to work while others rested and to deny himself indulgences which others enjoyed and again after (some two years since) satisfying the claims of his present owner's prospect of accomplishing this object, only secondary as resulting from it to the great object to which his efforts previously had been directed for years when he was prostrated the last summer at the Hot Springs of Virginia: by severe indisposition during which attendanse [*sic*] board and the Drs. Bills swallowed up a considerable part of his accumulations for that object and now—increased years enfeebled health prevent him from cherishing any such hope.[27]

Taliaferro's struggle illustrates how risky self-purchase could be. It also highlights some of the obstacles that most stranded families faced. Among these were old age, enslaved spouses, enslaved children, the specter of the slave market, and the long periods of labor required to complete transactions involving self-purchase or the purchase of a family member. Indeed, the lives of many people in Richmond's stranded families intersected with one or more of these issues. And the more these stranded families struggled with these issues, the fewer were the prospects of their ever applying for emigration. The result was that, just like Oscar Taliaferro, Jacob Prosser, Nellie Holmes, and John Winston, others like John Hope, John Elson, Judith Hope, Phillip Robertson, Clara Robinson, and Salley Dabney carved out lives for themselves between the porous borders of enslavement and manumission.

Living between the political borders of enslavement and manumission could be an extremely challenging task. Manumission in Richmond contained an unwritten class feature, wherein free coloreds without a regular income, property, or white allies to testify to their good character could quickly find themselves drawn into an unfree labor system that resembled indentured servitude. Richmond free coloreds who had firsthand encounters with the city's law enforcement system were exposed to this harsh reality. Lucy Briggs, "a free woman of color," was admitted to the Richmond city jail on April 25, 1841, for failing to register her status with local authorities. She was then denied a public hearing and compelled to remain in jail for nine months before a court released her to be "hired out at a public auction at the Old market to Benjamin Whopper." Whopper paid her jail fees of $59.38 in exchange for nine years of her labor. Polly Stewart, another free woman of color, received an even longer indentured sentence than Lucy, although Stewart spent less time in jail and accrued $1.74 less in jail fees than Briggs. Stewart was denied the right to a trial and "discharged from the Jail and carried to the old market and hired to Richard S. Whight Head . . . the lowis [*sic*] bidder for turm [*sic*] of 45 years." Louisa Brown suffered a similar fate. The jail fees she accumulated over a six-month period resulted in her being indentured for "fifty years." Finally, there was the case of Sally Ball, who received a sentence of "twenty five years" for her inability to pay $17.75 in jail charges. Each of these cases, in addition to the similar cases of Joe Ross, William Pleasants, and William Freeman, underscores the fact that manumission was not synonymous with freedom;[28] rather, manumission was an unstable bridge that linked together the social destination points of unfreedom and freedom. In this regard, manumission always had the potential to discourage persons who had access to it from emigrating to Liberia. For example, it would have been very difficult for indentured hires like Lucy Briggs and Sally Ball to emigrate to Liberia until their contractual labor obligations had been fulfilled.

Historians of Liberian colonization have often focused too much attention on the antislavery or proslavery tendencies of the American Colonization Society to explain why support for its Liberian colony began to decline in the 1830s. These historical approaches, along with others that have attributed the failure of Liberian colonization to abstract political and economic forces, have often alluded to the experience of free coloreds but have not placed it at the center of the discussion. This essay on black Richmond has attempted to shift the point of emphasis in this important discussion. The problem of manumission and the challenges faced by stranded families in Richmond demonstrate that the complicated process of living in a slave society was in itself a major inhibitor to Liberian emigration.

Notes

1. The nineteenth-century political and twentieth-century historiographical discussions on Liberian colonization have focused on the proslavery and antislavery proclivities of the American Colonization Society (ACS). Eric Burin's recent book complicates this discussion, but he too takes a side in this debate when asserting that ACS activities "undermined" slavery. See Eric Burin, *Slavery and the Peculiar Solution: A History of the American Colonization Society* (Gainesville: University Press of Florida, 2005), 2. Previous texts that portrayed the ACS as an antislavery or pro–free colored organization have included Archibald Alexander, *A History of Colonization on the West Coast of Africa* (Philadelphia, 1846), 78–79; Frederick Freeman, *Yardee: A Plea for Africa in Familiar Conversations on the Subject of Slavery and Colonization* (Baltimore, 1836), 149–86; Ralph R. Gurley, *Life of Jehudi Ashmun, Late Colonial Agent in Liberia* (Washington, 1835), chapter 6; Early Lee Fox, *The American Colonization Society, 1817–1840* (Baltimore: Johns Hopkins Press, 1919), 11–12; P. J. Staudenraus., *The African Colonization Movement, 1816–1865* (New York: Columbia University Press, 1961), 17–35; and George Frederickson, *The Black Image in the White Mind: The Debate on Afro-American Character and Destiny, 1817–1914* (New York: Harper & Row, 1971), 7–9. Texts characterizing the ACS as an anti-free colored or proslavery organization have included William L. Garrison, *Thoughts on African Colonization.*(New York: Arno Press, 1968; reprint 1832), 39–61; William Jay, *An Inquiry into the Character and Tendency of the American Colonization Society and Anti-Slavery Societies* (New York, 1835), 17–26; G. B. Stebbins, *Facts and Opinions Touching the Real Origin, Character, and Influence of the American Colonization Society.*(Boston, 1853), iii–iv; Charles Stuart, *A Memoir of Granville Sharpe* (New York, 1836), 75–82; Carter G. Woodson, *The Mind of the Negro as Reflected in Letters Written During the Crisis, 1800–1860* (New York: Russell & Russell, 1969; reprint of 1926 edition), 1–158; Douglas R. Egerton, " 'It's Origin Is Not a Little Curious': A New Look at the American Colonization Society," *Journal of the Early Republic,* 5 (Winter 1985): 463–64; and Amos Beyan, *The American Colonization Society and the Creation of the Liberian State: A Historical Perspective, 1822–1900* (Lanham, MD: University Press of America, 1991), chapter 1.

2. Carter G. Woodson, "Free Negro Owners of Slaves in the United States in 1830," *Journal of Negro History* 9 (January 1924): 41–85; Carter Godwin Woodson, *Free Negro Heads of Families in the United States in 1830, Together with a Brief Treatment of the Free Negro* (Washington, DC: Association for the Study of Negro Life and History, 1925), 176–78.

3. Tom Schick, *Emigrants to Liberia, 1820 to 1843: An Alphabetical Listing* (Newark: Department. of Anthropology, University of Delaware, Newark, 1971); Robert T. Brown, *Immigrants to Liberia, 1843 to 1865: An Alphabetical Listing* (Philadelphia: Institute for Liberian Studies, 1980).

4. In *Slave and Citizen* (1946), Frank Tannenbaum claimed that slaves were treated better in slave societies ruled by Euro-colonial empires in the Americas affiliated with the Catholic faith and ancient Roman systems of jurisprudence. It was therefore no coincidence that manumission policies were more flexible in Spanish, Portuguese, and French slave societies than in those ruled by English Protestants. See Frank Tannenbaum, *Slave and Citizen: The Negro in the Americas* (New York: A. A. Knopf, 1946). A growing body of secondary literature on slave societies in the New World, produced in the last thirty years, has implied that the flexibility of manumission was less the result of European legal policies or religious allegiances. Rather it was an outgrowth of a series of overlapping factors such as the type of crops grown, mortality rates among the slave, white, and free colored populations, the extent of free colored military service, the frequency of slave rebellions, and the speed at which free coloreds were able to acquire cash-crop producing lands before all-white planter regimes dominated these areas. Bodies of evidence marshaled by various scholars have contributed to this historiographic shift away from the Tannenbaum thesis. See Jack Greene and David Cohen, *Neither Slave Nor Free: The Freedmen of African Descent in the Slave Societies of the New World* (Baltimore: Johns Hopkins University Press, 1972), 1–18; Jane Landers, *Against the Odds: Free Blacks in the Slave Societies of the Americas* (London: Frank Cass, 1996), ix–xii; Gad J. Heuman, *Between Black and White: Race, Politics and Free Coloreds in Jamaica, 1792–1865* (Westport, CT: Greenwood Press, 1981), 7; Arnold Sio, "Marginality and Free Colored Identity in Caribbean Slave Society," *Slavery and Abolition* 8, no. 2 (September 1987): 166–82; Loren Schweninger, "The Fragile Nature of Freedom: Free Women of Color in the U.S. South," in David Barry Gaspar and Darlene Hine, eds., *Beyond Bondage: Free Women of Color in the Americas* (Urbana: University of Illinois Press, 2004), 106–24; Peter Voelz, *Slave and Soldier: The Military Impact of Blacks in the Colonial Americas* (New York and London: Garland Publishing, 1993), 24–25, 115; C. L. R. James, *The Black Jacobins: Toussaint L'Ouverture and the San Domingo Revolution* (New York: Dial Press, 1938), 9–26; Herbert Aptheker, *American Negro Slave Revolts* (New York: Columbia University Press, 1943), 71–72; Gwendolyn Midlo Hall, *Social Control in Slave Plantation Societies: A Comparison of St. Domingue and Cuba* (Baton Rouge: Louisiana State University Press, 1996; reprint 1971),130–31; Rebecca Scott, *Slave Emancipation in Cuba: The Transition to Free Labor, 1860–1899* (Pittsburgh: University of Pittsburgh, Digital Research Library, 2007), http://digital.library.pitt.edu/cgi-bin/t/text/text idx?idno= 31735055592343; view=toc; c=pittpress (accessed February 19, 2008), 11–14; Ada Ferrer, *Insurgent Cuba: Race, Nation, and Revolution, 1868–1898* (Chapel Hill: University of North Carolina Press, 1999), 15–42; Elsa Goveia, "The West Indian Slave Laws of the Eighteenth Century," in Verene A. Shepherd and Hilary Beckles, *Caribbean Slavery in the Atlantic World: A Student Reader* (Kingston, Jamaica, Oxford, and Princeton, NJ: Ian Randle Publishers, James Currey Publishers, and Marcus Wiener Publishers, 2000), 580; Arthur L. Stinchcombe, *Sugar Island Slavery in the Age of Enlightenment: The Political Economy of the Caribbean World* (Princeton, NJ: Princeton University Press, 1995), chapter 6; John Garrigus, "Blue and Brown: Contraband and Indigo and the Rise of a Free Colored Planter Class in French St. Domingue," *The Americas* 50, no. 2 (October 1993): 233–63; Kevin Mumford, "After Hugh: Statutory Segregation in Colonial America," *American Journal of Legal History* 43, no. 3 (July 1999): 280–305.

5. Midori Takagi, *Rearing Wolves to Our Own Destruction: Slavery in Richmond, Virginia, 1782–1865* (Charlottesville: University Press of Virginia, 1999), chapters 1 and 2.

6. Gregg D. Kimball, *American City, Southern Place: A Cultural History of Antebellum Richmond* (Athens: University of Georgia Press, 2000), chapters 1 and 2.

7. Bureell Mann to Ralph R. Gurley, Richmond, VA, June 21, 1847, and Bureell Mann to Ralph R. Gurley, Richmond VA, October 4, 1847, in "Letters to the American Colonization Society [Part 1], Abraham Camp; John Russwurm; John Jones; James Drew; Bureell W. Mann," *Journal of Negro History* 10, no. 2 (April 1925): 155–56 (hereafter cited as LACS 1).

8. Bureell Mann to Ralph R. Gurley, Richmond, VA, October 17, 1847, LACS 1.

9. Bureell Mann to Ralph R. Gurley, Richmond, VA, November 28, 1847, in "Letters to the American Colonization Society [Part 2], Bureell W. Mann; Lewis C. Holbert; George H. Baltimore; Cecelia D. Lyon; Peter B. Bolling; Branch Hughes; and E. Dustan," *Journal of Negro History* 10, no. 2 (April 1925): 154–80 (hereafter cited as LACS 2).

10. Bureell Mann to Ralph R. Gurley, Richmond, VA. November 9, 1847, LACS 1.

11. Bureell Mann to R. R. Gurley, Richmond, VA, March 28, 1848, LACS 2.

12. It would have taken Mann over five and half years to purchase himself, if his owner had allowed him to keep all of his yearly earnings. Mann knew that because he was denied his wages, earning enough to purchase himself was mathematically impossible. In February 1849, he notes that if someone had been kind enough to advance him the money for manumission in the spring of 1847 he would have been able to accumulate $250 for repayment by Christmas 1850. This never happened. Thus he remained trapped in a situation where he would "always" be hired out and his master would "get the money." See Bureell Mann to Ralph R. Gurley, Richmond, VA, February 14, 1849, LACS 2.

13. Bureell Mann to Ralph R. Gurley, Richmond, VA, September [?] 18, 1847; Bureell Mann to Ralph R. Gurley, Richmond, VA, October 4, 1847; Bureell Mann to Ralph R. Gurley, Richmond, VA, October 10, 1847, LACS 1; Frederic Bancroft, *Slave Trading in the Old South* (Columbia: University of South Carolina Press, 1996); Michael Tadman, *Speculators and Slaves: Masters, Traders, and Slaves in the Old South* (Madison: University of Wisconsin Press, 1989); and Robert H. Gudmestad, *A Troublesome Commerce: The Transformation of the Interstate Slave Trade* (Baton Rouge: Louisiana State University Press, 2003).

14. Bureell Mann to Ralph R. Gurley, Richmond, VA, November 9, 1847, LACS 1.

15. Bureell Mann to Ralph R. Gurley, Richmond, VA, December 6, 1847, LACS 1.

16. Bureell Mann to R. R. Gurley, Richmond, VA, January 2, 1849, *LACS 2*.

17. Ibid.

18. James B. Taylor, *Biography of Elder Lott Cary, Late Missionary to Africa* (Baltimore: Armstrong & Berry, 1837), 10–15; "The Rev. Lott Cary," *African Repository and Colonial Journal (1825-1849)*, October 1825: 1, 8; APS Online, 233; Joseph King to Thomas Tyson, December 30, 1823, *Benjamin Brand Papers*, 1779-1863, Virginia Historical Society, Richmond, Virginia.

19. "The Rev. Lott Cary," *African Repository*, October 1825: 1, 8; APS Online, 233; *Minutes of the First Baptist Church*, 1825-1830 (n.p.), 49. Virginia Baptist Historical Society, Richmond, Virginia.

20. Taylor, *Biography of Elder Lott Cary*, 24.

21. Ibid.

22. *The Code of Virginia. Second Edition. Including Legislation to the Year 1860* (Richmond, VA: Printed by Ritchie, Dunnavant & Co, 1860), 46.

23. In Luther Porter Jackson's masterwork on free coloreds in pre–Civil War Virginia, he argues that the 1806 law was largely ineffectual, based on the fact that more slaves were granted manumission in Virginia after it was passed than in the previous period (1782–1805). A sharp decrease in the growth of the free colored population compared to a sharp increase in the growth of the white population does, however, suggest that the 1806 law working in conjunction with other anti–free black laws effectively solved the problem of free colored population growth, which was the overarching purpose of these laws. The demography of antebellum Richmond reflects this trend as well. See Luther Porter Jackson, *Free Negro Labor and Property Holding in Virginia, 1830–1860* (New York: D. Appleton-Century Company, 1942), introduction, 142–43, 150–52, 197–99; *1820 Fourth Census of the United States*, Richmond City, National Archives microfilm publication M33, roll 131; *1830 Fifth Census of the United States*, Henrico County, National Archives microfilm publication M19, roll 195; *1840 Sixth Census of the United States, 1840*, Henrico County, National Archives microfilm publication M704, roll 561; *1850 Federal Population Census*, Henrico County, National Archives microfilm publication M432, roll 951; and *1860 Federal Population Census*, Henrico County, National Archives microfilm publication M653, rolls 1352 and 1353.

24. Loren Schweninger and Robert Shelton, *Race, Slavery, and Free Blacks: Petitions to Southern Legislatures, 1777–1867* (Bethesda, MD: University Publications of America, 1998), microform reel 17, accession no. 11681502.

25. Ibid., reel 18, accession no. 111682001.

26. Ibid., reel 20, accession nos. 11683304 and 11683610.

27. Ibid. reel 20, accession no. 11684703.

28. Richmond, VA, City Sergeant, Section 1 Register, 1841–46, Mss3R4156b1, Virginia Historical Society, Richmond, VA.

4

The Garvey Aftermath

The Fall, Rise, and Fall

Ibrahim Sundiata

Many excellent works have dealt with the meteoric rise and fall of Marcus Garvey's (1887–1940) Universal Negro Improvement Association (UNIA). The organization rode the crest of post–World War I cries for the "self-determination" of peoples. Emigration to Africa, specifically Liberia, offered a place to "be somebody," combined with the promise of untapped riches. Garveyism offered a most logical way out of the specifically American Dilemma. The abortion of Garveyism after 1924 has been attributed to many causes: the narrowness of its class aims; the opposition of the established African American elite; interference from the European colonial powers; harassment by the FBI. All of these played a part in the subversion of Marcus Garvey and the UNIA. None of them is, in and of itself, sufficient. The defeat (rather than the "failure") of Garveyism does not rest on the inherent illogic of its program. It rests on a failure to disentangle the claims of a national minority from those of pan-ethnicity. In Liberia, the site of the proposed West African experiment, the UNIA ran into issues of class and ethnicity that belied the very unity it proclaimed as its raison d'être.

This essay argues that Africa remained a potent force in the North American Diaspora until the advent of World War II. The continent was of concern to groups as divergent as the remnant UNIA and the National Association for the Advancement of Colored People (NAACP). For example, five years after the end of the Garvey plan, the United States accused Liberia of promoting "conditions analogous to slavery." Threatened with a loss of its independence, the Liberian government turned to the black Diaspora in the West. A varied group of white and black anti-imperialists, among them W. E. B. DuBois, took up the country's cause. The Liberian elite successfully looked for support among foreign pressure groups—as long as they eschewed emigrationism. But the impulse to leave the United States was not dead. By the late 1930s, the Peace Movement of Greater Ethiopia, a Garveyite spin-off, obtained support from Senator Theodore Bilbo and other avowed segregationists. Significantly, by 1940 a number of prominent African Americans, among them W. E. B. DuBois, briefly advocated a return to the "motherland." Far from being a single historical episode, as it is usually seen, emigrationism remained a prominent theme.

Marcus Garvey founded the Universal Negro Improvement and Conservation Association and African Communities League in Jamaica in 1914. Two years later he traveled to the United States to see Booker T. Washington for the purpose of raising money for a school in Jamaica. Unfortunately, his arrival came several months after the "Sage of Tuskegee's" death. However, Garvey's arrival in the United States was a turning point for him. Thrust into the wider ambit of North American society, he very quickly came to the conclusion that the organization of black enterprise must supersede his original plan to establish an educational institution. Garvey, once an optimist about the prospects of education and uplift in the Diaspora, was deeply affected by the wave of racial violence during and after World War I. Lynching and riots convinced him that the United States was essentially a "White Man's Country."

In Garvey's view, blacks could *never* be integrated into white society on the basis of *complete* equality. They were an exogenous body in the social and political life of a white polity. Inclusion would only produce a bastardized chaos. The white majority might one day "cast him [that is, the black man] off to die in the whirlpool of economic starvation, thus getting rid of another race that was not intelligent enough to live, or, you [whites] simply mean by the largeness of your hearts to assimilate fifteen million Negroes into the social fraternity of an American race, that will neither be white nor black!"[1] The only modus vivendi would be to abandon any idea of a modus vivendi. Garvey believed that in seventy to eighty years, race relations in the United States would be worse. Indeed, "the Problem of the Twentieth Century" would extend well beyond it. The Jamaican believed that competition from immigrants would pauperize blacks and increase racial hostility. In his worldview, informed by late-nineteenth-century social Darwinism, a group had to protect itself or die. "Power," Garvey said, "is the only argument that satisfies man. Except the individual, the race or the nation has POWER that is exclusive, it means that the individual, race or nation will be bound by the will of the other who possesses this great qualification."[2]

Garvey moved his headquarters to New York's Harlem after spending about fifteen months lecturing and fundraising across the United States. In May 1919 he announced the formation of the Black Star Line, a steamship company linking the scattered sons and daughters of Africa and supported by their investment. Garvey asked himself, "Where is the black man's

Government? Where is his King and his kingdom? Where is his President, his country, and his ambassador, his army, his navy, his men of big affairs?" He responded, "I could not find them, and then I declared, 'I will help to make them.'"[3]

The UNIA reached its apogee in 1919–20. Its message struck a chord with large numbers of African Americans, many of whom had migrated from the Deep South only to find their dreams of a better life cruelly betrayed. August 1920 was the organization's high point. Membership was affected by a downturn in the economy in 1920–21 and sales of stock in the Black Star Line fell off. In addition to suffering from financial problems, the movement was attacked from both the Right and the Left. Garvey had gained an enemy in the executive secretary of the NAACP. W. E. B. DuBois could not help but realize that Garveyism directly opposed his integrationism. Also, he had evolved his own version of Pan-Africanism; he organized congresses in 1919, 1921, and 1923 that directly competed for attention with the UNIA's annual conventions. In the pages of *The Crisis* magazine, the organ of the NAACP, DuBois increasingly questioned Garvey's methods. In his view, Garvey was as foolish as he was impolitic: "And finally, without arms, money, effective organization or base of operations, Mr. Garvey openly and wildly talks of 'Conquest' and of telling white Europeans in Africa to 'get out!' and of becoming himself a black Napoleon!"[4] Similar sentiments were voiced by the black socialist, A. Philip Randolph, who announced in his *Messenger* publication that "The whole scheme of a black empire, in the raging sea of imperialism would make it impossible to maintain power, nor would it bring liberation to Africa, for Negro exploiters and tyrants are as bad as white ones."[5] Eventually Randolph and William Pickens of the NAACP, calling themselves the "Friends of Negro Freedom," held four meetings with the central aim of removing Garvey from political life. From a completely different angle, J. Edgar Hoover of the Federal Bureau of Investigation was convinced that Garvey was "a notorious Negro agitator."[6]

The outlines of the American side of the saga of Garvey's fall are well known. A number of UNIA officials left in 1921 and 1922, and a number of prominent African Americans distanced themselves from the organization. Garvey purged his leadership in August 1922, but dissension continued. In New York on May 21, 1923, Garvey was tried for mail fraud; almost a month later the court declared him guilty. Garvey was given a $1,000 fine, made to pay court costs, and sentenced to five years in prison. The leader of the UNIA was imprisoned and then released on bond pending appeal. Garvey's judicial appeals proved futile and in February 1925 he was remanded to Atlanta Federal Penitentiary. In the final act of the U.S. phase of the drama, President Calvin Coolidge commuted the sentence in November 1927. Less than a month later, on December 2, Marcus Garvey was deported from the United States, never to return. The UNIA in the United States became the victim of factionalism and lost its cohesion, and Garvey's attempts to reestablish himself in Jamaica had little result. In 1935 he took up residence in London, the capital of the empire he had once hoped to topple. Garvey died there in 1940, a "Black Moses" who did not live to see the post-1945 triumph of anti-imperialism.

The African side of the Garveyite project is essential to understanding the movement. The intended West African center of a resurgent black race was already a semi-colony of U.S. capital. Liberia was an Ohio-sized country on the bulge of the West African coast in which an elite of approximately 15,000 souls descended from nineteenth-century immigrants ruled an indigenous population divided into at least sixteen indigenous ethnic groups. The polity had been established through the agency of the white American Colonization Society in 1822. The stated aim of the society was to provide a home for American freed persons; the more sinister goal was to rid the United States of an anomalous population of free blacks. In 1847, Liberia was granted de jure independence. The American government did not want direct responsibility for its black "stepchild," but was loath to let it fall to any European power. Between 1918 and 1922, during the formative period of the UNIA, the U.S. State Department attempted to secure an intergovernmental loan for its semi-ward. At first this was to be under the terms of wartime measures that allowed credits to be extended to allied nations. Although Liberia declared war on Germany in 1917, no loan had been authorized by the time of the armistice in November 1918. The State Department then tried to get Congressional approval for a loan of $5 million. The effort was unsuccessful and the Liberian loan was defeated in the Senate in November 1922.

It was against this backdrop that the UNIA approached isolated and insolvent Liberia. Unfortunately, the elite in Monrovia, Liberia's capital, was small, closed, heavily intermarried, and divided on the American loan, immigration, and "Native policy." At the time of the Garvey initiative, the political apparatus was increasingly in the hands of President Charles Burgess Dunbar King (1920–30), a man wary of emigration from America. Unfortunately for the Garveyites, King's authority expanded during the very period in which the association's plan was floated. The UNIA first approached King while he was in Paris for the 1919 peace conference. In September 1919, King was in New York and a group of Garveyite supporters again approached him on the subject of diasporic financial assistance. Subsequently, Hilary Johnson, the son of the mayor of Monrovia, appeared at Liberty Hall (the UNIA's New York headquarters) and encouraged UNIA members to visit Liberia. Reverend Dr. Lewis G. Jordan, secretary of the National Baptist Convention, informed a Liberty Hall audience in April 1920 that conditions were ripe. Jordan had just returned from Liberia, where President King had supposedly said that the UNIA was indeed welcome.[7]

It seemed that, finally, the rhetoric of Pan-Africanism would be realized. Garvey declared, "We of the UNIA at this moment have a solemn duty to perform and that is to free Liberia of any debt that she owes to any white government."[8] A UNIA mission set out in May 1920, headed by Elie Garcia, a striving Haitian entrepreneur. Once in Liberia, Garcia was outwardly effusive about prospects. He also succeeded in recruiting several prominent Liberians to the cause. Gabriel Johnson, mayor of Monrovia, was proclaimed "Supreme Potentate"—titular head of the world's black peoples. The UNIA's coup in coopting a prominent African politician promised to insure close collaboration between Harlem and Monrovia. The promise was illusory. Garcia confidentially informed Garvey that the Americo-Liberians were, in his judgment, rapacious and the parent UNIA should keep control in money matters. Garcia had hit upon a thorny problem that neither Garveyism nor later Pan-Africanism successfully surmounted: How did differences of class and culture fit within the conceptualization of a black world pursuing a common destiny?

The 1920 convention voted to raise $2 million for development projects. In January 1921, the UNIA in Liberia was incorporated under an act of the Liberian legislature, and the following month a second UNIA mission arrived. The emissaries met with the acting president of Liberia, Edwin Barclay, and the Liberian cabinet on March 22, 1921. Barclay claimed that the government would be glad to have the UNIA occupy certain settlements, which had already been laid out. The Liberians also set a number of restrictions. For one, even though money for the Black Star Line had largely been raised in America, the mission was informed that vessels flying the Liberian flag had to be manned and owned by Liberians. The Garveyites were also prohibited from setting up their own settlements. Since by law only Liberians could own real property, the parent body of the UNIA in New York could not directly purchase land. Under these somewhat onerous conditions, the UNIA team did begin to work. However, dissension soon erupted. The mission stopped its work after two months because of a lack of funds and by July 1923 all of its members had returned home.

Late in 1923 the UNIA sent a third mission to Liberia. An area of some five hundred square miles in the extreme south of the country (Maryland County) was selected as the site of a settlement. Representatives of the local UNIA and three delegates from overseas agreed on provisions regarding the prospective UNIA base in February 1924. Five hundred settlers were to emigrate from the United States later that year. It was agreed that settlers would swear an oath before departing from the United States declaring that they would respect the authority of the Liberian government. It was also agreed that each family would possess at least $1,500 and that each single person would have at least $500.

Like its predecessors, the third Garveyite mission was plagued by bad luck. Ill luck seemed to hover over the enterprise like a cloud. The Liberian president later maintained that he had spoken to the mission only unofficially. In addition, mission personnel either died or deserted the enterprise. In May 1924, a team of UNIA technical assistants was sent to prepare the projected UNIA settlement. Upon the team's arrival in Liberia in June, its members were seized and detained. On July 31, 1924, they were deported. The following month, the *Liberian News*, supporting the official line, published a stinging repudiation of Garvey's Pan-Negro assumptions: "this community both by tradition and inclination, is influenced rather by considerations which tend to secure and strengthen *national* existence, progress and stability than by *racial* Utopias." Furthermore, the article chided, it was idiotic to think "that Liberia can be used as the *point d'appui*, whence the grandiose schemes of the 'Negro Moses' may find their genesis."[9] In January 1925, the Liberian legislature ratified President C. D. B. King's exclusion of the UNIA from Liberia. It appeared that Garveyism was dead.

What killed the UNIA's chances with the Liberian government? Was it the blandishments of DuBois and his American backers that shifted the balance against the hope of any real emigration? Did the association's rabid anti-imperialism result in overwhelming pressure being brought to bear on the little black state? Indeed, some have sought to exculpate the Monrovia government by arguing just this point.[10] In his 1921 meeting with the UNIA delegation, Liberian Secretary of State Barclay did admit that the British and the French had inquired as to the Liberian attitude towards the UNIA. While agreeing that "There isn't a Negro in the world who, if given the opportunity and the power to do certain things, will not do them," Barclay had urged caution. He told the UNIA men, "It is not always advisable nor politic to openly expose our secret thoughts." In words pregnant with future meaning for the UNIA, he noted, "We don't tell them [people] what we think; we only tell them what we like them to hear—what, in fact, they like to hear."[11] Later, in the autumn of 1924, the Liberian consul general in the United States told the State Department that the UNIA's anti-imperialism brought forth complaints from the French in Ivory Coast and the British in Sierra Leone.[12]

No doubt Liberia knew of European hostility to Garveyism. Members of the association experienced difficulty in getting clearance to travel around the colonial empires. The UNIA paper, *The Negro World*, was banned in many colonies and mere possession of it was often treated as a criminal offense. Yet it was not pressure from Britain or France that sealed the fate of the UNIA venture in Liberia. American and French documents indicate that the Europeans were willing to let Monrovia itself dispose of Garvey. In September 1921, a draft memorandum by a member of the State Department's Division of Western European Affairs observed that "Officially the Liberian Government is not disposed to favor the political aspirations of the movement." This attitude seemed "to be largely based on fear that the UNIA might become powerful enough to take control of the Republic's government from the little group of Americo-Liberians who have run things for seventy-five years."[13] Two months later, R. Pêtre, French chargé d'affaires in Monrovia, wrote to his government that "The men currently in power have not failed to understand that the arrival here of partisans of MARCUS GARVEY would be the signal, not only of their rapid downfall, but of the disappearance from the political scene of representatives of all the old Liberian families."[14] The chargé was confident that the oligarchy was capable of destroying Garvey and Garveyism on its own. A year later, he reiterated that "Marcus Garvey has never had and cannot have influence in Liberia. The tiny oligarchy which holds power is too jealous to give any of it up."[15] In his analysis, Pêtre saw Gabriel Johnson, mayor of Monrovia, as the only real link between Liberian citizens and the American UNIA. Pêtre's successor agreed with these sentiments, maintaining that "The arrival here of colored people likely one day to take the power jealously held by a few Liberian families could not be agreeable to this country's statesmen."[16] The diplomat also reported that the government was offering Johnson the post of consul in the Spanish colony of Fernando Po, but only on condition he abandon the UNIA. When the Liberians hustled the last UNIA personnel out of the country, the British were caught off guard. A British Colonial Office functionary remarked in a minute, "I am rather surprised at the Liberians being so prompt to get rid of them. I suppose they were afraid of rivals in their running and exploiting of the 'broke' nation."[17]

Liberia and the UNIA had been ill matched. The settlement of Liberia, whatever gloss was later put upon it, was not part of the Pan-African project. Far from being the vanguard of the forces of African liberation, the settlers were initially the grateful servitors of whites. The Americo-Liberian elite was closed, conservative, and imbued with many of the values of Old Dixie. Separated by law from the "native" masses, the Americo-Liberians' Diasporic origins, rather than their color, defined them. Their reality was the diversity that was West Africa. In a world dominated by White Supremacy, a little bit of status goes a very long way. The Liberian ruling families were conscious of being simultaneously members of a despised race and citizens of an internationally recognized polity. In a world in which the majority of black people were subject to imperialism and/or racial segregation, the oligarchy was deeply conscious of its relatively "privileged" position within the world schema. Within Liberia, power meant the manipulation of congeries of ethnolinguistic units, all of them black. Economic survival depended upon squeezing benefit from a decrepit economy built on the backs of a disenfranchised native majority. Many Americo-Liberians seemed attracted to the UNIA as a way out of their individual financial difficulties. In 1921, Elie Garcia warned Garvey that "The Liberian politicians understand clearly that they are degenerated and weak morally and they know that if any number of honest Negroes with brains, energy and experience come to Liberia and are permitted to take part in the ruling of the nation they will be absorbed and ousted in a very short while."[18]

Even before the UNIA proffered its loan, the Liberian leader was deeply biased against the racial ideology embodied in it. The Garveyites first approached King while he was in Paris in February of 1919. The UNIA high commissioner in France, Eliezer Cadet, interviewed him; King supposedly said that, if conditions in America were so bad, African Americans might want to emigrate.[19] King repeated this sentiment during a visit to the United States in September 1919.[20] As Tony Martin, the most thorough of Garvey scholars, notes, "Yet, if these statements seemed favorable to UNIA aspirations, there were other indications to the contrary."[21] British intelligence sources reported that the Liberian president claimed not to feel any affinity with the struggles black people were waging in America.[22] More tellingly, on September 25, 1919, King visited the U.S. State Department and spoke candidly and off the record. He reportedly "felt that in view of the tendency of the American Negroes to look on problems from a local point of view and to fail to grasp international view points, it would be inadvisable to have an American Negro as minister of Liberia in Washington." The Liberian "observed that this was said without desire to criticize the American Negro, but this opinion was formed as a result of his observations while in the United States."[23] King's confidences somehow became known to a group of African Americans, who threatened that, unless King adopted a different attitude, African Americans would not interest themselves in the fate of the Black Republic.[24]

King's apparent vacillations must be seen against the background of his anti-Pan-Africanism. In June 1921, three months after he had received a UNIA delegation in New York, he wrote an open letter to DuBois' *The Crisis*, promising that under "no circumstances" would Liberia "allow her territory to be made a center of aggression or conspiracy against other sovereign states."[25] There is a grandly duplicitous quality in the pronouncements emanating from Monrovia. In July, Edwin Barclay wrote to the British consul that "Mr. Marcus Garvey's movements and activities are . . . of no practical interest to this Government as they have not given and will not give endorsement to his fantastic schemes. Steps have already been taken by President King to put an end [to] Mr. Garvey's unauthorized and unwarranted exploitation of Liberia."[26]

Garveyite Pan-Africanism was a black Diaspora echo of the grand nineteenth-century "pan" movements, such as Pan-Slavism. Establishing an African American homeland and uniting all of Africa in one superstate are not the same aim. The UNIA's Pan-Africanism took on the task of nation building in the real world. It was here that Garveyism faced the suspicions of both the white world and the Liberian oligarchy. More centrally, to be successful it would have to move from simple anticolonialism and confront the very nature of the continent itself. Although Garvey might maintain that there was "not even the semblance of government" in Africa, its leaders and peoples knew otherwise. Early in 1921, one African, Madarikan Deniyi, expressed his dismay: "How can Marcus Garvey and the U.N.I.A. redeem Africa without the consent and cooperation of the black kings, chiefs and presidents who were born and elected to rule the natives in Africa?"[27] In the following year another African, the Basuto M. Mokete Manoedi, critiqued the whole Garveyite enterprise in similar terms: "It is about as sensible and logical to speak of a president of Africa as it is to speak of a president or king of Europe or of all the Americas." Manoedi noted that Africa contained a multitude of polities and cultures, which were not "always at peace merely because they occupy the same continent. Witness the recent world war between nations, such as France and Germany, both European nations." Manoedi pointed out that not all of the inhabitants of Africa considered themselves "Negroes." In a pointed critique of the tendency to use "Africa" as a stand-in for "Black Man's Land," the African wrote that the continent was composed of diverse nations, races and religions and colors. Manoedi argued that "The term Africa is a composite one like Asia or Europe. It does not denote a nation or race." He attacked the leader of the UNIA, whom he accused of lumping "the population of Africa [with] the population of Negroes in the United States, the West Indies, South and Central America" in a vain attempt to reach the total of 400,000,000 "Black Folk."[28]

Specifically in the Liberian case, whatever the idea of universal black unity, the UNIA had to face the distinction between "Native" and "Civilized." Cyril Henry of the second UNIA mission had stumbled on the problem. Not surprisingly there were inherent difficulties, "when you imagine a mere handful of partly Westernized Negroes as compared with the millions of aboriginal inhabitants seeking to establish a government with all the virtues and defects of European and African ideals to contend with." The Americo-Liberian was "an off-shoot of the Westernized American in this conflict of ideas [and] strives to maintain himself in a class separate and distinct." The results were bitter, for the "Civilized . . . either draws [away] in sympathy or, given time, reverts to his [that is, his Native] ways."[29] Earlier, during the first mission to Liberia, Elie Garcia had observed to Garvey that "There are at this present time two classes of people: the Americo-Liberians, also called "sons of the soil," and the natives. The first class, although the educated one, constitutes the most despicable element in Liberia." Damningly, Garcia maintained that the Americo-Liberians "buy men or women to serve them, and the least little insignificant Americo-Liberian has half a dozen boys at his service."[30] It was the UNIA's potential impact on the delicate balance between the settlers and the indigenes that made it anathema in Monrovia. In March 1922, the London-based colonial organ *The African World* published a purloined copy of Garcia's secret report. The expected happened. The government-controlled *Liberian News* later claimed that the report "gave a clear picture of the revolutionary purposes of the UNIA in Liberia, and determined the Government's irrevocable attitude of opposition."[31] After vainly trying to placate the implacable Monrovia government, Garvey attacked "the Negroes of the Barclay and King type" who kept "the natives poor, hungry, shelterless and naked." Indeed, "In Liberia the Negroes of the Barclay and King type treat the natives like dogs, and with greater inhumanity than some of the most selfish whites."[32] In any contest between indigenous Africa and settlers, sympathies would now be with indigenous Africa.

After the Liberian fiasco of 1924, Garveyism appeared dead. It was, however, only dormant. In the late 1930s, emigrationism resurfaced as a beacon within a racial storm. The Great Depression and the rise of Fascism created a climate that made some question the long-term viability of Africa-America. For instance, in 1937, Arthur Schomburg opined: "I am becoming very doubtful of the Negro finding a place for himself in the next quarter of a century. . . . We will either be relegated to the level of the sidewalk or back to Africa in the spirit of the philosophy of Marcus Garvey."[33] Although DuBois spent part of the 1920s castigating Garvey's West African dream, his faith in the African American's permanent place in the American polity sometimes faltered. In the year of Garvey's death, DuBois commented on the possible future need for "eventual emigration" by "some considerable part" of the African American population. The American black, like the European Jew, might be "pushed out of his . . . fatherland."[34]

The desire to escape the Diasporic racial nightmare remained strong. In Garvey's calculus, the proximity of two races, black and white, must engender conflict, resulting in the elimination of the weaker. Even in the best of worlds, to Garvey, minority status resulted in an ongoing state of tension and disequilibrium. Even the granting of middle-class status to one segment of the black population would not be a final solution to the "Negro Question." In the Garveyite analysis, the greater (and darker) part of the race would be left to struggle even more intensely against increasing pauperization. Segregation was a halfway house on the road to race war. Separation by any means necessary was the key to racial survival. This was the absolute grand strategy before which all tactics and individuals were relative. Africa remained the lodestone of his program and, in the final years of his life, the continent claimed his attention more insistently than ever.

In the early 1920s, segregationist white America ignored or mocked Garvey and his movement. Fifteen years later, white America remained largely unconcerned. Interestingly, some people on the segregationist radical fringe sought to exploit African Americans' desire to flee discrimination and lynch law. As before, the desire for "repatriation" foundered on the tacit opposition of the federal government of the United States and the anxiously guarded sovereignty of the Liberian state. On the racist fringe, the rather unlikely godfather of this rebirth was the ardent segregationist, Senator Theodore Bilbo of Mississippi. At first glance, this legislator would seem a truly unlikely supporter of any form of black nationalism. In 1923, when Garvey's Liberian project still appeared viable, Bilbo mocked Maryland "Senator T. G. McCallum's scheme to move negroes of the United States to darkest Africa," as "wonderful to contemplate, a fact to be devoutly wished for, but . . . an idle dream."[35] Obsessed by the specter of interracial sex, Bilbo came to see black emigration as the final solution to his own American Dilemma. In the early 1930s, Bilbo became aware of the Peace Movement of Ethiopia, an emigrationist organization headed by a former UNIA member, Mittie Maude Lena Gordon. The Louisiana-born Gordon had been a delegate to the 1929 UNIA convention in Jamaica. She founded her single-issue lobbying movement in Chicago in December 1932. Its aim was federal "repatriation" of African Americans to Liberia. The movement's reasoning was that the cost of establishing African Americans in West Africa would be less than the cost of welfare in America. In 1933, the Peace Movement sent a petition with over four hundred thousand signatures to President Roosevelt, asking for help with its project. The petition was shunted to the State Department and then relegated to the Division of Western European Affairs, where it vegetated. Mistakenly, Bilbo believed that representatives of Gordon's group had visited Liberia, where now-President Edwin Barclay had guaranteed them large territories.

Bilbo was impressed by Garvey, who was "the most conspicuous [*sic*] of all the organizers of his race." Garvey had "definitely succeeded in establishing the fact that there is an overmastering impulse, a divine afflatus among the masses of Negroes in the United States for a country of their own and a government administered by themselves."[36] Garvey responded to the overtures. The Eighth International Convention of the UNIA met in Toronto in August 1938 and voted unanimously in favor of a motion supporting Bilbo's stance. Garvey wrote to Bilbo that "It is not necessary to comment on the vital importance of your motion, in that it strikes at the very future of the race in as far as its nationalistic aspirations are concerned."[37] The senator replied that he was "happy to know that your organization will give me fullest cooperation in the program that I am trying to project for the benefit of the Negroes in the United States."[38] Garveyites in various cities sent letters and delegations to the Mississippian. Mass meetings were organized and, by April 1939, the UNIA had collected 50,000 more signatures in support of emigration. From New York, Carlos Cooks, the president of the UNIA Advance Division, wrote the Southern legislator that "Our speaking staff is anxious, eager, and ready to swing into action."[39] Bilbo attempted to fund a speaking tour for the group, while Garvey in England set up a committee to pressure Washington. Garveyites in Cleveland, Philadelphia, and New York grouped themselves into a "Lobby Committee on [the] Greater Liberia Act."

In 1939, Bilbo introduced his Greater Liberia Act in the U.S. Senate. It called for the subsidized and voluntary emigration of African Americans to the Black Republic. The senator foresaw the exodus of from five to eight million African Americans over a period of fifteen to twenty-five years. The plan would favor persons in their reproductive years; Bilbo hoped that those who remained in the United States would die off. The legislation had two readings in the Senate and was buried in the Committee on Foreign Relations. Garvey said of the bill at the time it was proposed: "The Senator's desire for carrying out the purpose of his Bill may not be as idealistic as Negroes may want, but that is not the point to be considered."[40] What was important was "the opportunity of the Negro to establish himself and there is no doubt that this Bill offers such an opportunity." Garvey wholeheartedly supported the bill and attacked those members of the "Negro Press" who opposed it. He maintained that certain of the senator's comments on race in previous years were irrelevant in the present case. It was the bill that mattered. Bilbo's effort was "one that no Negro can make in America at the present time, because he [that is, the Negro] lacks the necessary influence in the Senate."[41]

Bilbo was not alone in his enthusiasm. More than a decade after Garvey's Liberian gambit, a handful of Southern racists rallied to the cause of "Greater Liberia." Perhaps the most notorious of Garvey's white racist supporters was Thomas Dixon, whose novel *The Clansman* had become the screen's *Birth of a Nation*. In 1939, Dixon published *The Flaming Sword*, a racist jeremiad centered on the specter of black sexuality. In the novel, the protagonist bequeaths $10 million for the purpose of establishing a Marcus Garvey Colonization Society to encourage the voluntary emigration of African Americans.[42] The title of the novel came from a line by DuBois: "Across this path stands the South with flaming sword." Dixon's novel attacked "the junta fighting for intermarriage" and heaped abuse on, among others, the Communists James W. Ford and Earl Browder, DuBois, James Weldon Johnson, A Philip Randolph, Claude McKay, Carl Van Vechten, J. E. Spingarn, and Moorfield Story. Garvey expressed himself "very much interested in Mr. Dixon's new work and more so when he has stated that his desire is to work in behalf of the repatriation of Negroes to Africa."[43]

Another segregationist, Bilbo's friend and fellow arch-segregationist Earnest Servier Cox dedicated a book, *Let My People Go*, to Garvey and was in communication with many UNIA branches. In 1932, he lobbied for an emigration resolution in the Virginia state legislature. The proposal died in committee. In 1934, Cox made contact with Mittie Gordon. Curiously, the white racist became the national representative of the Peace Movement of Ethiopia two years later. The semi-moribund American Colonization Society was contacted in an effort to get its sponsorship. Cox, acting as the white patron of Peace Movement activities, eventually got the Virginia legislature to petition Congress for federal aid to emigration. Later, Cox expressed his thanks to the state governor on behalf of the Peace Movement, the National Union of People of African Descent, and the Universal Negro Improvement Association.[44]

Garvey effusively praised Bilbo and Cox. "These two white men," he wrote, "have done wonderfully well for the Negro and should not be forgotten."

Politics does make strange bedfellows, but how do we account for the flirtation between militant black nationalism and the radical fringe of American racism? On the one hand, Garvey's reasoning makes perfect sense if one believes that the majority of Americans are capable of genocidal impulses. On the other hand, the sincerity of Bilbo's support for black emigration is suspect, especially his proposal that Eleanor Roosevelt be named "Queen of Greater Liberia." Segregationist flirtation with emigrationism may have been no more than a tactic to embarrass white liberal opinion by exposing a powerful countercurrent in the black community. A benefit of this tactic would obviously be division among African Americans themselves.

Except for this quixotic advocacy, expatriation of African Americans has never received much national support. No truly important twentieth-century conservative paladin ever emerged to champion total segregation through expatriation. Indeed, among members of the racial mainstream, the endeavor remained as ever: "Keep the Negro in his place." Nonexistent or tepid support from the American majority was matched by continuing opposition from the Americo-Liberian elite. The Peace Movement sent two representatives, David Logan and Joseph Rockmore, to Liberia in 1938. The American minister in Monrovia noted "that President Barclay does not take seriously the expressed hopes of the PME that financial support will be received from the United States."[45] The two emissaries did spend a month in Liberia, but Barclay dampened any emigration plans by asking that all immigrants have proof of at least $1,000 in assets.

Marcus Garvey died the year after Bilbo's Senate bill was proposed. What are we to conclude about his "rise and fall"? The Garvey plan in Liberia foundered not because it was *illogical* but because key members of the Liberian political class were opposed to it from the outset. Within the Diaspora, Garvey was intent upon carving out a safe place and a location for black people *to be somebody*. He realized that the legal end of slavery did not shatter the carapace of caste. Under legalized segregation, blacks remained economically discriminated against, endogamous, and residentially segregated. It is this perpetually liminal state that black nationalists before and after Garvey have found and find unacceptable. Until Africa and the African Diaspora have obtained equality in the world, the words and actions of the Universal Negro Improvement Association will reverberate.

Notes

1. Marcus Garvey, *Philosophy and Opinions; or Africa for the Africans* (New York: Viking, 1970). vol. 2, part 1, p. 2.

2 Quoted in Elome Brath, "Marcus Garvey: The First African Internationalist," *Caribe* 9, no. 1 (1987): 17.

3. Ibid.

4. Elliott Skinner, *African Americans and U.S. Policy toward Africa 1850–1924: In Defense of Black Nationality* (Washington, DC: Howard University Press, 1992), 442, citing *The Crisis*, no. 21 (January 1921), 112–15.

5. Kevin Gaines, *Uplifting the Race: Black Leadership, Politics and Culture in the Twentieth Century* (Chapel Hill: University of North Carolina Press, 1996), 240.

6. Skinner, *African Americans and U.S. Policy,* 442, citing *The Crisis,* no. 21 (January 1921), 112–15.

7. Tony Martin, *Race First: The Ideological and Organizational Struggles of Marcus Garvey and the Universal Negro Improvement Association* (Dover, MA: Majority Press, 1986), 123, citing *The Negro World,* May 8, 1920.

8. Judith Stein, *Race and Class in Modern Society* (Baton Rouge: Louisiana State University Press, 1986), 117.

9. Marcus Garvey, *The Marcus Garvey and Universal Negro Improvement Association Papers,* ed. Robert A. Hill (Berkeley: University of California Press, 1983–), vol. 10, Liberia, 113, article in the *Liberian News,* Monrovia, August 1924, enclosure in C. A. Wall to U.S. Secretary of State, August 8, 1924. These papers are henceforth cited as *Garvey Papers.*

10. Edmund Cronon, *Black Moses, The Story of Marcus Garvey and the Universal Negro Improvement Association* (Madison: University of Wisconsin Press, 1964), 130.

11. Martin, *Race First,* 124, quoting interview with the Acting President of Liberia by the Commissioners of the Universal Negro Improvement Association, Tuesday, March 21, 1921, Record Group (RG) 59, 882.001, United States National Archives at College Park (NACP).

12. Martin, *Race First,* 132, citing memorandum in Charles H. Hughes to President, n.d.

13. *Garvey Papers,* Liberia, vol. 9, 227, excerpt from draft memorandum by John Cooper Wiley, Division of Western European Affairs, ca. September 1921.

14. *Garvey Papers,* vol. 9, 89, R. Petre, French Chargé d'Affaires, Monrovia, to Aristide Briand, November 22, 1922.

15. *Garvey Papers,* vol. 9, 706, Georges Bouet to Governor-General of French West Africa, July 24, 1923.

16. *Garvey Papers,* Liberia, Georges Bouet to French Minister of Foreign Affairs, July 3, 1924 (forthcoming volume, material supplied by Robert A. Hill, editor in chief).

17. *Garvey Papers,* Liberia, citing Public Record Office (PRO), Colonial Office (CO) 532/289, September 5, 1925, note 1 to Francis O'Meara to British Secretary of State for Foreign Affairs, August 8, 1924 (forthcoming volume, material supplied by Robert A. Hill, editor in chief).

18. Garvey, *Philosophy and Opinions,* vol. 2, 399.

19. Martin, *Race First,* 122, citing C. G. Contee, "The Worley Report on the Pan-African Congress of 1919," *Journal of Negro History,* 55 (April 1970): 141.

20. Ibid., citing *New York Age,* September 20, 1919.

21. Ibid.

22. Ibid., citing "Unrest among the Negroes," October 7, 1919, RG 28, Box 53, Unarranged 398, NACP, and Contee, "The Worley Report," 141.

23. Memorandum, Division of European Affairs, September 25, 1919, RG 59, 882.00/630, NACP.

24. Memorandum, Third Assistant Secretary, Department of State, regarding Messrs. Emmett Scott, Louis Cobb, and William Lewis, November 24, 1919, RG 59, 882.00/630, NACP.

25. Martin, *Race First*, 125, citing *The Crisis* (June 1921), 53.

26. Ibid., 122, citing Edwin Barclay, "Minutes of Meeting, March 22, 1921."

27. *Garvey Papers*, vol. 9, 144, Madarikan Deniyi to the *Richmond Planet*, January 29, 1921.

28. Ibid., 651, pamphlet by M. Mokete Manoedi, New York, ca. July 1922, enclosure in Manoedi to Winston S. Churchill, September 30, 1922.

29. *Garvey Papers*, vol. 9, 69, Cyril Henry to O. M. Thompson, July 1, 1921.

30. Garvey, *Philosophy and Opinions*, vol. 2, 399–400.

31. Martin, *Race First*, 127, citing *Liberian News*, August 10, 1924.

32. Garvey, *Philosophy and Opinions*, vol. 2, 397.

33. Winston James, *Holding Aloft the Banner of Ethiopia: Caribbean Radicalism in Early Twentieth Century America* (New York: Verso, 1998), 211, citing Schomburg to Dabney, August 19, 1937, Schomburg Papers, reel 7.

34. W. E. B. DuBois, *Dusk of Dawn: An Essay toward an Autobiography of a Race Concept* (New Brunswick, NJ: Transaction, 1984; reprint of 1940 edition, with new introduction by Irene Diggs), 197–200.

35. Martin, *Race First*, 349, citing Thurston E. Doler, "Theodore G. Bilbo's Rhetoric of Racial Relations" (PhD diss., University of Oregon, 1968).

36. Martin, *Race First*, 349, citing Theodore G. Bilbo, *Take Your Choice: Separation or Mongrelization* (Poplarville, MS: Dream House Publishing Company, 1947).

37. *Garvey Papers*, vol. 7, 884, Marcus Garvey to Senator Theodore G. Bilbo, August 13, 1938.

38. Ibid., n. 2.

39. Ibid., 925, Carlos Cooks, President UNIA Advance Division, to Senator Theodore G. Bilbo, October 3, 1939.

40. Martin, *Race First*, 351, citing *The Black Man*, no. 3 (November 1938), 19.

41. *Garvey Papers*, vol. 7, 920, essay in *The Black Man*, "Bill Introduced into the United States Senate Aiming at Carrying Out the Ideal of the U.N.I.A., A Greater Government for the Negroes of the World in Africa."

42. *Garvey Papers*, vol. 7, 354; see Thomas Dixon, *The Flaming Sword* (Atlanta, GA: Monarch Publishing, 1939).

43. *Garvey Papers*, vol. 7, 893, Marcus Garvey to Earnest S. Cox, October 6, 1938.

44. Martin, *Race First*, 352, citing *Richmond Times-Despatch*, January 27, 1940, and Cox to Governor James H. Price, December 29, 1939, Box 8, d. 10, Universal Negro Improvement Association (UNIA) Central Division (New York) Files.

45. *Garvey Papers*, vol. 7, 822, n. 3, Charles Watkins, President, Peace Movement of Ethiopia, to Senator Theodore Bilbo, March 1938, footnote citing Lester A. Walton to the Secretary of State, January 14, 1939, RG 59, 882.5211, NACP.

5

Economic Relations between Nigeria and the United States in the Era of British Colonial Rule, ca. 1900–1950

Ayodeji Olukoju

Introduction

The economic relations between the British colony of Nigeria and the United States constitute a neglected theme in the literature. Until now, scholarly research has concentrated on political and social aspects of relations between Nigeria and the United States.[1] To be sure, aspects of economic contact between Nigeria and the United States have been examined in some scholarly publications,[2] but the present chapter sets out to examine some previously neglected but important aspects of the economic relations between Nigeria and the United States in the first half of the twentieth century, when the former was under British colonial rule.

The chapter focuses on maritime trade and shipping, agriculture, and transport within the framework of colonialism and globalization. The framework incorporates British colonial policies, especially in relation to foreign competition, and such issues as the vagaries of the global economy and the post–World War I global preeminence of the United States. The complementarity of the global and local—leading to the peculiarities of the Nigerian colonial political economy—provides the framework for this analysis of Nigerian-U.S. trade relations in the heyday of British colonial rule in Nigeria.[3]

The Colonial and Global Contexts of a Peculiar Relationship

The 1890s, the convenient point of commencement of our discussion, were remarkable for the formal establishment of British colonial rule over much of Nigeria, though the process lingered on till the first decade of the twentieth century in certain parts of the country. Beginning at Lagos, a major port of the transatlantic slave trade, which was formally annexed as a colony in 1861, the British proceeded to acquire the hinterland by treaties, shows of force, and outright conquest. The process was facilitated by a series of wars arising from the collapse of Oyo, the empire-building efforts of Ibadan, and the resistance of a broad coalition of Yoruba states in western Nigeria, the Islamic jihad that swept through much of northern Nigeria after 1804, the antislavery campaign, and the advent of Christianity.[4]

An immediate consequence of the imposition of British rule was the formal incorporation of the Nigerian colonial economy into the web of global trade networks largely through the "mother country," as Nigerian trade was channeled as far as was practicable to Britain. This was ensured through the domination of the external trade of the colony by British business firms, the provision of the infrastructure of trade (modern ports, steam shipping, railway and road networks aligned toward the ports, and British-controlled banking and currency systems), the institution of appropriate trade controls, and a regime of colonial law and order.[5]

With only a few exceptions, the dominant trading, mining, and shipping firms that controlled the Nigerian colonial economy were British.[6] The exceptions were the Germans, who dominated the pre–World War I trade in palm kernels, and the Dutch, who, together with the Germans and Austrians, controlled the trade in "trade spirits" (inferior liquor) during the same period.[7] In shipping, the dominance of the British line, Elder Dempster, was challenged by its German rival, Woermann Linie. The two came to terms by establishing in 1895 the West African Lines Conference, a cartel that dominated the trade, determined freight rates, and kept out competitors such as tramp shippers. World War I was a watershed in many respects, not least for shutting out German and Austro-Hungarian enterprises and ensuring the near-total dominance of the colonial economy by British nationals.[8] In spite of efforts to regain their dominance over the kernel trade, the Germans were never able to succeed in this, though they were more successful in the shipping business, where Woermann Linie (as well as the French and Dutch lines) managed to secure a portion of the trade.

Taking advantage of the war and its aftermath, the British imposed discriminatory tariffs on the trade of "foreign" (that is, non-British) countries where these posed a threat to British national economic interest. A differential export duty of £2 per ton of kernels exported outside the British Empire was imposed during World War I to ensure the diversion of Nigerian kernel exports to British mills; the duty was continued till 1919, when the object had been achieved. In the interwar period, discriminatory tariffs and quotas effectively curtailed the inroads of Japanese textiles into the Nigerian market.[9] It is against this background that we shall consider U.S. economic relations with Nigeria, with a focus on trade, agriculture, and transport.

U.S.–Nigerian Economic Relations, 1890s to 1918

Nigeria's external trade between the 1890s and the outbreak of World War I in 1914 was conditioned by several interlocking factors, both global and local. Among these were the provision of harbor and railway facilities, the establishment of colonial rule, and the concomitant expansion of the colonial economy; alternating weather conditions of drought (as in 1896–97) and rainfall; political and social developments, such as labor recruitment and military campaigning in the late 1890s as British colonial rule was being imposed, affecting trade by draining labor from the agricultural sector and disrupting peaceful economic pursuits; colonial policy, especially the imposition of tariffs on trade (see, for example, the depressing effect of high import duties on the volume of trade); and local and external economic developments, including booms and slumps in the economies of Europe and America, resulting in rises or falls in local prices in response to the forces of supply and demand in the metropolitan economies.[10]

Direct U.S.-Nigeria trade relations during this period were of little significance (see table 5.1). This was because, with the exception of hides and skins, there is no record of exports to the American market. It was only with the emergence of the cocoa industry in Western Nigeria in the second decade of the twentieth century that Nigerian exports to the United States received a major boost. However, if the United States had no direct economic impact on the Nigerian economy in the early years of the colonial period, it certainly had an indirect impact. This was due to the size of American cotton production and exports, which always impacted the prices offered to Nigerian cotton producers. Moreover, Nigeria was necessarily assailed by any adversity in the U.S. domestic economy, which had global repercussions given the rise of America as a world economic power by the opening decade of the twentieth century.

Thus, while the period from 1906 to 1914 in Nigerian economic history was characterized by commercial "prosperity," this was tempered by certain adverse developments. The financial crisis in the United States in the autumn of 1907 had caused a slackening of trade in Europe and a consequent fall in the prices of tropical products. This, coupled with an outbreak of drought toward the end of 1907, immediately affected the Nigerian cotton crop as well as affecting palm produce exports in 1908.[11] The reduction in producer prices naturally affected the people's purchasing power, which forced a decline in Nigerian imports.

On the whole, U.S.-Nigerian economic relations before 1919 were relatively insignificant. As is indicated in table 5.1, there were no recorded Nigerian exports to the United States till 1915, the first full year of World War I. The American percentage share of the import trade of Nigeria never hit double digits till the last two years of the war, though this level was

Table 5.1 Nigerian Imports from and Exports to United States, 1910–18, as
Percentages of Total Nigerian Imports and Exports

Year	1910	1911	1912	1913	1914	1915	1916	1917	1918
Imports	4.2	3.3	4.8	4.7	3.8	6.7	9.2	11.9	11.5
Exports	–	–	–	–	–	4.7	10.2	12.9	6.0

Source: The Nigerian Handbook, 1927 (Lagos: Government Printer, 1928), 43.

achieved for imports somewhat earlier. It was only in the interwar years that
American trade registered any significant impression on Nigerian trade statistics, even then, admittedly, only with regard to a few items of trade.

It is worth noting that, with the elimination of German competition during World War I, America was considered a suitable replacement for
Germany as a major trade partner for Nigeria. Frederick Lugard, Nigeria's
governor-general, had stated that foreign competition was "almost essential
to preserve a healthy trade and secure to the producer a reasonable value for
his produce." "If foreign competition is, therefore, to be encouraged," he
opined, "American is preferable to German, and it has the advantage of having more capital behind it than French enterprise would have."[12] We may
note in passing that Lugard's stance was hypocritical, given the government's
overt support for its own nationals, that is, Britons, in the form of discriminatory tariffs and protectionist policies.[13] The following section of this chapter examines developments in the postwar decade in the light of the
declaration in favor of American competition.

Shipping and Trade between Nigeria and the United States, 1919–29

A major feature of the wartime external trade of Nigeria, and one that was carried over into the postwar period, was the exclusion of German enterprise and
the concomitant predominance of British firms. It was in this context that U.S.
trade made a showing in a few lines of trade. "A prominent feature in the
returns since the outbreak of war," noted the Nigerian customs report of 1919,
"is the increasing trade with the U.S.A." While U.S. exports to Nigeria in 1913
amounted to a value of only £304,000, the figure for 1919 was £1,528,000, a
remarkable increase of more than 400 percent. Total exports from Nigeria to
the United States rose from zero in 1913 to £1,671,000 in 1919.[14] These
remarkable increases derived largely from the brief postwar boom of 1918–20,
the declining value of sterling, and the expanding American market for

Nigerian cocoa and hides and skins. "Exports to the United States," it was reported in 1922, "show a substantial increase due to larger shipments of cocoa, palm oil and hides and skins." In return, the United States was a major exporter of provisions, petroleum, and unrefined tobacco to Nigeria.[15] "Since the war," it was noted in 1919, "increasing quantities of provisions are being imported direct from the United States of America."[16]

A major import from the United States was the Ford motor car, 200 of which were delivered in September 1920 alone, a phenomenon described as the "Motor 'Boom.'"[17] The "boom" was a direct product of the commercial prosperity of the immediate postwar years, and it was boosted by the favorable customs tariff regime that was in operation. "There is no Customs duty on motor cars, lorries, vans etc.," it was reported in 1923, "nor on any parts thereof, nor on lubricating oil."[18] The only duty charged was on petrol at eight pence per imperial gallon and storage at one penny per month on a case of ten gallons or part of such a case. However, vehicles were required to obtain annual licenses based on their weight. The Customs Report for Nigeria in 1923 noted that the demand for motor cars, trucks, and motorcycles had increased in the postwar period, a significant trend since the boom of 1918–20 was effectively over. The report further stated that there were "agents for numerous American manufactures" and regretted that they did not "push the sale of the British light car." This was in view of the fact that there was "room for considerable development in motor traffic in Nigeria."[19]

The Nigerian market was attractive to vehicle importers because light vans were required for the door-to-door conveyance of goods that the railways could not provide. Short-distance runs between populous and rich commercial centers were said to offer prospects for profitable enterprise. The terrain was said to demand vehicles with "more ground clearance" than those produced and used in the United Kingdom (UK). The ground clearance had to be at least nine inches under the axles, twelve inches under the engine, and fifteen under the gearbox. The wheelbase was not to be less than eight feet, six inches, while the radius for the turning circle should not exceed twenty feet. Vehicles made in Britain did not meet these specifications, and this created room for appropriately designed American vehicles.[20] "The popularity of the Ford car for commercial purposes," it was noted in 1920, "has been established. Many of these arrive without bodies, and lorry platforms of stout native timbers are fitted locally. These make serviceable transport cars."[21]

The importation of American vehicles led to the development of an ancillary industry in repairs and sales of parts. A notable name in the importation, repair, and sale of spare parts for American Ford and Dodge cars during the 1920s was William Akinola Dawodu, a member of the renowned Mabinuori Dawodu family of Lagos Island. After obtaining the requisite technical training in Lagos, Dawodu pioneered the motor transport service and supply business in Nigeria, with a major focus on American vehicles. The slump of 1920–22, the spirited competition of European importers, and a series of personal and health crises dealt devastating blows to Dawodu's business.[22] The firm was forced to resort to aggressive sales tactics, mainly newspaper advertisements and price cuts, to cope with the biting effects of the depression of the 1920s. In January 1921, for example, its advertisement in a Lagos newspaper stated that the Dodge motor car's "steady growth in good opinion proves how readily the public appreciate real value." Customers were enjoined to visit the firm's premises at 21 Egerton Road in Lagos to inspect the cars, which were sold in Lagos for £480. There was the added advantage, according to the firm, that "Spare Parts for Dodge Cars are always in stock."[23] At its height, Dawodu's motor transport business spread into the hinterland to Oshogbo (in southwest Nigeria) and to Kano in the far north. As Dawodu's vehicle import business expanded, the American automobile industry penetrated the Nigerian market. In Lagos, thanks to pioneers like Dawodu, American vehicles formed the basis of the municipal transport service, which became well established in the interwar years.[24] Apart from the professional elite, indigenous royalty also developed a taste for such cars. The Deji of Akure and the Ogoga of Ikere, indigenous rulers of major towns in eastern Yorubaland, were reported to have bought cars in May 1921, ironically when the slump was worsening. A newspaper lauded these sales as "harbingers of many more."[25]

Messrs. A. H. Bull & Company and Messrs. Grace Brothers & Company of New York, which had established "a growing agency," were said to be the leading American firms in Nigeria. "In spite of abnormal differences in the exchanges," it was further noted, "American goods are being introduced into these markets and find a sale in competition with British manufactures." It was anticipated, however, that "when the financial consequences of the War have adjusted themselves, exports from America will be placed on easier conditions on these markets than they are today."[26] It is clear that there was a growing commercial relationship between Nigeria and the United States at least from 1919 onward.

Still, an analysis of the import and export figures for Nigeria during the early 1920s indicates that the United States was still only a marginal player in the Nigerian colonial economy.[27] U.S.-bound exports from Nigeria and U.S. imports to Nigeria in 1921 were valued at £114,594 or 1.18 percent and £811,237 or 7.53 percent of total Nigerian trade, respectively. In 1922 the figures were £774,175 or 7.41 percent and £645,079 or 5.91 percent, respectively, of total Nigerian trade. However, the apparently low figures for the United States masked the reality that the figures were much higher for certain specific items. Thus, the U.S. share of Nigerian exports of cocoa rose from 4 percent in 1921 to 15 percent a year later. For palm produce, the percentage rose from 2.5 to 19.4; and for raw hides from zero to 17 percent

Table 5.2 American Import and Export Trade with Nigeria, 1919–26, as Percentages of Total Nigerian Imports and Exports

Year	1919	1920	1921	1922	1923	1924	1925	1926
Imports	14.1	11.8	7.7	6.2	7.7	7.6	6.54	7.75
Exports	11.3	3.5	1.2	8.7	9.7	5.6	9.58	7.7

Source: The Nigerian Handbook, 1927 (Lagos: Government Printer, 1928), 43.

for the same years. However, the figures for certain goods exported from Nigeria to the United States plummeted: haired goatskins declined from 32 percent in 1921 to 17 percent in 1922, while the figures for haired sheepskins were 39 percent and zero for 1921 and 1922 respectively.

Table 5.2 conveys an idea of the dynamics of American trade with Nigeria after World War I. As in the prewar years, the U.S. share of Nigeria's external trade fluctuated wildly, not conforming to a discernible pattern. While the trends reflected fluctuations in the wider colonial and global economies, they may also have been responses to peculiar features of American trade, relating specifically to the demand for Nigerian produce in the United States and the demand for American imports in Nigeria. Thus, whereas in 1920, at the peak of the postwar boom, foodstuffs were imported into Nigeria "in larger quantities than ever," the severe slump of 1920–22 took its toll on Nigerian trade: there was a "serious falling off in the demand and the prices offered for the principal Nigerian products," with concomitant losses.[28] Shipments of hides and skins, a Nigerian export to the U.S., were reported in 1921 to "have nearly ceased owing to a lack of demand which is worldwide."[29]

Table 5.3 provides a statistical snapshot of steam shipping between 1920 and 1925. The most important American shipping enterprise was Messrs. A. H. Bull & Company of New York, which operated the Bull Line as an agent of the U.S. Board of Trade. A Lagos newspaper, probably chafing at the overwhelming influence of Britain's Elder Dempster line, applauded the entry of the U.S. shipping line into Nigerian maritime business. Commenting on the reported trial run heralding Bull's debut, the newspaper expressed the hope that the line would stimulate trade between Nigeria and America, asserting that Britain's Elder Dempster had "nothing to fear from any fair competition in the carrying trade between Lagos and New York."[30]

A report of 1920 indicated that American and other foreign shipping had begun to make some inroads into the near-monopoly position held by the British line, Elder Dempster. "Owing to the restrictions on shipping during the last few years," it noted, "the Customs wharf at Lagos had almost become

Table 5.3 Size and Character of Nigerian Shipping, 1920–25

Year	Tonnage Landed			Tonnage Shipped		
	British	Foreign*	Total	British	Foreign	Total
1920	601,616	115,939	717,555	586,389	121,0444	707,442
1921	570,264	262,456	832,720	554,959	263,864	818,823
1922	286,896	46,272	333,168	246,704	161,633	408,337
1923	286,715	57,023	343,738	315,791	171,155	486,946
1924	268,805	87,154	355,959	403,648	201,637	605,285
1925	355,242	74,205	429,447	552,082	208,561	760,643

* "Foreign" refers to French, American, Dutch, German, Italian, Norwegian, Swedish, Danish, Spanish, and Portuguese shipping.
Source: National Archives of Nigeria, Ibadan, *Nigeria, Annual Reports, Annual Report, 1921,* 10; *Annual Report, 1925,* 13.

the unintentional monopoly of the steamers of the Elder Dempster line. This week, we have had the spectacle of a Bull liner, a Holland liner, and a ship of the Elder Dempster line lying side by side discharging their cargo." This was seen as a pointer to the "coming prosperity of Lagos as a port of call for new shipping enterprises, and, incidentally, of the interest commercial men in the Continent and in America have in Nigeria as a market for the world's wares."[31] In November 1920, a Lagos newspaper reported the arrival of SS *Sangamon* of the Bull line in the harbor the previous Sunday and the ship's departure the following day. "During the evening of her arrival," it stated, "brisk trade went on between the sailors and Hausa petty traders."[32] The saga of a distressed American schooner, the *Allanwilde,* which was sold off in Lagos in 1922, indicates that the occasional American tramp ship also traded with Nigeria during this period.[33]

Despite the inroads made by American and other shipping enterprises, it is clear from the data in table 5.3 (taken from the official annual reports) that British dominance of the Nigerian shipping trade continued in the 1920s and that "foreign" (that is, non-British, including American) enterprises made only a modest showing. This is certainly a true reflection of the pattern of U.S. shipping and maritime trade with Nigeria in the decade after World War I. Yet not all of Nigerian trade with the U.S. during this period was recorded or licit. For example, one James Akiwunmi Bishopton was arrested in April 1920 for attempting to counterfeit a twenty shilling (£1) bill "with equipment ordered from America"![34]

American "Allen" Cotton in Northern Nigeria, 1912–29

The long tenure of O. T. Faulkner as Nigeria's director of agriculture during the interwar period witnessed several notable developments.[35] One of these was the steady infusion, from 1916 onward, of the American "Allen" cotton into Nigerian agriculture. This was an innovation that was intended to boost Nigerian cotton exports, primarily for the sake of the Lancashire textile industry, which was vulnerable to fluctuations in cotton imports from India and elsewhere. "The supply of cotton has never kept pace with the demand in recent years," *West Africa* reported in 1917, "and Lancashire, in the cruel grip of corner-operators, has been compelled to close its mills from time to time." Alluding to the impact of the United States on the Lancashire industry, the periodical added: "America is using year-after-year a larger proportion of her own crop, and in years of scarcity, is able to keep sufficient for her own needs whilst sending only the surplus to this country [that is, Britain]."[36] In an editorial on the subject, a Lagos newspaper pointed out that Great Britain had long depended on the United States for the greater portion of its cotton, but that reliance on the United States was no longer possible, due to certain developments: the high prices paid for labor in the United States; the unfavorable currency exchange rates; and U.S. internal consumption requirements. Hence, it was imperative to turn to other sources.[37] Consequently, increased cultivation of cotton in Nigeria was promoted and the indigenous variety in Northern Nigeria was to be displaced by the American "Allen" long-staple type.[38]

The British Cotton Growing Association (BCGA) had been set up to promote the cultivation of cotton in the colonies for export to Britain. For example, it promoted "Allen" cotton in Northern Nigeria, the area considered to be best suited to cotton cultivation. After several varieties of cotton had been tested between 1912 and 1916, the "Allen" variety was selected and distributed for planting in Northern Nigeria.[39] Initial problems were encountered by the producers in cultivating it, while spinners did not see any advantage over the indigenous variety. It was also not clear whether the Zaria region with its greater rainfall and less sandy soil was best suited to the cultivation of the new variety or, alternatively, whether the drier provinces of the extreme north were the best choice. Moreover, there were doubts as to whether cotton could compete with groundnuts, which were emerging as a major feature of the Northern Nigerian economy .

The BCGA report for 1917–18 stated that the Allen "improved staple cotton" had been "grown under supervision" but that no exports were recorded for 1913–14. In the three years from 1914–15 to 1916–17, there was a steady rise in export figures mainly from Northern Nigeria: 12, 110, and 461 bales respectively. The seed distributed for cultivation around Zaria reportedly yielded 100 bales in 1916–17. One hundred and thirty-eight bales of "Allen" cotton were distributed for cultivation in the districts bordering the Bauchi Railway, a notable center of production for export. It was declared that the future of the cotton industry was dependent upon the widespread cultivation of "Allen" cotton, 800 bales of which were expected to be exported in 1917–18. Accordingly, steps were taken toward achieving this target. First, to induce production, a price of two and a quarter pence per pound (lb) was guaranteed for the "Allen" crop around the railway and two pence at other places. Second, regulations were introduced under the Agricultural Ordinance of 1916 to prevent the mixing of "Allen" and local cotton.[40] Third, in 1920, the colonial government enacted a regulation forbidding the cultivation of other varieties of cotton in areas designated as "American cotton areas." The penalty for any breach of this regulation was a fine of £25.[41] This last measure produced contradictory results, as attested by a report of 1921: "the somewhat drastic regulations had achieved their end in keeping the cotton pure, but had incidentally resulted in reducing the area under cotton by some 50 percent. . . [thus underscoring] the inadvisability. . . of introducing a new variety of cotton to the compulsory exclusion of other time-honoured varieties."[42]

That said, the measures appear to have achieved their objectives, according to official reports. A report of 1923 stated that efforts had been made "in recent years" to boost cotton production in Northern Nigeria. "This has been achieved," it added, "by introducing a longstaple upland type of cotton producing cotton lint 1 13/16 inches in length. Not only does this improved type of cotton yield a heavier crop than the indigenous variety, but it commands a higher premium on the Liverpool market. This American cotton is rapidly superseding the local varieties."[43] The American "Allen" yielded 17,425 bales for export in 1923 compared with 16,443 bales and 22,527 bales in 1922 and 1921 respectively (see table 5.4).

The fluctuations in trade from the mid-1920s owing to local and global dynamics, however, caused a sharp drop in American "Allen" cotton exports from Nigeria, from 37,000 bales in 1925–26 to a little more than 16,000 bales in 1926–27.[44] This was ascribed to a combination of factors—the adverse weather, an increase in local consumption (that is, by the local textile industry), and "export by land," presumably to neighboring French colonies. Significantly, the increase in local trade was induced by the low prices offered by exporters. In any case, the expansion of "Allen" cotton cultivation was hampered by an "exceptionally heavy planting of grain crops."[45]

By 1926, the initial obstacles had been overcome and cotton growing, especially of the "Allen" variety, under state supervision had become well grounded. Yet Northern Nigeria was not going to be another cotton "haven" like Uganda, though there were hopes of steady increases in export figures, which were acknowledged to be contingent upon "the growth and movement of population, . . . [on] the extension of transport facilities . . . [on] the increase of ginneries . . . [and] on how far other exportable crops, such as groundnuts, are grown and found profitable." While the export goal was

Table 5.4 Exports of "Allen" Cotton from the Northern Provinces of Nigeria (with Prices), 1915/16–1925/26

Year	1915/16	1916/17	1917/18	1918/19	1919/20
Exports in bales of 400 lbs.	121	433	855	2248	3563
Prices per lb. of seed cotton	1¾d	1¾d	2½d	2¾d	3¾d

Source: National Archives of Nigeria, Ibadan, Nigeria, CSO 26 16690, vol. I, "Report on Cotton Growing Industry in Northern Nigeria," by Colonel N. French, 1926, 6.

still being pursued, the fundamental aim of supplanting the local species of cotton had been achieved. The latter, it was reported, had "now been practically eliminated from the gazetted cotton markets and [as far as could be ascertained] . . . none is purchased for export."[46] This was the ultimate triumph of "Allen" cotton in Nigerian agriculture.

The introduction of American "Allen" cotton resulted from the need to find new sources of raw materials for the Lancashire cotton industry, which could no longer rely on supplies from the United States. However, when the United States produced a bumper crop, Nigerian exports had to reckon with American exports on the world market. For example, "As a result of the extraordinarily big cotton crop in the United States of America last year," Nigeria's director of agriculture stated in December 1927,

> the world's prices for cotton, palm oil, palm kernels and groundnuts continued to fall during the first half of 1927. But as soon as a small American cotton and cotton seed production in the current year began to be anticipated, the price of all our export products steadied, and in August they began definitely to rise, and are now again at a fairly satisfactory level.[47]

In effect, Nigerian "Allen" cotton was competing with its mother stock (exported from the United States) on the world market, and this caused a decline in prices for the former if the latter was produced in considerable quantity. This point underscores the reality that Nigeria was becoming riveted to the evolving global economic system, in which the United States was becoming the key player.

U.S.-Nigerian Commercial Relations, 1929–39

The centrality of the United States in the emerging global economy of the inter-war years was confirmed by the New York Stock Exchange crash of

1920/21	1921/22	1922/23	1923/24	1924/25	1925/26
5405	9483	11,225	15,675	28,100	40,000
4½d	2d	2½d	4d	3d	2½d

September 1929, which precipitated the Great Depression of 1929–33. The global event had local repercussions in Nigeria, with conditions worsening as the Great Depression progressed.[48] The impact on Nigeria of developments in the United States is indicated by a report of 1933, which noted that

> the first few months . . . were clouded by the position in America which was steadily deteriorating, and in the spring resulted in the collapse of the banking system and the driving of the dollar off gold. This had a disastrous effect on all markets for Nigerian produce, of which the US is normally a large buyer, so that prices fell to £4 5s for palm kernels, £5 for soft oil and £11 10s for mid-crop cocoa. After a month or two of uncertainty there followed a wave of optimism in President Roosevelt and the United States and a rapid rise in the prices of almost all raw materials.[49]

However, when confidence in Roosevelt's plans waned by the end of the year, prices fell again; they finally stabilized but Nigeria was hardly any better off.

A somewhat different situation also illustrated the importance of domestic developments in the United States to the world economy. Sir Robert Waley Cohen, at the annual general meeting of the African and Eastern Trade Corporation Limited in January 1931, ascribed the decline in the volume of the cocoa export trade locally and globally to "the exceptionally hot weather in America this year during which period the consumption of chocolate was far below the normal level."[50]

Although the commercial outlook was generally dismal during the Great Depression, American trade with Nigeria was sustained. A striking example was the "New Ford" car, which was advertised in a Lagos newspaper in 1930 as the depression deepened. Versions of the popular American model marketed by Nigerian Motors Limited, a branch of the United Africa Company (UAC), were advertised as follows: a half-ton commercial truck with a covered body (priced at £100); a Ford touring car, or phaeton (£145); a Ford

Roadster (£145); a thirty-hundredweight chassis complete with covered "Lagos Body" (£195); and a thirty-hundredweight chassis complete with steel faced covered body (£225).[51]

Nigerian Motors Limited was the new dominant force in the motor import business. In a newspaper report of May 1930, this firm, which had been established in Lagos fourteen years previously, was said to have "done a yeoman service to push on the Motor trade." It was reported to have "[taken] over the Ford Cars from Messrs W. A. Dawodu & Co. and then started to import other Models—Reo, Willy's Knight, Dodge etc."[52] This is not surprising, as Dawodu's business did not survive his domestic crisis, terminal illness, and death in 1930. More striking, though explicable in view of the global economic adversity, was the sharp fall in automobile retail prices, from a height of £480 during the depression of 1920–22 to about a third of that price in 1930, the first full year of the Great Depression.

New or used Ford buses provided the basis of the municipal transport service in Lagos in the 1930s. The frontline motor transport entrepreneur of the times, J. N. Zarpas, who had himself acquired mainly British-made buses, lamented that his enterprise was being undercut by African operators, who employed "second hand old American cars converted for this type of transport but which are not safe and which are totally inadequate for this type of transport in a modern town."[53] It is significant that Zarpas, a Levantine merchant, sought to incite the British colonial government against his African rivals who put American buses on the road by arguing that, if they were not restrained, "my Company cannot undertake further extensions which means that further capital for the development of Nigeria must be restricted and *British productions must suffer to a corresponding extent.*"[54]

Meanwhile, as the Great Depression deepened, various independent states in the world instituted protectionist tariffs and other measures in their own economic interests.[55] Nigeria's oleaginous exports were especially vulnerable to such policies, some of which were enforced by the British government itself and its allies. For the British, a major dilemma was created when its interest in whale oil clashed with its interests in West African oleaginous produce, a subject that generated a major controversy in the 1930s. In addition, the protectionist tariff policy of the United States severely curtailed imports from Nigeria. First to be hit was the cocoa export trade, and this prompted a protest from Britain on the impact of protectionist restrictions on Anglo-American trade relations. The editorial column of a Lagos newspaper expressed what must have been a popular view on this subject:

> Whatever slight prospect there is for our cocoa is fast fading away with the introduction of new measures for the control of importation of cocoa, concerning what may or may not enter into America with particular reference to West African produce.

The new regulations are rather drastic and hard on the shipper. It will be a severe blow to the West African people if the American market is thus lost without any hope of its recovery at any future date.[56]

With regard to the oil seeds trade, the member for Rivers Division in the Nigerian Legislative Council, Mr. S. B. Rhodes, voiced the frustration of Nigerian producers when he called for the restriction of the importation of whale oil into Great Britain and the negotiation of a reduction of the U.S. import duty on Nigerian palm oil. The rate of duty was one cent on every pound weight of palm oil imported into the United States.[57]

U.S. policy was clarified for the affected colonial governments by the secretary of state for the colonies as follows. First, the policy was intended to promote domestic production of oils and fats in the United States. Second, it reflected a desire to give the United States' overseas territories and dependencies—in particular, the Philippines, a very important source of copra—a larger share of the remaining import market. These aims found expression in an act of the U.S. Congress that levied a processing tax "at an almost prohibitive rate" on the principal vegetable oils derived from imported raw materials. Arrangements were made to repay the Philippines government any amounts levied on Philippine copra. "In present circumstances," a top Nigerian official admitted, "it seems that very little besides Philippines copra will be imported" into the United States.[58] In view of this clarification, the Nigerian government could not pursue the options suggested by Mr. Rhodes. "The question of the U.S. Process[ing] Tax," the acting chief secretary wrote, "is of course one of world economics in which the interests of Nigeria unfortunately must play a very subordinate part, and it is a matter for world measures rather than local measures."[59]

As it happened, however, a string of unforeseen events forced a change in U.S. policy, even if only temporarily. In a review of the world economic situation at the beginning of 1935, the secretary of state for the colonies pointed out that the general rise in the price of certain products was "due almost entirely to widespread droughts in many parts of the world during the summer of 1934, which had reduced the supplies of alternative animal feeding stuffs, and to severe hurricanes in the Philippines which reduced the supply of copra from that source for the time being."[60] The persistence of this trend was revealed by an official report of September 1936, which referred to "another drought in America, almost as bad as the 1934 drought," which had caused shortages in wheat, oats, barley, rye, and maize. Maize shortages alone amounted to 834 million bushels or 21 million tons. "The shortage in cereal crops," the report concluded, "naturally affects Tallow and Lard, and the disappointing cotton crop naturally affects cotton oil."[61] Hence, Americans now had to import larger amounts of oil seeds, which worked to the advantage of Nigerian exports.

Table 5.5 Major U.S. Imports into Nigeria, 1930–35

Year	1930	1931	1932	1933	1934	1935
Leaf tobacco (lbs.)	4,105,430 (5,530,769)*	1,696,110 (2,355,578)	2,447,723 (3,872,034)	1,562,052 (2,375,873)	2,210,991 (2,278,597)	3,069,260 (3,122,885)
Motor spirits (imperial gallons)	6,592,345 (6,654,605)	3,869,286 (3,936,470)	4,024,597 (4,065,405)	2,258,387 (2,531,890)	2,105,556 (4,478,712)	1,864,357 (5,861,722)
Kerosene (imperial gallons)	4,630,973 (4,666,596)	3,152,073 (3,186,983)	2,095,289 (2,154,904)	1,448,970 (1,912,191)	1,098,515 (2,480,389)	1,134,732 (2,471,724)

*Figures in parentheses denote total imports for the year.
Source: National Archives of Nigeria, Ibadan, Nigeria: Colonial Reports—Annual: Annual Reports on the Social and Economic Progress of the People of Nigeria, 1931, 29–30; 1933, 9, 47; and 1935, 48.

The developments described above illustrate the central role of the United States and Nigeria's vulnerability to external or global dynamics. "The great recovery in [palm produce] prices since 1934," it was stated in 1936, "is probably due more than anything else to climatic conditions and Government policy in North America [the United States] which have combined both to reduce the production of cotton seed, an important competing vegetable product, and to depress the hog industry, the source of lard which is one of the most important animal products." This was complemented by the impact of developments in the whale oil industry, described as "possibly the most important single factor which may affect the industry in future," since "the interest of the [British] Empire in whaling is considerable."[62]

If figures for Nigerian exports to the United States fluctuated in the 1930s to the point of extinction during the Great Depression, the reverse was the case in the few imports to Nigeria in terms of which the position of the United States was unassailable: these were (unrefined) tobacco, motor spirits (gasoline), and kerosene. Less significant imports were flour, lubricating oil, motor cars, and trucks.[63] Though import figures for these commodities did fluctuate, the preeminence of the United States in the first three items was sustained, as may be seen from the figures in table 5.5. Still, the U.S. share of Nigerian trade was insignificant compared to the overwhelming dominance of the colonial power, Britain. The percentage figures for the U.S. share for the years 1929 through to 1936 were 12.4; 11.5; 8.9; 9.09; 7.72; 8.36; 8.15; and 6.67.[64] These trends persisted until the outbreak of

World War II in 1939 ushered in another period of global political, economic, and social dislocation.

World War II and Its Aftermath

World War II completely disrupted the prewar patterns of Nigerian trade. As in the earlier global war, the Germans were eliminated and a regime of controls and emergency measures was instituted.[65] U.S. trade and economic relations with Nigeria, which were precarious at the best of times, now declined. Various schemes for export and import controls were instituted to aid the war effort by curbing trade in order to conserve foreign exchange. "The British Empire and Nigeria are short of dollars," a commentator noted in 1944, "and Nigeria cannot therefore buy freely from United States. This is a matter of practical politics."[66] Nigerian external trade policy combined the principles of "Buy British" with "Sell Foreign"—to earn or save foreign exchange, as the case might be. The restriction of gasoline and other imports from the United States was designed to ensure that British trade deficits with the United States did not escalate, as the United States was the major foreign supporter of the British war effort. Still, U.S. trade with Nigeria was not totally extinguished, especially as gasoline, in particular, drove the war effort and was generally indispensable to daily life even in peacetime. This explains why the U.S. aggregate share of Nigerian trade for the duration of the war never fell below 6 percent: 10.32 in 1940, 9.95 in 1941, 6.79 in 1942, 8.26 in 1943, 13.25 in 1944, and 14.94 in 1945.[67]

The controls on trade lasted all through the war into the postwar years. The retention of controls after the war in aid of British war reconstruction was deplored by Nigerian nationalists. "The existence of [a] virtual embargo on trade between Nigeria and the United States of America," a Lagos-based newspaper declared, "was [at] one time looked upon as a war measure. Howbeit, the end of the war brought us to the realization that the control was more than that—it was also an expression of the economic impotency of Britain, which found it lucrative to trade Nigerian produce in exchange for US imports." The newspaper argued that since Britain had finally secured a loan from the United States, "African importers and exporters are eager to know when the existing barriers to trade with the Unites States will be lifted." It suggested that U.S. exporters were also anxious to take advantage of such a prospect. Arguing further in the same vein, the newspaper attributed the "perennial poverty" that had become "the curse of West Africa" to "a diabolical control on the sale and movement of her produce." "Now that the Britons have got their loan and are assured of a modicum of healthy living," the newspaper demanded, "are they not going to allow us to trade freely with the outside world?" "Free trade with the United States," it concluded, "must be the slogan."[68]

However, as late as 1948, the imperial government and the governments of the colonies still retained the controls on trade in defiance of the growing clamor for their abolition. The secretary of state for the colonies drew the attention of the governments of Nigeria and other cotton-producing colonies to statistics showing that "the United Kingdom has been largely dependent in the past on hard currency sources, and in particular, the USA, for its supplies of raw cotton. This dependence has, if anything, increased today while, at the same time, cotton has become of increasing importance to the United Kingdom, as one of its most important exports in the form of textiles and made-up goods." He explained to the governors of the colonies that "[any] increase in supplies of raw cotton from colonial sources, therefore, means, in many cases, a direct saving of dollars and in all cases will be of assistance to the U.K.'s export drive." Furthermore, "any improvement in the quality of the raw cotton exported from the colonies would enhance the quality of the textiles produced from it and hence of their exportable value."[69] In effect, Nigeria was a pawn in the wartime and postwar maneuvers of the imperial power as the latter fought for survival and sought to stay afloat after a devastating global conflict. Nigeria's trade with the United States accordingly fluctuated with the local and global dynamics in which it was conducted. The U.S. aggregate percentage share of Nigerian trade in the postwar years was as follows: 10.06 (1946), 16.73 (1947), 11.73 (1948), and 7.30 (1949).[70]

Conclusion

This chapter has highlighted some important but neglected aspects of the history of economic relations between Nigeria and the United States in the era of British colonial rule in Nigeria. The global context of the post–World War I economy, including rising U.S. preeminence and the interwar crises, joined with local conditions to shape the content and direction of trade relations. The American cotton crop always exerted a considerable impact on global demands for Nigerian produce, while the New York Stock Exchange crash of September 1929, which signaled the beginning of the Great Depression, had critical implications—even at the micro level—for the Nigerian colonial economy. American Ford cars of various types played a critical role in the evolution of modern (urban) transport in Nigeria, while the introduction of American "Allen" cotton seed into Nigerian agriculture was a major plank of colonial agricultural policy in the interwar years.

American involvement in the Nigerian colonial economy accentuated the globalization of that economy. Yet the impact of the United States was uneven and was affected by British colonial policy, especially when Britain was fighting for its survival during the two world wars. In both cases, British protectionist policies deliberately denied Nigerian produce access to the American market or Nigerian consumers access to American products. In

1916, for example, the Niger Company had requested a concession to export kernel oil to the United States, as French colonies were already doing so. The company highlighted the burden that the policy placed on Nigeria as a colonial dependency:

> With quantities of Kernels and Kernel Oil stored in this country [the UK], it does seem that the trade and interest of Nigeria are being allowed to suffer because the Government will not consent to the shipment of Kernels and Kernel Oil to America. . . . Already the United States are likely looking for a substitute in South America and have contracted for several thousands of tons of a similar seed from the Brazils [*sic*].[71]

As indicated above, the "Buy British, Sell Foreign" trade policy during World War II also took a toll on American imports to Nigeria, as Britain strove to minimize the imbalance in its trade with, and its indebtedness to, the United States.[72]

To be sure, the Great Depression of the 1930s also compelled the United States to enforce a discriminatory policy that almost extinguished Nigerian palm oil exports to that country, though natural disasters compelled America to abandon this policy. It is worth noting that though the percentage figures for the U.S. share of Nigerian trade were low throughout the period under discussion, the strategic value of U.S. exports to Nigeria—gasoline and kerosene—made the relationship a critical one. The Nigerian economy was heavily dependent upon petroleum imports from the United States during World War II.

In the final analysis, this chapter, in dealing with the neglected subject of U.S.–Nigerian economic relations during the heyday of British colonial rule in Nigeria, has highlighted the interplay of local and global dynamics in international trade relations in the peculiar context of colonialism. It has demonstrated that Nigeria, as a colony of Britain, was helplessly dependent on its colonial master, whose strategic interests superseded all other considerations, including the specific interests of the colony. This placed Nigeria, a mere pawn, at the receiving end of the vagaries of global trade and the dynamics of the peculiar relationship between an emerging global superpower and the colony of a declining power.[73] Trade with the United States accentuated the globalization of Nigerian trade without alleviating the colony's dependent status.

Notes

1. See, for example, Bassey Ate, *Decolonization and Dependence: The Development of Nigerian-US Relations, 1960–1984* (Boulder, CO: Westview Press, 1987); Kunle Lawal, "The United States and the Entrenchment of Democracy in Nigeria on the Eve of Independence," in *Governance and the Electoral Process: Nigeria and the United States of*

America, ed. Oyin Ogunba, 165–215 (Lagos: American Studies Association of Nigeria, 1997); and Ebere Nwaubani, *The United States and Decolonization in West Africa, 1950–1960* (Rochester, NY: University of Rochester Press, 2001).

2. Ayodeji Olukoju, "Tropical Terminus: The Distress and Disposal of the American Schooner, *Allanwilde*, in Lagos, 1920–22," *Lagos Historical Review* 1 (2001): 114–26; and Ayodeji Olukoju, " 'Getting Too Great a Grip': European Shipping Lines and British West African Lighterage Services in the 1930s," *Afrika Zamani*, nos. 9 and 10 (2001–2): 19–40.

3. See, for example, Ayodeji Olukoju, "Nigeria and the World Market, 1890–1960: Local and Global Dynamics in a Colonial Context," in *Globalisation and Its Discontents, Revisited* ed. K. S. Jomo and K. J. Khoo, 141–56 (Delhi: Tulika Press, 2003).

4. Studies of this subject are numerous. See Obaro Ikime, *The Fall of Nigeria* (London: Macmillan, 1977).

5. A few representative studies are Toyin Falola, ed., *Britain and Nigeria: Exploitation or Development?* (London: Zed, 1987); Ayodeji Olukoju, "The Impact of British Colonialism on the Development of African Business in Colonial Nigeria," in *Black Business and Economic Power*, ed. Alusine Jalloh and Toyin Falola, 176–98 (Rochester, NY: University of Rochester Press, 2002); and Ayodeji Olukoju, *The "Liverpool" of West Africa: The Dynamics and Impact of Maritime Trade in Lagos, 1900–1950* (Trenton, NJ: Africa World Press, 2004).

6. Ayodeji Olukoju, "Elder Dempster and the Shipping Trade of Nigeria during the First World War," *Journal of African History* 33, no. 2 (1992): 255–71; and Ayodeji Olukoju, " 'Helping Our Own Shipping': Official Passages to Nigeria, 1914–45," *Journal of Transport History*, 3rd ser., 20, no. 1 (1999): 30–45.

7. A. Olorunfemi, "German Trade with British West African Colonies, 1895–1918," *Journal of African Studies* 8, no. 3 (1981): 111–20; A. Olorunfemi, "The Liquor Traffic Dilemma in British West Africa: The Southern Nigerian Example, 1895–1918," *International Journal of African Historical Studies* 17, no. 2 (1984): 229–41.

8. Akinjide Osuntokun, *Nigeria in the First World War* (London: Longman, 1979).

9. Ayodeji Olukoju, "Slamming the 'Open Door': British Protectionist Fiscal Policy in Inter-War Nigeria," *Itinerario: European Journal of Overseas History* 23, no. 2 (1999): 13–28.

10. For details, see Olukoju, "Nigeria and the World Market."

11. Chief Secretary's Office (CSO) 1/19/14, 669 of October 6, 1908, Egerton to Crewe, encl. 2: Governor's Address to the Legislative Council, National Archives of Nigeria, Ibadan (NAI).

12. CSO 1/34/6, Confidential April 8, 1916, Lugard to Bonar Law, NAI.

13. Olukoju, "Slamming the 'Open Door.' "

14. CSO 21 CSO 1615, Trade and Customs of Nigeria, Annual Report on for 1919, p. 2, NAI.

15. *Annual Report on the Customs Department of Nigeria for the Year 1922*, p. 5, NAI; CSO 26/1 03688, vol. 4, Annual General Report, Comptroller of Customs to Chief Secretary to the Government (CSG), January 17, 1928, NAI.

16. *The Nigerian Handbook, 1919* (Lagos: Government Printer, 1920), 18.

17. *West Africa* (London), September 18, 1920, 1214.

18. Nigeria: Annual Report on the Customs Department of Nigeria, 1923, p. 41, NAI.

19. Ibid.

20. Ibid.

21. *West Africa*, September 18, 1920, 1214.

22. For more on W. A. Dawodu, see A. G. Hopkins, "An Economic History of Lagos, 1880–1914" (PhD diss., University of London, 1964), 370–72; and Ayodeji Olukoju, *Infrastructure Development and Urban Facilities in Lagos, 1861–2000* (Ibadan: IFRA, 2003).

23. "Random Notes and News," *Nigerian Pioneer* (Lagos), January 14, 1921.

24. Ayodeji Olukoju, "Urban Transport in Metropolitan Lagos," in *Nigerian Cities*, ed. Toyin Falola and Steven J. Salm, 211–36 (Trenton, NJ: Africa World Press, 2003).

25. "Ekiti Notes and News," *Nigerian Pioneer*, May 20, 1921.

26. CSO 21 CSO 1615, Trade and Customs of Nigeria, Annual Report on for 1919, p. 5, NAI.

27. Nigeria: Annual Report on the Customs Department of Nigeria for the Year 1922, pp. 5, 16–19, NAI, for the analysis that follows.

28. *The Nigerian Handbook, 1922–23* (Lagos: Government Printer, 1924), 29.

29. Nigeria: Annual Report on Trade, 1921, p. 13, NAI.

30. "New American Shipping Line," *Lagos Weekly Record*, August 2, 1919.

31. "Nigerian Notes and News," *West Africa*, September 18, 1920, 1214.

32. "Random Notes and News," *Nigerian Pioneer*, November 19, 1920.

33. For details, see Olukoju, "Tropical Terminus."

34. "Random Notes and News," *Nigerian Pioneer*, April 30, 1920. Of course, it is possible that the equipment was originally intended for legitimate use. Though this was probably the only instance in which currency counterfeiting involved equipment imported from the United States, currency counterfeiting in general was rampant in Nigeria during the interwar period. See Ayodeji Olukoju, "Criminality as Resistance? Currency Counterfeiting in Colonial Nigeria," *International Review of Social History* 45, part 3 (2000): 385–407.

35. For Faulkner, see Ayodeji Olukoju, "The Faulkner 'Blueprint' and the Evolution of Agricultural Policy in Inter-War Colonial Nigeria," in *The Foundations of Nigeria: Essays in Honor of Toyin Falola*, ed. Adebayo Oyebade, 403–22 (Trenton, NJ: Africa World Press, 2003).

36. *West Africa*, March 24, 1917, 143.

37. Editorial, "Empire Cotton," *Lagos Weekly Record*, May 1, 1920.

38. "AGM of BCGA, 1917," *West Africa*, August 4 1917, 455.

39. CSO 26 16690, vol. 1, Report on Cotton Growing Industry in Nigeria, by Colonel N. French, p. 1, NAI, for the discussion in much of this paragraph.

40. "Annual Report BCGA," *West Africa*, June 29, 1918, 349.

41. CSO 1/32/57, 980, of November 11, 1920, Clifford to Milner, encl. Regulations No. 18 of 1920 under "The Agricultural Ordinance, 1916," dated October 28, 1920, NAI.

42. CSO 1/32/60, 324, of March 30, 1921, Clifford to Churchill, encl. Report on Cotton Cultivation in Northern Nigeria, July–December 1920, by P. H. Lamb, Director of Agriculture, NAI.

43. Nigeria: Annual Report on the Customs Department of Nigeria, 1923, p. 42, NAI.

44. CSO 26/1 03688, vol. 4, Director of Agriculture to CSG, December 6, 1927, NAI.

45. Nigeria: Colonial, Report for 1927, No. 1384, 1928, p. 12, NAI.

46. CSO 26 16690, vol. 1, Report by Colonel French, pp. 5–6, NAI.

47. CSO 26/1 03688, vol. 4, Annual General Report, Director of Agriculture to CSG, December 6, 1927, Notes for Agricultural Report, 1927, NAI.

48. See Kehinde Faluyi, "The Impact of the Great Depression of 1929–33 on the Nigerian Economy," *Journal of Business and Social Studies* 4, no. 2 (1981): 31–44.

49. CSO 26/3 09512, vol. 10, Annual Report on the Colony of Lagos, 1933, p. 5, NAI.

50. "London Letter," *Nigerian Pioneer,* January 23, 1931.

51. *Lagos Daily News,* March 21, 1930.

52. Editorial, "The Nigerian Motors Ltd.," *Lagos Daily News,* May 19, 1930.

53. Comcol 1 1550, J. N. Zarpas & Co. Bus Service in Lagos Municipality, Zarpas to Chief Secretary to Government, August 28, 1933, NAI.

54. Ibid. Italics added for emphasis.

55. Olukoju, "Slamming the 'Open Door.' "

56. Editorial, "America and West African Cocoa," *Nigerian Pioneer,* May 6, 1932.

57. CSO 26/3 29777, vol. 1, Conditions of World Trade in Palm Products, Nigeria 1063 of December 7, 1934, Maybin to Cunliffe-Lister, encl. Legislative Council Debates, October 22, 1934, NAI.

58. Ibid., Cunliffe-Lister to Cameron, October 16, 1934.

59. Ibid., encl. Legislative Council Debates, October 22, 1934.

60. Ibid., Secretary of State to Colonial Governments (n.d.).

61. CSO 26/3 29777, vol. 2, Conditions of World Trade in Palm Products: Position of Nigeria in World Market for Oil Palm Products: Representation by AWAM, memorandum from Jasper Knight to Lord Trenchard, September 29, 1936, NAI.

62. Ibid., Report of a Discussion Concerning the Possible Developments in the African and Malayan Oil Palm Industries, September 24, 1936.

63. Nigeria: Annual Reports, 1937: Trade Report for 1937, p. 3, NAI.

64. *Nigeria: Colonial Reports—Annual* (published), NAI, for 1929–36.

65. See Ayodeji Olukoju, " 'Buy British, Sell Foreign': External Trade Control Policies in Nigeria during World War II and Its Aftermath, 1939–50," *International Journal of African Historical Studies* 35, nos. 2 and 3 (2002): 363–84.

66. DCI 1/1 4032/S.194, Import Controls: The Association of Merchants and Industrialists, Minutes of a Meeting on March 14, 1946, between Representatives of Association of Merchants and Industrialisation, NAI.

67. Trade Reports for 1940–45, NAI.

68. Editorial, "Trade between USA and Nigeria," *West African Pilot,* August 16, 1946.

69. IBMINAGRIC 18700, vol. I, Cotton: Export of, Nigeria No. 753, Savingram, Secretary of State, to Officer Administering Governments of Nigeria and all Cotton Producing Colonies, May 8, 1948, NAI.

70. Trade Reports 1946–49, NAI.

71. CSO 18/1 20, Nigerian Trade Restrictions on Certain Exports from the United Kingdom, Effects of—1916, Memorandum (by Niger Company) re Palm Kernel Industry, August 17, 1916, NAI.

72. Details of the operation of the licensing of American imports, especially the allocation of import licences and quotas among the leading firms, are contained in DCI 1/1 4032/S.162, Import Control: Goods from U.S.A., NAI.

73. A Lagos newspaper of the colonial era remarked ruefully in the context of the Great Depression that "as big countries fail the smaller States which are rightful appendages must also naturally fail"! See editorial, "Our Economic Problems," *Nigerian Pioneer*, May 25, 1934.

6

The United States' Economic and Political Activities in Colonial West Africa

Hakeem Ibikunle Tijani

Introduction

The central theme of this chapter is to detail the history of the United States' political and economic interests in West Africa after World War II. The United States was interested in political matters (including nationalist movements, political reforms, and decolonization); and the type of economic policy and development carried out by the colonial powers. Simply put, it consciously monitored the way colonial officials handled nationalist demands, colonial reforms, and the type of economic developmental plans put in place. This chapter reinvestigates the genesis of U.S. interests in West Africa; it reinterprets U.S. activities during the post–World War II period; and it presents a historical narrative of the Anglo-American entente during the colonial period (1945–60).

While the events that propelled the tactics of the Cold War are well documented, Africa's (indeed West Africa's) place in the scheme of the Western Allies' strategies is often misrepresented. While news of the strategies, tactics, and procedures regarding the Western powers' activities in colonial Africa did not make it to the front pages of leading newspapers or to the radio, official records indicate that Africa was never treated as a "backwater" in world affairs. This chapter argues that the focus of the United States' activities during the period under discussion was based on its Cold War goals. It was informed by the growing radicalism within Africa, international Communist activities, the role of the World Federation of Trade Unions (WFTU), the prevalence of Communist propagandist newsletters, the provision of funds and support by the Eastern bloc, and the presence of leftist nationalists and their sympathizers. As the leader of the Western world, the United States assisted the colonial powers (Britain in particular) to persuade West African nationalists to follow the "planned" decolonization process as a means to avoid a Communist takeover. This chapter focuses on British West Africa, emphasizing U.S. activities in Nigeria, the most populous British colony.

The Context

Contrary to general views, Anglo-American strategies and tactics against the inroads of Communists in West Africa predate 1950. The United States had understood the significance of British West Africa before the famous National Security Council Report, issued in 1950 and commonly known as NSC-68. As far as West Africa was concerned, the genesis of Anglo-American policy was the official 1946 meeting between British and U.S. officials at which procedures, tactics, and strategies for economic collaboration and the development of the untapped resources in West Africa for Cold War purposes were set up. As the following analysis indicates, this was followed by another meeting on January 3, 1950, when officials exchanged "notes" about economic cooperation and the resources of British West African colonies. This is the background to the January 27, 1950, signing of the Economic Cooperation Agreement in Washington, DC. The chapter also focuses on the relevance of the Mutual Security Act of 1951 as it relates to the development of the West African economy. The focus of the Economic Cooperation Agreement and the agreement approved by Congress as the Mutual Security Act of 1951 with regard to British West Africa is the United States' strategic interest in procuring raw materials, partly as a result of the outbreak of the Korean War in June 1950 but also as part of the covert measures taken during the Cold War period in general.

To fully grasp the economic activities of the United States during the 1950s in West Africa, it is necessary to identify the reasons for its political policy toward leftist groups south of the Sahara at the beginning of the Cold War. The U.S. consular offices and the United States Information Service (USIS) played an important role in West Africa during the 1950s. A major factor was the politics of the Cold War, including the determination to deny Communists worldwide any place under the sun. Suffice it to say that colonies were not insulated from Anglo-American anti-Communism. The success of anti-Communist efforts was important for the future of the Western bloc, as the history of Cold War politics has shown in recent times. I have identified three main reasons for the firm U.S. support of British anti-leftist policies in West Africa during the period under study. These are as follows:

(1) The identification of Marxist groups in West Africa (particularly in the Gold Coast and Nigeria) after World War II;

(2) An increase in shipments of Marxist literature from Cominform and the Communist Party of Great Britain (CPGB); and

(3) The supply of Cominform and Communist fronts' funds to notable leftists.[1]

To Louis Johnson (the U.S. secretary of defense in 1949), a major objective of U.S. policy was to contain leftist ideology in order to reduce its threat to the' security of the United States and its allies.[2] This was the guide for consular and intelligence officers throughout the period in their research and documentation of leftist activities, nationalism, the economic and strategic potential of the colonies, the capabilities of the Soviet Union, and its changing tactics toward the colonies.

U.S. officials in Accra, Lagos, and other parts of West Africa identified four principal stages of Communist penetration during the period under review. Stage one saw Communist Party member recruitment efforts among African students in the United Kingdom, followed by indoctrination and training either by the Communist Party of Great Britain itself, or in a university in the Soviet bloc, such as the University of Prague. Stage two involved concerted infiltration and control of nascent West African labor movements, focusing particular attention on such groups as the All-Nigerian Trade Union Federation (ANTUF); the agenda called for pushing such groups to obtain WFTU affiliation, while at the same time pushing them away from the International Confederation of Free Trade Unions (ICFTU) and British trade union influence. The third stage relied upon the distribution of propaganda, primarily printed matter, through direct mail or a certain small chain of bookshops in major West African cities. Finally, stage four turned upon efforts to place expatriate party members in influential official positions in the West African civil service, or on the staff of the university colleges at Accra or Ibadan, and in the quasi-official departments of extramural studies at these colleges.[3]

The United States' official position is well stated by Louis Johnson in a memorandum to the National Security Council in June 1949:

(a) Cooperate locally with security organizations to combat Communist subversive activities to the extent that this can be done without assisting in the repression of responsible non-Communist nationalist movements;

(b) Seek to prevent or at least curtail formal representation of Sino-Soviet bloc countries in Africa;

(c) Seek to provide constructive alternatives to Soviet blandishments but avoid trying to compete with every Soviet offer;

(d) Give general support to non-Communist nationalists, and reform movements, balancing the nature and degree of such support, however, with consideration of [our] NATO allies; and,

(e) In areas where trade unionism develops, guide it towards Western models by working with the International Confederation of Free Trade Unions, by direct advice and assistance, and by an exchange of persons program.[4]

In early 1951, A. W. Childs, the U.S. consul general in Nigeria, advised that the United States must render support to the governing authorities should the home country be unable to provide for internal security.[5] By the same token, Anglo-American officials at the United Nations (UN) agreed that nothing should be done at the UN to delay the achievement of self-government by colonies.[6] The U.S. position was to support liberal nationalists, encourage policies and actions of the colonial powers that would lead to self-government, and avoid identifying with metropolitan policies considered stagnant or repressive.[7] This was the United States' "clear political interest" in West Africa during the 1950s and afterward.

Understanding U.S. Economic Activities

Between 1948 and 1960, the United States and Britain shared the desire to deny the African continent to Communists.[8] The United States defined its position in Africa in terms of the Cold War and Communist threats, though nothing like the Marshall Plan was envisaged.[9] In fact, the American public and Congress were more responsive to issues of anti-Communist sentiments and mutual security than any other matters. As Henry Kissinger noted some decades later, "The United States possessed the full panoply of the means—political, economic, and military—to organize the defense of the non-Communist World."[10] It was in the national interest of the United States for Africa to be free of Communism, and that motivated its support for British anti-left policies.

The historical antecedent to U.S. Africa policy after World War II was the change from a policy of isolationism to one of containment. World War II changed the United States' global position, as it emerged as a super power. Immediate postwar American policy was aimed at preventing Communist inroads into developed economies and colonial dependencies (in collaboration with the governing powers). Perhaps the most significant intelligence report on Africa during the Truman era was the *Report on the Strategic Ports of West Africa*.[11] This was an attempt by the U.S. National Security Resources Board to observe at first hand and evaluate political, economic, and particularly port security situations and problems as they might affect the national security interests of the United States in the event of mobilization for total war, whether in the immediate future or over the longer term. The report recommended that West Africa should be preserved, by the colonial governments, as an integral part of the free world.

Contrary to what economist Andrew Kamarck has written, the United States had economic interests in Africa during and after World War II.[12] Its interests were both direct and indirect. The direct interests were based on the abundant labor and untapped natural resources in Africa. To the United States, West Africa was a strategic storehouse for American industry because of its resources. Contrary to existing views, the U.S. did not see West Africa as a foreign policy "backwater" and of "lowest priority." Rather it saw the area as significant in terms of collaborative exploitation of its untapped resources. The United States was dependent on West Africa, particularly Ghana and Nigeria, "for nearly all of our cobalt requirements, nearly all of our columbium, most of our palm oil, most of the critical bolt type of industrial diamonds, over half of our tantalum, a growing proportion of our manganese and an appreciable amount of our tin."[13] An official concluded as early as 1952 that "West Africa is the largest source of uranium in the world and most of the output comes to the United States. The national security of the United States and the fate of West Africa are closely interrelated."[14]

This conclusion should not be surprising because the United States (as well as Britain) depended on Nigeria's palm kernels, palm oil, tin ores, rubber, columbium ore, wolfram, and potash during the 1950s. A total of 73 percent of the total imports of columbium ore into the United States in 1950 was obtained from Nigeria. Columbium ore exports reached 1,092 tons in 1951, which represented an increase of 51 long tons over 1950. Also, in 1950, 17 percent of the palm oil imported into the United States came from Nigeria. Although most of Nigeria's rubber was exported to Britain, the United States remained the second largest importer of rubber from Nigeria during the 1950s.

The United States' indirect interest was also intertwined with its strategic interest in Europe as the main battleground against the Soviet bloc. As Vernon McKay put it at the time, "it is an economic interest in Europe which is affected by Africa's economic relations with Europe."[15] Certainly, one must look beyond official U.S. programs, given traditional American reliance upon private initiatives and free enterprise. The U.S. government encouraged (though covertly) private organizations to work with African entrepreneurs in the development of their economies.

In West Africa, the Rockefeller Brothers West African Fund was set up in 1957 to research and document feasibility studies about resources in the territory. Such studies served as the data bank for local and foreign investors during the transition to independence and later.[16] Sound economic development before independence was linked with political and educational progress in the colonies. The United States encouraged Britain to continue with its decolonization plans as a basis for a special relationship with the Nigerian leaders. Both liberal-political and labor leaders were sponsored, encouraged, and supported in their efforts against Marxist groups.[17] There is no doubt that the educated elites were of high priority because they personified the worst fears of the Anglo-American imagination regarding the nature of anticolonial protests and attempts by Marxist groups to make inroads into labor and nationalist politics during the decolonization years.[18]

The U.S. Department of State noted in 1946 that "it is thought that the eyes of certain of the more vociferous African exponents of early political independence have turned toward [the] USSR because of what they considered to be [the] Soviet Union's advanced attitude toward dependent people."[19] There was anxiety that the Soviet bloc could benefit from anticolonial sentiments in the colonies if the metropolitan government did not take the initiative.[20]

Attempt at Development or Economic Exploitation?

Records in England and the United States point to the fact that the basis of U.S. government interest in Africa during the colonial period (and afterward) was economic exploitation of its abundant resources. Leading officials did not hide the need for exploitation of the untapped natural resources that would be useful in technological and scientific undertakings in the United States and Britain. In 1950, for instance, it was realized that Nigeria supplied 95 percent of the world's columbium. Columbium is a metal derived from tin ore and used for armaments and industrial projects. It is also useful in the manufacture of gas turbines and jet engine components, as a carbide stabilizer in stainless steels, and in electrodes for stainless steels, alloys, and chemical equipment.[21]

The question is, how was the quest for the exploitation of the vital reservoir of minerals and natural resources that are critical stockpile items in the United States pursued during the colonial era? Collaboration with the colonial powers (Britain and France) through treaties and trade agreements was among the ways in which exploitation was carried out.

The collaborative efforts of the United States and the colonial powers in West Africa began in July 1946 when talks were held between British and U.S. officials in London. The officials agreed on economic cooperation between the two partners with a view to further developing their plans. The views on economic cooperation were amended by exchanges of "notes" between officials on January 3, 1950. On January 27, 1950, the two governments signed the Economic Cooperation Agreement in Washington, DC. This was approved by the U.S. Congress and was followed by another agreement, approved by Congress as the Mutual Security Act of May 25, 1951. The Mutual Security Act of 1951 was an amendment to the Mutual Defense Assistance Act of 1949, which specified mutual defense arrangements between Great Britain and the United States. The focus of the agreements as they relate to British West Africa was the United States' strategic interest in procuring raw materials. The British secretary of state for the colonies noted "the primary importance of strengthening the mutual security and individual and collective defenses of the free world."[22]

It was said that the goal was to develop resources in the interest of the security and independence thereby facilitating the effective participation of ally countries in collective security.[23] John Orchard, chairman of the Economic Cooperation Agreement (ECA) Advisory Committee, better summarized the exploitative nature of the agreement. To him, the ECA was to support European recovery and to ensure the possibilities of increasing raw material production, including the production of strategic materials for the U.S. stockpile.[24] Allan Smith, who was the acting director of the Overseas Territories Division of the ECA Advisory Committee in 1951, aired the same view. Smith was of the opinion that, "dependent overseas territories have generally been considered by ECA as appendages of European economy or as producers of strategic materials for the U.S. stockpile."[25]

To Her Majesty's Government, economic cooperation and other bilateral agreements with the United States were based on six aims. Under the agreements, Britain was to do the following:

(a) Join in promoting international understanding and goodwill, and maintaining world peace;
(b) Take such action as may be mutually agreed upon to eliminate causes of international tension;
(c) Fulfill the military obligations which they have assumed under multilateral or bilateral agreements or treaties to which the United States is a party;
(d) Make consistent with their political and economic stability, the full contribution, permitted by their manpower, resources, facilities, and general economic condition to the development and maintenance of their own defensive strength and the defensive strength of the free world;
(e) Take all reasonable measures which may be needed to develop their defense capacities;
(f) Take appropriate steps to insure the effective utilization of the economic and military assistance provided by the United States.[26]

It should not be surprising that the two governments established effective procedures suitable for the exploitation of vital resources in the colonies based on their mutual agreements under the ECA and MSA. Suffice it to say that there were hidden agendas concerning any human or physical capital projects embarked upon. Apart from the fact that the colonies indirectly paid with their vital resources for projects that were carried out, measures were put in place to protect British and U.S. finances.

For instance, Article IV of the ECA made the following stipulations:

(a) Expenditures of sums allocated to the use of the Government of the United States pursuant to paragraph 4 of Article IV of the Economic Cooperation Agreement will not be limited to expenditures in the United Kingdom.
(b) The government of the United Kingdom will so deposit, segregate, or protect their title to all funds allocated to them or derived by them from any program

of assistance undertaken by the Government of the United States that such funds shall not be subject to garnishee proceedings, attachment, seizure, or other legal process by any person, firm, agency, corporation, organization, or government.

(c) Pounds Sterling will be deposited pursuant to Article IV of the Economic Cooperation Agreement commensurate with assistance on a grant basis in the form of transfers of funds pursuant to Section III (*d*) of the Economic Cooperation Act of 1948, in the same way as amounts commensurate with the dollar cost [of] commodities, services, and technical assistance are deposited pursuant to that Article.[27]

The United States went a step further in its scheme to benefit from the economic cooperation and mutual security agreement as it related to the colonies' exports. It requested a tax exemption for "common defense effort and for aid programmes."[28] On their side, the British willingly agreed to facilitate such an exemption whenever it was requested. British officials believed the exemption should be seen as a form of relief rather than as direct refunds to the government of the United States. Members of the "Special United States Tax Delegation" were assured by the Colonial Office that at the request of the U.S. government, it would consult with the authorities of the dependent overseas territory concerned regarding the possibility of obtaining for the U.S. government appropriate relief or an exemption similar to that obtained in the United Kingdom.[29] That aside, it was also agreed that quarterly reports about projects carried out must be given to the U.S.-controlled Mutual Security Agency via the secretary of state for the colonies in London.

Taking Nigeria as an example, in that country, as elsewhere in British colonies, such projects were classified as the "Overseas Development Pool" (ODP). The most significant projects undertaken during the 1950s were the development of the Enugu Colliery and the construction of a road from Kano to Fort Lamy via Maiduguri using the Overseas Development Pool Fund (ODF). The Enugu Colliery had been a center of discontent among labor unionists in the late 1940s. The report of the government panel that looked into the uprising of 1949 had indicated a need, among other things, to improve the working conditions of employees of the colliery. Established by Ordinance no. 29 of 1950, the Nigerian Coal Corporation (NCC) engaged in coal exploration, exploitation, and marketing. The administration of the Enugu Colliery was transferred from the Railway Corporation to the NCC and its reconstruction fell under the ODP. With a population of 63,000[30] in 1953, Enugu was becoming not only a vibrant urban center but also an important labor and nationalist meeting point outside Lagos.

Out of the £365,000 and £162,000 spent on the Kano–Fort Lamy road and the Enugu Colliery, respectively, under the Development Pool Scheme in 1950/1951, £31,910 and £13,650 were considered to be grants by the

U.S. government. Various colonies adopted different formats in carrying out aid projects under the ECA, which by September 1952 was completely under the control of the MSA. The projects were approved in August 1951, with the British administering officer in Nigeria working closely with the director of audit, the inspector-general of public works, the director of commerce and industries, and the chairman of the Nigerian Coal Corporation. These were the agents of the effective actualization of the goals of the projects— that is, exploitation.

Since the ECA was prevented by law from making direct grants from the ODP to finance the non-dollar content of projects, the government of the colony of Nigeria and the Colonial Office worked out a formula that would benefit both the motherland and the United States. The following procedure was adopted:

(a) Nigerian importers of American wheat-flour and tobacco, when importing these commodities with dollars received through the medium of the Nigerian Exchange Control by import licenses in the normal way quote a special Procurement Authorization (P.A.) No; supplied to them by the ECA through the Secretary of State and the Director of Commerce and Industries, on all documents and correspondence with the U.S. supplier.

(b) The American supplier then forwards to the United Kingdom Treasury and Supply Delegation in Washington certain documents indicating the value of the dollar exports of wheat-flour and tobacco made [supplied] to the Nigerian buyers.

(c) The U.K. Treasury and Supply Delegation then claims on an E.C.A. form a refund of the dollars expended by Nigerian importers. This being made, an equivalent amount in sterling is paid by the United Kingdom Government into a special account at the Bank of England. Thereafter the Crown Agents are authorized to make grants up to the sterling equivalent of the ECA contribution towards the approved projects.[31]

Payment to the Crown Agents was subject to a satisfactory quarterly report from the inspector-general of public works (for the Kano-Lamy road) and the chairman of the Nigerian Coal Corporation (for the Enugu Colliery).[32] In addition, it was required that a final technical and financial report be sent through the secretary of state for the colonies to the MSA on every project.

Conclusion

This chapter has traced the history of U.S. activities in West Africa (emphasizing the case of Nigeria) after World War II. First, the analysis above clearly indicates that the United States was interested in colonial matters, and did not pretend to share the same opinion on colonial matters as its allied colonial powers, particularly Britain. Second, its political interests were backed by economic activities that became central to winning the hearts and minds of major nationalist leaders. Economic assistance by the United States thus aided the nurturing of a pro-Western economic structure that explains the anti-leftist policies of British officials and nationalist governments in Nigeria between 1945 and 1960. This "nurtured" capitalism was pursued by the Balewa government until its demise in a military coup in 1966.

Notes

1. See H. I. Tijani, "Britain and the Development of Leftist Ideology and Organisations in West Africa: The Nigerian Experience, 1945–1965" (PhD diss., University of South Africa, Pretoria, December 2004), chapter 6. The thesis is published as *Britain, Leftist Nationalists and the Transfer of Power in Nigeria, 1945–1965* (New York: Routledge, 2005).

2. Tijani, "Britain and the Development of Leftist Ideology," 202.

3. Ibid., 203.

4. Ibid., 202.

5. Ibid., 204.

6. Ibid.

7. Ibid.

8. Ibid.

9. R. W. Louis, "American Anti-Colonization and the Dissolution of the British Empire," *International Affairs*, no. 61 (1985): 395–420.

10. Henry Kissinger, *Diplomacy* (New York: Simon & Schuster, 1994), 31.

11. Tijani, "Britain and the Development of Leftist Ideology," 202–12.

12. A. Kamarck, "The African Economy and International Trade," *The United States and Africa* (New York: Praeger, 1958), 119. The most recent review of U.S. policy is contained in Peter J. Schraeder, "Reviewing the Study of US Policy towards Africa: From Intellectual 'Backwater' to Theory Construction," *Third World Quarterly* 14, no. 4 (December 1993): 775.

13. The attempt by Ebere Nwaubani, in *The United States and Decolonization in West Africa, 1950–1960* (Rochester, NY: University of Rochester Press, 2001), 28–55, to explain the significance of West Africa to the United States is unconvincing. His view that officials were not particularly interested in West Africa, or that their interest in the area was of "lowest priority," is not entirely true. The colonies of Africa, like any colonial territories, were treated within the context of their colonial status. The structure of the U.S. Department of State as it relates to African affairs during the period is not the only yardstick with which to measure policies or goals, as Nwaubani argued.

14. PSF/E.10501, E. T. Dickerson, "A Report of Strategic Ports of West Africa," p. 14, Harry S. Truman Presidential Library and Archive, Independence, Missouri.

15. Vernon McKay, *Africa in World Politics* (New York: Harper and Row, 1963), 248.

16. Rockefeller Brothers West African Fund, Box 3, 4, and 5, Rockefeller Archives (RF), New York. See Hakeem I. Tijani, "Rockefeller Brothers Fund and Modernization of Pharmaceutical Industry in Nigeria," in *Traditional and Modern Health Systems in Nigeria*, ed. T. Falola and M. Heaton, 147–60 (Trenton, NJ: Africa World Press, 2006).

17. Hakeem I. Tijani, "Communists and Nationalist Movements," in *Nigeria in the Twentieth Century*, ed. Toyin Falola, 293–313 (Durham, NC: Carolina Academic Press, 2002).

18. Ibid.; in addition, F. Ferudi, "Diagnosing Disorder: The Anglo-American Management of African Nationalism, 1948–1960" (paper presented at the ASAUK biennial conference, September 8–10, 1992), 12. H. Adi, West *Africans in Britain 1900–1960: Nationalism, Pan-Africanism and Communism* (London: Lawrence & Wishart, 1998).

19. British Colonies of West Africa: Policy and Information Statement, December 12, 1946, File RG (Record Group) 59 848K.00, National Archives at College Park (NACP).

20. Ibid.

21. American Embassy, London to the Department of State, Comment by Mining Journal on DMPA Columbium-Tantalum Guaranteed Purchase Program, July 22, 1952, RG 59 848K.00, NACP.

22. Colonial Office (CO) 26/10304/S5 vol. 1, Secretary of State for the Colonies to the Officer Administering the Government of Nigeria, December 29, 1951, Public Record Office, London (PRO).

23. Ibid.

24. See "Europe Program Division, 1949–1951", Box 3, August 9, 1950; RG 469, Memorandum from Allan Smith, Box 47, January 22, 1951, NACP.

25. Ibid.

26. CO 26/10304/S5 vol. 1, Economic Cooperation Act and Bilateral Agreements, p. 2, PRO.

27. Ibid., p. 3.

28. Ibid. See attached Circular 253/52, Mutual Security Act: Exemption from Taxation of the United States Expenditure under the Act, p. 1.

29. Ibid. See enclosed Agreed Minute, March 15, 1952.

30. NIGCOAL: 3–21, Correspondence of Nigeria Coal Corporation 1950–53, National Archives of Nigeria, Ibadan (NAI). Also see *Nigeria Yearbook, 1953* (Lagos: Government Press, 1953).

31. NIGCOAL: 3-21, "Overseas Development Pool Memo," September 29, 1952, pp. 1–2.

32. Details of projects carried out in other parts of West Africa are contained in Nwaubani, *The United States and Decolonization in West Africa*, chapters 3 and 4. Regrettably, Nwaubani did not use PRO documents, nor did he mention the Enugu Colliery and Kano-Lamy projects under the ECA/MSA. Tijani, *Britain, Leftist Nationalists*, chapter 7, for a full account.

Part Two

Forging Cultural Connections

America in Africa

7

Developing a "Sense of Community"

U.S. Cultural Diplomacy and the Place of Africa during the Early Cold War Period, 1953–64

Karen B. Bell

Introduction: African Independence Movements and the Beloved Community

"Americans killed Patrice Lumumba" proclaimed the headlines in Cairo, Egypt, early in 1961.[1] In response, U.S. State Department foreign service officer Zygmunt Nagorski assembled United States Information Service (USIS) personnel at the U.S. embassy in Cairo to develop a factual pamphlet using the text of speeches made by the secretary-general of the United Nations, Dag Hammarskjöld. The pamphlet also included remarks from the U.S. ambassador to the United Nations, Adlai Stevenson, and President John F. Kennedy. The publication, titled *The Truth about Congo* rolled off the presses and became the official response of USIS offices to the crisis in the Congo. The response of U.S. State Department foreign service officers and USIS personnel reflected a united effort in terms of activities aimed at influencing public perceptions and public attitudes in foreign countries in support of U.S. policies. Using the written word to influence mass attitudes on the controversial circumstances of Lumumba's death served the short-term and long-range U.S. strategic goals, which were to counter negative information and reinforce a favorable impression of the United States.[2]

The United States' provision of information, propaganda, and cultural activities has been a neglected area in the scholarship on U.S. foreign relations with Africa. The use of propaganda (white, true information; gray, distortion of the truth; and black, disinformation) encompassed a "range of information and psychological activities (such as films, news stories and broadcasts)" that purported to explain American foreign policies to non-Americans.[3] This brand of diplomacy joined with indirect methods involving cultural activities to profoundly shape U.S. cultural diplomacy during the early Cold War period. Through its information agency, the United States engaged in cultural diplomacy as a means of expressing and projecting its national identity abroad by seeking to build bridges and establish community with other nations. The early twentieth-century philosopher Josiah Royce proposed that a "community can only exist where individual members are in communication with one another so that there is, to some extent and in some relevant respect, a congruence of feeling, thought, and will among them." The ideal community, according to Royce, was the "Beloved Community," in which all members pursued the "cause of loyalty, truth, and reality."[4] One of the most complex and perplexing questions is that of ordering truth and reality within the total historical development of the Cold War. America's perceptions of truth and reality became instruments of cultural diplomacy and served to complement the high politics of power and security throughout the Cold War. The diffusion of truth, reality, and ideological loyalty by the exporter of cultural values to the recipient undergirded this form of diplomacy and formed the central feature of U.S. information, propaganda, and cultural programs. These programs served as a cultural matrix for expanding U.S. activities on the African continent.[5]

Propagating American ideas, images, and beliefs, and representations of American political values abroad played a significant role in the strategy used by the United States to enforce its conception of international order. The national ideals and values of America, which emphasized democracy, free enterprise, and freedom, were an integral part of the Cold War strategy designed to persuade, influence, and exert a measure of control over non-aligned countries. The promulgation of National Security Council Report 68 (NSC-68), issued on April 14, 1950, inaugurated military and economic policies designed to contain the spread of Communism; also, as Emily Rosenberg has argued in *Spreading the American Dream*, NSC-68 inaugurated polices to protect, preserve, and expand American values. Cultural diplomacy, a major subsection of public diplomacy, refers to "the use of culture and cultural tools by governments for the purpose of influencing and conducting foreign relations in a positive manner between peoples and nations."[6] The United States Information Agency (USIA), referred to overseas as the United States Information Service (USIS), implemented myriad cultural programs to transmit American political and cultural values abroad from 1953, the year of the agency's founding, through 1999, when the USIA merged with the U.S. Department of State. As an agency of the executive branch, the USIA advised the president, diplomatic personnel, executive independent departments, and agencies on the implications of foreign opinion for current and contemplated U.S. policies, programs, and official statements. To accomplish its goals, the agency conducted a variety of activities overseas. These activities included educational exchanges, international radio broadcasts, and television broadcasts. Additionally, by exporting

American literature, jazz, painting, sports, sculpture, and Hollywood films to the USIS resource centers overseas, the United States facilitated linkages between American and foreign nongovernmental institutions.[7]

President Lyndon B. Johnson advanced the position of establishing linkages and community with African nations in his 1963 address on Africa. President Johnson stated, "We in the United States are dedicated to the same goals as the people of Africa—justice, freedom, and peace. We want to help build a world in which all men have a better opportunity to improve their lives, both spiritually and materially. Thus, we will continue to press for equal rights for all—both in my country and abroad."[8] Concomitantly, the U.S. State Department in its analysis of the independence movements in Africa asserted that "it is also in the U.S. interest to seek the evolution of a sense of community between the United States and Africa, to develop that kind of racial relationship which will enhance our own influence and head off international confrontations and hostile alignments on a racial basis. This is of major importance because of the implications of the racial confrontation in Africa and the deep African interest in the US civil rights struggle."[9] It was during the American civil rights movement that Dr. Martin Luther King employed the concept of the "Beloved Community" to delineate the creation of an American society where the ideals of justice, freedom, and peace would serve as a bridge uniting a divided nation. The idea of establishing a "Beloved Community" extended into the realm of foreign policy as a political strategy used by the USIA and the U.S. State Department to establish community with African nations.[10]

In this chapter, I examine the instruments developed by the United States to influence African nations by exporting American civic culture and American identity in order to establish community with African nations. My analysis relies primarily upon records from the USIA's historical collection, the U.S. State Department's historical reports, and selected records from the State Department's Bureau of African Affairs. My research concentrates on the critical period from 1953 to 1964 when U.S. information, propaganda, and cultural activities became central to U.S. foreign policy. Drawing from the sources listed above, I first discuss the political context for the information, propaganda, and cultural activities in Africa, then examine the five critical information, propaganda, and cultural programs: the Voice of America (VOA), USIS publications in Africa, the English Language Teaching Program, educational exchange, and cultural exchange programs.

African Contexts: Cultural Diplomacy, African Independence, and the Cold War

During the early phase of the Cold War, the United States, through the Mutual Security Act of 1951, provided technical and economic assistance aimed at influencing "promising and receptive" independent African countries.[11] In North Africa, Libya gained its independence in 1951, and was followed by Morocco, Sudan, and Tunisia in 1956. By 1958, two sub-Saharan African nations, Ghana and Guinea, had gained their independence. Amidst the optimism and exuberance of African independence movements there loomed the question of whether to support the East or the West in the bipolar world of the Cold War. As the number of African nations increased steadily, reaching seventeen by 1961, the United States augmented its technical aid and economic assistance initiatives by inaugurating cultural relations with the newly emerging independent, politically nonaligned countries in Africa, as part of its propaganda efforts and intelligence activities designed to thwart the influence of the Soviet Union (USSR) and the People's Republic of China (PRC) on the African continent.[12]

Africa represented one of several territorial proving grounds in Sino-Soviet Cold War strategies. The USSR and the PRC both developed military assistance programs in East Africa and West Africa and both established an economic presence in several key African countries. The USSR had hoped to establish long-term assets in Africa and by the early 1960s established economic cooperation agreements (often involving credits) with twelve African countries, which included Algeria, Ghana, Guinea, Mali, and Tanzania. The Chinese Communists had established an economic presence in Guinea, Mali, Ghana, Congo-Brazzaville, Tanzania, Zambia, and to a lesser extent Algeria. Disagreement on the position the USSR and the PRC would occupy in the Communist world led to a formal Sino-Soviet split by 1962. The acrimonious ideological tensions between the USSR and the PRC served to sharpen each country's interest in Africa.[13]

The activities of both the USSR and the PRC in Africa shaped the character of U.S. relations with the continent. In an effort to meet the various political realities that had emerged with independence, the United States customized its policies toward the independent nations in Africa. By considering the cultural and social system of each country in formulating cultural relations, the United States sought to regionalize its influence in order to ensure its effectiveness. In most of the former French territories, historic relationships and the French capacity to provide substantial economic and other assistance made France the primary natural source of political and cultural ideas. Thus, the U.S. missions in French West and West-Central Africa were limited to establishing an American presence, engaging in small technical assistance programs, and engaging in what the State Department termed "educative diplomacy" through the English Language Teaching Program. In Gabon, Côte d'Ivoire, and Cameroon, the United States also provided bilateral aid in an effort to gain a measure of influence and leverage; however, both France and the European Economic Community (EEC) effectively limited U.S. trade agreements in order to protect French uranium, manganese, and iron ore interests, particularly in Gabon.[14]

In comparison, the situation in the former British territories produced an immersive response. A psychologically weakened Britain started to withdraw from its worldwide commitments, while at the same time the former British territories displayed an inclination to limit British influence. U.S. policy with regard to Britain's former colonies consisted of providing economic aid to the greatest extent that was feasible. To counter the Soviet presence, particularly in Ghana, where Kwame Nkrumah's relationship with Communist leaders stirred U.S. tensions, the United States provided financial and technical support to the Volta River Project. By the early 1960s, U.S. assistance to independent African countries was fairly substantial. Net obligations and loan authorizations in the economic and assistance fields for the fiscal year 1963 amounted to $473.2 million. This assistance consisted of Agency for International Development (AID) technical assistance, Food for Freedom, Export-Import Bank loans, and other programs such as the Peace Corps. U.S. assistance programs were primarily bilateral and aimed at long-range defense against Communist penetration. Economic assistance served other fundamental U.S. objectives such as providing an opportunity to introduce American values, institutions, people, and ideas.[15]

The independence movements in Africa produced a determination among African states to pursue independent foreign policies. Widening their trading links and diversifying their sources of foreign aid away from the former colonial powers conferred diplomatic legitimacy in relation to their power and position. However weak their bargaining power may have been, freedom from foreign domination directed the multilateral initiatives of African leaders, many of whom opposed direct Western influence on the continent. Leaders such as Kwame Nkrumah, Nnamdi Azikiwe, Sékou Touré, Kenneth Kaunda, and Julius Nyerere keenly assessed the political, economic, and social exigencies of the time and developed creative strategies in order to effectively negotiate with the USSR, the PRC, and the United States. Because of the ideological bipolarity of the post–World War II period, the United States viewed the advance of socialism in Africa as inimical to its economic and political interests. However, as William Tordoff has argued, "socialism was a loose concept in Africa and subject to varying interpretations."[16] African socialism reinforced communal traditions and communal identities and, in this context, differed from the socialist developments in the USSR and the PRC. Only a small number of African leaders were orthodox Marxists and even these leaders rejected key tenets of Marxist orthodoxy, such as the class struggle. African leaders adapted Marxist and other ideas to serve African conditions. The interests of leaders such as Julius Nyerere and Modibo Keita in socialism were accompanied by an affirmation of traditional African values.[17]

The strategic importance of Africa to U.S. foreign policy during the late 1950s is reflected in three areas: (1) statements in the USIA's "Third Report to Congress"; (2) President Dwight Eisenhower's Committee on Information Activities Abroad, also known as the Sprague Committee; and (3) statements by the U.S. Department of State's foreign policy analysts. In the USIA's "Third Report to Congress" (1954), the first director of the agency, Theodore Streibert, underscored the importance of "counteracting bad impressions created in [African] countries by American racial violence."[18] The report noted that USIS personnel in Africa concentrated heavily on combating Soviet propaganda on American racial injustice. Extensive coverage of the antisegregation decision of the U.S. Supreme Court was followed by news reports on the progress of desegregation in the United States and by a series of reports about eminent African Americans.[19]

In addition, the Sprague Committee in its analysis of political developments in Africa recommended drastically increasing information activities there to meet the demands of the changing times. In this context, Eisenhower's contention that the "battlegrounds of the Cold War had shifted to the economic and propaganda fields" reinforced the growing importance of Africa in Cold War politics. The ideological conflict between the United States and the USSR was a "total cold war" in which "trade, economic development, military power, arts, science, education, [and] the whole world of ideas [were] harnessed."[20] The National Security Council's Operations Coordinating Board, which developed the U.S. Ideological Program, underscored the warlike character of the Cold War by asserting that the United States "would use every opportunity to make clear to other peoples how the application of free world principles in their societies will work to their advantage and how the adoption of Communist principles will be to their detriment."[21]

With much of Asia lost to the West, Africa represented an important frontier in containing the spread of Communism. Discouraging trade agreements that tied the African economies too closely to the Soviet bloc became an integral component of U.S. foreign policy. In their assessment of African-USSR relations in 1959, foreign policy analysts in the Department of State postulated that "the loss of Africa to the Soviet Union would weaken capitalism in Europe."[22] Supporting the European metropoles and their former colonies with economic aid and technical assistance in order to negate Soviet influence became a policy objective of the United States. The United States not only recognized the centrality of African mineral resources and raw materials to the European economy, but also, in its official policy statements, integrated Africa into the American "mission" and program of cultural relations to counter the ignominy of southern resistance to the civil rights movement.[23]

U.S. strategic and economic interests on the African continent gained greater prominence during the 1960s. Economically, the United States sought to maintain access to the mineral and agricultural products of Africa, particularly rubber, uranium, bauxite, and copper, which were essential to the American economy and to American defense industries. The space age heightened the strategic importance of Africa. The National Aeronautic and Space Administration (NASA) maintained key facilities in the Malagasy Republic and southern Africa; and the trajectory for testing missiles from NASA's Cape Kennedy, Florida, space center ended near the tip of southern Africa.[24]

However, presenting a positive image of American culture to African nations and expanding American values to Africans was problematic for the USIA due to the persistence of racial discrimination and racial segregation in America. The Soviet Union's persistent coverage of racial incidents in America, particularly the Little Rock, Arkansas, desegregation crisis and the affront to Ghana's finance minister, Komla A. Gbedemah, who was refused service at a Howard Johnson's restaurant in Dover, Delaware, in 1957, underscored the problems faced by the agency in enhancing American credibility in Africa. Race relations in America had reached a critical turning point in the early 1960s. As civil rights activists and proponents of segregation collided in Alabama, Mississippi, and Georgia from 1961 to 1963, the international media questioned the authenticity of American democracy. The USSR, in particular, presented lynchings, school segregation, voting rights abuses, and antimiscegenation laws very effectively in its anti-American propaganda.[25]

Under the direction of USIA Director George V. Allen (1957–60), the USIA trimmed its Western European activities and appropriated more resources to cultural programming in Africa. The agency appropriated 35.4 percent of its $110 million budget for the fiscal year 1959 to its operations in Africa, compared with 11.5 percent to the Near East and South Asia; 10 percent to Eastern Europe; 5.5 percent to Latin America; and 1.6 percent to the Far East. Congress assigned 36 percent to Western Europe.[26] With the exception of Africa and Western Europe, USIA appropriations for cultural programming in all regions had been heavily reduced. In this context, Vice President Richard Nixon, following his return from an African state tour, reported to President Eisenhower that "funds for the information program in Africa should be substantially increased over the present level."[27]

Official visits to Africa underscored America's need to assess its informational activities. In December 1959, President Eisenhower visited Tunisia and Morocco, where he argued against "precipitate action" in granting independence to African nations. Eisenhower's cautious approach waned as African liberation movements intensified. Rapid social and political change in both the United States and Africa led to visits in 1961 by G. Mennen Williams, President John F. Kennedy's assistant secretary of state for African affairs, and the USIA director, Edward R. Murrow, in 1962. These visits

Fig. 7.1: President and Mrs. Eisenhower with His Excellency Sekou Toure, President of the Republic of Guinea, and Mrs. Toure in the White House, October 26, 1959. Source: RG 306, Records of the United States Information Agency, Photo Number PS-A-59-15292, National Archives and Records Administration, College Park, MD.

exemplified American interest in the process of nation building, as the number of independent African nations increased to thirty-four by 1964. Presidential identification with the independent nations of Africa also encouraged diplomatic visits to Washington, particularly during President Kennedy's administration, when twenty-eight African leaders visited America.[28] (See figures 7.1–7.3.)

One of the earliest USIA programs, the Voice of America (VOA), became an essential tool of U.S. foreign policy in Africa, beginning direct broadcasts to sub-Saharan Africa in 1956. Prior to 1956, VOA programs had been confined to the Arabic-speaking population of North Africa. The first fifteen-minute English news broadcast, "Report from America," began in 1957. The following year, the VOA English Service news broadcast to Africa expanded to thirty minutes in length and seven days a week and included new programming. By expanding its coverage and programming, the USIA sought to build its audience by implementing programs of interest to Africans and influencing African nations' perception of American policies, ideas, and culture. VOA news topics included science, medicine, and agriculture.

Fig. 7.2: President Eisenhower greets Prime Minister Kwame Nkrumah of Ghana at the White House, July 24, 1958. Source: RG 306, Records of the United States Information Agency, Photo Number PS-A-58-13073, National Archives and Records Administration, College Park, MD.

Additionally, the VOA featured special-focus topics on American history, women's activities, and education. The addition of two new broadcasting facilities enhanced the VOA's reception in Africa. In 1963, the USIA completed a 4.8 million–watt transmitter complex in Greenville, North Carolina, which became the most powerful long-range international broadcasting station in the world. In 1964, the agency constructed a transmitter relay complex of 1.6 million watts in Liberia that supplanted the Greenville relay station in Africa.[29]

Fig. 7.3: Assistant Secretary of State for African Affairs, G. Mennen Williams, (third from left) in Nairobi, Kenya with Jomo Kenyatta, Minister of State for Constitutional Affairs (far right), and Richard B. Freund, American Consul General, and Ronald Ngala, Minister of State for Constitutional Affairs and Administration, 1962. Source: RG 306 Records of the United States Information Agency, Photo Number PS-A-62-2912, National Archives and Records Administration, College Park, MD.

During the 1960s, the USIA diversified its cultural offerings in Africa through the development of more cohesive information programs. These programs expanded the ideological attack on the Soviet system through exploitation of the print media. The mass dissemination of information and propaganda in Africa was facilitated by the establishment of forty-eight libraries and twelve reading rooms in major cities by 1964. The print media used to carry the USIA message consisted of several notable publications that provided extensive coverage of African politics and visits of African leaders to the United States Additionally, coverage of the progress of civil rights in America, America's commitment to "peace and justice," and both African American and African athletic successes stressed harmony with African interests and U.S. identification with the process of nation building. The USIS produced *Topic, American Outlook,* and *American Perspectives* for African audiences in Ghana, Nigeria, Liberia, Sierra Leone, Gambia, Sudan, Ethiopia, and Tanzania. In these publications, American concepts of truth, reality, and loyalty to democratic-capitalist systems were sententiously expressed. The publication in French of *American Outlook* and *American Perspectives,* which began after 1960, expanded America's cultural reach into French West Africa and West-Central Africa during a pivotal period in the region, which witnessed the death of Patrice Lumumba and the secession of the Katanga province of the Congo. The city of Kinshasa, formerly Léopoldville, served as the cultural nexus for the production and distribution of USIS publications to French-speaking Africa regarding U.S. official policy on this crisis.[30]

The use of African languages in USIA publications, as well as in VOA broadcasts, began during the directorship of Edward R. Murrow (1961–64) and reflected a greater emphasis on the centrality of African languages to USIA programming. In addition to expanding VOA broadcasts in French, the USIA also implemented the use of Swahili, Hausa, Amharic, Igbo, and Yoruba in VOA programming. This new programming reflected the agency's strategy of targeting significant geographic regions and populations with programs highlighting African political developments, which were used on the English-to-Africa program *Voice of Africa.* By 1964, VOA programming had expanded to include several music, news, and reporters' roundup shows such as *Jazz Club USA,* African Panorama, *Africana,* and *Space and Man.*[31]

One contentious matter relating to USIS programs in Africa concerned the social level of the population that the information program should target. The question of whether to try to target and seek the support and sympathy of the elite or the masses represented a "dual of dialectics" during the tenure of Edward R. Murrow and Carl T. Rowan. USIS publications displayed self-conscious Americana designed to appeal to both the elites and the masses. In the area of USIS motion pictures, subsidized commercial newsreels, publicizing the activities of Africans in the United States, the activities of Americans in Africa, and self-help projects in African communities, served as collateral support for the same goal, that of reaching the masses and the elites simultaneously. In 1965, the USIA film list for Africa included *Africa in the Age of Independence, African Students Leave Bulgaria, Eisenhower Visits Morocco, President Sékou Touré Visits the U.S.,* and *Congolese Parliamentarians Visit*

Rural America. According to Carl Rowan (1964–65), the first African American director of the USIA, by 1964 *Africa Today* was seen by 30 million Africans each month in 746 theaters. This figure may well have been an exaggeration, since USIS posts reported technical and psychological difficulties with mass viewings of USIA films.[32]

The VOA was one of three international radio broadcasting tools that competed for audiences in Africa. By 1964, both the USSR and the PRC established effective broadcasting in Africa. In 1962, Communist broadcasts to Africa increased by 50 percent, and in that same year, the USSR's broadcasts introduced Bambara, spoken by nearly 3 million Africans in West Africa. Communist radio programming is said to have increased from 298 hours biweekly in 1962 to 332 hours biweekly at the end of 1963. Effective broadcasting in Africa was facilitated by the spread of transistor radios, which multiplied the number of listeners to U.S., USSR, and PRC radio broadcasts. By 1967, the USIA estimated that 4.3 million transistor radios were used in Africa.[33]

Explaining and advocating U.S. policies in credible and meaningful terms led to the implementation of the English Language Teaching program in non-English-speaking regions. In 1960 the USIA contracted with English Language Services, Inc. (ELS), to establish the first English language program in the Republic of Guinea. The ELS contract team in conjunction with the government of the Republic of Guinea conducted courses in English and provided teacher training through the establishment of an exchange program with American University, Georgetown University, and the University of Michigan. Sékou Touré's support of Communist positions in the United Nations initially limited the amount of aid the United States extended to Guinea. However, by 1962, U.S. economic interests in Guinea had grown, partly as a result of Olin-Mathieson's $61 million investment in FRIA, an international consortium operating a bauxite aluminum plant at Kimba, Guinea.[34] The USIA established similar English language teaching programs throughout West Africa and West-Central Africa from 1960 to 1965, and over the course of four years the USIA appropriated from $250,000 to as much as $500,000 to English language dissemination in the independent nations of West Africa and West-Central Africa. As one of several aggressive strategies that masked deeper truths about the realities of Cold War politics, the English Language Teaching Program served as a conduit for promoting American history, life, and culture.[35]

The effectiveness of the English Language Teaching Program, however, must be measured against the fact that African participants continually exploited cultural ties with the United States to fulfill their individual and collective objectives. The vast majority of Africans favored higher education in Europe because of cultural and institutional ties with former colonial powers. Prior to the implementation of educational and cultural programs targeting

African students and teachers, American institutions had not readily welcomed African students, and this constituted one of the major factors in the disparagement of American education by Africans. American-educated African leaders like Kwame Nkrumah and Nnamdi Azikiwe, who emerged during the struggles for independence, graduated from historically black Lincoln University in Pennsylvania, and experienced at first hand the indignity of racial discrimination in America. Both leaders, however, emerged as the "voice of the new Africa" with educational and cultural linkages to African American institutions. This fact informed the increased affinity of these institutions with Africa and African struggles for independence and represented an expanding interest in influencing American policies toward Africa. In this context, the African American Institute (AAI), founded by Dr. Horace Mann Bond of Lincoln University, Dr. Leo Hansberry of Howard University, and Etta Moton and William Steen, in 1953 served a significant role in promoting African interests in historically black institutions and advancing exchange opportunities. The AAI developed multilateral partnerships with the U.S. government, private foundations, and corporations to implement its African higher education and training programs and its educational outreach programs.[36]

The inexorable expansion of nationalist movements created opportunities for both the U.S. State Department and the USIA to initiate bilateral and multilateral aid to education. The Mutual Educational and Cultural Exchange Act of 1961 (the Fulbright-Hays Act) established the legislative framework for programs designed to strengthen patterns of informal two-way communication in ways that would favorably influence relations between the United States and other countries. The expressed objective of this act consisted of "increasing mutual understanding, cooperation, and community by direct and indirect methods."[37] As the fourth dimension of U.S. foreign policy, educational and cultural exchange enabled the United States to disseminate national ideas, images, and representations in order to transmit overtly political values. Challenges from the USSR with regard to extending academic educational opportunities to Africans threatened to undermine U.S. objectives. The overtures of the USSR in this area accelerated the pace of development of U.S. educational and cultural exchange programs in Africa. The opening of Peoples' Friendship University (renamed Patrice Lumumba University in 1961) in Moscow in 1960, primarily as a university for foreign students in Asia, Africa, and Latin America, underscored the importance the USSR attached to attaining a dominant role in the education-training process. Assistant Secretary of State for African Affairs G. Mennen Williams and U.S. State Department cultural affairs officers viewed the development of the USSR's programs as diametrically opposed to U.S. interests and they coordinated activities with the USIA to undermine Communist education. An effective counter to Soviet propaganda was to propagate printed media on racial discrimination in Soviet bloc countries.[38]

International and regional educational meetings on Africa, under the aegis of the United Nations Educational, Scientific, and Cultural Organization (UNESCO) and other UN agencies, provided the framework for the expansion of African and U.S. educational programs. The 1961 Conference of African States on the Development of Education in Africa, held in Addis Ababa, Ethiopia, laid the groundwork for wide-ranging programs of educational expansion. Similar conferences, such as the Tananarive Conference in 1961, stressed establishing a relationship with the Organization of African Unity's Educational and Cultural Commission. Cooperative programs with African governments and universities established a structure of mutual interdependency for undergraduate and graduate exchanges. Scholarship programs, such as the African Scholarship Program of American Universities (ASPAU) and the African Graduate Fellowship Program established by the AAI with funding from AID and the Bureau of Educational and Cultural Affairs, underscored the increasing importance of coordinating private American ideological efforts with U.S. government programs in Africa.[39]

Increasing levels of bilateral and multilateral aid to education through private organizations like the African-American Institute, the Ford Foundation, and the Benjamin Rosenthal Fund expanded during the first half of the 1960s. In 1962. the Bureau of Educational and Cultural Affairs allotted $4.7 million dollars to education grants and funding for educational exchange in Africa, an increase of 3.1 million over 1959. In previous years, under the Open Doors program, only a limited number of students from Africa studied in the United States, but increased funding for educational exchange led to an exponential increase in the number of students studying there. The early 1960s represented a significant watershed in the development of exchange programs in Africa. By 1963, 28,881 African students were enrolled in U.S. institutions, with the largest percentage enrolled at Howard University and the University of Southern California. In comparison, enrollment of African students in African universities increased from 18,000 to 21,000 during this same period.[40]

Cultural exchanges undergirded USIA efforts to take the offensive against Communist influence in Africa. In this context, the USIS "country team" played a pivotal role meshing the country programs of specific USIS posts with overall U.S. operations. Assisting and promoting foreign tours by American cultural groups in Africa served key political and psychological purposes. Cultural tours ostensibly aimed to express the desire of the United States for the peaceful evolution of African independence. These tours also putatively demonstrated the "ever-improving position" of African Americans in American society. African American entertainers stressed the bonds of mutual interest as they sought to achieve the agency's objective of promoting international understanding. Jazz artists such as the Wilbur de Paris Jazz

Band, the Herbie Mann Jazz Band, and Louis Armstrong served as international "race artists" who performed at venues in Kenya, Ghana, Nigeria, the Congo, Morocco, and Tunisia from 1956 to 1960. The "New Orleans" jazz played by the Wilbur de Paris Jazz Band featured original compositions with melodic improvisation that underscored a fusion of African and American instrumentation and intonation. African American theater groups from historically black colleges and universities, such as the Florida A&M Theater Group, which toured Nigeria and Uganda in 1958, provided added reinforcement to USIS country team objectives.[41]

The increased focus on educational and cultural exchange in Africa was consonant with the internationalization of civil rights issues. As a result, U.S. cultural policy during the 1960s witnessed a shift from "mutual understanding" to "political communication," which was characterized by an increase in the intensity of propaganda and information activities.[42] The USIA attempted to counter the influence of international criticism of civil rights abuses by sending American representatives abroad to promote positive race relations. From 1963 to 1964, American "ambassadors" of positive race relations traveled to several African nations to address social change in America and the democratic process. Second U.S. Circuit Court of Appeals Judge Thurgood Marshall and Berl I. Bernhard, staff director of the U.S. Commission on Civil Rights traveled to several East African countries to discuss civil rights with African officials. Howard University Professor Dr. Raleigh Morgan discussed the civil rights movement in several West African countries in order to provide what Carl Rowan called "perspective" on the race issue in America.[43] Entertainer Gene Kelly during a four-week visit to Senegal, Côte d'Ivoire, Upper Volta, and Ghana symbolically displayed American progressivism through the medium of dance. In the sports arena, Boston Celtics basketball stars K. C. Jones and John Havlicek and San Francisco Warriors star Thomas Mecherry were among the sports figures chosen by the USIA to conduct sports clinics in five West African countries. Despite the implicit political connotations of these activities, the international exchange program, with few exceptions, failed to provide outright support for American policies but did serve, in the short term, to preserve neutrality in key African countries, including Mauritania, Senegal, Kenya, Chad, the Malagasy Republic (where the United States positioned its NASA tracking station), and Zambia.[44]

The civil rights and foreign policy nexus became the cornerstone of America's efforts to secure a position of influence on the African continent. Cultural diplomacy failed to prevent the deepening of the Cold War in Africa, particularly in Congo (Brazzaville) and southern Africa; however, it did serve as an effective instrument in promoting foreign awareness and knowledge of American society, culture, and values. As an integral part of the U.S. strategy to win "hearts and minds," cultural diplomacy through

VOA broadcasting, USIS publications, the English Language Teaching program, and the educational and cultural exchange programs had a profound impact on African perceptions of America. From an official policy perspective, the U.S. State Department in 1964 asserted that it had succeeded in containing the spread of Communism in Africa, since out of 35 independent African nations not one had adopted Communism. The overall Communist effort in Africa, however, was considerable. From 1954 to 1967, the USSR extended $900 million in economic aid and $300 million in military aid. In comparison, the PRC extended some $350 million in economic aid, stationed 6,000 technicians in key African states, and provided an undetermined amount in military assistance.[45] The concerns of both the State Department and the Central Intelligence Agency regarding the influence of the USSR and the PRC in Africa persisted through the 1970s, primarily as a result of China's financing of the Tanzania-Zambia railroad. The co-linear relationship of the civil rights movement in America and the struggle for African independence during the early Cold War years moved Africa to the center of the bipolar conflict between East and West. The intensity of this conflict failed to create real "community" with African nations; however, cultural diplomacy served as an effective conduit for propagating American ideals, images, beliefs, and representations of American political values with the aim of enforcing American perceptions of truth and reality.[46]

Notes

1. "Lumumba Reverberations in Egypt," *United States Information Agency: A Commemoration* (USIA, 1999), p. 26, Box 25, Commemorative Books and Background Papers, MLR Entry A1–1064, General Records of the United States Information Agency (USIA), Historical Collection, Record Group (RG) 306, National Archives at College Park, Maryland (NACP); "How C.I.A. Put 'Instant Air Force' Into Congo to Carry Out United States Policy," April 26, 1966, *New York Times*; CIA Covert Operations, Agency History Program Subject Files 1926–75, MLR Entry A1–1072, Box 17, RG 306, NACP. For interviews with U.S. and UN officials during the Congo crisis, see the United Nations Oral History Collection Web site, www.un.org/Depts/dhl/dag/oralhist/htm. The author of this chapter would like to thank retired foreign service officers Richard Zorn and Ron Stewart for providing comments on an earlier version of this chapter. Several USIA public service officers disavow the use of the term "propaganda"; thus I distinguish between the different shades of propaganda and I note that black propaganda or complete disinformation was not a tool of the U.S. Information Agency.

2. Ibid.

3. Kevin V. Mulcahy, "Cultural Diplomacy: Foreign Policy and the Exchange Programs," pp. 270–92, Subject Files, MLR Entry A1–1066, RG 306, NACP.

4. Kelly Parker, "Josiah Royce," *The Stanford Encyclopedia of Philosophy*, Summer 2005 edition, ed., Edward N. Zalta, http:plato.stanford.edu/ archives/sum2005 /entries/ Royce/>. Charles Marsh and Ralph Luker's essays on King's theology establish the

roots of the "Beloved Community" in the philosophy of G. W. F. Hegel and Josiah Royce. See Ted Ownby's *The Role of Ideas in the Civil Rights South* (Jackson: University of Mississippi Press, 2002), 25; and A. J. Ayer, *Philosophy in the Twentieth Century* (New York: Random House, 1984), 71–72. White and gray propaganda were the foundation of U.S. information programs. White propaganda refers to the dissemination of information that represents American perceptions of truth. Gray propaganda is in the middle of the spectrum between white and black. Gray propaganda distorts the truth but does not reach the threshold of complete disinformation.

5. See Walter Hixson's *Parting the Curtain: Propaganda, Culture, and the Cold War, 1945–1961* (New York: St. Martin's Press, 1996), which discusses the use of cultural tools in U.S. foreign policy; Nigel Gould-Davies, "The Logic of Soviet Cultural Diplomacy," *Diplomatic History* 27, no. 2 (April 2003): 193–214, which provides a cogent argument for viewing cultural diplomacy as high politics; Robert E. Elder, *The Information Machine: The United States Information Agency and American Foreign Policy* (Syracuse, NY: Syracuse University Press, 1968); and Edward Barret, *Truth Is Our Weapon* (New York: Funk & Wagnalls, 1953).

6. Emily Rosenberg, *Spreading the American Dream: American Economic and Cultural Expansion, 1890–1945* (New York: Hill and Wang, 1982); John Tomlinson, *Cultural Imperialism* (Baltimore, MD: Johns Hopkins University Press, 1991), 4–5; Andrew J. Falk, "Reading between the Lines: Negotiating National Identity on American Television, 1945–1960," *Diplomatic History* 28, no. 2 (April 2004): 197–225; here: 208.

7. Mission Statements, 1945–67, Agency History Program Subject Files 1926–75, MLR Entry A1–1072, RG 306, NACP.

8. "The Place of Africa in U.S. Foreign Policy," *The Department of State during the Administration of President Lyndon B. Johnson*, vol. 4, November 1963–January 1969, 3–4, MLR Entry A1–5034, RG 59, General Records of the Department of State, NACP. For a discussion of the "Beloved Community" within the SNCC, see Clayborne Carson's *In Struggle: SNCC and the Black Awakening of the 1960s* (Cambridge, MA: Harvard University Press, 1981).

9. "The Place of Africa in U.S. Foreign Policy," *The Department of State during the Administration of President Lyndon B. Johnson*, vol. 4, November 1963–January 1969, 3–4, MLR Entry A1–5034, RG 59, General Records of the Department of State, NACP.

10. See Ownby, *The Role of Ideas*; Lewis Baldwin, *Toward the Beloved Community: Martin Luther King, Jr. and South Africa* (New York: Pilgrim Press, 1995); Martin Luther King, *Why We Can't Wait* (New York: New American Library, 2000), 1–38. Several scholars have examined race and Cold War politics in Africa during the 1960s. See, for example, James H. Meriwether, *Proudly We Can Be Africans: Black Americans and Africa, 1935–1961* (Chapel Hill: University of North Carolina Press, 2002); Gerald Horne, *From the Barrel of the Gun: The United States and the War against Zimbabwe* (Chapel Hill: University of North Carolina Press, 2001); Brenda Gayle Plummer, *Rising Wind: Black Americans and U.S. Foreign Affairs, 1935–1960* (Chapel Hill: University of North Carolina Press, 1996); Brenda Gayle Plummer, *Window on Freedom: Race, Civil Rights, and Foreign Affairs, 1945–1988* (Chapel Hill: University of North Carolina Press, 2003); Thomas Borstlemann, *Apartheid's Reluctant Uncle: The United States and Southern Africa in the Early Cold War* (New York: Oxford University

Press, 1993); Madeline G. Kalb, *The Congo Cables: The Cold War in Africa from Eisenhower to Kennedy* (New York: MacMillan Press, 1982).

11. U.S. Department of State, "Summary of Proposed Mutual Security Act of 1951," *Foreign Relations of the United States (FRUS)*, 313–334, 1951, vol. 1 (Washington, DC: Government Printing Office, 1979).

12. Africa Program, Historical Background, 1970, Agency History Program Subject Files 1926–75, MLR Entry A1–1072, Box 9, RG 306, NACP. See Philip Snow, *The Star Raft: China's Encounter with Africa* (New York: Weidenfeld & Nicolson, 1988) for a historical overview of Chinese-African relations; and Alan Hutchinson, *China's African Revolution* (Boulder, CO: Westview Press, 1975) for cogent analyses of China's economic interests in Africa; also see Laura Seay, "Misperception and Missed Opportunity: U.S. Policy and the Tanzania-Zambia Railway" (paper presented at the 2004 annual meeting of the African Studies Association, New Orleans).

13. Warren Weinstein and Thomas H. Henricksen, eds., *Soviet and Chinese Aid to African Nations* (New York: Praeger, 1980), 117–44; Alaba Ogunsanwo, *China's Policy in Africa, 1958–1971* (New York: Cambridge University Press, 1974), 61–111; The Gambia-China, 1966, Senegal-Soviet Bloc, 1966, CHICOMS, 1968, Subject Files Relating to The Gambia, Mali, and Senegal, 1965–73, MLR Entry A1–5683, Box 3, Bureau of African Affairs, Office of West African Affairs, RG 59, NACP.

14. "The Place of Africa in U.S. Foreign Policy," Nov. 1963–Jan. 1969.

15. Ibid., 57–58; Subject Files Relating to The Gambia, Mali, and Senegal, 1965–73, MLR Entry A1–5683, Box 3, Bureau of African Affairs, Office of West African Affairs, RG 59, NACP; Guidelines of U.S. Policy, Ghana: Guidelines for United States Policy and Operations, March 12, 1962, Bureau of African Affairs, Office of West African Affairs, Country Files, 1951–63, RG 59, NACP; "Memorandum from the Vice President's Military Aide (Burris) to Vice President Johnson, 31 January 1962," U.S. Department of State, *FRUS, 1961–1963*, vol. 21, *Africa*, 372; "Ghana: Assessment since Volta, June 13, 1962," *FRUS*, vol. 21, *Africa*, 375–77; "Memorandum of Conversation-African Unity and Guinean-American Relations," October 10, 1962, *FRUS*, vol. 21, *Africa*, 409–11.

16. "Memorandum from the President's Special Assistant for National Security Affairs (Bundy) to President Kennedy, 1 December 1961," *FRUS 1961–1963*, vol. 21, *Africa*, 365–68; William Tordoff, *Government and Politics in Africa* (London: Macmillan, 1984), 12–13; Records of the Foreign Service Posts of the Department of State, Classified General Records, 1956–58, Ghana, Ghana's Delicate Balance, Red Chinese Visit Ghana, MLR Entry 2597-A, RG 84, NACP; Andrew DeRoche, "Kenneth Kaunda and the Johnson Administration" (paper presented at the Society for Historians of American Foreign Relations conference, Austin, Texas, 2004).

17. Julius K. Nyerere, *Freedom and Socialism: A Selection from Writings and Speeches 1965–1967* (New York: Oxford University Press, 1968), 15; Guidelines of U.S. Policy, Ghana: Guidelines for United States Policy and Operations, March 12, 1962, Bureau of African Affairs, Office of West African Affairs, Country Files, 1951–63, RG 59, NACP.

18. Agency History Program Subject Files, Africa Program, Historical Background, 1970, MLR Entry A1–1072, Box 9, RG 306, NACP.

19. Ibid.

20. Roth, "Public Diplomacy and the Past: The Search for an American Style of Propaganda, 1952–1977," *The Fletcher Forum: A Journal of Studies in International Affairs* (Summer 1984): 368–369; "State of the Union Speech, January 9, 1958," *Public Papers of the Presidents: Dwight D. Eisenhower* (Washington, DC: Federal Register Division, 1958), 3. See Loyd Gardner's *Architects of Illusion: Men and Ideas in American Foreign Policy, 1941–1949* (Chicago: Quadrangle Books, 1970), which argues that the United States was responsible for the *way* in which the Cold War developed.

21. U.S. Department of State, *FRUS*, 1955–57, 522–23 (Washington, DC: Government Printing Office, 1989). The Operations Coordinating Board was abolished by President Kennedy. Roth, "Public Diplomacy," 369.

22. American Visits to the Soviet Union: Vice Presidential Documents, July–August 1959, Bureau of European Affairs, Bilateral Political Relations Subject Files, 1921–73, File 1631 (g), MLR Entry A1–5345, Box 12, RG 59, NACP; See Joyce and Gabriel Kolko, *The Limits of Power: The World and U.S. Foreign Policy* (New York: Harper & Row, 1972), which argues that the United States placed limits on independence and development in the Third World that might conflict with the interests of American capitalism.

23. See Michael L. Krenn, *Race and U.S. Foreign Policy during the Cold War* (New York: Garland Press, 1998); Michael L. Krenn, *Black Diplomacy: African Americans and the State Department, 1945–1969* (New York: M. E. Sharpe, 1999); Mary Dudziak, "Desegregation as a Cold War Imperative," *Stanford Law Review* 41 (November 1988): 80–93; Mary Dudziak, *Cold War Civil Rights: Race and the Image of American Democracy* (Princeton, NJ: Princeton University Press, 2000); Thomas Borstlemann, *The Cold War and the Color Line: American Race Relations in the Global Arena* (Cambridge, MA: Harvard University Press, 2001); Gerald Horne, *Black and Red: W.E.B. DuBois and the Afro-American Response to the Cold War, 1944–1963* (New York: State University of New York Press, 1986); and W. E. B. DuBois, *The World and Africa* (New York: Viking Press, 1947).

24. "The Place of Africa in U.S. Foreign Policy."; For a discussion of U.S. historical and contemporary interests, see J. Forbes Munro, *Africa and the International Economy, 1800–1960* (Totowa, NJ: Rowman & Littlefield, 1976); Henry F. Jackson, *From the Congo to Soweto: U.S. Foreign Policy toward Africa since 1960* (New York: St. Martin's Press, 1996); Peter Duignan and L. H. Gann, *The United States and Africa: A History* (New York: Cambridge University Press, 1984).

25. Worldwide Reactions to Racial Incidents in Alabama, Special ("S") Reports, 1953–63, RG 306, NACP; Borstlemann, *The Cold War and the Color Line*, 135–72; Cary Fraser, "Crossing the Color Line in Little Rock: The Eisenhower Administration and the Dilemma of Race in U.S. Foreign Policy,"*Diplomatic History* 24, no. 2 (Spring 2000): 233–64; Dudziak, *Cold War Civil Rights*.

26. Appropriations, 1954–74, Media Comment, Funding 1962–63, Subject Files, MLR Entry A1–1066, Box 9, RG 306, NACP.

27. Africa Program, Historical Background, 1970, Agency History Program Subject Files 1926–75, MLR Entry A1–1072, NACP.

28. Ibid. Although President Kennedy expressed a measure of goodwill toward both Africans and African Americans, Kenneth Janken has noted that Kennedy supported Portuguese colonialism and apartheid and branded members of liberation movements as "terrorists." See Janken, "Making Racial Change, Managing Radical

Change: The Civil Rights Movement, U.S. Foreign Policy, and Race Relations on the World Stage," *Diplomatic History* 27, no. 5 (November 2003): 713–23; here: 722.

29. Radio, Broadcasting to Near East, South Asia, and Africa, 1953–54, Broadcasting to Africa, 1954, Transmitting Stations, 1946–61, Subject Files, MLR Entry A1–1066, Box, 71, Box 88, RG 306, NACP; Africa Program, Historical Background, 1970, Agency History Program Subject Files, MLR Entry A1–1072, Box 9, RG 306, NACP; Facts about USIA, 1964, Communist Propaganda Expenditures, 1962, Agency History Program Subject Files, Box 16, RG 306, NACP.

30. USIS Centers, Africa 1954–91, Radio Program Schedules, 1963–64, Subject Files, MLR Entry A1–1066, Box 209, RG 306, NACP.

31. Radio Program Schedules, 1963–64, Subject Files, MLR Entry A1–1066, Box 109, RG 306, NACP.

32. Ronald Rubin, *The Objectives of the U.S. Information Agency: Controversies and Analysis* (New York: Frederick A. Praeger, 1966); 47–50; "An Era of Persuasion," Speeches, Carl T. Rowan, 1964, Agency History Program Subject Files, MLR Entry A1–1072, Box 13, RG 306, NACP.

33. Communist Broadcasting, 1963, USIA Reports Continued Rise in Communists Broadcasting, Communist International Broadcasting, 1966, Agency History Program Subject Files, MLR A1–1072, Box 16, Box 17, RG 306, NACP; Elder, *The Information Machine*, 6. The figures on Communist broadcasting are problematic. There are only 168 hours in a week. The figures may represent monthly totals, not biweekly totals.

34. English Language Teaching, Subject Files, MLR Entry A1–1066, Box 194, RG 306, NACP; "The Place of Africa in U.S. Foreign Policy"; USIA: English Language Teachers for Guinea, 1960, Bureau of African Affairs, Office of West African Affairs, Country Files, 1951–63, Guinea, RG 59, NACP; Gould-Davies, "The Logic of Soviet Cultural Diplomacy," 193–214.

35. English Language Teaching, Subject Files, MLR Entry A1–1066, RG 306, NACP; USIA: English Language Teachers for Guinea, 1960, Bureau of African Affairs, Office of West African Affairs, Country Files, 1951–63, Guinea, RG 59, NACP; Guinea: Technical Cooperation Bilateral Agreement, 1959, Bureau of African Affairs, Office of West African Affairs, Country Files, 1951–63, U.S.-Guinean Relations, RG 59, NACP; The "Place of Africa in U.S. Foreign Policy"; Gould-Davies, "The Logic of Soviet Cultural Diplomacy."

36. Margaret Y. Henderson and John P. Henderson, "The African Image of Higher Education in America," *International Educational and Cultural Exchange* (Spring 1967): 45–56, USIS Posts Publications, MLR Entry A1–1063, RG 306, NACP. See also Bureau of African Affairs, Office of Inter-African Affairs, Records Relating to Education and Educational Exchange, 1961–66, RG 59, NACP. Azikiwe attended Storer College in Harper's Ferry, West Virginia, and Lincoln University in Lincoln, Pennsylvania. Nkrumah attended Achimota College in Accra, Lincoln University in Pennsylvania, and the London School of Economics in England.

37. Mutual Educational and Cultural Exchange Act, 1960–62, Agency History Program Subject Files, MLR Entry A1–1072, RG 306, NACP; Friendship University Moscow: The Student Trap, 1965, Propaganda Country Files, 1953–91, MLR Entry A1–1068, Box 1, RG 306, NACP; "The Place of Africa in U.S. Foreign Policy."

38. Educational and Cultural Programs in Africa—Private and Public, Records Relating to Education and Educational Exchange, 1961–66, Bureau of African Affairs, Office of Inter-African Affairs, MLR Entry A1–5700, RG 59, NACP.

39. Educational and Cultural Diplomacy, 1964, Subject Files, MLR A1–1066, RG 306, NACP; Raymond L. Perkins, "ASPAU in French Speaking West Africa," *International Educational and Cultural Exchange* (Fall 1965): 2–5, USIS Posts Publications, RG 306, NACP. The *Washington Post*, in "O What a Tangled Web the CIA Wove," February 26, 1967, identifies the African American Institute, the Ford Foundation, and the Benjamin Rosenthal Fund as recipients of CIA funds. For a discussion of the CIA and the cultural Cold War, see Frances Stonor Saunders, *Who Paid the Piper? The CIA and the Cultural Cold War* (London: Granta Books, 1999).

40. The "Big Picture"—Basic Problems faced by the Department in Any Expansion of Our Educational Exchange Program in Africa, Bureau of African Affairs, Office of Inter-African Affairs, MLR Entry A1–5700, Records Relating to Education and Educational Exchange, 1961–66, RG 59, NACP; The Undergraduate Scholarship Program for African Students, Bureau of African Affairs, Office of Inter-African Affairs, MLR Entry A1–5700, Records Relating to Education and Educational Exchange, 1961–66, MLR Entry A1–5700, RG 59, NACP.

41. Ghana, Accra, Wilbur de Paris Jazz Band, Box 3, Records of Foreign Service Posts of the Department of State, RG 84, NACP; Educational and Cultural Programs in Africa—Private and Public, Records Relating to Education and Educational Exchange, 1961–66, Bureau of African Affairs, Office of Inter-African Affairs, RG 59, NACP; Exchange of Persons, Nigeria, Lagos Embassy, 1958, Classified General Records, 1956–63, RG 84, NACP; Elder, *The Information Machine*, 316–17.

42. Elder, *The Information Machine*, 42–43.

43. Speeches, Carl T. Rowan, 1964, Agency History Program Subject Files, MLR Entry A1–1072, RG 306, NACP; Exchange of Persons, Africa, 1960, African Students in the United States, Subject Files, MLR Entry A1–1066, RG 306, NACP; Bureau of African Affairs, Office of Inter-African Affairs, Records Relating to Education and Educational Exchange, 1961–66, MLR Entry 5700, RG 59, NACP.

44. Speeches, Carl T. Rowan, 1964, Agency History Program Subject Files, MLR Entry A1–1072, RG 306, NACP; Educational and Cultural Diplomacy, 1964, Subject Files, MLR Entry A1–1066, RG 306, NACP. For Soviet bloc interests in African athletics, see Classified Research Project Records, MLR Entry A1–1007-C, Requestor Only Reports, 1960, RG 306, NACP; Compilations of Cultural and Educational Exchanges between the Communist Countries and Africa, 1963, June 19 1964, Records Relating to Select USIA Programs, MLR Entry A1–1061, RG 306, NACP.

45. Subject Files, MLR Entry A1–1066, Educational and Cultural Diplomacy, 1964, RG 306, NACP; A Proposed US Policy toward Disaffection among Students from Developing Countries in the Soviet Bloc, May 24, 1963, Bureau of African Affairs, Office of Inter-African Affairs, Records Relating to Education and Educational Exchange, 1961–66, MLR Entry A1–5700, RG 59, NACP; "The Place of Africa in U.S. Foreign Policy."

46. Three Years of Progress: The Kennedy-Johnson Administrations, 1961–63, Subject Files, MLR Entry A1–1066, RG 306, NACP; Ogunsanwo, *China's Policy in Africa*, 61–111, 180–240; "Intelligence Memorandum/1/ No. 1393/67, Some Aspects of Subversion in Africa, October 19, 1967," *FRUS 1964–1968*, vol. 24, *Africa*,

Document 230 (Washington, DC: Government Printing Office, 1999); Seay, "Misperception and Missed Opportunity"; "The Place of Africa in U.S. Foreign Policy." Thomas J. Noer notes that the appointment of Averell Harriman in 1964 as ambassador at large for overseeing U.S. African policy was a development that "foiled G. Mennen William's attempts to make Africa a major priority in U.S. foreign policy following President Kennedy's assassination." See Thomas J. Noer, "Phone Rage: LBJ, Averell Harriman, and G. Mennen Williams," *Passport: The Newsletter of the Society for Historians of American Foreign Relations* 35, no. 3 (2004): 42–43; see also Records of the Assistant Secretary of State for African Affairs G. Mennen Williams, Bureau of African Affairs, MLR Entry 1485, Administrative and Organization File, 1961, RG 59, NACP.

8

African Americans in Ghana and Their Contributions to "Nation Building" since 1985

Kwame Essien

Introduction

Dr. W. E. B. DuBois, in *The Souls of Black Folk*, writes about the oppositional conflicts in black bodies: "Two souls, two thoughts, two unrecognized strivings, and two warring ideals in one dark body, whose dogged strength alone keeps it from being torn asunder."[1] DuBois' representation of the internal struggle within black bodies gave returnees the courage they needed to confront their fear over their multiple natures: one nature claiming African and American identity simultaneously; one accepting American citizenship but contemplating African citizenship at the same time; one embracing American cultural values and pondering African ethics at the same time; one feeling American and African all together; and most significantly, one living in America but romanticizing the "Motherland." A return to Africa epitomizes DuBois' notion of double consciousness and the crisis of identity.[2]

DuBois himself satisfied the yearning to return to the motherland when he left America in 1961 to take up Ghanaian citizenship. His home in Accra became a place of pilgrimage for black Americans and political activists who traveled to Ghana. The burial site of DuBois is like a shrine in Ghana.[3] Historical symbols and discourses such as this continue to bolster relationships between diaspora blacks and Ghanaians in a variety of ways. The study of African American history in Ghana encompasses a wide range of themes. Returnees in Ghana and local people have expressed mutual cultural and economic interests.

In my attempt to analyze this complex relationship and African Americans' profound attraction to their ancestral homeland, I will look at the following distinct elements: the historical forces that have shaped expatriates' and returnees' engagements with Ghanaians, the diversity within the returnee community itself, and the innovative contributions that members of this community have made to the socioeconomic landscape of Ghana. I ask what driving forces in the history of Ghana and the history of black America have led to the continuation and further development of a relationship between the two groups even after the horrific events of the transatlantic slave trade that gave rise to the New World blacks.

Three periods of migration to Ghana have occurred since 1950, creating groups of returnees with different objectives and sociocultural interests in Ghana. This chapter does not deny the effects of tensions between returnees and Ghanaians on local people or the conflicts between returnees and the Ghanaian government on the national level. For example, on the local front, returnees and Ghanaians have been influenced by their respective historical backgrounds, which tend to influence their views about each other; while on the national front, returnees have clashed with the Ghana Tourist and Monuments Board over how to preserve historical sites, especially the Cape Coast and Elmina slave castles.[4]

This chapter does not intend to address all the issues listed by Paschal G. Zachary in a 2001 article (for which, see below); neither does it seek to discuss in detail events in the expatriate community during President Nkrumah's reign and during the second period of migration after the fall of Nkrumah in 1966. Instead, it aims at casting new light on the fledgling relations between Ghanaians and returnees, as well as the implication of their engagements for socioeconomic reforms in Ghana. A sizable number of African Americans traveled to Ghana beginning in the 1980s to establish nongovernmental organizations. The various monetary and logistical contributions returnees have made toward Ghana's socioeconomic progress are worth mentioning. For instance, One Africa has created the Educational Sponsorship Program in the Central Region of Ghana,[5] Leon H. Sullivan has set up the Sullivan African Summit,[6] and Bryan Lowe has established and serves as the director of the Kwaku Kunta Kinte Orthopaedic Hospital Complex.[7]

The first wave of returnees, from 1950 to 1966, consisted of about eighty expatriates, whose mission in Ghana was to assist Dr. Kwame Nkrumah in his postindependence reforms. The availability of revolutionary projects in their ancestral homeland led individuals who were mostly intellectuals, doctors, nurses, and skilled professionals to flee their country during the Cold War hysteria.[8] From the oppressive environment in America that demanded revolutionary or radical reactions, they relocated to another environment that called for expertise to fill the social space created by the demise of British colonialism.

Due to political instability and economic hardships in Ghana between 1970 and 1985, the second period saw few black Americans migrate to

Ghana. Those who did travel to or live in Ghana during the military rule of Jerry John Rawlings (from June 4, 1979, to September 24, 1979, and from December 31, 1981, to January 8, 1993) used the country as a doorway to other African countries.[9] However, political and economic reforms in Ghana and the promise of Rawlings to grant them Ghanaian citizenship and free land attracted a third group, of approximately 1,000 returnees, from 1985 on.[10] The current population of African American expatriates in Ghana is believed to be the largest number of black Americans living in sub-Saharan Africa since the 1980s. A historical overview will be helpful in teasing out the elements that ignited the black American exodus to Ghana.

The early twentieth century witnessed a major transformation among blacks in the diaspora.[11] Marcus Garvey's United Negro Improvement Association (UNIA), established in 1917, called for the unification of blacks in the diaspora and for an end to white hegemony worldwide. Garvey's crusade was a precursor of Pan-Africanism, advocating a "Back-to-Africa" movement. Garvey's political rhetoric led to new consciousness, awakenings, and black assertiveness throughout the New World. His campaign influenced many blacks in the diaspora.[12] Although Garvey did not live long enough to see his vision come to fruition, his campaign had a lasting impact on the African diaspora. Garvey predicted that a return to Africa would not take "a day, a year, ten or twenty years."[13] The flamboyant Jamaican was right. New migrations fulfill Garvey's prophecy and keep his dreams alive. In Ghana, Garvey's symbol of freedom, the Black Star, sits at Independence Square, the heart of Accra. The location has become a tourist attraction in Ghana.

As blacks became more conscious of similarities in their struggles, they launched a vigorous crusade that Paul Robeson called "a mighty blow on the side of real democracy for our people here as well as our brothers on the continent of Africa to end white oppression of blacks."[14] Nonetheless, this attempt to unite under one umbrella in order to topple white supremacy came with a price. White power structures in America, Europe, and the colonies sought to silence the authentic voices of black leaders such as Marcus Garvey, C. L. R. James, Paul Robeson, W. E. B. DuBois, Kwame Nkrumah, Jomo Kenyatta, and scores of black nationalist leaders in the diaspora. However, the attacks on these leaders increased the momentum in the struggle to end white domination across the globe and later sparked black American migrations to Africa.[15] From the 1930s, the concept of Pan-Africanism resonated strongly throughout Africa and the New World, increasingly shaped political discourse and black consciousness, and spurred black activism and militancy worldwide.[16]

Something even more extraordinary happened in the 1950s, during the process of decolonization in Africa and desegregation in black America. Blacks in America and other parts of the New World embarked on emigration campaigns to relocate in independent African nations.[17] Historian

Kevin K. Gaines notes that at the beginning of the 1950s, some people saw Ghana as a symbolic site reinforcing Pan-African ideals. In his recent book, *American Africans in Ghana: Black Expatriates and the Civil Rights Era,* Gaines argues that the demise of Nkrumah's regime in 1966 influenced black American expatriates to return home to infuse new passion into the civil rights movements.[18] Numerous other historians such as Robert Johnson and Ernest Dunbar have examined relationships between black Americans and Ghanaians during the same period.

Through oral interviews, in *Why Blacks Left America for Africa,* Robert Johnson Jr. carefully sketches the factors that drove black Americans to Africa between 1971 and 1999.[19] Ernest Dunbar follows a similar thread by thoroughly examining the flow of black people from the United States to West and East Africa in his book *The Black Expatriates: A Study of American Negroes in Exile.*[20] However, scholarship in the past has not seriously examined the contributions African American returnees have made to socioeconomic change. While academics have largely neglected the returnees, more popular accounts have even looked at them with disdain. African Americans' involvements in Ghana in the last two decades deserve scholarly attention and recognition. I provide that recognition by highlighting returnees' contributions in this chapter.

An article entitled "Tangled Roots: For African Americans in Ghana, the Grass Isn't Always Greener—Seeking the Motherland, They Find Echoes of History and Chilly Welcome," published in *The Wall Street Journal* in 2001 by Paschal G. Zachary, found no traces of any constructive relationship between Ghanaians and returnees. Like others who have written about relationships between African American expatriates and Ghanaians, Zachary failed to provide a balanced report on the conditions in Ghana and made no mention of the contributions and sacrifices that African Americans were making there. He illuminated some tensions and washed dirty linen in a newspaper read daily by millions of people around the world, but found no constructive engagement between the two groups.

In addition, Zachary portrayed Ghanaians as desperate people who despise their own country. In his words, "nobody wants to live in Ghana anymore. . . . Nobody, that is[,] except African Americans."[21] He concluded that "many black Americans living in Ghana find they aren't particularly welcome—and wonder whether they need a new civil rights movement to secure a place in their adopted home."[22] Zachary claims that "Ghana forbids American residents from taking jobs. Hospitals charge them higher fees. Americans can't vote in elections or participate in local politics. It is virtually impossible for them to obtain citizenship or permanent 'right of abode,' even after marrying a Ghanaian."[23] The implication is that there is no constructive engagement between the two groups. The article alleges that Ghanaians discriminate against African Americans and prevent them from achieving their dreams. It ignores the ongoing cultural dialogue between returnees and the Ministry of Tourism in Ghana about using Emancipation Day and the Panafest celebration to cement the ties between Ghanaians, African American tourists, and returnees.[24] Recently, Jake Obetsebi Lamptey, Ghana's minister of tourism, has inaugurated the Joseph Project to showcase the historical cultural bonds between Ghanaians and blacks in the New World.[25]

Zachary's misleading information ignores Ghanaians' hospitality and their tolerance for the people of diverse ethnic, racial, cultural, and religious backgrounds who travel to Ghana. The article did not escape the attention of returnees. Akhbar Muhammad, a spokesman for the African American Association in Ghana, claims that it threatened the relationships returnees have established with Ghanaians in the past fifty years. Leaders of the African American Association in Ghana denounced the piece and called it "a derogatory statement." They argued that it was "part of the old tricks perpetuated by whites . . . and a calculated attempt to put fear in African Americans about what to expect in Ghana. It is simply an old neo-colonial modus operandi to frustrate attempts by Africans to unite."[26] The returnees sought avenues of redress. They urged the Ghanaian government to set up a quick response department to deal with foreigners who disseminate deceptive and divisive information about Ghana and its people. The Ghanaian government pursued this idea as the leaders of the community requested.[27]

Historicizing Expatriates and Returnees and Their Choice of Ghana

The sociopolitical and racial conditions in America in the middle of the twentieth century compelled a number of black Americans to resist racial oppression through exile.[28] Many of those who could afford to travel around the world hoped that if they left America their conditions would improve. Black American intellectuals, such as James Baldwin and others, who visited Ghana during this period, encouraged black Americans at home to migrate to Ghana because it was relatively free of racial tensions.[29] That is not to say, however, that all black Americans who left America were victims of government attacks or were under close government surveillance, as we can say of DuBois, Robeson, and Alpheus Hunton.[30] A variety of factors motivated those who migrated to Africa. For example, although racial and economic problems in America created waves of migration, various historical events, foremost among them the Pan-African conferences and the demise of colonialism in Africa, also influenced migration patterns. Accra became a Mecca for African nationalist leaders and freedom fighters after the Fifth Pan-African Congress in Manchester, England, in 1945, at the height of black radicalism and nationalism.[31] Also, once Ghana gained independence from Britain on March 6, 1957, it became famous as the first colonized nation in sub-Saharan Africa to reclaim self-governance, and its role in Pan-Africanism paved the way for oppressed people across the globe.[32] Other political factors also aided the black exodus.

Kwame Nkrumah gained experience in mobilizing people as a result of his participation in the black American freedom struggle during his college days at Lincoln University. Later, he associated with many black American leaders such as W. E. B. DuBois, Paul Robeson, and others who invited him to work with the Council on African Affairs and the National Association for the Advancement of Colored People. Nkrumah's experiences triggered migrations decades later.[33] When Nkrumah became the president of Ghana in 1960, he extended invitations to a number of black American activists, radicals, and intellectuals whose services were greatly needed after the end of British rule in Ghana. For example, in 1961, DuBois was invited to begin the *Encyclopedia Africana* project to document African history. The Ghana Academy of Sciences and the University of Ghana sponsored the project.[34] It is against such a backdrop and, overall, against the backdrop of the quest for freedom from white hegemony that evolved within the New World and especially in black America that the first migration to Ghana emerged.[35] Unfortunately, the expatriates' participation in Nkrumah's revolutionary projects was interrupted by tragic events in the 1960s.

The attempts on Nkrumah's life in 1962 and 1964[36] caused many Ghanaians to suspect black American expatriates of engaging in subversive activities in the interest of the Central Intelligence Agency.[37] This was a watershed moment because it was the first time in the history of the two groups that such cynicism had surfaced publicly. For many Ghanaians during this period, Nkrumah was the messiah and the only leader who could set the nation free from colonial oppression and repair the economy of the country,[38] so they perceived an attack on Nkrumah as one directed at them. Although there was no substantial evidence linking the expatriates with the attacks, the rising frenzy caused some of the expatriates, including Wendell Jean Pierre, a black American lecturer at the University of Ghana, to be deported. This was to signal a warning to the expatriate community.[39] The fall of Nkrumah's government and the political chaos in Ghana in 1966 forced many expatriates, including Alpheus Hunton, to relocate to other African countries.[40] Despite the setback in relations between the hosts and the returnees, however, various cultural and social elements deeply embedded in the psyche of the returnees encouraged fresh migrations and visits to Ghana.

Certain sites in Ghana have historical value that also encourages tourism. During the period of the transatlantic slave trade, thirty-two of the forty-five forts and slave dungeons along the West African coastline were built in Ghana. This encouraged blacks in the diaspora to trace their ancestry to this region. For example, in 1956, Louis Armstrong, the famous jazz musician, traced his ancestry to Komantse and Abandzie, twin fishing towns in the

Central Region of Ghana. Armstrong gave a concert in Accra during his visit.[41] Over the years, the nation has continued to parley its historical significance into tourism. As anthropologist Brempong Osei Tutu argues, Ghana continues to be a place of pilgrimage for many African Americans because of the importance of historical monuments to blacks in the diaspora.[42] Other cultural and social elements have also been important in attracting diaspora members.

Today, political stability and a low cost of living also attract many returnees and tourists to the region. In addition, as violence in the streets of America increases, many African Americans contend that Ghana is a safer environment, conducive to raising their children. According to Janet Butler, a leader in the returnee community, the social environment in the United States does not offer a safe nurturing space in which children can develop confidence and a sense of worth. She contends that Ghana provides the opportunity to develop both of these.[43] For Benjamin Robinson, another leader in the returnee community, the chaotic conditions and the escalation of violence in the streets of America have caused many of the returnees to "run like hell from New York straight to Afrika."[44]

Few returnees settled in Ghana between 1970 and 1985, however, because of political instability and economic hardships, especially under the structural adjustment programs (SAPs) that were introduced in Ghana in the 1980s.

How did Flt. Lt. Jerry John Rawlings, the Ghanaian military leader, involve African Americans in Ghana's economic recovery programs when he became president in 1992? Flt. Lt. Rawlings, a junior air force pilot, staged a bloody coup on June 4, 1979, to overthrow General F. W. K. Akuffo's military government. Rawlings handed over power to Dr. Hilla Limman, a democratically elected president, in December of the same year. Dissatisfied with the new administration, Rawlings took over the government again in 1981 and headed a military government until he was elected president in 1992. Most Ghanaians perceived Rawlings, like Nkrumah, as their redeemer, whose mission was to save the country from its corrupt leadership. Both leaders had a long history of engaging with black Americans to benefit the country, and there are striking resemblances in the ways they did this. Rawlings continued to foster close ties with blacks in the diaspora, just as Nkrumah did in the 1950s and 1960s.[45] Rawlings' invitation to African Americans to resettle in Ghana led to another paradigm shift in the later years of his military regime and during his tenure as a civilian president from 1992.[46] This was the first time since the fall of Nkrumah's government in 1966 that any Ghanaian leader had officially reconnected with people of African ancestry in the diaspora. Both Nkrumah and Rawlings saw African Americans as the richest and most highly educated black population in the Americas, and they took advantage of this by tapping into African

Americans' resources and expertise.[47] Furthermore, the fact that Nkrumah had an Egyptian wife and the fact that Rawlings was of mixed background (his father is Scottish and his mother is Ghanaian) may have prompted them to associate or identify closely with African Americans.

For Rawlings, the journey to economic reforms began with an international approach. To set the new relationships in motion, Rawlings carried his plans around the African continent. In 1993, during the Organization of African Unity (OAU) conference in Cairo, Egypt, Rawlings attempted to convince other African heads of state to grant unconditional African citizenship to African Americans and other blacks in the diaspora who chose to relocate to their ancestral homeland. To push his agenda even further, the Ghanaian leader proposed African American seats and representation at future OAU conferences.[48] Rawlings introduced the Right of Abode Bill to Ghana's Parliament in April 1995. If passed, this would guarantee security for investors and full Ghanaian citizenship to blacks in the diaspora. Rawlings forced the Ghanaian Parliament to form a committee to study the bill, which gained media coverage, especially in the *Ghanaian Times* and the *Daily Graphic*.[49] The new Ghanaian Parliament is still working out details about the Right of Abode Bill.

In October 1995, Rawlings visited America to discuss Ghana's economic progress and reforms with African American leaders; he invited them to invest in Ghana's economy. During his trip, he repeated his promise to grant Ghanaian citizenship to African Americans.[50] The idea of taking Ghanaian citizenship is foreign to many African Americans, due to their limited knowledge of and interest in Africa, but this did not deter Rawlings from making his offer.

The Ghanaian leader's trip to the United States was productive in terms of articulating his economic plans as he traveled to Harlem, Philadelphia, Atlanta, Chicago, Detroit, Los Angeles, and other cities. Speaking at the Chicago Town Hall during his investment promotion tour, he urged investors to make Ghana their target because of the opportunities available. Newspaper reports on his trip indicate that many investors expressed an interest in Ghana and were pleased with its leadership. In fact, Rawlings' trip did more than encourage investment: it elevated Rawlings' own image in America. During the two-week visit, Rawlings and his wife were honored with doctorates at Lincoln University in Pennsylvania, Nkrumah's alma mater, in recognition of their services to society. One citation read: "President Rawlings is one of the leaders to whom the world is looking to help the African continent achieve equitable and sustainable development in the 21st Century."[51] Such public acknowledgments energized Rawlings.

To attract more African Americans to Ghana and sustain them there, Rawlings asked local Ghanaian chiefs to provide land incentives to returnees. The chiefs welcomed this idea and selected wealthy returnees as honorary or development chiefs in their towns and villages. The returnees responded by funding social activities in these locales.[52] It is believed that Nkrumah also made available free land to black Americans and other political activists while he was in power.[53] The primary goal of both leaders was to win the hearts and minds of blacks in the diaspora, and in doing so to elevate Ghana's image worldwide.

Finally, in 1998, during the first Emancipation Day celebration in Ghana, commemorating the official abolition of chattel slavery in Jamaica in 1834, the Ghanaian president emphasized the urgency of attracting returnees to Ghana, encouraging African Americans to pool their resources to invest in Africa's economic progress.[54] Thereafter, Rawlings embraced Panafest and Emancipation Day as methods of cementing relations with the diaspora. Both celebrations became part of his political agenda.[55]

The first Emancipation Day celebration in 1998 witnessed emotional scenes and attracted more than 5,000 visitors. To climax the occasion, and to reemphasize the connections between all blacks, two caskets containing the remains of descendants of slaves from the diaspora were returned to Ghana. After traditional rites, the bodies of Samuel Carson, a U.S. Navy officer from New York; and Crystal, a native of Jamaica, were reinterred at Assin Manso, a former slave market in the Central Region. According to Nana Kwame Nkyi XII, paramount chief of Assin Apinim, the reburial of the remains fulfilled a prophecy in the village, a prophecy asserting that one day the dead in the New World would be brought back home for a royal burial.[56] The burial site has become another tourist center in Ghana.[57]

Rawlings' unending efforts to develop economic relations and his relentless dialogue with the returnees bore some fruit in 1999 when Rev. Leon Sullivan, an African American philanthropist and founder of the Leon Sullivan African–African American Summits, selected Accra as the venue for his fifth summit. The theme of this Millennium Summit was "Business, Trade, and Investment." Rev. Sullivan declared that "Ghana is the flagship for African nations. We are proud of President Rawlings and the work he has done."[58] The goal of the summit was to emphasize globally the opportunities for investments and other economic opportunities in Africa. Previous summits had been held in Ivory Coast, Gabon, Senegal, and Zimbabwe. More than forty African nations were considered to host the Millennium Summit. However, Ghana was chosen as a result of its growing economy and Rawlings' success in building bridges between Ghana and the diaspora.

Rawlings made his economic intentions quite clear and emphasized on many occasions that Ghanaians already had enough problems at home and did not want to see returnees jumping on the bandwagon empty handed. For example, during his trip to America in 1995 he declared, "Do not come to that continent [Africa] without appropriate skills and resources because [if you do] you will only be contributing to its poverty."[59] During the Fifth African–African American Summit, he underscored this point.[60]

In November 2001, after the end of Rawlings' regime, the Ghanaian Parliament passed legislation allowing blacks in the diaspora to work in Ghana indefinitely and to own property.[61] Although the promises that they would be granted citizenship have not materialized, they continue to show their commitment by using their expertise and skills to benefit the nation. It is against this background and in the circumstances created partly by Rawlings that the current wave of migrations evolved.

Members of the third group of returnees have a twofold ambition: to use their professional skills by engaging in entrepreneurship, and to reconnect with their ancestral homeland. They differ in economic status, politics, religion, and education. The group includes Rastafarians living in mud huts in remote villages, middle-class retirees seeking safe environments to invest in, and lower-middle-class returnees who usually form partnerships with Ghanaian entrepreneurs or create their own small-scale businesses. One such business is Asaase Pa, a company that sells whole food products in Tema and Accra.[62]

Because the local people overwhelmingly outnumber the returnees, the returnees' presence in Ghana is not very visible. Most of them settle along the coast in places such as Cape Coast, Elmina, Accra, and Tema because of easy access to historical sites, industries, the international airport, Tema Harbor, and the availability of business opportunities in the cities.

Ghana's projected population for July 2005 is more than twenty-one million, while the number of returnees is only 1,000-plus.[63] There are more than seventy local Ghanaian languages, many of them being Akan languages.[64] Although English is the official language, less than 40 percent of the people speak it fluently. Returnees' inability to communicate fluently in local languages hinders their ability to interact more effectively with the local people, especially when they come into contact with people who have little Western education. In addition, the cultural backgrounds of the returnees are imbued in part with Western values, and their views on racism create barriers and sometimes tensions between them and Ghanaians. For example, most local people tend to see both black and white tourists as their guests, and therefore offer them equal hospitality as traditions demand. This means that tourists from the diaspora and returnees are not given any special treatment in many situations.

Some African Americans prefer that they be given special attention because of their ancestral links with Ghana. But since the local people do not provide this, the returnees tend to see the equal friendliness that Ghanaians extend to European tourists as elevating the white race above the black race. Some returnees would like the local people to distance themselves from white tourists, as they themselves do, in order to create a stronger bond between blacks.[65]

The returnees are terribly frustrated by the language barriers because of their earnest desire to reconnect culturally with their roots. After living in

Ghana for more than forty-eight years, Dr. Lee, a respected member of the returnee community, had this to say: "We need to stop trying to be Fante, Ashanti, Ewe, Ga [these are the most common languages]. We have our own tribe of Afrikans born in America, Europe, the Caribbean and other parts of the Diaspora."[66] This profound but troubling statement helps to explain the complexity of fitting into new cultures. In fact, returnees' frustrations reflect the double consciousness and crisis of identity that DuBois described. Lee's assertion may be comforting to the returnees but it defeats the purpose of reclaiming their African past. The implication is that they do not need to absorb a native language to reconnect with their ancestry.

Languages have always been vital ingredients of African societies and were an issue of contestation during the colonial era. In fact, throughout the colonial period, language was used as a tool against white domination as well as a vehicle for uniting local communities. Because of the influential nature of language, colonial powers imposed Western languages in the colonies to divide and rule their subjects. In New World plantations, the same shrewd tactics were used to strip slaves of their mother tongues. Michael Gomez, in *Exchanging Our Country Marks: The Transformation of African Identities in the Colonial Antebellum South*, devotes an entire chapter to the theme of language, retentions, and lost identities among slave communities. Gomez argues that local languages bound the slaves even when English was imposed on them.[67] Zaline Makini Roy-Campbell, in *Empowerment through Languages: The African Experience*, contends that languages and power are closely linked themes in African history.[68] The importance of verbal communication cannot be overstated here.

Language has remained a core component of African cultures. In Ghana, it is through shared languages that ethnic groups embrace, identify, and communicate well with each other. Lee's advice to other returnees is deeply disturbing and misleading. Returnees and local people are similar in looks. It is the returnees' inability to speak a local language fluently that sets them apart. To put it in simple terms, Lee's recommendation could undermine and in some ways weaken returnees' yearning to belong to their homeland. Such utterances as his, if encouraged, would not facilitate the process of assimilation; instead these utterances would isolate returnees and discourage them from creating deeper relations with Ghanaians in the future. If suggestions such as Dr. Lee's persist, the returnees will remain on the periphery of Ghanaian cultures. In my view, African Americans in Ghana are becoming a new black nation within a larger nation, not only because of language barriers but also due to their inability to fit together their Western values and Ghanaian culture.

Indeed, one cannot fully grasp the complex relations between African Americans and Ghanaians without interrogating the tensions and contradictions between memory and reality. "Racial" and cultural difference remain a problem. To put it another way, returnees' memory of their ancestral homeland and their attempts to assimilate have been obstructed not only by their inability to speak Ghanaian languages fluently but also by the color line. For instance, some Ghanaians, known as "gatekeepers of identity," have challenged returnees on many levels. They call African American returnees, tourists, and pilgrims *obroni*, a local Akan word that literally means a white person, a stranger, or a foreigner. In some situations, *obroni* extends beyond phenotype or skin color and is also associated with behaviors or manners colored largely by Western cultures and values. According to Janet Butler, the president of the African American Association in Ghana, returnees' interactions with Ghanaians are sometimes marred by racial comments by the local people.[69] Nana Ababio II (formerly known as Benjamin Harrison Robinson Jr.), a returnee who was formerly a firefighter in New York, sums it up this way: "I was an African when I was captured, I was converted from an African to an American so much that when I returned home my brothers, sisters, and family call me a stranger, *obroni*."[70] As I have shown, therefore, relations between expatriates, returnees, and Ghanaians have sometimes been troubled. Nonetheless, the returnees have thrived in some areas.

The third group of returnees has solidified and unified its ties with Ghanaians through financial investments, educational programs, voluntary associations, and cultural celebrations. The associations and institutions associated with this solidifying of ties include the African American Association of Ghana (AAAG), One Africa (OA), and nongovernmental organizations (NGOs) such as Rev. Sullivan's African–African American Summit, Kwaku Kunta Kinte Orthopaedic Hospital Complex, the Sankofa Educational Foundation, Inc., and the International Leadership Development Academy. Since 1990, a growing number of returnees have been engaging in entrepreneurship and competing with other investors in Ghana to provide jobs for Ghanaians and revenue for the government. Their businesses include restaurants, grocery stores, health food stores, car rental services, construction firms, real estate agencies, Internet cafés, technological services, and private schools.[71] A few of the returnees are shareholders in various businesses using franchise names, such as Avis car rental in Accra. These and many other examples show how African Americans have acted to support Ghana's progress. Other individuals have established chiropractic and wellness businesses to provide job opportunities for local people and to support Ghana's growing economy.[72]

Since the returnees are not a homogeneous group, which aspects of African American ideology should be emphasized in their new environment? Most of the returnees diverge in their objectives but converge on one basic principle. As Benjamin Robinson declares, their overarching goal in Ghana is to "to reclaim our African Citizenship which we never voluntarily surrendered."[73] The current returnee community is divided into three categories:

AAAG, OA, and those that do not affiliate directly with these two groups, for example, those married to Ghanaians, those who work for foreign institutions such as the United Nations, and those who work for the American Embassy or the American Information Services in Accra. AAAG and OA are the most active and best-known returnee groups. They have intertwined objectives: acting as networking systems and educational information or service centers, both groups have created havens for new returnees and are actively involved in social programs in their communities.[74]

The major difference between them is that AAAG does not espouse any particular religious position because of the diverse backgrounds of its members. On the contrary, most returnees who associate with OA are Black Afrikan Hebrew Israelites. While AAAG members operate within Accra and some suburbs of Tema, OA members, on the other hand, organize their programs around Cape Coast and other areas in the Central Region. In fact, because of the influence of OA in the region, its members work hand-in-hand with the Ministry of Culture and Tourism in planning Panafest and Emancipation Day celebrations each year. As a result of these relationships, the Ministry of Culture and Tourism offers One Africa a space at the Cape Coast Castle compound in which to organize the Juneteenth celebration each year, a celebration that attracts both traditional chiefs and the public.[75] Juneteenth memorializes the end of slavery in America on June 19, 1865, but there is another twist to this celebration.

The returnees echo the enslavement of their forebears through the enactments of the Juneteenth celebration, as an outlet for sharing their New World experiences and to forge deeper relationships with the audience. During the celebration the participants, who are mostly African Americans, pour a libation, a traditional practice in Ghana, to call the spirits of their ancestors. Unlike their forebears who walked through the "Door of No Return" into ships that dispersed them across the New World, the participants walk through the slave dungeons, through the same doors, but they reenter the castle. This symbolizes African Americans' return to their ancestral home, echoing Garvey's cry for a return to Africa almost a century ago.[76]

The most striking aspects of the ceremony are the emotions and drama that surround it. The returnees believe that it is through such discourses Ghanaians can better relate to the returnees' earnest desire for acceptance in the motherland. On the other hand, the celebration has opened new doors for squabbles. As anthropologist Edward M. Bruner relates, highlighting the horrors of the slave trade at the very place where their ancestors were kept in inhumane conditions portrays whites as oppressors and diaspora blacks as victims. There have been some objections to Juneteenth celebrations in recent years because of the emphasis on the atrocities that were committed against Africans. In fact, some Ghanaians identify African Americans as racist because they exclude local people and European tourists from the performance. Ceremonies that were designed to inform, educate, and strengthen the cultural ties between Ghanaians and people of the African diaspora have rather increased tensions between local people, returnees, and tourists who visit the castles.[77]

The African American Association in Ghana

The AAAG has existed for almost half a century, since the first period of migration to Ghana in the mid-1950s.[78] Currently, it has about fifty-two permanent members. Among the aims of the association, as stated in its constitution, are the following: to create a positive image of African Americans in Ghana and the diaspora, to reintegrate diaspora blacks into African culture and society, to encourage respect for the civil and human rights of all Africans, to embrace Pan-African ideals, and to "educate" Ghanaians about the African American experience.[79] The AAAG's head, Janet Butler, is originally from New York City and is a mechanical engineer who worked for Procter and Gamble for twenty-three years. She is now the managing director of the Pioneer Aluminum Company in Tema, an industrial city in Ghana. Butler has declared that "We have skills, many of us have capital, and some of us find it far more rewarding to continue to take our skills that [we] have acquired and help Ghana move forward."[80] They do not do this alone.

The AAAG recognizes the skills and knowledge of Ghanaians, sees the local people as partners in the nation-building process, and seeks to carry out the daunting task of providing expertise for both Ghanaians and returnees who are interested in setting up businesses. This is an important element for the returnees in their pursuit of building bridges, because of the cultural implications. As a networking base, the AAAG links returnees with Ghanaian entrepreneurs in social services, hospitals, transportation systems, entertainment, educational facilities, and cultural festivities, and informs them about immigration procedures.[81] Both Ghanaians and returnees are aware of the umbilical cord that links them to a common ancestral heritage, and therefore they create a base from which to learn about their cultural differences. Several of these issues are underscored during African History Month, a program organized each year to coincide with Black History Month in America.[82]

Although the Kwanzaa celebration is not part of the cultural festivities in Ghana, the returnees organize programs on December 26 of each year to foster unity. Also, Panafest and Emancipation Day celebrations are major sites for bridging the gap between returnees and locals and for dispelling myths and stereotypes.[83] Furthermore, the AAAG provides television documentaries about experiences of blacks in America while the local Ghanaian newspapers and radio talk shows serve as channels for disseminating information. The contributions the expatriates are making in Ghana, as the president of the AAAG claims, have manifested themselves in various ways. To begin with, the association has been initiating and participating in social programs countrywide. When the AIDS and HIV menace spread across the entire continent of Africa in the 1990s, members of the AAAG organized activities and educational programs to help combat the epidemic in Ghana.

Led by Pamela Bowen, an executive member of the AAAG, a new organization known as African Americans against AIDS in Africa (A5) was founded in 2000 to improve the quality of life of people living with HIV/AIDS. Their motivation was to provide hope, comfort, and counseling to lessen the traumatic impact of the disease on victims. A5 activities were held at the Korle-Bu Teaching Hospital in Accra. In addition, the AAAG has made invaluable contributions to the educational system in Ghana. Helen Akuley, another leading member of the association, has led educational programs in various towns. A librarian by profession, Akuley relocated to Ghana about forty-five years ago and since her relocation has taken a keen interest in providing library services and books to Ghanaian children. Akuley played an instrumental role in establishing a library at Kpone, a coastal town near Tema, that now serves about one hundred students. In the past, most children in this locale had to travel to nearby towns to use library facilities.[84] The AAAG also helps to facilitate activities initiated by other organizations in the returnee communities that are not directly linked with the AAAG, because such coordination is in line with the association's broader vision of embracing Pan Africanism's ideals. In fact, this endeavor has propelled AAAG to contribute logistical and financial support to the Pan-African Student Summits (TPASS) that have been held in Ghana since 2003.

TPASS is the initiative of the International Leadership Development Academy (ILDA) and the Sankofa Educational Foundation (SEF), which are composed of African American returnees. The SEF has supported various projects in Ghana and donated medical supplies to many towns and villages to support development projects.[85] The annual summit is co-sponsored by the University of Ghana, Legon, and other Ghanaian institutions. TPASS brings students and black youth from the diaspora together in the spirit of Pan-Africanism. The long-term goals of the summit, as the organizers have announced, are to encourage the youth to be conscious of issues confronting Africa and the diaspora. Beside ILDA and SEF, other returnee groups in Ghana share some of the views held by the African American Association in Ghana, but they are unique in terms of their religious and political ideology. One such group is OA, an NGO.

One Africa

OA is an embodiment of the notion of the "Back-to-Africa" movement in terms of its members' resilience, their rhetoric, their popularity, and their involvement in the lives of the people of the Central Region. One Africa literally means unity for all black people. Another outstanding element of OA members is their ability to define who they are and their belief systems. OA is located at Iture, a village near Elmina in the Central Region. Vienne Hines Robinson, now Seestah Imahkus, who is a former assistant personnel director in a major teaching hospital in New York, established the organization in 1990. Her husband is Benjamin Harrison Robinson Jr., a taxicab owner and a former firefighter in the New York Fire Department.[86] Benjamin Robinson has now been enstooled as *nkosohene* (development chief)[87] at Iture. His stool-name is Nana Ababio I. One Africa was registered as an organization in 1996, initially as a way station or a rest stop in a metaphorical sense, for Africans returning to their ancestral homeland. As Nana Ababio I has pointed out, "We have come [home] to set up an arena for those of us who have survived the African Holocaust."[88] This daunting task is carried out in various ways through members' interactions with new returnees and Ghanaians.

In its efforts to enlighten and inform Ghanaians about African American culture and history, OA has built a photo library and museum at the One Africa House complex to highlight the roles of the pioneers in the black diasporic struggles. Besides meeting the needs of returnees, the organization is actively involved in the lives of Ghanaians, especially the people of Iture. Seestah Imahkus argues that nation building is deeper than erecting physical structures; it includes the establishment of more "intimate" ties with needy people in their locale. OA has a unique vision in this regard.

According to Imahkus, the concept of nation building is larger than being assertive in one's philosophy or political and cultural convictions. She claims that nation building means "talking about oneness, joining together with our brothers and sisters"[89] in Africa. With this view in mind, OA has established the Educational Sponsorship Program. This nonprofit program selects children in the Central Region and equips them with mathematical, scientific, and technical skills to empower them to compete in the global economy. Individuals and organizations in the United and other parts of the world sponsor the children through pledges, donations, and voluntary contributions.[90] The funds raised each year go to meet the educational needs of the students from nursery to technical education level.

Although the government subsidizes public schools in Ghana, its support does not meet all the educational needs of students. More than two hundred Ghanaians have benefited from the innovative effort initiated by OA. Sponsored children remain in the program until they are twenty-one years old. As the director explained during an interview, the program initiated by OA has successfully educated many youth who are currently attending universities in Ghana and around the world.

One Africa gained international prominence and media attention when it successfully solicited funds to save the life of one of its students, Prince

Edmund Otibu, who was combating a life-threatening disease and needed urgent medical treatment abroad. The returnees mobilized medical doctors from St. Thomas, America, Ghana, and Ethiopia to assist in the surgical operation to remove a tumor at Howard University Hospital, Washington, DC, in 1993.[91] Some of the donations for the surgery came from Christian churches in the Washington area, from the Nation of Islam Muhammad's Mosque No. 4 in Washington, DC, from students in a summer work training program, and from the Abundant Life Clinic in Washington, DC. Concerned individuals who heard about the student in their local newspapers and on television news also contributed.[92] Socially, OA plays a prominent role in the lives of the people of Iture by supporting developmental programs, for example, funding electricity projects in the village. Sometimes OA pays families' medical bills; at other times they provide food to sustain the community.

The returnees are greatly influenced by their spiritual obligations and ties to the people in their ancestral homeland. They associate their benevolence with their religion. As Imahkus explained, the organization provides the people of Iture with medicine not because OA is wealthy but because of its members' God-given obligation to "Mother Africa."[93] Culturally, while other black American expatriates in Ghana identify themselves as African Americans, the members of the OA community and those who associate closely with them are characterized as Afrikans. They hold the view that their forefathers did not migrate to the Americas willingly, and that their African identity was stripped from them after years of bondage in a strange land. Another reason for bearing a unique name is to set them apart from other returnees who claim to be Americans as well as Africans. Imahkus describes the OA's ideology more eloquently: "We are talking about clearing the misinformation that has been put up there about us as African people. That's why I tell people we are not African Americans. No I am not. I am an Afrikan first and foremost. I was born in America."[94] Referring to another returnee from the Caribbean, Imahkus continued: "He is an Afrikan born in Jamaica. . . . We are Afrikans first, we come from Ghana, Nigeria etc."[95] Members of the OA community often say such things.

Other elements also separate OA from the rest of the returnees. The members of the group call themselves the Black Afrikan Hebrew Israelites of Jerusalem. They maintain a dual identity: On the one hand, they trace their cultural roots through their African ancestry. On the other hand, they claim their spiritual lineage through the ancient land of Israel, and associate the slave trade with the Holocaust. They claim that both the slave trade and the Holocaust were part of God's divine plan.[96] OA's position on white oppression during the transatlantic slave trade and their claim of God's divine plan seem to contradict and contend with each other.

Because their spiritual beliefs and practices are closely connected to the Hebrew faith, members of OA draw their inspirations from the Bible, especially books of the Old Testament such as Genesis, Exodus, Jeremiah, and Psalms.[97] These biblical writings are important to them because of the emphasis on creation, forced migration, oppression, and redemption. They support this statement with Bible references. For example, they often cite this following reference: "And God spoke on this wise, that his seed should sojourn in a strange land; and they that should bring them into bondage and entreat them evil for four hundred years [a period covering the transatlantic slave trade]."[98] The dual identity is also embodied in their clothing; they wear both African and Hebrew dress in their daily lives. Since a large portion of the Ghanaian people are Christian, they embrace some of the Christian teachings that are linked with the Bible and attend religious programs that are organized by members of the Black Afrikan Hebrew Israelites.[99]

A great many of the OA members are vegetarians and have established businesses in Tema and Accra marketing health and health food products, serving vegan-vegetarian cuisine, and featuring whole wheat products, yoghurt, ice cream, tofu, milk, foods that are high in protein, high in fiber and calcium, low in fat, and free from genetically modified ingredients, and other natural food items that are made from soya beans. According to Richard Simons-Atur, a Black Afrikan Hebrew Israelite and the production manager of Asasse Pa ("good soil") Natural Food, the health food business was established in August 2003 with the aim of improving the eating habits and health conditions of Ghanaians. More importantly, he points out that the retail health stores and restaurants in Accra and Tema provide more than two hundred jobs for Ghanaians.[100] In addition, the company also provides free meal services to local public hospitals and elementary schools in Ghana.[101] Most of the company's employees are Black Afrikan Hebrew Israelites, and the company holds weekly Bible meetings, camps, and worship services in Accra that provide opportunities for converting Ghanaians to the Black Afrikan Hebrew Israelite group. According to Atur, Asasse Pa is jointly owned by members of the Black Afrikan Hebrew Israelites and some Ghanaian entrepreneurs who are not associated with their faith.[102]

This discussion of the ongoing contributions of African American expatriates to nation building in Ghana would not be complete without drawing attention to other NGOs and to the development chiefs or *nkosohenes*. Bryan Oswald Lowe, the director of Kwaku Kunta Kinte Orthopaedic Hospital Complex, is an outstanding figure. The hospital complex, which originated in the 1970s, is located at Akropong Akwapim in the Eastern Region. Although the Ghanaian government has structures in place to cater for the needs of the disabled, it has not traditionally been able to supply most of their needs. Lowe and his sister, Dorothy Lowe-Wilbekin, spend half of the year in Ghana managing the complex and the other half soliciting funds in America to manage the project. Most of the funding comes from African American churches, private agencies, and philanthropists, both black and white.[103]

The Lowes have invested in and contributed to health services in Ghana in diverse ways. According to Bryan Lowe, the goals and objectives of the organization, among others, are to engage in research, dissemination of information, and action aimed at improving the conditions of disabled people; to rehabilitate disabled people, to assimilate them into their communities, to combat discriminatory practices in their workplaces and their communities; and most importantly, to defend the rights of the disabled under the Ghanaian constitution and the United Nations Human Rights Convention.[104] The Lowes' organization provides equipment and mobility gadgets for handicapped people in Ghana, and shares information with Ghanaians. The Lowes have raised more than two million dollars and built a hospital complex with a capacity of 200 beds. On February 5, 2004, President John Kufuor, the new leader of Ghana, commissioned the orthopedic project, which gained front-page news coverage in the *Daily Graphic*, the major newspaper in Ghana.[105]

In the 1980s, Rawlings and some local chiefs invented the concept of honorary or development chiefs to strengthen ties with blacks from the diaspora. Armed with this vision, Rawlings embarked on a campaign to involve people of African descent in expanding local projects. As a result of these interests and ties, many descendants of African slaves from the New World have been enstooled as honorary or development chiefs in Ghanaian locales.[106] Indeed, such initiations and the royal treatment given to the new chiefs to show Ghanaians' appreciation for them have led to a growing number of African Americans being named honorary chiefs. They include Isaac Hayes, Molefi Kete Asante, and Rita Marley, the widow of Bob Marley the legendary reggae musician.[107]

In addition to the people mentioned above, since 1985, more than fifty African American expatriates have been enstooled as subchiefs in various areas. Dr. Beryl Dorsett, a retired educator and administrator from New York who was enstooled as development queen mother in July 1997 at Atwima Apatra, a village in the Ashanti Region of Ghana, is one of them. Her stool name is Nana Ama Serwah-Nyarko. As part of her contribution toward nation building in Ghana, Dr. Beryl Dorsett obtained funds of over $50,000 in the United States to provide medical supplies, school buses, and other items for the people of Atwima Apatra. Other contributions Dorsett has made include the provision of wells, a health clinic, and a school.[108]

The African–African American Summit (AAAS) movement has also had a positive impact on Ghana and other African countries. Rev. Leon Howard Sullivan, a pioneer in the civil rights movement and an African American Baptist Zion Church minister from Philadelphia, established the summit movement in 1991. He is also the founder of Opportunity Industrialization Centers (OIC), which provides education, technical skills, and training to the underprivileged around the world. The objectives of the summit are fourfold: to build new bridges between blacks around the world, to create effective partnerships between Africa and the global world, to usher the continent of Africa into trade and investment opportunities, and to negotiate debt relief and fight economic injustice.[109]

The recurring theme of the summits is the importance of African and African American unity as a means toward increasing investment in Africa. Some of AAAS's achievements in Africa include the following: the establishment of fifteen OICs including one in Ghana; the construction of more than 5,000 irrigation projects to provide good drinking water; a role in the establishment of democratic governments with the aim of stabilizing investments; the cancellation of $30 billion in African debt; and the additional investment of $12 billion by Shell Oil Company.[110]

More than 4,000 delegates, including a Ghanaian government delegation, students, African heads of state, African American activists, and members of the returnees' community, attended the Fifth African–African American Summit, which was held in Ghana. Others attending the summit included high-powered representatives from the World Bank, the United Nations, and other international bodies. Miss Alexis Herman, then U.S. secretary of labor, Andrew Young, and Rev. Jesse Jackson, U.S. special envoy, led the American delegation[111] How did Ghana benefit from the summit? During the closing stages, Rev. Sullivan pointed out that Ghana would be the first beneficiary of new funding instituted by the summit organizers to set up small-scale entrepreneurial projects, mostly in animal husbandry and crop farming.[112] Also the Coca-Cola Company was planning to open a $12 billion plant in Ghana because of its political stability and economic progress.[113] According to African American participants in the summit, not only did their involvement open business links for them, but also their visit to Ghana eradicated some of the myths about Africa that they had accepted in the past and made them aware of their ancestral ties with Ghanaians.[114]

Conclusion

The evidence, for example, on associations, interactions, and dialogue, that I have presented in this chapter suggests that there have been long-term, positive mutual relations between descendants of slaves in America and citizens of West Africa. Cultural observances such as Panafest and Emancipation Day, as well as expatriates' contributions to Nkrumah's revolutionary project between 1950 and 1966 that worked toward nation building, have exposed two paradigms: a unified mutual spiritual and ideological interest shared by the two groups, and compelling cultural, political, and economic ties.[115] I have shown that African Americans and Ghanaians have cultivated strong ties in their relationships, even as they have faced various challenges across the decades.

In fact, as the contributions of the returnees have become more visible in Ghana, the new government has taken steps to legislate to provide other incentives, such as tax breaks for African American investors in Ghana. According to Kwabena Agyepong, a public spokesperson for President John A. Kufuor, the new government is interested in stabilizing old links and creating a new economic and cultural dialogue with the returnee community.[116] The poignant voices and profound themes that emerged from my interviews, interactions, and investigations within the returnee communities in Ghana buttress my argument that the relationships between returnees and local people need to be recognized.

Various trends that I have pointed out suggest that positive relations exist between Ghanaians and African Americans. The returnees joined a long history of black American exodus to Ghana and powerfully evoked the philosophy of both Dr. W. E. B. DuBois and Marcus Garvey with regard to double consciousness and "Back-to-Africa," the two themes that bind the returnees to their ancestral roots. Although the returnees have not completely resolved their identity crisis, they are resolved to pursue their dream and have stationed themselves in a good space to do so. Furthermore, the newest period of emigration to Ghana provides fertile ground for exploring the following issues: What are the effects of the black diaspora returnees on the west coast of Africa? What if all the blacks in the diaspora return to Africa? How would they impact the socioeconomic and cultural space in their ancestral homeland? How will Garvey's dream be accomplished if Africans do not carry their share of the burden? What reforms are needed in the educational curricula in Africa to educate Africans about the African diaspora, in order to ease the homecoming of the sons and daughters of Africa?

One compelling question remains: are Africans ready or adequately prepared to receive the descendants of the transatlantic slave trade? The chronicles of the ongoing relationships between blacks in West Africa and the Americas, initiated by the trailblazers of black diaspora migration, have left an indelible mark, have remained a beacon of hope for the new generation in America, the Caribbean, and Africa. The migrants have carved a path for tracing the unending routes of the black diaspora, as the phenomenon of Pan-Africanism, unity, and reconnections constantly produces, reproduces, and recycles itself in black history. The ending to this story therefore depends on the next generation as it analyzes the historical links and the patterns of interaction between people of African descent and Africa.

Notes

This chapter was developed after two conferences: the annual meeting of the African Studies Association in New Orleans, November 2004; and the U.S–West African

Conference at the University of Texas, Arlington, April 2005. I would like to express my sincere thanks to Dr. Ibrahim Sundiata, Samuel and Augusta Spector Professor of History and Professor of African and Afro-American History at Brandeis University, for his constructive feedback. My deep appreciation also goes to Dr. Maurice Amutabi, formerly of the History Department at the University of Illinois, Urbana-Champaign, and now an assistant professor of history at Central Washington University, for reviewing and commenting on my paper. They are not responsible for any errors in this chapter.

1. Quoted in Robert Johnson Jr., *Why Blacks Left America for Africa: Interviews with Black Repatriates, 1971–1999* (Westport, CT: Praeger, 1999), xvii.

2. David W. Blight and Robert Gooding-Williams, eds., *The Souls of Black Folk* (Boston: Bedford/St. Martin's, 1997), 1–3.

3. Leslie Alexander Lacy, *The Rise and Fall of a Proper Negro* (New York: Macmillan, 1970), 143.

4. Edward Bruner, "Tourism in Ghana: The Representation of Slavery and the Return of the Black Diaspora," *American Anthropologist* 98, no. 2 (June 1996): 292–93.

5. Kim Trent, *Detroit News*, September 13, 1992, 1. See also Seestah Imahkus, *Returning Home Ain't Easy but It Sure Is a Blessing* (Cape Coast, Ghana: One Africa Tours and Speciality Ltd., 1999).

6. Ibrahim Awal, "The African-African American Meeting in Accra Opens Today: Over 4,000 Delegates will Attend," *Daily Graphic* (Accra, Ghana), May 17, 1999, 1–3.

7. Samuel Adjei Boateng, "Orthopedic for Mampong-Akwapim," *Daily Graphic*, February 6, 2004, 1.

8. Kevin Gaines, "From Black Power to Civil Rights: Julian Mayfield and African American Expatriates in Nkrumah's Ghana, 1957–1966," in *Universities and Empire: Money Power in Social Sciences during the Cold War*, ed. Christopher Simpson (New York: The New Press, 1998), 264. See also Maya Angelou, *All God's Children Need Traveling Shoes* (New York: Vintage Press Books Edition, 1991), 18–23.

9. Curtis J. Kojo Morrow, *Return of the African* (New York: Kroshka Books, 2000), 59–72.

10. Paschal G. Zachary, "Tangled Roots: For African Americans the Grass Isn't Always Greener—Seeking the 'Motherland,' They Find Echoes of History and Chilly Welcome," *Wall Street Journal* (Eastern edition), March 14, 2001, sec. 1A, 1–2.

11. Tiffany Ruby Patterson and Robin D. G. Kelley, "Unfinished Migrations: Reflections on the African Diaspora and the Making of the Modern World," *African Studies Review* 43 (April 2000): 11. See also John Davis, ed., *Pan-Africanism Reconsidered* (Berkeley: University of California Press, 1962), 88–89.

12. Amy Jacques Garvey, ed., *Philosophy and Opinions of Marcus Garvey*, vol. 2, *1923–1925* (New York: Athenaeum, 1969), 122, also 70–78; and Joseph E. Harris, ed., *Global Dimensions of the African Diaspora* (Washington, DC: Howard University Press, 1982), 10–13.

13. Joseph E. Harris, ed., *Africans and their History* (New York: Penguin, 1987), 215.

14. Penny Von Eschen, *Race against Empire: Black Americans and Anticolonialism, 1937–1957* (New York: Cornell University Press, 1997), 103.

15. Mario Azevedo, ed., Africana Studies: *A Survey of Africa and the African Diaspora* (Durham, NC: Carolina Academic Press, 1993), 162.

16. Brenda Gayle Plumer, ed., *Window on Freedom: Race, Civil Rights, and Foreign Affairs* (Chapel Hill: University of North Carolina Press, 2003), 26–29. See also Anthony Bogues, *Black Heretics, Black Prophets* (New York: Rutledge, 2003), 76–77.

17. Isidore Okpewho et al., *The African Diaspora: African Origins and New World Identities* (Bloomington: Indiana University Press, 1999), 526–30.

18. Kevin K. Gaines, *American Africans in Ghana: Black Expatriates and the Civil Rights Era* (Chapel Hill: University of North Carolina Press, 2006), 245, 266. See also Gaines, "From Black Power to Civil Rights," 257–61.

19. Robert Johnson, *Why Blacks Left America for Africa: Interviews with Black Repatriates, 1971–1999* (Westport, CT: Praeger, 1999), xviii–xix.

20. Ernest Dunbar, *The Black Expatriates: A Study of American Negroes in Exile* (New York: E. P. Dutton, 1968), 25–88. For earlier works on emigration to Africa, see Elliot Skinner, *African Americans and US Foreign Policy toward Africa, 1850–1924* (Washington, DC: Howard University Press, 1991), 349–56.

21. Paschal G. Zachary, "Tangled Roots: For African Americans the Grass Isn't Always Greener—Seeking the 'Motherland,' They Find Echoes of History and Chilly Welcome," *Wall Street Journal* (Eastern edition), March 14, 2001, sec. 1A, 2.

22. Ibid.

23. Ibid.

24. Seth Nunno, "All Hail Emancipation Day," *Daily Graphic*, July 30, 1998, 1–8.

25. Bridget J. Katsriku (chief director, Ministry of Tourism and Diasporan Relations, Accra), interview by the author, March 8, 2007. See also Nii Addokwei Moffat, "Jake's Coat of Many Colors," *Daily Graphic*, August 13, 2005, 19.

26. "African American Association of Ghana Condemn WSJ," *Ghana News* (Accra), March 22, 2001, 1.

27. Ibid.

28. David Jenkins, *Black Zion: Africa, Imagined and Real as Seen by Today's Blacks* (New York: Harcourt Brace Jovanovich, 1975), 132. For other scholars who have added the dimension of race to explain why black Americans migrated to Africa in large numbers in the 1960s, see the work of Emmanuel Akyeampong. Akyeampong argues that some black Americans moved to Africa because they regard Africa as their true home and the place of their ultimate return. See Akyeampong, "Africans in the Diaspora: The Diaspora and Africa," *African Affairs* 99, no. 395 (2000): 185.

29. "There Is no Racism in Ghana," *Daily Graphic*, August 18, 1962, 3. See also Johnson, *Why Blacks Left America for Africa*, 78.

30. Gerald Horne, *Black and Red: W.E.B. Du Bois and the Afro-American Response to the Cold War, 1944–1963* (New York: State University of New York Press, 1986).

31. K. B. Asante. "Looking into the Future," *Daily Graphic*, October 13, 1995, 5.

32. Joseph E. Harris, ed., *Global Dimension of the African Diaspora* (Washington, DC: Howard University Press, 1982), 187.

33. In addition, when Nkrumah visited the United States in 1958, after Ghana became independent, he recalled that the political atmosphere in the United States and the crusades by the NAACP and the Urban League during his college days gave him a deeper appreciation for democracy. James Meriwether, *Proudly We Can Be Africans: Black Americans and Africa, 1935–1961* (Chapel Hill: University of North Carolina Press, 2002), 152–54.

34. Lacy, *The Rise and Fall of a Proper Negro*, 143–46.

35. Angelou, *All God's Children Need Traveling Shoes*, 20–23, 39–41, 46. See also Bill Sutherland and Matt Meyer, *Guns and Gandhi* (Trenton, NJ: Africa World Press, 2000), 42; and Dunbar, *The Black Expatriates*, 89.

36. "Another Attempt on Nkrumah's Life: Osagyefo Triumphs over Assailant," *Daily Graphic*, January 3, 1964, 2. See also F. K. Buah, *A History of Ghana* (London: Macmillan Education, 1998), 185.

37. Relationships between Ghanaians and expatriates reached a crossroads after the assassination attempts on Nkrumah's life in 1962 and 1964. Recounting her experience in Ghana, Maya Angelou points out that some Ghanaians accused the black American expatriate community of working for the CIA to overthrow Nkrumah's government. She highlights the tensions and the divisions that surfaced in the expatriate community after some of the expatriates were deported to the United States. Angelou, *All God's Children Need Traveling Shoes*, 78–81. An article in a local newspaper, the *Ghanaian Times* (Accra), generalized about black Americans and warned Ghanaians about the threat the expatriates posed to Nkrumah's government. "There are emerging from the Negro (American) community in Ghana, and possibly in other parts of Africa, dangerous Afro-American elements who appear to mortgage their consciences for neocolonialists' dollars and favors in service of collective imperialism. There is an enemy ion your doorstep, the Negro student, technical aid worker who is equally dangerous as the peace-looking white Peace Corps meddler, or white C.I.A. agent or embassy stooge." Quoted in Elliot P. Skinner, "The Dialectic between Diasporas and Homelands," in *Migration, Diasporas and Transnationalism*, ed. Steven Vertovec and Robin Cohen (Northampton, MA: Edward Elgar, 1999), 35–36.

38. "Kwame Is Our Shepherd: We Shall Not Want," *Ghanaian Times*, September 14, 1962, 2.

39. Lacy, *The Rise and Fall of a Proper Negro*, 166–70.

40. Von Eschen, *Race against Empire*, 257, 268.

41. "Louis Gets the Biggest Welcome of His Life," *The Gold Coast Today* 1, no. 2 (June 1956): 3.

42. Brempong Osei-Tutu, "African Americans' Reaction to the Restoration of Ghana's Slave Castles," *Pubic Archaeology* 3 (2004): 196–99. See also Brempong Osei-Tutu, "The African American Factor in the Commodification of Ghana's Slave Castles," *Transactions of the Historical Society of Ghana*, new ser. 6 (2002): 121–22.

43. Janet Butler, interview by the author, June 21, 2004, 1.

44. Imahkus, *Returning Home Ain't Easy*, 18.

45. During the All-African Conference in Ghana in 1958, Nkrumah urged Africans to show their appreciation of black Americans for the support they gave to the African struggle. Such appeals resonated in America and inspired other migrations to Africa. Harris, ed., *Global Dimensions of the African Diaspora*, 350. Nkrumah also invited black American teachers to work in Ghana. See also Jacob Drachler, ed., *Black Homeland/Black Diaspora: Cross-Currents of the African Relationship* (New York: National University Publications, 1975), 25; Akyeampong, "Africans in the Diaspora," 213.

46. Imahkus, *Returning Home Ain't Easy*, 274–75.

47. Divine Komlah, "President Praised in Harlem: Hints on dual citizenship for Americans of African Descent," *Daily Graphic*, October 23, 1995, sec. 1D, 1. See also Joe Bradford, "Africa Needs Economic Freedom: President Declares," *Daily Graphic*, July 31, 1998, 1.

48. Akbar Muhammad, "President's Initiative at OAU Meeting Was Bold," *Daily Graphic*, July 9, 1993.

49. "Right of Abode Being Studied," *Daily Graphic*, April 5, 1995, 1.

50. Komlah, "President Praised in Harlem," 1. See also Imahkus, *Returning Home Ain't Easy*, 298.

51. Joe Bradford Nyinah, "Lincoln Honors President and Wife," *Daily Graphic*, October 27, 1995, 1. See also Ghana News Agency, "Chicago Mayor Praises Ghanaians," *Daily Graphic*, November 1, 1995, 1; Divine Koblah, "President Opens African Trade Expo," *Daily Graphic*, November 2, 1995, 1; Divine Koblah, "Top Los Angeles Stars Roll Carpet for J-J," *Daily Graphic*, November 3, 1995, 3.

52. Imahkus, *Returning Home Ain't Easy*, 80. See also Godfrey Mwakikagile, *Relations between Africans and African Americans: Misconceptions, Myths and Realities* (Dar es Salaam, Tanzania: New Africa Press, 2007), 264; also Seestah Imahkus, interview by the author, July 12, 2004, 3.

53. Lacy, *The Rise and Fall of a Proper Negro*, 157.

54. Joe Bradford, "Africa Needs Economic Freedom: President Declares," *Daily Graphic*, July 31, 1998, 1.

55. Nunno, "All Hail Emancipation Day," 1–3.

56. Janet Quainoo, "Remains of Two African Slaves Buried," *Daily Graphic*, August 1, 1998, 13.

57. Akosua Adoma Perbi, *A History of Indigenous Slavery in Ghana: From the 15th to 19th Century* (Accra: Sub-Saharan Publishers, 2004), 152–54.

58. Charles W. Corey, "We Are Not Here for Fun," *Daily Graphic*, May 17, 1999, 1, 3.

59. Koblah, "President Praised in Harlem," 1.

60. Joe Bradford Nyinah, "Implement Summit Decision—Rawlings," *Daily Graphic*, May 20, 1999, 17.

61. Imahkus, interview; Imahkus, *Returning Home Ain't Easy*, 273–84.

62. Richard Simon Atur (production manager, Asaase Pa), interview by the author, January 10, 2005, 1.

63. Although many newspaper articles state that there are over 1,000 returnees in Ghana, I could not obtain any new data from the Immigration and Naturalization Services in Ghana or the American Embassy in Ghana that would verify new migrations to the country. This is due to the fact that American citizens in Ghana are not identified statistically by race (black or white) when they arrive in Ghana. According to some members of the African American Association of Ghana, the number has doubled since it was first reported in newspapers over five years ago. Ken Porter (CEO, West African Diamond Cutting Company), interview by the author, March 12, 2007, 1.

64. U.S. Library of Congress, http:www.odci.gov/cia/publications/fact book/print/gh.html.

65. Bruner, "Tourism in Ghana," 292–96.

66. Imahkus, *Returning Home Ain't Easy*, 137.

67. Michael Gomez, *Exchanging our Country Marks: The Transformation of African Identities in the Colonial and Antebellum South* (Chapel Hill: University of North Carolina Press, 1998), 6–7.

68. Zaline Makini Roy-Campbell, *Empowerment through Languages: The African Experience—Tanzania and Beyond* (Trenton, NJ: Africa World Press, 2001), 20–21.

69. Butler, interview.

70. Stephen Buckley, "U.S., African Blacks Differ on Turning Slave Dungeons into Tourist Attractions," *Washington Post,* April 1995, A1–2.

71. Johnson, *Why Blacks Left America for Africa,* 58–60.

72. Mealer. "Some African Americans Returning to Ghana," 1.

73. Imahkus, *Returning Home Ain't Easy,* 275.

74. Imahkus, interview.

75. Imahkus, *Returning Home Ain't Easy,* 48.

76. Imahkus, interview.

77. Bruner, "Tourism in Ghana," 291–96.

78. Maya Angelou, *All God's Children Need Traveling Shoes,* 42, 128–32.

79. Janet Butler, "African American Association of Ghana," *E-Board Special Edition,* no. 1 (September 2003), 1.

80. Butler, interview.

81. Ibid.

82. Ibid.

83. Butler, "African American Association of Ghana," 4. See also Sandra L. Richards, "What Is to Be Remembered: Tourism to Ghana's Slave Castle-Dungeons," *Theatre Journal* 57 (2005): 617.

84. Butler, interview.

85. *FACTS: Life Style Magazine,* June 10, 2004, 18–19.

86. Imahkus, *Returning Home Ain't Easy,* 18–22.

87. Ibid., 115; 249–50.

88. Nana Ababio I, interview by the author, July 12, 2004.

89. Imahkus, interview.

90. Ibid.

91. Imahkus, *Returning Home Ain't Easy,* 180. For detailed discussions of the coordination between One Africa, President Rawlings, Ghana Airways, and Louis Farrakhan, see ibid., 178–87.

92. Ibid., 193.

93. Imahkus, interview.

94. Ibid.

95. Ibid.

96. Ibid.

97. The Black Afrikan Hebrew Israelites of Jerusalem and One Africa draw heavily on these biblical writings to explain the connection between the oppression of Jews and blacks in the African diaspora. For example, Genesis 15:13: "And he said to Abram, know a surety that thy seed shall be a stranger in a land that is not theirs and shall serve them; and they shall afflict them for four hundred years," and Jeremiah 16:14–15: "Yahowah says, the time is coming when people will no longer swear by me as the Living Elohim [God] who brought the people of Israel out of the land of Egypt. I will bring them back to their own country, to the land that I gave their ancestors. I Yehowah have spoken." Imahkus, *Returning Home Ain't Easy,* 275.

98. Imahkus, *Returning Home Ain't Easy,* 271.

99. Richard Simons-Atur (production manager, Asaase Pa), interview by the author, January 10, 2005.

100. Ibid.

101. Ibid.

102. Ibid.

103. The work of the Lowes has been widely recognized by the media in Ghana as well as by black organizations and institutions in the United States. See Elise B. Washington, "Cousins." *ESSENCE* 23, October 1992, 100.

104. Bryan Oswald Lowe, interview by the author, July 18, 2004, 1.

105. Samuel Adjei Boateng. "Orthopedic for Mampong-Akwapim," *Daily Graphic*, February 6, 2004, 1.

106. Imahkus, *Returning Home Ain't Easy*, 79–82.

107. Ibid., 253. See also Johnson, *Why Blacks Left America for Africa*, 131–32.

108. Imahkus, *Returning Home Ain't Easy*, 249–50.

109. Nana P. Amoah and Kojo Sam, "Rev. Sullivan and African-African American Summits," *Daily Graphic*, May 19, 1999, 11.

110. Nana P. Amoah and Kojo Sam, "Supplement on African-African American Summit: Sullivan Initiative Yields Positive Results," *Daily Graphic*, May 19, 1999, 11.

111. Victoria Odoi and Albert K. Salia, "Time for Africa to Wake Up—Sullivan," *Daily Graphic*, May 22, 1999, 3.

112. Editorial, "Ghana to Benefit from PIFA—Sullivan," *Daily Graphic*, May 24, 1999, 1.

113. Joe Bradford, "Reforms Have Boosted Investments Confidence," *Daily Graphic*, May 22, 1999, 13. The Coca-Cola plant has not yet been opened.

114. Victoria Odoi, "Summit Must Help Sustain Africa's Goals," *Daily Graphic*, May 22, 1999, 3.

115. Nunoo. "All Hail Emancipation Day," 1–8.

116. Mealer. "Some African-Americans Returning to Ghana," 2.

9

Perspectives on Ghanaians and African Americans

Harold R. Harris

Introduction

People of African ancestry who have been scattered throughout the world as a result of forced or voluntary migration have felt, to a greater or lesser degree, a desire to return to their roots. Although this motivation has many similarities with those of other diasporic groups such as the Jews, the Irish, or the Italians, its primary difference lies in the psychical disorientation that was the result of the system of slavery imposed upon these diasporic blacks by their Western masters. This disorientation is also evidenced among non-diasporic blacks, inasmuch as the domination of Africa by Europe reduced Africans to similar positions of subservience, though with some differences.

One of my major arguments in this chapter is that Ghanaians and African Americans, although they are derived from the same basic roots and both have suffered the dehumanizing effect of Western domination, are differentiated especially by the dominance of the role of the family and community in Ghanaian life and the dominance of individualism in the lives of African Americans. For the Ghanaian, communalism is inseparable from life itself, and personal happiness is secondary to that of the community. For the African American, individual concerns dominate within a wider framework of an increasingly fractured communal structure.

This dilemma of communalism vs. individualism is famously described by W. E. B. DuBois as "double consciousness." According to him, African Americans strive for the individualism of the West, but cannot separate themselves from a tendency toward communalism, which is African. They yearn for the success that capitalism promises, but are unable to separate it from a basically socialist outlook. They claim the rights of citizenship in a country that still refuses to give them all of their entitlements, yet they cannot justify returning to their "homeland." They feel lost without their

African past, but are reluctant to claim it because they have accepted a belief system that denigrates that past.[1]

By extension, then, my argument is that the identities of Ghanaians and African Americans, though both are affected by Western depredations, have evolved along different trajectories. When these groups interact, there are therefore massive hindrances to cooperation, understanding, and trust, which have to be overcome, and are being overcome as the root causes of some of the differences are examined and understood.

The main source material for this chapter is a series of interviews, conducted during June 2003, with Ghanaians and repatriated African Americans from different social, economic, and cultural backgrounds, as well as a series of lectures conducted by specialists on the staff of the University of Ghana at Legon in Accra, Ghana.

Perspectives on Ghanaians and African Americans

The Ghanaian identity, for the most part, tends to be influenced more by concerns about family, clan, community, and nation than by concerns about personal growth for its own sake. Local clan chief Kofi Jackson affirms that a Ghanaian is a nonperson without his family, that families form clans, and clans form the nation.[2] For example, the education of those family members showing the greatest potential is aggressively pursued for the benefit of the family as a whole. A logistical result of the family-oriented mindset is reflected in the architecture in such places as Kumasi, where homes are enlarged in order to accommodate several generations of family members under the same roof. Remittances sent home by family members who have migrated to the United States and other economically progressive countries constitute important statements of prosperity and help preserve family cohesion.

The impact of the communalistic approach is felt in a number of ways. Growth of the kinship network necessarily retards individual growth, which is a more desirable outcome from a Western perspective. At the same time, health issues, particularly the spread of social and communicable diseases, have wreaked havoc and continue to do so because the communalistic system serves as an incubator. On the other hand, social welfare systems, which include state-funded nursing and retirement establishments and are necessary but less productive outcomes of capitalism, are missing from the Ghanaian system since the family and clan absorb the responsibility.

African Americans are survivors of an unsurpassed holocaust, larger, longer, and more deeply damaging than any other the world has ever known. Their survival is inseparably linked to the failure of the system of slavery to destroy their notions of family connectedness. These notions gradually gave way to individualism, as migration, increased competition, unionization, and other factors tended to favor family splintering and devolution. Blacks soon realized the frustration of living in one of the most progressive countries in history while being forced to accept a system designed to demoralize them. In the midst of plenty, they had but little. In education, sports, entertainment, employment, housing, travel, and other aspects of life, they experienced the true meaning of the term camouflage (as used by Fanon). They understood painfully the multilayered definition of the term ambition, even as they were criticized for not demonstrating it. They developed a deeper appreciation of their wretchedness even as they struggled to extricate themselves from its inexorable grip.

Black success in the United States could not have been achieved without white support despite all of blacks' efforts. Booker T. Washington would have been ineffectual without the support of Samuel Chapman Armstrong, President Theodore Roosevelt, and Andrew Carnegie, although some of their support was double-edged. The National Association for the Advancement of Colored People (NAACP) would not have been born without the approval and financial support of whites of that time. Similar statements may be made about Marcus Garvey's Universal Negro Improvement Association (UNIA) movement, and about hundreds of other movements, including the civil rights movements of the 1960s that led to the final dismantling of institutionalized racism.[3] The paradoxical nature of the black-white relationship is more of a dilemma for blacks from their position of relative weakness; and it compounds their duality with uncertainties as well as frustrations.

It is not surprising, therefore, that vast chasms of cultural, psychological, and other differences separate Ghanaians and African Americans, and present tremendous difficulties in communication and understanding between them. In addition to the distancing inherent in their geographical separation, many American perceptions of Africa have been reinforced through educational institutions, the media, and the foreign policy of the United States, which seem designed to cast the black people of Africa in a most unfavorable light. Thus, the impression of Africa as a place to avoid is very prevalent among African Americans and therefore becomes a psychological barrier that must be overcome in order that understanding may be fostered.

Ghanaians consider the United States a country abounding in wealth.[4] It follows then that all Americans, including blacks, as inheritors of this wealth, possess the means of lessening the burdens of those who are less well endowed, particularly Ghanaians. Of less importance to Ghanaians are the barriers that African Americans must overcome in their efforts to acquire this wealth. Because Ghanaians are aware of the wealth of prominent African Americans in business, entertainment, and sports, and the influence of those in power, they tend to see black success in the United States as a given. Thus, they tend to denigrate those African Americans who become mired in the welfare system, regarding them as opportunists that prey upon a system designed to help them.[5]

Since the rate of exchange between the cedi—the Ghanaian currency—and the U.S. dollar is heavily weighted in favor of the latter, Ghanaians aggressively pursue the movement of dollars into their country. It is therefore understandable that in the area of Akosombo, a local chief donated 3,500 acres to African Americans desirous of taking up permanent residence in Akosombo. This chief and others are cognizant of the impact on their local economies of the infusion of U.S. dollars.[6]

Acquisitiveness is a characteristic that is inseparable from the issue of economic growth. It is one of the pillars of capitalism or any economic system based on accumulation of resources. However, depending on the context, it may be configured to justify excessive greed and exploitation or aligned to corruption. In fact, the two extremes, positive acquisitiveness and acquisitiveness characterized by greed, exploitation, and corruption, are not really far removed from each other, the difference quite often being determined by forces that are beyond the control of the players involved in the drama.

One's ability to borrow in the West might be determined by measurable standards such as one's credit rating, performance history, financial status, and ability to earn and less on one's connections, which are more subjective. In Ghana, determining factors such as family connections, gender, and clan speak to a more communalistic orientation. In addition, because the determining factors in Ghana tend to be based more on kinship relationships rather than on non-kin-based relationships, there is an increased potential for misunderstanding. This is especially the case when bartering, attitudes toward credit default, and other accommodations foster the widening of the pervading arc of nebulosity surrounding business transactions instead of constricting and crystallizing it.

Ghanaians are deeply concerned about foreigners' perception of rampant corruption and greed at all levels of their society. In 2003, in a featured article in the *Evening News,* former ambassador and current director of gold mining operations for the government Joseph G. Amamoo highlighted corruption and violation of individuals' rights as the two major issues facing Ghana that need to be addressed by the government. In the article as well as in a personal interview, Amamoo excoriated recently departed President Rawlings for atrocities committed during his tenure in office. He also expressed dismay about the view of Ghana taken by outsiders, and the extent to which these views impact their inclination to travel to, or invest in, Ghana.[7]

Ghanaians are culturally different from African Americans. Even though African Americans have retained many aspects of African traditions in their cultural forms, they have also absorbed many Western patterns of behavior. Thus, there exist significant differences in their spiritual outlook, religious practices, patterns of worship, and so on. These differences affect the ways in which Ghanaians perceive and react to African Americans. Generally, Ghanaians see African Americans as selfish, demanding, impatient, and not easygoing. These perceptions are softened somewhat with respect to repatriated African Americans who, of course, have returned to live in the country, and would not have done so unless they had made important decisions about specific cultural accommodations. However, according to Kofi Bempong, a graduate student and tour guide, and other Ghanaians interviewed informally on the street, Ghanaians quite often prefer to interact with whites because they find them less demanding, more patient and accommodating, and more situationally flexible.[8]

Music in Ghana generally follows the pattern found in the rest of sub-Saharan Africa. American and Caribbean music is very popular, and the sound of reggae, calypso, pop, jazz, rhythm and blues, ragtime, neo-soul, rap, and hip-hop can be heard everywhere. Michael Jackson is a folk hero, and so also is Bob Marley. The ready availability of electronically produced music in all genres, combined with the shift from rural to urban living, has resulted in the decreasing popularity of traditional music and is a major concern, particularly among Ghanaian students of music. This concern is not only for the loss of sensitivity to the nuances in the sounds, textures, and lyrics that give traditional music its life, but also for the concomitant loss of the meanings and messages encoded in the rhythms, cadences, patterns, and other dynamics. In addition, the intrinsic richness of the music is lost during reproductions of performances, since a true deepening of one's appreciation can only be obtained through experiencing live performances. The recording process robs music of its unmistakable naturalness to which the psyche of the listener becomes bound. Ghanaians therefore have a very deep respect for musicians from the United States and the Caribbean who travel to their country for the purpose of learning, through interactions with Ghanaians, the foundational sources of their music. Such interactions have been mutually beneficial and continue to be a bridge toward cultural understanding.

African American and other musical groups that visit Ghana not only constitute a source of inspiration to their Ghanaian counterparts from the standpoint of diversity but also serve as reminders of the absolute necessity of the survival of traditional music. During 2001, a black group, among whose members were Antonio Parker and Vince Evans, as well as a white trio consisting of Scott Robinson, Pat O'Leary, and Larry Ham, conducted tours of Ghana.[9] Many other African American musicians have visited Ghana in the general capacity of music ambassadors, including the late Duke Ellington, Louis Armstrong, and Ella Fitzgerald, as well as Stevie Wonder and others who are still very much alive. As a result of these interactions, the cultural divide has narrowed perceptibly. In fact, Ghanaians regard music as an area where true common ground has been reached through mutual respect and appreciation, despite differences.

Ghanaians quite often use the term *obruni*, which means white man or foreigner, when referring to African Americans. The term *bibini* on the other hand is much more palatable because it means African or black person. Some African Americans take offense when referred to as *obruni*, because they infer from its use a coded warning that they are not a part of Africa. In other words, they have not fully arrived nor have they been fully accepted. In fact, what the term implies, according to Nana Okofu, is that the person addressed looks like, speaks like, dresses like, or walks like someone from the West. This is merely a way of saying that the one addressed is being acknowledged. Any sense of not belonging is therefore in the mind of the addressee. Nana Okofu recommends the use of another term, *ababui*, which is less commonly used and which means "he who has returned."[10]

It seems unlikely that Ghanaians are aware of the affront that African Americans perceive in the use of *obruni*, as Ghanaians seem to retain considerable respect for the United States and its people. This is shown by the deep desire to migrate to the United States that Ghanaians have demonstrated and the many strategies they use to accomplish this, including marriage. Marriages between Ghanaians and African Americans increased during the 1960s and 1970s. These marriages were driven by many desires, including educational and economic opportunities and the search for self that may have been prompted by a Pan-Africanist awakening, as well as social and political necessity.

Ghanaians have become increasingly aware of the problems that African Americans face in the United States and the coping mechanisms that they utilize in solving them. The new diasporans in the United States therefore focus on avoiding these problems. Many Ghanaian immigrants to the United States work several jobs simultaneously to secure better lives for themselves and their immediate and extended families in the United States and Ghana. Many of them have returned "home" to establish businesses: these include the Yaws, who own a desalination plant just outside Accra. Others, such as the Adarkwahs, who still reside in Arlington, Texas, fund primary and occupational schools in Ghana where children and young adults are given opportunities to prepare themselves for better lives. Many return to Ghana after purchasing a home there and establishing small businesses from savings amassed during years of employment in the United States.[11]

From views expressed by Ghanaians in interviews, it seems that they do not mix easily with most African Americans. Marriages between Ghanaians and African Americans tend to be beset by problems; and divorces and separations are fairly common. Marriages usually occur between Ghanaian men and African American women, since Ghanaian women generally prefer not to marry African American men. In the Dallas–Fort Worth metroplex there are roughly a half dozen Ghanaian organizations, none of which claim any African American members. Both groups seem to use avoidance strategies, for the most part, in dealing with one another and freely employ adjectives such as resentful, jealous, lazy, and opportunistic in describing each other.

On the other hand, Ghanaians hold those African Americans who have succeeded in their chosen fields, ranging from sports and entertainment to science, medicine, education, and religion, in very high esteem. For this reason, they have converted what used to be the DuBois family compound located in Accra into the W. E. B. DuBois Center. It houses DuBois' works, his personal library, and his correspondence, as well as medals and photographs commemorating exceptional moments in his life and the honors he received. Guided tours are conducted by trained individuals who are professional, informed, and enthusiastic about their work. This site also marks DuBois' final resting place.

All of this speaks to the deep respect and veneration in which Ghanaians hold his memory. DuBois is regarded as the father of Pan-Africanism. He is remembered as the man who gave up his U.S. citizenship and chose to live out the last years of his life as a citizen of Ghana while he worked on the still incomplete *Encyclopedia Africana*. Most of all he is lionized as the man who tutored Kwame Nkrumah on the rationale for Ghanaian independence; he is therefore regarded as vital to the birth of the Ghanaian nation.

Martin Luther King is honored as a symbol of the struggle for civil rights during the 1960s in the United States. He is venerated because, despite calls for reprisals for atrocities committed against blacks, he stood firm on the question of nonviolence. While it is generally known that King was influenced by Mahatma Gandhi's nonviolent philosophy, what is less known but can be ascertained through an examination of his writings is that the focus of King's mission changed as a result of his trip to Ghana in 1957. There, he participated in the celebration of Ghanaian independence.[12]

Although the Martin Luther King Center in Accra is not nearly as impressive as the W. E. B. DuBois center, the fact that such a place exists in Ghana with its small size and limited resources is testimony to Ghanaians' respect for King's achievements in the cause of freedom and justice. King's birthday is commemorated yearly, as are Black History Month, Panafest, and other Pan-African festivals. Ghanaians interviewed by the author were not impressed by the large number of cities in the United States that do not have a Martin Luther King center, and are horrified by the thought that several U.S. cities and states initially refused to observe King's birthday as a national holiday.

What is significant about the commemoration of DuBois and King is the desire to remember these personages not so much because of their fame but because of their contributions to the history of the black race. For example, although Malcolm X and Marcus Garvey both spoke to the uplifting of the race, there was a crucial difference in the Ghanaian perception of their approaches. While Malcolm X appears to be less highly regarded because of his perceived antiwhite militancy, Marcus Garvey's memory is more tangibly preserved and iconic because his focus is regarded as positively uplifting for the entire black race.

Among the many areas in which the United States has impacted the lives of Ghanaians, the Peace Corps has maintained an enduring positivity with very minor reversals. During its forty-four-year history, the Peace Corps has functioned in many countries throughout the world, but Ghana stands alone as the country in which this organization has had a continuous presence. Interviews with Peace Corps volunteers and administrators, including the country director, Dr. C. Howard Williams, revealed that they saw no sharp differences in Ghanaian perceptions of black or white Peace Corps volunteers. Both were called *obruni* for reasons already stated, although black volunteers, according to Dr. Williams and his assistants, would have much preferred not to be so identified. Aside from the other benefits of being a Peace Corps volunteer, blacks in the organization were also motivated by the desires to return to their roots and to establish long-severed kinship bonds.

Differences in expectations between black Peace Corps volunteers and Ghanaians impacted both the pace and the depth of the relationships that they developed. Additionally, the psychological baggage each side brought to the table sometimes intensified their misapprehensions. For example, Ghanaians tended to show what could be perceived as preferential treatment of white volunteers over black volunteers. This showed itself mainly in situations where a choice had to be made with regard to some kind of living accommodation, and the white volunteer was given the better of two options. According to Williams, whereas the Ghanaian was simply extending to the white stranger a deference required by African and Eastern traditions of hospitality, black volunteers tended to regard this act as a slight, and a submission to racism and the notion of white supremacy.[13]

Although Peace Corps volunteers were sometimes looked upon as likely to be spies for the U.S. Central Intelligence Agency (CIA), according to Dr. Williams, there never seems to have been any substantive proof of their involvement in anything remotely clandestine.[14] The impression of complicity was prevalent mostly during Nkrumah's tenure as president. This is understandable since at the time, there were Soviet and Chinese and other advisors in Ghana, and, in the parlance of the Cold War, the term *advisor* was usually a euphemism for *clandestine operative*. Given this state of affairs, it is possible that some Peace Corps volunteers were in fact CIA operatives.[15]

Professor Robert Addo-Fenning, who worked with Peace Corps volunteers, asserts that they were in great demand by school principals and administrators, especially those in rural schools. Their uncommon enthusiasm and willingness to suffer the hardships associated with living in deep rural areas, in contrast to the reluctance shown by Ghanaians, made them a sought-after commodity. They were regarded as status symbols, raising the level of respect for the schools where they were placed, and thus increasing Ghanaians' desire to attend these schools. Addo-Fenning is supported in his position by Kofi Bempong and Kofi Jackson, both of whom had close associations with Peace Corps volunteers.

Generally, Peace Corps volunteers were perceived by Ghanaians as contributors to their personal and their country's well-being. In addition, they were respected for what was seen as their sincerity in wanting to learn from and about Ghanaians instead of attempting to impose their culture and preconceptions upon Ghanaians. There were a few marriages between Peace Corps volunteers and Ghanaians. Of these, the failures tended to be among those couples who decided to live in Ghana. The main reason for these failures, according to Kofi Jackson, seems to have been intrusion into the couple's affairs by the Ghanaian spouse's extended family. On the other hand, successful marriages tended to occur among those who returned to the United States, as this arrangement presented opportunities for the Ghanaian spouse's extended family members to emigrate to the United States and make "better" lives for themselves.[16] Family members would not wish to jeopardize these opportunities by intrusions into the couple's affairs.

The history of Ghana is inextricably bound to religion; and the African Methodist Episcopal Zion Church of Ghana, which was established in 1898, holds a place of distinction among all churches. Initiated by the Reverend Thomas Birch Freeman Jr., who was appointed by Bishop Small in the United States, it overcame its many difficulties through financial assistance received from the United States, the material and moral support of the Nyaho Tamakloe family, and a donation of land by Chief Joachim Acolaste.[17] This church is arguably the only religious organization sent to Africa that was not intent on the exploitation of the African. In fact, its emphasis seemed to have been placed equally on the uplifting of the minds as well as the souls of Ghanaians. Ghanaians' realization of this bolstered the church's popularity and also made it easier for other denominations to gain footholds. In fact, by the end of World War II, denominational schools had an enrollment of some 286,688 students.[18]

Those Ghanaians who were fortunate enough to receive the full measure of training available in these schools became members of the elite. The early leadership in Ghana came out of the missionary school system, particularly the "Big Six": Dr. J. B. Danquah, Kwame Nkrumah, E. A. Akuffo Addo, W. E. Ofori Atta, Ako Adjei, and Obetsebi Lamptey, as well as the famous Dr. James Kwegyir Aggrey. Thus, Ghanaians regard the AME Zion church and its parent institutions in the United States, particularly Livingstone College in North Carolina, and other similar institutions, as potential pathways, then and now, to a better life, both spiritually and materially. Later efforts by Nkrumah to nationalize the denominational schools because of ideological disagreements with them were only partially successful. The fact that denominational schools are still flourishing in Ghana is testimony to the strength of the religious fervor of Ghanaians even in the face of Nkrumah's determination.

A very important aspect of the attitudes of Ghanaians toward African Americans has been African Americans' repatriation to Ghana, which has a long and varied history. Repatriation was most significant during the presidencies of Nkrumah and Rawlings. Maya Angelou in *All God's Children Need Traveling Shoes* discusses four distinct categories of returnees. There were teachers and farmers who tended to blend into the Ghanaian landscape, people who came under the aegis of the U.S. government, members of the business community, and an assortment of people who felt that they were citizens of the universe, and would have felt at home in Ghana or any other place.[19]

Nkrumah and Rawlings offered many advantages to those, primarily of African ancestry, who wanted to relocate to Ghana. Many diasporans responded to his call, in particular about 200 repatriates from St Louis, Missouri, including doctors, dentists, businessmen, and other professionals. One has only to look at the life lived by Angelou in Ghana as depicted in her book to have a reasonably accurate idea of the mixture of emotions experienced by these émigrés. A look at the same book will reveal that the attitude of most Ghanaians was generally one of positive acceptance.

The move toward nationalization under Nkrumah was justifiable under the socialist program that he instituted. However, this rechanneling of the country's resources for the benefit of the mass of the population was counterproductive from the standpoint of many repatriates. It was also unfulfilling for the members of the population, who failed to realize the benefits that they had been promised while instead they witnessed widespread political corruption.

Ghanaians have become increasingly aware of the need to become more attractive to foreigners, whether they are "lost cousins," potential investors, nomads, cultural connoisseurs, tourists, or members of a study-abroad group. During his interview with me, Joseph Amamoo argued that the move toward privatization, the increased availability of assistance with raising local capital, the search for one's roots, the easy way of life, and new investment opportunities are all reasons for African Americans and others to settle in Ghana. The government has commissioned studies of the increase in the size of the black American middle class in an effort aimed at boosting tourism in Ghana. Such efforts are reaping dividends as the number of first-time and repeat visitors to Ghana has shown a steady increase over the years.[20]

In addition, Ghanaians have a great deal of respect for African American cultural institutions and have adopted several of them. These include Juneteenth, African History Month, and Panafest. "Through the Door of No Return: The Return Ceremony," another of these celebrations, is a gift from repatriated African Americans to Ghana. The increase in the number of Ghanaians attending these celebrations, augmented by returnees and visitors from the diaspora, speaks to the manner in which Ghanaians have embraced these festivals. It is fairly obvious that most Ghanaians both value the economic advantages to be gained from the West and treasure the cultural diversification that they are experiencing. However, it seems that their priority is the movement of resources toward Ghana.

The African–African American Organization (AARO) is a highly respected organization that was established by African American repatriates in Cape Coast in 1998. One of its main purposes is to emphasize the importance of Africa to persons born in the diaspora. It highlights the uniqueness of the Africans-abroad experience, and compares it with other diasporic groups throughout history. It has taken the struggle for reparations for Africans to courts in the United States and in other countries in the West whose economic development was in any way tied to African slavery and the extraction of resources from Africa. This aspect of its work is being carried out by a subgroup known as the Reparations and Reparations Truth Commission. The purpose of this subgroup is to bring the issue of reparations to Western and world courts, as well as to Africans throughout the diaspora. Its members believe, for example, that since the United States defends its support of the state of Israel, in the face of strong opposition and in the absence of substantive justification, then it should be ten times as willing to extend its support to African countries.

A large number of African Americans and African American organizations interact with Ghanaians on a regular basis. In some cases, delegations are sent by the U.S. government to forge new links with the government of Ghana for mutual benefit. Envoys such as the Reverend Jesse Jackson have paid official visits to Ghana in order to help stimulate U.S. investments there. Representatives of the legal, medical, political, educational and other professions visit Ghana to get firsthand views of the country's health, judicial, and other systems at work. In addition, African Americans such as Secretary of State Condoleezza Rice, as well as her immediate predecessor, Colin Powell, are very highly regarded by Ghanaians. Their opinions of these individuals are in direct correlation to perceptions of how well they have performed or continue to perform on the job and the extent to which they have supported and still support African issues. irrespective of the outcome. According to a prominent Ghanaian, K. B. Asante, Ghanaians are somewhat apologetic with regard to U.S. policy and actions toward Iraq because of the positions held by Powell and Rice in the Bush administration.[21]

There is no denying that both Ghanaians and African Americans need to make adjustments in order to reach a middle ground that will promote deeper harmony. While Ghanaians generally might need to be more assertive and become less accepting of the inefficiencies that seem to bedevil them daily, visiting and returning African Americans might consider shedding some of the characteristics that they have brought with them from the West, for example, aggressiveness, arrogance, selfishness, and the impatient desire for immediate results. These and similar behaviors tend to impede progress toward richer and longer-lasting relationships.

Conclusion

It is evident from the foregoing discussion that there are common threads in the experiences of African Americans and Ghanaians. Both have suffered from the effects of Western domination and despoliation, which, on the one hand, changed Ghanaian economic, cultural, and political institutions and, for the diasporans, replaced a communal outlook with one that was essentially individualistic. Despite the efforts of totalitarian regimes to dehumanize them, these groups, developing along different trajectories, began to shake off the cloaks of domination imposed on them.

The two groups, Ghanaians and African Americans, in the course of emerging from the shrouds of silence in which they had been embedded, necessarily regarded each other with varying degrees of jealousy and suspicion. The removal of these roadblocks and the positive engagement of these groups in cultural, economic, intellectual, and religious endeavors has opened up new vistas for understanding and respect.

Notes

1. W. E. B. DuBois, *The Souls of Black Folk* (New York: Modern Library, 2003), 4–7.

2. Kofi Jackson, chief of a clan that numbers in excess of 3,000 persons, interview by the author, Accra, June 4, 2003.

3. John White, *Black Leadership in America: From Booker T. Washington to Jesse Jackson* (London: Longman, 1985), 1, 2.

4. Kofi Bempong, interview by the author, Accra, June 19, 2003.

5. Ibid.

6. Ibid.

7. Joseph G. Amamoo, "The Twin Evils: Corruption and Human Rights Violations— As I See It," *Evening News* (Accra, Ghana), June 23, 2003, 7; Joseph G. Amamoo, interview by the author, in Mr. Amamoo's office in Accra, Ghana, June 24, 2003.

8. Bempong interview.

9. *Amanee* (U.S. Information Service, Accra), July 2001, 8, and September 2001, 1.

10. Nana Okofu Iture Kweku I Abibio, interview by the author, Cape Coast, June 11, 2003.

11. Gyassi Yaw, interview by the author, Accra, June 2, 2003; and Rosemarie Cobbina, interview by the author, Arlington, Texas, July 10, 2003. The Yaw family returned to Accra after spending several years in the United States, where they earned enough money to build two large homes and start a business in Accra. The Cobbina family still resides in the United States, but continues to fund the operation of two elementary schools in Kumasi.

12. Carson Clayborne et al., *The Papers of Martin Luther King Jr.*, vol. 4 (Berkeley: University of California Press, 1969), 192–97.

13. Dr. C. Howard Williams, interviewed by the author, Accra, June 6, 2003.

14. Ibid.

15. John Stockwell, *In Search of Enemies: A C.I.A. Story* (New York: Norton, 1978), 160n., 201n.

16. Robert Addo Fenning, professor of history at the University of Ghana, Legon, interview by the author, Accra, June 3, 2003; Jackson, interview; Bempong interview.

17. "History of the AME Church in Ghana," www.netministries.org/see/churches/ch13091?frame=N,1/15/04, p. 2.

18. Ibid.

19. Maya Angelou, *All God's Children Need Traveling Shoes* (New York: Random House, 1966), 22.

20. Amamoo, interview.

21. K. B. Asante, interview by the author, Accra, June 5, 2003. Dr. Asante is the author of several books, a former ambassador to Switzerland and Belgium, high commissioner to the UK and principal secretary of the African Affairs Secretariat under President Nkrumah. He has held several additional offices, including that of head of administration of the OAU in Addis Ababa.

Part Three

Forging Cultural Connections

Africa in America

10

The Chasm Is Wide

Unspoken Antagonisms between African Americans and West Africans

Fred L. Johnson III

In his controversial 1998 book, *Out of America: A Black Man Confronts Africa*, journalist Keith Richburg articulated the vast array of differences that separate Africans and African Americans. From 1991 to 1994, Richburg served as bureau chief for the *Washington Post*, reporting on Daniel Arap Moi's tyranny in Kenya, the post–Cold War carnage in Somalia, the brutal excesses of Liberia's civil war, and the incomprehensible horrors of Rwanda's 1994 genocide. Being an eyewitness to so many tragedies left Richburg traumatized and despairing; it also left him thankful that he was an American. "There but for the grace of God go I," he reflected, adding that he was glad his enslaved African ancestor had survived the nightmarish transatlantic voyage. "Does that sound shocking?" Richburg pointedly asked. "Does it almost sound like a justification for the terrible crime of slavery? Does it sound like this black man has forgotten his African roots?"[1] Richburg's wrenching questions underscore the historical tensions that have frequently characterized relations between Africans and African Americans.

It is sad but true that between Africans and African Americans there are striking numbers of misconceptions regarding history, race, culture, class, and identity. There are also large numbers of factors connecting the two groups. For Africans and African Americans, an obvious point of relational intersection is the continent of Africa and its history, especially that pertaining to the transatlantic slave trade. The forced amalgamation of so many ethnically different Africans into an American social context in which Africans became generally known as "black" was just one of many series of events that forever changed the reference points of understanding between Africans and their Americanized counterparts. Naturally, blacks in America, existing as an oppressed and despised nation within a nation, were left no choice but to focus upon the element that America selected as the key to full national political and socioeconomic inclusion: *race!* For Africans, admittedly left with scorching memories of racism from the experience of colonialism, their remaining on the African continent and reasserting their power after independence diminished the importance (and presumed superiority) of whites in their daily affairs.[2]

George B. N. Ayittey notes in his book *Africa in Chaos* that a "large part of the problem" between Africans and African Americans "derives from differences in perception, attitude, and historical experiences."[3] While blacks in America have historically been oppressed by whites, in Africa the oppressors are just as likely to have been black. Black Americans, vilified because of their racial origin, have focused upon racism as the major source of their historical troubles; black Africans have instead been plagued by ethnic antagonisms. American blacks have often looked to the government for relief and corrective action; for black Africans, repressive government has more often been the problem. Black Americans, traditionally barred from positions of social and political power, celebrate the presence and power of black African leaders on the African continent; those same leaders, however, have often brutalized and plundered their nations.[4]

Bill Berkeley underscores this last point in *The Graves Are Not Yet Full: Race, Tribe, and Power in the Heart of Africa.* "Among African Americans . . . there has been great sensitivity about publicly criticizing the black leadership of independent black countries. There has also been a sense . . . that a measure of" African Americans' "self-esteem . . . is somehow tied to the success or failure of independent black governments running their own shows."[5] Placing racial solidarity as a priority concern above tyrannical despotism, African Americans have often reacted to criticism of black African leaders with the charge of racism.[6]

Although the different perceptions of the "historical experiences" of Africans and African Americans are apparent in the modern world, the legacy of the slave trade is a wound that continues to fester. African Americans returning to Africa to visit slave pens and other relics of the trade necessarily confront contradictions. The forts that housed their ancestors were sanctioned, supported, and made viable by Europeans who stood to profit most from their misery. Those same ancestors, however, were often sold to Europeans by other Africans, the hapless "merchandise" being people who were traded as a result of raids or the settlement of debts, or were the losers of conflicts who were exported into the oblivion of the New World.[7]

African Americans seeking to find some measure of reconciliation with a stolen and suppressed past are thus confronted with the ugly reality that that same past was lost due to the complicity of people who were supposedly their brethren. African Americans' assumption that they will be able to find solace is often supported by a simplistic (maybe naïve) romanticizing of past, mystical connections to Africa, and by conjured visions of a period in which peace and harmony were the presumed norm. Those assumptions do not allow for the realities that among Africans there were, and are, strong ethnic identities. For African Americans, their American experience having forged them into a community of millions, there are few such sharp distinctions. This mass of generality clashes with the African perspective wherein there were (and are) cultural, linguistic, and historical differences between people that offered powerful incentives for selling off those whose black skin was incidental to the larger fact that they were still considered foreign.[8]

The troubling bewilderment African Americans might experience, compounded by an inability to comprehend the African worldview of the transatlantic slave trade period (that is, the people sold were dealt a dreadful blow, but it was in accordance with the rules and practices of the day), reflects bitter historical realities. There remain questions regarding an atrocity that led to African Americans being deposited as strangers in a strange land while simultaneously creating a spatial distance between them and the continent of their ancestry.[9] That dynamic limited their connection with Africa, and centuries later restricted them to being mere spectators of both the past and the present.

For contemporary Africans, there is the acknowledgment that their ancestors participated in the commission of an atrocity, but one that cannot be undone and, in any case, would most likely have been deemed appropriate at the time. The assumption of a universal identity and purpose for African peoples clashes with the reality that there were legitimate differences between people on the continent (differences and antagonisms no less potent than those that have historically separated other people), creating expectations that have been nurtured and dashed. In ancient (as well as modern) Africa, the overwhelming diversity of physical environments militated against the development of a continent of people sharing similar cultures, lifestyles, morals, and systems of politics and economy. The insistent presumption by many African Americans that racial solidarity should have trumped other societal practices and worldviews of profound importance to Africans adds to the continued strain between the two communities.[10]

Among the significant reasons causing that strain, none is perhaps as potent as the realization for many African Americans that their historical "otherness" in America is also a reality in Africa. Perceiving themselves as having been previously rejected by their mother continent and being perpetually harassed in the land of their forced adoption, they discover that mere blackness is not enough of an entry visa to enable them to blend back into the myriad cultures, histories, traditions, and peoples of Africa.[11] Africa's numerous strong ethnic and national entities are not readily predisposed to accept strangers any more than other people on other continents would be thus predisposed. Thus, African Americans are often confronted with the reality that they must return "home" to America, their spiritual and historical quests having been less than resolved (if at all).[12]

Certainly, success has eluded African Americans in their attempts to find relief within the historic cultural context of the United States. Since the establishment of the American republic, the nation has generally communicated a desire for African Americans to either return or be sent back to Africa. The message has not gone unnoticed. Numerous African Americans have rejected the nation and culture that through its multicentury repression and harassment has, at worst, rejected them or, at best, confined them to the margins. "One ever feels his twoness,—an American, a Negro; two souls, two thoughts, two unreconciled strivings," wrote W. E. B. DuBois at the start of the twentieth century.[13] DuBois further noted that

> The history of the American Negro is the history of . . . strife. . . . He . . . simply wishes to make it possible for a man to be both a Negro and an American, without being cursed and spit upon by his fellows.[14]

The anger and anguish resulting from the "twoness" and "strife" that have bedeviled generations of African Americans have repeatedly found expression, emphasizing the persistence of their struggle to find a secure place within America's mainstream. In the 1920s, Marcus Garvey's nationalist "Back-to-Africa" movement was an attempt to achieve self-sufficiency by confronting the "racially based political and economic oppression in America." In the 1960s, the Black Panthers stressed that African Americans needed to achieve "self-determination for the black community,"[15] themes that echoed earlier exhortations. Derek Bell, in his book *Gospel Choirs: Psalms of Survival in an Alien Land Called Home*, offered a fictional spin on the matter, suggesting that, given the chance, America would agree to a proposal for trading its African descendants to space aliens (that is, "Space Traders") in exchange for "sufficient stores of gold to pay off its debts, chemicals to cleanse the environment, and a safe nuclear engine and fuel to replace disappearing fossil fuels."[16]

> The response: horror from virtually all blacks and some whites; barely restrained glee from many whites; much ambivalence from everyone else. After two weeks of furious debate, there was a national referendum on the issue: 70 percent of the citizenry voted yes, and the Trade went forward.[17]

"There is always some joy to be found in the black American circumstance," wrote Bruce Wright in *Black Robes, White Justice*. "It is a perishable joy," since African Americans "are a people without a country and, at the same time, quintessential Americans."[18] Summing up the challenge presented

by the historical chasm separating Africans and African Americans, Wright
states that

> It is virtually impossible for [American] blacks to look homeward, except with nos-
> talgia for a place they have never been. The critical element of kinship is painfully
> missing. . . . We have only wonderment for the historical divorce from what we
> never knew. We cling to America in a pathetic kind of urgency and with the des-
> peration of those without national options.[19]

The identity crisis African Americans have struggled to resolve represents
another aspect of the peripheral drifting zone they have occupied in
American culture. Staunchly courageous scholarship attesting to the significant presence of Africans and their descendants in Western and American
history has debunked earlier assertions that perverted, obscured, and outright denied those facts. Conversely, the overemphasis upon Africa, Africans,
and African history and heritage so that it elevates rather than illuminates
their substantial role in the historical record has also proven problematic.

In *Not Out of Africa: How Afrocentrism Became an Excuse to Teach Myths as Fact*,
Mary Lefkowitz stands firm when she says that, like the problems created by
Eurocentric historical interpretations, Afrocentric viewpoints prevent "students from learning about real . . . African civilizations."[20] The glorification
of African history as an antidote to the suppression, dismissal, and convolu-
tion of the African legacy, especially its significance in contributing to the
overall history of Western civilization, "not only teaches what is untrue; it
encourages students to ignore known chronology, to forget about looking
for material evidence, to select only those facts that are convenient, and to
invent facts whenever useful or necessary."[21]

From the African perspective, there often exists much confusion about
the apparent dissatisfaction articulated by African Americans concerning
their condition in America. Seen from afar as beneficiaries of a major power,
a land rich in opportunity and wealth in which anything is seemingly possible, African American' focus upon historical inequities is puzzling. Indeed,
it seems as though African Americans are simply whining about past injustices rather than focusing upon succeeding in a marvelous land that offers
such vast material comfort and reward. Given this perspective, it becomes
easier to deduce that such resentment could also result from so many contemporary Africans having to struggle against problems like crushing
poverty, civil war, and predatory government while African Americans com-
plain of what may appear to be the low-threat irritants of racism and
discrimination.[22]

This oversimplified perspective exposes one area of Africans' misunderstanding of the African American experience. It fails to account for the
stresses resulting from a people knowing that their ancestors were sold into

the horrors of the Middle Passage, were brutalized through more than two centuries of one of the worst slave systems in modern history, were violently suppressed in their first century of emancipation, and continue to fight systems and attitudes that have restricted their social, economic, and political mobility.[23]

Even so, from afar it appears that African Americans are engaged in a never-ending pity party. Difficulties notwithstanding, it is presumed that being in the midst of such opportunity is sufficient reason to consider most problems surmountable. Misunderstandings worsen when African Americans, exhibiting a cultural chauvinism deeply rooted in their American experience, confront Africans with malicious, insulting questions about, for example, the availability in Africa of modern conveniences like indoor plumbing and electricity, and the nature of dress habits (for example, people wearing shoes) in contemporary African societies.[24]

Such corrosive inquiries are consistent with the generally shallow, negatively skewed perspective that Americans (of African descent and otherwise) have of Africa. In his book *Free at Last: U.S. Policy toward Africa at the End of the Cold War*, Michael Clough indicates that as late as 1979 many Americans still perceived Africans as being animalistic and primitive. Many others had their perspectives tainted as a result of consistently damaging media coverage that focused upon the continent's worst aspects. This reinforced old ideas of "darkest Africa" as a place of savagery, unforgiving jungles, and chaos.[25]

Those tainted perspectives and old ideas have migrated into the twenty-first century, exemplified by a continued American failure (or refusal) to recognize something as fundamental as the wonder of Africa's ethnic diversity. On those occasions when Americans attempt to learn more about the continent and its people, the information is subjected to filters of Western judgment that stand ready to indict African societies, religions, cultures, traditions, and sociopolitical structures.[26]

The difficulty that some contemporary Africans have in comprehending the African American experience is perhaps best resolved by comparing that experience to the multiple hardships and indignities that Africans endured during colonialism.[27] Colonialism was its own brand of slavery. It robbed Africans and African nations of material and human resources, subjected people to persistent assaults upon their self-esteem and identities, and did everything possible to deny Africa's rich historical past. Indeed, the colonizers propagated the belief that there had been *no* African history (certainly none worth preserving or studying) prior to the arrival of the Europeans.[28]

In the postcolonial era, many African nations and people continue to cite neocolonial factors (e.g., globalization) as the reason for their continued difficulties. From the American side of the Atlantic, questions arise as to how this state of affairs can persist after colonial domination has been removed. The answer is that while the colonizers have been physically removed, they continue meddling through hidden controls buried in politics and economics. African Americans are challenged to comprehend Africa's colonial experience just as Africans are have similar difficulties relative to African Americans' long fight to overcome slavery, Jim Crow segregation, and contemporary difficulties in the United States. The historical experiences of colonialism and slavery have both left legacies. Both are cited, by Africans and African Americans respectively, as causes of contemporary ills.[29]

For those African Americans intrepid enough to speak out, there is a great deal of risk when they point out that, in many instances, corrupt, tyrannical African leaders are also responsible for a nation's ills. The absence of white overlords where Africans retained their familial connections, their culture, religions, traditions, and languages (that is, everything African Americans lost as a result of their ancestors being sold into slavery) results in questions of accountability that are as compelling as when they are focused upon African Americans regarding their fixation upon race in the United States.[30]

The challenge of deconstructing the dangerous distortions that have added to the difficulties of drawing all peoples of African descent together is, perhaps, best met by examining the histories of the various dispersed communities.[31] This offers the hope that a forthright analysis of past and present inequities, determining how, where, and to what extent Europeans, Africans, and African Americans participated in creating contemporary difficulties, will ease tensions between people who, after all, historically have much in common.

Notes

1. Keith B. Richburg, *Out of America: A Black Man Confronts Africa* (New York: Harcourt Brace & Company, 1998), xv–xvi.

2. Serge Badiane, interview by the author, May 2005. At the time of the interview Serge, a former student at Hope College in Holland, Michigan, was working toward a master's degree in aerospace engineering at the University of Michigan in Ann Arbor. Serge noted that since he had grown up in Senegal, where all persons in authority were black Africans, and where the best and worst members of society were also black Africans, he did not arrive in the United States in awe of whites. He also did not feel any urgency to take sides in the ongoing friction between black and white Americans, seeing the struggle of black Americans as being a problem very different from the issues that were of importance to him in the pursuit of his studies and the choices he made in establishing friendships and other matters of social consequence.

3. George B. N. Ayittey, *Africa in Chaos* (New York: St. Martin's Griffin, 1999), 287–89.

4. Ibid.

5. Bill Berkeley, *The Graves Are Not Yet Full: Race, Tribe, and Power in the Heart of Africa* (New York: Basic Books, 2002), 90–91.

6. Ibid.

7. John Reader, *Africa: A Biography of the Continent* (New York: Penguin Books, 1998), 384. In chapters 35–38, Reader effectively narrates the grim details of the process, risks, and profit-making potential of the transatlantic slave trade. Regarding the Africans and their role in the trade, on page 384 he states: "to their eternal shame, Africans . . . conducted slave raids on behalf of the European interlopers," with "no thought for the wider implications and long-term consequences of their actions."

8. This information is derived from a February 2004 interview by the author with Reverend David Ballah who is from Liberia. From 2002 through early 2004, Rev. Ballah served as an associate pastor at the Messiah Missionary Baptist Church in Grand Rapids, Michigan. At the time of the interview, he was preparing to return to Liberia and focus his energies on a church school building project. In his comments, Rev. Ballah provided a historical overview of the significant role played by ethnicity in precipitating the Liberian civil war of the 1990s. He also noted that ethnicity had significantly impacted the attitudes of Africans toward each other during the transatlantic slave trade.

9. In 1903, the prolific African American scholar, writer, journalist, and philosopher W. E. B. DuBois asked: "Why did God make me an outcast and a stranger in mine own house?" He posed this question in his book, *The Souls of Black Folk* (New York: Bantam Books, 1989), 2. The book was first published in 1903.

10. John Hope Franklin and Alfred A. Moss, Jr., *From Slavery to Freedom: A History of African Americans*, 8th ed. (New York: McGraw-Hill, 2000), 18. Also interviews and discussions by the author with Rev. David Ballah; Winston Edun, a Nigerian who works as an automotive parts manager and resides in Columbia, Maryland (interviewed July 2004); and Lilian Ringera of Meru, Kenya (interviewed August 2004). These interviewees all acknowledged that the notion that racial solidarity should have trumped ethnic association in the history of relations between Africans and African Americans is one more likely to be held and perpetuated by African Americans. Present-day Africans in the diaspora, however, recognizing the global similarities faced by all peoples of African descent, are also more likely to elevate race over national or ethnic identity, since African people have faced hardship in most countries based on their race.

11. This paragraph is a synthesized analysis taken from numerous discussions and interviews that were conducted by the author between 1990 and 2004 with Africans pertaining to the issues examined in this article. The Africans who graciously shared their perspectives include Cyrus Mad-Bondo from the Central African Republic who graduated from Malone College in Canton, Ohio in the mid-1990s; Lilian Ringera from Kenya, a participant in the Great Lakes College Association's summer 2001 "East Africa in Transition" conference held at the University of Nairobi and also a research associate at the University of Denver through 2004 while working on her doctoral degree; Rev. David Ballah, associate pastor of Messiah Missionary Baptist Church in Grand Rapids, Michigan, 2002–4; Rev. Isaac Wheigar who in 2003 was invited to Hope College in Holland, Michigan to give a presentation on Liberia's rebuilding efforts; Sheila Dicks, a friend from South Africa who has been living in the United States since the early 1980s; and Winston Edun of Nigeria who resides in Columbia, Maryland and has been in the United States since the late 1980s.

12. See note 11, above.

13. DuBois, *Souls of Black Folk*, 3.

14. Ibid.

15. Floyd W. Hayes III, ed., *A Turbulent Voyage: Readings in African American Studies,* 3rd ed. (San Diego: Collegiate University Press, 2000), 432–33, 454, and 548. The references to Marcus Garvey's movement are found in section 7 of this work, under the subheading "Political Economy of the African American Situation." The article "The Demand for Black Labor: Historical Notes on the Political Economy of Racism," by Harold M. Baron, which also discusses Garvey, is also located in section 7. Garvey, a Jamaican, was the founder of the UNIA (Universal Negro Improvement Association), which, unlike organizations that sought to obtain equality for African Americans in the United States, urged blacks to return to Africa. Reference to the Black Panthers is taken from the article "All Power to the People: The Political Thought of Huey P. Newton and the Black Panther Party" (546–61), by Floyd W. Hayes III and Frances A. Kiene III.

16. Derek Bell, *Gospel Choirs: Psalms of Survival for an Alien Land Called Home* (New York: Basic Books, 1996), 17–18.

17. Ibid.

18. Bruce Wright, *Black Robes, White Justice* (Secaucus, NJ: L. Stuart, 1987), 51–52.

19. Ibid.

20. Mary Lefkowitz, *Not Out of Africa: How Afrocentrism Became an Excuse to Teach Myth as History* (New York: Basic Books, 1996), 156–58.

21. Ibid.

22. The information presented here is a synthesized analysis taken from numerous interviews and discussions conducted by the author with Africans pertaining to this issue. See note 11, above.

23. Ibid.

24. During a July 30, 2005, question-answer session that followed a presentation given by the author to members of ULICAF (the United Liberian Inland Church Associates and Friends, an Indianapolis-based organization) on building closer relations between the African and African American communities, Liberian participants expressed the pain, frustration, and anger they felt on those occasions when their American counterparts asked questions like "Do some Africans have tails?" "Do your huts have roofs?" and "Do you cook your food before eating it?"

25. Michael Clough, *Free at Last: U.S. Policy Toward Africa at the End of the Cold War* (New York: Council on Foreign Relations Press, 1992), 20–23.

26. During a research tour in Cameroon from June 7 to July 9, 2005, as part of a U.S. Department of Education–sponsored Group Studies Abroad Project it was observed that, while extremely curious about the languages, history, culture, and people of Cameroon, many Americans were also perplexed and, on occasion, repulsed by that society's cultural norms. This was particularly true regarding the practice of polygamy by ruling fons, who are hereditary rulers, some with lineages extending back to the thirteenth century. In complete contradiction of the deep diversity that exists in the country, American officials were sometimes overheard derisively describing Cameroonians as having various "typical" characteristics or behaviors.

27. In various interviews and conversations with the author, Kenyan Leecox Omollo (interviewed in spring and fall 2003), Liberian Tonzia Buor (January through May 2006), and Senegalese Serge Badiane (May 2005), all of whom are former Hope College students, expressed a mixture of compassion and confusion with

regard to their African American counterparts who seemed far too obsessed with matters of race and racism. They generally felt that life would be better for African Americans if they paid more attention to their work rather than focusing on instances of being offended. However, they also noted that during their time in the United States, they had often been grouped into the same category as African Americans. As such, they have experienced discrimination, prejudice, and racism and, therefore, they have a heightened understanding of the difficulties African Americans have faced historically. Note also that at a "cluster presentation and discussion" pertaining to this issue at the University of Nairobi in summer 2002, most of the Kenyan students participating expressed the opinion that African Americans, while certainly facing challenges during their long sojourn in America, were nevertheless squandering opportunities not available in Kenya and other African nations. In short, African Americans were pampered and, not having to confront the potentially lethal challenges that are a reality for so many in Africa, they needed to celebrate their good fortune.

28. Lecture notes from the course "Africa: 1880–Present," given by Dr. Felix Ekechi of Nigeria, professor of history, Kent State University, Kent, Ohio, August 31, 1988. In this presentation, Dr. Ekechi emphasized that prior to the 1950s there were few, if any, courses offered in American colleges or universities that looked in depth at African history. The history of the continent and its people was deemed unimportant, which resulted from Europeans' determination that Africans were nonliterate. They had no awareness of, or appreciation for, the oral tradition. The result of this intellectual misguidedness was a Eurocentric perspective that articulated the history of Africa as being the history of the white man in Africa (or, to a lesser extent, the history of the activities of Arabs). Either way, black African history was omitted or minimized).

29. This information was extracted on May 20, 2005, from the Web site for SORAC (the Society for the Research of African Culture), located at Montclair State University in Montclair, New Jersey. The information described a November 2002 conference, organized by Dr. Daniel Mengara, executive director of SORAC, that focused upon emerging schools of thought that conflicted over issues pertaining to the persistence of Africa's political, cultural, and economic problems. In the Web site's description of the conference, it was noted that the "externalists" attributed much of the continent's current predicament to the ongoing pervasive influence of colonialism. However, the "internalists," while acknowledging colonialism's impact, emphasized the significance of African-related influences that have hampered the continent (for example, the activities of Mobutu Sese Seko in Zaire/Democratic Republic of Congo, Charles Taylor in Liberia, and Foday Sankoh in Sierra Leone). Indeed, it was pointed out that "Africans alone must be held responsible for the slave trade because they freely sold their own into slavery" and that "African people should start to acknowledge their own historical and contemporary failures." The Web site's address is http://picard.montclair.edu/~sorac/events/conferences/upcoming/sorac2002/.

30. Richburg, *Out of America*, 140–41. Richburg notes that when "black [American] leaders . . . venture into Africa" they "go through a bizarre kind of metamorphosis," in which "Dictators are hailed as statesmen, unrepresentative governments are deemed democratic," and "corrupt regimes are praised for having fought off

colonialism and brought about 'development.' " Bill Berkeley also observes, in *The Graves Are Not Yet Full*, that "many liberals and African Americans . . . for reasons of their own," have avoided condemning "black African tyrants."

31. Dr. Sei Buor of Liberia, interview by the author, April 2005. Dr. Buor, who lives in Indianapolis, has for the last few years directed the efforts of ULICAF (the United Liberian Inland Church Associates and Friends) to build stronger connections between African Americans and Liberians (in the United States and Africa). During the interview he stressed that one way for Africans and African Americans to build stronger bonds was to "learn each others' history."

11

Double Consciousness and the Homecoming of African Americans

Building Cultural Bridges in West Africa

Bayo Lawal

Introduction

An attempt is made in this chapter to explore the validity of DuBois' thesis of "double consciousness," which has naturally been motivating African Americans to know more about Africa, visit Africa, rediscover their roots, and if possible live in Africa. But this psychological phenomenon is not peculiar to African Americans alone. It is common to various diasporic groups all over the world. Hence the longing for one's place of birth after relocating either voluntarily or involuntarily to faraway countries is natural and human. According to DuBois, the African American

> lives in a world which yields him no true self-consciousness. One ever feels his two-ness—An American, a Negro: two souls, two thoughts, two unreconciled strivings, two warring ideals in one dark body. The history of the American Negro is the history of this strife—this longing to attain self-conscious manhood, to merge his double self into a better and truer self.[1]

DuBois' thesis of double consciousness raises the question of other forms of consciousness. Is double consciousness synonymous with split consciousness? Are both conditions associated with modernity? Is self-awareness the same thing as self-image? What role did the spread of visual culture in the late nineteenth and twentieth centuries play in creating or reinforcing double consciousness? How are race, class, gender, sexuality, and ethnic consciousness different from other consciousnesses? Is there any possibility of multiple consciousness?[2] Answering these questions is not the focus of this chapter. But the questions are raised for consideration in further studies.

DuBois' thesis challenged and still challenges African Americans to discover their roots and know who really they are, to refute the cultural and racial labels imposed by the whites. Thus the longing for a thorough knowledge of Africa can only be satisfied by education, information, and cultural contact with Africans and Africa to build a cultural bridge and establish a cultural identity. To a large extent, DuBois' thesis has had a positive and rewarding impact, because Africans in the diaspora are still nostalgic about their roots and globalization has further reinforced the trend toward the reestablishment of cultural connection and interaction with Africa.[3]

The "double consciousness" of African Americans emanated from their experience of slavery and its history. In its career, the peculiar institution of slavery dehumanized and brutalized the uprooted Africans and their descendants, who were called all sorts of derogatory names even though they had dignified African names. They were made to believe that their ancestors were criminals and vagabonds who roved in barbaric African environments until they were captured as slaves and brought to the civilizing American society; this was the justification of slavery and racism put forward by some whites.[4]

Despite the legal abolition of slavery in 1865 and the official recognition of African Americans as American citizens by the American Constitution, the battle for equality, equal rights, and freedom was fought until the civil rights movements of the 1950s and 1960s.[5] The monumental success of these movements is well known. But the consciousness of the 1960s created in African Americans an overwhelming urge to visit Africa and rediscover their cultural and historical roots in reaction to the disparaging remarks and publications of many whites.[6] Henceforth, African American scholars began to research into their African past and into African history from the African point of view. In the process they jettisoned the existing racist historical interpretation of African culture and value systems and succeeded in introducing black studies, African history, and African American history into the universities in the 1960s.[7]

It must however be stressed that the thoughts, ideas, lectures, and publications of the exponents of Pan-Africanism motivated and are still motivating African Americans and other Africans in the diaspora to assert their African identity with confidence by maintaining regular cultural contacts with Africa and thereby deemphasizing the evils of slavery and racism that have impinged on their minds. The more they identify with African culture, the more they promote Africanness and acquire a worthy liberating experience that is tied to pride in their heritage.[8]

The project of cultural contact and promotion is a continuing one, fostered by various groups such as traders, missionaries, scholars, tourists, and publishers who have satisfied their curiosity and carried a number of cultural items and mementos to North, Central, and Latin America. Thus, many artists have visited West African towns and cities to give public performances during various Pan-African festivals of arts and culture. Many have been drawn to West Africa by Peace Corps experiences[9] and postings by the American consular service and multinational corporations. By and large, they have served as American cultural ambassadors who have motivated their peers to visit West Africa. In recent times, there has been a marked increase in the rate at which they have relocated and settled in various parts of West Africa.[10]

The African Diaspora in Postcolonial Studies

Very germane to the topic of this chapter are the concepts of the African diaspora, diasporic hybridity, and consciousness of cultural identity. Recent research and postcolonial discourses have justified a rethinking of the definition of the African diaspora, its changing meanings, nature, and composition. Thus we can identify one diaspora with scant contact with the homeland (Africa) and another that is characterized by frequent contacts with the homeland.[11] But the focus here is the impact of regular contacts of African Americans with West Africa on the promotion of African culture from the twentieth century to the present.

An African diaspora is any group of Africans and descendants of African ancestors who are alien residents, expellees, refugees, expatriates, immigrants, or ethnic minorities sharing spaces with other racial groups outside Africa. Like other diasporic groups, African Americans are largely descendants of ancestors who were forcibly dispersed from Africa to North America,where they retained a collective memory, vision, or myths about their original homeland (Africa), its history and achievements. They received hostile treatment from their host society and therefore regarded themselves as strangers; hence the crucial role of the memory of their ancestral homeland, to which they should eventually return at an opportune moment.[12]

They are convinced they should corporately develop their homeland by investment of their capital and constant visits, and this can be facilitated only by the ethno-communal consciousness and solidarity fostered by an Africanist ideology. According to Joseph Harris, several phases of the African diaspora have occurred in time and place. There are primary, secondary, tertiary, and circulatory phases of the African migration. Much has already been published on African cultural "survivals" or "transformations" in the United States during the period of slavery and thereafter. However, fresh academic attention is now being paid to the re-creation of African cultures as a result of the frequent contemporary exchanges and contacts between African Americans and West Africa.[13]

Paul Cuffe, Lott Cary, Martin R. Delany, Daniel A. Peyne, Alexander Crummell, and Colin Teague were most outstanding figures among the blacks who visited West Africa in response to the policy and program of the

American Colonization Society.[14] The society established the colony of Liberia in 1822 and shipped about 15,000 blacks there. Later, more shiploads of emancipated Southern slaves and nonslaves triggered the demographic transformation of the colony. The independence of Liberia and the material support of the U.S. government attracted more black returnees, who became educators traders, importers, exporters, artisans, missionaries, and administrators.[15] Edward Blyden exemplified the caliber of Liberian intellectuals who influenced anticolonial protests against the imposition of Western culture. His thoughts and comments about the abuses of colonialism were disseminated among his peers in the *Liberia Herald* and other newspapers.[16]

The Impact of Pan-Africanism

Pan-Africanism began in the nineteenth century as an evolving ideology designed to attack the colonial world order. Its exponents, in speeches and writings, included George Padmore, W. E. B. DuBois, Marcus Garvey, Kwame Nkrumah, Jomo Kenyatta, Nnamdi Azikwe, Dr. Martin Luther King Jr., and Julius Nyerere, to mention but a few. In the twentieth and early twenty-first centuries, Pan-Africanism has become a multidimensional concept that embraces all the positive forms of African redemption, restoration, reparation, political and economic development, and the reintegration of the all the various diasporic Africans into their homeland. It is a life-changing worldview, teaching us that the world should be a peaceful place for the development of human potential, mutual respect for others, cooperation, and recognition of the significant contributions of the various groups of Africans and their descendants toward the progress of mankind.[17]

Pan-Africanism glorifies and appreciates the ancient African civilizations and their enduring legacies to the world. It educates us about the origins and consequences of colonization and neocolonialism, exploitation and underdevelopment, and the evolving relationship between the diaspora and continental Africans. Its realistic set of goals have included decolonization and independence, the establishment of the Organization of African Unity (OAU), which is now the African Union (AU), and the reshaping of the current and future circumstances of Africa for the purpose of development by the collaborative efforts of Africans in the diaspora.[18]

Pan-Africanism has promoted frequent interactions, cooperation, common understanding, and cultural exchanges through numerous roundtables, conferences, and symposia in Europe, Africa, and the Americas over the years. It was Pan-Africanist sentiment that stimulated scholarly research by African Americans into African history, culture, and society, to educate Africans in the diaspora about the necessity for the study of Africa, the reconciliation of diverse interests and views, the cross-fertilization that has taken place, the promotion of understanding, and the need to appreciate the rich and glorious African cultural heritage. The same movement mobilized wide-ranging protests against racism in America, Africa, the Caribbean Islands, and South America and insisted that black people should be accorded their due respect everywhere in the world.[19]

So far, the African Union (AU) has maintained the expected contacts with Afro-descendants in the diaspora through the Sixth Region Initiative. In the process, Afro-descendant institutions have proliferated all over the world to promote African culture and organize unity conferences that draw together in one forum Africans, African Americans, Afro-Latin Americans, Afro-Brazilians, Afro-French, and Afro-Caribbeans. Thus they build bridges for cultural, social, and economic development.[20]

The effective articulation of Pan-Africanism in the United States was one of the factors that accounted for the unprecedented civil rights movements of the 1950s and 1960s, the emergence of Black Power and the Nation of Islam led by Malcolm X, and protests at American universities by African American students against Eurocentric education. The collective black consciousness was mobilized with the introduction of African studies, black studies, and African American studies.[21]

Edward Wilmot Blyden, one of the proponents of such studies, argued that "a disciplined focus on the issues concerning the people of African descent globally required an autonomy of disciplined thought and dedication to the topic." For Blyden and his peers, the purpose of intellectual inquiry was to educate a race of people who were by law denied education in the United States and Africa. By implication, Africans and African Americans were denied access to the technological and global benefits of the study of scientific discoveries in the West.[22] There was therefore an urgent need to correct the distorted worldview of Africa and its peoples held by Euro-Americans. Indeed, Pan-Africanist campaigns stimulated African nationalists to advocate the decolonization of the teaching of all disciplines in schools and colleges. To the exponents of Pan-Africanism, culture and history were the cornerstones of African development and the development of Africans in the diaspora. Black studies was regarded as an educational channel for the development of self-knowledge and liberation, by which blacks would take responsibility for the development of their own knowledge base with which to acquire the new technologies, rather than depend on Euro-Americans who would not transfer their technologies. Black studies is, then, an Africa-centered form of scholarship, designed to properly address the issues of development confronting peoples of African descent.[23]

Postcolonial Contacts and Cultural Exchanges

Apart from helping to lead African colonies to independence in the 1950s and 1960s, Pan-Africanism continued to stimulate a growing interest among activists and scholars seeking political, socioeconomic, religious, educational, and cultural self-determination for Africans and for blacks in the diaspora, imbuing them with pride in African history and culture. African Americans freely came to various countries in West Africa and other parts of Africa for trade, research, tourism, festivals, workshops, conferences, and seminars. In recent years, many Pan-African nongovernmental organizations (NGOs) have sprung up in America and Africa to promote Pan-African ideals.[24]

These organizations include the Pan-African Strategic and Policy Research Group (PANAFSTRAG, Nigeria), the Pan-African Organizing Committee (PAOC, USA); the Institute for Research on African Diaspora in the Americas and the Caribbean (IRADAC, USA); United African Artists (UAA, USA); the African Heritage Research Library (AHRL, Ibadan, Nigeria); the Organization of Afro-American Unity (OAAU, USA); and several others around the world with Web sites that showcase the glorious diversity of African cultures.[25]

The UAA, for example, promotes the growth, unity, and sustenance of African artists around the world by providing exposure and support services to them. Such artists include actors, writers, directors, singers, dancers, performers, poets, instrumentalists, and others who are sponsored to develop African artistic culture and heritage in the diaspora for the entertainment of the world at cultural festivals, concerts, and public ceremonies. The African Heritage Research Library (AHRL, located in Adeyipo Village, Lagelu Local Government Area, on the outskirts of Ibadan, Nigeria) is the first private, rural-community-based library on the African continent. Apart from serving the educational needs of students, researchers, scholars, documentalists, and archivists, it also caters for the sociocultural needs of the local community. It houses all the publications on Africa and Africans in the diaspora of the Americas, Europe, Asia, the Pacific, and the Caribbean islands. The chief librarian is Mrs. Yeye Akilimall Funua Olade, an African American married to a Nigerian for more than twenty-five years. She always appears in the typical Yoruba *buba* and *iro* dress with matching headgear.[26]

Among the Pan-Africanist societies on the Internet is Africa: One Continent, Many Worlds, with its extensive site featuring traveling art exhibits from the Field Museum, the Natural History Museum of Los Angeles, and others. Its collection includes videos and photographs on the following: the history and art of the royal palace of the Bamum (Cameroon), conflict resolution among the Bakongo (Congo-Brazzaville, Congo-Kinshasa, and Angola), Benin history through elephant tusks and Benin bronzes, metal working, the use of gold weights, commerce across the Sahara, the market in Kano (Nigeria), men's hats, combs, jewelry, rock art, and much more.[27]

The African Performance Clearing House, under the auspices of the African Studies Program, University of Wisconsin–Madison, promotes access to visiting African performers or troupes in North America by listing their schedules according to their country and genre, that is, music, dance, or the-ater.[28] Dr. George F. Kojo Arthur and Dr. Robert Rowe, both of the Art Department, Marshall University, West Virginia, direct the Akan Cultural Symbols Project to "utilize the pictograms and ideograms encoded in the arts of the Akan to decode some aspects of the history, beliefs, social organi-zations, social relations, and other ideas of the Akan of Ghana." The site is rich in illustrations of Akan symbols used in architecture, cloth (*adinkra, kente, asafo* flags, and so on), cosmology, economics, knowledge, political beliefs, gold weights, jewelry, and wood carvings.[29]

At the University of Iowa, professor of art Christopher Roy directs a pro-ject on Art and Life in Africa. This site introduces a CD-ROM project and serves as an online searchable catalog of the University of Iowa's Stanley Collection of African Art. The "Key Moments in Life" section describes events such as infancy, childhood, initiation, marriage, religion, leadership, elderhood, and death and illustrates them with art in a mini-slide show. While the "Countries Database" provides some basic facts, the "Types of Art Database" describes the art of each ethnic group, including the Ashanti, Bamana, Baule, Bwa, Dogon, Fang, Hemba, Ibibio, Kongo, Kota, Kuba, Lobi, Luba, Lwalwa,[30] Makonde, Mbole, Mossi, Pende, Suku, Tabwa, Woyo, Yaka, and Yoruba. Several other Web sites on African cultures and institutions are managed by American universities. It is rather ironic that similar Website projects are yet to be developed in Africa, and so African scholars must use the Web sites of Euro-American institutions and organizations.

Apart from the initiatives of private organizations, the Organization of African Unity (OAU; now the AU) has sponsored many Pan-African cultural festivals in different parts of Africa since the 1960s. Such festivals have been hosted by Senegal, Ghana, Nigeria, and Algeria to provide opportunities for cultural exchange, social interaction, and continental integration. As expected, the attendance and participation of Africans in the diaspora at these festivals have been conspicuous. Indeed, the contingents of African Americans have always been spectacular by reason of their enthusiasm and eagerness to reunite with Africans in their cultural environments. In 1966, Cheikh Anta Diop and W. E. B. DuBois were honored for exerting the great-est influence on African people in the twentieth century at the World Festival of Arts in Dakar.[31]

The Second Festival of Black Arts and Culture (FESTAC), held in Lagos in 1977, was spectacular in scale, diversity, and content. It attracted hundreds of African American artists like Stevie Wonder and Isaac Hayes, tourists, scholars, and publishers from Latin America. The published proceedings of the FESTAC Colloquium are kept at the National Theatre, Lagos, in the Centre for Black and African Arts and Civilization (CBAAC).[32] The themes of the published proceedings include black civilization and arts, pedagogy,

African languages, literature, philosophy, religion, history, government, mass media, science, and technology. Since FESTAC, CBAAC has been organizing regular public lectures and international conferences on different Pan-African themes.[33]

Since 1992, the Pan-African Historical Theatre Festival (Panafest), a biennial cultural celebration in Ghana, has replaced FESTAC. Each time the festival has been held, in 1994, 1997, and 1999, it has attracted people of African descent in the diaspora. African Americans have seen it as an opportunity for cultural education, reunion, entertainment, and sightseeing, and as an occasion for exploring and exploiting business opportunities through contact and exchange of ideas with African business concerns.[34] Cultural and theater displays, musical concerts, and dances have been held in Cape Coast, Elmina, Accra, Koforidua, Takoradi, and Kumasi. African Americans have participated in the grand durbar of traditional chiefs, carnivals, reverential events, the Pan-African colloquium, and visual art exhibitions, and have seized the opportunity to purchase ladies' attire, men's suits, and beautifully embroidered dresses made of *kente* cloth and various local textile materials.[35]

Although Senegal, Nigeria, and Liberia have been attractive destinations for African Americans, Ghana, in recent years, has been their most attractive destination as a result of the continuation of the Ghanaian policy of hospitality and accommodation inaugurated by late Kwame Nkrumah. DuBois relocated to Accra, which he claimed was the home of his ancestors, in the 1950s. He died and was buried there in 1963. The late Louis Armstrong, the great jazz musician, traced his ancestry to Kromantse and Abenze, twin fishing villages in the Central Region of Ghana.[36] Malcolm X, who firmly believed in uniting people of African descent throughout the world, visited Ghana and Nigeria. Professor Maulana Karenga, of the Department of Black Studies at California State University, Long Beach, served as the chairman of the African American delegation to FESTAC in 1977. He is widely known as the creator of Kwanzaa, an African American and Pan-African holiday celebrated in African communities throughout the world.[37]

Thousands of African Americans already live in Ghana for at least part of the year. Stevie Wonder and Isaac Hayes have some landed property, and to encourage others to come to Ghana, the African American Association of Ghana has been formed, with Valerie Papaya Mann as its president. The government of Ghana has proposed to offer a special lifetime visa for members of the diaspora and to relax citizenship requirements in order to enable peoples of African descent to receive Ghanaian passports.[38] Publicity campaigns and slogans are being promoted to encourage Ghanaian people to change their attitudes toward African Americans, who hitherto have been regarded as rich tourists rather than long-lost relatives. Advertising campaigns urge Ghanaians to drop the label *obruni*, which means "white foreigner," a label that is applied to African Americans regardless of their skin color. Instead, the public are to say, *akwaba anyemi,* meaning "Welcome, sister or brother."

African Immigrants as Cultural Ambassadors

It is not surprising that the reception that has been accorded African Americans in Ghana has been adequately reciprocated in the United States. In recent years, Ghanaians who have migrated to North America have out-numbered the nationals of other African countries apart from Nigeria. The most successful are academics, professionals, football players, and musicians who marry Caribbean and African American women. This trend in African immigration has been attributed to the Immigration Diversity Lottery.[39]

African immigrants have formed various ethnic and cultural associations in American cities like their counterparts in Europe. Their Internet and Web site facilities have widened the cultural networks for unity and cooperation in education, trade, and social events. There are Asante associations all over the United States with their kings, queen mothers, and wing chiefs modeled on the traditional Asante political system. Their conferment of traditional titles is always endorsed by the *asantehene* (king of Asante in Ghana), who is represented by a chief.[40] In 1998, the Asante Association of Chicago spon-sored a traditional durbar for the Ghana Studies Council at the African Studies Association conference. In like manner, the Yoruba of Nigeria have chapters of Egbe Omo Oduduwa all over the United States that admit many African Americans as members. Apart from their regular cultural activities, these chapters promote the economic and educational development of the Yoruba in the diaspora. Recently, a chapter in Florida requested applications for scholarships from students in Nigerian universities who come from eight Yoruba-speaking states.[41]

The chiefs of the Asante associations are indeed cultural ambassadors in the United States, making efforts to strengthen cultural ties between African Americans and Africans. So far they have sponsored the visit of two of their kings from Ghana. Several years ago Asantehene Otumfo Opoku Ware II vis-ited the New York Museum of Natural History. In November 2005 his suc-cessor, Otumfo Osei Tutu II, made a visit to the Museum of Fine Arts, Boston, accompanied by a delegation of his palace officials and with tradi-tional Asante drumming, horn blowing, and dancing provided by the Ghanaian community in the United States.[42] It is likely that before long other groups of African immigrants will emulate their Ghanaian peers in inviting their kings to the United States, in order to honor the time-honored African political institutions that have survived the ravages of imperialism and colonialism.

Both African immigrants and African Americans now engage in the business of importing many cultural items from Africa for retail in the United States.

Thus we have private museums, art galleries, shops, and supermarkets selling African clothing material, ready-made clothes, bangles, hats, shoes, leather belts, bags, slippers, and necklaces. Eateries are spread across many American towns and cities for African tourists with a desire for African cuisine.[43]

Sports, music, films, and religion are other viable channels of cultural contact and exchange. These have been fully explored and exploited to optimal advantage over the years. African American boxers, wrestlers, and basketball players have visited West Africa and have influenced sports development there.[44] The names of African American singers are household names in West Africa, as thousands of their records, DVDs, and videos sell rapidly. Since its premier showing in 1977, the movie *Roots* has had a profound impact on the psyche of both whites and Africans in the diaspora. The epic drama, which chronicled seven generations of Kunta Kinte's family, motivated African Americans and whites to investigate their family histories and names. *Roots* made Alex Haley, who died in 1992, and his ancestors Kunta Kinte and Kizzy, household names; African Americans have given these names to their children. The movie not only led to frequent visits to West Africa by African Americans but it also served as a stimulus for impassioned discussion on American history and race relations. It reawakened in African Americans a sense of pride and a genuine knowledge that their heritage did not begin with slavery and its stereotypes.[45]

Conclusion

The recurring theme of this chapter has been the role of Pan-Africanism in fostering the nationalist struggle for colonial disengagement in Africa and in mobilizing Africans in the diaspora for moral support. Thus Pan-Africanism has stimulated political and cultural interaction and generated an awareness of the necessity of identifying with the glorious African past and Africa's contributions to the development of the ancient world.

Many exponents of Pan-Africanism have been celebrated and honored for their ideas, publications, public addresses, and activities, which have stimulated cross-cultural conferences and congresses hosted by various countries to mobilize support for unity and cooperation in promoting African culture for purposes of development. Thus Pan-Africanism has positively transformed the attitudes of Africans in the diaspora, encouraging them to regard one another as brothers and sisters, and as belonging to African ancestral roots.

Pan-Africanism was highly influential in awakening the nationalist spirit of the educated elite in Africa, encouraging them to agitate for the independence of their colonial states. The achievement of independence for many states since the 1950s, and the establishment of a continental forum known as the Organisation of African Unity (now the AU), opened the floodgates of immigration into Africa for Africans in the diaspora, especially African Americans. In like manner, Africans became free to emigrate to various parts of the world since colonial restrictions had been removed.

Scholars, researchers, publishers, traders, and tourists among Africans in the diaspora from North, Central, and South America have visited various African countries to learn more about the legendary riches of African culture. Their efforts have yielded some appreciable dividends in portraying Africa in its true colors, destroying the Western stereotypes that had hitherto discouraged people from learning about or visiting Africa. All this has further promoted the program of the Pan-Africanist movement.

Under the auspices of the OAU, transcontinental cultural festivals of arts and culture in various countries have brought together Africans in the diaspora, and opened up more opportunities for friendships, marriages, cultural exchange, employment, business, trade, and permanent settlement. Indeed the AU is encouraging nongovernmental organizations to complement its efforts in this direction.

Notwithstanding the arguments of such schools of thought as Afrocentrism, Atlanticism, and Essentialism,[46] Africans in the diaspora and African immigrants abroad are becoming more united and culturally integrated. In fact, they are not daunted by those who attempt to differentiate African Americans from such Afro-descendants in the diaspora as Afro-Latinos and Afro-Caribbeans. Rather than live separately as assumed by the Atlanticists and Essentialists, they intermarry with each other as well as with African immigrants, even though their offspring inevitably reflect a diasporic hybridity. Indeed representatives of the Afro-Latino and Afro-Caribbean diasporas have been visiting West Africa, although they have not done so in such large numbers as the African Americans.

The AU has designated the Afro-descendants in the diaspora as its official Sixth Region, because of the potential to increase global trade and open commercial opportunities for entrepreneurs to foster economic development. Thus African member states are encouraged to get in touch with those in the diaspora in order to achieve a positive response to the AU initiative through regular national and international dialogues.

Notes

1. W. E. B. DuBois, *The Souls of Black Folk* (New York, Vintage Books/Library of America, 1990), 8–9.

2. The information and ideas in this paragraph are taken from a Google search on "double consciousness" http://...db/conc.htm+double+consciousness&hl=en&ie =UTF-4/23/2005.

3. Isidore Okpewho, Carole Boyce Davis, and Ali A. Mazrui, eds., *The African Diaspora: African Origins and New World Identities* (Bloomington: Indiana University

Press, 1999), xv, xvi. See also Paul Gilroy, *The Black Atlantic: Modernity and Double Consciousness* (Cambridge, MA: Harvard University Press, 1993).

4. Kenneth, M. Stampp, *The Peculiar Institution: Slavery in the Ante-Bellum South* (New York: Vintage Books, 1956), 111, 177–91, 204, 219; John Hope Franklin, *From Slavery to Freedom: A History of Negro Americans*, 4th ed. (New York, Alfred A. Knopf, 1974), 140–42, 155–59.

5. Thomas A. Bailey and David M. Kennedy, *The American Pageant*, 8th ed. (Lexington, MA, D. C. Heath and Company, 1987), 459, 460–61, 472–73, 865–66.

6. George B. Tindall and David E. Shi, *America*, brief 2nd ed.(New York: W. W. Norton, 1989), 880; Joseph E. Harris, "The Dynamics of the Global African Diaspora," in *The African Diaspora*, ed. Alusine Jalloh and Stephen E. Maizlish (College Station: Texas A&M University Press, 1996), 7–8.

7. Gary Y. Okihiro, "Education for Hegemony, Education for Liberation," in *Ethnic Studies*, vol. 1, *Cross Cultural, Asian and Afro-American Studies*, ed. Gary Y. Okihiro (New York: Marcus Wiener, 1989), 1–5; St. Clair Drake, "Prospects for the Future," in *Key Issues in the Afro-American Experience*. vol. 1, ed. Nathan I. Higgins, Martin Kilson, and Daniel M. Fox (San Diego: Harcourt Brace Jovanovich, 1971), 281–83; Charles H. Wesley, "Creating and Maintaining an Historical Tradition," in *Understanding Negro History*, ed. Dwight H. Hoover (Chicago: Quadrangle Books, 1968), 17–19, 20–26.

8. J. B. Webster and A. A. Boahen, eds., *The Revolutionary Years: West Africa since 1800*, 4th impression (London, Longmans, 1969), 300, 302; Molefi Kete Asante, *Afrocentricity* (Trenton, NJ: Africa World Press, 1989), 5–27.

9. Jonathan Zimmerman, "Beyond Double Consciousness: Peace Corps Volunteers in Africa, 1961–1971," *Journal of American History* (December 1995): 1000–1003.

10. Since W. E. B. DuBois' relocation to Ghana and claim of Ghanaian citizenship in the 1950s, more African Americans have visited and settled in West Africa. More research needs to be done on this topic.

11. Bill Ashcroft, Gareth Griffiths, and Helen Tiffin, *Post-Colonial Studies: The Key Concepts* (London: Routledge, reprint 2005), 70.

12. William Safran, "Diasporas in Modern Societies: Myths of Homeland and Return," *Diaspora* 1, no. 1 (1991): 83–99.

13. Joseph E. Harris, "Introduction," in *Global Dimensions of the African Diaspora*, ed. Joseph E. Harris (Washington, DC: Howard University Press, 1982), 8–9.

14. John Hope Franklin, *From Slavery to Freedom: A History of Negro Americans*, 4th ed. (New York: Alfred A. Knopf, 1974), 114, 186, 187.

15. M. K. Akpan, "The Return to Africa—Sierra Leone and Liberia," *Tarikh* 5, no. 4 (1980): 96, 98, 99; J. B. Webster and A. A. Boahen, *The Revolutionary Years: West Africa since 1800* (London: Longmans, 1969), 159, 160.

16. Hollis R. Lynch, ed., *Selected Letters of Edward Wilmot Blyden* (Millwood, NY: KTO Press, 1978), 54–59, 60–69, 70–79, 80–81.

17. James de Jongh, "The Diaspora's Role as the World Re-Awakens to Africa: The Perspective From Harlem USA" (paper presented at an international symposium on "Pan-Africanism and the African Diaspora," organized by the Centre for Black and African Arts and Civilization [CBAAC], University of Lagos, Nigeria, August 1–5, 2005), 1–2.

18. De Jongh, "The Diaspora's Role," 4–6.

19. James de Jongh, "African Literati and Pan-Africanism." (paper presented at an international symposium on "Pan-Africanism and the African Diaspora," organized by the Centre for Black and African Arts and Civilization [CBAAC], University of Lagos, Nigeria, August 1–5, 2005), 1–10.

20. James de Jongh, "The Diaspora Role as the World Re-awakens to Africa: The Perspective from Harlem USA" (paper presented at an international symposium on "Pan-Africanism and the African Diaspora," organized by the Centre for Black and African Arts and Civilization [CBAAC], University of Lagos, Nigeria, August 1–5, 2005), 4.

21. Diedre L. Badejo, "A Challenge for Pan-Africanism and Pan-African Studies in the 21st Century: Gender Ideology in the Advancement of Global Africa" (paper presented at an international symposium on "Pan Africanism and the African Diaspora," organized by the Centre for Black and African Arts and Civilization [CBAAC], University of Lagos, Nigeria, August 1–5, 2005), 21.

22. Ibid., 21–24.

23. Ibid., 26

24. For more information, see Hakim Adi and Marika Sherwood, *Pan-African History: Political Figures from Africa and the Diaspora since 1787* (New York: Routledge, 2003).

25. De Jongh, "The Diaspora's Role," 3, 4.

26. Information brochure, African Heritage Research Library, Ibadan, Nigeria, 2005.

27. "Africa: One Continent. Many Worlds," http://www/Iam.mus.ca.us/africa/main.htm.

28. "African Performance Clearing House," http://polyglot.Iss.wisc.edu/afrst/clear.htm/.

29. "Akan Cultural Symbols Project," http://www.marshall.edu/akanart/.

30. "Art and Life in Africa," University of Iowa, http://www.uiowa.edu/~africart.

31. John Henrik Clarke, "Cheikh Anta Diop and the New Light on African History," http://www.nbufront.org/html/MastersMu.

32. *Information Bulletin of the Centre for Black and African Arts and Culture* (CBAAC) (Lagos: National Theatre, 1978).

33. Ibid.

34. *Official Souvenir Brochure of PANAFEST '99* (Accra, Ghana: PANAFEST Foundation, 1999); Emmanuel Akyeampong "Africans in the Diaspora: The Diaspora and Africa," *African Affairs* 99, no. 395 (April 2000): 212.

35. *Official Souvenir Brochure of PANAFEST '99*, 13. The author was a member of the Nigerian delegation at this cultural event.

36. *Official Souvenir Brochure of PANAFEST '99*, 13.

37. Maulana Karenga, "Kwanzaa: A Celebration of Family, Community and Culture," http://www. Official Kwanzaawebsite.org/ka.

38. Lydia Polgreen, "Ghana's Uneasy Embrace of Slavery's Diaspora," USA-Africa Dialogue 1436, http://us.509.mail.yahoo.com/ym/showletter?

39. Akyeampong, "Africans in the Diaspora," 211.

40. Ibid., 210.

41. Adewale Alonge, Chai, the Egbe Omo Oduduwa of South Florida, Inc. (E001), 2005/2006 Academic Scholarship Application Form, for the scholarship program

for sixteen final-year students, from Yoruba-speaking states, at the University of Lagos, Nigeria.

42. Christraud Geary, "His Majesty the King of Asante, Otunfuo Osei Tutu II from Ghana, Makes First Visit to Boston," http://us.f509.mail.yahoo.com/ym/showletter?

43. Akyeampong, "Africans in the Diaspora," 210.

44. Notable sportsmen include Mohammed Ali, Joe Frazier, and Michael Jordan. Some of the singers are Diana Ross, Stevie Wonder, James Brown, and Isaac Hayes.

45. Monica L. Haynes, "The Power of 'Roots': Special Celebrates 25th Anniversary of Landmark Miniseries," January 15, 2002, http://www.post–gazette.com/life style//20020115rootso115fnp4.asp.

46. Isidore Okpewho, "Introduction," in *The African Diaspora*, ed. Okpewho, Davis, and Mazrui, xiv, xv, xviii; Michael I. C. Echeruo, "An African Diaspora: The Ontological Project," *The African Diaspora*, ed. Okpewho, Davis, and Mazrui, 10, 11–16; Bill Ashcraft et. al., *Post-Colonial Studies*, 77, 118; Asante, *Afrocentricity*, 58, 59, 60–64.

12

Sierra Leoneans in America and Homeland Politics

Alusine Jalloh

Introduction

This chapter examines the Sierra Leonean diaspora in the United States and its interconnection with homeland politics during All People's Congress (APC) rule under President Siaka Stevens from 1968 to 1985. The Stevens era is arguably the most decisive period in the postindependence history of Sierra Leone. For seventeen years, power was concentrated in the hands of President Stevens.[1] The chapter focuses on why and how diaspora Sierra Leoneans in America exerted an influence on the politics of the country they had physically, but not emotionally, abandoned. In addition, the chapter examines how President Stevens and the APC responded to the Sierra Leoneans in America who brought pressure to bear on the government of their adopted country to influence politics at home. In attempting to exert their influence at home, diaspora Sierra Leoneans were not unique. In fact, diasporans have long sought to influence governments in their adopted countries and politics at home.[2]

Over the past three decades, the study of the African diaspora, an ongoing dynamic process, in the United States and elsewhere, including Europe, Latin America, and the Caribbean, has become a growing multidisciplinary field of inquiry. In particular, historians, anthropologists, sociologists, economists, and political scientists have collectively produced several major works dealing with various aspects of the black experience outside of Africa. Themes such as the voluntary and involuntary migration of black peoples, their settlement in and adaptation to the complex political, social, economic, and cultural environments they have encountered in their host countries, and their relationship with Africa as their ancestral homeland have dominated the literature. But more research is needed to expand our knowledge of the postindependence political contributions of diaspora Africans to their homeland. This chapter therefore seeks to advance our understanding of this theme from the perspective of the Sierra Leonean diaspora in the United States.[3]

This chapter is divided into three sections. The first traces the postindependence transnational migration of Sierra Leoneans to America. The second section examines the Sierra Leonean community in America from the 1960s to the 1980s. The third discusses why and how diaspora Sierra Leoneans in America responded to seventeen years of APC rule under President Stevens.

Sierra Leonean Migration to America

The transnational migration of Sierra Leoneans to the United States in the postindependence period may be understood in three contexts. The first was the pursuit of American higher education. For the Sierra Leoneans who migrated to America in the 1960s and 1970s, the "American dream" was to acquire higher education and return to their homeland to pursue diverse careers in such areas as politics, education, and business, as well as eventually retire in comfort. However, for many of the Sierra Leonean immigrants of the 1980s, the American dream became the pursuit of money through work in America and the eventual return to their homeland to retire in comfort and wealth. A large number of the Sierra Leoneans who came to the United States as students remained in the country after their visas expired. Many obtained permanent residence permits to stay and work in America through marriage with Americans. But a small number were arrested as illegal aliens and faced deportation hearings.[4]

The Sierra Leoneans who went to the United States in the first three decades of the postcolonial period were a minority compared to those who went to Britain during the same period. Britain had colonized Sierra Leone since 1808. Often, Sierra Leoneans traveling to the Western world went to Britain, especially its capital, London. Evidence of higher education acquired in Britain often resulted in higher social prestige and better-paying jobs for Sierra Leoneans in their homeland. For a long time there was the perception in Sierra Leone that British higher education was superior to that of the United States.[5]

The pursuit of higher education by Sierra Leoneans in America was aided by direct and indirect U.S. support in the form of scholarships, as well as travel and research grants obtained through governmental agencies like the United States Agency for International Development (USAID) and nongovernmental institutions such as the African American Institute (AAI). Funding agencies such as the Ford and Rockefeller Foundations also awarded scholarships and grants to Sierra Leoneans for travel and research. American education aid should be seen in the context of the Cold War: a major goal was to influence the minds of young Sierra Leonean intellectuals to appreciate certain models of development based on American culture. American educational assistance was an effective propaganda tool in Sierra Leone.[6]

The second context in which Sierra Leoneans migrated to America revolved around oppressive political conditions in their homeland. During APC rule under President Stevens, violence, corruption, and human rights abuses characterized national politics. Public criticism and opposition to Stevens' government was largely silenced through violence or intimidation. However, in 1977 the Stevens government was brought close to political extinction by an unprecedented nationwide civil disturbance involving University of Sierra Leone students, primary and high school students, and workers. The demonstrators demanded that President Stevens resign. The president responded by declaring a state of emergency and imposing a national curfew. He later dissolved Parliament and called a general election, marked by considerable violence, which paved the way for the declaration of a one-party state in 1978. All official political opposition was outlawed in Sierra Leone in 1978 following a nationwide referendum conducted by Stevens' APC, the country's only legal party. Stevens had said that a multi-party system would only exacerbate ethnic tensions and had confused traditional ethnic rulers. Following the questionable national referendum on a one-party state, public opposition to APC rule became virtually nonexistent, except for a small group of Sierra Leoneans using the medium of a Freetown-based newspaper, the *Tablet*.[7]

The third context for transnational Sierra Leonean migration to America was related to the rapid decline of the Sierra Leone economy from the 1970s onward. The economic crisis created conditions in which a cross-section of the Sierra Leonean population, including academics, business owners, students, and ordinary people, decided to leave for the United States in search of better-paying jobs. The economic crisis was marked by currency devaluation, high inflation, a decline in the production of export crops, rising interest rates, and the increased intervention of the International Monetary Fund (IMF) and the World Bank in the Sierra Leone economy. The World Bank, for example, called for the rationalization of the University of Sierra Leone, which involved a reduction in the number of students and teachers as well as a diversion of funds to secondary education. The university also suffered because the weakened economy led to the migration of many academics and students to other regions of Africa, particularly South Africa and Nigeria, and the West, especially Britain and the United States.[8]

The evidence suggests that instead of improving economic conditions in Sierra Leone, IMF structural adjustment programs exacerbated Sierra Leone's crisis and deepened poverty across the country. During the 1980s, poverty expanded markedly, and living standards deteriorated for the vast majority of Sierra Leoneans. All segments of Sierra Leonean society experienced hardships because of the declining availability and quality of basic services such as health and education. In rural areas, peasants were squeezed by low prices, rising inflation, and deteriorating infrastructure. For urban wage earners too, inflation steadily eroded incomes. Consequently, many urban wage earners were pushed into the informal economy or back to rural areas. Fixed salaries, when paid at all, depreciated rapidly. Because of budget problems and mismanagement, the APC government, which was the largest employer, was delinquent in paying wages to its employees. As fiscal pressures mounted, the government embarked on austerity measures involving cutbacks that removed many employees from the public sector payroll altogether. In the private sector, decreasing profits and a growing tide of business failures put many employees out of work as well.[9]

With the failure of the formal economy in Sierra Leone, much of the local population moved to informal activities or parallel markets for survival. In the capital city, Freetown, this often meant a turn to petty trading and questionable activities like smuggling and the parallel currency markets that characterized the "second economy." In rural areas, many Sierra Leoneans shifted to subsistence activities, localized commerce, or cross-border trade. These coping mechanisms, however, had negative consequences for APC government revenues, national savings, investment, and the institutions of the formal economy. By the 1980s, a large number of Sierra Leoneans were dependent on the second or parallel economy for their livelihood.[10]

The rise of a parallel economy in Sierra Leone was connected with another important feature of the country: the decline of the state. As public resources waned and fiscal pressures grew, the APC government was unable to sustain basic functions or services. Also, the government was unable to raise additional revenues from its dwindling economy, and it could not adequately compensate for fiscal shortfalls through external borrowing or aid. Consequently, spending on such basic services as infrastructure, administration, and social services declined noticeably. The failure of public institutions aggravated the course of economic decline and undermined the legitimacy of the APC government. These conditions contributed immensely to the outbreak of a long and bloody civil war in Sierra Leone.[11]

By the end of the Stevens era in 1985, many of the Sierra Leonean immigrants who arrived in America, unlike those of the 1960s and 1970s, were in search of an American dream that centered on self-enrichment and economic independence, as well as the transfer of assets to their homeland to start business enterprises or retire in comfort. For these Sierra Leoneans, the American dream was the achievement of economic prosperity that transcended America and carried over into their homeland, where they were convinced their future lay. This dream was held in common by Sierra Leoneans in the American diaspora who represented diverse career ambitions, political ideologies, and ethnicities, and skilled and unskilled backgrounds.

The Sierra Leonean Community in America

From the 1960s to the 1980s, the Sierra Leonean community in America evolved from a small group of about forty people to over ten thousand spread out geographically but concentrated in major cities such as Philadelphia, Washington, DC, Boston, New York City, and Los Angeles. It was not altogether a closely bonded community. Instead, over three decades, the Sierra Leonean diaspora community became fragmented along homeland-derived ethnic, political, religious, and regional lines as the population grew with new arrivals from Sierra Leone. Also, over this period, the main concentration of the Sierra Leonean diaspora population shifted from Philadelphia to the Washington, DC, area, extending across the District of Columbia and outlying suburban areas in Maryland and Virginia. In these communities, Sierra Leoneans developed and expanded networks, institutions, and resources to help in their adjustment to America and to help them retain meaningful social, cultural, economic, and political links with their homeland.[12]

Once in America, Sierra Leoneans were both disunited and united in their intragroup relations. They experienced rivalries and tensions as well as cooperation. Religious activity was a very important part of daily life in Sierra Leone, and this cultural tradition was continued when Sierra Leonean immigrants made their new homes in America. Although Sierra Leoneans were one of the most educated immigrant groups, there was a broad spread of income within the group, whose members ranged from wealthy to poor. But the American environment provided an opportunity for Sierra Leoneans to redefine their social identities, particularly through education. Some were even able to overcome the social liabilities of their birth. Often, class distinctions Sierra Leoneans brought from their homeland were erased as the educated and the semi-educated, the high-born and the low-born rubbed shoulders as they pursued the American dream.

The Sierra Leonean presence in America was significantly shaped by an urban-based associational life that provided an important social environment providing for survival and nurture for Sierra Leonean immigrants. The transethnic and transregional cooperation that characterized the Sierra Leonean diaspora community in the 1960s was gradually replaced in the 1970s and 1980s by the growth of ethnic-based organizations that functioned as cultural and benevolent entities. The ethnic associations provided social networks and services, as well as re-creating Sierra Leonean culture in the American diaspora. Often, Sierra Leonean rites of passage were celebrated, and bereaved members found membership in these organizations a particularly comforting experience. The ethnic-based organizations also served as information networks in the search for jobs and housing. They were thus an important substitute for the kinship and family networks that were important aspects of social life in their homeland.

Examples of the ethnic-based Sierra Leonean groups included Sakoma (Temne), Rokel (Krio), Tegloma (Mende), the Kono Association, and the Fula Youth Organization (FYO). Ethnicity gradually replaced higher education as the organizational basis of Sierra Leonean social and political groups. However, there were a few Sierra Leoneans, such as Samuel G. E. Tucker, who continued on the path of transethnic and transregional partnerships among diaspora Sierra Leoneans. In the 1970s, Tucker formed Citizens for a Better Sierra Leone and the Coalition of Sierra Leone Organizations in the United States and Canada.[13]

In the 1960s, the Sierra Leonean community in America was made up mostly of students who were spread across the country. The Sierra Leonean students attended American universities such as Harvard University, Howard University, Hampton University (then called Hampton Institute), Syracuse University, Boston University, and the University of Maryland. Some of the students received scholarships directly from the universities while others were privately funded. In a few instances, the Sierra Leone government assisted the students with some of their educational expenses. Prominent among the 1960s students were Tucker, who attended Syracuse University, and Ted Roberts, who attended the University of Maryland. Tucker was initially privately funded but was later supported by the Sierra Leone People's Party (SLPP) government. Upon completion of his undergraduate studies at Syracuse, Tucker worked for the Sierra Leone Embassy in Washington, DC, and New York as an information attaché between 1965 and 1967.[14]

During this period, the Sierra Leonean community was less ethnically, regionally, and politically fragmented than it later became. Although the students were scattered across America (with large numbers in Philadelphia), they would travel to Washington, DC, where the Sierra Leone Embassy was located, at the end of the academic year. Students came together annually in Washington to meet with embassy officials, especially the education officer, and to share experiences with fellow Sierra Leonean students from across America. The embassy played a pivotal role in providing students with scholarship information and assisted with admission to American universities, for example, providing letters of recommendation. It was then common for American universities to channel scholarship information through the embassy. The 1960s were the period that marked the end of European colonialism in Africa, and American universities provided scholarships to young African nationals of newly independent countries like Sierra Leone.[15]

During the 1970s, the Sierra Leonean diaspora population in America increased substantially, numbering in the thousands, with the arrival of more students and also opponents of APC rule, especially after the APC's declaration of a republic in 1971 and a one-party state in 1978. Still, the vast majority of the diaspora Sierra Leoneans were students. They studied at various American universities as before. Although the Sierra Leonean population was concentrated in Philadelphia, it was during this period that it started to shift toward the Greater Washington area. Even though the Sierra Leonean community was divided along ethnic, religious, political, and regional lines, there was a considerable degree of convergence on national issues such as the promotion of democracy and the improvement of the economy in their homeland.[16]

As the student population increased, the students formed a new organization, the Sierra Leone Students Union of the United States and Canada, to promote their interests. Sierra Leonean student politics in America reflected homeland political differences: for example, there were APC, SLPP, and United Democratic Party (UDP) groups among the student population. Some of the prominent Sierra Leonean students of the 1970s were Ted Roberts, M. Alpha Bah, William Lewis, Bill Kallon, Almami Taylor-Kamara, Issa "Catco" Kamara, Abubakr Timbo, Haroun Bangura, Sadu Bah, Sulaiman Forna, Alex Koroma, Dennis Sankoh, Suleiman Tejan-Jalloh, Bob Farmer, Tom Shar, Sam Sankoh, Francis Pettiquoi, Emmerson Koroma, Bob Thomas, and Hamid Fullah. M. Alpha Bah was president of the Students Union between 1972 and 1975.[17]

Besides students, the 1970s Sierra Leonean diaspora population was made up of opponents of Stevens' government who had fled their homeland. One such opponent was the former editor of a Sierra Leonean opposition newspaper, Alimamy Hamed Conteh. When he came to the United States in 1971 at age thirty, after editing the newspaper *Unity*, Conteh worked as a cab driver in the Greater Washington area where he settled. In October 1981, Conteh was found shot to death near his home in Langley Park, Maryland. Prior to his death, Conteh had been attempting to organize a branch of the SLPP in the metropolitan area.[18]

Another prominent opponent of the Sierra Leonean government was Pious Foray, who arrived in New York City (having escaped through Liberia) in 1981. Like Conteh, Foray became a cab driver when he arrived in America. He worked mainly in the New York City metropolitan area. In an interview with the *New York Times* in 1984, Foray expressed his commitment to return to his homeland when political conditions became favorable. He saw an important role for himself in a new Sierra Leonean government that he said would soon replace the Stevens government.[19]

Before arriving in America, Foray had escaped from APC government officials who wanted to kill him. Foray said he went into hiding when the offices of his newspaper, the *Tablet*, which was antigovernment and the country's only independent newspaper, were bombed. According to Foray, he had been warned of the danger to his life from elements within the government of President Stevens. The *Tablet*'s feisty and irreverent style guaranteed an almost immediate sellout of its biweekly press run while the government-owned *Daily Mail* and the government party newspaper *We Yone* were relatively

easy to come by on Freetown's streets. According to Foray, the APC government was beginning to interpret the *Tablet* as an opposition in the absence
of an opposition party. The *Tablet* was a perpetual thorn in the side of
President Stevens. According to Stevens, Foray was the "tool" of a clandestine opposition, paid to attack the APC government by his relative Cyril P.
Foray, whom Stevens had fired as foreign minister in the early 1970s. Pious
Foray acknowledged that the *Tablet*'s offices were once the headquarters of
the opposition SLPP and the office for their now-defunct newspaper, the
People, but denied the other charges made by Stevens.[20]

According to *Tablet* columnist Ibrahim Kargbo, the problem was that the
APC leadership did not believe in public forums to discuss problems and did
not believe that the *Tablet* was just trying to alert the government to its mistakes or unpopular policies. Not only did Stevens deny the fact that there
were no forums for dissent under his government, but he claimed that the
Tablet would not be shut down during his time because he did not see any
benefit from doing that.[21]

Diaspora Sierra Leoneans and APC Rule

In this section I will discuss why and how multiethnic Sierra Leoneans in the
diaspora in America tried to exert influence on the Stevens government.
Clearly not all diaspora Sierra Leoneans took part in political activities or
were members of organizations that challenged APC rule under President
Stevens. For the majority who were politically active, however, their response
to the Stevens government was largely one of sustained opposition centered
on two issues.

The first issue was President Stevens' despotic rule, which was marked by
violence in their homeland. Freedoms such as those of expression, association, and the press were severely curtailed. Also, there were human rights
abuses, especially against opposition politicians, the press, and students.
Stevens, who led Sierra Leone for seventeen years before retiring as president in 1985, was born at Tolobu, in the southern Moyamba district, on
August 24, 1905. He joined the colonial police force in 1923. Seven years
later, he joined the Sierra Leone Development Company, a subsidiary of the
British firm William Baird, which then had a monopoly over the country's
iron resources. Concerned over Sierra Leonean miners' conditions, Stevens
organized the United Mine Workers' Union in 1943 and became its first
secretary-general. He was a local councilor and was appointed as a workers'
representative in Sierra Leone's protectorate assembly, set up in 1945. In
1953, he became minister of lands, mines, and labor but lost his assembly
seat in the 1957 general election.

As British colonial rule came to an end, Stevens refused to join the three-
party coalition that was to assume power. Instead, he formed the opposition

APC in October 1960. The APC party was born, in part, as a response to the Mende hegemonic politics that was growing in Sierra Leone. From its inception, the APC was led mainly by northerners who were largely Temne and Limba. Both Stevens and the secretary-general of the APC, C. A. Kamara-Taylor, were Limba. Other prominent members of the party, such as M. S. Forna, Ibrahim Taqi, M. O. Bash-Taqi, S. I. Koroma, and S. A. T. Koroma, were Temne. The northern composition of the APC leadership demonstrated northerners' opposition to Mende hegemonic politics.

President Stevens was on the sidelines on April 27, 1961, when Sierra Leone became independent from British colonial rule and Sir Milton Margai became its first prime minister. In the first postindependence elections in 1962, Stevens, a persuasive speaker, became opposition leader in Parliament. Prime Minister Margai died a day after the third anniversary of Sierra Leone's independence and was succeeded as prime minister and head of the governing SLPP party by his brother, Sir Albert Margai. Elected to the influential post of Freetown mayor in 1964, Stevens led the APC party to a narrow win in the controversial general election of 1967. Following the election, the APC under the leadership of Stevens assumed the reins of government. Stevens was appointed prime minister but almost immediately he and other APC officials were arrested by the army chief, Brig. David Lansana, who declared martial law. After a month of military infighting that saw power change hands at least three times, a military-led National Interim Council took control and returned the leadership of the country to Stevens' civilian government in April 1968.

In 1971, there were two unsuccessful assassination attempts against Prime Minister Stevens. He assumed the presidency on April 21, 1971, two days after Sierra Leone became a republic. After nine years of political rule, President Stevens proposed the introduction of a one-party system in 1978. Calls for the introduction of a one-party constitution were not new in the postindependence history of Sierra Leone. As early as 1965, Prime Minister Sir Albert Margai proposed a constitutional amendment to create a single-party form of government. But he encountered strong national opposition, resulting in his abandonment of the idea. At that time, Stevens was one of the foremost critics of the proposed one-party system. In 1978, however, Parliament passed a bill allowing one-party rule, later supported by a referendum. In June 1978, Stevens was sworn in as head of state for seven years under the new system.

The one-party system was perhaps the single most important political legacy of the Stevens era. At the state opening of Parliament in June 1978, President Stevens put forward his reasons for the introduction of the one-party system. For Stevens and the APC, the one-party system was the outcome of political evolution in Sierra Leone, not a political imposition on the people. Stevens stated that support for the single-party form of government as an alternative to the British-derived multiparty system was not confined to the APC government. He maintained that by introducing one-party rule, the APC was merely responding to the political desires of most Sierra Leoneans. He characterized the period of political experimentation with the multiparty system as one in which ethnic cleavages were reinforced and ethnic violence increased considerably. He attributed this to the actions of ethnocentric politicians who exploited the weaknesses of the multiparty system to further their personal interests. He noted that ethnic conflicts within the context of Sierra Leone's multiparty democracy had almost brought the country to civil war.

One of Stevens' strongest criticisms of the multiparty system was that the SLPP opposition had continuously frustrated "constructive government policies" at a critical time of national development. While opposition criticism was welcome, he stated, that of the SLPP was designed to destabilize the APC government and pave the way for SLPP rule. President Stevens concluded by stating that unlike older Western democracies such as Britain, which had had time to experiment with different political systems in solving national problems, African countries such as Sierra Leone were compelled by history to devise an immediately viable political system. Given Sierra Leone's enormous socioeconomic problems, originating largely from its colonial past, he argued that the one-party system would create a stable political and social environment conducive to the resolution of these problems. Stevens emphasized that one-party rule was imperative if the pressing task of national development was to be successfully carried out.[22]

The APC party reinforced President Stevens' position by arguing that the one-party system would further political integration by increasing political participation and expanding cross-ethnic interaction. The party argued that unlike the "patron parties" of the early nationalist era, the single-party system was concerned with more than attracting influential people. Instead, it supported political education and encouraged mass participation, thus bridging the elite-mass gap. By bringing together leaders from diverse ethnic groups and socioeconomic backgrounds, the one-party system provided a framework that would transcend particularistic ethnic interests.

In spite of seven years of APC one-party rule, the Stevens government did not eliminate the roots of ethnic political rivalry and tensions in Sierra Leone. This was evident on a number of levels. First, there was no equitable democratic representation of ethnic groups within the APC party decision-making structure. Second, political rewards—power, services, and wealth—were largely ethnically and regionally biased. The APC party and the government hierarchy were ethnically dominated by northerners: Temnes and Limbas. The consolidation of Temne and Limba political hegemony within the APC contributed to the political alienation of other ethnic groups such as the Mende and Krio.

One of the ways in which President Stevens attempted to minimize ethnic conflicts within the framework of the one-party system was his use of political patronage. Recognizing that the Mende posed the greatest threat of political opposition to the APC, Stevens appointed a few Mende SLPP leaders such as Salia Jusu-Sheriff to cabinet positions in the APC government. While this exercise in political patronage considerably reduced the tensions between the Mende political leadership and the APC, it would be misleading to conclude that it ended Mende political alienation under APC single-party rule. A large number of ordinary Mendes remained politically apathetic because of the absence of political options.

Ethnic political rivalry was not exclusive to the relationship between the APC and SLPP supporters. In addition, it manifested itself in the APC leadership. To end the rivalry between the Temne and Limba in the party, Stevens created two vice presidential positions, to which he appointed S. I. Koroma, a Temne, and C. A. Kamara-Taylor, a Limba. The Limba argued that in spite of their minority status they were entitled to a leadership role in the APC alongside the Temne, because of their consistent loyalty to the party. But although Stevens appeased the political leaders of the two founding ethnic groups of the APC, he did not eliminate the underlying distrust between their followers.

During President Stevens' period of single-party rule there was a relatively low incidence of ethnic conflicts on a national scale. This can be attributed in part to Stevens' divide-and-rule political strategy and his personality. He exploited his provincial background, humble beginnings, old age, and multilinguistic ability to foster ethnic reconciliation at both local and national levels. Also, Stevens used his broad executive powers, including control over the armed forces, especially the Special Security Division (SSD), to intimidate and suppress actual and potential political dissenters from various ethnic groups. This was often justified as necessary for the survival of the state.

In spite of the low incidence of ethnic conflicts, neither President Stevens nor the APC party was able to create a national consciousness that transcended ethnicity. Ethnocentricism and ethnic particularistic interests remained strong. The APC under Stevens' political leadership was only partially successful in balancing competing ethnic interests within the framework of the one-party system.[23]

The second major reason why Sierra Leoneans in the diaspora in America attempted to exert an influence on the Stevens government was the rapid economic decline in their homeland. The vast majority of diaspora Sierra Leoneans blamed President Stevens and the APC government for the economic crisis because of massive corruption and mismanagement. In the years just before independence in 1961, Sierra Leone appeared to be headed for a prosperous future. It had a Krio educated class and mineral resources such as diamonds, gold, and bauxite. And as recently as 1972,

Sierra Leone was still a net exporter of rice. Like many countries in sub-Saharan Africa, however, Sierra Leone was hit hard by rising prices for oil and manufactured goods, as well as falling prices for its commodity exports such as cocoa and coffee.

In 1978, Stevens' government devalued the leone by 5 percent on the instructions of the IMF. As a result, according to Stevens, traders and other Sierra Leoneans doubled their retail prices for consumer goods and almost got the government into domestic trouble. Afterward, President Stevens told IMF officials that Sierra Leoneans did not understand devaluation and that the IMF should come and explain it to the Sierra Leonean people. Stevens was among the first voices in what has become a chorus of protests in Africa over the lending policies of the IMF, which normally demands that would-be borrowers cut subsidies, devalue their currency, and take other unpopular measures. He called such moves "political suicide." Sierra Leone was in a severe economic crisis by the time of Stevens' retirement in 1985.[24]

The country's oil imports had more than doubled between 1978 and 1979, rising to $60 million, while its alluvial surface diamond fields, which provided 70 percent of the $220 million that was collected in government revenue, had begun to dry up. The country was also losing about $140 million per year in cross-border diamond smuggling, black market activities, and corruption. Underground kimberlite diamond mining would have been a major boost to the country's economy, but the government had been unable to raise half of the $60 million required to purchase mining equipment. The other half reportedly would have been supplied by the private firm Sierra Leone–Selection Trust, a subsidiary of DeBeers Diamond Company of South Africa and a diamond-mining partner of the Sierra Leone government. [25]

In 1980, Sierra Leone's deficit exceeded $100 million. Because of the country's deteriorating economic situation, Western creditors were forced to reschedule the repayment of $350 million in loans in February 1980. In March, the country erupted into four days of rioting that spread from Freetown to the northern city of Makeni after the government raised the price of gasoline 33 percent, from $2.25 a gallon to $3. The police killed at least two persons.[26]

It was against the background of Sierra Leone's long-standing economic crisis that many diaspora Sierra Leoneans in America, including the Coalition of Sierra Leone Organizations in the United States and Canada, opposed Sierra Leone's hosting of the Organization of African Unity summit in June 1980. They argued that it would compound their homeland's economic problems. However, some members of the Sierra Leonean diaspora supported the proposed summit. In January 1980, a five-member delegation from the U.S. branch of the APC party paid a visit to President Stevens, during which the benefits accruing to Sierra Leone through hosting the summit were discussed.

Stevens said that projects connected with the forthcoming summit were geared toward the overall development of the country. Their practical usefulness would continue after the conference was over, he said. He then informed the delegation of the opportunities for employment that existed outside the civil service and also briefed them on development projects.

The vice president of the APC's U.S. branch, Alex Koroma, told the president that APC members in the United States commended Sierra Leone's decision to host the summit. He said that the venture would be to the country's advantage both economically and politically. Thanking the president for the fair distribution of development programs throughout the country, he mentioned the Siaka Stevens Stadium, the Freetown-Waterloo road, the Kambia Bridge, the extension of the Freetown International Airport, and the Taiama-Bo road as examples of practical development.[27]

Following the OAU summit, the Sierra Leone economy experienced a further sharp decline. Both Sierra Leoneans at home and those in the diaspora in America were expressing anger at static wages and spiraling costs just after an estimated $200 million (two-thirds of the country's annual budget) had been spent to host the OAU summit in June. In reply to his critics, Stevens argued that hosting the OAU summit was a popular decision. "This OAU business was passed by parliament. Everyone was happy. I put them on the map." Stevens served as chairman of the OAU from June 1980 to July 1981.[28]

Financial problems, worsened by corruption, forced President Stevens to adopt the austere economic policies, which he termed "political suicide," that were recommended by the IMF. Minerals, principally diamonds, accounted for more than half of Sierra Leone's exports. But with diamond smuggling endemic, foreign exchange earnings were badly hit. At the same time, import costs, particularly the cost of oil, rose sharply, causing balance of payments problems and budget deficits.

At the time of President Stevens' retirement in 1985, Sierra Leone had a battered economy. Nearly a third of the rice consumed locally was imported, diamond exports brought in less than 25 percent of the foreign exchange that they had brought in four years earlier, and inflation was about 40 percent a year. Sierra Leone owed tens of millions of dollars to foreign companies, and borrowing money commercially was no longer possible. According to the director of research of the Central Bank, Sierra Leone was blacklisted as not credit worthy. As much as 75 percent of the country's economic activity took place outside the formal economy. Lack of foreign exchange meant that spare parts were scarce. This led, for example, to frequent power outages. Some parts of Freetown received power only a few hours a day, and telephone service had become sporadic at best. There was no longer a functioning railroad to tie the country together, and the roads were increasingly in disrepair. There was little new foreign investment unless it was an aid project of some kind financed from outside. The wealthiest Sierra Leoneans, including those in government, had long been transferring their money to safer currencies in banks in safer countries like Britain and the United States, thus contributing to the impoverishment of Sierra Leone. President Stevens, who appeared to be more feared than loved, was generally given credit for the fact that all these problems had not led to a revolt. However, the potential for increased volatility did not lie far beneath the surface. In 1984, student protest over living conditions at Fourah Bay College had quickly spread to the streets. Shops were looted and several people were killed before order was restored by the security forces.[29]

I will now examine how Sierra Leoneans in the diaspora in America attempted to influence the Stevens government. Several methods can be identified. The first approach, which was pursued in America, was to organize and articulate opposition through public protests, the media, and lobbying the U.S. government. Many of the public demonstrations against the Stevens government occurred in the 1970s and 1980s on university campuses, at the Sierra Leone Embassy in Washington, DC, at the U.S. State Department, and at the United Nations headquarters in New York City. Public protests often coincided with visits to the United States by members of the Stevens government.

In organizing opposition to Stevens' government, Sierra Leoneans in America also pursued a second approach, which was to forge transatlantic partnerships with Sierra Leoneans in Britain, which had a larger Sierra Leonean diaspora presence. For centuries Britain had been the home of diaspora Sierra Leoneans. Many Sierra Leoneans had been sent to Britain for schooling and higher education that was not available in Sierra Leone. In fact, London was where many anti-APC Sierra Leonean politicians settled, including the former prime minister, Sir Albert Margai, a London-trained lawyer.[30] Among the diaspora Sierra Leoneans who entered into transatlantic anti-APC partnerships with fellow Sierra Leoneans in Britain was Samuel Tucker, founder of Citizens for a Better Sierra Leone. He worked very closely with Ambrose Ganda, a British-trained lawyer based in London. Ganda was a political commentator and an influential advocate for Sierra Leone. He was the founder or co-founder of several Sierra Leonean newspapers, including the *Sierra Leone Report*, the *Watchman*, and the *New Patriot*. According to Ganda, "the papers had one common theme running through them: the welfare and defense of the underprivileged, disadvantaged and long exploited ordinary citizens of the country, and the articulation of their views as one saw them, since they themselves did not have the means to do so."[31]

Returning to the approach of organizing public protests in the United States, a number of such protests can be identified. One major Sierra Leonean protest against the Stevens government occurred on October 29, 1979, when the Coalition of Sierra Leone Organizations in the United States and Canada organized a public demonstration, involving about 400 individuals, against President Stevens when he received an honorary doctorate in civil law at Lincoln University in Pennsylvania. Stevens, who was in the United States for talks with American and world organizations, including the IMF, received the degree in recognition of more than twenty years of service to Sierra Leone. In a speech of thanks to the university's board of trustees, Stevens said that his doctorate was not only an honor for him and for the people of Sierra Leone but was also a token of the solidarity that existed between the United States and Africa. He commended the role the university had played in the emancipation of blacks in the United States as well as its policy of opening its doors to Africans and Caribbeans, and he compared it to Fourah Bay College, University of Sierra Leone, the first institution of Western higher learning south of the Sahara.[32]

The key figures in the demonstration against President Stevens included Samuel Tucker and Ted Roberts. There was some booing during the degree ceremony itself. This came when Stevens spoke about human rights and the dignity of man. Pictures of people like Mohamed Sorie Forna and Ibrahim Taqi, who had been executed by the Stevens government, were displayed. The main demonstration took place outside the cafeteria in which Stevens was entertained to luncheon. Placards and banners were displayed, calling for his resignation and making various accusations against him. Slogans were shouted as Stevens arrived at the university and as he left it. At the invitation of members of Stevens' delegation, a committee from the coalition headed by Tucker met with all of Stevens' group, including Stevens himself, to explain the reasons for their demonstration and to present Stevens, through the delegation members, with a twenty-point petition outlining their grievances and concerns. The coalition questioned the distribution of rice, the staple food, by politicians; they asked that the size of the cabinet and the size of constituencies be drastically reduced to pave the way for a fair and open election; and they argued that they saw no clear plan to improve agriculture and the economy and therefore suggested that a "think tank" of international experts in these areas be created to help the Stevens government.[33]

The coalition also pleaded for the return of freedom of speech, the press, association, and movement in Sierra Leone. Mohamed M. Turay, Sierra Leone's ambassador to the United States, agreed to present the twenty-point petition to Stevens. The coalition pledged to continue its nonviolent protests in the United States and elsewhere until visible changes came to Sierra Leone through well-reasoned policies and programs.[34]

The OAU summit scheduled for Freetown in 1980 was of great concern to the coalition. Its members protested that it was another international program or prestige project that militated against the interests of Sierra Leoneans who were poor and oppressed. But, according to President Stevens, Sierra Leone would not be deterred by its economic difficulties from hosting the OAU summit. Stevens explained that much of the expenditure was on development projects that would be of permanent benefit to the country. It was not simply a matter of prestige, he said.[35]

Another major public protest organized by diaspora Sierra Leoneans in America against the Stevens government was over the abortive attempt in 1980 by an American company, Nedlog Technology Group, Inc., of Arvada, Colorado, to export millions of tons of hazardous chemical waste from the United States to Sierra Leone for processing and disposal. Diaspora Sierra Leoneans first learned about the proposed shipment from a prominent Sierra Leonean in America, Dr. John Karefa-Smart, who had himself been briefed by the U.S. State Department. Protests against the Stevens government were held at the Sierra Leone Embassy, the State Department, and the United Nations headquarters.[36]

Nedlog was primarily involved in developing technology to recover minerals from mining and smelting waste. It was also involved in recycling and recovery projects in Missouri and Arizona. Faced with the prospect of disposing of millions of tons of toxic waste generated in the United States each year, companies like Nedlog offered hundreds of dollars for every 55-gallon barrel that could be dumped legally. A number of private U.S. companies had approached West African countries like Sierra Leone seeking permits to dump the waste.[37]

The abortive waste shipment deal between President Stevens and Nedlog originated, according to Godfrey Harris, a Los Angeles consultant to Nedlog, when he and Nedlog Vice President James R. Wolfe approached President Stevens in fall 1979, when Stevens was attending the United Nations General Assembly meeting in New York, and offered "up to $25 million" for permission to dispose of the hazardous waste in Sierra Leone. Harris, a former State Department employee, reported that the company submitted two memos to Sierra Leonean officials outlining the plan. He said that Nedlog planned to ship "all forms of hazardous waste except radioactive waste" to the country. According to Harris, the payment of up to $25 million was offered to President Stevens "in lieu of fees or taxes. It was to be more or less of a license." Stevens' reaction to the offer, Harris said, "was one of great interest, but also one of mature political caution." Under the plan, Nedlog would ship waste of an undetermined nature to the Sierra Leone port of Pepel, about thirty miles northwest of the capital, Freetown. The port was equipped with unloading facilities and a rail line leading into the interior. According to Nedlog, Sierra Leone was one of a half-dozen countries that the company was looking at. Nedlog planned to export a million tons of hazardous waste annually for processing and dumping abroad. In 1980, Nedlog already had contracts for waste recovery and disposal with two U.S. mining firms. Nedlog had been primarily involved with processing mining waste from the western part of the United States but had declined to state what kind of hazardous material it planned to ship to Sierra Leone.[38]

Diaspora Sierra Leoneans picketed the Sierra Leone Embassy opposing Nedlog's proposal, while both Nedlog and the Sierra Leone Embassy reported threatening telephone calls and bomb scares because of the plan. In a cable to the Sierra Leone Embassy, Stevens said that U.S. Ambassador John Linehan had warned him earlier of possible hazards from the disposal scheme. Stevens said in the cable that acceptance of the waste would be "foolhardy" in light of the dangers. Following the protests, the Nedlog president, Thomas Clerk, said he did not expect approval of the plan after news reports about the dumping proposal caused a sharply negative reaction in the United States and West Africa. A newspaper in Lagos called the proposal "nauseating" and accused President Stevens of a willingness to poison the population of Sierra Leone.[39]

In February 1980, President Stevens, after intense pressure from the Sierra Leonean diaspora in America, as well as concerns from State Department officials, rejected the Nedlog proposal. At an APC convention, Stevens stated that no arrangement had been made by his government for toxic wastes to be deposited in Sierra Leone.[40]

A further example of diaspora Sierra Leonean public protest against Stevens' government was seen in September 1981, when the U.S. Federal Bureau of Investigation (FBI) arrested eleven Sierra Leoneans outside the Sierra Leone Embassy after a takeover of the embassy had been planned. Following the arrests on charges of violating the Protection of Foreign Officials Act, Ted Roberts of Concerned Citizens of Sierra Leone told a press conference that the takeover was planned for two reasons: to alert the world about the recent labor unrest and the jailing of labor officials in Sierra Leone, and to take over the telephones at the chancery so the protesters could send messages back home and find out what was really going on.[41]

Another approach through which diaspora Sierra Leoneans in America attempted to exert influence on the Stevens government was by returning to their homeland temporarily or permanently and trying to work from within to bring about reform. But it was also the strategy of the Stevens government to co-opt the Sierra Leonean diaspora opposition by inviting them to return to their homeland and take up civil service employment. In official visits to the United States and through delegations sent to America, President Stevens encouraged and facilitated the return of diaspora Sierra Leoneans to their homeland to contribute to national development. In the 1970s, the secretary to the president and head of the Sierra Leone civil service, G. L. V. Williams, traveled to America to encourage diaspora Sierra Leoneans to return to their homeland with their knowledge, skills, and experience to help bring about national development.[42]

Sierra Leonean returnees, from the Stevens era, included prominent figures like Tucker and Roberts. Although they left America with great optimism, they soon experienced serious problems, including political problems and difficulties with homeland Sierra Leoneans over professional jealousy, nepotism, and alleged spying.

Roberts left for Sierra Leone at age thirty-three in 1974 after resigning his faculty position in the Department of Communications at Howard University. In fact, he was recruited by G. L. V. Williams to return to his homeland to work for the Stevens government. Roberts was offered the position of media adviser to President Stevens but the position was changed to that of deputy chief information officer after he arrived in his homeland. He worked under a European expatriate and assumed the position of chief information officer after the expatriate left the post. In the discharge of his professional duties, Roberts encountered problems with some Sierra Leonean government officials who perceived him as a CIA spy because he had worked for Voice of America, which was under the United States Information Agency. Roberts was also perceived, as were many Sierra Leonean returnees, as displaying an attitude of superiority because he had come from America. This problem was evident in his relationship with his political boss, the minister of information and broadcasting, A. B. M. Kamara. To supplement his modest government income, Roberts set up a band, Zapata, which was run by his brother. He was encouraged by President Stevens and Stevens' deputy S. I. Koroma to become involved in national politics. Following this advice, Roberts campaigned in East II constituency where he had family roots but was not given the party endorsement by the Stevens government. Instead, the Stevens government placed a travel ban on Roberts because of political disagreements with him.

In 1977, Roberts returned to Howard University as a faculty member in the Department of Communications. He continued his activism and his protests against the Stevens government. Between 1979 and 1981, he published in America a newspaper, *Lehpet*, which included contributions from diaspora Sierra Leoneans like Tucker as well as APC ministers like D. F. Shears and S. H. O. Gborie using pseudonyms. In 1980, Roberts sent an open letter to the independent Freetown-based newspaper the *Tablet*, criticizing the Stevens government for its corruption and human rights abuses.

Conclusion

Between the 1960s and the 1980s, the Sierra Leonean diaspora in America evolved from a community of less than fifty individuals to a community of several thousand. The diaspora reflected homeland political, ethnic, religious, and regional differences. However, it was united by its common pursuit of the American dream. For the Sierra Leoneans in America in the 1960s and 1970s, the American dream centered on the pursuit of higher education. But with further economic decline in their homeland in the 1980s, many of the Sierra Leoneans who migrated to America during this period pursued an American dream that revolved around self-enrichment and economic independence, as well as the transfer of assets to their homeland with the aim of starting businesses or retiring in comfort.

Although diaspora Sierra Leoneans in America did not bring about the end of authoritarian APC rule under President Stevens, they did exert an influence on their homeland politics. Through their organizational efforts, using means such as public protest, they were able to provide some of the few checks on the seventeen-year rule of the Stevens government. A clear example of the Sierra Leonean diaspora's influence on homeland politics is provided by the occasion on which President. Stevens was pressured to turn down the hazardous chemical waste deal.

Notes

1. President Stevens retired in November 1985. At the 1985 conference of the APC party, Stevens persuaded other presidential hopefuls to stand down in favor of Maj. Gen. Joseph Momoh, a forty-eight-year-old soldier. Momoh's election as party leader was seen as a triumph for Stevens. Momoh took over in November 1985, in an unusually smooth transfer of power. Stevens was only the fourth black African head of state to retire from office, after Léopold Senghor of Senegal in 1981, Amadou Ahidjo of Cameroon in 1982, and Julius Nyerere of Tanzania in 1985. In May 1988, Stevens died in his Juba Hill home after a brief illness. He was eighty-two years old.

2. See "Special Report: Diasporas," *Economist,* January 4, 2003, 41–43.

3. For diaspora studies, see, for example, Isidore Okpewho, Carole Boyce Davies, and Ali A. Mazrui, eds., *The African Diaspora: African Origins and New World Identities* (Bloomington: Indiana University Press, 1999); Nicholas Van Hear, *New Diasporas: The Mass Exodus, Dispersal, and Regrouping of Migrant Communities* (Seattle: University of Washington Press, 1998); Alusine Jalloh and Stephen E. Maizlish, eds., *The African Diaspora* (College Station: Texas A & M University Press, 1996), and Joseph E. Harris, ed., *Global Dimensions of the African Diaspora* (Washington, DC: Howard University Press, 1982).

4. There are no official government statistics for the number of Sierra Leoneans residing in the United States from 1968 to 1985. The only available figures are those for African immigrants as a whole until the late 1970s, when separate figures for Egypt and Nigeria began to appear. Thereafter, figures for Ethiopia and Ghana were added. For Africa as a whole, the numbers are as follows: 16,600 for 1951–60; 39,300 for 1961–70; 91,500 for 1971–80; and 192,300 for 1981 to 1990. Also see *Washington Post,* January 29, 1982, A29.

5. See David Killingray, ed., *Africans in Britain* (Portland, OR: Frank Cass, 1994).

6. See Trevor Coombe, *A Consultation on Higher Education in Africa: A Report to the Ford Foundation and the Rockefeller Foundation* (London: Institute of Education,University of London, 1991).

7. See Abdul K. Koroma, *Sierra Leone: The Agony of a Nation* (Freetown: Andromeda Publications, 1996); and Ibrahim Abdullah, ed., *Between Democracy and Terror: The Sierra Leone Civil War* (Dakar: CODESRIA, 2004).

8. See Thandika Mkandawire and Charles C. Soludo. eds., *Our Continent Our Future: African Perspectives on Structural Adjustment* (Dakar: CODESRIA, 1999); and World Bank, *Adjustment in Africa: Reforms, Results and the Road Ahead* (New York: Oxford University Press for the World Bank, 1994).

9. See C. Magbaily Fyle, ed., *The State and the Provision of Social Services in Sierra Leone since Independence, 1961–1991* (Senegal: CODESRIA, 1993); and Earl Conteh-Morgan and Mac Dixon-Fyle, *Sierra Leone at the End of the Twentieth Century* (New York: Peter Lang, 1999).

10. For more information on Sierra Leonean entrepreneurship, see Alusine Jalloh, *African Entrepreneurship: Muslim Fula Merchants in Sierra Leone* (Athens: Ohio University Press, 1999).

11. See Sahr J. Kpundeh, *Politics and Corruption in Africa: A Case Study of Sierra Leone* (Lanham, MD: University Press of America, 1995); and William Reno, *Corruption and State Politics in Sierra Leone* (New York: Cambridge University Press, 1995).

12. Samuel G. E. Tucker, interview by the author, Arlington, Texas, February 26, 2005. Tucker was a key member of the Sierra Leonean diaspora in the United States.

13. Ibid.

14. Ibid.

15. Ibid.

16. M. Alpha Bah, interview by the author, Arlington, Texas, March 13, 2005. Bah was a prominent member of the Sierra Leonean diaspora in the United States.

17. Ibid.

18. See *Washington Post*, October 7, 1981, C12.

19. See *New York Times*, March 18, 1984, section 1, 44.

20. See *Washington Post*, July 14, 1980, A21.

21. Ibid.

22. See Siaka P. Stevens, *What Life Has Taught Me* (Bourne End, Buckinghamshire, UK: Kensal Press, 1984).

23. See *The Rising Sun: A History of the All People's Congress Party of Sierra Leone* (Freetown: APC Secretariat, 1982); and Stevens, *What Life Has Taught Me.*

24. See *New York Times*, May 30, 1988, section 1, 28.

25. See *Washington Post*, July 14, 1980, A21.

26. Ibid.

27. See *Sierra Leone, 1968–1980*, 541.

28. See *Washington Post*, July 14, 1980, First Section, A21.

29. See *New York Times*, June 21, 1984, section 1, 2; also see Abdullah, ed., *Between Democracy and Terror.*

30. Sir Albert Margai died as a political exile while visiting a relative in the United States in December 1980.

31. See Ambrose Ganda's obituary on Peter Andersen's Sierra Leone Web site, www.sierra-leone.org; also Tucker, interview.

32. See *Sierra Leone, 1968–1980*, 527–28.

33. See *West Africa*, November 19, 1979, 2135.

34. Ibid.

35. See *West Africa*, November 5, 1980, 2023.

36. Dr. John Karefa-Smart, interview by the author, Arlington, Texas, March 29, 2005. Dr. Karefa-Smart was a senior SLPP cabinet minister and a strong opponent of Stevens.

37. See *Washington Post*, February 22, 1980, A10.

38. See *Washington Post*, January 26, 1980, A4.

39. Ibid.

40. See *Sierra Leone, 1968–1980*, 549.

41. See *Washington Post*, September 10, 1981, C8.

42. Ted Roberts, interview with the author, Arlington, Texas, February 26, 2005. Roberts was a very influential member of the Sierra Leonean diaspora in the United States.

Part Four

U.S. Political and
Economic Interests in West Africa

13

The United States and West Africa

The Institutionalization of Foreign Relations in an Age of Ideological Ferment

Peter A. Dumbuya

Introduction

This chapter situates relations between the United States and West Africa within the historical context in which overall responsibility for African affairs in the organizational structure of the Department of State (DOS) began to evolve separately from responsibility for European affairs. It then explores the nexus between ideology and the institutionalization of U.S. foreign relations with Africa in the critical interwar and Cold War decades. The restructuring process began in 1937 and culminated in the establishment of a separate Division of African Affairs within the DOS in 1958.

Prior to World War II, U.S. relations with Africa were shaped by a dual strategy: tacit recognition of Europe's colonial interests and pursuit of economic, cultural, and strategic interests in key areas of the continent. When Africa mattered, it was often in response to crisis situations involving rival European claims to African territories, or when Nazism and Fascism aligned themselves with the colonial lobby, in Germany and Italy respectively, to challenge key provisions of the post–World War I peace settlement. In the Cold War years, the United States often overreacted to the threat posed by Soviet Communism in Africa by supporting repressive/racist regimes in South Africa and Rhodesia and corrupt strongmen like Joseph Mobutu in Zaire (now the Democratic Republic of Congo, DRC) because of their anti-Communist rhetoric.

Historical Context of U.S. Relations with Africa

Although 12 percent of the U.S. population (about 30 million people) claim descent from Africa as a result of the transatlantic slave trade, overall, <u>foreign</u>

policy and national security planners in Washington have treated Africa as a marginal area of the world. Henry Serrano Villard, a foreign service officer (FSO) with firsthand knowledge of the bureaucracy created on the eve of World War II to coordinate African affairs within the DOS, has written of the relationship in very somber terms: "With the exception of independent Liberia, for whom we acted as 'next friend and attorney,' we had no particular interest in what was to all intents and purposes an appendage of Europe and therefore a blind spot in our view of the international scene, where even the conventional duties of protecting American citizens and promoting American commerce were at a negligible low."[1] Russell Warren Howe concurs, referring to Africa as "a vast region where America had a special responsibility," but admitting that "At the Washington level, Africa was still seen, principally, as being distant."[2]

According to Elliot P. Skinner, "the United States government and most of its citizens sought to dissociate themselves from the plight of Africans" by adopting a "noninterventionist policy toward Africa."[3] This stood in sharp contrast to U.S. policy toward Europe. As H. G. Nicholas has written with regard to Britain, "A shared language and a common historical inheritance of 'Anglo-Saxon' polity created, for British and Americans alike, a set of immediately recognizable and axiomatically accepted habits of thought and behavior—especially in the conduct of public affairs."[4] The major preoccupations of Anglo-American relations included trade and investment policies and the 2.8 million British immigrants who entered the United States between 1815 and 1860. According to Nicholas, between 1821 and 1837, Britain invested more in the United States than in any other country in the world, and bought 80 percent of U.S. cotton, accounting for three-fifths of total U.S. exports by the 1850s.[5]

Prior to World War II, the United States had no clearly designated office in the DOS with responsibility for African policy. The nearest Washington came to recognizing Africa's importance was the assignment of North Africa, long regarded as the gateway to the commerce of the East, to the Division of Near Eastern Affairs, and the transfer of sub-Saharan African affairs to the Division of European Affairs. This organizational setup underscored the reality that by 1914, Africa, with the exception of Ethiopia and Liberia, was under European colonial domination. By designating the DOS's European division as the authority responsible for African affairs, the United States gave tacit recognition to Europe's colonial empires on the continent.[6]

Furthermore, the nature of U.S. interests and the extent to which they were pursued are highly disputed. Immanuel Wallerstein has argued that there was not much overlapping between the economic histories of Africa and the United States in the period 1789 to 1960. U.S. "indifference" toward Africa was linked to industrial Europe's perception of the African continent as a "peripheral area of the world economy,"[7] even though prior to the abolition of the transatlantic slave trade, African slave labor provided the much-needed backbone of the cotton and sugar plantations of the Americas and the Caribbean islands. Industrialization and the abolition of the slave trade and slavery brought "legitimate trade" and European and American naval, cultural, and diplomatic influences to the shores of West Africa.

As Paul A. Varg has observed, cultural contacts, underscored by the presence of American missionaries, cannot be separated from U.S. foreign policy objectives.[8] The intersection of religion and foreign policy informed Samuel Hopkins' 1772 plan for the training of free blacks as colonizers and missionaries, especially in Africa. This prompted the U.S. Congress, in 1821, to empower the president to make "proper negotiations" with the coastal peoples of Africa for the repatriation of people of African descent. In the following year, President James Monroe chose Dr. Eli Ayers to head the mission that later founded the settlement of Monrovia. Between 1822 and 1827, the American Colonization Society (ACS) shipped more than 6,000 free blacks to the West African settlement, and in 1847 the Republic of Liberia came into being.[9] The founding of Liberia encouraged former President John Quincy Adams to support the extension of education and "the true religion" (Christianity) as "the best and only means by which the prosperity and happiness of nations can be advanced and continued."[10]

This religious and cultural imperative in West Africa stood in sharp contrast with U.S. policy toward North Africa, which was shaped in large part by commercial interests. For their own economic survival, many European states, including Spain, France, and Britain, had concluded bilateral treaties with the Barbary states of Morocco, Algeria, Tunisia, and Libya. In 1787, the United States dispatched Thomas Barclay, its consul general in Paris, to Morocco, where he signed a treaty with Sultan Sidi Muhammad XVI (reigned 1757–90), who agreed to curb piracy on the Mediterranean Sea.[11] In 1825 the United States established a consulate general in Tangier to oversee its interests in the North African kingdom. The United States made similar efforts in Zanzibar and the Congo.

Partition of Africa and U.S. Foreign Policy

Modern African nationalism had its genesis in the Berlin Conference. Hosting the conference was German Chancellor Otto von Bismarck. Even though prior to 1884 Bismarck had expressed no interest in African colonial ventures, he nonetheless spearheaded the creation of German protectorates over Togo (July 5, 1884) and Cameroon (July 12, 1884), in addition to the colonization of Southwest Africa (now Namibia; August 1884 and German East Africa (now Tanzania; February 27, 1885). The "Iron Chancellor" was motivated to colonize these African territories by domestic concerns (electoral gain) and foreign policy concerns (peace at home and prestige abroad) stemming from Germany's triumph over France in the Franco-Prussian War of 1870.

The Berlin Conference met from November 15, 1884, to February 26, 1885, without any African representatives in attendance. The conference dealt with such issues as free trade in the basin and mouth of the Congo River, freedom of navigation on the Congo and Niger Rivers, and the formalities to be observed when taking possession of new coastal territories. The agenda of the conference reflected a desire on the part of Germany and King Leopold's Belgium to forestall implementation of the Anglo-Portuguese Treaty of February 26, 1884. The treaty, by which Britain was to recognize Portuguese sovereignty over the mouth of the Congo River, threatened the treaty interests Henry M. Stanley had negotiated on behalf of King Leopold, albeit fraudulently, with more than two thousand Congolese chiefs between 1879 and 1884.

The United States, which had recognized King Leopold II's claim to the Congo (Kinshasa) in April 1884,[12] urged John Adam Kasson, its minister in Berlin, not only "to fight for free trade in the Congo, and to have the Congo basin defined as widely as was possible—against the competing Portuguese and the commercial 'dead hand' of the French," but also to fight for "humanitarian policies" that included access for missionaries to the Congo (renamed the Congo Free State in May 1885), a ban on the sale of illicit liquor, and the peaceful settlement of conflicts in the region.[13]

The Final Act of Berlin (February 26, 1885) created two free trade areas known as the "conventional Congo basin," offered protection to Christian missions, banned the slave trade, and authorized the regulation of the liquor trade by local authorities. Furthermore, the Final Act sanctioned the "effective occupation" of new coastal territories and required notification of such actions to be made to the other signatories. With this requirement, the Berlin Conference sought to minimize conflicts between and among rival European claimants to African territories.

Historians were quick to point out that the Berlin Conference did not ignite the partition of and scramble for Africa. According to H. L. Wesseling, this historic event began in Senegal, where the French had established a foothold during the Second Empire and from where they continued their colonial expansion soon after their defeat at the hands of the Germans in the Franco-Prussian War.[14] However, the events that stirred most Europeans to action were the establishment of a French protectorate in Tunisia (and Algeria) in 1881 and the British occupation of Egypt in 1882. The scramble for and partition of Africa ended in 1912 with the establishment of a French protectorate over the kingdom of Morocco. Wesseling has argued that French sailors and geographers championed the late-nineteenth-century colonial movement while Jules Ferry and Léon Gambetta provided its economic (the colony as a market for industrial goods), social (the colony as a dumping ground for social outcasts), humanitarian (the civilizing mission), and political (international prestige) justifications.

West African Nationalist Stirrings

This section of the chapter provides a typology of African resistance to European colonial rule.[15] The first form of resistance, primary resistance, took the form of armed revolt against the imposition of colonial rule. By 1914, most of the armed resistance had been suppressed by imperial military and police forces. The Sierra Leone Hut Tax War of 1898 was one of many examples of primary resistance to European colonial rule. The war was precipitated by the imperial and tax policies of Governor Frederic Cardew who, from his appointment in 1894, set out to curb the excesses of the Frontier Police Force (established in 1890) and suppress the slave trade by proclaiming a protectorate over the territories adjacent to the Colony of Sierra Leone (Freetown and its environs) in 1896. As Arthur Abraham has written, "The Protectorate Ordinance took away the independence of the rulers, [and was] justified neither by the treaties they had signed, nor by conquest."[16]

Financing the new protectorate administration of five districts (Karene, Koinadugu, Ronietta, Bandajuma, and Panguma) proved problematic. Cardew proposed a scheme of taxation that levied an annual tax of ten shillings on houses with a minimum of four rooms, and five shillings on houses with less than three rooms. The governor empowered the chiefs to collect the tax (beginning on January 1, 1898) in cash or kind; the chiefs received a 5 percent commission from the revenue thus collected. Villages of fewer than twenty huts were exempted, as were the districts of Koinadugu and Panguma, because of manpower and logistical difficulties. Attempts to collect the tax sparked the Hut Tax War in April 1898. The war in the north ended with the capture and exile of its leader Bai Bureh, in November, while the southern resistance petered out in December with the capture, trial, and execution of individuals connected with indiscriminate acts of violence against "Unsuspecting officials, missionaries, traders and their families."[17]

The second form of resistance occurred in the interwar years and involved the formation of elite educational, political, and religious parties or movements that sought to influence colonial policies by operating within the colonialist structures. Among the prominent elite formations were the London-based West African Students Union (founded in 1925), and the National Congress of British West Africa (NCBWA). Formed in 1920 by J. E. Casely Hayford of the Gold Coast (now Ghana), the NCBWA demanded civic rights and African political participation in the colonial political process. Its formation led to constitutional reforms in the British colonies of Nigeria, Sierra Leone, and Ghana, which included the appointment of Africans to the colonial legislative councils in these territories. The use of colonial institutions and platforms to effect changes in policy was a feature of elite political and social formations in the interwar years.

The rise of various forms of political parties and movements was crucial to modern African nationalism. This third form of resistance to colonialism came into its own during and after World War II, when African nationalist leaders sought to take over the political apparatus of the colonial state itself. This period coincided with the initial overhaul of the DOS bureaucracy responsible for African affairs, but the extent to which African nationalist movements influenced U.S.-African relations remains an open question. Dominated by educated elites, these political parties, such as Kwame Nkrumah's Convention People's Party (CPP) of Ghana, Nnamdi Azikiwe's National Council of Nigeria and the Cameroons (NCNC), and French West Africa's Rassemblement Démocratique Africain (RDA) were often organized along ethnic or regional lines. Encouraged by the recapture (mainly by troops from West, East, and South Africa) of Ethiopia from the Italians in May 1941 and the deployment of more than 500,000 African troops by the Allied Powers, anticolonial nationalist movements mobilized the aspirations of Africans for political change leading to independence from colonial rule.

Versailles Peace Conference

The United States' deferential policy toward its European allies undermined its commitment to African self-determination. Nowhere was this more evident than during the Versailles Peace Conference of 1919. President Woodrow Wilson believed that World War I had been ignited by, inter alia, European colonial rivalries in places like Africa. Therefore, on January 8, 1918, in the fifth of the Fourteen Points that he presented to a joint session of the U.S. Congress, he called for an "impartial adjustment of all colonial claims," and also suggested that "the interests of the populations concerned must have equal weight with the equitable claims of the government whose title is to be determined."[18] In speeches in May and July 1918, Wilson continued to refer to national self-determination and the rule of law as "this great enterprise of liberty," while Secretary of State Robert Lansing warned that the president's statement on self-determination was "loaded with dynamite," would create impossible demands on the peace conference, and raise false expectations among colonial peoples.

At the peace conference itself, the Allied powers (Britain, France, Italy, and Japan) crafted a colonial settlement based not on the principle of self-determination but on security and geopolitical considerations. These had been spelled out in two secret treaties in which the powers undertook to divide the German and Turkish colonies among themselves should they win the war: the Anglo-French treaty of August 30, 1914, relating to the division of Cameroon and Togoland, and the Treaty of London of April 26, 1915,

[handwritten: manipulation of Africa as a commodity, resource to use at disposal]

whereby the Allies (including Russia) promised Italy substantial lands in Africa as an inducement to join their war effort. In his memoirs, David Lloyd George, British prime minister from 1916 to 1922, characterized the Treaty of London as a "very distinct violation of the principles of nationalities."[19]

After protracted negotiations, Wilson conceded the right of the Allies not only to maintain their respective colonial empires intact, but also to administer the German colonies they had occupied in Africa during the war subject to international supervision by the League of Nations.[20] Article 119 of the Treaty of Versailles demanded that Germany hand over its colonies to the Allied and Associated Powers. South Africa's Jan Christian Smuts offered the blueprint for the League's mandate system: *The League of Nations: A Practical Suggestion* (1918). Established by Article 22 of the Covenant of the League of Nations, the mandate system created three categories of mandates on the assumption that these territories were "inhabited by peoples not yet able to stand by themselves under the strenuous conditions of the modern world," and "that the well-being and development of such peoples form a sacred trust of civilisation and that securities for the performance of this trust should be embodied in this Covenant." The "A" mandates, colonies of the former Turkish Empire in the Middle East, received recognition, albeit provisionally, as independent states subject to administrative supervision by Britain and France. The victors considered the "B" mandates (the German colonies of Togoland, Cameroon, and Tanganyika; and Ruanda-Urundi, awarded to Belgium for its war efforts) to be politically less advanced than those in the Middle East. The "C" mandates (German Southwest Africa and scattered German island colonies in the Pacific Ocean), viewed as politically the least advanced of all the former German colonies, were administered as "integral portions" of the mandatory powers.

U.S. Reactions to Nazism and Fascism

The focal points of Nazi Germany's African policy were the colonies (Tanganyika, German Southwest Africa, Togo, and Cameroon) it had ceded to Britain, France, and Belgium as mandates under the League of Nations. Due to its size and location on the Indian Ocean, Tanganyika lay at the core of a future German Central African empire or *Mittelafrika*.[21] Throughout the interwar period, various German colonial associations and individuals denounced the Treaty of Versailles in general and the mandate system in particular. The Italian Fascist leader Benito Mussolini's support for the return of the former German colonies forced the government of British Prime Minister Ramsay MacDonald to issue a statement on the "permanence" of the mandates. As the U.S. ambassador to Norway noted at the time, "Britain is adamant, and at present is determined not to yield the colonies—under any circumstances."[22]

[handwritten: the colonists become the colonizers]

However, following Germany's withdrawal from the League of Nations in October 1933, Adolf Hitler, who in May 1933 had announced that "our fate is not bound up with coasts or dominations, but with the east of our own frontiers," told the Reichstag in 1934 that Germany wanted its former colonies as a source of raw materials, an outlet for German migrants settling in the colonies, and a market for German goods.[23] The Reichsführer's instructions to Joachim von Ribbentrop, then ambassador at large, "to take up the colonial matter generally—but not to press the issue" induced Britain to counter with an offer to sell raw materials to Germany through the League of Nations, and as "Part of the price of a general European settlement" that "will involve no territorial changes."[24]

Critical steps in the institutionalization and regularization of U.S. policy toward the "dependent" areas of Africa by President Franklin D. Roosevelt's administration came in the wake of the Italian invasion of Ethiopia in 1935. Ignoring offers from the United States and Britain "to settle the dispute if that could be arranged,"[25] Mussolini ordered the invasion of Ethiopia to safeguard or develop Italy's "legitimate interests," which included establishing an Italian mandate over Ethiopia, fostering "amity" and "collaboration" with Ethiopia under the Treaty of 1928, minimizing French influence, and avenging the Italian defeat at Adowa in 1896.[26] As Villard noted: "When the thunderheads of Nazi imperialism began to rise over Africa—Hitler's grand design was to take over the continent's resources for the New Order in Europe—the way was paved for recognition of another area. The European Division, which had jurisdiction over the European colonies on the African land mass, transferred them—for want of a better place—to the Division of Near Eastern Affairs."[27]

In 1938, the administration began this process by transferring responsibility for African affairs (with the exception of Algeria, South Africa, and Madagascar) within the DOS from the Division of European Affairs to the Division of Near Eastern Affairs, created in 1937 with responsibility for Ethiopia and North Africa, among other places. Villard headed the new African section. In July 1940 he became assistant chief of the African section, and in January 1944 he became chief of the newly created Office of African Affairs in an expanded Division of Near Eastern, South Asia, and African Affairs. Villard assumed the position of acting deputy director of that office in April 1946. As Loy W. Henderson has observed, the administration effected these institutional changes "In recognition of the increasing importance of Africa to the United States and the dynamic developments which were beginning to take place in the continent."[28]

West Africa and World War II

World War II not only highlighted Africa's role in the defeat of the Axis Powers (Germany, Italy, and Japan) but also facilitated the eventual de-linking of African affairs from the European Division. On November 7, 1942,

President Roosevelt articulated U.S. military objectives in Africa, which were "to prevent an occupation by the Axis armies of any part of northern or western Africa and to deny to the aggressor nations a starting point from which to launch an attack against the Atlantic coast of the Americas."[29] Nevertheless, Roosevelt's administration rejected the establishment of a military base in Dakar (Senegal). Even though "Climate, health conditions, communications, base facilities and ease of defense, all favor Dakar" over Freetown (Sierra Leone), the operation would have required, among other assets, 100,000 army troops and 500 planes, and the earliest the troops could have deployed was November 1941.[30] The War and Navy Departments concluded that "This operation would not contribute materially toward winning the present war and it is not vital to hemisphere defense," indicating that "For our participation in [the] present war, a base in West Africa would be useful only in the protection of friendly shipping in the South Atlantic."[31]

In December 1941, the War Department had acknowledged West Africa's strategic significance in the "North Atlantic as our principal theatre of operations should America become involved in the war."[32] The West African theater featured prominently in the scheme of things because it could be used to protect air and sea communications and supplies to Egypt, the Persian Gulf, and the Far East generally (including Australia, Singapore, and China) and "as a means of preventing Germany from reaching Dakar from which she would both block the trade route around Cape Horn and also threaten the South American continent."[33] *never about THEIR good...*

According to Villard, the United States settled for a policy ensuring that the French North and West African colonies remained friendly toward and supportive of the Allied cause. This was achieved in part by the Murphy-Weygand agreement (1941), under which France purchased consumer goods (tea, sugar, cotton cloth, petroleum, and so forth) and durable goods (agricultural machinery) with funds frozen in U.S. banks. To make sure that these commodities did not fall into the hands of General Erwin Rommel, the commander of German troops in North Africa, General Maxime Weygand, supreme French commander in North Africa, allowed the United States to station intelligence officers posing as vice consuls in Morocco, Algeria, and Tunisia. The Murphy-Weygand agreement, initially condemned because it seemed as if the United States was collaborating with Vichy France, cleared the way for "Operation Torch," the Allied landing in North Africa on November 8, 1942. This was followed by the Casablanca Conference of January 1943, where Roosevelt announced the "unconditional surrender" of all enemy forces as an Allied war aim.

African Nationalism and the Truman-Eisenhower Doctrines

Between the Roosevelt and Dwight D. Eisenhower administrations, the United States responded more to national security crisis situations than to

the aspirations of Africans, often stepping in to bolster or replace the departing European colonial powers, much as it did in southern Europe and the
Middle East. As Undersecretary of State Chester Bowles remarked in April
1961, "for the first time in 200 years the British were really thoroughly inca-
pable, simply by lack of power and capacity to balance out the power of
Europe."[34] The collapse of the European balance of power system was evident in Greece and Turkey, where the United States began to be "exposed to
all the force and ferocity of a new and revolutionary world."[35]

Whereas in the Monroe Doctrine of 1823 the United States had asserted
its hegemony in Latin America as Europe's colonial empires crumbled, the
Truman (1947) and Eisenhower (1958) doctrines provided the rationale for
U.S. entry into the countries and regions that were being vacated by Britain
and France and that Washington considered prime targets of Communist
subversion.[36] The Truman Doctrine was crafted to aid Greece, in the throes
of a civil war, and Turkey, being pressured by the Soviet Union for territorial
concessions and the right to erect naval bases on the Bosporus. By 1950,
both countries had been stabilized by U.S. economic and military assistance.
Similarly, the Eisenhower Doctrine was predicated on the extension of U.S.
economic and military assistance to ward off the threat of Communist
aggression in the Middle East following the withdrawal of Britain and
France.

Of all the communist parties in Africa (in Morocco, Algeria, Tunisia, the
Sudan, Senegal, and Nigeria) in the first decade of the Cold War, the most
effective was said to be the South African Communist Party (SACP). Though
banned, the SACP was committed, along with other political groups like the
African National Congress (ANC), to the dismantling of South Africa's
apartheid structures and laws. Communist countries struck the right chords
in the 1950s by offering an alliance of mutual interest and an alternative
source of badly needed development assistance. However, as shown below,
such assistance as the Communist states offered was far smaller than that
provided by the United States and its Western allies. West African leaders
such as Ahmed Sékou Touré of Guinea and Kwame Nkrumah of Ghana
embraced communist/socialist ideology not only as an economic system but
also as a means of ridding the continent of colonialism and fostering pan-
African unity.[37]

Economic Aid, Trade, and Education

Faced with an upsurge in African nationalism on the one hand and the need
to contain Communism on the other, the United States and its Western allies
began to find ways to increase development aid while preventing what they
considered to be a hasty and unwise transfer of power to African nationalists.
It was feared that Africa's domestic problems could be exploited by

manipulation based on our gain

Communist agitators at the beck and call of Moscow and Beijing. Almost overnight, Africa became "not only a fascinating part of the world, but what happens there is of very great importance to all of us."[38] Africa became an "emergent colossus" with great economic potential.[39] As George Fielding Elliot pointed out, Africa's storehouse of strategically important resources (including industrial diamonds, cobalt, gold, and palm oil) had enhanced America's fighting capabilities during World War II.[40] The Congo's uranium was much sought after by the United States in the 1940s as it developed the atomic bomb.

Concern over the spread of Communism was not reflected in the fields of economic and technical assistance. Compared with aid to other parts of the world, U.S. aid to Africa was very modest, in part because most of the continent was still under European colonial rule. In the 1950s, pursuant to the Eisenhower-Acheson foreign policy commitment to roll back Communism, the United States accorded preferential treatment to those nations that renounced neutralism, which John Foster Dulles adjudged "immoral," and joined the crusade against Communism. For Dulles, development was not an end in itself but a tool for shielding the newly independent nations of Africa from Communist subversion. Beyond that, aid was meant to promote sound economic development as an important factor contributing to democratic political evolution.[41] This East-West perspective had dominated the thinking of the foreign policy and national security establishment since the enunciation of the Truman Doctrine in 1947.

The rhetoric of anti-Communism, however, far outstripped the amount of aid provided to African countries that were supposedly the targets of Communist machinations. For instance, between July 1, 1945, and December 31, 1955, the United States disbursed, without requiring the recipients to pay back, $46,142,423,000; African states received $71,595,000 or 0.15 percent of that amount. Of $16,140,524,000 in U.S. loans, Africa netted $342,713,000 or 2.12 percent. South Africa alone received $151,714,000, and Northern and Southern Rhodesia (now Zambia and Zimbabwe respectively) received $60,686,000. In 1956, less than $25 million of approximately $1,546,700,000 that was set aside for foreign aid for fiscal year 1957 went to Africa.[42]

Between 1945 and 1961, the United States provided $24 million in technical cooperation and $23 million in economic assistance to various African countries. Liberia, described by President Roosevelt as "the historic, unwritten protectorate,"[43] received $5.5 million (out of the total of $24 million) in technical assistance during the same period. By the end of the fiscal year in 1961, the United States had furnished special assistance to advance military and political interests in Morocco ($302.2 million), Tunisia ($254.7 million), Libya ($179 million), and Ethiopia ($180.4 million).[44] For the rest of Africa, the United States awarded $50 million in mutual security funds.

Military aid to Africa from the Communist bloc countries was, however, far less than that provided by the United States and Western Europe. It totaled $101 million from 1959 to 1963. This figure did not include aid for paramilitary training and military assistance to nationalist groups. Most of the aid went to Algeria, Ghana, Mali, Morocco, Guinea, and Somalia. In the same period, 1,340 African military personnel were trained in the Communist bloc countries.[45]

As in the provision of development aid and technical assistance, overall U.S. investments in Africa represented but a small percentage of the world total. Between 1943 and 1950, U.S. investments rose from $104 million to $298 million. In 1954, investments stood at $568 million, and in 1959 they rose to $834 million. The lion's share went to South Africa, which, it was estimated, had a more developed, stable, and profitable market than the rest of Africa.[46]

Prior to 1960, U.S. trade with sub-Saharan Africa amounted to $1 billion annually. In 1955, the United States imported $618,702,000 worth of goods from Africa, representing 5.4 percent of its total imports from all countries. It exported $587,577,000 worth of goods to Africa, or 3.8 percent of all U.S. exports. The shortfall in trade and investments was offset by the activities of missionary and philanthropic organizations, universities, and organized labor. The African-American Institute, the American Society of African Culture, and the American Committee on Africa helped to create and sustain awareness in the United States of African issues. In 1958, philanthropic grants totaled $7 million. The economic indicators demonstrated that propaganda was more important than trade.

On the Soviet side of the equation, trade with Africa was minimal. In 1956, for instance, the Soviet Union's exports to Africa were valued at $24 million, while its imports were valued at $29 million. Between 1954 and 1963, the total Communist economic aid to Africa was $857.7 million in credits and $160.3 million in special drawings. Much of the aid went to Algeria, Ethiopia, Ghana, and Guinea. Most of these were independent states by 1959, the exception being Algeria, which gained its independence from France in July 1962 after a bloody war of independence.[47]

On May 8, 1950, Assistant Secretary of State George C. McGhee drew attention to the fact that there was "no comprehensive program of African area studies in any American university."[48] Therefore, as part of U.S. interest in stimulating greater involvement in the continent, McGhee appealed to private financial interests, educational institutions, and foundations for help in promoting an awareness of Africa. The result was the setting up of African studies programs in more than 2,000 universities and other institutions of higher learning. By 1961, there were more than 2,800 students from Africa (out of a total of 47,000 foreign students) enrolled in American educational institutions. In 1963, the figure jumped to 6,000. In 1957, a $50,000

AFL-CIO scholarship program for trade union leaders was inaugurated. The aim of these various programs was to maintain a high profile that would discourage African reliance on the Soviet Union, China, and those countries' allies.[49]

Even in the field of education, Communist bloc countries did not have an edge over the United States and its Western allies. The Communist bloc hosted 6,135 students, 3,385 of whom were in the Soviet Union. Students from West Africa constituted 52.8 percent of the total.[50] In fact there were more African students in Britain (18,000) and France (12–15,000) combined than in the Communist bloc states.[51]

The Politics of Self-Determination

As the "wind of change" swept across Africa in the post–World War II period, the United States continued to advocate a policy of containment of Communism. This policy stimulated greater American involvement in those parts of the continent where the United States perceived a Communist threat. More often than not, the United States exaggerated the threat Communism posed to Western, as opposed to African, interests. Inevitably, this resulted in the crafting of a policy, in reaction to real and putative Communist threats, that supported the continuation of European colonial rule in places like Mozambique, Guinea-Bissau, and Angola.

When decolonization occurred in most of the continent in the 1950s and early 1960s, the United States was poised, as in Vietnam when the French withdrew, to step in and take the place of the departing colonial powers. This angered many African nationalist leaders, who felt that the United States had turned its back on the support for independence endorsed in the Atlantic Charter of 1941. Demands for independence became even more persistent after World War II, with the Soviet Union lashing out at European imperialism. The war itself, fought largely to curb the threat posed to world peace by the Axis powers, became a rallying point for anticolonial forces in Africa.

Certainly the United States and its allies expressed sympathy for the national aspirations of individual African states. Nonetheless, such sentiments were muted, in favor of larger Cold War concerns and the unity of the Western world in the North Atlantic Treaty Organization (NATO).[52] What the United States wanted to see was a continent emerging from colonial rule in an orderly fashion and in cooperation with Britain, France, and the other European colonial powers. American thinking was based on what was perceived to be a symbiotic relationship between Europe and Africa dating back to the dawn of imperial rule in the nineteenth century and centering on investments, trade, and the procurement of raw materials for Europe's industrial development.[53]

Another U.S. foreign policy determinant was containment. The goal of containment in Africa was to deny the Sino-Soviet bloc any access to markets and sources of raw materials. In an address at Northwestern University (in Evanston, Illinois) on June 27, 1951, McGhee spelled out U.S. policy toward African decolonization in the post–World War II era. It was premised on the achievement of individual and national aspirations in concert with what he called the free world. In caustic and paternalistic words, McGhee warned that independence for "primitive, uneducated peoples," unprepared to stand up to aggression, would have a negative effect on Western interests. He argued that the immediate concern of African colonies was not political independence but improvements in health, sanitation, education, and living and working conditions, and training for successful participation in government.[54]

From the outset the United States and its NATO allies overestimated Communist interests in order to strengthen their influence throughout Africa during the decolonization period. No American politician expressed the U.S. viewpoint on decolonization better than John Foster Dulles, President Dwight D. Eisenhower's secretary of state. In a speech on June 1, 1953, following a tour of the Near East and South Asia, he presented this candid assessment:

> Most of the peoples of the near east and Southern Asia are deeply concerned about political independence for themselves and others. They are suspicious of the colonial powers. The United States too is suspect because, it is reasoned, our NATO alliances with France and Britain require us to preserve or restore the old colonial interests of our allies.
>
> I am convinced that the United States policy has been unnecessarily ambiguous in this matter. The leaders of the countries I visited fully recognize that it would be a disaster if there were any break between the United States and Great Britain and France. However, without breaking from the framework of Western Unity, we can pursue our traditional dedication to political liberty. In reality the Western powers can gain, rather than lose from an orderly development of self-government. I emphasize, however, the word "orderly." Let none forget that the Kremlin uses extreme nationalism to bait the trap by which it seeks to capture the dependent peoples.[55]

Dulles's statement revealed the primacy of U.S. relations with its European allies, which for the United States far outweighed the importance of self-determination for Africans under colonial rule. For instance, the White House Office of National Security expressed concern that U.S. abstention on the Algerian vote in 1960 in the UN General Assembly would strain the NATO alliance. France, the colonial power, would view it as a betrayal of a friend. Also, the United States would not come down too heavily against South Africa's apartheid laws and its illegal occupation of Southwest Africa (Namibia) because of defense, trade, and investment considerations.[56] The need to maintain cohesion with its allies influenced America's equivocal attitude toward decolonization even when all signs pointed to its inevitability.

When the inevitable happened, the United States established and maintained diplomatic and cultural ties with Africa's independent states. The number of embassies, legations, and consulates jumped from sixteen before 1959 to forty-one in 1960 and sixty-one by the end of 1962. As Undersecretary of State Douglas Dillon put it, "no matter how admirable our intentions, no matter how well-conceived our policies and programs, our success in the final analysis depends upon people" who would adequately represent the United States in Africa.[57]

Self-determination and decolonization continued to fuel the East-West rivalry and influence peddling. The political transformation of the continent from the outbreak of World War II to the 1960s was extraordinary and unsurpassed in the history of the modern world. In 1945, Egypt, Ethiopia, Liberia, and South Africa were the only independent states in Africa. By the end of 1958, six more colonies (Ghana, Guinea, Libya, Morocco, the Sudan, and Tunisia) had regained their independence. In 1960, fourteen more colonies became independent, constituting the largest number of sovereign states ever to join the ranks of free nations.

By the end of the 1950s, the United States could no longer ignore the shrinking European colonial empires in Africa, and the strident anticolonial stance of the Communist bloc states. These developments led to the establishment of a separate Division of African Affairs on July 1, 1958. Joseph C. Satterthwaite became the first assistant secretary of state for African affairs. The wind of change swept through Africa in the 1950s, bolstered by the rise of independent states like Egypt, the Sudan, Libya, Morocco, Ghana, and Guinea. These factors were responsible for the decision by the Eisenhower administration to upgrade the African section of the DOS.

Conclusion

This chapter has shown that the United States has not always pursued its relations with Africa with a great deal of enthusiasm. In the period under review, as now, foreign policy planners in Washington treated Africa as a marginal area of the world in spite of the historical ties that bind the two regions together. Part of the explanation lies in the fact that U.S. relations with Africa were predicated upon the recognition of Europe's colonial empires. As the Berlin Conference amply demonstrated, the United States acquiesced in the existence of those empires and sought to further its own economic interests by cooperating with the colonial powers. Woodrow Wilson realized the shortcomings of the old diplomacy characterized by the balance of power, colonial rivalries, and secret alliances, but was isolated on the issue of self-determination at Versailles in 1919.

Before the 1930s, the United States had no clearly designated office in the DOS with responsibility for African policy. Instead, the DOS's Division of European Affairs handled matters relating to Africa. The Italian invasion of Ethiopia in 1935, among other things, convinced the Roosevelt administration to rethink its African policy. In 1938, the administration began to institutionalize its relations with Africa by transferring responsibility for African affairs within the DOS from the European division to the Division of Near Eastern Affairs.

The chapter has also explored the nexus between ideology and the institutionalization of U.S. foreign relations with Africa in the critical interwar and Cold War decades. The aim has been to provide as detailed an analysis as possible of the origins and the central themes of that relationship, the particular circumstances in which foreign relations were crafted, and the impact of U.S. policies on relations between the United States and Africa.

Notes

1. Henry Serrano Villard, *Affairs at State* (New York: Thomas Y. Crowell, 1965), 65.

2. Russell Warren Howe, *Along the Afric Shore: An Historic Review of Two Centuries of U.S.-African Relations* (New York: Barnes and Noble, 1975), 3, 40.

3. Elliot P. Skinner, *African Americans and U.S. Policy toward Africa 1850–1924: In Defense of Black Nationality* (Washington, DC: Howard University Press, 1992), 95, 104.

4. H. G. Nicholas, *The United States and Britain* (Chicago: University of Chicago Press, 1975), 1.

5. Ibid., 11–12, 23–24.

6. Peter J. Schraeder, *United States Foreign Policy toward Africa: Incrementalism, Crisis and Change* (Cambridge: Cambridge University Press, 1994), 12–15.

7. Immanuel Wallerstein, "Africa, the United States and the Third World Economy: The Historic Bases of American Policy," in *United States Policy toward Africa*, ed. Frederick S. Arkhurst (New York: Praeger, 1975), 14.

8. Paul A. Varg, "Missionaries," in *Encyclopedia of American Foreign Policy*, vol. 2, ed. Alexander DeConde (New York: Charles Scribner's Sons, 1978).

9. James K. Penfield, "The Role of the United States in Africa: Our Interests and Operations," *The Department of State Bulletin* 60, no. 1041 (June 8, 1959): 842.

10. Varg, "Missionaries," 569.

11. Luella J. Hall, *The United States and Morocco, 1776–1956* (Metuchen, NJ: Scarecrow Press, 1971).

12. Adam Hochschild, *King Leopold's Ghost: A Story of Greed, Terror, and Heroism in Colonial Africa* (Boston: Houghton Mifflin, 1998), 80–81.

13. Howe, *Along the Afric Shore*, 34–39.

14. H. L. Wesseling, *Divide and Rule: The Partition of Africa, 1880–1914*, trans. Arnold J. Pomerans (Westport, CT: Praeger, 1996), 9.

15. Philip Curtin, Steven Feierman, Leonard Thompson, and Jan Vansina, *African History*, 8th impression (New York: Longman, 1990), 575.

16. Arthur Abraham, *An Introduction to the Pre-Colonial History of the Mende of Sierra Leone* (Lewiston, NY: Edwin Mellen Press, 2003), 186.

17. Ibid., 191–94.

18. "Address of the President of the United States Delivered at Joint Session of the Two Houses of Congress, January 8, 1918," Woodrow Wilson Papers, Bierce Library, University of Akron.

19. David Lloyd George, *Memoirs of the Peace Conference* (New Haven, CT: Yale University Press, 1939), 1:8–9, 14–15.

20. Peter A. Dumbuya, *Tanganyika under International Mandate, 1919–1945* (Lanham, MD: University Press of America, 1995), 24.

21. For an analysis of the German position on the lost colonies in the post–World War I era, see ibid.

22. A. J. Drexel Biddle Jr., "Memorandum: A Digest of Opinion of Norwegian Informed Observers Bearing on European Outlook and War Tendencies," President Franklin D. Roosevelt's Office Files, 1933–45, Part 2: Diplomatic Correspondence File, Library of Congress, Washington, DC. Hereafter FDR's Office Files, followed by the part number. Biddle served as U.S. ambassador to Norway from 1935 to 1937.

23. Dumbuya, *Tanganyika under International Mandate*, 197, 199.

24. Biddle, "Memorandum."

25. Telegram from U.S. Embassy in Paris to Secretary of State, July 13, 1935, FDR's Office Files, Part 2.

26. Telegram from U.S. Embassy in Rome to Secretary of State, August 19, 1935, Franklin D. Roosevelt's Office Files, Part 2.

27. Villard, *Affairs at State*, 18.

28. Loy W. Henderson, Letter to the Editor of the *Boston Herald*, December 1956. Original in American Foreign Service Association Papers, Library of Congress, Washington, DC. Henderson was deputy undersecretary of state for administration.

29. Memorandum for Hon. John J. McCloy, February 6, 1943, FDR's Office Files, Part 2.

30. Brief of Study on Occupying a Base in West Africa, May 7, 1941, FDR's Office Files, Part 2.

31. Ibid.

32. War Department: Memorandum for the President, December 20, 1941, FDR's Office Files, Part 1.

33. Ibid.

34. Remarks by Chester Bowles, Under Secretary of State, to the Foreign Service Association, April 27, 1961, 4, American Foreign Service Association Papers, Library of Congress, Washington, DC.

35. Ibid., 5–6.

36. Schraeder, *United States Foreign Policy toward Africa*, 28–32.

37. Kwame Nkrumah, *Class Struggle in Africa* (New York: International Publishers, 1970), 84–88.

38. Penfield, "The Role of the United States in Africa," 841.

39. Basil Davidson, "Africa: Emergent Colossus," *The Nation*, September 8, 1951, 187–89.

40. George Fielding Elliot, "Africa, Key to Western Security," *American Mercury*, April 1955, 147–52.

41. N.S.C. 5818, "U.S. Policy toward Africa South of the Sahara Prior to Calendar Year 1960," White House Office of the Special Assistant for National Security Affairs,

August 26, 1958, *The Declassified Documents Quarterly Catalog* 7, no. 3 (Washington, DC: Carrollton Press, 1981): 2.

42. Walter Goldschmidt, *The United States and Africa* (New York: Columbia University Press, 1958), 17.

43. The White House: Memorandum for the Secretary of State and the Under Secretary of State, June 11, 1941, FDR's Office Files, Part 2.

44. Vernon McKay, *Africa in World Politics* (New York: Harper and Row, 1963), 365.

45. Thomas L. Hughes, "An Outline Guide to Communist Activities in Africa," Department of State, Bureau of Intelligence and Research, May 15, 1964, *The Declassified Documents Retrospective Collection* (Washington: Carrollton Press, 1976), 7.

46. Ibid.

47. Thomas L. Hughes, "An Outline Guide to Communist Activities in Africa," Department of State, Bureau of Intelligence and Research, May 15, 1964, *The Declassified Documents Retrospective Collection* (Washington: Carrollton Press, 1976), 4.

48. McKay, *Africa in World Politics*, 289.

49. Ibid., 249.

50. Hughes, "An Outline Guide to Communist Activities in Africa," 7.

51. Ibid.

52. Piero Gleijeses, *Conflicting Missions: Havana, Washington, and Africa, 1959–1976* (Chapel Hill: University of North Carolina Press, 2002), 195. Gleijeses has argued that the John F. Kennedy administration attached more importance to the U.S. base in the Portuguese territories of the Azores than to African self-determination.

53. N.S.C. 5818, "U.S. Policy toward Africa South of the Sahara Prior to Calendar Year 1960," 3.

54. George C. McGhee, "Africa's Role in the Free World Today," *The Department of State Bulletin* 25, no. 629 (July 16, 1951): 97–101.

55. Wallerstein, "Africa, the United States and the Third World Economy," 16.

56. Discussion Paper: "National Security Implications of Future Developments Regarding Africa," White House Office of Special Assistant for National Security Affairs, 1960, *The Declassified Documents Quarterly Catalog* 6, no. 4 (Washington, DC: Carrollton Press, 1980): 11.

57. Ibid., 12.

14

U.S. Foreign Policy toward West Africa

Democracy, Economic Development, and Security

Andrew I. E. Ewoh

Introduction

U.S. foreign policy toward West Africa during the Cold War was, by most accounts, aimed at isolating the region and the continent from Communist expansion. As a result, the United States provided aid indirectly through multinational institutions such as the World Bank, and directly through agencies such as the U.S. Agency for International Development (USAID). However, in the absence of African sentiments against the former Soviet Union, the multifaceted socioeconomic and political-military problems facing the continent provided the impetus for U.S. policymaking institutions to leave West African nations at the mercy of their former European colonial masters.[1]

In the twenty-first century, U.S. policy toward West Africa is being driven almost entirely by geopolitical and economic interests, principally interests in oil and other natural resources.[2] In recent years, the United States has tried new strategies to promote economic development and political reform in West Africa. An example of such a strategy is the African Growth and Opportunity Act, now being supplemented with a new worldwide program known as the Millennium Challenge Account.

U.S. relations with West Africa have many stakeholders, including federal bureaucracies, Congress, many special interest groups, and individuals involved in the making of U.S. policy toward West Africa. The process of policymaking is often a struggle between various stakeholders whose ideas often clash on policy issues.

The purpose of this chapter is to examine U.S. foreign policy toward West Africa in the twenty-first century. The analysis begins with an exploration of the policy actors. This is followed by a discussion of key U.S. policy priorities, focusing on democracy, economic development, and security issues. Critical issues that cut across national boundaries, such as the fight against HIV/AIDS and terrorism, are also explored. The analysis concludes with recommendations on how to better craft future U.S. foreign policy toward West Africa.

U.S. Policy in West Africa: An Exploration of the Actors

In this section, it is important to raise some questions underlining the earlier stated purpose of this chapter, as follows: Is U.S. policy toward West Africa actually made by the president, by Congress, by joint executive and congressional actions, or by other actors? In other words, who is actually involved? While the U.S. Constitution gives both the executive and the legislature a role in the foreign policy process, answers to these questions will unfold here through an exploration of the roles played by the actors within policy process. Whereas there are other stakeholders in the foreign policy process it is important to note that the president plays a major role.

Specifically, Article II, Section 2, of the U.S. Constitution gives the president the power to make treaties with other nations, with the approval of two-thirds of the members of the Senate. In addition to his formal treaty power, the president can deploy an executive agreement, which does not require congressional approval, in order to reach an accord with the leader of another country.

In terms of the presidential role, the period from 1946 to 1976 was one of limited involvement, because the major goal of U.S. foreign policy was centered on the global containment of Communism. While U.S. presidents varied in style, they were similar in adopting a limited, hands-off approach toward Africa in general and West Africa in particular. However, the decolonization of West Africa between 1957 and 1961 compelled the United States, under Dwight D. Eisenhower, to build diplomatic relationships with sub-Saharan countries, especially Ghana. President Eisenhower saw Ghana's 1957 independence and its prime minister, American-educated Kwame Nkrumah, as crucial instruments not only in combating Communism in Africa but also in influencing other African leaders to embrace the Western powers.

On the basis of Eisenhower's view, the State Department focused on stopping Communist infiltration by courting various African liberation movements, leading "to the paradoxical policy of espousing self-determination and decolonization while supporting the European colonial powers."[3] While John F. Kennedy supported African nationalism and policies of nonalignment, he also worked to build support for the containment of Communism. Kennedy's immediate successor, Lyndon B. Johnson, preferred instead to establish policy subsystems with moderate African leaders in Ghana, Nigeria, and elsewhere on the continent, but he did not accomplish much in terms of substantive policy because of his preoccupation with the Vietnam War.

[handwritten note: Africa as an exotic, faraway place we interact with only when necessary]

While both the Richard Nixon and Gerald Ford administrations pro-moted ties with more conservative African leaders, the Carter administra-tion's policy coupled liberal objectives with a special emphasis on restraining Communist expansion in Africa. The Carter administration acknowledged support for Africa's objectives with regard to self-governance and democracy as the most effective means of denying opportunities to Communist diplo-macy. For example, the Carter administration took several measures, in the form of trade embargoes, to indicate the administration's disapproval of the apartheid policies in South Africa.[4]

U.S. foreign policy toward the West African region and the African conti-nent became more assertive with the election of Ronald Reagan in 1980. Because of its commitment to a realist agenda on foreign policy issues, the Reagan administration tried to advance U.S. national interests by restoring America's sense of purpose, prestige, military credibility, and economic dynamism. While the Reagan administration restricted its foreign policy agenda to effective responses to the Communist threat, it turned to a serious constructive engagement with South Africa. For example, by the summer of 1985 the Reagan team took stronger measures against white dominance there, including the withdrawal of the U.S. ambassador over South African military raids into neighboring countries, and the imposition of a ban on computer exports to government agencies involved with the implementa-tion of apartheid policies.[5]

The Reagan administration was of course not the only stakeholder with regard to U.S. policy on South Africa. Other stakeholders such as the Congressional Black Caucus and TransAfrica were instrumental in influenc-ing U.S. policy when sanctions were imposed on South Africa's apartheid government in 1986. This resulted from years of daily protests in front of the South African embassy in Washington, DC, led by TransAfrica and supported by African American legislators such as Ronald Dellums, Charles Rangel, and Julian Dixon. Other African Americans who aided the drive for sanc-tions against South Africa through the Free South Africa Movement included Randall Robinson, Walter Fauntroy, Mary Frances Berry, and Eleanor Holmes Norton.[6]

After Reagan's assertive engagement in Africa came George H. W. Bush's more consensus-oriented style. Bush accepted the reality of U.S.-Soviet coop-eration and took a pragmatic view of the options available under Mikhail Gorbachev's new thinking. In his effort to cope with the challenges of the post–Cold War era, Bush encouraged the conflicting parties in Sudan, Ethiopia, Angola, Mozambique, Namibia, and South Africa to negotiate their differences, mediating between adversaries and promoting the imple-mentation of agreements where necessary. For example, Herman J. Cohen, Bush's assistant secretary of state for African affairs, engaged directly in mediation in Ethiopia and Sudan.

In the period between his assumption of office in 1993 and the 1994 Republican midterm congressional victory, Bill Clinton established an activist humanitarian agenda in Africa. Clinton promoted and supported multilateral peacekeeping, democratization, economic development, and the reorganization of economic assistance programs. His administration responded to calls for more effective U.S. leadership and invited more than 160 political leaders, businessmen, and academics to a White House conference on Africa in June 1994. This conference provided the guideposts for the formation of Clinton's presidential policy group. However, the African American policy group, composed of members of the Congressional Black Caucus (CBC) and various individuals, was ineffectual in its efforts to impose oil sanctions on Nigeria during General Sani Abacha's repressive military regime.[7] The failure to pass the Nigerian Democracy bill, introduced by Congressman Donald Payne, was largely due to the divisions among members of the CBC with regard to the potential impact of the oil embargo on Nigerian citizens and Abacha's antisanctions campaign against the United States. Clinton's visit to Lagos, Nigeria, in July 2000, following Nigeria's triumphant return to civilian rule, helped to restore his project of promoting democracy. He used the opportunity of his visit to praise the emergence of democratic values in Africa and promised his administration's support in enhancing efforts to build real democratic institutions there.[8]

When President George W. Bush took office in January 2001, some critics doubted whether he would take an active interest in Africa given the many challenges facing the continent. Indeed, Bush indicated during the 2000 presidential campaign that Africa would not be part of his foreign policy agenda. It was therefore a surprise when, in his 2003 State of the Union address, he promised to spend $15 billion over the following five years to fight HIV/AIDS in Africa and the Caribbean. While this promise was the major focus of Bush's African visit in July 2003, the United States' initial contribution was only $200 million. Generally, Bush's foreign policy toward Africa focuses on three themes: the establishment of peace and security, the struggle against AIDS, and economic development through trade.

The preceding review of various presidents' policy perspectives toward Africa provides the foundation for further exploration of the current U.S. policy priorities in West Africa, such as promoting democracy, bolstering economic development through trade and investment, and enhancing security. These substantive policy issues are discussed in turn, focusing on the policies of the Clinton and George W. Bush administrations.

Promoting Democracy

In the post–Cold War era, it is the president who defines the core objectives of U.S. foreign policy strategy, which always include the promotion of

democracy overseas. Promoting democracy was one of the Clinton administration's major claims to a distinguishable African policy strategy. This writer
contends that the spread of democracy to West African nations is in the
interest of the United States because democratic governments are inclined
to work toward peaceful relations with each other, thereby making it easier
for the United States to cooperate with these countries in countering any
threats to mutual security. In its effort to further democratization, the
Clinton administration encouraged regular elections and good governance
and promoted strong party systems and civil societies. This was symbolized
by the integration of democratic governance into the core aims of USAID
and the appointment of Reverend Jesse Jackson as the presidential envoy on
democracy and human rights in Africa.

Despite Clinton's efforts, critics[9] argue that the United States did not spend
much on development assistance in its attempt to achieve its democratization
objectives. For example, Harbeson shows that the United States spent only 8
percent (about $244.24 million) of USAID development funds in 1995–96 on
democratization projects, with 90 percent of its support going to 13 nations in
eastern and southern Africa, and the remaining 10 percent to western African
countries. A subsequent study, using 1997–2000 data, revealed a similar pattern, except that the money spent on the U.S. commitment to democratization in Africa fell by 5.4 percent. Although some countries had their
democracy assistance suspended for human rights abuses, others such as
Guinea in West Africa and Ethiopia in East Africa continued to receive assistance despite their undemocratic activities.[10] Nonetheless, there has been an
increase in funding for development assistance in democracy and governance
to West Africa during the Bush administration. In the 2001 fiscal year, for
instance, about $418,000 of the USAID budget was allotted to supporting con-
flict monitoring and mitigation activities in West Africa, while $462,000 of the
2002 fiscal year budget was used to expand and institutionalize the administration's democracy objectives in the region.[11] This money is related to democracy and governance in the sense that much of it goes toward capacity building
for civil society, which is required for democracy to triumph.

Available evidence on U.S. democratization efforts in West Africa and the
rest of the continent demonstrates that Africans prefer elected and account-
able government—even when they disagree with its constitutional structures, with the degree of regional and ethnic autonomy provided, and even
on citizenship and national boundaries. Figures from the International
Foundation for Electoral Systems show that voter turnout in African national
elections declared free and fair in the late 1990s ranged from 60 to 94 percent. As noted by Chege, "Success in one country will serve as a beacon to
activists in the next, as witnessed by the public routing of General Robert
Guei in Abidjan, Cote d'Ivoire, in October 2000 following the example set
by the Serbians in ousting Slobodan Milosevic."[12]

In 2001, it became evident that the George W. Bush administration is committed to helping African countries to become democratic, following in Clinton's footsteps. According to Freedom House reports, nineteen African countries are listed as elected democracies. Bush's policies and programs encourage good governance and the rule of law through the development or strengthening of democratic institutions such as independent media, effective parliaments, and independent judiciaries. The Bush team also supports anticorruption programs and respect for internationally recognized human rights all in efforts to deepen the fragile roots of new democracies in West Africa and throughout Africa.[13] Progress toward the spread of democracy in West African states under the Bush administration includes peaceful transitions from one party to another in Senegal, Mali, and Ghana, undergirding the growing maturity of African leaders and their electorates. This success follows the progress witnessed in Benin, Nigeria, and other African countries in the 1990s. This success was aided by African leaders' efforts to adopt economic reform measures imbued with transparency as mandated by U.S. foreign policy.

However, while voting and elections are good signs of democracy, there are signs of human rights violations in the new African democracies. For example, the Nigerian police, army, and security forces have committed extrajudicial killings or used excessive force to apprehend criminals and to quell incidents of ethno-religious violence.[14] Governments have been suspected of murdering journalists in The Gambia, Sierra Leone, and Equatorial Guinea, and this interference with the media prompted the International Press Institute to demand freedom of the press in Africa during its 54th World Congress and annual general assembly on May 21–24, 2005, in Nairobi, Kenya.[15]

The situation in Togo, where the military illegally compelled the Togolese legislature to amend the constitution to allow the son of the late President Eyadema to succeed his father as the president of Togo amounts to a travesty of the rule of law. It is expected that the United States and the international community will not recognize the government of Togo until it goes through the process of constitutional and democratic transition that will bring in a democratically elected government.

Bolstering Economic Development through Trade

The Clinton administration viewed trade as a catalyst for African growth as well as a symbol of America's partnership with the continent. In view of this, the administration initiated the African Growth and Opportunity Act (AGOA), which was signed into law on May 18, 2000, as Title 1 of the Trade and Development Act of 2000. Basically, AGOA provides that certain African products, such as textiles and apparel, can enter the United States market duty-free for a ten-year period, provided that such exports do not exceed 1.5 percent of U.S. imports, rising to 3.5 percent over an eight-year period. The AGOA provisions include debt relief, access to loans and credits through U.S. government-backed equity funds and insurance schemes, and technical assistance. President Bush signed amendments to AGOA—also known as AGOA II—into law on August 6, 2002. AGOA was further modified under the AGOA Acceleration Act of 2004, or AGOA III, which was signed into law by Bush on July 12, 2004, substantially extending preferential access for imports from beneficiary sub-Saharan African countries until September 30, 2015. AGOA III provides additional congressional guidelines to the Bush team on how to administer the textile provisions.[16] It is possible that recent protests from U.S. textile manufacturers against AGOA may result in its modification in the near future.

Since AGOA authorizes the president to designate the countries that are to receive benefits, President Bush identified 36 African countries as being eligible for economic and trade benefits under AGOA on December 21, 2004. These countries include twelve West African states: Benin, Cape Verde, The Gambia, Ghana, Guinea, Guinea-Bissau, Mali, Mauritania, Niger, Nigeria, Senegal, and Sierra Leone. Burkina Faso was determined to be eligible on December 10, 2004. Côte d'Ivoire was removed as of January 1, 2005, from the list of eligible countries because of the political instability and violent conflict in that country, while Liberia and Togo were deemed ineligible for similar reasons.[17] The president can designate countries as eligible if they are determined to have established, or are continuing to make progress toward establishing, the following:

- Market-based economies;
- The rule of law and political pluralism;
- Elimination of barriers to U.S. trade and investment;
- Protection of intellectual property;
- Efforts to combat corruption;
- Policies to reduce poverty, increasing the availability of health care and educational opportunities; and
- Protection of human rights and worker rights, and elimination of certain child labor practices.[18]

While AGOA is described as the cornerstone of the Clinton and Bush administrations' trade and investment policy toward Africa, critics, including the Congressional Black Caucus, contend that AGOA has brought very limited benefits to only a small number of countries and has not promoted sustainable economic development. Africa's share of total world trade stands at 1 percent, less than half of what it was in 1980. This leaves African countries in a precarious condition, since most of them are dependent on primary commodities that are vulnerable to even minor fluctuations in market prices. In addition, Booker and Colgan[19] contend that most U.S. trade with Africa is with only a handful of countries.

The success of AGOA in two West African nations should, however, be mentioned here. Charles R. Snyder, acting secretary of state for African affairs, remarks that in Ghana, the Heinz Corporation, an American company, is investing to expand a tuna-processing plant; in Senegal, U.S. investors are working with Asian and Senegalese partners to revitalize factories to spin yarn, weave fabric, and manufacture garments, thereby creating more than 2,000 new jobs.[20]

Another new initiative in Bush's economic assistance is the Millennium Challenge Account (MCA), designed to support African countries' efforts to meet the United Nations' Millennium Development Goals. This initiative, crafted in 2002, is supposed to make $1.3 billion available to Africa and other countries that qualify, but only $1 billion was appropriated by the Republican-controlled Congress in 2004 because of the politics of budgetary constraints. The program is administered by the newly created Millennium Challenge Corporation. As it is a highly selective economic aid program, only Ghana and Senegal in West Africa and Uganda in East Africa are projected to receive aid through the MCA based on their strong commitment to the principles of just government, their investment in people through health and education, and their promotion of economic freedom.

Before Bush's visit to Africa in July 2003, many analysts and activists were worried that the administration's search for more secure sources of oil was leading him to the doorsteps of some of the world's most troubled and repressive regimes, the petroleum-rich countries of West Africa.[21] Although it was centered on a macroeconomic and humanitarian-based agenda, Bush's visit to Nigeria, Senegal, and other sub-Saharan African nations also involved underlying U.S. economic concerns pertaining to the strategic importance of U.S. energy security. The United States' preoccupation with energy security makes the West African region especially crucial because of its oil reserves. The region supplies 14 percent of all U.S. oil imports, and the National Intelligence Council predicts that the region's share will rise to 25 percent by 2015.[22]

Since West African oil production is projected to increase from 4.9 million barrels a day in 2003 to 8.2 million barrels a day in 2010, U.S. policy toward the region ought to be focused on massive economic development in West Africa in recognition of its strategic importance to U.S. energy and national security. Nigeria and Angola are expected to account for the lion's share of the region's oil production, but others, like Guinea and possibly Niger as well as São Tomé and Principe, are expected to contribute to oil production. In view of this, routing funds through multinational financial corporations or general economic aid programs may not work well in the region; rather, the U.S. government ought to be committed to securing the oil resources; this will require commitment to certain economic and political reforms as well as to the military security of the region. The section that follows focuses on the issue of security enhancement.

Enhancing Security by Increasing Peace and Stability

Violent internal and cross-border conflicts have disrupted economic, social, and political development in West Africa, with substantial costs to human life and property. These conflicts began in 1989 in Liberia when Libyan-trained and Burkina Faso–backed militants started a civil war with the aim of overthrowing Liberian dictator Samuel Doe. The fighting extended to Sierra Leone in 1991, to Guinea in 2000, and to the Ivory Coast thereafter. Although the now ousted president of Liberia, Charles Taylor, was the epicenter of this conflict system, public cynicism also contributed to the crisis.

Development programs cannot be sustained in the absence of peace and security. The U.S. State Department's International Affairs Strategic Plan recognizes that the prevention and elimination of conflict is a major foreign policy goal. As a result, major responses to violent conflicts in West Africa have been through the Economic Community of West African States' Monitoring Group (ECOMOG), which has tried to fill the power vacuum in the region. ECOMOG has conducted both military and peacekeeping operations in Liberia, Sierra Leone, and Guinea-Bissau, with logistical and material support from the international community. Although ECOMOG has been effective in containing the spread of war, it lacks a successful strategy for preventing regional conflicts.[23]

Since the late 1990s, American foreign policy toward West Africa has been preoccupied with efforts to contain and isolate Charles Taylor's regime. This goal was achieved when Taylor exiled himself in Nigeria in 2003. In the case of the Sierra Leone and Ivory Coast conflicts, the U.S. government provided financial and political support to the British and French efforts, backing the former European colonial powers. To end conflict in the region, the United States is supporting the development of the capability of regional organizations such as the Economic Community of West African States (ECOWAS) to oversee and support regional peace and meet humanitarian response requirements, thereby encouraging ECOWAS member states to resolve their conflicts.

Nowhere in West Africa is stability more important to the United States than in Nigeria, the continent's most populous country, where 137 million of the region's 240 million people are living.[24] Nigeria is the sixth largest producer of oil in the world and is also one of the two (along with South Africa) focal points of American foreign policy in sub-Saharan Africa. The U.S. government has supported the democratic government of Olusegun

Obasanjo and has established strong military cooperation with Nigeria, which has resulted in the training of five battalions of Nigerian soldiers. Partnership with Nigeria has positive policy implications for the United States: it will not only improve the chances for domestic and regional stability in West Africa but will also signal to other African countries that U.S. engagement in the region is especially important in countering the deleterious effects of the activities of corrupt nonstate actors (for example, diamond, timber, and arms traffickers), the potential growth of militant Islam, and Libyan expansionism. It is important to note here, for example, that Libya was implicated in training Charles Taylor and Sierra Leone's Revolutionary United Front, which participated in cross-border attacks in Guinea in the late 1990s.[25]

However, U.S. partnership with the Nigerian military is very problematic. On the one hand, Washington expects Nigeria to shoulder much of the peacekeeping burden in West Africa (for example, in Liberia) and has provided aid for this purpose. But on the other hand, a recent congressional initiative suspended some military financing and a program of international military education and training for Nigeria, worth more than $3 million, until the Nigerian government accounted for its military's human rights violations in Benue and Niger Delta communities. Booker and Colgan[26] contend that a long-term view of U.S.-Nigerian relations must confront fundamental issues of democracy, conflict resolution, resource use, the environment, and poverty. In view of this, any effort to promote stability and development in Nigeria must include the protection of the environment from oil externalities and the preservation of human rights.

Fighting HIV/AIDS and Terrorism

The HIV/AIDS pandemic has been the greatest challenge facing Africa and the international community. Africa has lost more than 18 million lives, about 72 percent of the global loss of live. In his January 2003 State of the Union address, Bush announced plans to spend $15 billion to fight AIDS, tuberculosis, and malaria, overwhelmingly in Africa and the Caribbean. Unfortunately, the Bush pledge was quickly undermined by his own budget request of only $450 million for the 2004 fiscal year instead of the promised $3 billion installment, although Congress appropriated $2 billion.[27]

The Bush AIDS initiative was assigned to the State Department immediately following its creation in 2003 and was headed by a former pharmaceutical executive, Randall Tobias. Critics argue that the new AIDS bureaucracy competes with and may duplicate the efforts of other, much more important agencies such as the Global Fund, an international nongovernmental agency created in 2001 to fight AIDS, tuberculosis, and malaria. Consequently, the new bureaucracy is likely to pose a challenge to other aid providers and recipient countries because its approach favors prevention over treatment and abstinence over sex education and condoms, and its close ties with the pharmaceutical industry place it in opposition to the ensuring of access to treatment for HIV/AIDS using low-cost generic drugs.[28] While the fight against AIDS is a difficult one, the signing of the HIV/AIDS Act of 2003 into law is the administration and Congress's way of addressing one of the most urgent needs of the world.[29]

West Africa is home to almost 130 million Muslims and has some small-scale grassroots support for terrorism. Nonetheless, Middle Eastern issues do not generally affect relationships between the United States and West African countries to any great degree. Predominantly Muslim West African countries such as Senegal, Mali, and Niger with functional democracies have close ties with the United States, and they have been engaged by that country in the Pan Sahel Initiative, a program designed to enhance security and intelligence along the southern border of the Sahara.

Generally, the terrorist threat in West Africa comes less from religion and politics than from lack of sovereign control and general frailty. The Bush team acknowledged this linkage in its 2002 National Security Strategy, which argued that poverty, weak institutions, and corruption can make weak states vulnerable to terrorist networks and drug cartels within their borders. The wars that Charles Taylor initiated around neighboring countries during his presidency underscore this contention. It was reported that al-Qaeda colluded with the governments of Burkina Faso and Liberia to buy diamonds marketed by rebel forces in Sierra Leone during the civil war that affected that country and neighboring Liberia in the 1990s. What is needed is for the United States to offer a strong commitment to the region and make it a part of its global antiterrorist strategy.

Conclusion

The call to spread democracy is logical and appealing to most Africans, but the United States has to commit more financial resources to the daunting task of promoting democratic institutions and civil society in West Africa. Otherwise any effort to nurture political reform will be problematical. While an integrated U.S. foreign policy encompassing all of Africa may be advocated by some of those involved in international relations, Africa is too broad and complex to accommodate in this way. However, in the twenty-first century, it is imperative to craft U.S. foreign policy for clusters of African countries that show promise in key U.S. policy priority areas, such as security, prevention of terrorism, and international crime, control of disease pandemics, democratization, and free trade.

In sum, in promoting economic and political reforms in West Africa, the United States should concentrate more of its efforts on Nigeria as the economic and political driving force for the region because of its strategic position and resources. In addition, each country in the region should be encouraged to adopt economic and political reform measures that are specific to its citizens, given the heterogeneous nature and ethnic composition of each country. To end the endemic civil unrest in some pockets of the region, the United States should help military and police forces through its International Military Education and Training program and continue to support the peacekeeping efforts of the Economic Community of West African States.

Notes

1. Anyu J. Ndumbe, "West African Oil, US Energy, and Africa's Development Strategies," *Mediterranean Quarterly* (2004): 93–104; Okbazghi Yohannes, "America's New Frontier: Oil in the Gulf of Guinea," *Black Scholar* 33, no. 4 (2003): 2–21; Human Rights Watch, "Bush Trip to Africa," September 12, 2004, http://www.hrw.org/bagrounder/africa/bush-africa2k3.htm.

2. Yohannes, "America's New Frontier," 21.

3. Roger A. Davidson, "A Question of Freedom: African Americans and Ghanaian Independence," *Negro History Bulletin* 60, no. 3 (1997): 6–12.

4. Donald Rothchild, "The US Foreign Policy Trajectory on Africa," *SAIS Review* 21, no. 1 (2001): 179–211.

5. Ibid.

6. Adebajo Adekeye, "Africa, Africans, and the Avuncular Sam," *Africa Today* 50, no. 3 (2004): 92-110.

7. Ibid.

8. Gilbert M. Khadiagala, "The United States and Africa: Beyond the Clinton Administration," *SAIS Review* 21. no.1 (2001): 259–73.

9. John W. Harberson, "The Clinton Administration and Promotion of Democracy: Practical Imperatives for Theoretical Exploration," *Issue: A Journal of Opinion* 24, no. 2 (1998): 36–46; Rothchild, "The US Foreign Policy Trajectory on Africa."

10. Harberson, "The Clinton Administration and Promotion of Democracy"; Rothchild, "The US Foreign Policy Trajectory on Africa."

11. U.S. Agency for International Development, *Activity Data Sheet*, 2002, http://www.usaid.gov/pubs/cbj2002/afr/warp/624–007.html.

12. Michael Chege, "A Realist's Minimal US Policy toward Africa," *SAIS Review* 21, no. 1 (2001): 225–37.

13. U.S. Department of State, "U.S. Partnership of the 21st Century," Remarks to the Pacific Council on International Policy by Charles R. Snyder, Acting Secretary for African Affairs (November 17, 2003), http://www.state.gov/p/af/rls/rm/26772.htm.

14. U.S. Department of State, *Nigeria: Country Reports on Human Rights Practices— 2002*, released by the Bureau of Democracy, Human Rights, and Labor, March 31, 2003, http://www.state.gov/g/drl/rls/hrrpt/2002/18220.htm.

15. Benjamin Bruehwiler, "Freedom of Press in Africa," *African News Digest* 16, no. 22 (June 1-7, 2005): 1, 5.

16. African Growth and Opportunity Act, "Summary of AGOA I," 2004, http://www.agoa.gov/agoa_legislation/agoa_legislation.html.

17. White House, "Statement on the African Growth and Opportunity Act," 2004, http://www.whitehouse.gov/news/releases/2004/12/2004/20041222–1.html.

18. African Growth and Opportunity Act, "General Country Eligibility Provisions," 2005, http://www.agoa.gov/eligibility/country_eligibility.html.

19. Salih Booker and Ann-Louise Colgan, " 'Compassionate Conservatism' Comes to Africa," *Current History* 103, no. 673 (2004): 232–36.

20. U.S. Department of State, "U.S. Partnership of the 21st Century."

21. Warren Vieth, "US Quest for Oil in Africa Worries Analysts, Activists," *Los Angeles Times*, January 13, 2003, http://www.commondreams.org/headlines03/0113–06.htm.

22. "General Interest," *Oil and Gas Journal Online* 101, no. 45 (November 24, 2003), http://www.ogj.onlinearticle.printhis.clickability.com.

23. U.S. Agency for International Development, *Activity Data Sheet.*

24. World Fact Book, *Nigeria* (2005), http://www.cia.gov/cia/publications/factbook/geos/ni.html.

25. U.S. Institute of Peace, *Responding to War and State Collapse in West Africa, Special Report 81* (2002), http://www.usip.org/pubs/specialreports/sr81.html.

26. Booker and Colgan," 'Compassionate Conservatism' Comes to Africa," 232–36.

27. Ibid., 233.

28. Ibid., 232–36.

29. White House, "President Signs HID/AIDS Act," 2003, http://www.whitehouse.gov/news/releases/2003/05/print/20030527–7.html.

15

U.S. Economic Assistance to West Africa

Abdul Karim Bangura

Introduction

This chapter begins by examining the West Africa Regional Program (WARP), the bilateral economic assistance program geared toward helping the citizens of the following countries in West Africa: Benin, Burkina Faso (formerly Upper Volta), Cape Verde, Côte d'Ivoire, The Gambia, Ghana, Guinea, Guinea-Bissau, Liberia, Mali, Mauritania, Niger, Nigeria, Senegal, Sierra Leone, and Togo. Administered by the United States Agency for International Development (USAID), the program was provided through capital transfers and technical assistance.

As can be seen in table 15.1, U.S. economic assistance has been given to every country in West Africa. Also evident is the fact that aid disbursements have not been consistent over the years, either in terms of level of funding or in terms of continuity; such factors can make development planning quite difficult. The four biggest recipients of aid overall have been Ghana, Liberia, Mali, and Senegal. However, since 2000, Nigeria has emerged as the biggest recipient of aid to West Africa.

An examination of tables 15.1 and 15.2 reveals that four West African countries began receiving U.S. economic assistance even before they got their independence. The first recipient was Nigeria in 1953. It was followed by Benin, The Gambia, Sierra Leone, and Togo, all receiving their first aid packages in 1959. This was during their periods of limited self-rule before achieving independent status. The countries receiving aid included both those colonized by Britain and those colonized by France.

As shown in table 15.3, WARP was launched in 1998. The funding lasted only until 2002, and the short-term nature of the program was a potential source of difficulty in development planning. The objective of the program was to promote economic growth through regional economic integration by providing technical assistance for the following:[1]

(a) promoting the expansion of cross-border trade among member countries (Benin, Burkina Faso, Cape Verde, Côte d'Ivoire, Ghana, Guinea, Guinea-Bissau, Liberia, Mali, Niger, Nigeria, Senegal, Sierra Leone, The Gambia, and Togo) of the Economic Community of West African States (ECOWAS);
(b) strengthening regional private actor business and trade associations in the areas of organizational design, financial management, and activity implementation;
(c) increasing awareness of issues associated with World Trade Organization (WTO) requirements and globalization with a view to expanding trade between the United States and ECOWAS countries;
(d) creating a policy and regulatory environment that would encourage trade and investment throughout the region; and
(e) furthering the establishment of a gas pipeline and power pool in the ECOWAS region for electrical energy exchange and trading.

In order to delineate those factors that might have led to the developments sketched above, at least four major questions can be posed: (1) What political perspectives and traditions shape the way Americans look at West Africa and other developing regions? (2) What are the purposes of American foreign assistance to West Africa and other developing regions? (3) How is U.S. foreign aid policy toward West Africa shaped? (4) What type of foreign aid doctrines has the United States espoused? The following sections explore these questions. In conclusion, a call is made for a West African Marshall Plan.

American Political Perspectives and Traditions

The following words from E. R. May are quite apt in describing what drives American policymakers as they design U.S. foreign aid policy toward West Africa:

> Framers of foreign policy are often influenced by beliefs about what history teaches or portends. Sometimes, they perceive problems in terms of analogies from the past. Sometimes, they envision the future either as foreshadowed by historical parallels or as following a straight line from what has recently gone before.[2]

John Sewell and John Mathieson suggest four factors—abundance, individualism and democracy, revolution and social change, economic liberalism and attitudes toward poverty—that shape the ways in which Americans look at African and other developing countries and their development.

Table 15.1 United States Economic Assistance to West Africa, 1953–2005 (in 2005 US$ Millions)

Year	Benin	Burkina Faso	Cape Verde	Côte d'Ivoire	The Gambia	Ghana	Guinea	Guinea-Bissau
1953	0.0	0.0	0.0	0.0	0.0	0.0	0.0	0.0
1954	0.0	0.0	0.0	0.0	0.0	0.0	0.0	0.0
1955	0.0	0.0	0.0	0.0	0.0	0.0	0.0	0.0
1956	0.0	0.0	0.0	0.0	0.0	0.0	0.0	0.0
1957	0.0	0.0	0.0	0.0	0.1	0.5	0.0	0.0
1958	0.0	0.0	0.0	0.0	0.1	0.2	0.0	0.0
1959	0.1	0.0	0.0	0.0	0.0	1.7	1.7	0.0
1960	0.0	0.0	0.0	0.0	0.0	1.0	2.1	0.0
1961	3.0	0.2	0.0	2.1	0.1	22.6	0.2	0.0
1962	2.1	1.2	0.0	2.5	0.0	65.1	10.4	0.0
1963	1.0	1.0	0.0	3.1	0.0	3.0	15.9	0.0
1964	1.1	0.9	0.0	8.9	0.0	4.0	16.7	0.0
1965	0.8	0.7	0.0	4.8	0.1	2.9	20.8	0.0
1966	1.2	1.5	0.0	2.7	0.2	9.4	7.3	0.0
1967	1.3	2.9	0.0	1.5	0.4	35.2	1.3	0.0
1968	1.0	1.7	0.0	0.9	0.2	34.6	4.5	0.0
1969	0.9	1.0	0.0	2.9	0.7	24.6	8.4	0.0
1970	0.5	2.2	0.0	0.7	0.3	31.1	0.5	0.0
1971	0.5	5.0	0.0	2.1	1.3	22.0	12.5	0.0
1972	11.6	3.3	0.0	0.8	0.5	15.1	0.7	0.0
1973	0.8	3.1	0.0	1.9	0.9	24.4	4.8	0.0
1974	16.0	8.9	0.0	1.9	1.9	6.0	5.7	0.0
1975	1.2	9.6	1.1	2.6	1.9	7.5	11.5	1.0
1976	1.4	6.2	3.1	2.2	1.5	19.6	8.9	0.1
1977	1.2	12.5	5.5	1.3	1.1	13.5	1.9	2.5
1978	1.2	20.7	11.4	1.5	2.8	12.2	13.6	6.9
1979	1.3	26.9	7.4	1.6	5.8	24.2	8.4	2.4
1980	3.7	22.8	5.8	1.5	7.4	27.5	11.4	2.1
1981	7.5	30.7	6.6	1.3	7.7	25.8	10.5	7.4
1982	2.3	19.6	6.0	0.0	3.1	16.9	5.9	4.0
1983	1.5	8.9	4.9	0.0	5.2	7.3	6.9	2.6
1984	3.0	17.7	6.5	0.0	7.9	20.3	6.6	5.1
1985	3.1	26.7	5.0	1.6	9.3	25.2	9.7	4.1
1986	2.7	23.6	7.2	1.9	8.4	24.1	19.6	2.8
1987	3.0	14.9	4.4	1.0	13.0	29.5	14.4	1.9
1988	3.7	9.5	5.0	1.4	9.0	18.9	28.3	2.8
1989	4.6	13.0	4.9	8.5	8.3	30.9	23.7	3.5
1990	4.9	9.8	7.3	27.2	7.3	31.5	16.5	5.4
1991	25.8	16.7	7.4	25.5	17.9	45.9	43.1	5.3
1992	13.5	17.0	7.3	21.8	13.3	50.8	37.6	5.8
1993	23.2	15.1	7.4	17.8	12.9	67.3	38.8	8.0

Table 15.1 (continued)

Year	Benin	Burkina Faso	Cape Verde	Côte d'Ivoire	The Gambia	Ghana	Guinea	Guinea-Bissau
1994	25.4	11.5	6.6	6.6	10.6	55.2	31.4	6.4
1995	20.4	13.7	8.2	1.6	5.1	39.1	19.7	6.5
1996	16.2	12.1	7.4	21.6	4.2	43.8	15.7	7.2
1997	17.3	13.3	4.8	12.1	3.2	48.1	32.2	6.7
1998	23.1	16.4	8.2	2.5	3.4	49.1	46.6	0.7
1999	28.7	17.9	3.3	13.1	3.7	76.5	27.6	2.3
2000	20.7	16.1	5.8	7.4	4.4	65.5	33.2	0.2
2001	21.7	13.1	5.2	3.1	3.4	64.9	33.7	.03
2002	24.7	15.8	5.7	13.0	2.1	48.6	45.2	1.4
2003	30.5	14.1	5.6	22.7	4.3	77.6	48.9	1.7
2004	18.3	5.2	4.0	0.0	0.0	47.7	26.1	0.0
2005	19.3	11.5	3.5	0.0	0.0	47.2	21.5	0.0

Year	Liberia	Mali	Mauritania	Niger	Nigeria	Senegal	Sierra Leone	Togo
1953	0.0	0.0	0.0	0.0	0.2	0.0	0.0	0.0
1954	0.0	0.0	0.0	0.0	0.7	0.0	0.0	0.0
1955	0.0	0.0	0.0	0.0	0.3	0.0	0.0	0.0
1956	0.0	0.0	0.0	0.0	0.4	0.0	0.0	0.0
1957	1.7	0.0	0.0	0.0	0.5	0.0	0.0	0.0
1958	2.4	0.0	0.0	0.0	0.1	0.0	0.0	0.0
1959	6.4	0.0	0.0	0.0	1.6	0.0	0.1	0.1
1960	5.5	0.0	0.1	0.0	1.9	0.0	0.3	0.4
1961	6.7	2.5	0.1	2.0	13.2	3.6	0.6	1.4
1962	11.9	2.6	0.1	1.2	23.0	3.4	2.6	2.5
1963	41.7	3.9	0.2	1.4	30.1	3.5	4.0	1.4
1964	16.5	3.0	0.8	2.7	51.0	4.2	3.7	2.0
1965	19.1	2.0	0.0	1.7	32.9	1.6	5.6	1.4
1966	11.7	1.9	0.2	2.1	30.2	2.7	5.5	2.8
1967	10.2	3.1	0.3	2.3	26.8	6.5	3.9	1.5
1968	8.5	1.1	0.0	2.2	25.7	2.6	3.8	0.8
1969	13.0	4.0	0.0	1.5	87.1	3.1	2.9	1.2
1970	8.0	1.0	0.0	1.2	48.3	4.2	2.4	1.0
1971	8.0	3.9	1.8	1.4	37.1	3.2	2.8	1.7
1972	17.3	1.8	1.4	3.9	25.1	1.9	3.5	1.1
1973	18.6	13.0	1.5	5.3	11.0	2.5	2.3	1.8
1974	6.0	16.4	8.6	21.4	6.5	8.8	2.8	2.2
1975	15.7	22.7	4.3	9.2	9.3	9.4	4.9	3.0
1976	7.0	4.6	5.1	13.6	0.6	6.3	5.0	3.9
1977	21.4	10.6	3.5	8.4	0.0	13.1	4.5	4.2
1978	7.2	16.1	9.2	14.8	0.0	21.5	7.1	4.2

Table 15.1 (continued)

Year	Liberia	Mali	Maurita-nia	Niger	Nigeria	Senegal	Sierra Leone	Togo
1979	17.2	19.0	8.7	12.8	0.0	22.7	8.6	6.1
1980	23.5	17.3	11.6	12.7	0.0	26.9	7.1	5.6
1981	55.2	15.8	15.8	17.4	0.0	35.6	9.5	10.0
1982	65.5	11.9	11.2	17.8	0.0	31.1	10.5	7.7
1983	62.9	15.4	12.5	24.0	0.0	33.1	8.7	7.7
1984	66.0	24.2	14.0	29.3	0.0	51.2	8.5	8.9
1985	69.1	53.5	20.3	51.0	0.0	53.2	9.0	8.5
1986	58.8	21.5	7.9	31.6	2.0	66.3	12.5	15.9
1987	42.7	16.7	8.6	30.5	20.9	53.6	14.5	10.1
1988	20.5	35.0	9.0	39.1	5.5	37.1	10.2	10.9
1989	32.0	36.3	8.2	31.2	43.7	58.7	11.5	11.2
1990	16.6	27.0	6.9	26.1	11.7	46.8	14.1	9.6
1991	43.5	50.7	5.0	36.7	8.0	31.2	5.0	14.8
1992	53.3	44.9	2.5	37.4	5.5	55.3	19.4	20.1
1993	49.0	41.9	5.3	20.8	13.0	31.7	12.7	8.8
1994	60.2	41.4	3.1	26.7	7.3	35.5	12.8	5.4
1995	51.8	34.8	2.7	18.9	3.4	24.4	10.2	3.0
1996	69.0	31.0	2.1	4.9	2.3	19.8	28.2	1.9
1997	37.6	38.5	5.6	8.0	2.4	21.0	17.3	2.0
1998	43.4	46.7	4.0	7.8	10.7	22.3	33.6	1.7
1999	25.8	41.1	2.5	3.7	33.1	29.4	17.1	5.3
2000	14.2	43.3	3.4	5.7	93.0	36.6	30.3	1.7
2001	11.2	40.3	6.6	9.5	75.3	28.1	50.7	6.1
2002	14.4	39.9	6.2	13.9	99.6	34.5	77.8	2.2
2003	39.9	52.6	20.0	15.1	93.4	48.4	41.6	5.3
2004	12.9	38.6	7.5	6.2	61.1	27.1	13.2	0.0
2005	27.5	34.6	3.4	9.0	64.3	31.4	13.6	0.0

Source: U.S. Agency for International Development, *Green Book Online*, http://qesdb.usaid.gov/gbk/ (accessed March 5, 2005)

They add that these four factors are, in turn, shaped by attitudes and values rooted in the American political system and institutions.[3] The following discussion of the four factors is based especially on Sewell and Mathieson's essay.

Table 15.2 West African Independence

Country	Date of Independence	Colonizer
Benin	August 1, 1960	France
Burkina Faso	August 5, 1960	France
Cape Verde	July 5, 1975	Portugal
Côte d'Ivoire	August 7, 1960	France
The Gambia	February 18, 1965	United Kingdom
Ghana	March 6, 1957	United Kingdom
Guinea	October 2, 1958	France
Guinea-Bissau	September 10, 1974	Portugal
Liberia	July 26, 1847	None (U.S. influenced)
Mali	September 22, 1960	France
Mauritania	November 28, 1960	France
Niger	August 3, 1960	France
Nigeria	October 1, 1960	United Kingdom
Senegal	April 4, 1960	France
Sierra Leone	April 27, 1961	United Kingdom
Togo	April 27, 1960	French-administered UN trusteeship

Source: U.S. Central Intelligence Agency, *World Factbook Online,* http://www.cia.gov/library/publications/the-world-factbook/ (accessed March 5, 2005).

Table 15.3 West Africa Regional Program (WARP) (in 2005 US$ Millions)

Year	Amount
1998	19.9
1999	29.4
2000	17.4
2001	29.3
2002	33.0

Source: U.S. Agency for International Development, *Green Book Online,* http://qesdb.usaid.gov/gbk/ (accessed March 5, 2005).

Abundance

The political and economic traditions that are prevalent today in the United States were shaped by settlers on a continent with enormous space, rich natural resources, a sparse population, and no rigid social structure. This combination encouraged individual initiative. As long as existing assets were limitless and differences over the redistribution of wealth rarely arose, there was little need to confront the difficult choice of how to divide the riches.[4]

As a result, American social development began over and again on the frontier. "This perennial rebirth, this fluidity of American life, this expansion westward with its new opportunities, its continuous touch with the simplicity of primitive society," unleashed the forces that dominated the American character.[5]

Given their national experience of relative physical abundance and few political and social controls, American citizens tend to assume that change and development are relatively easy. Consequently, a lack of initiative is frequently seen as the culprit when economic progress does not take place at home or in developing countries. Very little blame is accorded to determinants such as scarce national resources or inadequate social structures.[6]

Individualism and Democracy

The United States escaped a rigid class structure mainly because the European immigrants (and their descendants) who shaped the nation's socioeconomic structure had fled economic calamities, oppressive governments, and restrictive class structures. Thus, the individual emerged as the cornerstone of the American social and economic order. Individual rights and participation became the foundation of America's political democracy. This propels the United States to check the sometimes arbitrary central governments in developing countries.[7] On certain occasions, however, the American government ignores calls by opponents of ruthless central governments that are strong allies of the United States. A case in point is the government of late dictator Joseph Désiré Mobutu Sese Seko of Zaire (now the Democratic Republic of Congo).

A recent American president who championed the notion of individualism and democracy in U.S. foreign policy was Ronald Reagan. When Reagan first ran for the presidency, the global economy was in a serious recession. Reagan took office questioning the assumptions that undergirded economic assistance from the Western industrialized countries to the developing countries of Africa. The global economic recession offered Reagan the opportunity to preach the blessings of the free market system. He sought to unleash the energies of the free market on the American economy. Reagan promised to "get the government off the backs of hard-working Americans" to allow them to reap the full benefits of their labor with as few government regulations as possible. As time went by, he tried to sell this cause to the rest of the world.[8]

Revolution and Social Change

Even though Americans like to think of their country as a former colony, a state created by revolution, their revolution was different from others. The

American Revolution was neither radical nor ideological. Instead, it was a "practical" revolution that sought self-determination.[9]

Americans generally look at revolutions, such as the one that took place in Cuba under Fidel Castro, as bad. They believe that the costs of violent social upheaval outweigh the gains. This notion hinges on the idea that moderate reformist solutions to political conflict are good for economic prosperity.[10]

It is no surprise, therefore, that the United States observed the passing of colonialism in Africa with a mix of approval and apprehension. On the one hand, the American heritage was anticolonial; the national instinct was to applaud Africa's advance from European colonial rule to self-government. On the other hand, the fact that African nationalism emerged during the Cold War made the United States apprehensive about the challenge to the hegemony of the Western alliance on the continent. Rather than whole-heartedly supporting independence movements throughout Africa, American policy leaned toward damage limitation. When the Congo crisis erupted in 1960, the Eisenhower administration feared major damage to Western interests. Much of U.S. policy towards Africa since then, according to some observers, has been influenced by the "Congo syndrome": that is, the fear of radical nationalism in Africa.[11]

Economic Liberalism and Attitudes toward Poverty

Classical liberal economic thought remains strong in the United States mainly because Americans believe that the market mechanism should not be impeded, although occasional government interventions are welcomed. Consequently, large segments of the American public are against most forms of governmental regulation and planning.[12]

This preference for economic liberalism and free-market economies made American government officials reluctant to discuss proposals for a new international economic order (NIEO) during the 1980s. While the facilitating of equality of opportunity is considered a praiseworthy objective, any attempt to level incomes, however, is seen as a fruitless and needless endeavor. Thus, Americans are never enthusiastic about calls for tackling income inequalities, either within a country or between countries. Americans' support for basic human needs programs in developing countries and their opposition to proposals for a NIEO are consistent, therefore, with their deep-seated belief in economic liberalism.[13]

One of the earliest postcolonial links between the United States and African nationalism came in the area of American education. This link was bolstered by John F. Kennedy on the eve of his election. Kenya's Tom Mboya saw Kennedy in 1960 in connection with attempts to raise money for 260 Kenyan students who had been admitted to American colleges but did not have the money for their fares. Kennedy took up the matter with the Kennedy Foundation, and a $100,000 grant was provided.[14]

As soon as he took office, Kennedy appealed to the missionary strain in the American temperament. He said to his fellow Americans:

> Since this country was founded, each generation of Americans has been summoned to give testimony to its national loyalty. . . . Now the trumpet summons us again—not as a call to bear arms, though arms we need—not as a call to battle, though embattled we are—but a call to bear the burden of a long twilight struggle, year in year out, "rejoicing in hope, patient tribulation"—a struggle against the common enemies of man: tyranny, poverty, disease and war itself.[15]

However, the missionary factor in the American temperament is not without its dangers. Sometimes it takes the form of an ideological crusade. American anti-Communism, for example, is akin to the doctrine of manifest destiny—the combination of missionary zeal and patriotism that creates a militancy that is both outward looking and self-centered.[16]

Kennedy attempted to isolate the boy scout from the ideological crusader within the American missionary when he stated the following in his inaugural address:

> To those peoples in the huts and villages of half the globe struggling to break the bonds of mass misery, we pledge our best efforts to help them help themselves, for whatever period is required—not because the Communists may be doing it, not because we seek their votes, but because it is right.[17]

Indeed, Kennedy's inaugural address was an approximation to his real intentions. But a complete separation of the boy scout from the ideological crusader was an overly ambitious goal. Kennedy brought forward a new emphasis on the boy-scout side, but his Peace Corps and, even more clearly, his Alliance for Progress could not be completely separated from motives of ideological proselytism.[18]

The Purposes of American Foreign Aid

In examining the debate over the purposes of American foreign assistance to Africa and other developing countries, one is able to discern at least two major contending schools of thought, the classical and the critical.

The Classical School

Proponents of the classical school see American foreign aid as important if used appropriately: that is, if it can contribute to break bottlenecks (massive poverty, illiteracy, low life expectancy, malnutrition, unemployment, and so forth) in development and encourage innovation. This presupposition, Hettne suggests, is a "missionary assumption" that the United States and other Western countries are going to save the world—the idea of nature as an object to be mastered and exploited.[19] This thinking is generally ingrained in U.S. development aid policy. As an annual report of President Gerald Ford, transmitted to Congress in May 1975, for example, boldly asserts:

> Over the past decade, the economies of the developing countries have grown at an encouraging rate. This was particularly because of American assistance. Consequently, many nations no longer need assistance on the concessional terms we once extended.[20]

This school of thought can be traced to the "Western" model of development. In the words of Nisbet, "developmentalism is one of the oldest and most powerful of all Western ideas." The central idea of this development thinking is the metaphor of growth. Thus, development, according to Nisbet, is conceived as being "organic, immanent, directional, cumulative, irreversible, and purposive. Furthermore, it implies structural differentiation and increasing complexity."[21] Certainly, the emphasis within this perspective has shifted and new elements have been introduced during the history of Western civilization. The emergence of capitalism and of the bourgeoisie as the dominant class must have given a certain shape to Western developmentalism. This is one reason why some observers have branded the intellectual movements of seventeenth-century Europe as the birthplace of Western development thinking. In the twentieth century, the successes of the Marshall Plan[22] in Europe helped to set the stage for the early discussion of modern economic development.

The discussion of modern economic development in the 1950s and the early 1960s had an optimistic tone that cannot be replicated today. This optimism hinged on two factors: (1) the dynamic economic growth experienced by the industrialized countries themselves under the Marshall Plan as a successful demonstration case in development; and (2) the philosophic tradition in the West that looked upon growth as more or less inevitable. The Keynesian "revolution" in economics had taught Western economists that the state sometimes had to give a helping hand, but few doubted that the future of the developing countries was on the whole reflected in the experience of the industrialized countries. The simple formula was the following: just find out the incremental capital–output ratio and the desired rate of growth. Then one can (after giving due consideration to the rate of population growth) arrive at the appropriate level of investment needed for economic growth. Foreign capital inflows were seen as a pump-priming mechanism intended to help a recipient country's savings and tax receipts as well as investment to rise steadily.[23]

More sociologically minded authors also stressed the importance of a leading sector (private or public) and the emergence of an entrepreneurial elite as stimuli for economic development. Growth, as expounded by scholars such as Rostow,[24] was, thus, seen mainly as a function of investment, and not too many observers doubted that a process of economic growth through a series of "stages" would in the end benefit an entire country. This is why the 1960s were called the First Development Decade, in anticipation of what was expected to follow.

During the early 1970s, however, many African and other developing countries began to encounter difficulties in pursuing this development strategy. Even those economists trained in formal theory began to sense new realities. I. Adelman and C. Taft Morris, for example, capture this idea quite well:

> We had shared the prevailing view among economists that economic growth was economically beneficial to most nations. We had also greatly questioned the relevance today of the historical association of successful economic growth with the spread of parliamentary democracy. Our results proved to be at variance with our preconceptions.[25]

It is evident from this quotation that these scholars exemplified a renewed interest in the connection between economic growth and income distribution. One reason for this emphasis was the visible aspects of the extent of poverty: recurrent starvation, mass unemployment, political unrest, and so forth. What was taking place in many African and other developing countries during the development decade was growth with poverty, instead of development.

As the special report on poverty and inequality in *World Development* (1978) reveals, poverty is in fact enormously multidimensional. It may, therefore, be asked whether one can actually get a better insight into this problem with the aid of ordinary income analysis, since poverty can also be identified with reference to social and economic classes, rural and urban residence, regions, ethnic groups, and so on. A distinction should also be made between poverty on the one hand and political inequality on the other. Policies directed toward the elimination of poverty may not necessarily be the same policies as those aimed at reducing inequality. Whereas the former are concerned with irreducible and minimal issues, the latter must go deeper into the structured patterns of access to wealth, knowledge, and decision-making institutions. The former policies can be included in conventional growth models (redistribution with growth), but the latter policies are of qualitatively different types.

There are, however, those who have also argued that poverty should be structurally defined if the underlying causes of poverty are to be removed. Proponents of this view include Keith Griffin and Azizur Rehman Kahn.[26] On this level, policies of poverty elimination and policies of inequality reduction converge. This is where the main division between different schools of how to eradicate poverty can be found.

The new strategy implied in the "redistribution with growth" discussion exemplified a modification of, rather than a clear break with, previous strategies. First, the analysis retained much of the optimism of the earlier "trickle down" models in asserting that the benefits of growth, empirically, had a tendency to be concentrated in the early stages but that further increases in concentration were by no means inevitable. Second, the social engineering approach to development, as H. B. Chenery and his partners[27] claimed, was still adhered to, in that they believed that to deal with the problems of groups in poverty, governments needed to design overall programs or policy packages rather than isolated projects. This is simply a continuation of the old approach of "balanced growth," extended to include social development as well.

The rather dismal postwar record (up to the 1970s) of development plans propelled the Institute of Development Studies (at the University of Sussex, in England) to bring together a large number of experts to probe the difficult questions raised by the planning experience.[28] As emphasized by D. Seers in a contribution to this study, a plan has to take account of the government's economic and political aims, and politicians are busy people: "They have to keep an eye on the parliamentary situation and on the balance of power within the cabinet, not to speak of pondering rumors of invasion or threats of assassination."[29] Intellectuals, on the other hand, are more concerned with reaching a "correct" decision from a logical or theoretical perspective. After that, they usually lose interest.

Occasionally, as Hettne points out, politicians are intellectuals. Julius Nyerere of Tanzania, for example, was extremely interested in planning and implemented his *Ujamaa* (socialist) villages program.[30] By 1975, however, Nyerere and his government had largely backed down from the idea of communal production.

Such difficulties led Leys to suggest that planning is to be thought of in terms that require the world to be other than it is, if planning is to work. This type of situation, still according to Leys, may be said to mark the end of the dominance of a certain paradigm and initiate a heterodox search for another.[31] This search led to the critical school of thought.

The Critical School

This school sees the whole complex of American and other development aid, in many respects, to be a typical example of quasi-reform. The functions of American and other aid are perceived to be many: to make "weak" economies capable of joining the international capitalist market, to make them more able to suppress internal rebellions, to link them to one or the other of the main political blocs, and to facilitate the spread of the Western model of development.[32]

This school emerged as a cry for Marxist and non-Marxist alternatives to the classical school. The call for the "indigenization" of social sciences, particularly development theory, in developing countries is a further development of this thought. This was an outcome of the confrontation between "Western" concepts and theories on the one hand and the social reality in developing countries on the other. Obviously, the intensity of this confrontation has varied from country to country, mainly depending on the extent of Western intellectual penetration. The theories that have developed in the developing countries ("New International Economic Order," "dependencia," "self-reliance," and "indigenization") have dealt with imperialism as a Western problem connected with the accumulation process in mature capitalism. These theories have provided an antithesis and a healthy corrective to Western thought, stating that Asia and Africa contained within them legacies of European colonial systems (and by implication, legacies of American neocolonialism) that continue to retard their development processes.[33]

However, going through the later literature on development and underdevelopment (that is, from the early 1970s to the mid-1980s), one is struck by the fact that one paradigm dominated a large number of analyses, namely, what has been referred to as the "dependence paradigm." The dependence paradigm, according to a common view, emerged as a result of the merger of two intellectual trends: one can be referred to as neo-Marxism, and the other is rooted in the Latin American discussion on development. The concept of neo-Marxism has been seen as creating a certain dualism in Marxist thinking, between the traditional approach focusing on the concept of development and taking a basically Eurocentric view, and the neo-Marxist approach focusing on the concept of underdevelopment and expressing a view from the developing world. Consequently, a great deal of controversy has arisen as to the continuity or discontinuity in these two approaches.[34]

The second important trend contributing to the breakthrough of the dependence paradigm in development theory has been the Latin American "dependencia" school, rooted in the specific economic and intellectual experiences of Latin American countries, particularly during the depression of the 1930s. A development strategy emphasizing *desarrollo hacia adentro* (inward-looking development) as opposed to *desarollo hacia afuera* (outward-looking development) was made popular by the United Nations Economic Commission for Latin America (ECLA), headquartered in Santiago de Chile from 1948. The main theme that was put forward by the ECLA team of economists was that economic theory as expounded in developed capitalist countries was inadequate and there was a need for more structural approaches, including an appreciation of different historical situations and national contexts.[35] The remedy on the level of economic policy was thought to be industrialization based on import substitution. A number of observers have demonstrated that the import substitution strategy was, if not wrong, at least inadequate.[36]

This situation provided the incentive for the elaboration and extension of the dependency approach, resulting in a variety of dependency schools. Some of these views were continuations of the old ECLA strategy, while others were oriented toward Marxism.

These ideas, which so clearly emerged from the empirical reality of Latin America (and the Caribbean region), constituted the most formidable challenge that the Eurocentric concepts and theories of development had faced so far. They had a strong impact on Western scholars working in the area (notably Andre Gunder Frank)[37] and, thus formulated, they began to conquer the Western academic community from the late 1960s to the 1980s. In this way, two conflicting paradigms in development theory arose.

That the two schools of development theory ("from tradition to modernity" and "dependence to underdevelopment") constitute competing and incompatible paradigms can be seen in the obvious lack of communication between them. This is taken to be an important criterion of paradigmatic shift (in Thomas Kuhn's usage). As suggested by Foster-Carter and Hettne, this communication gap problem could be studied in the editorial policies of various journals. The new paradigm (dependency) has been reflected in the contributions to journals such as the *Journal for Contemporary Asia*, the *Review of African Political Economy*, and the *Monthly Review*. Gradually, it received a kind of mainstream legitimacy by getting fairly generous treatment in such regular development journals as *World Development*, the *Journal of Development Studies*, and the *Journal of Peace Research*. Somewhat surprisingly, one article by Dos Santos, member of the "dependencia" school, can be found in the *American Economic Review*,[38] but this appears to be an exceptional case. Dependence was never able to conquer the stronghold of the old paradigm: economic development and cultural change.

According to the classical school, an empirical analysis of the effects of American foreign aid to West African countries should find that as the level of U.S. development assistance increases to those countries, overall economic development in those countries will also increase. But according to the critical school, such an empirical study should find that increases in American development assistance to West African countries will lead to negative economic effects in those countries. Unfortunately, the quantitative exercise required to test these propositions is beyond the scope of this essay.

The Shaping of U.S. Foreign Aid Policy toward West Africa

In order to examine those factors that shape U.S. foreign aid policy toward West Africa, a conceptual framework is suggested, as presented in figure 15.1. In the framework, the key variables are political and strategic interests, economic interests, the political process, and the type and level of U.S. aid to West Africa. These serve as inputs to the transformational/political process, with feedback performing the function of continuity.

Political and Strategic Interests

American political and strategic interests in West Africa, in a general sense, are a reflection of the global interests that have shaped U.S. foreign policy since World War II. As Sewell and Mathieson suggest, although these objectives are shared by the overwhelming majority of the American population, numerous differences of opinion emerge as to their relative merits and the best way to achieve them.[39] What is frequently not clear is whether or not it is in the best interest of the United States to aid dictatorial allies, such as Mobutu and now Yoweri Museveni in Uganda, with arms and funds they go on to use to suppress their people.

It is obvious that the pursuit of any goal can be a taxing exercise for any country, even the United States. It is equally obvious that U.S. relations with African countries have been less predictable than those of, say, Western Europe, simply because of the fact that no serious Communist threat in Africa was perceived by the United States. However, there were certain African countries that were perceived by the United States as "stooges" of the former communist bloc and, therefore, received a certain amount of attention in Washington: Libya, Egypt (under President Gamal Abdel Nasser), Angola, Mozambique, and Ethiopia. While no African country has threatened the sanctity of American borders in a military sense, the United States has historically viewed the security and stability of major maritime areas (the Suez Canal, Cape Horn, the Cape of Good Hope) and mineral-rich and strategically located countries such as the Democratic Republic of Congo, Sudan, Kenya, Egypt, Somalia, South Africa, Namibia, Morocco, and Nigeria as important to its international and economic stability.

Expansionism and retrenchment in America's political and strategic interests are the results of perceived threats to the country's national interests and support or opposition at home.

A. U.S. Expansionism. Discounting the period of slavery, the United States first became actively involved in Africa in the late nineteenth and early twentieth centuries when it emerged from relative isolation and began acting as a global power, intervening in the affairs of other countries when

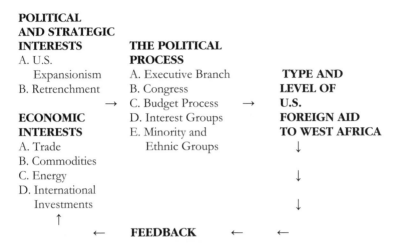

POLITICAL
AND STRATEGIC
INTERESTS
A. U.S.
  Expansionism
B. Retrenchment

THE POLITICAL
PROCESS
A. Executive Branch
B. Congress
→ C. Budget Process →

ECONOMIC
INTERESTS
A. Trade
B. Commodities
C. Energy
D. International
  Investments
↑

TYPE AND
LEVEL OF
U.S.
FOREIGN AID
TO WEST AFRICA
↓

D. Interest Groups
E. Minority and
  Ethnic Groups

↓

↓

← FEEDBACK ← ←

Figure 15.1 The making of U.S. foreign aid policy toward West Africa.

this suited its interests. There are many reasons for the shift from isolationism to expansionism. Sewell and Mathieson suggest the following: (a) a desire to emulate the Europeans who had colonized Africa and Asia; (b) the end of the seemingly limitless open frontier; (c) the transformation of the American economy from agriculture to manufacturing; (d) the increasing acceptance of Darwin's theory of evolution with its supposedly biological evidence of Anglo-Saxon supremacy; (e) the growing concept that sea power was essential for world power, which prompted the United States to build a large modern navy.[40] Evidence of U.S. expansionism is provided, for example, by the United States' evocation of the Monroe Doctrine to plant its flag in the Caribbean, Latin America, Hawaii, Puerto Rico, Cuba, and elsewhere. A later example of U.S. expansionism is provided by its forcible removal of residents from Cabo Delgado in 1981 as part of its efforts to monitor the Soviet navy in vital sea lanes in the Pacific Ocean.

B. Retrenchment. U.S. strategic thinking about African countries began to change in the late 1960s, influenced strongly by unrest at home and humiliation in Vietnam. The emphasis shifted from the direct use of U.S. troops to an increased reliance on friendly governments and local forces. This new policy had a corollary: the United States would continue to supply arms, equipment, and other forms of support necessary to help its African allies counter external aggression or internal subversion led or inspired by the Soviet Union or China.

As Volman points out, between 1973 and 1978 the volume of arms transfers to Africa increased tenfold, from $300 million to more than $3 billion
annually, making Africa the second largest arms market in the developing
world (the largest being the Middle East). Most of the arms received by
African countries came from three major sources: the Soviet Union, France,
and the United States. The Soviet Union provided about 50 percent of the
arms, France about 25 percent, and the United States about 13 percent. The
remaining 12 percent were supplied by several European producers (Great
Britain, West Germany, Italy, Switzerland, and Sweden), by the People's
Republic of China, and by two developing-world arms producers (Israel and
Brazil).[41]

The Reagan and Bush administrations in particular gave a higher priority
to providing military and security-related assistance than to providing economic aid to African countries. This was at a time when there was a sharp
decline in overall development aid to the continent and its economic and
political woes were mounting.

Economic Interests

As stated earlier, before 1960, U.S. economic activities in West Africa were
relatively insignificant (if we discount the Atlantic slave trade, of course). As
the U.S. economy matured, American businesses became more active in the
region.

A. Trade. Following years of rapid expansion, in the first half of 1982, U.S.
exports to Africa abruptly reversed their high pace of growth. Shipments
were off 8 percent in the first six months of 1982, and total American
exports to sub-Saharan Africa fell below the $6 billion mark.[42] Many factors
were responsible for this reversal.

One was the fact that West Africa, like other regions, was in economic crisis. Continued stagnation in export earnings, high rates of population
growth, and mounting burdens of international debt plagued many countries in the region. In some cases, these problems were exacerbated by poor
policy decisions.

Furthermore, most West African countries are monocrop or single-
mineral economies. Because of the economic reorganization in the developed countries in the 1980s (due to recession, unemployment, stagnation,
and economic uncertainties), some West African countries could not find
suitable outlets for their goods.

Nigeria and South Africa were suffering the effects of soft world markets
for oil and minerals. In Nigeria, the worldwide oil glut of 1981–82 caused a
drastic shortfall in export revenue. Oil sales to the United States, Nigeria's

leading customer, were off by nearly 40 percent in the first five months of 1982 alone. South Africa's export earnings experienced a similar decline due mainly to the drop in the price of gold.[43] Both Nigeria and South Africa, therefore, took firm steps to restrict their imports in order to protect their balance of payments.

Also, U.S. exports to West Africa declined because of the strong dollar. The dollar appreciated nearly 15 percent against the special drawing right (SDR) between April 1980 and April 1982, cutting deeply into U.S. export competitiveness worldwide, and especially in the capital-scarce markets of Africa. The strong dollar also cut into the profits the oil-exporting African countries would have gained.[44]

B. Commodities.   In spite of the economic problems West Africa faces, the United States continues to be dependent on some of the region's minerals. And as Jackson suggests, the Arab oil boycott of 1973–74 demonstrated the usefulness of a vital natural resource as a weapon of political policy among developing world producers. African minerals have also become essential to the American economy and have established their role in the future of America as the sole super power. Certain minerals are concentrated in just a few regions of the world. Southern Africa, for example, has 86 percent of the world reserves of platinum group metals, 53 percent of manganese, 52 percent of cobalt, 64 percent of vanadium, and 95 percent of the world's reserves of chromium.[45] It comes as no surprise, thus, that the United States supported the racist government in South Africa for many years.

Jackson also notes that American vulnerability in terms of minerals has become as acute as its oil dependency in many respects. The point was underscored in the 1980 Santini Congressional Report, cited by Jackson, which concluded that "no issue facing America in the decades ahead poses the risks and dangers to the national economy and defense as US dependency on foreign sources for strategic and critical minerals."[46] The American Society of Metals reiterated this view when it suggested that "A cutoff of our chromium supply could be even more serious than a cutoff of our oil supply. We do have some oil but we have almost no chromium."[47]

C. Energy.   Since U.S. consumption of energy is higher than its production of energy, it seeks a sufficient supply of energy at predictable prices (which is not necessarily the same as low or unchanging prices) for adequate but prudent use by industries and individuals. But historically, U.S. consumption has been less than prudent. Decades of abundance and declining real prices led to wasteful consumption. In 1979, for example, per capita consumption of energy in the United States, the equivalent of about 12,350 kilograms of coal, was more than 56 percent higher than average consumption in industrialized countries (7,892 kilograms), and nearly a hundred times higher than that in low-income countries other than China and India (129 kilograms). The reduced supply of oil and price rises of the 1970s altered this pattern.[48]

In West Africa, Nigeria emerged as one of the richest countries in the world in terms of natural resources in the 1970s and the 1980s, and oil represented the key to its new wealth. Concomitant with this wealth came an emergent position of political leverage vis-à-vis the United States and other industrialized countries.

Nigerian petroleum production in 1980 yielded a daily average of 2.2 million barrels of crude. It was prized by Americans for its high-quality, low-sulfur content, which can yield more gasoline per barrel than the heavier Middle Eastern crude. American importers bought a million barrels, or almost half of the production, every day. U.S. imports of Nigerian oil grew so rapidly in the decade between 1970 (when the United States imported none of it) and 1980 (when Nigeria provided as much as 16 percent of American oil imports) that Nigeria emerged as a creditor to the United States.[49]

D. International Investments. U.S. investments in Africa are highly visible and important to both the sending and the receiving countries. Despite the fact that these investments further the "dependency" of African countries upon the United States, it is obvious that the investments provide the host countries with the capital and technology needed to create some jobs. But clearly, South Africa has emerged as the biggest winner in terms of American investments in Africa.

The increased level of U.S. investments in South Africa provides a substantial benefit to U.S. economic interests. The favorable balance of trade with South Africa is particularly important in view of the continuing U.S. deficits in its international balance of payments and its troubles with economic recession at home. The favorable terms of trade are attractive, too: largely because of cheap African labor, the annual rate of return on direct American investments in South Africa, for instance, ranged from 17 percent in 1968 to 19 percent in 1976.[50]

The trade needs of the two countries are also compatible. The United States sells industrial goods that significantly benefit South Africa's economic expansion in such areas as computer technology, heavy-capital goods, oil exploration, and chemical industries. In return, the United States imports crucial minerals, such as platinum, chromium, and gold from South Africa. All these U.S. activities helped to perpetuate the racist South African system for a long time, since South Africa viewed them as partial approval of its social, economic, and political systems.

The Political Process

A. The Executive Branch. This branch of the American federal government has no centralized structure for making decisions or implementing policy on the broad range of issues that concern West African countries. Functional areas of responsibility are widely dispersed among federal departments and agencies, each of which jealously guards its independence and influence. Interdepartmental rivalries and conflicts are inevitable and often result in fundamental policies.

For example, as Sewell and Mathieson note, the State Department oversees relations with individual governments in West African countries. As a group, it assigns them a lower priority than either the industrialized countries or Russia and its former allies. The State Department maintains control over bilateral development assistance through the United States Agency for International Development (USAID). Because economic development is only one of the State Department's foreign policy concerns, it often views development assistance as primarily a political instrument, a view that at times has caused major conflicts within the agency.[51]

With authority so diffused, the role of the individual USAID policymaker often becomes exceedingly crucial. Who does or does not dominate the bureaucracy varies from time to time and from administration to administration.

B. Congress. Congress plays a role in determining foreign policy that is perhaps unique among industrial countries. It shares authority over foreign policy—including power over war, treaties, appointments, and commerce—with the executive branch. In addition, Congress has effective control over budgetary authorizations and appropriations (fondly referred to as "the power of the purse"), including foreign aid expenditures. This wide range of powers makes it possible for Congress to negate executive branch initiatives if it so wishes or, alternatively, to put forward its own programs. Power is, however, more dispersed within Congress than within the executive branch. For example, 13 of 19 standing committees have some responsibility for foreign economic expenditures and legislation, and almost 50 subcommittees have some jurisdiction over issues significantly affecting West African countries.

However, Congress's contemporary record in foreign affairs is mixed. The executive branch maintains that legislators have been mainly obstructive. Congress claims that on some issues, particularly in the area of international development policy, it has taken a constructive lead. It was Congress, not the executive branch, that initiated the reforms of the American foreign aid program in 1973 designed to make the program focus on basic human needs.[52]

C. *The Budgetary Process.*   Decision making within the American government is closely tied to the process of formulating, authorizing, and appropriating the annual federal budget. The budget itself has become the main vehicle for determining federal defense and domestic social policy. The process works well, except for those areas of public policy that are not large budgetary items. Although foreign aid is only a small part of the overall transactions between the United States and West African countries, the annual foreign aid legislation tends to dominate discussions of policies toward those countries. As the aid bill goes through the legislative process, it consumes an inordinate amount of the time and attention of both the executive branch and Congress.[53]

D. *Interest Groups.*   A variety of organized groups affect American policies toward African countries. Trade unions, for example, which generally have played a leadership role in social reform efforts in the United States, remain a potent political force despite the fact that the overall rate of unionization of the labor force has declined. However, many unions in recent years have hardened their outlook on relations with developing countries for reasons involving both self-interest and altered domestic economic conditions.

Until the mid-1960s, when the United States still enjoyed a monopoly in the manufacture of capital- and technology-intensive products, the trade unions favored free trade and open markets. As the trade balance swung into deficit and the United States' manufacturing sector diminished relative to the service sector, some unions altered their position. Organized labor continues to support foreign aid to developing countries, but it would like to see it focused more narrowly on the poorest countries. Labor is worried because of the fact that the transfer of technology leads to loss of American jobs. Indeed, outflows of private capital, whether government subsidized or not, are seen as exporting American jobs to developing countries, and technology transfers are seen as selling the "United States heritage."[54]

E. *Minority and Ethnic Groups.*   American policies toward African and other developing countries are very much influenced by minority and ethnic groups that have more impact than their sizes might indicate. The growing interest of African Americans in U.S. policies toward Africa, for example, is a result of raised consciousness over civil rights within the country. There was a growing unwillingness among African Americans to see the United States continue to support the once white-dominated regime in South Africa. This type of position facilitated President Carter's decision in 1977 not to lift economic sanctions against Rhodesia (now Zimbabwe). It also forced President Reagan to implement Congress-designed economic sanctions against South Africa in the 1980s. African American sentiment is deeply rooted in the history of the African diaspora.

As Jackson reminds us, a significant stratum of African Americans has always been stimulated by the foreign policies of the United States because they have considered Africa as their homeland. They have identified the slave labor of their ancestors as the capital that built and enriched the Southern plantation economy that was fundamental to the later industrialization of the North; this slave labor represented their investment in America's national development. It was a stake not to be surrendered at any cost. After the end of slavery, African Americans began their entry into the foreign policymaking process determined to play a significant role.[55]

Their pursuit of power has been indefatigable. From the American Colonization Society (ACS) of the nineteenth century to TransAfrica today, African Americans have continued their efforts to influence American policies toward Africa, not always in union, sometimes in a contradictory fashion, and infrequently with success. Like other Americans of foreign (though not enslaved) descent, African Americans have sought to use American power in the interest of their ancestral homeland. These African Americans have also looked incredulously at the ease with which immigrants born a generation ago in Europe have risen to the commanding heights of American decision making, while African Americans, rooted in America for more than three centuries, have until recently been so systematically excluded that they had never gotten close to the levers of executive power (and we are now learning that even the once well-liked and respected Colin Powell was being marginalized as Secretary of State by white males in the George W. Bush administration).

The United States' Foriegn Aid Doctrine in Sub-Saharan Africa

Characterizing the United States' foreign aid doctrine in Sub-Saharan Africa as one that mostly promotes America's self-interests is not far-fetched. On the one hand, when the United States wants certain African countries to respond favorably to its political and economic interests, there is an increase in the amount of aid going to those countries. On the other hand, when the United States perceives certain countries to be antagonistic toward its interests or sees them as "communist" countries, the amount of American aid going to those countries decreases, with the exception of a few humanitarian crises.

The United States, while never a true colonial power in the region, has sought repeatedly to use the continent of Africa for its vast resources or for strategic purposes. The United States used African slave labor as fuel for continental expansion and agricultural development in the earliest years of American development. During the Cold War, the United States valued

Africa for strategic purposes. American policy focused on encouraging governments that claimed to be democratic, while deterring and hindering the development of socialist countries sponsored by the USSR. In the post–Cold War era, the United States has again turned to Africa for its natural resources.

One example of recent U.S. policy in the region is the African Growth and Opportunity Act, which was signed into law by President Bill Clinton on May 18, 2000. This bill authorized a new trade and investment policy for sub Saharan Africa. Proponents of this bill claimed that the intent was to enhance economic stability and growth in the region through free trade and private investment, which would then raise the overall well-being of the people.

Opponents of the bill cited six major shortcomings that would hurt, rather than assist, African nations in their development: (1) the bill did not mandate debt reduction; (2) it did not protect or mandate an increase in development assistance funding; (3) it continued the emphasis on conditionalities; (4) it did not mandate any human rights standards; (5) it lacked any measures to ensure African leadership and direction and ensure that poor households would benefit from investment; and (6) it would have the effect of shrinking the public sector.[56]

It is my position that the measure is an example of the efforts of political elites and big business to promote American economic interests and hegemony in the region rather than the well-being of West Africans, a position that seems to be in congruence with the position of critics of the bill.

Walters concludes, similarly, that the motives behind the act are the self-serving efforts of the power elites in America to promote their largely economic interests over and above the social interests of Africans. Walters cites an increase in the economic viability of Africa as the impetus for the act. He argues that signs of increased democratization and political stability have made Africa more inviting to U.S. economic interests: in Africa, "25 countries [have] experienced elections since 1990."[57]

In his analysis, Walters claims that the United States has a strong and increasing interest in African economies. "What made the sudden economic interest in Africa possible . . . [were] the new signs that some parts of the continent were experiencing significant rates of economic growth."[58] The rate of economic growth in Africa from 1994 to 1997 showed a steady increase in the viability of African markets. In 1994, the rate of growth was 2.6 percent; in 1995, 3.2 percent; in 1996, 4.4 percent; and in 1997, 3 percent.[59] Furthermore, the return on the rate of investment in Africa reached 33.3 percent, more than doubling the rate of 14 percent found in Asia.[60]

As a result of this growth, "American export sales to Africa increased by 13.5% between 1995 and 1997, reaching $6.1 billion." According to Walters, it is this growth and the increased political stability of Africa that triggered the African Growth and Opportunity Act.[61]

The ideology behind the African Growth and Opportunity Act, the idea that increased American investment and business in Africa will promote socially beneficial change, is by no means new. Under the Carter administration, a similar ideology was applied to ending apartheid in South Africa. Carter held that "economic development, investment commitment and the use of economic leveragee . . . seems to [be] the only way to achieve racial justice [in South Africa]."[62] According to Kevin Danaher's analysis, "this was no blind belief in the impersonal forces of the market. Carter recognized that the dependence of the South African economy on Western capital conferred political leverage on U.S. corporations."[63]

Carter assumed that American economic influence on South Africa would be beneficial in ending apartheid. However, Danaher refutes this assumption: "Throughout South African history, economic growth and racial oppression have been remarkably compatible. The editors of *The Wall Street Journal* acknowledged that South Africa itself is the best argument against the notion that economic growth necessarily brings political liberalization."[64]

The Reagan-Bush victory at the polls over the Carter-Mondale ticket in 1980 revealed a shift in attitude toward the use of American power in foreign relations. Unlike the Carter-Mondale administration, which was sensitive to criticisms and to the ambivalence of American power overseas, the Reagan-Bush administration took office with a clearly articulated and internally consistent view of the United States' political and economic role in global affairs. This had implications both for the international political struggle between the United States and the Soviet Union, and also for American policies in international economic matters and toward development.[65]

According to an Overseas Development Council (ODC) communiqué of 1982,[66] four major themes were dominant in shaping the Reagan-Bush foreign aid doctrine. These themes were (1) the meaning of power in the 1980s; (2) the nature of the Soviet Union's foreign policies; (3) the causes of the developing world's instability; and (4) the divergent and common goals of the Western alliance.

The point behind the first theme was that an increase in American military power was necessary to reestablish American security and permit the United States to exercise its hegemony. The Reagan and Bush administrations believed that one of the most significant challenges to American foreign policies in the 1980s was the notion that the United States had to establish relations with a broad range of developing countries. It was believed that if such relations were constructive enough, U.S. security would be protected and enhanced.

The second theme hinged on the notion that the Soviet Union's enhanced strategic and conventional military capacities made it possible for it to become "aggressive and expansionist," thereby threatening vital American security interests. The belief here was that the Soviet Union was intent on spending as much money as possible to reach overall military superiority over the United States. Consequently, the call was made for the United States to outspend the Soviet Union if America was to put a check on that country's "aggressive and expansionist" behavior.

The presupposition behind the third theme was that the developing world was the most likely terrain for what was then referred to as the "East-West conflict." Two reasons were suggested for this. The first was that the developing world was the arena for an increasing degree of political instability and potential regional conflicts. The second was that the Soviet Union would capitalize on such developments in the developing world to expand its (the Soviet Union's) power and influence at the expense of the West. It was, thus, believed by the Reagan and Bush administrations that the United States should in effect attempt to raise the cost of the adventurism of the Soviet Union by instituting policies that supported indigenous efforts in the developing world to preclude Soviet intervention.

The fourth proposition emerged from the idea that the Western alliance must pay whatever price necessary to increase its military capacity in the European theater and coordinate anti-Soviet policies in the developing world. It was perceived by Reagan and Bush that there was a growing divergence between the United States and Western Europe on East-West matters and on the potential results of détente. For Western Europe, détente meant peaceful relations and rapid growth in East-West trade. For the United States, in contrast, détente meant a strong Soviet military machine making gains in Africa, Asia, Latin America, and the Middle East.

These premises led Reagan, especially, to embrace the philosophies of Presidents Roosevelt and Truman in overseas economic policy, for which Reagan's critics were quick to label him a reactionary. Reagan emphasized his return to earlier principles during his speech in Philadelphia on international economic development in October 1981.[67]

During the speech, Reagan called for a reexamination of American assistance efforts to assure that they were promoting private enterprise as opposed to merely reinforcing the growth of the public sector. He went on to suggest five major principles that would guide his administration's foreign aid programs. The first was that international trade had to be stimulated by opening up markets within and among countries. The second involved the proposition that development strategies had to be tailored to the specific needs and potential of individual countries and regions. The third suggested that development assistance be guided toward self-sustaining productive capacities, particularly in food and energy. The fourth called for improving the climate for private investment and the transfer of technology accompanying such investment. And the fifth was that a political atmosphere be created that would facilitate practical solutions instead of "relying on misguided policies that restrain and interfere with the international marketplace or foster inflation."[68]

It is no surprise, therefore, as Rondinelli points out, that four of these themes were reflected in USAID's Development Administration Strategy Paper issued in 1981.[69] As Rondinelli also notes, USAID development administration goals included the following:

1. Sector-specific institutional development—improving institutional performance in policy formulation, technology transfer, and program management and strengthening the capacity of institutions in high-priority sectors to provide public services and promote private investment in order to achieve "sustainable benefits for broad groups of people."

2. Strengthening local initiative—improving the managerial performance of local enterprises in developing countries and assisting governments to strengthen local entrepreneurship, group cooperation, local government, and provincial development "in ways that stimulate local initiative and self-help, but avoid imposing burdens on the poor."

3. Improving capacity in management service institutions—strengthening the capacities of selected institutions in developing countries to provide relevant and practical management training, education, consulting, and applied research.

4. Policy reform—selectively supporting the reform of economic, financial, and administrative policies and government structures through technical assistance and the application of new management technologies.[70]

This strategy clearly emphasized the improvement of managerial performance in developing countries' institutions and the expansion of administrative capacity in the private sector. But as Eberstadt observes, the actions of the Reagan administration[71] were contrary to its stated objectives. And as Eberstadt puts it,

> Instead of bringing America's foreign aid policies back into alignment with the goals and ideal that had originally animated them under Roosevelt and Truman, the Reagan Administration allowed American programs to continue down the path charted in the 1970s. So smooth, in fact, was the trajectory that it would be difficult to tell which administration was in power from the statements and actions of its development apparatus. No less than during the Carter years, American development programs under Reagan seemed to be at systematic variance with the objectives of the international order we nominally supported. The administrators of these programs, moreover, appeared increasingly intent upon concealing the discrepancy from the American public.[72]

The interests of American investors and businesses became intertwined with the interests of the ruling elites. American investors catered, for example, to the white government in South Africa and relied on cheap black labor in their firms. According to Danaher, "although a small minority of South African Blacks attained some affluence, capitalist growth [was] quite compatible with white supremacy."[73]

A stratification theory analysis can be applied to the African Growth and Opportunity Act. The upper class is defined totally in economic terms. The upper-class members are the big business owners who seek African markets for expansion and cheap labor. They own their own businesses, or have invested heavily in their corporations and control large amounts of capital. The big businesses have gained influence over political elites in America through campaign contributions and lobbying groups. Political leaders are subordinate to these elites because they rely on their campaign donations for reelection. The capitalist nature of these businesses means that they are heavily profit seeking, in order to increase their own financial resources and stay competitive with other businesses. According to stratification theory, all this will lead to social problems. However, the problems will not be felt in America; rather, they will occur in Africa. Capitalist investments will greatly benefit a small minority and have only limited effects on the majority, as in South Africa during apartheid, because the African Growth and Opportunity Act did not mandate sufficient social controls on the investments. As Walters states, the African Growth and Opportunity Act "does not go far enough. It does not mandate a balanced strategy that alone would achieve the goals of trade and investment; it does not mandate debt relief; it does not mandate labor standards that would spread the fruits of such economic activity to the common person."[74] Rather, the act makes African nations dependent on American investment.

According to Ann Louise Colgan, in the 1990s Clinton became known as a great friend to Africa, thanks to his administration's successful public relations efforts. He made a well-publicized trip to the continent, the first really major trip by an American president in U.S. history. Clinton expressed great concern for Africa's challenges and a commitment to help the continent reach its potential by encouraging trade, promoting debt relief, and supporting democracy. The symbolism of Clinton's African policy in many ways succeeded in masking the real damage that was done by his administration's indifference to the genocide in Rwanda, its failure to address the growing HIV/AIDS crisis, and its negligence in terms of peacekeeping efforts in West Africa and elsewhere.[75]

During the presidential debate at Wake Forest University on October 11, 2000, George W. Bush declared that Africa was important but not a priority. As he put it, "Africa's important. And we've got to do a lot of work in Africa to promote democracy and trade. It's an important continent. But there's got to be priorities. And the Middle East is a priority for a lot of reasons as is Europe and the Far East, and our own hemisphere."[76] Bush had hinted at his position earlier that year when he was asked about appropriating $300 million out of the surplus to help fight AIDS in Africa. His response was that the United States could rally the world to help fight AIDS, as long as it was not with American funds. In his own words, "Oftentimes we're well intended when it comes to foreign help, but the money never makes it to the people that we're trying to help. And so I think before we spend a dime, we want to make sure that the people we're trying to help receive the help necessary. But this is a compassionate land. And we need to rally the people of compassion in the world to help when there's terrible tragedy like this in Africa."[77] All that changed with the terrorist attacks on the World Trade Center in New York City and the Pentagon in Washington, DC, on September 11, 2001. Since then, Bush has acted in consistency with U.S.-African relations with Africa since decolonization, in which successive administrations have been driven by calculations of Africa's geostrategic significance, with the United States seeking to foster military and security relations that advance its own interests. Bush's policies have, similarly, been motivated by the need for Africa's natural resources and have been geared toward the promotion of closer trade and investment ties with key African states.

As Colgan observes, 2005 was another year of George W. Bush's "compassionate showmanship" rather than a year of sea change. Colgan adds that while George W. Bush pursues policies toward Africa similar to those of his predecessors, the aspects that set him apart and harm Africa's interests in significant ways are two key tenets of his foreign policy philosophy. The first has to do with Bush's rejection of the process and principle of multilateralism when it comes to addressing urgent global issues. The second has to do with Bush's embrace of the ideology of the religious right and his promotion of this ideology in his domestic and international policies. These tenets undermine Africa's priorities, especially the fight against HIV/AIDS. Meanwhile, Bush's White House likes to point out that he met with 25 African heads of state in his first two years in office, that he announced new initiatives on HIV/AIDS and aid and pledged to significantly increase U.S. funding for both, that he traveled to five African countries in five days in 2003, and that his administration recognized that genocide was taking place in Darfur, Sudan, and claimed to be addressing the issue. However, with duplicity, Bush has been promoting his own economic and military agenda while portraying himself as a great friend to Africa.[78] Salih Booker has dubbed all this "Bush's lackluster Africa policy."[79]

The 100 percent multilateral debt cancellation for impoverished countries called for by civil society groups and some governments in Africa was put on the table for the first time during discussions among the Group of Eight leaders in June 2004, and then during discussions among their finance ministers in the fall. Despite statements supporting the initiative, an agreement remains elusive, due to differences between the United States and the United Kingdom. The United States, on the one hand, claims that it supports multilateral debt cancellations for forty-two countries, to be paid for by the World Bank and the International Monetary Fund (IMF), and argues that a move from loans to grants at the World Bank is one key to breaking the debt cycle. Nonetheless, the United States Treasury Department refuses to recognize the illegitimate nature of the debts and has indicated that its main concern is "debt sustainability." This concept refers to the amount of debt a country can carry without inhibiting economic growth, but it does not take into account the fact that no amount of debt can be sustainable for African countries at a time when they are dealing with the worst health crisis in human history. The United Kingdom, on the other hand, supports a less ambitious debt deal for about twenty impoverished countries, but it opposes the idea of the World Bank's using its own resources to cover the debts. Instead, the United Kingdom wants the G 8 countries to take over the debt service payments on behalf of eligible countries for an initial ten years, but without debt cancellation. In January 2004, the United Kingdom launched this new plan when the finance minister, Gordon Brown (now the prime minister) signed a deal with Tanzania to take over more than 10 percent of the debt payments it owes to the World Bank and the African Development Bank for ten years.[80]

The Millennium Challenge Account (MCA) set up by George W. Bush in 2002 was to increase American foreign aid over three years by an additional $10 billion, so that by 2007 the United States would be spending 50 percent ($15 billion) more on foreign aid than in previous years. However, by 2005, the MCA had disbursed nothing. In 2004, $1 billion was appropriated for the account; for 2005, the amount was slightly increased to $1.25 billion, which is only half of what the White House requested. Even more disturbing is the fact that the MCA was set up to direct aid only to a handful of countries that meet specific political and economic conditions, meaning that the initiative does very little to support poverty reduction in the world's most impoverished countries because most of them are ineligible for its funding. In contrast, over the three years ending in 2004, flows of American aid to Israel, Egypt, Jordan, Iraq, Turkey, and Afghanistan have been equal to the flows of aid of the rest of the world combined. In addition, development efforts in African countries will be undermined because 70 percent of the aid is tied to an obligation to use the money to buy goods and services from the United States.[81]

While multilateral trade negotiations such as those at the World Trade Organization (WTO) ministerial meeting in Doha in 2001 and the Cancun trade meeting in 2003 have proved difficult, the United States remains focused on securing bilateral and regional trade agreements that can facilitate greater access for American corporations to African markets. It continues to push for a free trade agreement with the five nation Southern African Customs Union (SACU), which will give preferential access to American businesses. In 2004, the African Growth and Opportunity Act was amended and extended, and Bush announced that 37 countries would be eligible for the program in 2005.[82]

The 2006 U.S. African trade profile indicates that the trade between the United States and Africa remains highly concentrated, both in terms of partners and in terms of products. A very small number of African countries account for a significant amount of exports and imports. The United States' major trading partners in Africa are the main oil producers on the continent: Angola, Gabon, and Nigeria. These countries are also the largest recipients of American investments in Africa. In 2003, 70 percent of all U.S. imports from Africa were of oil, and 80 percent of the African Growth and Opportunity Act imports were petroleum products.[83]

The Bush administration's policies on HIV/AIDS in Africa are completely inadequate in light of the magnitude of the crisis. The President's Emergency Plan for AIDS Relief (PEPFAR) began disbursing money in 2004, with a focus on only a dozen countries. For 2005, Congress approved $2.9 billion for HIV/AIDS, tuberculosis, and malaria programs globally, a slight increase on the amount for 2003 but still less than needed and very far from Bush's original promise of $3 billion per year for HIV/AIDS in Africa alone.[84]

Beyond the inadequate funding levels, the United States' policies on HIV/AIDS have been in contradiction to the most important ways of combating the pandemic. Placing priority on its ties with the pharmaceutical lobby, the Bush administration has approved only the use of expensive name brand drugs instead of promoting access to cheaper, generic versions of essential HIV/AIDS medications. The brand name drugs generally cost three times as much as the generics, thereby reaching only about one third of the potential beneficiaries. Moreover, the Bush administration's embrace of the ideology of the religious right has led it to promote an abstinence only approach to HIV prevention strategies in the United States and overseas. This approach dangerously places a premium on ideology over science and undermines the most effective ways for combating the spread of the disease in Africa and other parts of the world. An abstinence only prevention program can do little to meet the needs of women, when most of those contracting HIV are staying faithful to one partner, and when effective prevention clearly hinges upon women's sexual and reproductive rights.[85]

Far more significant to the Bush administration has been its war on terrorism. U.S. military activities have been growing, particularly in East Africa, where military bases and access to ports and airfields have become more and more strategically important. Meanwhile, the new $100 million antiterrorism initiative announced by Bush in 2003 will not even offset the money being lost by the tourist industry in Kenya as a result of frequent terror warnings from Washington, DC.[86] Particularly controversial was Bush's claim in his 2003 State of the Union Address that British intelligence had discovered that Iraq was seeking to buy uranium from the West African nation of Niger. Officials and diplomats disputed the evidence for this claim, especially after the document describing the alleged attempted purchase, which was presented to the United Nations Security Council by Colin Powell, was found to be a forgery.[87]

Conclusion: A Marshall Plan for West Africa

American foreign aid to West Africa has been geared toward reinforcing long-standing U.S. economic, moral, and political objectives throughout the continent, because these objectives have been considered to be fundamentally sound. It has been a widely held belief among American policymakers that if such objectives are sound, then U.S. power in itself can be a beneficial and effective form of foreign aid.

American economic aid to West Africa has been used to promote development in a few countries because it has dovetailed with the desire to maintain existing international economic relations and at the same time to garner political influence in the region. Aid, however, has been a second-best solution for West Africa: It has meant neither a change in the management of U.S.–West African relations nor a real distribution of economic benefits. In addition, because American aid has been dependent on domestic and international conditions, it has been an unreliable source of capital and technology in West African countries. Thus, I conclude here that only a Marshall Plan–type aid program will be a viable means to help West Africa get out of poverty and move toward economic development.

In 1947, America announced the Marshall Plan. This was an economic aid package given by the United States to the Western European countries to rebuild their economies after the devastation caused by World War II. This aid package was considered both economically and politically motivated. America, politically and strategically, hoped to maintain a firm political relationship with Western Europe, thereby widening its sphere of influence in the Cold War system. The economic gain would come in the form of increased trade that would be formalized in the 1947 General Agreement on Trade and Tariffs (GATT) signed in Geneva. The Marshall Plan also helped the United States confirm its economic dominance, which at the end of the war was reflected in the fact that it held two-thirds of the world's gold stock.[88]

One of the conditions of the plan was that the aid would not be presented as individual aid packages for the different countries but would be presented as a whole, to be administered through coordination of economic activities among the European nations. Thus, the United States insisted on the creation of the Committee of European Economic Cooperation (CEEC) and its maintenance as a permanent organization:

> This was the origin of the Organization for European Economic Cooperation (OEEC), which was to be one link in the intermeshing chain of obligations that Western European governments accepted in these first post-war years. As such it is part of the story of European Integration.[89]

This brief history reveals the role of the Marshall Plan in the integration of Western Europe and reveals it as a model for the economic aid package that I am suggesting for the development of West Africa.

The model proposed for West Africa is a mirror image of the Marshall Plan that would "force" the West African nations to work together in the administration of aid by coordinating economic structures and activities. After a proper adjustment period, this could eventually lead to further integration, especially integration of political structures and activities. This could ultimately lead to peace and economic development in the region.

The basis for the notion that region-wide integration will lead to peace has its roots in the theory presented by Said and myself in the article, "Ethnicity's Threat to Peace."[90] In this article, we present the idea that "ethnicity has become a force of political instability."[91] We analyze the role of ethnicity, the nation-state, and conflict in the following way:

> The nation-state is the typical arena of ethnic conflict. State governments often try to ignore and suppress the aspirations of individual ethnic groups or impose the values of the dominant elite. In response, ethnic groups mobilize and place demands upon the state, ranging from representation and participation to protection of human rights and autonomy. Ethnic mobilization takes on a variety of forms, ranging from political parties to violent action.[92]

This is clearly the situation found in West Africa, which exhibits conflict due to ethnic schisms that can only be solved by letting go of ethnic and state divisions to allow for region-wide neofederalism, hence moving from "statehood" to "peoplehood" in order to create a working peace system.[93] We propose this in our article:

> Given the inadequacies of African nation-states in the face of ethnic challenges, there is a need for discussion and action that does not assume the continued utility and viability of the nation-state system. We should explore moving away from conceptual regimes of "statehood" to "peoplehood" and from "state rights" towards "rights of people." We should explore recognizing the legitimacy of cul-

tural differences and instituting structures with local geographical authority with regard to social and religious affairs.[94]

This perspective lays the foundation for the idea that the integration of the political structures of the various nation-states in West Africa will lead to peace. This concept goes hand in hand with that of the functional integration of political, social, and economic structures to achieve a "working peace system" proposed by integration theorist David Mitrany.[95]

Mitrany's approach to integration calls for an "overlay of political divisions with a spreading web of international activities and agencies, in which the interests and life of all the nations would be gradually integrated."[96] Mitrany goes on to state that functional integration would be "pragmatic, technocratic and flexible. . . . As functional agencies are formed and joined, national divisions would become . . . less important."[97]

This would work in the West African case because, if the functional theory of integration actually does yield flexible structures, they would constitute the element in the supranational governmental structure that would give the various ethnic groups the consideration and autonomy they need in order to be able to live peacefully along with other ethnic groups. In terms of economic development, this political and social integration would lead to an integration of interests that would consequently lead to various agents working in unison to achieve a common goal: economic development.

Economic development and modernization, on the other hand, lead to increased conflict, not only between ethnic groups but among social classes as well. This perspective is presented by Ted Gurr in his revolutionary theory that modernization leads people to migrate from rural areas to urban centers in search of jobs, and that this, in turn, leads to overpopulation and declining living standards. As a result, the concept of relative deprivation comes into play, leading to conflict. Furthermore, if government structures are not flexible enough to adapt to ethnic and socioeconomic diversity, then political instability and totalitarian regimes emerge.

Therefore, for the successful application of the African Marshall Plan, the supranational structure created must be rooted in democracy. James Robert Huntley's theory of *pax democratica* suggests that peace and international order can be achieved only through democracy, and this will also be true for economic interdependence and development.[98] A democratic system will develop, and it will ultimately lead to peace through the assimilation of the various West African ethnic groups into government.

The theory of *pax democratica* presents the common interests of democracies, which include the following: "Promotion and consolidation of the spread of democratic ideals and practices, including the protection of human rights and the Rule of Law. . . . [and] . . . Giving better form and rules to the global economy: furthering free market systems, unfettered trade, international investment, monetary integration and harmonized economic policies."[99] This ideally would lead to peace and increase economic development in the West African area.

Notes

1. United States Agency for International Development (USAID), *Economic Assistance Loans and Grants Online* (2005), www.usaid.gov.

2. E. R. May. *"Lessons" of the Past* (New York: Oxford University Press, 1978), ix.

3. J. W. Sewell and J. A. Mathieson, *The Ties That Bind: US Interest and Third World Development* (Washington, DC: Overseas Development Council, 1982), 5–8.

4. Ibid., 5.

5. F. J. Turner, *The Significance of the Frontier in American History* (New York: Frederick Ungar, 1963), 28.

6. Sewell and Mathieson, *The Ties That Bind*, 5.

7. Ibid., 5–6.

8. V. B. Khapoya, *The African Experience*, 2nd ed. (Englewood Cliffs, NJ: Prentice Hall, 1998), 293.

9. Sewell and Mathieson, *The Ties That Bind*, 6.

10. Ibid.

11. N. Chazan et al., *Politics and Society in Contemporary Africa* (Boulder, CO: Lynne Rienner), 372–73.

12. Sewell and Mathieson, *The Ties That Bind*, 6.

13. Ibid., 7.

14. A. A. Mazrui, *Africa's International Relations* (Boulder, CO: Westview Press, 1977), 156.

15. Ibid., 156–57.

16. Ibid., 157.

17. Ibid.

18. Ibid.

19. B. Hettne, *Current Issues in Development Theory*, SAREC Report R15 (Gothenburg, Sweden: SAREC, 1978), 44–45.

20. U.S. Development Coordinating Committee, *Development Issues* (Washington, DC: Government Printing Office, 1975), i.

21. R. A. Nisbet, *Social Change and History* (New York: Oxford University Press, 1969), 7.

22. On June 5, 1947, at the commencement exercise at Harvard University, Secretary of State George C. Marshall announced what came to be known as the Marshall Plan: America's intention of making a significant financial contribution to rebuild a wartorn Europe. The major goal of the plan was to promote economic integration and cooperation among European countries. Between 1948 and 1952 (when the plan ended), $13.3 billion had been spent on the plan, with over half of this amount going to England, France, and Italy. For details, refer to H. T. Nash, *American Foreign Policy: A Search for Security*, 3rd ed. (Homewood, IL: Dorsey Press, 1985), 42–44.

23. For more on this perspective, see A. I. MacBean and V. N. Balasubramanyam, *Meeting the Third World Challenge* (New York: St. Martin's Press, 1976), 147–48.

24. W. W. Rostow, *The Stages of Economic Growth: A Non-Communist Manifesto* (Cambridge: Cambridge University Press, 1960).

25. I. Adelman and C. T. Taft Morris, *Economic Growth and Social Equity in Developing Countries* (Stanford, CA: Stanford University Press, 1973), vii.

26. K. B. Griffin and A. R. Kahn, "Poverty in the Third World: Ugly Facts and Fancy Models," *World Development* 6, no. 3 (1978).

27. H. B. Chenery and M. Bruno, "Development Alternatives in an Open Economy: The Case of Israel," *Economic Journal* 72, no. 285(1962): 79–103; H. B. Chenery and I. Adelman, "Foreign Aid and Economic Development: The Case of Greece," *Review of Economics and Statistics* 48, no. 1 (1966); H. B. Chenery and A. M. Strout, "Foreign Assistance and Economic Development," *American Economic Review* 56, no. 4 (1966).

28. M. Faber and D. Seers, eds., *The Crisis in Planning* (University of Sussex, Brighton, England: Institute of Development Studies, 1972).

29. D. Seers, "The Prevalence of Pseudo-Planning," in ibid., 21.

30. Hettne, *Current Issues in Development Theory*, 25. The *Ujamaa* (socialist) villages program was part and parcel of Tanzania's Arusha Declaration, drawn up by Julius Nyerere in February 1967 as a means for the country to achieve self-reliance.

31. C. Leys, "Underdevelopment and Dependency: Critical Notes," *Journal of Contemporary Asia* 7, no. 1 (1977).

32. Hettne, *Current Issues in Development Theory*, 25.

33. T. Hodgkin, "Some African and Third World Theories of Imperialism," in *Studies in the Theories of Imperialism*, ed. R. Owen and B. Sutcliffe (London: Longman, 1972), 106.

34. A. Foster-Carter, "Neo-Marxist Approaches to Development and Underdevelopment," in *Sociology and Development*, ed. E. de Kadt and G. Williams (London: Oxford University Press, 1974); A Foster-Carter, "From Rostow to Gunder Frank: Conflicting Paradigms in the Analysis of Underdevelopment," *World Development* 4, no. 3 (1976).

35. P. J. O'Brien. "A Critique of Latin America Theories of Dependency," in *Beyond Sociology of Development*, ed. I. Oxaal (London: Routledge and Kegan Paul, 1975).

36. World Bank, *World Development Report* (Washington, DC: World Bank Publications, 1977).

37. A. G. Frank, "The Development of Underdevelopment," in *The Political Economy of Development*, ed. K. Wilbur (New York: Random House, 1979).

38. T. Dos Santos, "The Structure of Dependence," *American Economic Review* (May 1970).

39. Sewell and Mathieson, *The Ties That Bind*, 9.

40. Ibid., 10–11.

41. D. Volman, *A Continent Besieged: Foreign Military Activities in Africa since 1975* (Washington, DC: Institute for Policy Studies, 1980), 4.

42. U.S. Department of Commerce, *Business America* (Washington, DC: Government Printing Office, 1982), 22.

43. Ibid.

44. Ibid.

45. H. F. Jackson, *From the Congo to Soweto* (New York: William Morrow, 1982), 169–70.

46. Ibid., 182–83.

47. Ibid., 183.

48. Sewell and Mathieson, *The Ties That Bind*, 28.

49. Jackson, *From the Congo to Soweto*, 171.

50. M. A. El-Khawas and B. Cohen, *The Kissinger Study of Southern Africa* (Westport, CT: Lawrence Hill, 1976), 28.

51. Sewell and Mathieson, *The Ties That Bind*, 28.

52. Ibid., 31.

53. Ibid., 32.

54. Ibid.

55. Jackson, *From the Congo to Soweto*, 121.

56. R. Walters, "The Africa Growth and Opportunity Act: Changing Foreign Policy Priorities toward Africa in a Conservative Political Culture," in *Foreign Policy and the Black (Inter)national Interest*, ed. C. P. Henry (Albany: State University of New York Press, 2000), 21–26.

57. Ibid., 20.

58. Walters, "The Africa Growth and Opportunity Act," 19–20.

59. Ibid., 20.

60. Ibid.

61. Ibid.

62. K. Danaher, *In Whose Interest? A Guide to US–South African Relations* (Washington, DC: Institute for Policy Studies, 1984), 42.

63. Ibid.

64. Ibid., 51.

65. N. Eberstadt, *Foreign Aid and American Purpose* (Washington, DC: AEIPR, 1988), 44.

66. Overseas Development Council, *The Reagan Administration's Foreign Aid Policy* (New York: Praeger/ODC, 1982).

67. Eberstadt, *Foreign Aid and American Purpose*, 49; see also J. Herbst, *US Economic Policy toward Africa* (New York: Council on Foreign Relations, 1992).

68. D. A. Rondinelli, *Development Administration and US Foreign Aid Policy* (Boulder, CO: Lynne Rienner, 1987), 99. For the decline in the level of Africa's share of U.S. aid during Reagan's presidency, consult TransAfrica, "Developing Africa: The Shrinking US Share," in *TransAfrica Forum* (Washington, DC: TransAfrica Publications, 1982).

69. Ibid., 100-101.

70. Ibid.

71. This is also true for the Bush-Quayle administration, mainly because Bush was afraid of diverging from the course already set by Reagan. Some observers have cited Bush's timidity in similar matters (especially in the economic sphere) as one of the major reasons why he lost the 1992 presidential election.

72. Eberstadt, *Foreign Aid and American Purpose*, 50–51.

73. Danaher, *In Whose Interest?* 48.

74. Walters, "The Africa Growth and Opportunity Act," 32.

75. A.-L. Colgan, "Dark Continent? Poverty, AIDS and War: The Everyday Tsumani," *Africa Policy Outlook 2005* (March 1, 2005), 3, www.africaaction.org.

76. Issues 2000, *George W. Bush on Foreign Policy*, www.4president.org/issues/Bush2000/Bush2000foreignpolicy.htm (accessed March 26, 2005).

77. Ibid.; see also Export-Import Bank, "Ex-IM Bank Provides $1 billion to Finance Sub-Saharan African Purchase of HIV/AIDS Medicines from US Pharmaceutical Firms," EXIM.gov, October 23, 2000, Gopher:exim/gov/press/jul1990.html.

78. Colgan, "Dark Continent?" 3.

79. S. Booker, "Bush's Lackluster Africa Policy," *Chicago Tribune,* July 3, 2003, http://www.chicagotribune.com.

80. Colgan, "Dark Continent?" 4.

81. Ibid., 5.

82. Ibid., 6.

83. Ibid.

84. Ibid., 7.

85. Ibid.

86. Booker, "Bush's Lackluster Africa Policy."

87. "Foreign Policy of the George W. Bush Administration," Wikipedia, http://en.wikipedia/org/wiki/foreign_policy_of_the_george_w._bush_administration (accessed March 26, 2005).

88. D. Urwin, *The Community of Europe: A History of European Integration since 1945,* 2nd ed. (New York: Addison Wesley Longman, 1995), 17.

89. Ibid., 19.

90. A. A. Said and A. K. Bangura, "Ethnicity's Threat to Peace," in *Rethinking Peace,* ed. R. Elias and J. Turpin (Boulder, CO: Lynne Rienner, 1994).

91. Ibid., 98.

92. Ibid.

93. Ibid., 103.

94. Ibid.

95. B. F. Nelsen and A. C.-G. Stubb, eds., *European Union: Readings on the Theory and Practice of European Integration* (Boulder, CO: Lynne Rienner Publishing, 1998), 93.

96. Ibid.

97. J. R. Huntley, *Pax Democratica: A Strategy for the 21st Century* (New York: St. Martin's Press, 1998).

98. Ibid., 11.

99. Ibid.

16

The West African Enterprise Network

Business Globalists, Interregional Trade, and U.S. Interventions

Anita Spring

Introduction

This chapter discusses the "new generation" of African entrepreneurs who were organized into the West African Enterprise Network (WAEN) between 1993 and 2003, as a result of a project funded by the United States Agency for International Development (USAID) and other donors. The aim was to "strengthen private sector capacity to pursue regional and international business opportunities and to develop and implement a reform agenda targeting trade and investment."[1] There was not an absence of trade between the United States and various African countries before this intervention, but some of the changes that this intervention accomplished (for example, enhancing interregional communication and changing cumbersome trade regulations) were helpful to the participant network members themselves and to subsequent trade and interaction between West African countries and the United States. The changes also helped regional trade.

Unlike small-scale informal-sector vendors and other large formal-sector African businesses, WAEN members were and continue to be business globalists. WAEN at its height included thirteen West African country networks. (Two other regional enterprise networks, in East and southern Africa, and a Pan-African network also were formed between 1998 and 2003.) This chapter discusses the collection of data from a sample of male and female network members in Ghana, Mali, and Senegal (interviews were also carried out with members from ten additional African countries in East and southern Africa). An analysis of these data shows that WAEN members, like their counterparts in the other regional networks, differ from many other formal-sector entrepreneurs within their own countries because they stress financial accountability and transparency, hold to good business ethics, hire employees outside of kinship affiliation, stress efficient business management and organization, and use the latest technology. They view themselves as players in the global economy and advocate for changing trade regulations. The findings show that WAEN aimed to be an engine of development through private sector expansion using global business methods and ethics.

In the 1980s, one kind of development intervention funded by donor agencies focused on improving the capabilities of government policymakers as a means of enhancing trade capacity to strengthen the private sector.[2] However, this brought little success. In the early 1990s, there was a change of focus and U.S. project interventions targeted young, successful entrepreneurs in order to build business networks as a means of enhancing the private sector. Another aim was to enhance Anglophone and Francophone business connections and break down trade barriers between countries that often looked to former colonial powers and/or only to their English- or French-speaking partners. The type of interventions changed again in the late 1990s and the early years of the twenty-first century to partnering of businesspersons (business matchmaking) between business owners in the United States and West African countries.

This chapter discusses the formation of a West African business network and its characteristics. It queries WAEN's efficacy, and assesses how it functioned as a role model for modernity and development. Finally, the achievements and weaknesses as perceived by network members, the U.S. donors, and the researchers are discussed. The reasons for the demise of the formal networks are also discussed.

Origin of the Networks

The creation of an African network of businesspersons stems from a 1991 conference sponsored by the Africa Bureau of the U.S. Agency for International Development (USAID), the Organization for Economic Development (OECD), and the Club du Sahel, a unit within it.[3] The OECD had carried out a study of private enterprise in the late 1980s in Francophone West Africa. It found that there was mistrust of the private sector by government; financial lending was limited and short-term; "modern-sector firms" did not do cross-border trade; national markets were small; and private sector organizations were weak (for example, chambers of commerce and employers' federations were influenced by government). The conference brought together participants from Francophone and Anglophone West Africa, and at its conclusion, participants asked for donor assistance to establish a private sector businesspersons' network in West Africa.[4] Funding came from two USAID Africa Bureau divisions, and the Implementing Policy Change Project (IPC) began at the end of 1992. As the intervention

Table 16.1 USAID and Other Donor Funding for WAEN and the Other Networks

	WAEN	EAEN	SAEN
1993 (USAID)	$400,000 (7 networks)		
1994 (USAID)	$450,000 (10 networks)*		
1995 (USAID)	$450,000 (13 networks)		
1996 (USAID, France, Canada, European Union)	$550,000 (13 networks)*		
1997 (USAID, France, Canada)	$550,000 (13 networks)*		
1998 (United States, France, World Bank, Switzerland, Belgium)	$300,000	$200,000 (4 networks)	$230,000 (7 networks)
1999 (United States, France, World Bank, Switzerland, Belgium)	$250,000	$225,000 (6 networks)*	$250,000 (10 networks)*
2000 (United States, France, World Bank, Switzerland, Belgium)	$300,000	$430,000 (6 networks)**	$490,000 (11 networks)**
2001 (proposed)	$200,000*	$210,000 (6 networks)	$275,000 (11 networks)
2002 (proposed)	$160,000	$175,000 (6 networks	$225,000 (11 networks)
Total	$3,610,000	$1,240,000	$1,470,000

*This includes funds for regional conference, ranging from $40,000 (EAEN) to $100,000 (WAEN) per conference.
**This includes a USAID technical assistance contract of $112,500 each for EAEN and SAEN.
Source: Deborah Orsini, "Case Study of: EAEN, SAEN, WAEN," Organization of Economic Cooperation and Development (OECD) DCD (2001), 10/ANN5, www.oecd.org/dataoecd/16/37/1886229.pdf: 25.

continued, additional funding came from the other main donors, the World Bank, and the Club du Sahel of the OECD. In total, there were six bilateral and two multilateral donors involved, as shown in table 16.1. This was the beginning of a ten-year run for WAEN in an intervention project that subsequently spawned the East African Enterprise Network (EAEN, 1998–2002) and the Southern African Enterprise Network (SAEN, 1998–2003/4) composed of thirty-one national chapters, as well as a Pan-African network (AEN, 2000).

*econom.
politic.*

The IPC's goals for WAEN were as follows: (1) to create a West African regional network and at least twelve national networks; (2) to formulate strategic plans "for achieving policy reforms favorable to the private sector"; (3) to formulate financial plans for sustainability; and (4) to aid in information exchanges between the country networks.[5]

The timing of this project coincided with the liberalization of the political environment. Deborah Orsini noted that "formal private sector organizations . . . [had] . . . lost much of their credibility and the younger generation [was] seeking an effective forum for discussion and action."[6] Governments in the decades following independence operated state-owned enterprises (SOEs) and parastatals. They often imposed legal and regulatory frameworks on private enterprises, both to collect revenues and to control them. For indigenous Africans, the private sector was limited, and the brightest and the best chose to enter government service or the education sector. When the state divested some of its SOEs, government bureaucrats often were the first to buy them. Orsini and coauthors wrote that the "state's bureaucracy, run by an educated administrative class, enjoys a great deal of discretionary control over the formal private sector through an array of regulations and licenses. This educated elite often used its power to extract 'rents' from the private sector, which had to beg favors to escape government control."[7]

By contrast, under the IPC, regional economic integration was a main objective of the networks; there was also hope for West African–U.S. trade. Before this time, there had been nothing like a private sector network; the Economic Community of West African States (ECOWAS) and West African Economic and Monetary Union (UEMOA) were strongly criticized in the 1990s as being ineffective (although WAEN subsequently became a member of both). Most formal-sector transactions were with European markets rather than with neighboring countries, while the informal sector, by contrast, did much of the regional trade "outside the legal framework."[8] National priorities and the Anglophone and Francophone division contributed to a focus on national markets.

The IPC intervention provided ten years of technical assistance in West Africa to create recognizable national networks that could also have "active liaison with interested donors and U.S. and European private sector groups."[9] The country networks of Ghana, Mali, and Senegal (the three most successful networks) were constituted in 1993, followed by those of Benin, Burkina Faso, and Nigeria, while those of The Gambia, Guinea, Mauritania, Niger, and Chad were constituted in 1994. In Nigeria and The Gambia the political situation was not as favorable as in Ghana, Senegal, and Mali, but the chapters endured, unlike the networks in Chad, Guinea, and Togo that died out.[10] Networks in East and southern Africa were created in 1998 and lasted until about 2003. A Pan-African network was founded at the

Millennium Conference in Addis Ababa, Ethiopia, in 2000, where 300 delegates from the three regional networks, as well as donors, agencies, and others, met to elect officers and sign incorporation documents.[11]

A two-person team (one person from the United States and the other from France) established the country and regional networks and also worked with the three-person WAEN executive committee. Representatives of the networks went to the United States for international trade symposia. By the end of 1995, there were four regional network conferences in West Africa. With start-up funds to support country and regional secretariats, the consultants helped the country and regional networks to hold meetings and conferences, develop newsletters and websites, draft supporting documents, and act as business presences in their country and region. The Ghana network, the first one formed in 1993, became the site of the secretariat for West Africa. The regional network secretariat coordinated donor and business programs as well as all aspects of association maintenance. The country networks maintained Web sites and membership lists, promoted Internet connectivity, and disseminated information/newsletters. They involved themselves in providing capacity-building services (management audits and training), and a few raised venture capital funds (VCFs).

Network members were carefully selected to participate first by the donor team and then by members themselves. Orsini and Courcelle noted the characteristics of the network members who were recruited as being between 30 and 45 years old, employing ten to fifty persons, averaging a turnover of $1,000,000, and not being active in other private sector organizations. Many had been educated in the United States and Europe and returned to start their own firms, usually by investing personal equity in their businesses. Others left salaried positions within their countries and also used their own funds to start their businesses. Still others were managing directors of large businesses. Many already had their own international networks. Many, but not all, had traveled abroad to study and work, but returned to Africa to pursue business opportunities rather than remaining in well-paying jobs overseas.

WAEN country chapters worked with their governments as advocates for the private sector and viewed themselves as players in the global economy. Participants saw the networks and themselves as engines of development through private sector expansion. They had strong views on the need for financial accountability, the utilization of global methods, and the ethical conduct of business; these were also criteria for network membership. Some had learned and learned to believe in such techniques and concepts from university education and formal-sector positions abroad; others had learned them in their own countries.

Another major criterion was that network members be apolitical. McDade and Spring found that network members were often personally acquainted and frequently met with presidents, cabinet ministers, and other important officials. They queried how such contacts could be apolitical.[12] The answer, repeatedly mentioned by members, was that they initiated and maintained dialog with powerful officials to reform the regulatory environment and that they rejected government patronage. A Senegalese member met with the president and other government officials in his role as head of a national professional association. He was hired by the government as a consultant on urbanization projects and was able to provide an independent opinion that differed from the government's. WAEN members sought to interact with officials who supported good business ethics and financial transparency, and who were against "rent-seeking." This made sense, because these were criteria for network members themselves. One Senegalese member headed his country's chapter of Transparency International. These characteristics set network members apart from other business people. Both the donor team and the members themselves sought out for network membership like-minded business people who were trustworthy in their financial dealings.

Most members served as advocates for the private sector and employed global business practices. Some had learned these practices in other formal sector employment, both outside and inside their countries. The Senegalese member of the WAEN secretariat said the larger issues of global strategies and informed economic policies were more important than simply brokering business deals (other members thought that business deals were more important, as explained below). A Ghanaian network member affirmed, "We want to achieve a voice and do business without being appendaged to government." In 2000, the Ghanaian network highlighted the visibility of the private sector business community and presented recognition awards, including one to the president, Jerry Rawlings.

Ghanaian members stated that one advantage of being a network member was the cooperation with other business owners. The network chair commented: "one of the benefits of the network is that members do not feel that they are working in isolation." Data from a survey of sixty members from all regions carried out at the Millennium Conference in 2000 by the U.S. Corporate Council on Africa reiterated this point; the data showed that network members kept in frequent communication by e-mail and telephone, and consulted each other frequently about business problems.[13]

The literature on WAEN and the other regional networks includes works of several types: journal articles,[14] book chapters,[15] and a book in which several members were featured.[16] Additional published materials included the networks' own newsletters,[17] magazine articles by network members,[18] and the regional networks' Web sites.[19] The Web sites provided information on the networks in general, specific country networks, and individual members. As well, there were reports from conferences and funding agencies.[20] WAEN also left "footprints" on the Internet.[21]

There have been other USAID-funded projects and initiatives that focused on U.S.–West Africa trade. The West Africa International Business Linkages Program (WAIBL), implemented from 1998 to 2005, focused on investment in seventeen West African countries including Ghana, Mali, and Senegal, and was responsible for $220 million worth of trade between the United States and West Africa.[22] It sponsored fifteen conferences, on agribusiness, shea butter, handicrafts, financing, renewable energy, marketing, and infrastructure, as well as forging public-private partnerships.[23] It also recorded 611 business transactions between U.S. and African firms and business persons.[24] USAID's Trade and Investment Policy Program (ATRIP) project matched individual businesspersons with U.S. partners between 1998 and 2001. The National Summit on Africa (1997–2001) took as one of its causes lobbying for and making Americans aware of the passage of the Africa Growth and Opportunity Act (AGOA). It organized forty-eight state chapters and held a national summit in Washington, DC, to build an American constituency for issues related to Africa in terms of trade and development.[25] AGOA was passed in 2000 and accelerated in 2004 (AGOA Acceleration Act of 2004).[26] Annual progress reports on AGOA (for example, the 2005 AGOA Competitiveness Report, the 2005 Annual Report to Congress) and success stories highlight West African countries and particular entrepreneurs, but WAEN members are not mentioned. In 2000–2001, the WAEN newsletters urged network members to attend meetings held by the U.S. embassy trade unit explaining AGOA's provisions. However, no data were collected either by WAEN or for this study on whether and how network members may have benefited from AGOA.

Finally, in 2005, the African Global Competitiveness Initiative (AGCI) was initiated by USAID. Its objectives were to improve the policy, regulatory, and enforcement environment for private sector–led trade and investment; to improve the market knowledge, skills, and abilities of workers and private sector enterprises; to increase access to financial services for trade and investment; and to facilitate investment infrastructure. In West Africa, AGCI was operating in Accra, Ghana, and Dakar, Senegal.[27] Progress reports will appear in future years.

Methods Used and Data Collected on WAEN

Spring and McDade collected interviews with sixty-two network members from all three regions and ten countries that constituted a sample of over 10 percent of the entire Pan-African network (about 550 members in total).[28] Table 16.2 gives information only for the interviewed members of WAEN (thirteen from Ghana, two from Mali, and five from Senegal). Ghanaian members were interviewed in 2000, both in their country by McDade and Spring and by Spring at the Millennium Conference in Ethiopia, at which

Table 16.2 WAEN Members Interviewed by Business Position, Business Acquisition, and Business Enterprise

Country	Members inter-viewed	National network member-ship	Business position (n = 20)		Business acquisition (n = 19)			Business enterprise (n = 19)	
			Owner	Manager	Self	Family	SOE*	Single	Multiple
Ghana	13	44	13		9	3	1	9	4
Mali	2	17	1	1	1			1	
Senegal	5	18	5		5			3	2
Total	20	79	19	1	15	3	1	13	6
%	25%	95%	5%	79%	16%	5%	68%	32%	

* SOE (state owned enterprises)

Source: Data for Ghana, Mali, and Senegal taken from McDade, Barbara, and Anita Spring, "The New Generation of African Entrepreneurs: Changing the Environment for Business Development and Economic Growth," *Entrepreneurship and Regional Development* 17 (2005):1–26.

WAEN was well represented; some were reinterviewed by Spring in 2006. McDade also interviewed network members in Botswana in 2000. Individual members from Madagascar, Swaziland, Zambia, and Zimbabwe were interviewed by Spring at the Ethiopian conference, a time when there was great anticipation of the Pan-African event. Spring also interviewed Ethiopian and South African members in their countries in 2000, and then again in 2004 and 2006, respectively. The Malian network interviews were conducted by Delores Koenig in 2001 as part of her research there, and Spring also conducted interviews in Tanzania in 2005.

Interviewees visited in their own countries, as opposed to those who were interviewed during conferences, were contacted by e-mail, fax, and cell phone. Lists of network members and their businesses were obtained from the WAEN Web site and secretariat in Accra. Data on individual entrepreneurs and their businesses were obtained by administering surveys and asking narrative questions, as well as through profiles that were in the newsletters and websites. The head of the Ghanaian chapter and the regional executive committee members from Ghana and Senegal were interviewed for their perspectives on network structure, operational activities, and organizational constraints. Data from the surveys and narratives were analyzed using WINMAX^R (a software program that organizes qualitative data into designated categories) to construct profiles of members and country networks. Summary statements were based on demographic characteristics, business activities and behavior, and network relationships. To understand the business climate in the countries involved, other businesspersons, financial officers, and donors were interviewed in the countries visited. Secondary data were collected from the publications and documents of these diverse sources, as well as through Internet searches.

Findings from the Interviews

Network members primarily financed their business start-ups with their own equity. They used savings from professional jobs and previous businesses, many of which were in the United States. Their formal-sector employment facilitated their ability to obtain loans and credit. Some received loans and gifts from parents, other family members, and spouses. None reported receiving start-up funds from government agencies, although some received grants for product development and marketing from government business promotion units and international donors.

Almost all network members had bachelor's degrees, and some had graduate degrees (MBAs, JDs, and PhDs). About 60 percent had received these degrees in the United States or Europe. Many interviewees worked in major corporations outside Africa after completing their education. Others worked in their own countries in family, local, and international firms before venturing off on their own. A Ghanaian member received his MBA in the United States, and then worked for a Fortune 500 financial services corporation in New York. After returning home, he founded a financial services company and was a co-founder of the Ghanaian Stock Exchange.[29] Some Ghanaian members earned high salaries in firms such as Morgan Stanley and Goldman Sachs before returning to Ghana to start their own businesses. The Ghanaian chapter kept a list of "returnees" from the United States in particular, and over half of the network members were part of this reverse diaspora.

The Ghanaian network, being the oldest and largest, had the most diverse businesses. These included manufacturing (glass bottles, furniture, toys and wood products), real estate and housing development, information technology (IT), public relations, agro-business (poultry, timber), consultancy services (educational, environmental impact, and so forth), financial and investment services, and office services and specialty printing. Of the Malian members interviewed, one headed a travel/tourism company and the other was a bank official who did not own his firm. Senegalese members' businesses included manufacturing (chemicals, furniture, and sanitation facilities), construction, consultancy services, IT, and professional firms (accounting, architecture, and law).

A common image of African entrepreneurs is ownership of several businesses to avert financial risks in uncertain economic environments.[30] However, this practice was not prevalent among the network members interviewed. Table 16.2 shows that the majority (68 percent) owned and operated only one enterprise. The other 32 percent owned multiple enterprises, primarily in manufacturing, transportation, and agro-business, industries that may be associated with greater financial risks. However, instead of avoiding risk, some of these multiple enterprise owners said that they sought to expand their company's original function. This included a consultant who added manufacturing, and an accountant who added real estate, both in Senegal.

Revenue data were not requested because they were awkward to collect and often unreliable, although some owners volunteered this information. During site visits, information was gained on the value of company revenues and assets by observing physical facilities and equipment, type of products or services, and reported marketing and distribution strategies. The national coordinator of WAEN stated that revenues of members' businesses ranged from US$300,000 to $10 million annually, although several newly established businesses had not reached $300,000.

As noted previously, members considered transparency and ethical business practices the most important criteria in evaluating prospective new members. In Senegal, a network member also headed Transparency International's national chapter, which had 250–300 members. He helped write and implement a code of financial and accounting practices that was adopted by businesses in twenty Francophone countries. The networks created trust among members within each country, and between members in different countries and regions. The primary reason for the small numbers of members was that membership was selective; all members were carefully scrutinized in each country network to evaluate backgrounds and business practices to ensure that new members had good character and ethics.[31] Hence, members felt that they could trust the advice of a network member in another country, even one whom they had never met. Members who desired market expansion aimed to visit other WAEN countries and interact with network members whom they trusted, "not only for business, but for everything." Members often noted that the main asset of the network was "the ability to pick up the phone and get the information you want from a network member, and that is forever, it doesn't go away." One Senegalese member gave the example of being able to send his children to Ghana for a visit with a network member's children. These sentiments were expressed repeatedly, and members believed that a major advantage of the networks was their help in building trust among African businesspersons. (Many still maintain these contacts, even though the networks have been dissolved.)

The networks led to interactions between Anglophone and Francophone country members. "We don't know the other African countries. We're always trying to get things from Europe or America," was a common refrain. One

Senegalese member located Arabica coffee, not through Europe but in Uganda and Ethiopia. For water bottling, he dealt with network members from Ghana and Ethiopia. Another cooperated with a company in The Gambia to manufacture vinyl doors, and helped two network members in Mali do business feasibility surveys free of charge.

Women comprised 23 percent of the total network membership but comprised 40 percent of the forty-five members in Ghana and 20 percent of the twenty-five members in Senegal. However, some national chapters, such as Mali, had no women members. Women network members were in all business sectors, and most said their sex was not a disadvantage in terms of their business or network status. They knew women faced gender issues such as childcare responsibilities, restrictions in credit access, lack of land ownership, and other gender biases, and they wanted mechanisms to address these topics. Some acted as spokespersons for women's issues in their countries, while others sponsored training courses for women entrepreneurs (from micro- to medium-scale businesses) and hired female managers. Still others assisted market women and traders with bookkeeping skills.[32] In general, women network members focused on business innovations and the expansion of their own businesses, like their male counterparts. All were in formal-sector, urban businesses but were aware of the large number of women in informal-sector enterprises. They believed that improvements in the business climate, such as eliminating corruption, benefited all levels.

Most men and women network members were married and had children. In the Ghanaian chapter, many had spouses who were also in business, and some worked together. In a few instances, both spouses were network members but had separate businesses. About a third had parents who were business owners, while some had parents who were professionals or in management. Others came from families in which the parents were civil servants, political officials, or teachers. Social and professional relationships among members were more likely to cut across kinship, ethnic group, and local area lines. Those interviewed in Senegal took time to explain the religious diversity in their network, in terms of Muslim and Catholic members as well as members from the four Islamic sects in Senegal.

Network members believed they were in a position to effect changes to stimulate the private sector and impact economic growth in their country and region. Their outward-looking global business perspective and inward focus interpreted Africa's economic crises as fertile ground for business opportunities. As well, they were interested in developing markets outside Africa; as noted above, there was much discussion of AGOA in WAEN's *Trade Flash*, a monthly e-mail newsletter, however, no data were collected on the members' participation in AGOA, which may have occurred after the network's demise.

Network members lauded the following: (1) being financially transparent and having good business ethics; (2) having efficient business management and organization; (3) using the latest technology in business and professional lives; (4) trusting fellow network members; (5) doing intra-African and South-South commerce/trade; (6) having an optimistic, "can-do" attitude; and (7) cooperating with government, but not accepting patronage or being in a parasitic relationship. More than half also viewed themselves as players in the global economy.[33]

Those who had studied or worked in the United States were more likely to think of business methods that worked in the United States and some brought them back to their countries. A fascinating example was a Ghanaian member who put together the idea of an electronic trade discount service for Ghanaians who had access to the Internet. He started one of the first Web sites (bestbuyghana.com) where people could purchase goods without the use of credit cards (there were no credit card services operating in Ghana, although some people had "international" credit cards).[34] Local firms (most were in Accra) paid to list their retail stores, products, and services on this Web site. Anyone with Internet access could download a discount coupon (the business owner and the vendor received copies). The buyer could then go to the business location and pay for the items or services and receive a 20 percent discount. The site owner noted that, unlike American companies, the businesses involved did not have to worry about merchandise being damaged in shipping or deal with returned merchandise, the downfall of many "dot coms" in the United States in the late 1990s and the early years of the twenty-first century.

WAEN members discussed the idea of constituting a number of subnetworks (for example, for accounting, law, transport, consultancy services, and so forth) that would link the Anglophone and Francophone countries together to solve common problems and become more in line with U.S. standards.[35] However, only one subnetwork, NetForce, was actually constituted. Beginning in 1994, a woman network member from Senegal (who owned one of Senegal's largest accounting firms) set up a professional subnetwork of accounting firms across seven countries. There was one participating firm per country (Benin, Burkina Faso, Ghana, Guinea, Niger, and Nigeria) and two from Senegal, making a total of eight members. NetForce standardized training, procedures, and formats across the region, essentially harmonizing formal accounting standards and methods for firms throughout West Africa. It trained trainers and produced manuals on quality control and auditing in both French and English. By 2003, NetForce no longer met, but it still functioned to enable members and their firms to cooperate on business services.

In 2000, WAEN established the West Africa Enterprise Fund (WAEF), to raise $30 million for investment in network member businesses. Borrowers who agreed to abide by global standards could access it.[36] Two years later, WAEF invested capital in a bank in The Gambia, the Trust Bank Ltd. This investment was the first cross-border listing on the Ghana Stock Exchange, and within a year's time, it almost doubled in value. However, after three years in which only $6 million were raised, WAEF was abandoned.[37]

WAEN members paid dues and expended their own funds to attend network conferences, another criterion for membership. They were optimistic and enthusiastic about their businesses, network contacts, and business prospects. Until 2001, they were enthusiastic about the networks. Compared to network members, other entrepreneurs interviewed expressed the feeling that they were pushing against government entrenchment, their country's poverty, and many business constraints (for example, corruption, the lack of a trained workforce, or the effects of HIV/AIDS on employees).[38] In difficult situations, by contrast, network members felt both empowered and self-confident, and able to carry out their realistic business plans.

Achievements of WAEN

From 1995 to 2001, a combination of WAEN newsletters and donor agencies' reports were produced, evaluating the country networks and WAEN itself. Both network members and donors (table 16.3) acknowledged all types of successes, such as changes in regulations/policy reform, membership in organizations and agencies, business deals, provision of a country presence for commerce, and information dissemination.

WAEN members pointed mostly to the accomplishment of business activities, the formation of a private sector business network, and the making of social/business friends. Some mentioned the subnetwork, NetForce, attempts at a VCF, regulatory changes, and memberships in various agencies. WAEN gained official observer status at regional economic organizations (for example, ECOWAS and UEMOA) and signed memoranda of understanding with multilateral agencies. Others mentioned how country chapters lobbied for and succeeded in achieving changes in government regulations in selected countries and sectors.

By contrast, project reports for USAID tended to focus on private sector activities in terms of regulatory reform, policy work, studies undertaken and information disseminated, and linkages and memberships in regional economic bodies and agencies; some business deals were mentioned.[39] The emphasis reflected the differences between business people who need to show profits and keep their companies functioning, in spite of being project participants, and the United States' goal of changing the business climate for regional and international trade. Generally the network members' lists of achievements and the implementing donor's list (table 16.3) vary in emphasis.

Table 16.3 Achievements of WAEN According to Implementing Agency

---

A $15 million, privately capitalized West African Enterprise Fund set up to promote regional trade and investment in the ECOWAS region;

WAEN organized four regional conferences to promote intraregional trade linkages and debate regional integration issues;

WAEN created NetForce, a professional cluster of indigenous auditing firms in the region, to improve professional standards and obtain regional contracts;

WAEN members utilized the network to identify skilled labor in other countries (managers, construction supervisors);

WAEN was active in the launching of a regional consultative entity on economic integration policy, the Forum West Africa (FOWA), a body that brings together key regional players—ECOWAS, Union Economique et Monétaire Ouest Africaine (West African Economic and Monetary Union [UEMOA]), Comité Inter-Etate pour la Lutte contre la Sécheresse au Sahel (Permanent Inter-State Committee for Drought Control in the Sahel [CILSS]), and WAEN—to share information on regional integration initiatives, to discuss, research, and establish positions on technical aspects of regional integration, and to make preliminary designations and commitments to action among the entities;

WAEN carried out a special study on the cost and speed of intraregional monetary transfers, via regional banks such as the Bank of Africa (BOA) and Ecobank, to encourage more efficient transfers within the ECOWAS region;

WAEN proposed to the Forum West Africa and interested donors the creation of an observatory of border-crossing practices, to track anomalies and report them to national authorities (customs, immigration, police, etc.), and participated in its implementation;

WAEN was asked to contribute to the debate on the proposed redesign of the ACP-EU convention and on the UEMOA unified investment code;

WAEN created a Regional Trade Information Center (RTIC) in 1995, to collect and disseminate trade information at the request of its members, create a Web site, and publish a quarterly bilingual newsletter, the *Networker*.

Source: Deborah Orsini, "Case Study of: EAEN, SAEN, WAEN," Organization of Economic Cooperation and Development (OECD) DCD (2001), 10/ANN5, www.oecd.org/dataoecd/16/37/1886229.pdf: 20.

Weaknesses of the Networks

WAEN members, donors, and researchers had differing ideas of the weaknesses and successes of all three networks. The donors and implementers of the IPC tended to focus on successes and recommendations for the future, while the members themselves mentioned both problems and accomplishments.[40]

McDade and Spring considered the stated views of network members and the literature about business networks in Africa and elsewhere.[41] The weaknesses WAEN members identified included the following. First, the number of members at country, region, and Pan-African levels was too small. Ghana was the largest country network with forty-five members, while Senegal had twenty-five. Other country networks varied from eight to fifteen members. Second, network members' businesses were not representative of the main sectors of their country's economy. More service-sector than manufacturing businesses were represented. Third, there were countries that had no women members or too few women members in the national networks, even though there were women company owners and managers who met the membership criteria (for example, Ghana and Senegal had women members, but Mali did not). Fourth, network members expended little effort to establish linkages with traditional entrepreneurs through such mechanisms as membership in chambers of commerce. WAEN members believed that large inclusive organizations like chambers of commerce included too many business levels to be useful. Fifth, network members' businesses did not have enough sustainable large-scale business activity with each other, probably because there were too many service-sector businesses in the networks. Finally, network members' lofty goals may not have made enough impact, and their impacts at country levels were difficult to measure.

WAEN members were disturbed by the demise of the networks. First, they pointed to the implementers' contracting methods, in terms of the ways in which interventions concerning the networks were contracted. Members were upset with the donors (USAID and OECD) when they realized that most of the IPC funds went to the implementing agencies in the form of salaries for consultants and overhead charges (both are standard procedures for development implementing firms). In most projects, participants do not have the ability to provide their own technical assistance. But WAEN members were a highly educated group, and many had consultancy businesses themselves. Second, WAEN members commented that the donors recruited more network members with service-oriented businesses, when there should have been more manufacturers who produced goods, purchased inputs, and required market outlets. Such manufacturers would have produced jobs, supplier networks, and marketing channels.

Third, WAEN members criticized the donors' interest in conferences and meetings, rather than in concentrating on business transactions. By definition, the implementing consultants were not business owners and did not have expertise in business transactions. WAEN network members tired of the meetings and conferences and wanted to "do actual business." (Some of the other USAID projects focused on business matches and "deals.") Fourth, they noted that the accounting of network funds was not transparent. They wanted each network to be run by the members, rather than the donor support unit. Each national network collected membership dues and contributed annually to the support of the secretariat. The donors wanted to use these funds to pay for conferences, while WAEN members wanted to use them to operate the secretariat and the national chapters. A final problem was structural: only the secretariat, not the individual country chapters, could negotiate with the donor support unit. Some country chapters wanted direct access to the support team. To change the situation, WAEN reorganized the secretariat and tried to redirect the funds to its operations. At this point, according to WAEN members, the IPC decided to focus on the Southern African Enterprise Network (SAEN).

The donor support group wanted to focus on change issues, while the network members wanted to do more practical business. They also became less interested in changing the macro-environment after the first four or five years of the network, and much less interested in conferences and network meetings once they were already acquainted and networking in dyads. However, the two "sides" were not completely at opposite poles, since their interests overlapped in terms of taking advantage of business advocacy opportunities. WAEN lasted ten years, a relatively long life span for USAID and other donor-financed projects. Donor agencies' policies alter due to changes in their personnel as well as to the political situation. Hence, it was not surprising that the IPC ended, and new interventions and projects were begun.

Conclusion

Business constraints in WAEN countries included poor physical infrastructure and utilities, little land reform and security of property investments, limited foreign exchange and capital, and inadequate production capacity. As a result, both U.S. companies and network members saw constraints to Africa-U.S. trade. For some, it was difficult to obtain U.S. visas for business and trade shows (especially mentioned by Malian network members); there was a lack of information about U.S. markets; a lack of linkages to and contacts in the United States; there were difficulties in servicing large U.S. orders; and there was a lack of information among U.S. business persons about market opportunities in Africa. The IPC focused on creating networks within Africa and could not change in midstream to address these issues or to move into increased trade with the United States after AGOA was passed. The IPC had ten years of donor funding, and other USAID projects such as ATRIP and WAIBL were begun during its final years, while new initiatives continue to be created (for example, AGCI). ATRIP and WAIBL were mostly concerned with matching trade partners between the United States and Africa and changing bilateral tariff regulations, while the AGCI continued with networking but added trade and investment. Hence, many of the issues that

WAEN and the other regional networks had with regard to the IPC were never resolved.

However, for the decade starting in 1993, it seemed from the U.S. business technical assistance perspective that changes in regulations would help open the private sector in Africa. The United States was also keenly interested in the harmonization of laws, and WAEN through NetForce and other actions accomplished some of this. From the data collected from the participants in WAEN, it seemed that their businesses were special in terms of financial transparency and ethical and global business practices, the criteria for membership. The enterprise networks helped them meet like-minded private-sector businesspersons who could open the door to regional trade, business interaction, and communication. Building a cadre of like-minded, successful, global entrepreneurs throughout the continent proved to be an interesting intervention with a variety of accomplishments.

Many lessons were learned in the IPC for both West Africans and USAID. First, the idea of building national, regional, and Pan-African business networks was successful in that it was carried out in thirty-one countries, three regions, and a continent. The networks were exclusive (not inclusive like large chambers of commerce). Members were chosen because they were medium- to large-size firm owners and managers, were practitioners of good business ethics, and held to financial transparency. They had global perspectives and avoided government rent-seeking and political patronage. Second, this group of young businesspersons was easy for the donors to work with, and it was easy for participants to work together because of their education, formal-sector work experience, and shared values in terms of global practices and forward-thinking methods. Third, women were members of many country networks with total acceptance as businesspersons.[42] Fourth, the networks provided a visible private sector presence that was substantial, although difficult to measure numerically in such terms as effect on GDP and international trade. Finally, in a number of countries, trade regulations and policies affecting the private sector were improved, studies were carried out, business information was disseminated, venture capital funds were generated, and the networks gained membership in important regional economic entities (table 16.3).

Network members and their businesses continued through time, and some interacted after the IPC ceased to exist. As in such networks everywhere, members maintain social and business ties when convenient and mutually remunerative. For a ten-year project to accomplish this is a tribute to the participants. In the end, other activities/projects concerning U.S.–West African trade and West African interregional trade followed. AGOA became a U.S. focus, and partner-matching was the mechanism for its accomplishment. Future research is necessary to determine whether or not the new projects and activities also produced desired results, and whether or not network members were participants.

Notes

I would like to thank the Opportunity Fund and Center for International Business Research and Education (CIBER) at the University of Florida for funding, and the enterprise network members for sharing their information. My colleague, Dr. Barbara McDade, and I worked together on collecting and analyzing much of the data.

1. Deborah Orsini, "The Enterprise Network Initiative: A New Generation of African Entrepreneurs Emerges" (paper presented at the USA-Africa Trade and Investment Symposium, Orlando, Florida, 1999; Deborah Orsini, "Case Study of: EAEN, SAEN, WAEN," Organization of Economic Cooperation and Development (OECD) DCD (2001) 10/ANN5, www.oecd.org/dataoecd/16/37/1886229.pdf.

2. Orsini, "Case Study of: EAEN, SAEN, WAEN," 20.

3. Deborah Orsini, Michel Courcelle, and Derick Brinkerhoff, "Increasing Private Sector Capacity for Policy Dialogue: The West African Enterprise Network," *World Development* 24, no. 9 (1996): 1453–66.

4. Ghanaian and Senegalese WAEN members mentioned to me in both 2000 and 2003 that some of them had already been meeting in 1991, so the time was right.

5. Orsini, Courcelle, and Brinkerhoff, "Increasing Private Sector Capacity for Policy Dialogue," 3.

6. Orsini, "Case Study of: EAEN, SAEN, WAEN," 4.

7. Orsini, Courcelle, and Brinkerhoff, "Increasing Private Sector Capacity for Policy Dialogue," 5.

8. Ibid., 6.

9. Ibid., 8.

10. Orsini, "Case Study of: EAEN, SAEN, WAEN," 26.

11. OECD/Club du Sahel, *Engaging African Entrepreneurs for Global Competitiveness,* Working Paper 3 (Addis Ababa: OECD/Club du Sahel, 2000), 98; Anita Spring, field-notes on the conference.

12. Barbara McDade and Anita Spring, "The New Generation of African Entrepreneurs: Changing the Environment for Business Development and Economic Growth," *Entrepreneurship and Regional Development* 17 (2005): 17–42. I draw on this article for some of the analysis here.

13. On the Frontier (OTF), "Report of a Survey of Entrepreneurs at the Millennium Conference, Addis Ababa," Powerpoint presentation prepared by Tim McCoy, personal communication, 2000.

14. Orsini, Courcelle, and Brinkerhoff, "Increasing Private Sector Capacity for Policy Dialogue"; McDade and Spring, "The New Generation of African Entrepreneurs."

15. K. Wohlmuth and M. Wauschkunh, "West African Enterprise Network WAEN," *The African Development Perspectives Yearbook,* vol. B, *Africa's Reintegration into the World Economy* (New Brunswick, NJ: Transaction Publishers, 2001); Anita Spring, "Gender and the Range of Entrepreneurial Strategies: The 'Typical' and the 'New' Generation of Women Entrepreneurs," in *Black Business and Economic Power,* ed. by Alusine Jalloh and Toyin Falola (Rochester, NY: University of Rochester Press. 2002), 381–401; Anita Spring, "Empowering Women in the African Entrepreneurial Landscape: Microentrepreneurs to Business Globalists in the Informal and Formal Sectors," in

Power, Gender and Social Change in Africa and the Diaspora, ed. Muna Ndulo (forthcoming); Anita Spring "Conventional and 'Modern' African Women Entrepreneurs: Diversity in the Landscape," *Journal of African Business* (forthcoming).

16. David Fick, *Entrepreneurship in Africa: A Study of Successes* (Westport, CT: Quorum Books, 2002).

17. WAEN publications include *The Networker,* the West African Enterprise Network newsletter (Accra, Ghana, 1993–98); WAEN, *Presenting the West African Enterprise Network: Mission, Objectives, Organization and Activities* (Accra: WAEN, 1998–2000); *Trade Flash,* a monthly electronic newsletter (WAEN Secretariat, Accra, Ghana, dates not available); and *Facing the Issues: Final Report on the Regional Conference on the West African Private Sector* (Accra: Enterprise Network of Ghana, 1993).

EAEN publications include "EAEN Takes Flight," *EAEN Newsletter* 2 (1998): 2; *Meeting the Challenge of Regional Economic Cooperation in East Africa: Final Report on EAEN First Regional Conference* (Kampala: EAEN, 1999); "New Generation Entrepreneurs Address Regional Cooperation in East Africa," *EAEN Newsletter* 2, no. 5 (2000).

SAEN publications include *Building a Southern African Regional Market: Issues for the Private Sector: Final Report on SAEN First Regional Conference* (Mauritius: Mauritius Enterprise Network, 1999).

18. "Networking West Africa," *Business in Ghana,* January 1996, 23–35; Peter Kibiriti, "Entrepreneurship in East Africa," *EAEN Newsletter* 2, no. 3 (1999): 2; *Enterprise Africa Magazine,* nos. 1–4 (2000), ed. Peter Kibiriti.

19. The original Web sites of the three regional enterprise networks were as follows: for WAEN, http://www.waenonline.com; EAEN, http://www.ugandacapitalmarkets.co.ug; and SAEN,www.saen.net. Since 2002, the sites have not been active. The WAEN domain name was put up for sale in 2002.

20. Michel Courcelle and Anne de Lattre, "The Enterprise Impulse in West Africa," *OECD Observer,* no. 203 (1996): 32–34; Orsini, "The Enterprise Network Initiative"; OECD, http://www.oecd.org/dataoecd/53/26/2536659.pdf.

21. Corporate Council on Africa, 2002, 55, http://www.africacncl.org/downloads/WAGEnglishFinal.pdf. On SAEN, also see Anock Janssens-Bevernage, *Capacity-Building for Private-Sector Development: The Southern African Enterprise Network (SAEN), ECDPM Discussion Paper 38* (Maastricht: ECDPM, 2002).

22. See West Africa International Business Linkage Program, http://www.africacncl.org/Linkages/WAIBL.asp.

23. See ibid.; also http://www.ccawaibl.com.

24. See West Africa International Business Linkage Program, http://www.africacncl.org/Linkages/WAIBL.asp; also http://www.usaid.gov/missions/warp/ecintegration/waibl/index.htm.

25. I chaired the State of Florida delegation during this time period, as well as serving as one of the reporters for the national meetings.

26. See Africa Growth and Opportunity Act, http://www.agoa.gov.

27. See National Summit on Africa, http://www.usaid.gov/locations/sub-saharan_africa/initiaives/agci.html.

28. McDade and Spring, "The New Generation of African Entrepreneurs."

29. He was also discussed in Fick, *Entrepreneurship in Africa: A Study of Successes,* 24–25.

30. Anita Spring and Barbara McDade, eds., *African Entrepreneurship: Theory and Reality* (Gainesville: University Press of Florida, 1998); Jalloh and Falola, eds., *Black Business and Economic Power.*

31. McDade and Spring, "The New Generation of African Entrepreneurs."

32. Spring, "Gender and the Range of Entrepreneurial Strategies."

33. McDade and Spring, "The New Generation of African Entrepreneurs."

34. The website is currently inoperative.

35. Wohlmuth and Wauschkunh, "West African Enterprise Network WAEN."

36. *Enterprise Africa Magazine*, ed. Kibiriti.

37. Personal communication with WAEF founder, 2003. Several other countries' networks (for example, those of Kenya and Zambia) also had venture capital funds, but these too were smaller than desired.

38. McDade and Spring, "The New Generation of African Entrepreneurs."

39. Orsini, "The Enterprise Network Initiative"; Orsini, "Case Study of: EAEN, SAEN, WAEN."

40. OECD, "Engaging African Entrepreneurs for Global Competitiveness"; Orsini, "Case Study of: EAEN, SAEN, WAEN."

41. McDade and Spring, "The New Generation of African Entrepreneurs."

42. Spring, "Gender and the Range of Entrepreneurial Strategies."

17

Poverty Alleviation in Sierra Leone and the Role of U.S. Foreign Aid

An Institutional Trap Analysis

Stephen Kandeh

Introduction

The nature of poverty in Sierra Leone is particularly unusual. A small country with a size of approximately 27,699 square miles and a moderate population size estimated at 6.4 million in 2004, this West African country is endowed with a reasonable supply of natural resources such as diamonds, rutile, gold, iron, timber, cocoa, coffee, and fish. In spite of these resources, Sierra Leone's economy has continued to perform dismally since the country attained independence. Having won the unenviable status of "poorest nation" several times in the last two decades, and with a human development index consistently estimated as the worst in the world, Sierra Leone is rated as one of the worst development cases in the developing world. The nature of poverty in Sierra Leone defies simple analysis.

While standards of living have continued to improve for many countries in the world, Sierra Leone has made little progress in this area. According to United Nations Development Program (UNDP) reports, life expectancy for Sierra Leoneans actually declined from 38.9 years in 2001 to 34.3 years in 2004. This does not compare well to a life expectancy of 46 years for an average West African. With the average person in Sierra Leone expected to live for 35 years in 1970, this country has barely shown any signs of improvement in the quality of life of its people. In 2001, undernourishment was said to affect up to 50 percent of the population, while the adult literacy rate, albeit measured in terms of elementary educational attainment, oscillated between 33.3 percent and 36 percent of the adult population between 1999 and 2004. In 2004, 74 percent of the population in Sierra Leone were said to live on less than $2 a day, while more than half of the population lived on less than $1 a day. UNDP reports show that only about 0.5 percent of people in this country had access to a telephone in 2002, and only 57 percent had access to improved water systems. More and more people continue to fall into the snares of extreme poverty and deprivation, with the poorest 20 percent of the population of Sierra Leone sharing a meager 1 percent of the income by 2003. It is estimated that between 1985 and 2002, 1,800 out of 100,000 women who had live births died as a result of birth-related complications, and that at least 27 percent of all babies born alive were also born underweight.[1]

In addition to these depressing figures, the level of human vulnerability to health risks and violence continued to increase tremendously in recent years. As a result of a ten-year civil war that lasted from 1992 to 2002, conservative estimates of the numbers of victims record violent deaths at over 50,000 while millions became victims of displacement, maiming, and rape. Today, thousands of orphans who have little hope of surviving to the next day populate the cities and countryside of Sierra Leone. In a country where human cruelty has done its worst, individual vulnerability to violence has increased tremendously. In analyzing the impact of the war on society, Margaret Lebbie-Moebiyor explains how "a decade of mistrust, war, bitterness, destruction, hatred and looting in the entire country, has created an entirely new generation of dangerous, deprived, misused, abused, and poorly motivated children and youth who are traumatized."[2]

As disastrous as this war has been for Sierra Leoneans, however, the conditions of human misery and degradation have causes that go deeper and are more long term than the war. The depth of poverty in Sierra Leone is such that decades of development efforts have not helped to loosen its grip. In fact, some observers believe that misguided development efforts have actually added to the mix of the poverty complex.[3]

Throughout the decades following independence, Sierra Leone like many other developing nations, has received increasing amounts of foreign aid in efforts to stimulate economic growth. As shown in table 17.1, the United States has emerged as the largest donor to Sierra Leone with donations totaling about $441.44 million between 1961 and 2003. The United Kingdom follows closely behind with donations totaling $429.33 over the same period. Other donor countries such as Japan and China are increasing their contributions toward economic development in this country. In spite of these efforts, poverty continues to increase for Sierra Leoneans. Even in the face of ambitious U.S. policy instruments such as the African Growth and Opportunity Act (AGOA) and the United Nations' millennium goals, accompanied by multiple debt rescheduling and partial debt cancellations, the prospects for sustained development in Sierra Leone continue to be slim. In short, Sierra Leone represents a development puzzle, a special case of state paralysis that requires urgent attention.

Table 17.1 Foreign Aid to Sierra Leone

Year	All foreign aid (in US$ millions)	U.S. foreign aid (in US$ millions)	U.S. aid as a percentage of all foreign aid
1961	14.81	1	14.81
1962	7.28	2	3.64
1963	9.5	3	3.166667
1964	9.59	4	2.3975
1965	16.98	12.98	1.308166
1966	9.09	4.84	1.878099
1967	6.36	4.34	1.465438
1968	10.73	4.46	2.40583
1969	9	4	2.25
1970	6.91	3	2.303333
1971	10.49	4	2.6225
1972	10.3	3	3.433333
1973	14.27	2	7.135
1974	10.46	3	3.486667
1975	18.06	4	4.515
1976	15.15	3	5.05
1977	26.23	4	6.5575
1978	40.28	4	10.07
1979	53.54	6	8.923333
1980	90.93	8	11.36625
1981	60.11	8	7.51375
1982	82.19	8	10.27375
1983	65.27	10	6.527
1984	58.68	9	6.52
1985	64.87	10	6.487
1986	91.31	12	7.609167
1987	66.73	12	5.560833
1988	102.36	9	11.37333
1989	99.96	11	9.087273
1990	60.86	3	20.28667
1991	104.11	8	13.01375
1992	133.47	13	10.26692
1993	207.88	8	25.985
1994	275.55	10	27.555
1995	206.36	8	25.795
1996	184.11	11	16.73727
1997	118.64	13	9.126154
1998	106.43	13.19	8.068992
1999	73.59	17.39	4.231742
2000	182.4	7.97	22.88582
2001	344.97	26.36	13.08687
2002	353.38	70.12	5.039646
2003	297.37	58.79	5.058173
Total	3730.56	441.44	

Source: Based on data from the Organization for Economic Cooperation and Development, oecd.org.

In view of the difficult development problems that this country faces, this chapter examines the claim of economic development models that the provision of large amounts of foreign investment and development capital is fundamental to the eradication of poverty in Sierra Leone and countries in similar situations. According to the various stipulations of the capital infusionist development approach, substantial amounts of foreign capital will stimulate economic growth, create jobs, and increase workers' earnings. This in turn will stimulate local savings and investments that will begin the process of national development in impoverished countries.[4] Based on recent research findings, however, some capital infusionist scholars are realizing that the foreign investment aspect of the development equation is not working well for countries with unpredictable socioeconomic and political conditions like Sierra Leone. A new approach, recently popularized as the "poverty trap" model, is shifting the burden of capital infusion from private investors to wealthy foreign governments.[5] It can be inferred from this economic model that the role of the United States in overcoming the intractable poverty in Sierra Leone should be crucial because of its donor potential and its long history of assistance to Sierra Leone. However, the increasingly dismal economic performance of Sierra Leone in spite of increasing foreign assistance provides little confidence in the claims of the poverty trap model.

Foreign aid as a means of economic growth has been challenged on numerous fronts. The resource distribution problem, an institutional problem that makes it difficult for aid to reach targeted populations and groups, has been identified as a major difficulty with foreign aid as an effective poverty alleviation tool.[6] Similarly, Amartya Sen in his seminal discussions about democratic principles and economic growth concluded that in a society where institutional structures unabashedly support undemocratic practices regarding problems of modernization, foreign aid is ineffective as an instrument for poverty eradication.[7] Richard Joseph makes a similar claim, stating that "without a minimally effective state, there will be no sustainable development or democracy, regardless of the financial resources available to Africa"[8] In agreeing with the aid-failure thesis, however, Joseph Hanlon places the responsibility on donors who give aid to corrupt governments in their own self-interest and yet expect a positive outcome.[9] In Sierra Leone, institutional delivery methods are constrained by the patronage system that makes foreign assistance part of elite accumulation. It has also been suggested that foreign aid inherently reinforces corruption and dependence on external powers and politicians. In any case, there are reasons to believe that the United States is not likely to step up to the plate as the "big push" financial sponsor for poverty alleviation in Sierra Leone that the poverty trap model so passionately advocates.

A careful analysis will reveal that foreign capital is not the crucial missing element in the war against poverty in Sierra Leone, even though capital is

important in development. Instead, social change involving drastic changes
in norms, values, and social expectations within the culture and institutional
arrangements in Sierra Leone holds greater promise as a first step in the war
against poverty. An alternative view of the complexity of poverty in Sierra
Leone, the "institutional trap" model, is presented in this chapter to explain
the nature of this country's unyielding economic predicament. The model
explains the historical roots and contemporary foundations of the
intractable poverty in Sierra Leone as offshoots of a syncretic institutional
system that holds development initiatives captive and promotes irrational
responses by elites and masses alike.[10]

Political and Economic Decadence in Sierra Leone

Since Sierra Leone's independence in 1961, the political and economic
drama has often served to catapult the nation further into the abyss of
poverty and dependence on international assistance. While many developing countries experienced sustained growth in the late 1970s and 1980s, the
economy of Sierra Leone saw an overall degradation. By the late 1990s, this
country had become so notoriously poor that it earned the infamous United
Nations' title of "least developed nation" in the world. According to UNDP
human development reports, Sierra Leone remains at the bottom of the list
of countries in terms of Human Development Index (HDI) measures, and
there is no sign of the country's losing that position. In 2006, Sierra Leone
still occupied 176th position among 177 countries on the HDI ratings. In
terms of political corruption, Transparency International has consistently
given Sierra Leone one of the worst rankings in the world based on perceptions of corruption.[11] Although the limited ability of the state to maintain
peace, security, and a semblance of sanity suddenly evaporated in 1992 with
the invasion by rebel fighters, the process of state collapse was in the making
for a very long time. Indeed, it is difficult to support the much touted contention that Sierra Leone ever started on a path of sustained economic
development before or after independence.

Some scholars have tended to paint a glamorous picture of precolonial
Sierra Leone so as to blame the problems of this troubled region on colonial
policies. Similarly, others have attempted to pinpoint the downward spiral as
a trend beginning during the early years of independence. More often, scholars locate the beginnings of economic and political turbulence in specific
postindependence political periods such as the Albert Margai era, or the era
of the All People's Congress political party under Siaka P. Stevens or his pro-
tégé, Joseph Momoh. The postwar regimes of Presidents Ahmed Tejan Kabba
and Ernest Bai Koroma, like all the interim civilian regimes and juntas before
them, receive their share of the blame. A closer examination of this country's
history would reveal, however, that failures to support the ideals of equality,

transparency, accountability, and economic development are due largely to systemic problems, to a pattern of structured behavior and expectations that is here labeled syncretism, than to any single fleeting moment or any single policy event. Although it is more convenient to lay the blame on specific persons or events, the complexity and significance of the economic development question demands an investigation of fundamental institutional problems that will truly contribute to a solution to chronic poverty in Sierra Leone. Relevant questions for development theorizing are why the people of Sierra Leone consistently produce incompetent leadership and why Sierra Leoneans have such a high tolerance for exploitative social relations.

Many precolonial societies in the region were largely preliterate, so a review of institutional development must proceed with caution as most of the evidence is speculative and superficial. This difficulty notwithstanding, oral traditions, archaeology, and the social characteristics of relatively unchanged communities today serve as moderately reliable sources of some information about precolonial cultures. Based on the little evidence available to them at the time, Meyer Fortes and E. E. Evans-Pritchard were able to establish in their study of several African political and social systems that the precolonial African social milieu had multiple and disparate institutional structures and values, some of which were incompatible.[12] With the establishment of a colonial regime in the Sierra Leone region in the early 1800s, however, these precolonial communities were gradually homogenized into a state system called Sierra Leone. A fundamental misunderstanding of and disregard for precolonial social systems as separate social entities in the institutional homogenization process marked the beginnings of a misguided culture mixture whose repercussions still reverberate two hundred years later.

Before the establishment of colonial rule, different ethnic communities evolved diverse political, economic, and social systems in the territory that now constitutes the Republic of Sierra Leone and parts of the neighboring countries of Liberia and Guinea. Archaeological and oral historical evidence suggest that these groups engaged in diverse activities that included farming, fishing, trade, and nomadic life. While some communities maintained simple social organizations with councils of elders providing governmental functions, others evolved more complex and centralized political systems with royal courts, standing armies, and diplomatic corps.[13] Some of these societies employed dynastic leadership patterns that raised natural successors to the throne through kinship structures, while others devised complex administrative systems that trained leaders through apprenticeship and service. Still others evolved different forms of representational political systems with different degrees of gender equality. In some of these societies, queens, princesses, and councils of women comprised formidable political constituencies. Even along the lines of popular consent and the degree to which religion influenced political action, these societies showed remarkable differences. Different patterns of power relations and social structures ensured that some societies were more or less susceptible to the rise of despotic leadership than others. This is exemplified by Sheikh Umarr Kamarah in his interpretation of linguistic data, showing that institutionalized individualism and competitiveness were normative values among the Northern Temne people who also organized centralized political systems.[14] At the other end of the spectrum, my own interpretation of ethnographic data on the Kono people of the eastern province indicates that these people organized themselves in decentralized societies that were essentially communal.[15]

In utter disregard of these important cultural and institutional differences, however, and in an eagerness to develop a system that would deliver maximum economic benefits to Britain, the British Colonial Office blended forms of traditional social systems and Western values into a hybrid system called "indirect rule." Under this system, a state system was created in which political power was concentrated in the hands of colonial elites who rationed out authority to local leaders known as paramount chiefs. Some of these chiefs were prepared to subvert their own societies and cultural systems for the power conferred on them by colonial elites. A kinship-based chieftaincy structure, an alien power structure in many of the societies under discussion, became the channel for colonial dictatorship because the chiefs concerned held power purely at the discretion of the Colonial Office. As long as they remained faithful to the colonial elites and were able to enforce colonial policies on local people, chiefs remained in office for life and could easily pass this acquired privilege to their own children. Since most of these dynasties were co-opted to replace legitimate traditional rulers who refused to cooperate with colonial officers, and because the hybrid colonial system greatly expanded the scope and depth of the new chiefs' power, they depended on the coercive forces of colonialism and constructed myths of legitimacy to maintain political control. In this way, the foundations of the patronage on which present-day syncretic, dysfunctional social institutions rest gained preeminence.

To further embed these new social realities in social processes, the structure and function of the educational system was set up to promote patronage privileges. Social privileges were conferred on a select group of African elites who were trained to benefit from and sustain the patronage stratification system as future leaders of their own communities. Colonial policy encouraged and fostered ethnic rivalry among prospective elites as a means of maintaining colonial control.[16] In the wider society, as in the educational institutions, values of exploitation promoted a policy of divide and rule that also promoted ethnic rivalry.

The ordinary people of Sierra Leone were not innocent bystanders in all these developments. Throughout the colonial period and beyond, people collaborated with power brokers in exchange for material gain, political positions, and prestige. Others, out of apathy, fear, or ignorance, acquiesced to political corruption and violence by looking the other way or sometimes by actively contributing to it. Public officers were expected to accumulate public resources and to garner the support of a network of followers to facilitate colonial administration. The masses accepted and helped to operate a system that granted favors to those who cooperated with power holders and neglected or even punished those who refused to cooperate. Corruption, bribery, and intimidation by public officers were promoted as the way modern society operated. In these ways, the patronage system was normalized. In more than a century of conflicted value systems, the nation was ordered according to misplaced priorities and distorted views of modernization. Social institutions that functioned to repatriate local resources and relied on a fragile suboptimal educational system to perpetuate elitist principles were entrenched.

The granting of independence in 1961 did not change this situation. Political elites and political parties sustained norms and values of leadership and social relations handed down by their predecessors. Throughout the local and global political turmoil and economic turbulence of the decades that followed independence, the syncretic infrastructure remained intact and the norms and expectations of syncretism were taken to new heights. Having been mentored in the oppression and patronage of colonialism, the new political elites were not inclined to dismantle the leadership structures that promoted their own newfound authority. The interests of national political elites also converged with those of local chieftains in terms of extracting resources at the expense of the masses and sharing in elite plunder. The people acquiesced to this structure by actively promoting "di pa" (literally, "the father") culture of dependence.[17] This culture promotes the dependency of the masses on wealthy people and elites.

To many people in Sierra Leone, the end of colonialism signaled optimism: optimism in terms of an oppression-free society, of economic prosperity, and of inheriting the wealth and prestige enjoyed by the European colonial authorities. However, the consequences of economic degradation, including intense feelings of personal worthlessness, hunger, and starvation had become the daily realities for millions of Sierra Leoneans. In this age of modern technological interventions, Sierra Leone continues to languish in labor-intensive production systems that become increasingly less rewarding and more inefficient. After decades of government policies targeting agricultural revolution in this country, for example, a majority of farmers still use the hoe and axe for crop cultivation. The slash and burn technique remains the primary method of land clearing for farming. In spite of the progress around the world in land tenure systems, land is still communally owned and distributed in many areas of Sierra Leone.[18]

Yet the true picture of poverty in this country is worse than numbers can ever demonstrate. Research data grossly underrate the extent of poverty in

Sierra Leone because vast areas of the country are completely removed from the eyes of data collectors, foreign observers, and development agents. In a country where urbanization is still in its infancy, most people reside in rural village communities that are located as many as three days on foot away from the nearest towns that vehicles can reach.[19] The great majority of communities in Sierra Leone do not have access to schools, medical centers, or pure water supplies. Thus, it is safe to assume that the poverty statistics for Sierra Leone are gravely underestimated. Census workers in this country unabashedly admit to "data doctoring" because they do not get paid enough to undertake the long and arduous journeys to reach many remote communities. When census workers do eventually visit some of these communities, the residents are nowhere to be found because traditional farming activities keep them on farms all day and sometimes for several days at a time.[20] Some residents flatly refuse to take the time to provide information to "city idlers" because they find it a waste of their time to spend hours with census personnel whose efforts are completely meaningless to local people. The combination of large-scale illiteracy, intractable poverty, and neotraditional ideologies of power and prestige produces a society that seems to conspire against its own development. As a result, efforts to understand the depth and breadth of poverty in Sierra Leone are always shallow and sometimes fruitless.

The Failure of Development Theory

Since the most obvious condition of poverty is a lack of material resources, the focus for many poverty reduction approaches is increasing access to material resources. Neoclassical perspectives, theorizing development in terms of economic growth and the trickle-down effect, have become the most authoritative development approaches. Because neoclassical developmentalism centers on capital infusion as necessary and sufficient to reverse poverty, national development initiatives in poor countries as well as international programs for poverty alleviation depend heavily on world capitalist centers for development aid. Foreign aid has adopted many forms for the delivery and utilization of capital by recipient nations, however, the driving spirit has always been the belief that if more capital is spent then development will happen. The one-size-fits-all neoclassical models therefore emphasize that modernization entails catching up with Western European and North American countries in lifestyle and consumption patterns that include ever-increasing technology-driven activities. However, relentless efforts to acquire modern lifestyles without the requisite institutional support have not led to economic development. While elites in Sierra Leone continue to implement strategies that promote their acquired Western tastes, Western lifestyles continue to create problems in terms of the accumulation of the very capital that neoclassicists insist is indispensable for development. In the past, for instance, most people would seek effective traditional methods of healing for simple ailments. However, the uncontested acceptance of prohibitively expensive Western medicine as the only source of any effective cure contributes to the increasing incidence of disease among the poor and to the causes of capital flight as elites outsource medical services for themselves and their cronies to wealthy countries. This strategy comes at the expense of local capital accumulation and investment and at the expense of domestic development of medical facilities and infrastructure.

The strategies for modernizing Sierra Leone have not produced the required results either. During the latter days of colonialism in Sierra Leone and in the early years of the independent state, export-led growth was emphasized as the way to obtain capital for domestic growth. As was made clear earlier on, this policy did not lead to economic development. In the 1960s and early 1970s, import substitution replaced export-led growth as the new development style. At this time, low national income and growth rates were emphasized as poverty indicators. Sierra Leone began to request foreign capital to build industries for the manufacturing of basic necessities and for the marketing of produce. In spite of this policy change, poverty continued to grow, and industrial development never happened. As recently as 2004, for example, only 7 percent of all merchandise exported from Sierra Leone was composed of manufactured goods. During the same year, the country experienced a negative growth rate estimated at -5.5. By the mid-1970s, development wisdom shifted to agriculture and rural development. The rationale for this switch was to increase food production that could then sustain industrial development. Nonetheless, by the early 1980s, Sierra Leone had become almost dependent on Chinese and Burmese rice, and hunger soon became the most important characteristic of poverty. The average Sierra Leonean could no longer afford to eat more than one meal a day, while many people literally starved.[21] Between the 1980s and the outbreak of the civil war in 1992, spiraling foreign debt was added to the poverty complex to produce a debt burden of over $1.5 billion by 2005.

As needed to meet the needs of political elites, development wisdom continued to vacillate between various program objectives with flamboyant titles that included women in development, urban poverty reduction, green revolution, institution building, governance, and grassroots projects. The World Bank and the International Monetary Fund also designed structural adjustment programs that focused on the fiscal and financial policies of the government.[22] The structural adjustment programs, in addition to the many other development ideas, only continued to intensify the adversities of the masses. The failures that continued to accompany development policies in Sierra Leone are evident in the speedy descent of the nation into hunger, bankruptcy, indebtedness, and social chaos that culminated in a bloody civil war, beginning in 1992 and lasting until 2002. No matter the name of the game, development initiatives in Sierra Leone have consistently asked for more and more foreign assistance, and yet increasing assistance has not lent itself to poverty alleviation.

As one policy after another failed to show positive results in Sierra Leone, the need to explain the failures became more intense. Some observers suggest that the intervention of the state in economic development in Sierra Leone is the primary reason for the economic development failures.[23] However, in what has come to be known as the statist development model, state interventionism has been shown to work in the development of Singapore, Japan, China, and Taiwan. In fact, many of the development approaches used in Sierra Leone, including the notorious structural adjustment programs, have succeeded in other development arenas.

In the eyes of other observers, classical economic schools of thought are missing the point. According to many critical perspectives, economic development is context sensitive and therefore development must focus on country-specific needs because different societies have fundamentally different ideas of human nature and society. Among other factors, historical conditions such as colonialism and the nature of capitalist profiteering are blamed for poverty. These views, however, generally present developing countries as passive elements in the social drama of colonialism and capitalism. While some of these positions call for reform in structural conditions to facilitate effective participation in the capitalist system, others propose inward-looking strategies such as de-linking from global economic and political arrangements. Others call for reparations for colonial exploitation.[24]

Still others look for development answers in individual characteristics. Some suggest that Sierra Leoneans suffer from an inferiority complex, while others advance "weak leadership" and "moral uprightness" hypotheses to suggest that success in economic development depends on the individual personality of leaders.[25] An analytical extension of this argument, in some instances, relies on the "failed states" hypothesis, which suggests that the best development path for poor countries lies in surrendering their sovereignty to foreign powers that have the moral fortitude to build capitalist empires.[26] Building on the assumption that capitalist leadership is built on moral character, these psychological perspectives have a tendency to invoke the notorious racial superiority myth. Although these perspectives are somewhat promising as clinical therapy for some development agents, and certainly for many African elites, the subjectivity involved makes them unsatisfactory models for understanding persistent poverty in Sierra Leone.

In spite of the spirited criticisms of the traditional economic approach, capital infusion is again gaining the spotlight. In the aftermath of the New York World Trade Center terrorist attacks of September 11, 2001, capital infusion is increasingly gaining salience in the discussions of why groups around the world living in poverty might serve as labor reserves for terrorist recruiters. Suddenly, foreign aid as a means of pacifying the poor if not ultimately solving poverty problems is receiving renewed support in the development literature and in U.S. policy halls. Additionally, poverty is gaining attention as a push factor leading to increased illegal migration into the United States. As illegal immigration, refugee problems, and poverty issues become increasingly tangled up with terrorist movements and activities, the old wisdom of promoting economic development in poor countries through capital supply is gaining new currency in U.S. foreign policy.[27] The "poverty trap" perspective, a view that has recently been in the limelight in the World Bank, gathers momentum from the frustrating twenty-first-century global issues.

The poverty trap perspective, as popularized by Jeffrey Sachs and his colleagues in a recent study conducted for the United Nations millennium project, assumes capital infusion as being the means to solve poverty problems. The contribution of this perspective, as stipulated by Sachs and his colleagues, is in the "big push" hypothesis, which suggests that a massive capital infusion into poor economies beyond a certain threshold is the magic bullet that will finally cause economic development.[28] This big push represents significantly large sums of foreign capital that would be used to build the infrastructural basis of economic development. The idea of large-scale foreign investment or aid is not a new idea in the economic development literature. As far back as the 1960s, when the American economist and theorist Walt Rostow popularized his stages of economic growth, the idea of foreign aid for Third-World development had been sacrosanct. Like other neoclassical economic theories, however, the poverty trap model puts old wine in new bottles by creating a stir around capital as the central development imperative.

Accordingly, the big push of capital infusion above the "threshold" is said to be required to stimulate economic growth in Sierra Leone, a country in which the basic infrastructure for productivity is lacking. Capital infusion will lead to productive investments, which in turn will lead to better pay and increasing levels of discretionary income for many people. As people's level of discretionary income increases, their levels of savings will consequently increase. This will have the effect of removing the "savings trap" that excludes poor people in Sierra Leone from profitable investments. As well as removing the savings trap, increasing income will remove the debilitating barrier of the "demographic trap," which makes reproduction a problem for profitable economic activities. The big push, according to the poverty trap perspective, will remove multiple barriers to economic growth in Sierra Leone, barriers that include high transportation costs, small market sizes, low-productivity agriculture, the burden of disease, slow technology diffusion, and adverse geopolitics.[29] Sachs and his colleagues also outline an elaborate process for national planning that will require tremendous expertise, and the participation of groups and organizations at both local and international levels, including the national government, donor governments, national and international nongovernmental organizations, the World Bank, and the IMF.[30] This line of thinking assumes that lack of capital is the primary reason why, for instance, women in poor countries have too many children. Capital can therefore save them from self-destructive behaviors or structural barriers. Without Western capital, therefore, Jeffrey Sachs and his colleagues emphatically see no other way for Sierra Leone to step out of poverty.[31] This is the typical classical economic view that patronizingly stipulates a single, one-way path for poor nations that shuts the door to all other possibilities.

The United States is the single largest donor to Sierra Leone. Even more important for the poverty trap analysis is the fact that the United States has the greatest potential for large-scale capital infusion into Sierra Leone and the potential political constituency to make such capital infusion possible. In 2003, for example, the United States provided $58.79 million net in aid to Sierra Leone, about 20 percent of all aid received by that country during that year. However, this was only 0.4 percent of all U.S. aid to developing countries. Instead of giving foreign aid in small amounts that have little net effect on poverty, proponents of capital infusion suggest that the United States should target its allocation to a small number of poorer countries at a time. This targeting will lead to larger amounts of aid that will be sufficient to jumpstart development. A 5 percent increase in total U.S. allocations to developing countries would translate into $735 million to Sierra Leone in terms of 2003 foreign aid disbursement. This amount exceeds Sierra Leone's annual budgetary needs and can ostensibly serve to launch economic development. Several years of this level of support, according to infusionists, would start the economic growth engine just as it did for Western Europe after World War II. Because the United States provides the smallest proportion of gross national product in aid (estimated at 0.17 percent of GNP in 2006) in comparison with other donor countries, simply doubling that amount would provide the big push to many countries simultaneously.

In practical terms, therefore, the poverty-trap model calls for a substantial increase in U.S. capital flow into Sierra Leone and the use of these funds on building roads, power sources, schools, and other forms of infrastructure that are clearly needed for development. It also calls for substantial foreign involvement in the planning, implementing, and assessing of development efforts, in addition to local participation. These policy prescriptions require great expertise, knowledge, and awareness among local people to make their involvement in the planning, implementing, and assessing of development efforts meaningful. The prescriptions therefore presume that citizens have high levels of awareness and education, and that they are able and willing to monitor development policies and projects. The prescriptions also demand that social institutions are functioning correctly, that the mandate of the legal and justice system, for example, is clearly defined, and that the institution of justice is independent and competent. Successful development also demands that resources are actually allocated to viable projects and that citizen participation ensures transparency.

Building on the neoclassical foundation that "aid that is ambitious enough would actually end Africa's dependency," Jeffrey Sachs and his fellow researchers employ two fundamental assumptions that demand attention.[32] First, that Sierra Leone has the necessary institutional capacity to effectively utilize huge amounts of foreign capital for development in ways that will lead to poverty alleviation, and second, that the United States can be persuaded to provide an enormous capital flow to Sierra Leone as required by the big push theory.

Institutional Syncretism

The assumption of institutional capacity in the poverty trap model fails to address the power of cultural elements such as values, norms, and expectations to impact and control social action and response. It fails to stipulate mechanisms for normative changes that will enable the legal-rational criteria of economic development to operate in a society that is largely arranged according to syncretic modes of social relations. Recent scholarship in development studies, however, shows that social institutions are the primary vehicles through which economic development occurs, and that social institutions in many poor countries are also the mechanisms through which poverty is reinforced.[33] In many recent research reports, the need for an institutional-change model is suggested. I attempt to show that institutional capacity is central to poverty alleviation by proposing a theory of institutional syncretism.

At the core of social life and development activities are social institutions. In an attempt to understand the nature of these institutions, therefore, Roland defines them as "constraints on behavior imposed by rules of the game."[34] Because social institutions are the result of the habitual nature of the social relations that are the critical element in the experiences of a community, argues Roland, they comprise the systems of organized social behaviors and expectations that are held together by social values in the fulfillment of important social goals. However, social institutions can be counterproductive in meeting the social needs of its people. Nicholas Abercrombie and Stephen Hill explain that social systems that are based on feeble formal institutions give rise to patronage systems and "remain in opposition to the central principles of modern society."[35] By inference from Paul Bush, therefore, the goals of economic development for poverty alleviation inherently entail the rearrangement of human habits and the value structure of a culture, because the need for poverty alleviation presupposes the existence of cultural values that are in conflict with the norms of capital accumulation and investment.[36] When patronage is present, therefore, the need for institutional change is clear.

Cultures and their institutional frameworks, however, do not exist in isolation, nor are they static. Because cultural change is normally a continuous process, cultures are usually developed in the context of, in reference to, and in admixture with other cultures. In the cultural change process, therefore, different cultures meet, interpenetrate, and blend. During this change process, inherent differences in value systems and normative structures produce institutional strains. The intensity, duration, and effect of the strain depend largely on the characteristics of the colliding values and on how members of society manage these strains and subsequent change. As the change process progresses, hybrid institutions evolve in order to fulfill the function of mediating social problems. In a normal change process, these emerging institutions are continually changing to provide optimum conditions for resolving contradictions. However, if major players in changing societies do not perceive social change as in their best interest, these hybrid institutions can be trapped in the middle passage, in a state of perpetual cultural adolescence of contradictions and conflicts. This is the syncretic state of institutional development.

Institutional syncretism defines infantile social institutions that are functionally inadequate and that continually exhibit contradictions due to their inability to change dysfunctional values and normative patterns of society.[37] As hybrid systems, syncretic institutions are characterized by conflicts and contradictions between opposing values and norms inherited from parent cultures.[38] When these contradictions and dysfunctionalities are perceived to operate in the interests of powerful elites, the processes of social change are captured and impeded, and thus syncretism is perpetuated. As opposed to normal institutional development where social institutions are constantly evolving to gain maturity, syncretic institutions, unusually, are held in development adolescence, promoting social values or responses that are largely ceremonial rather than instrumental.[39] Ceremonial responses provide nonrational evaluations that are usually based in myths and neotraditional explanations because they tend to solve today's problems with yesterday's explanations and they provide no channels for judging the validity of these explanations. Reverence for traditional authority and maintenance of the status quo are important elements of ceremonial response. Ceremonial responses comprise attitudes to and justifications for behavior or states of affairs based on habitual and emotional reasoning in which logical reasoning for explaining cause and effect is usually of little significance. Instrumental value systems, on the other hand, are rational ways of evaluating institutional rules, performance, and constraints. A social system that relies on instrumental responses is likely to utilize scientific standards for drawing conclusions and testing alternatives or competing explanations for validity. These value systems are inherently deliberative, critical, and forward looking.[40]

Although instrumental and ceremonial responses exist in varying degrees in institutional development, social change in the direction of economic growth and increasing social justice requires greater dependence on instrumental responses. In a syncretic institution, however, the core values that modulate social behavior and expectations tend to be ceremonial. The essence of neotraditionalism, for example, is the provision of ideological cement for the patronage system by providing explanations for behaviors, attitudes, and values that seem inconsistent with aspirations to economic growth, prosperity, equality, and justice but are nonetheless incontrovertible. The control and manipulation of information, myths, and perceptions through the employment of various rhetorical strategies, forms of imagery, and tales are particularly instrumental in the process by which elites influence the masses into accepting the status quo of their own subordination and exploitation.[41] In Sierra Leone, for example, the neotraditional arguments for the institutionalization of a single-party state are that multiple political parties are alien cultural elements because they lead to differences in ideology, and that true African government is based on unifying themes and cooperative politics. In reality, however, syncretic politics produces and sustains class, gender, ethnic, and regional inequalities through the patronage system.

Formal syncretic institutions are characteristically incompetent in performing the functions of a state in protecting its citizens, providing for their needs, and equitably distributing access to resources. The system is further characterized by severe inequalities and social insecurities. To fill this functional gap, the patronage system rises as a functional alternative. It establishes patron-client relationships that are built on loyalty and allegiance. These relationships are established to gain preeminence over formal institutions in terms of loyalty. The patron accumulates resources by all means available to him and redistributes these to clients, who in turn offer their loyalty, political support, praise, and esteem to the patron instead of loyalty to formal institutions.

Patronage in contemporary Sierra Leone is characterized by a structurally bifurcated class system of elites and masses. Elite groups, which comprise political, economic, and military elites, have privileged access to political power, economic resources, and the coercive powers of the state. They are often born into powerful elite families, or they are related to elite families through ties of marriage or adoption, but less often they are recruited into elite circles as a reward for loyalty. At other times, elites are recruited as a result of their educational achievement, or because they belong to a potential counter-elite group. In the Sierra Leone syncretic system, political elites quite often dominate access to state resources to gain economic power. In fewer instances, military elites are able to capture political and economic power. Although elite groups have diverse regional, ethnic, religious, linguistic, and economic backgrounds, commitment to the syncretic system is the tie that binds them. Another trait of elites in a syncretic system is their commitment to consumption standards and lifestyles that burden national resource capacity.[42] By retaining control of public resources, elites perpetuate patronage structures by recruiting clients into their entourage and bestowing "privileges" on the masses. Through this show of grandiosity and largesse, the members of the elite elicit compliance from the masses.

The masses, on the other hand, represent the large majority of people in Sierra Leone who are alienated from resources and occupy social positions and statuses that provide little or no opportunity for advancement.[41] Because of their socioeconomic conditions, the masses are vulnerable to economic, political, and social upheavals. The syncretic culture forces the masses to cognitively and emotionally acquiesce in exploitation by joining the clientele of elites in order to protect themselves and their relatives.[43] In time, the demoralized masses see the lifestyles of the elites as the model for modern life and see their own station as the consequence of some cosmic order or bad luck. Nonetheless, they maintain an enduring aspiration, for themselves, their children, their relatives, and even their grandchildren, to join the ranks of the elites. As such, any activity that upsets the patronage order is generally perceived as working against their best interests.

Paradoxically, the fortunes and survival of the masses and the elites are delicately intertwined, as the daily survival of the masses is heavily influenced by elite behaviors and attitudes while the fortunes of the elite depend on the acquiescence of the masses. Daloz saw this as the "big man" syndrome that allows elites to scavenge resources and redistribute these to their followers and clients. The interdependence is characterized by several contradictions that sustain ceremonial responses and limit the opportunity for rational social responses in addressing institutional dysfunctions.[44] For the purpose of understanding poverty in Sierra Leone, three major contradictions are presented here.

First, there is the class size contradiction. Syncretic institutions impose an artificial limit on the size of the elite class to minimize resource competition. One way of achieving this is by reducing the rate of upward class mobility by restricting access to quality education among the masses while imposing ascribed status as the primary means of gaining certain social rewards and positions. This contradicts elite theories of economic growth that demand increasing numbers of elites that would promote economic investment and accumulation. On the other hand, increasing the size of the elites' clientele is promoted to enhance elite prestige and political survival. However, as the size of the elites' clientele increases, it imposes a burden on available elite resources. In a culture in which elites are forced to fend for themselves, elites scavenge for resources by any means to sustain their prestigious patron lifestyle in an atmosphere of lax monitoring, producing a culture of blatant bribery and embezzlement. In a contemporary society where the continued survival of patronage paradoxically depends on resource investment and accumulation, the increasing size of the elite clientele creates accumulation problems for elites. This class size contradiction threatens the status of elites, and consequently, the entire social system.

Second, the problem of resource redistribution in a syncretic system creates a source of conflict and tension that threatens elite status as well as economic growth. While economic rationality requires investment and accumulation, syncretic patronage demands resource redistribution for the maintenance of a clientele that will continue to support the syncretic system.[45] Similarly, the syncretic system forces elites to concentrate opportunities in areas of influence where they can effectively control their protégés. In Sierra Leone, for example, under the "green revolution" policy, the private accounts and home towns of elites effectively became the redistribution centers for public resources.[46] One effect of patron allocation schemes in a syncretic system is that rural and remote areas are permanently impoverished and forgotten. As with the class size contradiction, the redistribution contradiction provides a perfect medium for institutional malfunction and underdevelopment. Third, syncretic societies face the locus-of-power contradiction. Whereas elites rely on vast state resources and power to perpetuate their patronage, the need to accumulate resources and extend their own personal spheres of influence stands in contrast to the need to increase the power of an impersonal state for economic growth.

The interdependence of the elites and the masses is further mediated by conflict mechanisms to sustain syncretic institutions that provide a structure within which elites and masses stay committed to syncretic principles. Lewis Coser explains that the degree of functional interdependence and social differentiation between these classes is essential in understanding the intensity of class conflict.[47] Whereas the socioeconomic and political gap between the elites and the masses in Sierra Leone has historically been wide, and continues to grow wider, the level of class interdependence is also high. As a result, the interclass conflicts that arise from the alienation of the masses are generally of low intensity and are easily suppressed and defused by the paraphernalia of state power and the personal influence of elites. The submission of the masses is further achieved through dogmatic neotraditional principles and the instrumentality of ignorance and illiteracy. The numerous but virtually inconsequential outbreaks of social unrest among workers, students, and women traders in Sierra Leone are examples of low-intensity interclass conflict. On the other hand, conflicts among elite groups are fewer but more intensive, as observed by Augustine Kposowa and J. Craig

Jenkins, who concluded that military coups are extremely destructive because they "are largely driven by elite rivalries inside the military and civilian government."[48] Military coups and the disastrous civil war in Sierra Leone between 1992 and 2002 exemplify high-intensity elite conflicts.

In addition to an explanation of how systemic contradictions and conflict mechanisms provide syncretic institutions with their staying power, four principles of syncretism, namely, reproduction, irrationality, blame attribution, and collective inaction are stipulated in the institutional trap model to explain how the syncretic system promotes patronage and subdues the masses.

According to the reproduction principle, elites maintain existing structures of patronage by means of the dynastic entitlements and recruitment methods outlined earlier. These methods of recruitment control class size and reduce the risk that people with alternative political ideals will gain power. When, for example, the leadership of the Sierra Leone People's Party became vacant with the death of Milton Margai in 1963, Albert Margai, a brother of the late prime minister, succeeded him in spite of opposition. Once in power, Milton Margai started to pursue the goal of a single-party political system. His failed attempt to establish a single-party system at that time was only a temporary setback for the syncretic structure. His opponent and successor, Siaka Stevens, eventually established a one-party system in 1978. After seventeen years of relatively uninterrupted and unchallenged plunder, oppression, and exploitation, Siaka Stevens recruited his replacement, in the person of Joseph Momoh, who in turn protected elites in the Stevens regime from prosecution. During these years, even university teaching positions served as incentive tokens for political elites. Scholars whose academic outlook challenged the status quo were easily removed and replaced with individuals with the right political connections and outlook, questionable credentials notwithstanding. Civil society activists were similarly co-opted into positions of power, making protest activities in Sierra Leone organizationally chaotic and politically ineffective. The position of chiefs recruited through dynastic principles and holding their offices at the pleasure of the president became positions for elite recruitment in support of syncretism.

The irrationality principle stipulates that syncretic elites will resist changes in institutional arrangements if the gains made by elites will be less than those made by other participants, even if the net benefits to themselves and society are increased. As described in the distribution contradiction, the main focus of syncretic elites is to accumulate resources and redistribute these both to increase their political power and to increase their clientele. Any other alternative institutional arrangement that will allow greater gains to other actors and to society threatens the patronage structure. To this effect, the syncretic system opposes economic transformation and political democratization and therefore promotes investment disincentives through irrational responses to important issues. In an environment of political instability and high political risks, political entrepreneurship is actively discouraged, thus weakening the formation of revolutionary groups or an energetic civil society. Such irrationalities are exemplified in government loan policies, frivolous luxuries like the "pajero culture" and the hosting of the Organization of African Unity conference under the Stevens regime.[49]

According to the principle of blame attribution, syncretic institutions provide a psychological escape for elites and convince the masses to support the status quo. Leaders in a syncretic system provide a justification for failed policies and programs by blaming external factors such as colonialism, global capitalism, and the policies of rich nations such as the United States. The principle of collective inaction, on the other hand, explains the inability of the masses in a syncretic system to collectively identify with their own class interests. Like the Marxist class consciousness problem, dysfunctional institutions persist because the masses are unable, unwilling, and unmotivated, and are apathetic about actions against elite interests mostly because they are unable to see past their dependence on elite privileges.[50] In the eyes of many Sierra Leoneans, bribery, public corruption, and affluence are simply the benefits of public office in a contemporary society.

From the point of view of institutional trap analysis, therefore, the assumption of institutional capacity in Sierra Leone by the poverty trap model of development is overtly simplistic. Like many failed development models implemented in Sierra Leone, the institutional trap model puts too much faith in the power of money to transform society. According to the institutional syncretism analysis presented here, however, institutional contradictions, social values, and expectations are formidable barriers to economic growth and poverty alleviation. The predominance of ceremonial responses to poverty issues, issues that arise from attempts to fit into the mold of a modern society, clearly demonstrates the need for an institutional change. In the absence of institutional changes in Sierra Leone, no amount of money will fix the systemic contradictions of the patronage system or negate the syncretic principles that sustain exploitation, corruption, and inefficiency.

The U.S. Foreign Policy Framework

The second assumption of the poverty trap economic model suggests that it is possible to persuade the U.S. government to provide free capital to serve as the big push to launch economic development in Sierra Leone. This is a faulty proposition, not because money is not important in poverty alleviation but because the policy environment within which U.S. foreign aid allotment is decided is not sympathetic enough to the poverty conditions in Sierra Leone to provide the level of aid required by this approach.

Table 17.2. Import and Export Data for Sierra Leone–U.S. Trade (US$ millions): 2000–2006

	2000	2001	2002	2003	2004	2005	2006
Export	3,824,157	4,573,846	3,832,840	6,537,180	10,856,649	9,439,745	36,133,793
Import	18,677,522	27,879,626	25,459,491	28,250,318	40,433,703	37,808,011	39,246,151
Trade Balance	−14,853,365	−24,040,786	−21,626,651	−21,713,138	−29,577,054	−28,368,266	−3,112,358

Source: Based on U.S. International Trade Commission data, www.usitc.gov.

It can be argued that the relationship between Sierra Leone and the United States has important cultural and economic dimensions that might suggest that the United States can serve as an important ally and sponsor in the war against poverty. Indeed, substantial diplomatic, cultural, and economic relations between Sierra Leone and the United States date back at least to late colonialism in Sierra Leone. During this period, U.S. policy was deeply committed to the containment of Communist ideology around the world. It can be argued that Sierra Leone received a U.S. consulate in 1959 and subsequently gained access to U.S. economic assistance primarily in furtherance of this containment policy. Since then, Sierra Leone has continued to receive U.S. foreign aid in varying amounts comprising anywhere from 1 to 28 percent of Sierra Leone's total aid package. In 1990, for example, it was over 20.3 percent, in 1999 it was 4.2 percent, in 2000, it was 23 percent, and in 2003, it was 5 percent (see table 17.1). Even though the level of U.S. aid to Sierra Leone may not be sufficient, from the point of view of the poverty trap, to provide the requisite big push capital flow to eradicate poverty, the contribution of the United States is still very generous. It is not unreasonable to expect occasional large-scale aid from the United States in the future, either. In addition, Sierra Leone is a beneficiary of the food for development initiative under Title II of U.S. Public Law 480. The program is administered by the U.S. Department of Agriculture to provide food aid to hungry populations in poor countries. Additionally, Sierra Leone benefits from the Peace Corps program, which was authorized under U.S. Public Law 87-293 to help poor countries in meeting manpower needs. Indeed, the United States has emerged as one of the most important financial contributors to Sierra Leone. Table 17.2 provides trade data that reflect the economic relations between Sierra Leone and the United States.

In 2000, the Clinton administration authorized the African Growth and Opportunity Act (AGOA), which was modified and reauthorized by the Bush administration. This arrangement allows Sierra Leone to participate in a limited form of free trade with the United States, providing Sierra Leone with opportunity to export its products to a market that can offer higher prices. Since 2000, the export capacity of Sierra Leone to the United States has steadily increased, rising from $3.8 million to $36.1 million in 2006. However, imports from the United States have increased at a faster pace, creating a substantial negative balance of trade for Sierra Leone (see table 17.2). The economic returns of AGOA trade to Sierra Leone, however disappointing they may seem now, constitute an opportunity for the country to open up to international competition and face the challenges of building competitive industries. However, the meager returns for Sierra Leone from this trade relationship speak to the institutional incapacity of Sierra Leone to take advantage of an economic opportunity. The future is not gloomy, however. The AGOA data shows a steady declining unfavorable balance of trade for Sierra Leone since 2005. The huge increase in export to the United States in 2006 is a sign of hope. In spite of the promise that AGOA and U.S. aid status holds for Sierra Leone, however, a careful examination of the U.S. foreign policy environment is likely to suggest that hopes for a big push from the U.S. government are unrealistic and that this, therefore, is an ill-fated policy for poverty alleviation.

U.S. foreign policy does not exist in a vacuum. It is principally informed by economic, political, and strategic self-interest.[51] Within this policy framework, foreign aid is disbursed on the basis of considerations that are related to the strategic importance of the recipient country to America's hegemonic interests. In addition, U.S. foreign policy is affected by the public mood, which is in turn affected by the American worldview and social values. The role of individualism as an imperative ideology in the American social system, coupled with faith in the forces of the liberal marketplace, has a significant impact on America's responses to poverty. The implication of American individualism and the American perception of poverty is that there is a dearth of sympathy for a country that is steeped in poverty seemingly because of mismanagement, inefficiency, and misplaced priorities. This perception is further complicated, unfortunately, by the fact that Sierra Leoneans belong to the darker end of the racial spectrum. Many scholars have observed that racial prejudice is fundamental to American perceptions and value systems, and that this prejudice is influential in international policy matters.[52] It has been suggested that the United States' halfhearted reaction to disasters in Africa, such as its indifference to apartheid in South Africa and dictatorships in the Sudan and the Democratic Republic of Congo, and its indifference to wars in Rwanda, Liberia, and Sierra Leone compared to its more dedicated and often preemptive role in the Middle East, Eastern Europe, and Asia, is an indicator of the effect of racial perceptions on foreign politics in the United States.

Even though one would expect that the African American constituency could provide the needed policy advocacy group, the black constituency in America is not likely to provide much political capital for a big push capital infusion into Sierra Leone. This is because the black constituency is itself faced with many domestic problems for the solution of which it cannot get funds and is itself a victim of racist attitudes. Furthermore, Sierra Leone is just one among many African nations in severe poverty, making African poverty a dull issue to the American public.

In addition to these unfavorable conditions, the "Bush Doctrine," which took center stage after the September 11, 2001, terrorist attacks, is not particularly responsive to issues in Sierra Leone. It is an ideology that appeals to emotions about the security and independence of the American people and resonates with the resolve of Americans to defeat terrorism. This doctrine is at once uniquely unilateral as well as intrinsically assertive and interventionist in promoting U.S. hegemonic interests. The neorealist philosophy of this doctrine rests on state militarism, the use of force, preemptive strikes, and disengagement from international coalitions as long as these actions are useful in orchestrating and perpetuating U.S. hegemony. It is a foreign policy environment that prioritizes U.S. strategic concerns above all other considerations and encourages capitalist norms in the protection of U.S. economic interests. This approach to foreign policy, in spite of its grandiosity, fits so neatly into the general American policy framework that many foreign actions under a conservative administration such as that of George W. Bush are likely to be similar to actions under more liberal administrations. This same policy framework allows liberal administrations such as those of Clinton and Carter to fail to live up to their rhetoric of helping African nations out of poverty, just as it gives cover to the conservative Bush administration to renege on promises to provide drugs for the HIV/AIDS epidemic in Africa. This same policy framework allows attacks on Afghanistan and Iraq in the security interests of the United States, while the United States provides increased foreign aid to countries that fit into its strategic configuration of its security concerns.[53]

Within this U.S. policy framework, Sierra Leone is unlikely to benefit from war on terror assistance compared to states like Pakistan, Indonesia, Israel, Palestine, Iraq, or even North Korea and Iran. Sierra Leone is not located in a hotbed of cultural conflict like the Middle East or East Asia, nor is it overflowing with fundamentalist religious movements that are likely to cause concern for the United States. Sierra Leone does not have the capability to develop weapons of mass destruction that could pose a threat to world peace; it does not have strategic minerals and oil in quantities that would make its economic and political environment of consequence to the United States. Sierra Leone's remoteness and virtual communication disconnect with the capitalist nerve centers of the world make it a less than attractive candidate for organizations that have significant influence on U.S. policies. Consequently, the country finds itself one of the least favored nations on earth with regard to U.S. foreign policy priorities.

Increased foreign aid allotment to Sierra Leone between 2001 and 2004, as shown in table 17.1, is best explained by a humanitarian action of the United States to help the war recovery efforts rather than a commitment to increasing aid for development in Sierra Leone. One possible area for modestly increasing U.S., aid to Sierra Leone remains in the domain of trade liberalization, yet Sierra Leone's response to the AGOA initiative is, at best, feeble (see table 17.2). Yet the significance of a free trade approach to persistent poverty in Sierra Leone, barring institutional rearrangement, is contentious. As is evident so far, the impact of AGOA on the Sierra Leonean economy is insignificant. Although experience under AGOA is too short to be symptomatic of development failures, the Doha rounds of trade talks would suggest that tremendous structural barriers exist for sustained significant benefit for Sierra Leone under AGOA.[54] Besides, syncretic institutional barriers are likely to negate any benefit of free trade for Sierra Leone. Without drastic institutional restructuring in postwar Sierra Leone, even the benefits of the United States' AGOA policy will accrue to a few privileged members of society who will use these resources to continue to entrench and fortify their positions, effectively backing political elitism with economic oligopoly.

Conclusion

With respect to the theoretical arguments, it is reasonable to submit that the evidence does not support the assumption by the poverty trap theory that the United States is likely to provide the "big push" capital to Sierra Leone to engage in a dramatic economic recovery. The U.S. foreign policy environment is not amenable to a huge development capital infusion into Sierra Leone. Huge amounts of capital assistance by the United States, of the magnitude required by the poverty trap perspective or of a magnitude that can actually lead to economic development, are possible only if there are fundamental changes in the U.S. foreign policy framework accompanied by fundamental changes in U.S. social values. This is an audacious expectation but certainly unlikely to materialize. Additionally, due to media obsession with "crisis Africa," the American public has developed a high tolerance level for poverty in Africa. Given this compassion fatigue, it will take humanitarian needs of colossal proportions in Sierra Leone for U.S. public opinion to rally in support of significant foreign aid to the country. Having found no convincing grounds to believe that the United States would undertake capital infusion in Sierra Leone, and more importantly, having found no evidence to support the contention that Sierra Leone's institutional arrangements have the capability to utilize a big push capital infusion for sustained economic development and poverty reduction, the only conclusion is that the poverty trap economic theory does not provide a model that is appropriate for poverty alleviation in Sierra Leone.

The poverty trap perspective, like many development theories, assumes capital infusion as the final solution. This is the weakest link in the theoretical framework. The institutional trap analysis outlined in this chapter clearly demonstrates the inherent contradictions in a syncretic system that sets up capitalist accumulation against the elite resource redistribution imperative. Even though the poverty trap perspective identifies weak institutional capacity as an issue, this weakness is treated more as a symptom than as a cause of endemic poverty. The failure of the big push theory to link structural bottlenecks to institutional weakness that requires institutional restructuring makes the theory ineffective in addressing poverty alleviation in Sierra Leone. A dangerous implication of the capital infusionist perspective in development theory is one that provides political elites in Sierra Leone with a convenient cover and a scapegoat. Rather than examining their own twisted ideas of modernity and institutional arrangements, elites in Sierra Leone blame persistent poverty on rich nations such as the United States while using neotraditional arguments to sustain syncretic structures.

Economic development and sustainable poverty alleviation are possible in Sierra Leone. This possibility, however, resides in social institutional reconstruction and cultural changes that will emanate largely from within rather than from without. Focusing on increasing the quantity of the U.S. aid to this country is futile, and in any case, ineffective. The bottlenecks to sustained economic growth in Sierra Leone are mostly ingrained in syncretic institutions. Institutional change strategies that will permit broad democratic participation and encourage opportunities for self-reliance and self-realization are more likely to effectively channel local resources in ways that will lead to investment confidence. This change is already in the works.

The postwar period in Sierra Leone has witnessed a number of positive steps toward institutional development that, if sustained, will eventually help to reverse the poverty trend. One such step is the decentralization program that is allowing power to devolve to local people in city and district councils, enabling them to make and implement strategic decisions about their own affairs. After decades of centralized power, however, this project is not without major challenges that are related to the tenacity of syncretism. The need for elites to influence policy matters at local levels, the potential conflict issues between councilors, chiefs, and other traditional power brokers, and the corruption in high and low places are among the pitfalls. The task of overcoming the expectations ordinary people have of "di pa" patronage culture is also formidable. Indications are, so far, that local councils and citizens are awakening to the challenge of managing their own lives. Other steps toward institutional rearrangement include educational reform and streamlining as well as reforms in the civil service. In addition, external aid to Sierra Leone for institutional rebuilding is taking shape. In fulfillment of their promise to Sierra Leone upon completion of the IMF/World Bank requirements for the enhanced Heavily Indebted Poor Country (HIPC) initiative, the United States and the creditor countries of the Paris Club have announced substantial debt cancellation for Sierra Leone in 2007.[55] The United States, for its part, has provided a 100 percent debt cancellation. This has relieved Sierra Leone of a heavy debt of over $1 billion, a burden that has contributed to so much misery over the years. These efforts, placed within the context of evolving instrumental social institutions, have the potential to begin the process of sustained poverty alleviation. There is no doubt that people in this country are already raising questions about how funds saved due to this huge debt relief will be utilized. Time will tell whether these initial institutional reforms will translate into bigger reforms that will institutionalize transparency and accountability as part of the culture in Sierra Leone.

As these developments and the analysis in this chapter show, development theory that is built on unrealistic expectations is likely to repeat the disappointing results of developmentalism of the past. Sierra Leone cannot afford to continue to fail in its efforts to overcome persistent poverty. A focus on institutional reforms, on the other hand, holds great promise for defeating persistent and endemic poverty.

Notes

1. UNDP, *Human Development Index* (New York: Oxford University Press, 1999–2006), http://www.undp.org.

2. Margaret Lebbie-Moebiyor and Credo (Community Research and Development Organization), "Sierra Leone: A Country Report," National *Women Studies Association Journal* 15, no.1 (2003): 133, http://muse.jhu.edu/journals/nwsa_journal/vo15/15.1lebbie-moebiyor.html.

3. Alejandro Portes and Kelly Hoffman, "Latin American Class Structures: Their Composition and Change during the Neoliberal Era," *Latin American Research Review* 38, no.1 (2003): 41–82; and Jerry Kloby, *Inequality, Power and Development: Issues in Political Sociology*, 2nd ed. (Amherst, NY: Humanity Books, 2004).

4. Sushanta Mallick and Brigitte Granville, "How Best to Link Poverty Reduction and Debt Sustainability in IMF–World Bank Model," *International Review of Applied Economics* 19, no. 1 (2005): 67–85

5. Jeffrey D. Sachs et al., "Ending Africa's Poverty Trap," *Brookings Papers on Economic Activity* 1 (2004): 117–240, http://www.unmillenniumproject.org/documents/PEAEndingAfricasPovertyTrapFINAL.pdf.

6. Frances Moore Lappe et al., *World Hunger: Twelve Myths* (New York: Grove Press, 1998).

7. Amartya Sen, "Democracy as a Universal Value," *Journal of Democracy* 10, no. 3 (1999): 3–17, http://muse.jhu.edu/demo/jod/10.3sen.html; and Amartya Sen, "A Decade of Human Development," *Journal of Human Development* 1, no. 1 (2000): 17–23, http://hdr.undp.org/docs/training/oxford/readings/Sen_HD.pdf.

8. Richard Joseph, "Africa: States in Crisis," *Journal of Democracy* 14, no. 3 (July 2003): 161.

9. Joseph Hanlon, "Do Donors Promote Corruption? The Case of Mozambique," *Third World Quarterly* 25, no. 4 (2004): 747.

10. Syncretic institutions are hybrid social institutions that exhibit severe symptoms of disfunctionality because of their inability to change values and norms that are inefficient, unproductive, or clearly destructive to society.

11. For more information on the Corruption Perception Index (CPI) as used by Transparency International, see Transparency International's Web site, http://www.transparency.org/.

12. M. Fortes and E. E. Evans-Pritchard, *Introduction to African Political Systems* (London: Oxford University Press, 1940), 3.

13. Ibid., 5.

14. Sheikh Umarr Kamarah, "The Individual and Society: Political Philosophy in the Themne Proverb," *Sierra Leone Studies and Review* 1, no. 1 (2000): 121–33.

15. Stephen Kandeh, "The Growth of a Church amidst Conflicts and Crisis: The Case of God Is Our Light Church in Sierra Leone" (bachelor's thesis, University of Sierra Leone, 1989), 7–30.

16. Jimmy D. Kandeh, "Politicization of Ethnic Identities in Sierra Leone," *African Studies Review* 39, no. 1 (1992): 81–99.

17. In Sierra Leone, people who are called "di pa" are typically wealthy and powerful elites. In a sense, the title implies reverence for one considered to be a sustainer. The desires and orders of "di pa" basically have the force of law to all those whose livelihoods depend on the benevolence of this sustainer.

18. Stephen Kandeh, "Agricultural Technology and Rice Availability in Sierra Leone"(bachelor's thesis, University of Sierra Leone, 1989).

19. According to the UNDP *Human Development Report* of 2004, only 21 percent of the population were urban in 1971. Over 30 years later, in 2003, only 38.1 percent of the population lived in urban areas. It is reasonable to assume that urbanization is overestimated because census data gravely underestimate rural population due to the data collection problems discussed in the text. Additionally, a large number of people who live in urban areas in Sierra Leone are seasonal migrant workers in mines and industries.

20. Stephen Kandeh, "Structural Adjustment Programs and Democratization in Sierra Leone" (master's thesis, Ohio State University, 1995).

21. Ibid., 44.

22. C. Melamed, *Adjusting Africa: Structural Economic Change and Development in Africa* (Oxford: WorldView, 1996); D. P. Forsythe and B. A. J. Rieffer, "US Foreign Policy and Enlarging the Democratic Community," *Human Rights Quarterly* 22 (2000): 988–1010; M. McFaul, "Democracy Promotion as a World Value," *Washington Quarterly* 28, no. 1 (2004): 147–63; and Kandeh, "Structural Adjustment Programs and Democratization in Sierra Leone."

23. John Mukum Mbaku, "Military Coups as Rent-Seeking Behavior," *Journal of Political and Military Sociology* 20, no. 3 (1994): 241–84.

24. F. Michael Higginbotham, "A Dream Revived: The Rise of the Black Reparations Movement," *NYU Annual Survey of American Law* 58 (2003), http://www.nyu.edu/pubs/annualsurvey/articles/58%20N.Y.U.%20Ann.%20Surv.%20Am.%20L.%20447%20(2003).pdf; Martha Biondi, "The Rise of the Reparations Movement," *Radical History Review*, 87 (2003): 5–18; and Marx du Plessis, "Historical

Injustice and International Law: An Exploratory Discussion of Reparation for Slavery," *Human Rights Quarterly* 25 (2002): 624–59.

25. Barba M. Koroma, "Inferiority Complex: A Deterrence to Development in Sierra Leone and Sub-Saharan Africa," *Sierra Leone Studies and Reviews* 1, no. 1 (2000): 33–53; and George B. Ayittey, *Africa Betrayed* (New York: St. Martins Press, 1993).

26. Stephen Krasner, "Sharing Sovereignty: New Directions for Collapsed and Failing States," *International Security* 29, no. 2 (2004): 85–120. A discussion of radical alternative methods that fly in the face of traditional Westphalian ideologies for addressing failing states has gained momentum in recent development literature. These views generally elaborate development policy failures in terms of political regime failures due to elite exploitation, and they present alternative approaches that include the sharing of sovereignty with developed nations instead of the nonintervention diplomacy that has resulted, these views claim, in entrenching poverty and instability around the world.

27. Jeffrey Sachs, "Resolving the Debt Crisis of Low-Income Countries," *Brookings Papers on Economic Activity* 1 (2002): 257–86; Jeffrey Sachs, "The Strategic Significance of Global Inequality," *Washington Quarterly* 24, no. 3 (2001): 187–98; and Michael O'Hanlon, "Doing It Right: The Future of Humanitarian Intervention," *Brookings Review* 18, no. 4 (2000): 33–37.

28. Sachs et al., "Ending Africa's Poverty Trap," 122.

29. Ibid., 149–51. Poverty trap theorists note that the "big push" will be effective only in regimes of good governance. Sierra Leone is ranked as average in their analysis, making this country eligible for the big push initiative.

30. Ibid., 171–74.

31. Ibid., 144; Gerhard Lenski, "Marxist Experiments in Destratification: An Appraisal," *Social Forces* 57, no. 2 (1978): 364–83; and Hanlon, "Do Donors Promote Corruption?" In his discussion of the failures of macroeconomic indicators of development, Hanlon shows that there are no visible signs of economic success among ordinary citizens, in spite of the IMF's declaration of Mozambique as a structural adjustment success story. Hanlon points to institutional change as the best path to a solution.

32. Sachs et al., "Ending Africa's Poverty Trap," 124.

33. O'Hanlon, "Doing It Right"; James H. Street, "The Institutionalist Theory of Economic Development," *Journal of Economic Issues* 21, no. 4 (1987): 1861–87; Daron Acemoglu, "A Theory of Political Transition," *American Economic Review* 91, no. 2 (2001): 938–63; Daron Acemoglu, "Oligarchic versus Democratic Societies," *Journal of the European Economic Association,* forthcoming (2007), http://econ-www.mit.edu/faculty/download_pdf.php?id=1493; Daron Acemoglu, "A Simple Model of Inefficient Institutions," *Scandinavian Journal of Economics* 108, no. 4 (2006), http://econ-www.mit.edu/faculty/download_pdf.php?id=1389.

34. Gerald Roland, "Understanding Institutional Change: Fast-Moving and Slow-Moving Institutions," *Studies in Comparative International Development* 38, no. 4 (2004): 111.

35. Nicholas Abercrombie and Stephen Hill, "Paternalism and Patronage," *British Journal of Sociology* 27, no. 4 (1976): 417.

36. Paul Bush, "The Theory of Institutional Change," *Journal of Economic Issues* 21, no. 3 (1987): 1075–99.

37. Abercrombie and Hill, "Paternalism and Patronage," 419.

38. Violet Bridget Lunga, "Mapping Africa's Postcoloniality: Linguistic and Cultural Spaces of Hybridity," *Perspectives on Global Development and Technology* 3 no. 3 (2004): 291–326; Olantunji A. Oyeshile, "Communal Values, Cultural Identity and the Challenge of Development in Contemporary Africa," *Journal of Social, Political and Economic Studies* 29, no. 3 (2004): 291–303.

39. Bush, "The Theory of Institutional Change," 1091.

40. Carol Myers-Scotton, "Elite Closure as a Powerful Language Strategy: The African Case," *International Journal of the Sociology of Language* 103 (1993): 149–63; Alejandro Portes, "Neoliberalism and the Sociology of Development: Emerging Trends and Unanticipated Facts," *Population and Development Review* 23 no. 2 (1997): 229–59.

41. Portes, "Neoliberalism and the Sociology of Development," 229–59.

42. Kloby, *Inequality, Power and Development*.

43. Ibid.

44. Jean-Pascal Daloz, "Big Men in Sub-Saharan Africa: How Elites Accumulate Positions and Resources," *Comparative Sociology* 2, no. 1 (2003): 272.

45. Ibid.

46. At the trial of the former inspector general of police, Mr. Bambay Kamara, it was alleged that thousands of bags of PL 480 rice and millions of leones (Sierra Leonean currency) were discovered on his farm, a place used by politicians planning political campaigns and thuggery.

47. Augustine J. Kposowa and J. Craig Jenkins, "The Structural Source of Military Coups in Postcolonial Africa, 1957–1984," *American Journal of Sociology* 99, no. 1 (July 1993): 126.

48. Jonathan H. Turner, *The Structure of Sociological Theory* (Belmont, CA: Wadsworth, 1978), 216–28.

49. Kandeh, "Structural Adjustment Programs," 98. Political regimes in Sierra Leone that lasted longer than a year almost invariably arranged and collected foreign loans in the name of the country for some development project or other. Between 1970 and 1989, the debt of Sierra Leone grew from $60.5 million to $727 million. By 2006, the debt was said to be in excess of $1.5 billion. Some of the reasons advanced for taking loans included agricultural projects and the building of roads, stadiums, government buildings, and hotels. In 1980, for example, the government of Siaka Stevens secured a $95 million loan to sponsor the hosting of the Organization of African Unity (OAU) summit in Freetown. Against the advice of many observers, and in the interest of becoming the chairman of the OAU, Siaka Stevens undertook an elaborate project involving the building of a village and conference centers to accommodate the African heads of states attending the summit. In 1984, the Siaka Stevens government had plunged the country into another $25 million debt in order to purchase a fleet of Pajero Mitsubishi sport utility vehicles for his ministers and top civil servants, even though these officials had official Mercedes Benz cars already at their disposal.

50. Peter Evans, "The Eclipse of the State? Reflections on Stateness in an Era of Globalization," *World Politics* 50, no. 1 (1997): 62–87.

51. John Ndumbe, "West African Oil, U.S. Energy Policy, and Africa's Development Strategies," *Mediterranean Quarterly* 15, no. 1 (2004): 93–104

52. Sarah White, "Thinking Race, Thinking Development," *Third World Quarterly* 23, no. 3 (2002): 101; and Paul M. Sniderman and Philip E. Tetlock, "Reflections on American Racism," *Journal of Social Sciences* 22, no. 2 (1986): 173–87

53. Stephen M. Walt, "Beyond Bin Laden: Reshaping US Foreign Policy," *International Security* 26, no. 3 (winter 2001): 56–78

54. Trade talks between the rich and poor countries that are members of the World Trade Organization (WTO) have highlighted the opposing, and probably irreconcilable, interests of the rich and poor nations. These unproductive meetings, to which many poor countries cannot afford to send representatives, have failed to reach agreement on core issues such as export competition, market access, and domestic support. The United States, for example, refuses to cut subsidies to its farmers. This policy, poor nations claim, gives an unfair advantage to American farmers in the world market because they can afford to sell for less, making them more competitive. Poor nations, on the other hand, are resisting attempts to cut tariffs, which, rich nations claim, are unfairly protecting poor nations' producers from fair market competition. Visit the following Web sites for more information: http://www.bread.org/about-us/institute/trade-sidebars/one-kenyan-voice.html (accessed May 17, 2007); http://www.voanews.com/english/archive/2006-10/2006-10-26-voa1.cfm (accessed May 17, 2007).

55. For more information on HIPC relief efforts, visit the IMF at http:/www.imf.org or the World Bank at http://www.worldbank.org.

18

Post–Cold War U.S. Foreign Policy toward Liberia and Sierra Leone

Osman Gbla

Introduction

The Mano River Union States of Liberia and Sierra Leone offer appropriate case studies for critical reflections on the impact of post–Cold War U.S. foreign policy on the peace and security of West Africa. The plunging of these two states into violent conflicts in 1989 and 1991 brought to the fore the horrendous character of post-Cold War intrastate conflicts and the half-hearted international response to the attendant catastrophes.[1] The realities of these situations contradict two major post–Cold War arguments: (a) that the post–Cold War era would elongate the corridors of peace in Africa,[2] and (b) that the post–Cold War period would be marked by active U.S. involvement in tackling the intractable problems of economic development, conflict resolution, and democracy in Africa.[3]

These counter-arguments are largely informed by the halfhearted response of the United States to the atrocious nature of these two West African conflicts. The period under review witnessed international peace-keeping involvement in African conflicts.[4] In the Liberian case in particular, the American response to the conflicts seems incredible to many West Africans, considering the long-standing historical relationship between the two states. The skeptic's view that, in spite of the end of the Cold War, perceived national interests will always influence states' responses to international development deserves serious consideration.[5]

This chapter argues that the halfhearted post–Cold War foreign policy of the United States toward Liberia and Sierra Leone impacts in diverse ways on the peace and security of the West African subregion. Accordingly, it seeks to provide answers to some of the following questions: What factors influenced post–Cold War U.S. foreign policy toward Liberia and Sierra Leone? What is the impact of this policy on the peace and security of the

West African subregion? In what ways could the Liberian and Sierra Leonean states respond to this U.S. policy in order to ensure peace and security?

Background

The Upper Guinea region of West Africa, also known as the Mano River Union Basin, is made up of Guinea, Liberia, and Sierra Leone. The three countries have very small populations in relation to those of other West African states, none of them having more than eight million people. They are also endowed with rich natural resources. Liberia is blessed with diamonds, gold, iron ore, rubber, and timber. Sierra Leone has diamonds, gold, iron ore, rutile, and bauxite. Sierra Leone also boasts of having the oldest university in West Africa, that is, Fourah Bay College, opened in 1827. This achievement earned it the prestigious title of the Athens of West Africa. Guinea, like Liberia and Sierra Leone, also has rich mineral resources.

Liberia and Sierra Leone share a similar historical origin.[6] The American Colonization Society (ACS) founded Liberia in 1822, and British merchant-philanthropists founded Sierra Leone in 1787. The ACS, a philanthropic organization in the United States, vigorously spearheaded the repatriation of freed Negro slaves to Liberia. The first settlers, known as the pioneers, landed at Providence Island, near Monrovia, on January 7, 1822. It is however historically incorrect to pinpoint 1822 as the beginning of Liberian history. Prior to the arrival of the settlers in Liberia in 1822, there had existed, for at least a hundred years, along what used to be called the Grain Coast about one and half dozen ethnic groups. This group included the Bassa, Belle, Dan (Gio), Dey, Gbandi, Kissi, Gola, Grebo, Kpelle, Krahn, Kru, Mano, Mandingo, Mende, and Vai. Available evidence suggests that these groups coexisted in relative peace with one another before the arrival of the settlers, though occasionally destabilized by minor conflicts.

Early attempts by the settlers to dispossess the indigenes of their lands and to subject them to the settlers' authority met stiff resistance that sometimes culminated in minor wars. The coastal Krus, Grebos, and Golas, for example, engaged the colonists in a series of battles, for example, in November and December 1822. These confrontations between the settlers and the indigenes compelled the settlers to form a cohesive force, as a minority group, to ensure their continued survival. As a result, the settlers, through the ACS and its assistant organizations in New York and Pennsylvania, created the Commonwealth of Liberia in 1839. This union consisted of Grand Bassa County and Montserrado County. Three years later, in 1842, Mississippi in Africa joined the commonwealth as Sinhoe County. The Constitution of the Commonwealth provided for a legislature known as the Liberian Colonial Council; the executive branch was headed by a governor, who was appointed by the ACS, and there was also a judiciary. The first governor of the commonwealth was Thomas

Buchanan, who ruled from 1838 to 1841. The Commonwealth of Liberia was, however, not recognized by European powers such as Britain and France.

On July 26, 1847, Liberia became a free and independent state called the Republic of Liberia, making it the first republic in Africa. A historic document—the Declaration of Liberian Independence—was written by Hilary Teague, a settler from Massachusetts County. Eleven people from the three counties of Montserrado, Grand Bassa, and Sinhoe signed it. A constitutional convention in Monrovia drafted a new constitution in January 1847. On July 26, 1847, the convention adopted and proclaimed Liberia's Declaration of Independence. Joseph Jenkins Roberts was elected as first president of the Republic of Liberia and ruled from 1847 to 1876.

From 1847 until 1980, a small group of expatriates—the Americo-Liberians—dominated the social, economic, and political landscape of Liberia. This predominance was accompanied by a well-orchestrated scheme to marginalize the majority of indigenous Liberians, who constituted more than 90 percent of the country's population. This and other factors laid the foundation for the Liberian crisis that erupted in 1989.

Sierra Leone is an ex-British colony. Its colonial history can be traced as far back as 1787, when a group of British philanthropists acquired a piece of land in the western part of what became Sierra Leone to be used as a haven for freed slaves. These former slaves (liberated Africans) came mainly from England, America, Nova Scotia, the West Indies, and the West African high seas. The Sierra Leone Company, a British trading company, was entrusted with the administration of the settlement in the early period of its establishment. Owing to financial and other problems, the company in 1808 handed over jurisdiction to the British government, and the settlement became a British crown colony. The hinterland was declared a British protectorate in 1896 and was added to the colony, a development that finally saw the rest of what is now Sierra Leone come under British rule.

In order to ensure the smooth running of the country, the British introduced two systems of administration: the crown colony system for the colony and indirect rule for the hinterland. The former entailed direct administration of the colony by the British through a resident governor, while in the latter, the affairs of the hinterland were run by the indigenous people, supervised by British officials such as district commissioners.

Sierra Leone gained independence from Britain on April 27, 1961. Sir Milton Margai of the Sierra Leone People's Party (SLPP) headed the first postindependence government (1961–64). Sierra Leone was declared a one-party state under All People's Congress (APC) rule in 1978, a development that helped lay the foundation for the outbreak of war in 1991.

The historical connection between the states of Liberia and Sierra Leone is discernible in the name of the capital city of Sierra Leone—Freetown—and in the name Liberia itself, which literally means the land of liberty/freedom.[7]

It is therefore unsurprising that descendants of former slaves are among those who live in both countries—the Krios in Sierra Leone and the Americo-Liberians in Liberia.

Sierra Leone, Liberia, and Guinea share certain similarities especially in ethnographic terms. There are, for example, common ethnic groups along their common borders, and these include the Mandingoes, Kissis, Vais, and Fullahs. This situation helps to explain why it was relatively easy for refugees to be absorbed into any of the three states when the subregion imploded in 1989.

Geopolitical realities compelled Sierra Leone and Liberia to establish a subregional grouping, the Mano River Union (MRU), in October 1973.[8] Guinea joined in 1980. The MRU aimed at strengthening existing ties, promoting trade, and fostering social integration.

Relations between the United States and the two MRU states of Liberia and Sierra Leone had deep roots in history. As already discussed, the American Colonization Society founded Liberia in 1822 as a haven for freed slaves. Prominent American figures including Presidents James Monroe and Thomas Jefferson played a leading role in the establishment of the settlement. As far back as 1819,[9] the U.S. Congress had provided $100,000 for the effort. Even the country's capital—Monrovia—was named after President James Monroe. The country's constitution and other major state institutions including its security forces are based on the U.S. model. About 5 percent of Liberia's population are made up of descendants of freed slaves from America—the Americo-Liberians, who dominated the country's socioeconomic and political scene from 1822 to 1980. In order for the indigenous Liberians to conveniently move up the social ladder, they had to belong to the famous triangle: the True Whig Party (TWP), the Masons, and the Church.[10]

Liberia was also a key ally of the United States during World War II, as its territory was used as a resupply center for the campaign in North Africa.[11] During the Cold War, Liberia served as a relay station for Voice of America broadcasts, for the tracking of shipping, and for communication surveillance. American companies such as Firestone, Bethlehem Steel, and B. F. Goodrich were very active in the exploitation of Liberian resources.

This background was important in shaping U.S. foreign policy toward Liberia, especially during the Cold War. Even at the height of Samuel Doe's appalling human rights violations in the late 1980s, America was still willing to pump huge sums of money into the country as foreign aid assistance.[12] American policy toward Liberia was at the time guided by three major objectives. These were to protect uninterrupted access to American facilities and American military use of Liberian airspace and ports; to promote political stability; and to help bring about financial and economic stability to foster an atmosphere conducive to growth and development.

Relations between America and Liberia took a negative turn in late 1988, following Doe's decision to renounce treaty obligations and to revise the cost structure of the Voice of America relay station, the Omega navigation station, and other extensive communications facilities in Liberia.[13] American access to most of these facilities was drastically curtailed before the outbreak of war in 1989. However, in the early 1990s, the United States was not prepared to seriously engage in Liberia. It did very little, for example, to stop the escape of Charles Taylor from an American jail, from where he came to unleash terror and mayhem in the MRU subregion. This lack of American action may have been caused by the U.S. desire to use Taylor to highjack the Gadhafi-initiated National Patriotic Front of Liberia (NPFL) to the advantage of America. The ploy initially worked, but later backfired as Taylor refused to sever his links with Gadhafi.

Sierra Leone, like Liberia, had deep historical links with the United States. The Gullahs, a distinctive group of black Americans in South Carolina, are the descendants of African slaves from the rice coast of Sierra Leone. They speak a Creole language similar to Sierra Leonean Creole, use African names, tell African folktales, and make African-style handicraft products such as baskets.[14] African Americans of Sierra Leonean background are increasingly becoming interested in Sierra Leone's affairs in their search for identity, although they are far away from the country. Unsurprisingly, they have played and are continuing to play a crucial role as bridges of understanding between the United States and the increasingly race-conscious people of Africa.[15]

However, while Sierra Leone was under British control, U.S. foreign policy makers and businessmen had hesitated to offend the colonial master, since Britain was a friend to the United States and a fellow member of the North Atlantic Treaty Organization (NATO). There was therefore relatively little U.S. involvement in Sierra Leone until the country gained its independence in 1961. The fact that Sierra Leone's closest neighbor, Liberia, was America's first ally in West Africa was fully utilized to establish friendly ties. In 1959, even before the achievement of independence, the United States appointed a consul in Freetown.[16] Such developments facilitated other U.S.–Sierra Leone ties including the active involvement of U.S. investment companies like Nord Resources at Sierra Rutile. In 1991, Sierra Leone agreed to send a contingent to serve in the allied forces during the Gulf War when requested by the United States. In addition, it had allowed its territory to be used as a staging base for the evacuation of American nationals from Liberia when war broke out in 1989.

Liberia and Sierra Leone were plunged into violent armed conflicts in 1989 and 1991 respectively. Both conflicts, like many others in Africa, were triggered by a number of interrelated internal and external factors. Prominent among the internal causes of the wars was the failure of governance and the concomitant socioeconomic, political, ethnic, and generational exclusion

experienced by many people in both countries. Sierra Leone's political landscape, especially between 1967 and 1997, exhibited long periods of authoritarian civilian and military rule. During those years, members of the political
class and their cohorts not only attempted to annihilate the opposition but
also perfected the arts of political patronage, intolerance, corruption, and
nepotism, which inevitably led to socioeconomic decline in the country.

As in Sierra Leone, Liberia's political system was characterized by long
years of oppressive, oligarchic, and ethnically centered leadership.
Beginning in 1847 when Liberia became a politically independent republic,
the political, economic, and even religious structures were controlled predominantly by the minority Americo-Liberian group made up of former
slaves and their descendants (1847–1980). During this long period, the
indigenous African groups—including the Gios, Krahns, Manos, and
Mandingoes—were not only cruelly oppressed but also politically excluded.
This experience played a crucial role in triggering the Liberian civil war in
1989.

The Sierra Leonean conflict, like the Liberian one, was triggered and sustained by a combination of subregional, regional, and international developments. Initially, the Sierra Leonean conflict was interpreted as an offshoot
of the Liberian crisis. Charles Taylor of the National Patriotic Front of
Liberia (NPFL) had, since the early 1990s, nursed a grudge against Sierra
Leone for a number of reasons including the country's pivotal role in the
operations of the ECOWAS Ceasefire Monitoring Group (ECOMOG) in
Liberia. As the headquarters of ECOMOG were in Freetown, Sierra Leone
was used as a launching pad from which to restore peace and stability in
Liberia. Taylor therefore became convinced that ECOMOG, through the
facilitation of Sierra Leone, was determined to frustrate his political ambition of becoming president of Liberia. Consequently, Sierra Leone became
a target of Taylor's war of terror; a fact he demonstrated by threatening that
Sierra Leone, too, would taste the bitterness of war. Sadly, the Sierra Leone
government did not treat the threat seriously and no adequate security measures were taken, especially along the border with Liberia. Sierra Leone's
diamonds also attracted Taylor's attention as a valuable war-funding
resource. Liberia therefore provided not only the fighting forces but also the
training and launching pad for the Sierra Leonean war in 1991.

Libya, Burkina Faso, and the Ivory Coast also played a role in fueling and
sustaining the conflicts in Liberia and Sierra Leone. The mission of Col.
Gadhafi, Libya's leader, of spreading the philosophy of his Green Book all
over the world, including West Africa, saw the establishment of centers for
the study of his philosophy, for example, at Fourah Bay College (FBC),
University of Sierra Leone. Thus the foundation for the genesis of the idea
of the Revolutionary United Front (RUF) was laid. Visits to Libya by prominent student leaders from FBC were designed to raise the consciousness of

young Sierra Leoneans on the Third World Universal Theory as contained in the Green Book. Foday Sankoh and his cohorts later hijacked the revolution from the students.

Libya's role in the Liberian conflict that erupted in 1989 is partly attributable to Samuel Doe's decision to sever relations with Libya in favor of the Americans. Against this background, Libya threw its support behind Taylor in a bid to see the end of Doe's regime. It provided training facilities as well as logistic support for both the NPFL and the RUF. The role of Burkina Faso in the Liberian and Sierra Leonean conflicts can be traced to the long-term relationship between Taylor and President Blaise Compaoré. Burkinabes were among the NPFL fighters in Liberia and the RUF fighters in Sierra Leone. Côte d'Ivoire was spurred to throw its support behind the NPFL and RUF because of the Doe regime's brutal killing of Liberian President William Tolbert's son, the son-in-law of the Ivorian president, Félix Houphouët-Boigny. It is therefore not surprising to learn that Taylor's attack on Liberia in 1989 was launched from the Ivorian border with Liberia.

The Liberian and Sierra Leonean conflicts were also over the years fueled and sustained by super- and middle-power political actors including France. In the case of Liberia, French commercial companies established contacts with Taylor at a very early stage in the conflict. French private commercial firms supported the NPFL and undermined ECOWAS by negatively influencing official Ivorian policy. The role of West African countries like Guinea and Nigeria in both countries was also crucial. Both countries contributed troops to the ECOMOG forces that played a crucial role in ending the two conflicts.

As already discussed, the Liberian and Sierra Leonean wars were brought about by a combination of many factors. To attribute both wars to any one particular cause will obfuscate any objective analysis of their true nature and manifestations.

The long years of war in both countries (Liberia 1989–2003, and Sierra Leone 1991–2002) were accompanied by massive destruction of lives and property. The wars also contributed significantly to the dislocation of the economies as well as the physical infrastructure and social facilities of both countries. Additionally, the conflicts adversely affected the legitimacy of the governments of both countries and their capacity to govern effectively. The spillover effect of the conflicts on neighboring West African countries was also great. The influx of Liberian and Sierra Leonean refugees into Guinea, for instance, had devastating effects on that country's fragile economy, social infrastructure, and political stability. The refugees brought to the fore the fundamental issues of insecurity, the fragility and porosity of state borders, and the flagrant abuse of human rights, especially of children and women.

Post–Cold War U.S. Foreign Policy toward Liberia and Sierra Leone

The Liberian and Sierra Leonean conflicts brought into question not only American foreign policy in Africa but also the supposition that the end of the Cold War would elongate the corridors of democracy and peace in the continent. Both conflicts erupted at a time when Africa was generally considered very marginal in the strategic calculations of big powers like the United States.[17] No longer confronted with the thorny problem of containing Communism in Africa but now preoccupied with the Iraqi invasion of Kuwait, American strategic thinking put West African issues on the back burner.[18] Accordingly, the U.S. exhibited permissiveness, marginal involvement, and a hands-off African policy. Underscoring the marginality of the African continent, the United States in the post–Cold War era moved decisively to trim approximately seventy positions from its Bureau of African Affairs and closed consulates and embassies in Cameroon, the Comoros, and Nigeria. This was largely done in order to staff the growing numbers of consulates and embassies in Eastern Europe and the newly independent republics of the former Soviet Union.[19] This American foreign policy stance contradicts the professed American spirit of promoting democracy, human rights, trade and investment, conflict resolution, and preservation of the environment in Africa.[20]

The United States' post–Cold War African foreign policy stance was amply demonstrated in both the Liberian and Sierra Leonean conflicts. In the case of Liberia, in spite of the strong historical ties, America displayed a hands-off policy with regard to resolving the crisis. Herman J. Cohen, then assistant secretary of state for African affairs, underscored this American position in noting that U.S. policy was not to permit U.S. troops to shoot at Liberians or be shot at by Liberians.[21] He further noted that there was no role for either the United States or the United Nations in Liberia as their respective agendas were full, and that neighbors might be more able to help.[22] Washington made it abundantly clear that the Liberian crisis was an African problem to be solved by Africans.[23]

The memory of the deaths of eighteen U.S. marines in Somalia in 1993 contributed to a U.S. determination not to involve its forces in peacekeeping operations abroad, and led the United States to make a historic declaration in Presidential Decision Directive 25 (PDD 25, May 3, 1994). This declaration points to a desire for virtual withdrawal from UN peacekeeping operations. It stipulates among other things that the objectives of an operation must be in America's interest, cannot be open ended, must include a clear exit strategy, and must ensure American involvement under command and control management.[24] There was also the Powell Doctrine, arguing that America would intervene only if it could win decisively and with minimal losses through the introduction of overwhelming force.[25] Programs like the African Crisis Response Initiative (ACRI), set up in 1996, were therefore designed by the United States to enhance the capacity of African peacekeeping organizations like the Organization of African Unity (OAU), now the African Union (AU), and the Economic Community of West African States (ECOWAS).

The U.S. State Department and the U.S. National Security Council agreed, therefore, that the role of the United States was merely to support the position of Nigeria and ECOWAS on the Liberian situation. At the height of the crisis in Liberia, the U.S. State Department urged ECOWAS to "take the lead in efforts to bring the Liberian parties peacefully together and discourage a military solution. . . [and] called on other states in the region to refrain from supplying military assistance to the parties."[26] The apparent U.S. indifference to the Liberian situation seriously undermined efforts to bring the Liberian crisis before the United Nations for serious consideration in 1990. No permanent member of the Security Council was willing, without American agreement, to sponsor any UN resolution that would have salvaged the situation. As it happened, Côte d'Ivoire, which initially opposed the presentation of the Liberian case in the United Nations, turned around later to table the case in the UN, hoping that it would lead Nigeria to withdraw from playing a key role in the peace process.

Although the United States offered to airlift Doe to Togo in the early period of the crisis, America did little to resolve the Liberian conflict. Even the signals given by Charles Taylor to Herman Cohen, then assistant secretary of state for African affairs, asking the United States to broker peace in the country fell on deaf ears, as the U.S. administration was skeptical of Taylor's intentions.[27] Instead of helping to salvage the situation, the United States was busy organizing the evacuation of its citizens and protecting its interests in Liberia. It stationed U.S. marines to protect the Omega military communications station and the transmitter used by the Central Intelligence Agency (CIA) to communicate with its stations throughout the world. Six ships of the U.S. Atlantic fleet anchored off Liberia, merely observing the mayhem.[28] Initially, some U.S. military advisers, who were supposed to advise the Liberian government, were present, but they disappeared when some human rights groups in the country got wind of their presence. Beyond these initial moves geared toward the interests of America, very little was done by the United States to contain the Liberian problem.

However, as the suffering of Liberians increased, some pressure to review U.S. policy toward Liberia in particular and Africa in general arose. National Review 30, carried out by the administration of George H. W. Bush in the final months before Clinton's assumption of office, was an indication of some moves to review American foreign policy toward the African continent. This triggered some limited American action toward resolving the Liberian crisis. Realizing the embarrassing nature of American policy given the atrocities committed in the Liberian conflict, America decided to play a role in efforts to widen the circle of players in the resolution of the crisis. One of the most noticeable moves in this direction was the facilitation of the active involvement of Senegal, a major Francophone state, in the ECOMOG operations in Liberia, with a view to defusing the idea of a Nigerian-dominated peacekeeping force in Liberia. In September 1991, the United States invited President Diouf of Senegal on a formal state visit to Washington, where he was strongly urged by President Bush and Secretary of State James Baker to contribute forces to ECOMOG. As an incentive, the U.S. administration pledged to pay a major portion of the operation's cost and to provide logistic support. As proof of the United States' intentions, the Pentagon immediately came up with $15 million worth of military equipment for the Senegalese peacekeepers.[29] Furthermore, the United states forgave Senegal's $42 million debt.[30] This U.S. strategy not only ensured that Senegal would support the peace process but also enhanced ECOMOG's capacity.

Another positive step in facilitating the Liberian peace process was President Clinton's appointment in July 1996 of Ambassador Howard F. Jeter to succeed Ambassador Dane Smith as special envoy to coordinate U.S. government support. In this capacity, Ambassador Jeter attended ECOWAS meetings as an observer and participated in dialogues with the regional leaders including President Abacha, who was then the ECOWAS chairman. This cooperation with ECOWAS leaders played a significant role in facilitating the U.S. assistance to ECOMOG. After the visit of a joint Department of State/Department of Defense Mission to Liberia for consultations with ECOMOG, U.S. support for the regional peacekeeping force was increased. Realizing that ECOMOG was a capable force with able leadership but lacking in certain capacities, the United States provided ECOMOG with helicopters, commercial helicopter lifts, significant quantities of communications equipment, generators, vehicles, nonlethal field equipment, rations, medical supplies, and many other items. The United States also provided ECOMOG checkpoints throughout Monrovia and a full maintenance service to be carried out by Pacific Architects and Engineers (PAE), a U.S.-based company. Between August and December 1996, the U.S. government provided $40 million toward the above-mentioned equipment.[31] In June 1997, it announced a contribution of $7.4 million to support the electoral process in Liberia and also pledged additional support for ECOMOG. The only source of friction was the requirement that ECOMOG had to seek the authorization of the U.S.-based PAE to lease helicopters and gain flying hours.[32] Although the United States' financial assistance was appreciable, it was small in comparison to what the United States spent in Bosnia and Kosovo.

The United States also played a crucial role in facilitating the tough United Nations Security Council Resolution 1509 of September 19, 2003, which established the United Nations Mission in Liberia (UNMIL) and the Taylor exit strategy. UNMIL was given the toughest possible UN mandate with Chapter VII powers. UNMIL was envisaged eventually to comprise a force of about 15,000 military personnel excluding 250 observers and international police. Through the persuasive skills of Paul Klein, an American and the special representative of the UN secretary-general (SRSG) in Liberia, the Security Council later approved 1,115 observers. UNMIL was empowered to take full control of the strategic infrastructure of the country including the airports and seaports. It was also given powers to investigate actions against the peace process but no guidelines on what to do with the results of their findings on these matters.[33] In a practical demonstration of its support of the Liberian peace process at the time, America supplied nine officers to UNMIL (two headquarters staff members and seven military observers). The United States also committed itself to helping in the setting up and training of a new Liberian army.[34] Though laudable, this American effort also had its flaws, mainly because of the American military preoccupation with Iraq and Afghanistan, which meant that the United States was not willing to send its military into Liberia. Furthermore, the United States could have provided an over-the-horizon force, as the British did in Sierra Leone, in a show of confidence for UNMIL.

There is evidence that the United States was highly instrumental in Taylor's exit from Liberia, especially through the Department of Defense. After realizing the destabilizing role of Taylor in the West African subregion and hearing about his alleged business connection with al-Qaeda in 2001, the Pentagon became worried. Consequently, it moved on various fronts to destabilize Taylor through some form of support to Liberians United for Reconciliation and Democracy (LURD) and the Movement for Democracy in Liberia (MODEL).[35] Although various anti-Taylor Liberians were at the time already working very hard in both Liberia and Sierra Leone to oust Taylor, America's indirect support was crucial. But one is left wondering why the United States left it until 2003 to assist in setting up an exit strategy for Taylor. It is also puzzling to learn that before the inauguration of Liberia's interim administration on 14 October, Liberia's then minister of state for foreign affairs, Lewis Brown, signed an agreement with the U.S. government. This agreement provided that the Liberian government would not turn over American citizens to the International Criminal Court. Considering that most of the former officials in the Taylor government were American citizens, the agreement made it difficult to achieve serious transitional justice in postwar Liberia.

America also displayed its halfhearted post–Cold War foreign policy in the Sierra Leonean conflict. The United States was on the priority list of countries that Sierra Leone approached for assistance when war broke out in March 1991. But the American response to the request was halfhearted. Sierra Leone, like Liberia, was at that time perceived as a small, strategically insignificant country as compared to others like Bosnia.[36] The UN's consolidated humanitarian appeal for Kosovo in July 1999 was for $690 million, of which 58 percent was promptly met, in addition to $2.1 billion pledged for regional reconstruction. Following the conclusion of the Lomé Accord in the same month, the UN's appeal for Sierra Leone was for $25 million, of which only 32 percent was met and not covered. Furthermore, the United States saw Sierra Leone as within the British sphere of interest and therefore believed that the British government should take the lead in mustering international support to end the crisis. Instead of engaging in diplomatic and military moves to help end the crisis, the United States urged the Sierra Leone government to introduce far-reaching political liberalization as a way of undercutting the rebels' activities. Even this limited U.S. gesture was negated with the seizure of power by the National Provisional Ruling Council (NPRC) in 1992, which led to the suspension of all U.S. aid to Sierra Leone. However, in furtherance of its quest for democratic civilian rule in Sierra Leone, the United States decided to work closely with the British government to convince the military junta to hand over power to a democratically elected government. The U.S. government provided $4.5 million toward the $8.5 million total coming from the international community for the elections of 1996. It also contributed greatly to disengaging the NPRC junta from power by opening up a scholarship opportunity for its members willing to go and study abroad.[37]

As it was in Liberia, U.S. policy in Sierra Leone was focused on supporting the regional peacekeeping body, ECOMOG. It provided logistics and other nonlethal support. This was, however, a belated development, starting in 1998 with the provision of $3.9 million. Although this support was crucial to ECOMOG's efforts in battling the rebels, it was inadequate as compared to the United States' $60 million daily expenditure on bombing Serbia. This comparison does not support the idea that the United States is eager to protect the interests of conglomerates in the country, including Nord Resources, which owns a majority of shares in Sierra Rutile. While the West has always been involved in the exploitation of the wealth of developing countries, it has not always been willing to help such states when trouble erupts. In fact, when Rutile fell under rebel attack, the immediate American response was simply the speedy evacuation of its nationals. These and many other contradictions involving the Western powers' policies in developing countries like Sierra Leone led to assertions that the West's grievance against the RUF was triggered more by political concerns than the need to promote peace and democracy. This assertion is supported by the West's desire to weaken the RUF's links with Libya, Liberia, and Burkina Faso.

Gradually, the strong Anglo-American alliance, especially the cordial relationship between Tony Blair and Bill Clinton, led to the adoption of a U.S. foreign policy that was favorable toward Sierra Leone. As the British government expressed a willingness to play a leading role in resolving the Sierra Leone crisis, America became disposed to backstopping such an initiative, especially in the United Nations Security Council. Other advocates for a positive U.S. role in the Sierra Leone crisis included former congresswoman Cynthia McKinney, who called on President Clinton to declare the Revolutionary United Front (RUF) an international terrorist organization. McKinney even interpreted the U.S. pressure on the Sierra Leone government to negotiate with the rebels as evidence of U.S. reluctance to assist Sierra Leone and ECOMOG.[38] These and many other developments were crucial in shaping a favorable U.S. foreign policy toward the Sierra Leonean conflict. The U.S. government under Bill Clinton began to view the Sierra Leone conflict through the prism of American commitment to the enhancement of democracy and human rights in Africa. Clinton's special envoy, Reverend Jesse Jackson, drew attention to the United States' differential responses to different conflicts and advocated equal treatment of both European and African civil wars. He reminded Americans that the foreign policy of the United States must be driven by a single set of shared values and that more lives had been lost in Sierra Leone than in Kosovo. Accordingly, he urged Americans to take seriously the efforts to end civil wars in Africa.

One of the most contentious U.S. foreign policy strategies in Sierra Leone's war resolution efforts was its crucial role in facilitating the signing of the Lomé Peace Accord in July 1999. Through Jessie Jackson, the United States assisted in pushing through the accord. American officials drafted the agreement and pressured President Ahmed Tejan Kabbah of Sierra Leone to sign it. The United States employed various diplomatic tactics to lure the Sierra Leonean government into signing the accord, even at the cost of ignoring the views of the majority of Sierra Leoneans who were against a power-sharing formula that would include rebels in the government.[39] The agreement gave many concessions to the RUF, including key cabinet positions, chairmanship of the Commission for the Management of Strategic Resources for National Reconstruction and Development (CMRRD), and a general amnesty. In spite of all these incentives, the RUF was still reluctant to give Sierra Leoneans the peace they yearned for.

The United States also played and is still playing a significant role in strengthening the United Nations Mission in Sierra Leone (UNAMSIL). In voting for the progressive expansion of UNAMSIL for example, the United States committed itself to paying a quarter of UNAMSIL's operating cost, which according to official UN estimates was approaching US$782.2 million. President Clinton also authorized the Pentagon to spend up to US$20 million in support of the mission. Most of this assistance was provided for the training of Nigerian peacekeepers and the U.S. airlifting of Jordanian and Indian forces. In close working cooperation with the United Kingdom, the United States developed the three key Security Council initiatives of a diamond embargo, an international tribunal, and the strengthening of UNAMSIL in Sierra Leone. There is no doubt that the United States is now concerned for peace and stability in Sierra Leone in particular and the West African subregion in general, to prevent their being used as terrorist bases. In this connection, the United States was uncomfortable with President Kabbah's development of closer links with Libya and other Arab states. President Kabbah's relationship with Libya, for example, was probably triggered by the need to positively engage Colonel Gadhafi and to convince him of the need to terminate support to the RUF and Taylor. Indeed, the Sierra Leone government endeavored in diverse ways to explain to Gadhafi the negative role of the RUF and NPFL in the subregion, and this helped influence Gadhafi's severance of links with the RUF and Taylor.

Summary, Conclusions, and Recommendations

This chapter has examined the critical post–Cold War U.S. foreign policy toward West Africa with particular focus on the two MRU states of Liberia and Sierra Leone. It has not only discussed the background to the U.S.-Liberian and Sierra Leonean relations but also shed critical light on the U.S. response to the conflicts that engulfed the two states during the period under review. A major conclusion of the chapter is that the end of the Cold War undermined the strategic significance of peripheral African states like Liberia and Sierra Leone in the foreign policy calculations of big powers like the United States. Further, this undermining of African states' significance gives the lie to the argument that the post-Cold War era will ensure the positive engagement of big powers in the consolidation of peace and democracy in Africa. The situation warrants serious attention to home-grown initiatives in Africa to ensure peace and security.

Notes

1. Charles Ukeje, "State Disintegration and Civil Wars in Liberia," in Amadu Sesay, ed., *Civil Wars, Child Soldiers and Post-conflict Peace Building in West Africa* (Ibadan: College Press and Publishers, 2003).

2. Ibid.

3. Ibid.

4. "Limits Set on US Peacekeeping Role," *Guardian Weekly*, February 11, 1994.

5. Amadu Sesay, "Between the Olive Branch and the AK 47: Paradoxes of Recent Military Interventions in West Africa," ISSU Bulletin No 6 of 1999, 18.

6. Osman Gbla, "An Analysis of Selected Conceptual Issues for A Mano River Strategy Paper," Consultancy Report to Action Aid Sierra Leone, 2004.

7. Ibid.

8. Walter H. Kansteiner, Assistant Secretary of State for African Affairs, Testimony to House Committee on International Relations on Africa, Washington, DC, October 2, 2003.

9. Sesay, "Between the Olive Branch and the AK 47."

10. Kansteiner, Testimony to House Committee on International Relations on Africa, October 2, 2003.

11. S. Tarr Byron, "The ECOMOG Initiative in Liberia: A Liberian Perspective," *Issue* 21, nos. 1–2 (1993): 75.

12. Joseph Opala, *The Gullah: Rice, Slavery and the Sierra Leonean Connection* (Freetown: USIS, 1987), 1.

13. Tarr Byron, "The ECOMOG Initiative in Liberia," 81.

14. Seven Kertesz, *American Diplomacy in a New Era* (Notre Dame, IN: University of Notre Dame Press, 1961), 43.

15. Osman Gbla, "The Impact of United States Foreign Policy on the Socio-economic Development of Sierra Leone (1961–Present)" (master's thesis, Fourah Bay College, 1993).

16. M. Ali Taisier and Robert O, Mathews, *Civil Wars in Africa: Roots and Resolution* (Montreal: McGill-Queens University Press, 1999), 106.

17. Kwesi Aning, *Managing Regional Security in West Africa: ECOWAS, ECOMOG and Liberia*, Working Paper 94 (Copenhagen: Centre for Developmental Research, 1994), 9; Amadu Sesay, "Indigenous Military Interventions in West Africa," in *Managing African Conflicts: The Challenges of Military Interventions*, ed. Michael Hough and Louis du Plessis (Pretoria, South Africa: Human Sciences Research Council, 2000).

18. "Liberia: An American Tragedy?" *ECOWAS NOW*, November–December 1998, 33.

19. P. Schrader, "Removing the Shackles? U.S. Foreign Policy Towards Africa, After the End of the Cold War," in Edmund Keller and D. Rotchild, eds., *Africa in the New International Order* (Boulder, CO: Lynne Rienner), 94.

20. Aning, *Managing Regional Security in West Africa*, 9.

21. Cited in ibid.

22. *West Africa*, August 20–26, 1990, 2309.

23. Kramer Reed, "Liberia: 'A Casualty of the Cold War End,'" allafrica.com, October 24, 2000.

24. "Toward a Pax West African: Building Peace in a Troubled Sub-Region, IPA-ECOWAS Conference Report, September 2001," 18.

25. *International Herald Tribune*, 13–14 May, 1993, 9.

26. Press statement, U.S. State Department, September 14, 1992, quoted in Tarr Byron, "The ECOMOG Initiative in Liberia," 81.

27. Taisier and Mathews, *Civil Wars*, 81.

28. Robert O. Mortimer, "ECOMOG, Liberia, and Regional Security in West Africa," in *Africa in the New International Order: Rethinking State Sovereignty and Regional Security*, ed. Edmund J. Keller and Donald Rothchild (Boulder, CO: Lynne Rienner, 1996), 155.

29. Ibid.

30. Adekeye Adebajo, *Liberia's Civil War: Nigeria, ECOMOG and Regional Security in West Africa* (Boulder, CO: Lynne Rienner, 2002), 213.

31. Ibid.

32. United Nations Security Council Resolution 1509 of September 19, 2003.

33. "Liberia: Security Challenges," International Crisis Group (ICG) *Africa Report*, no. 71, November 2003, 14.

34. Ibid, 16.

35. John Hirsch, *Sierra Leone Diamonds and the Struggle for Democracy* (Boulder, CO: Lynne Rienner, 2001), 64.

36. Osman Gbla, "The Crisis of Globalization and Its Impact on Democracy and Good Governance in Post-Colonial Africa: Case Study of the March to Multiparty Democracy in Sierra Leone (1990–1998)," *Journal of Development Alternatives and Area Studies* 20, nos. 1 and 2 (March–June 2001: 8.

37. Ibid.

38. Ibid.

39. Ibid.

Part Five

Looking toward the Future
U.S.–West African Linkages in the
Twenty-first Century

19

The United States and Security Management in West Africa

A Case for Cooperative Intervention

Olawale Ismail

The August 2003 berthing of an American warship—the USS *Iwo Jima*—off the coast of Monrovia was greeted with huge expectations of a much-needed American presence, expectations held by Liberians and international public opinion. The optimistic expectation of a positive and perhaps decisive American military intervention parallels the United Kingdom's deployment of special forces in neighboring Sierra Leone three years earlier. However, the expectations and optimism proved unfounded, given the limited nature of the deployment (if any), the perceived or real short-term nature of active American intervention, and the continued practice of subcontracting the leadership role (especially in military terms) to less capable African states. Yet this singular event in August 2003 challenges us to reexamine the nature, scope, and commitment of the United States to conflict and security management in West Africa, especially in the post–September 11, 2001, era.

Underlying any analysis of the American role in conflict and security management in West Africa are certain historical, political, and military dynamics. Prior to 2001, the American role in conflict management in sub-Saharan Africa (SSA), including West Africa, was shaped by Cold War dynamics and a colonial legacy under which American ideological and strategic interests were subordinated by and contracted to European allies—the United Kingdom (UK) and France. This engendered a policy of minimal or avoidable military engagement in conflict management, except in the case of U.S. intervention in Somalia, whose outcome further diminished the already tenuous rating of Africa in the American strategic calculus, and also compounded the skepticism about the potential of American active military intervention in conflict management in Africa. Thus, the "US has been able to avoid a significant presence in Africa, in support of shifting sets of priorities and interests, powered by unexpected, and intermittent requirements to intervene."[1]

However, since September 11, 2001, events have changed the strategic importance of SSA (especially West Africa) in the context of the War on Terror (WoT), given SSA's geographical location as a back door to the Persian Gulf; and the emerging potential of the Gulf of Guinea as an alternative source of energy needed to reduce overdependence on the Middle East. Against the backdrop of a near-consensus about a greater and more active American focus on security in Africa, especially West Africa, and the Gulf of Guinea in the post–September 11, 2001, period, the appropriateness of Washington's post-Somalian reluctance to commit troops to West Africa for conflict management becomes questionable. Yet crucial questions arise about possible new types and forms of engagement in conflict management (beyond past and current patterns) and the availability of a model or models to guide new possible forms of engagement.

Accordingly, this chapter identifies an emerging pattern of external intervention, as typified by the British and French in Sierra Leone and Côte d'Ivoire respectively, as a practical and increasingly effective conflict and security management model. It contends that this emerging pattern of partnership between regional and extra-regional actors in active military deployment for conflict management represents a guiding pattern that could be adapted to American national interests and peculiarities in conflict management in West Africa. This model is viewed conceptually as "cooperative intervention." It encapsulates the long- and short-term (physical and diplomatic) commitments of states, often outside Africa, that are viewed as having (mythical or real) historical, cultural, socioeconomic, and political ties with imploding states. The need for American cooperative intervention is underscored by the multilayered security challenges in the region, its increasing strategic importance in global oil production, and the reality that "if the U.S. chooses to remain on the periphery of these conflicts, the prospects for future Rwandas, Liberias, and Sierra Leones are high."[2]

The focus of this chapter is restricted to an analysis of emerging patterns of conflict and security management in West Africa, especially the division of labor between regional and extra-regional actors (especially the UK, France, and the United States). While I draw important insights from American foreign policy in Africa, an exhaustive analysis of overall American foreign policy in SSA is beyond the scope of this chapter. I divide the rest of this chapter into four sections: the first undertakes a conceptual exploration of cooperative intervention, highlighting its background, components, advantages, and limitations. In the second section, I review the past and present American roles in conflict and security management in West Africa, using Liberia as a case study. The third section reconciles the changing or changed American national interest in West Africa with the current scope of engagement in conflict and security management in the subregion. The concluding section summarizes the arguments.

Understanding Cooperative Intervention

The concept of cooperative intervention, although still emerging, is rooted in the recent historical, political, and military experiences of Third World countries, especially in West Africa. It captures the comprehensive use of diplomatic, economic, political, and military tools in the management of conflict and insecurity. It is a partnership arrangement between regional and extra-regional actors in containing the spread of conflicts and insecurity and the attendant humanitarian consequences through covert and overt political and military pressures on warring parties to observe imposed and self-declared ceasefires and eventual comprehensive peace agreements.

Historically, external intervention in any form cannot be said to be new, given the precolonial, colonial, and even postcolonial interventions in intercommunity warfare in SSA, especially by European states—Britain, France, and Portugal. Even in the post–Cold War era, direct intervention by both regional and extra-regional actors, as exemplified by the multiple interventions by South Africa and Botswana in restoring constitutional order in Lesotho during the 1990s, the multiple interventions by neighboring states and allies—Zimbabwe, Rwanda, Namibia, Angola, and Uganda—in the war in the Democratic Republic of Congo (DRC) in 1998, and the complicated intervention by Ethiopia, Uganda, and Eritrea in Sudan, has been a common phenomenon.[3] In fact, West Africa recorded the first form of organized regional intervention with the deployment of a subregional peacekeeping force (ECOMOG) in Liberia, Sierra Leone, and Guinea Bissau in the 1990s.[4] Moreover, conventional intervention under the rubric of United Nations (UN) peacekeeping is not new in Africa, as evidenced by UN peacekeeping missions in the Congo, Liberia, and Sierra Leone.[5] Also not new is direct military intervention by external actors, especially France, whose long history of direct military intervention in postcolonial Africa dates back to its 1964 and 1968 interventions in Gabon and Senegal, respectively, to prop up pliant regimes.

What is new, however, is the much more integrated use and the comprehensive nature of direct intervention in West Africa since the late 1990s. Also notable is the increased formalization of a tripartite division of labor involving regional actors, the United Nations, and a leading extra-regional actor, often a permanent member of the UN Security Council, in conflict management. The concept of cooperative intervention is markedly different from neocolonialism and dependency, given cooperative intervention's emphasis on humanitarianism, peace, and security as opposed to the neocolonialism and dependency's assumption of a necessarily negative quartet alignment involving Gramsci's organic intellectuals (senior state bureaucrats), political classes, domestic bourgeoisies, and their foreign counterparts, centered on resources and their control.[6] In understanding the nature of the emerging tripartite division of labor, it is important to highlight the five components of cooperative intervention.

Five Pillars of Cooperative Intervention

Conceptually, cooperative intervention is a progressive mix of various components: orthodox preventive action; institutional capacity building of the security sector; active support for two-track diplomatic negotiation by third parties; consensus building and multilateral involvement (multitrack diplomacy) in peace negotiation; and direct military deployment. Preventive action involves efforts, assistance, and pressures on Third World states, including those in West Africa, to democratize, observe human rights and good governance, increase accountability and transparency, and develop the infrastructural needs of the citizenry in order to counteract the socioeconomic and political sources of conflicts.[7] This underlines the age-old contention of relative deprivation theorists that it is "the upsetting of expectations [that] provokes the sense of relative deprivation which may in turn provide the impetus for drastic change [especially political violence]."[8] Hence, the outbreak of internecine conflict (political violence) is a function of the extent and intensity of shared discontent among members of a society and the degree to which such discontents are blamed on the political system and its agents or beneficiaries.[9] Clapham, in his valuable profile of insurgency movements in Africa, confirms the conclusion that blocked political aspirations, reactive desperation, and rural resistance to the exploitative exactions and extractions of centralized governments underlie insurgencies in Africa.[10]

Institutional capacity building, especially in the security sector, is encapsulated in attempts since 1992 to transform the security sector of most Third World states into benign structures that are subservient to constituted democratic authority, "right-sized" and reprofessionalized to meet the peculiar security challenges of their environment.[11] The security sector reform agenda came out of the need to mainstream security issues into development planning, adopt a holistic interpretation of the security sector to encompass civilian and military aspects, and fulfill the optimistic expectations of a post–Cold War peace dividend in the developing world.[12] Institutional capacity reform is a preventive action as much as it is a transformative tool for stabilizing the security environment in countries that are politically volatile or emerging from conflicts. The role of Britain in helping to transform the security sector in Sierra Leone after over eight years of civil war illustrates this.

The third component is perhaps the most common and the oldest approach to conflict management. It is defined by the overt and covert involvement of third parties, within and outside the region, to persuade, encourage, and support warring parties to sign binding and effective cease-fire agreements, followed by more comprehensive peace agreements. This component is actively used at any point along the conflict-peace continuum, including postconflict settings, where political tensions and military actions and counteractions are either occurring or looming. Closely connected to the third pillar, but distinct from it, is the multilateral effort toward conflict management, mostly in the context of multilateral peacekeeping and peace negotiations. This, otherwise known as multitrack diplomacy, is centrally driven by international organizations, either at the regional level by such bodies as the African Union (AU) and ECOWAS, or by the United Nations. Extra-African states play the crucial role of encouraging and sponsoring such arrangements beyond the regular support for peace efforts. A good example of multitrack diplomacy was the 1999 Lomé Peace Accord, which was actively supported by the United States in the run-up to the peace process in Sierra Leone.

The fifth pillar consists of direct military intervention by external actors in containing and managing civil conflicts and insecurity. This involves the deployment of special forces, up to brigade level, by a state to contain the size of a humanitarian emergency, defined as a "profound social crisis in which large numbers of people unequally die and suffer from war, displacement, hunger, and disease owing to human-made and natural disasters."[13] This definition expands the scope of cooperative intervention to other crisis situations beyond violent conflicts and puts humanitarianism, as encapsulated in the United Nations' "Responsibility to Protect" principle, at the heart of military intervention. The recent deployment of military personnel by the United States in the tsunami-hit countries of Indonesia, Thailand, Malaysia, and Sri Lanka is a practical example.

It is important to state that, although the five pillars of cooperative intervention might appear to be in a progressive, incremental order in which direct military intervention could be judged to be at the apex, however, in reality the employment of these components does not rest on any permanent order; rather, it is governed by considerable flexibility, which allows the use of any component at any point in time, relative to the circumstance at hand. It is possible, for example, that direct military intervention could be used at very early stages of a conflict as a form of preventive action, especially when the anticipated scale of a humanitarian emergency is judged to be enormous. Also, the overarching goal of conceptualizing this form of intervention is to comprehensively define the whole range of actions and inactions, mechanisms and tools available to and used by third parties in a crisis situation. More importantly, it is a robust attempt to holistically unpack and seek greater coordination between the various actions and mechanisms used in conflict management. I acknowledge that all the pillars have been used and continue to be used by third parties, but with very little emphasis on or acknowledgment of the need for greater coordination. So what are the benefits of the coordination encapsulated in cooperative intervention?

The Benefits of Cooperative Intervention

The institutional lack of capacity of the UN in peacekeeping and peace-support operations was highlighted in the 1992 Agenda for Peace Report and restated in the 2000 Brahimi Report.[14] This finding mirrors larger legal, administrative, and bureaucratic restrictions on effective peacekeeping and peace-support operations at the multilateral level. Based on this finding, cooperative intervention becomes a faster, more effective, and perhaps better-focused form of conflict management. The presence of an extra-African lead-state, with considerable capacity to project force and possibly coerce factions into peace settlements, makes the intervention and peace process in Sierra Leone a milestone in peace operations. This contrasts sharply with the role and failure of multilateral deployment to prevent the 1994 genocide in Rwanda. Worse still, the reality that multilateral intervention comes when the conflict is already intensified and it is too late, does not come at all, results in resounding failures, or is narrow in scope has made the role of a lead-state more central to conflict management since the late 1990s.[15]

In addition, cooperative intervention since the late 1990s has proved to be an important tool for preventing or containing large-scale humanitarian emergencies in West Africa. To date, a major effect of the direct early and continuous deployment of French military actors to safeguard a buffer zone and humanitarian corridor in Côte d'Ivoire has been a reduction in the scale of the humanitarian emergency, defined to include the destruction of life and property and the refugee outflow. This reinforces the current emphasis on sovereignty as responsibility, with humanitarianism increasingly overriding political and legal boundaries.[16] The long-term gain of this lies in forestalling greater destruction and, by implication, downscales the cost and needs in postconflict rebuilding.

Cooperative interventions complement rather than undermine or complicate multilateral intervention. In fact, multilateral mechanisms are part of the tools available to and used in cooperative intervention. This explains why the UK and France sought UN support (through a Security Council cover-mandate and the eventual deployment of peacekeepers) for their interventions in Sierra Leone and Côte d'Ivoire, respectively. More often, cooperative intervention advocates for a lead extra-African state to provide background support (a robust force less constrained by the legal and political inhibitions of multilateralism) for multilateral peace efforts. The active military presence of a cooperating lead-state alone carries huge psychological potential and advantages for conflict management, especially sending warning signals of punitive actions to renegade factions should they violate ceasefires, intensify humanitarian crises, or even attack third parties' military personnel (both direct and multilateral deployments). The threat of and actual punitive sanctions against the rebel Revolutionary United Front of Sierra Leone (RUFSL) following military assaults against multilateral deployments in January 1999 (against ECOMOG) and May 2000 (against UNAMSIL) by a combination of ECOMOG and British forces illustrates this. In fact, the use of peacekeeping and peace-support mechanisms outside the formal UN machinery was advocated by the Agenda for Peace report.

A further advantage of cooperative intervention is enhanced coordination and strategic leadership for postwar reconstruction processes. This is where the social, economic, political and diplomatic commitment of a lead-state (external actor) is crucial to the immediate postwar disarmament, demobilization, and reintegration (DDR) of combatants, and to long-term commitment, over a ten- to fifteen-year horizon, to postwar socioeconomic recovery, political restructuring, and overall institutional capacity building.[17] The lead extra-African state is particularly central to the organization of special conferences to mobilize international political, diplomatic, and financial support for peace processes, and to the harmonizing of differing perspectives among key external actors.[18]

The fifth advantage of cooperative intervention lies in the acute (African) regional incapacity to fully project effective force and undertake independent multilateral peacekeeping. This contrasts sharply with the current emphasis on solely building and using regional actors and capacity for managing conflicts in West Africa. While it is important to promote the use of Africans and African solutions for African problems as the long-term peace and security strategy, it is crucial to acknowledge the importance of external actors and assistance. Cooperative intervention facilitates the use of African solutions by providing the logistical, financial, political, and diplomatic requisites for the successful implementation of African solutions. Also, while force deployment is one aspect of the conflict management jigsaw covered by cooperative intervention, it is hardly even effective when used as an isolated tool of conflict management. It is extremely hard to find any regional actor in SSA with the viable institutional capacity for all the five components of cooperative intervention.

Specifically in West Africa, all the cases of regional intervention from the 1982 Nigerian-led intervention in Chad (on behalf of the Organization of African Unity) to the more recent examples of intervention by ECOMOG in Liberia (1990–97 and 2003), Sierra Leone, and Guinea Bissau have demonstrated logistical weaknesses, poor funding, inadequate capacity to project robust force, and tenuous political will.[19] The rationalization that "African armies have the manpower to participate in every kind of operation"[20] underlines the current argument about a division of labor in which extra-regional actors provide the operational needs. Yet I argue that force deployment is only one aspect of conflict management, and effective conflict management is enhanced only when the full range of options and tools are used simultaneously or in different contexts. Thus, rather than capitulate to the cheap argument that all that is required is logistical support and hardware for effective force deployment by regional actors,[21] it is important to restate the desirability of efforts to develop regional capacity for conflict management and, crucially, the continued active military and nonmilitary involvement of extra-regional actors to neutralize the limitations of regional actors. The active military involvement of two extra-regional actors in conflict management in two West African countries illustrates this better.

Since the late 1990s, Britain and France appear to have embodied a comprehensive, multidimensional attempt, encapsulated in cooperative intervention, to manage conflict and insecurity in West Africa. This is rooted in their long socioeconomic, political, and diplomatic engagement with the region since colonialism and reinforced by bilateral and multilateral treaties and institutions, especially the Commonwealth, Franco-African summitry, and strings of defense cooperation agreements (military pacts). The British involvement in transforming the conflict situation in Sierra Leone is a classic case of cooperative intervention. The involvement combined elements of preventive action, as contained in the Commonwealth's 1991 Harare Declaration aimed at democratization and improving good governance;[22] sponsorship of the security sector reform agenda (belatedly and more intensively as part of the postwar reconstruction agenda) to build the capacity of the security sector; active covert and overt roles in peace negotiations; involvement in multilateral efforts through ECOWAS, the AU, and the UN to transform the conflict situation, including the deployment of multilateral peacekeepers through UNAMSIL; and active direct military intervention (the deployment of 800 troops) for humanitarian purposes and to bolster UNAMSIL with more punitive and robust force projections. The comprehensiveness of British involvement was particularly evident after the January 1999 and May 2000 incidents in which the rebel RUFSL overthrew the elected government and captured multilateral peacekeepers, but joint British–ECOMOG military action restored the status quo, and Britain's continued military presence contributed to the eventual capitulation of RUFSL.

France, on the other hand, after more than thirty years of classical neo-colonial military intervention, masked by the contentious defense pacts agreed to and perhaps imposed on former colonies across Africa at independence, appears to have remodeled post–Cold War military interventions after the British example, as illustrated in Côte d'Ivoire since 2002. The erstwhile foreign minister, Dominique de Villepin, the foreign minister, articulated this change as three new principles of French policy in Africa: first, support for legitimate powers and regimes; second, respect for national sovereignty and territorial integrity; and third, systematic support for African peace talks and mediation.[23] As a result, the remaining 6,500 French military personnel and the few functional military installations in Africa were redesignated for humanitarian and peacekeeping roles and the retraining of African military forces. The new approach is institutionalized under the Reinforcing Africa's Capacity to Maintain Peace (RECAMP) project and the Guidimakha military exercise designed to professionalize and build the capacity of African military forces in peacekeeping roles under the joint UN-AU mandate, as part of a regional brigade-level component.[24]

Still, the 2002 direct military intervention in Côte d'Ivoire, first to impose a ceasefire and contain the humanitarian crises, and second to facilitate the deployment of a separate multilateral (African) peacekeeping force as well as to facilitate diplomatic peace negotiations between the Southern-based incumbents in power and the Northern antigovernment rebel alliance, has proved to be an early window through which to observe France's new conflict management approach in Africa. Although the scale of the current intervention in Côte d'Ivoire is hardly new, especially with the 1983 deployment of over 3,000 troops in Chad under "Operation Mantra," the use of military means as part of an overall strategy in conflict management, the extent of the effort to seek and obtain international legitimacy for such a deployment, and the increasing recourse to more convincing and obvious humanitarianism appear unprecedented. Moreover, France's insistence on peace negotiations and its robust defense of the buffer zone, even after massive provocation, especially by the incumbents in power and allied militias in 2004, differentiates current engagement from those of the Cold-War era when France directly intervened to impose solutions or to give outright support to pliant regimes.

The Limits of Cooperative Intervention

I have already noted that direct military intervention and the other pillars of cooperative intervention are hardly new, but what sets apart the new and emerging forms of direct intervention by third-party states, typified by Britain in Sierra Leone and France in Côte d'Ivoire, is the impressive coordination of the five components of cooperative intervention, with the deployment of military force when necessary and the recognition that military solutions hardly engender sustainable peace and security. However, given past patterns of use of the individual pillars of cooperative intervention, it is possible to hypothesize potential limitations. First, cooperative intervention is considered to be prone to failure or complications when only a single component is used or the pillars are employed in an isolated manner.

Hence, cooperative intervention requires active coordination of the many components in different phases of peace building.

Second, cooperative intervention, as much as any form of third-party involvement, must necessarily involve regional actors in order to surround the theater of conflict and insecurity, thereby undercutting proximate sources of support and supply to warring parties. It was the failure to involve regional actors, especially neighboring states, that undercut the American-led "Operation Restore Hope" in Somalia in 1993 and led to the extension of the Liberian and Sierra Leonean conflicts in the 1990s. In the first place, intervening parties need the diplomatic and political support of regional actors for staging-post purposes, and to build regional and international public opinion in favor of interventions. Even with the emerging division of labor, regional actors are expected to contribute troops, host refugees, and put pressure on warring factions to commit to peace negotiations.

Third, the intervention being advocated requires long-term planning and engagement on the part of intervening states. Without this, intervening parties risk underestimating or misunderstanding the sociocultural, political, and historical contexts of a conflict, thereby jeopardizing the outcome of intervention. Crucially, this point highlights the existence of an interlocking web of socioeconomic, political, and diplomatic relations between a cooperative state and host (threatened) states well before the outbreak of conflict and other security challenges as an important component of cooperative intervention. The British in Sierra Leone and the French in Côte d'Ivoire already reflect this, with their colonial past and their close engagement and close relations with postcolonial governments.

Finally, direct military deployment, although the highest-profile component of cooperative intervention, should not be favored above the other pillars. In essence, sustainable peace and security lies in long-term socioeconomic and political empowerment, rather than in the symbolic cessation of hostilities, the signing of ceasefire agreements, and the holding of national elections.[25]

The United States and Conflict and Security Management in Post–Cold War West Africa

The sweeping post-1990 optimism about global consensus and responsibility prompted the December 1992 American-led military intervention in Somalia, but the complicated outcome of this intervention has become a watershed in terms of the form and scope of American involvement in conflict management in Africa. The killing, media outrage (perhaps embarrassment), and political expediency that accompanied American casualties in Somalia resulted in a hasty withdrawal and a subsequent high-level Presidential Review (PDD-25) of American peacekeeping policy by the

Clinton administration in 1994. PDD-25 demands that the objectives of American peacekeeping should clearly reflect U.S. national interests, with public and congressional support; with definite entry and exit strategies; and with a command and control structure acceptable to Washington.

The August 2003 deployment of American marines off the coast of Monrovia has been the closest to any form of overt, active, direct American military intervention in West Africa and SSA in the post-PDD-25 era. Yet this does not help to predict other forms of involvement in conflict management in West Africa. Throughout the 1990s, Washington's involvement in conflict management in West Africa, even before the PDD-25 review, was largely restricted to continuing the Cold War practice of either delegating such duties to European allies or seeking to build the capacity of African countries to undertake such military roles. The only other form of engagement relates to support for diplomatic and peace negotiations (the 1999 Lomé peace talks) and substantial material and financial support to humanitarian relief operations. I use the first and second periods of civil war in Liberia as a template for interrogating the form, scope, and composition of U.S. involvement in conflict management in West Africa, not least because of important sociocultural, historical, economic, and perhaps strategic linkages.

The Republic of Liberia was founded in 1847 following the resettlement of freed and recaptured slaves from North America by the American Colonial Society (ACS).[26] The American culture of liberty and freedom was "ostensibly" to define the character of the independent Liberian state, as it draws its name from "liberation" and named its capital Monrovia, after the influential President James Monroe. The strong ancestral linkage to the United States translated into a substantial socioeconomic, political, and strategic partnership before 1990. It is estimated that by the 1980s, American private investment was worth over $350 million, signposted by American firms including Firestone, Goodrich, Bethlehem Steel, Chase Manhattan, and Citibank Group. Until 1989, Liberia was Washington's main trading partner in West Africa, and in 1982 two American firms accounted for about 52 percent of central government revenue in Monrovia. Strategically, Liberia's enviable record of having the world's largest ship registry resulted in important military cooperation and the delivery of American military aid (hardware) averaging about $14 million per annum and worth $500 million between 1980 and 1989.[27]

However, a combination of internal dissent, caused mainly by the marginalization of indigenous Liberians by the Americo-Liberians, and economic decline snowballed into political volatility in the 1980s, especially with the April 12, 1980, military putsch of Master Sergeant Samuel Doe. The subsequent dictatorship of the Doe regime heralded the final collapse of the Liberian state with the outbreak of the civil war, spearheaded initially by the

Charles Taylor–led National Patriotic Front of Liberia (NPFL), in December 1989. The revolt (the first Liberian civil war) endured for more than seven years, costing more than 200,000 lives including that of Samuel Doe. A ceasefire mediated by the United Nations (UN) and the Economic Community of West African States (ECOWAS) in 1996 led to democratic elections and Charles Taylor's presidency in 1997. The circle of violence, however, continued under Taylor, given his inability to change from a war-lord into a statesman, his continuation of wartime shadow-state practices, neopatrimonialism, and warlord politics in the brief post period. Large-scale fighting resumed in 2000 when a dissident rebel group called Liberians United for Reconciliation and Democracy (LURD) revolted against Taylor (the second Liberian civil war). The Liberian war led to the first case of direct subregional multilateral military intervention by West African states under the aegis of ECOMOG. In both rounds of violence, it was military personnel from subregional countries that monitored or imposed ceasefires that enabled subsequent progress in peace negotiations.

An examination of Washington's role in conflict management in Liberia reveals that only two, at best three, of the five tools of conflict management under cooperative intervention were used, and even then disjointedly. First, the United States used heavy covert pressure and revealed a preference for peace negotiations by offering to airlift former president Doe to exile in Togo during the first civil war.[28] The fact that more than sixteen peace accords were signed during the first round of violence also suggested American support for peace negotiations. This trend was repeated during the second civil war with Washington's open call for the resignation and exil-ing of President Taylor and support for the Accra peace talks (even if the United States was paradoxically seeking to sabotage all this with an indict-ment of Taylor and an attempt to arrest him by the Washington-sponsored Sierra Leonean War Crimes Tribunal on the eve of the peace talks).

Second, Washington tends to provide logistical support for peacekeeping operations, as evidenced by its support in 2003 for ECOMOG's intervention. Yet such support is always ambivalent as it is often conditioned by larger political and diplomatic calculations, especially with regard to Nigeria. For example, the ambivalence of U.S. support for ECOMOG in its intervention in the first and second rounds of violence in Liberia is explained by the ascendancy and exit of the Abacha regime in Nigeria.[29]

Finally, the United States, in both periods of the conflict, provided sub-stantial financial support to aid relief agencies, especially the United Nations High Commissioner for Refugees (UNHCR), providing more than $500 mil-lion during the first civil war and $10 million in July 2003, in addition to $81 million to the UNCHR Africa-wide program.[30]

Although the United States outwardly projects democratization, good gov-ernance, human rights protection, and accountability as core values in its foreign policy, very little has been done to actualize these in Liberia. In the pre-1990 period, the Cold War obsession with alliance building and the containment of Libyan and Communist influence in Africa was allowed to obscure the human rights abuses by the Doe government. Similarly, while Washington was more vociferous in its objection to Taylor's dictatorship, it still lacked any coherent policy to constructively engage the Taylor regime. Also, the United States, even at the height of the post–Cold War peace optimism, failed either to intervene militarily or to support the ECOMOG intervention during the first civil war. It is ironic that this was before its intervention in Somalia, and thus made the allegedly close link between Washington and Monrovia a myth, rather than reality. A similar pattern is noticeable in the second Liberian civil war, where strong local and international public opinion demanding direct American military intervention could generate only the pseudo-deployment of three warships off the coast of Monrovia and the deployment of 200 troops in Liberia to protect the American embassy and provide background logistical support to the ECOMOG forces.

Since the presidential review, the African Crisis Response Initiative (ACRI; now renamed African Contingency Operations Training and Assistance, or ACOTA) has been the linchpin of post-Somalia American policy and roles in conflict and security management in West Africa. The program, funded by the peacekeeping operations account (at an annul rate of $20 million), trains military trainers and equips African national armies to conduct peace-support and humanitarian operations (as in envoy escort, logistics, protection of refugees, command and control, and negotiation techniques), thereby increasing their capabilities in human rights, international law, and civil-military relations.[31] In July 2000, for example, the United States, under "Operation Focus Relief," trained Nigerian peacekeepers who were subsequently deployed in Liberia, in August 2003. So far, more than 8,000 African military personnel have been trained.

The ACOTA program has also been integrated into President Bush's September 2002 National Security Strategy (NSS), as the hub of Washington's plan to empower Africa to address its myriad conflict and security problems,[32] emphasizing that "Africa's capable and reforming states and sub-regional organizations must be strengthened as the primary means to address transnational threats on a sustained basis."[33] The NSS seeks to use three interlocking security strategies for West Africa and the larger SSA region: partnership with core states (Nigeria in West Africa) with huge impact in the region; increased coordination with allies and international institutions for constructive conflict mediation, conflict resolution, and successful peace operations; and reform of institutions in and across states to enhance their capacity to meet transnational threats.[34] Thus, the overarching goal, as articulated by Paul Wolfowitz, then the influential deputy secretary of state for defense, is "to increase the capacity of . . . [African states] to provide for their own security," a security that is only possible with a high degree of military professionalism, suited to the challenges of the twenty-first century.[35]

While the current scope and level of engagement must be commended, especially in its efforts to increase the institutional and military capabilities of African countries to meet their individual and common security needs, it is limited in four important ways. The first is the apparent overreliance on African personnel, with routine logistical and financial support, to manage conflict and insecurity situations. Admittedly, this may be adequate in certain instances; however, the overall record of conventional peacekeeping on the continent by both regional and extra-regional forces is less than impressive. More importantly, reliance on African intervention is still limited by intra-African incapacity to sustain long-term military engagement or even to project credible force in the short term.[36]

Second, most neighboring African countries are interested parties in conflict situations at both regime and individual levels. The complicated invasions and interventions by neighbors of the DRC in the 1990s typify this. The cross-border social formations and divisions of ethnic nationalities further accentuate the problem. Third, the ACRI-ACOTA plan appears to be a way of regionalizing African crises, thereby avoiding any serious deployment of American troops.[37] In short, only African blood could and should be shed in managing and resolving conflict and security in Africa. Finally, as recent examples in Sierra Leone and Côte d'Ivoire suggest, an early, decisive direct deployment needs to be considered in managing conflict and security in West Africa, because "experience has shown that when early and decisive action is not taken to help resolve a dispute, the problem can turn destructive, resulting in the loss of hundreds and thousands of lives and the expenditure of millions of dollars."[38] It is quite possible that a modest early cooperative intervention in Liberia in both rounds of violence could have prevented or limited the bloodshed, the length of the violence, and the humanitarian emergencies. Yet the interventions that are advocated under cooperative intervention need to be integrated into an overall, comprehensive strategy.

The absence of direct American intervention in Liberia, despite the historical, humanitarian, cultural, and political linkages, is an indicator of America's aversion to military intervention in West Africa, in comparison to the Middle East. Yet there are at least five logical reasons to justify possible intervention in West Africa. The first is the moral imperative to contain the complex humanitarian emergencies, not least because the refugee problem in the Third World has global socioeconomic, cultural, and political reverberations. Second, intervention in Liberia would serve the broader purpose of stabilizing the region, especially in light of the region's increasing energy-related and strategic importance to America. Third, U.S. intervention would have been welcomed by all parties to the conflict and even by local people, all of whom had openly solicited American intervention. Fourth, such intervention could signal a change in American policy thinking about Africa, especially after Somalia, thereby demonstrating a new commitment to Africa. In fact, it could be argued that even the pseudo-deployment produced important psychological effects that contributed to the resignation of President Taylor, reduced the tendency to violate peace treaties that had been a trademark of the warring parties in Liberia, and helped to kick-start the peace process. Finally, intervention in Liberia would have been easily covered under President Bush's September 2002 National Security Strategy, which reaffirmed the important nexus between American strategic and moral interests in exporting democratic values and the ending of state failure.

Accordingly, what is the potential for greater, more robust involvement in light of the past, current, and future security challenges in West Africa? Examining the potential and adequacy of the current American approach to security management in West Africa becomes more expedient in light of the War on Terror and the energy (and strategic) profile of the region, as represented by the Gulf of Guinea. I now turn attention to this.

Changing U.S. National Interests and West Africa

Following the terrorist attacks of September 11, 2001, a major redirection of American national interests and overseas security strategy, based mainly on the War on Terror (WoT) and the diversification of energy supplies, appears to have consequences for West Africa. The WoT emphasizes retribution for suspected or real terrorists, outlaws negotiation with terrorist groups, exerts diplomatic, economic, political, and military pressure on states that sponsor terrorism to renounce such policies, and aims to bolster the counterterrorist capabilities of the antiterror coalition. Politically, the United States seeks support for the WoT at bilateral and multilateral levels. The UN's Security Council, for example, passed resolutions 1377 and 1368 to condemn the attacks of September 11, 2001, reaffirmed the threats terrorism poses to international peace and security, and pledged its readiness to combat terrorism within and across nations. Economically, the United States provides financial assistance to coalition partners, through the Millennium Challenge Account, to increase official American development assistance to $5 billion by 2006.[39] Militarily, the WoT emphasizes preemption as opposed to containment—the decisive preemptive use of force instead of its limited retaliatory use. The preemptive strategy covers the gathering of high-quality intelligence, the destruction of terrorist facilities and cells, and the selective use of targeting to limit the ability of terrorists to launch attacks similar to those of September 11, 2001.[40] The proactive nature of the WoT and its emphasis on alliance building appear to upgrade the strategic importance of West Africa in post-2001 American strategic thinking.

Consequently, a U.S. antiterror program—the Pan Sahel Initiative—was designed to help the West African states of Mali, Chad, Mauritania, and Niger to deal with terrorism, especially terrorism associated with militant Islam.[41] Moreover, the continued threat and presence of collapsed states in the region (Liberia, Guinea) and the strong linkage between state failure and terrorism also make the subregion and the rest of the SSA region important to American policymakers.[42] This explains the major realignments of American military forces and the increased military engagement with the subregion; from 2004, top-ranking American military personnel, under the European Command (EUCOM), which oversees West Africa, made several visits and initiated new military planning for the region.[43] In January 2005, in an unprecedented fashion, American warships were deployed to the Gulf of Guinea for a month-long joint military exercise with West African states (Ghana, Gabon, Cameroon, and others) to "enhance the security cooperation between the US and participating Gulf of Guinea nations," and also to bolster their deep sea (naval) capabilities.[44]

However, the plan to diversify American energy sources and reduce dependence on the Middle East, as set out in the May 2001 National Energy Plan, appears to be a more convincing explanation for increased American military engagement with West Africa. This is underscored by the energy profile of the Gulf of Guinea. In this context, I define West Africa and the Gulf of Guinea geopolitically. West Africa covers the sixteen member states of ECOWAS, while the Gulf of Guinea spans the Atlantic littoral from Mauritania to Nigeria and south to Angola.[45] The political map of Africa reveals that the Gulf of Guinea includes non–West African states, such as Angola, the DRC, Congo, Gabon, and Cameroon, among others. Yet West African states are in a majority and are the major players in the politics, energy potential, and security of the Gulf of Guinea region. Thus, Nigeria becomes central in diplomatic, energy, and security terms, while Liberia, given its recent turbulent political history and extensive ship registry, is central to security within the region.

Although there are other energy suppliers in Africa outside the Gulf of Guinea (for example, Tunisia, Algeria, and Sudan), the Gulf of Guinea remains central to American energy policy in Africa. Africa currently produces about 9.1 million barrels per day, of which 4.7 million come from the Gulf of Guinea, and African oil currently accounts for 11 percent of the global supply. Importantly, Africa currently supplies 18 percent of U.S. net oil imports, with Nigeria and Angola among the top ten suppliers to the United States. Africa is proven to hold about 7 to 9 percent of the total 80 to 100 billion in global reserves, but this percentage is set to rise with ultra-deep-water discoveries that could increase daily output by 4 to 6 million barrels per day over the next decade. Nigeria, Angola, Gabon, Congo, and Equatorial Guinea have the potential to increase production by about 3 to 5 million barrels per day, with states such as Senegal, São Tomé and Principe, and Sierra Leone harboring great potential for oil exploration. U.S. Vice President Dick Cheney, in the May 2001 National Energy Policy Report, reinforces the centrality of West Africa in the energy plan for the Gulf of Guinea, asserting that "West Africa is experiencing the fastest-growing sources of oil and gas for the American market."[46] This is underlined by the fact that the ECOWAS region of the Gulf of Guinea holds 33.8 billion barrels of proven reserves, equal to 3.1 percent of total global estimates, but able to increase to 7 percent of the world's total reserves if unproven reserves are added. Accordingly, the National Intelligence Council (NIC) notes that the African share of U.S. oil imports, currently at 15 percent, is expected to rise to 25 percent by 2015.[47] In short, the burgeoning competition for oil and gas exploration rights in the Gulf of Guinea by American, Chinese, Australian, and European multinationals has been likened to a new "Scramble for Africa."[48]

The energy profile of the region and increased American military engagement also reveal the interconnectedness of American national security and energy policy. This was articulated by the influential African Oil Policy Initiative Group (an advisory panel composed of oil executives and Pentagon officials) in a report to Congress in 2002, urging that Africa should be declared a priority in American foreign and security policy.[49] In light of this, how adequate is the current U.S. role in and plan for conflict and security management in West Africa? Before answering this question, it is imperative to highlight present and future security challenges in the region. There are four current and potential security challenges in the region. The first is the continued large-scale incidence of subnational violence, constructed along ideational contours of ethnicity, religion, and communal identity. The continued occurrence of intrastate violence and political volatility has made internally displaced persons (IDPs) and requests for humanitarian aid into recurring phenomena. Between 1999 and 2003, Nigeria alone produced more than a million IDPs and several thousand human casualties in more than a hundred cases of subnational violence.[50] Similar occurrences have been recorded in other supposedly stable countries, including Ghana. This makes the threat of state implosion a huge possibility in the region.

The second challenge is the increasing scale of maritime piracy, feeding into the proliferation of small arms, the black-market trading in stolen crude oil, secessionist movements, and armed threats to oil and gas exploration in the region, specifically in the Gulf of Guinea. The challenge is spearheaded by armed groups that emerged initially to protest the lack of environmental governance connected with multinational oil exploration in Nigeria but were increasingly transformed into criminal networks and gangs. One of the groups confessed to the illicit tapping and selling of a substantial portion of the total 100,000 barrels per day of stolen crude oil from Nigeria's daily production. The total worth of stolen crude (put at $1.5 million per day) has inevitably attracted arms dealers (smugglers) to the region, thereby making the Gulf of Guinea waterways some of the most dangerous in the world.[51] The International Maritime Bureau Report for 2004 notes that while the total number of pirate attacks fell in 2004, the disaggregated number of attacks on, and deaths of, seafarers increased in Nigeria, with 13 attacks and 15 deaths (out of the total number of 30 seafarers murdered).[52]

The third challenge is the often-cited threat, even if latent at this point, of militant Islam and international terrorism, given the historic ties between a majority of the states in the region with substantial Muslim populations and North Africa and the Middle East through the age-old trans-Saharan trade routes. Moreover, the more than 75 million Muslims in Nigeria alone, as well as those in Niger, Chad, Mauritania, and Mali among others, appear to generate both real and unfounded fears of militant Islam in the region. In fact, the fears appear real given the recent emergence of a self-styled Taliban movement in Nigeria and minor uprisings in the border states of Yobe and Borno in northern Nigeria since late 2003.[53] Finally, there is the prospect of interstate clashes that are likely to arise as a result of territorial and counter-territorial claims along overlapping and poorly demarcated littoral borders, often harboring huge energy reserves. The Nigerian-Cameroonian clashes over the oil-rich Bakassi Peninsula are a credible example of this. These territorial claims, underlined by the desire to control oil reserves and their exploration rights and accompanying rents, could actually reverse the conflict and security trend in the region, with possible increases in interstate conflicts as opposed to the dominance of insecurity from within. Thus, the Gulf of Guinea appears to be the hub of future security challenges in West Africa. The complex nature of the multiple security challenges facing the subregion, as already advanced in this chapter, requires a long-term comprehensive and holistic approach that combines various elements of cooperative intervention.

I have already identified major strands in U.S. policy and roles in conflicts and security management in West Africa. Current policy thinking emphasizes building and rebuilding the capacity and capabilities of countries in the region to meet current and future security challenges. This is augmented by active contributions to aid and relief efforts, and support for peace negotiations. Above all, the United States has actively supported the strengthening of the conflict management mechanisms of subregional and regional bodies, including ECOWAS, the African Union, and the Gulf of Guinea Commission.[54]

Thus, American policy continues to support the 1999 ECOWAS conflict management mechanism that created a tripartite council—mediation and security, defense and security, and council of elders—to coordinate conflict management efforts in the region. The plan is to have a standby ECOMOG intervention force composed of fifteen battalions (one from each member country). A cursory look at the current policy framework shows an impressive conflation between the ECOWAS plans and the American focus on strengthening allies to undertake collective security roles.

However, serious limitations are apparent. First, the WoT and its emphasis on alliance building, intelligence gathering, and proactive military action seem to crowd out the emphasis on and the measures capable of preventing the outbreak of conflict. Thus, there appears to be a trade-off between supporting democratization, human rights, and good governance and fighting the WoT. Second, the reliance solely on African capacity and capabilities in conflict management, notwithstanding Washington's professed but disproportionate "support role," loses sight of a core lesson from the UNAMSIL operations in Sierra Leone, where even with a robust mandate, some national units were not prepared to act according to the rules.[55]

Third, while there has been a recalibration in American forces' deployment (from large troop concentrations to small troop concentrations closer to trouble spots), the extent to which this reflects the security and energy profile of West Africa is unclear. With a record number of 37 of the 48 countries in SSA under its command, EUCOM oversees West Africa. Admittedly, EUCOM's plan for the subregion, revealed in part by a high-profile visit by EUCOM personnel, includes the promotion of regional stability, democratization, and military professionalism. However, the extent to which these goals and plans will address the specifics of current and future conflicts and security challenges are unclear. Moreover, West Africa as part of the overall SSA region continues to attract the lowest priority in EUCOM's plans and resources. It is reported that the United States through EUCOM is trying to negotiate the long-term use of a group of military bases capable of housing up to 5,000 brigades, for the provision of a robust military presence and for the use of special forces, across the region.[56] Yet EUCOM's operational plan, mirroring a majority of other Defense Department deployment plans, has consistently lacked adequate funding, systematic planning, sufficient intra-agency coordination, and effective measures for its evaluation. The inadequacy of current plans has prompted calls for a "unified command for Africa, similar to CENTCOM in Middle East" that would safeguard oil (from the Gulf of Guinea), provide an anchor for intra-agency effort, and reinforce economic, political, and security objectives.[57] Finally, the ever-present need to integrate and coordinate political, economic, security, and energy policies in preventing and managing conflicts and insecurity in the subregion receives little attention, at least in official proclamations. This reinforces the need to use a comprehensive, five-pillar approach to conflict and security management in the region.

Conclusion

This chapter has reviewed the history and evolution of the current American policy and role in conflict and security management in West Africa. It identifies a carry-over of the Cold War policy of subcontracting a leadership role in conflict and security management to European allies and, lately, to African countries. The chapter observes that while the multilateral approach to conflict and security management is crucial, the American leadership role remains central to security and stability in West Africa. This is poignantly reinforced by the post–September 11, 2001, security and energy policy that targets West Africa's Gulf of Guinea as an alternative source of energy. This chapter argues for a comprehensive and integrated policy framework, encapsulated in the cooperative approach based on five components: (1) preventive action (democratization, good governance, and the rule of law); (2) institutional capacity building to respond to security challenges; (3) support for peace negotiations by third parties; (4) cooperation with and support for multilateral institutions in conflict and security management; and (5) direct military deployment. While the current American role and policy already contain substantial elements of the first four components, it is important to overcome the post-Somalian "hangover."

Notes

1. Herman, Cohen, "The United States and Africa: Non-vital Interests Also Require Attention," American Diplomacy, August 30, 2003, http://www.unc.edu/depts/diplomat/archives_roll/ 2003_0709/cohen_africa/ cohen_africa.html.

2. David Goldwyn and Stephen Morrison, *A Strategic U.S. Approach to Governance and Security in the Gulf of Guinea* (Washington, DC: CSIS, July 2005), 7.

3. Adebayo Adedeji, "Comprehending African Conflict," in *Comprehending and Mastering African Conflicts: The Search for Sustainable Peace and Good Governance,* ed. Adebayo Adedeji (London: Zed Books for ACDESS, 1999), 3–6.

4. Festus Aboagye, *ECOMOG: A Sub-regional Experience in Conflict Resolution, Management and Peacekeeping in Liberia* (Accra: SEDCO Press, 1999), 1–3.

5. Margaret Karns and Karen Mingst, "The Evolution of the United Nations Peacekeeping and Peacemaking: Lessons from the Past and Challenges for the Future," in *World Security: Challenges for a New Century,* 3rd ed., ed. Michael Klare and Yogesh Chandrani (New York: St. Martin's Press, 1998), 206.

6. Tunde Zack-Williams and Giles Mohan, "Theories of the State/State of Theories," in *The Politics of Transition in Africa,* ed. Tunde Zack-Williams and Giles Mohan (Oxford: James Currey for ROAPE, 2004), 4–5. See also Naomi Chazan et al., *Politics and Society in Contemporary Africa,* 3rd ed. (Boulder, CO: Lynne Rienner, 1999), 18.

7. The Nigerian vice president alluded to this, noting that "There is no security and certainly there will be no energy security in the Gulf of Guinea without good governance and democracy in the sub-region." See Atiku Abubakar, vice president of the

Federal Republic of Nigeria, "Keynote Address" (presented at the Conference on Security in the Gulf of Guinea, organized by the Center for Strategic and International Studies, Washington, DC, July 20, 2005), http://www.csis.org/media/csis/events/050720_atiku.pdf.

8. Walter Runciman, *Relative Deprivation and Social Justice* (London: Routledge and Kegan Paul, 1966), 22.

9. Ted Robert Gurr, *Why Men Rebel* (Princeton, NJ: Princeton University Press, 1970), 8.

10. Christopher Clapham, "Analysing African Insurgencies," in *African Guerrillas*, ed. Christopher Clapham (Oxford: James Currey, 1998), 5.

11. Rockyn Williams, "Africa and the Challenges of Security Sector Reform," *ISS Monograph 46* (South Africa: Institute for Strategic Studies, February 2000), 2–3.

12. Olawale Ismail, "Rolling Back the Clock: The War on Terror and Security Sector Reform in Africa" (paper presented at the 19th congress of the International Political Science Association, Durban, South Africa, July 2003), 12.

13. Raimo Vayrynen, "Complex Emergencies: Concepts and Issues," in *War, Hunger and Displacement: The Origins of Humanitarian Emergencies*, vol. 1, ed. Wayne Nafziger, Frances Stewart, and Raimo Vayrynen (New York: Oxford University Press, 2000), 49.

14. United Nations, *Report of the Panel on United Nations Peace Operations, UN Doc A/55/305-S/2000/809* (August 2000), http://www.un.org/peace/reports/peace_operations/.

15. Amadou Toumain Toure, "Mastering African Conflicts," in *Comprehending and Mastering African Conflicts*, ed. Adedeji, 22.

16. Thomas Weiss, "Internal Exiles: What Next for IDPS," *Third World Quarterly* 24, no. 3 (2003): 442.

17. International Crisis Group, "Liberia and Sierra Leone: Rebuilding Failed States," *Africa Report No 87* (Dakar/Brussels: ICG, December 2004), http://www.crisisgroup.org/home/index.cfm?id=3156.

18. United Nations, *The Causes of Conflict and the Promotion of Durable Peace and Sustainable Development in Africa* (April 1998), paragraph 24, http://www.un.org/ecosocdev/geninfo/afrec/sgreport/conflt2.h.

19. Adekeye Adebajo, "Pax West Africana? Regional Security Mechanisms," in *West Africa's Security Challenges*, ed. Adekeye Adebajo and Ismail Rashid (Boulder, CO: Lynne Rienner, 2004), 292–95. See also David Leatherwood, "Peacekeeping in West Africa," *Joint Force Quarterly*, Autumn/Winter 2001–2, 78.

20. Toure, "Mastering African Conflicts," 28.

21. Herbert Howe identifies the political nature of the state, the nature of politics, and lack of military professionalism as critical challenges inhibiting the capacity of African countries to counteract threats to their individual and collective security. See Herbert Howe, *Ambiguous Order: Military Forces in African States* (Boulder, CO: Lynne Rienner, 2005), 1–5.

22. See the full text of the Commonwealth's Harare Declaration at http://www.thecommonwealth.org/Templates/Internal.asp?NodeID=35773.

23. Kaye Whiteman and Douglas Yates, "France, Britain, and the United States," in *West Africa's Security Challenges*, ed. Adekeye Adebajo and Ismail Rashid (Boulder, CO: Lynne Rienner, 2004), 366.

24. Ibid., 365.

25. Adedeji, "Comprehending African Conflict," 7.

26. Eghosa Osaghae, *Ethnicity, Class and the Struggle for State Power in Liberia,* CODESRIA Monograph Series 1/96 (Dakar: CODESRIA, 1993), 27.

27. Whiteman and Yates, "France, Britain and the United States," 360.

28. Herman Cohen (former U.S. assistant secretary of state for African affairs), "Liberia: The Bush Doctrine Comes to Africa" (paper presented at a seminar organized by the American Enterprise Institute, Washington, July 2003), http://www.aei.org/events/eventID.468,filter./event_detail.asp.

29. Several authors writing on the ECOMOG operations in West Africa note that the character of the ruling regime in Nigeria strongly influenced American support for the ECOWAS monitoring group. In one instance, it is claimed that the demise of the Abacha regime ushered in a diplomatic rapprochement in Nigeria-U.S. relations, with an impact on U.S. support for ECOMOG. See, for example, Funmi Olonisakin, *Reinventing Peacekeeping in Africa: Conceptual and Legal Issues in ECOMOG Operations* (The Hague: Kluwer Law International, 2000).

30. U.S. Department of State, "US Contributing Additional $10m to Humanitarian Agencies to Aid Refugees in West Africa," press release, July 2003, http://www.state.gov/r/pa/prs/ps/2003/22224.htm.

31. U.S. Department of State, "Africa Crisis Response Initiative (ACRI)," daily press briefing, July 2, 2003, http://www.state.gov/r/pa/prs/ps/2003/22237.htm.

32. See U.S. House of Representatives, "African Crisis Response Initiative: A Security Building Block," hearing of the Sub-committee on Africa of the Committee on Internal Relations, U.S. House of Representatives, 107th Congress, 1st session, July 12, 2001, serial number 107–120, http://commdocs.house.gov/committees/intlrel/hfa73778.000/hfa73778_of.htm.

33. U.S. Dept. of State, *The National Security Strategy of the United States* (September 2002), 11, http://www.whitehouse.gov/nsc/nss.pdf.

34. James Carafano and Nile Gardiner, "U.S Military Assistance for Africa: A Better Solution," *Backgrounder No. 1697,* Heritage Foundation, October 15, 2003, www.heritage.org/Research/Africa/ bg1697.cfm.

35. Embassy of the United States in Japan, "Wolfowitz Cites Importance of Africa in U.S. Security Policy," press release, November 2, 2004, http://www.tokyo.usembassy.gov/e/p/tp-20040212-01.html.

36. Howe, *Ambiguous Order: Military Forces,* 2.

37. Whiteman and Yates, "France, Britain and the United States," 373.

38. Johnnie Carson, "Shaping U.S. Policy on Africa: Pillars of a New Strategy," *Strategic Forum No. 210* (Washington, DC: Institute for National Strategic Studies, National Defense University, September 2004), 5.

39. Raphael Perl, "Expert Sees More Proactive US Policy against Terrorism," July 2, 2002, http://usinfo.state.gov/topical/pol/terror/02070204.htm.

40. Raphael Perl, "Expert Says Adjustments Needed to Combat Terrorism," April 26, 2002, http://usinfo.state.gov/topical/pol/terror/02042605.htm.

41. Carson, "Shaping U.S. Policy on Africa," 4.

42. In 2001, the United States under the Terrorist Exclusion List (TEL) classified eight of the twenty-eight terrorist groups in the world as existing in Africa. See U.S. Department of State, *Patterns of Global Terrorism: 2001 Report* (Washington, DC: Department of State, May 2002), 113–30.

43. Ellen Kickmeyer, "U.S. Military Shows Interest in Africa," Associated Press, February 24, 2004, www.independent-media.tv/item.

44. See "U.S. Deploys Warship to Oil Rich African Gulf," January 26, 2005, http://english.people.com.cn/200501/ 26/eng20050126_171940.html.

45. Rudolf Traub-Merz, "Introduction: Oil Policy in the Gulf of Guinea," in *Oil Policy in the Gulf of Guinea: Security and Conflict, Economic Growth, Social Development,* ed. Rudolf Traub-Merz and Douglas Yates (Lagos: Friedrich Ebert Foundation, 2004), 12.

46. Cyril Widdershoven, "West African Oil: Hope or Hype?" Institute for the Analysis of Global Security, July 16, 2003, http://www.iags.org/africa.html.

47. National Intelligence Council, *Global Trends 2015: A Dialogue about the Future with Nongovernment Experts* (December 2000), 73, http://www.fas.org/irp/cia/product/globaltrends2015/index.html), 73.

48. Helmut Dietrich, "Will Oil Spoil This African Paradise?" *Fortune,* September 6, 2004, 20, http://www.earthinstitute.columbia.edu/cgsd/STP/documents/Fortune_STP.pdf.

49. Julian Borger, "US to Lock Africa in a Military Embrace," *Guardian Weekly,* July 10, 2003, 6.

50. Olawale Ismail and Jeremy Ginifer, *Armed Violence and Poverty in Nigeria: A Case Study for the Armed Violence and Poverty Initiative* (Bradford, UK: CICS, Department of Peace Studies, University of Bradford, November 2004), 4.

51. See "Piracy Report Says Nigerian Waters the Most Deadly," Naijanet, July 28, 2004, http://www.naijanet.com/news/ source/2004/jul/28/1000.html.

52. BBC News, "Murders by Pirates on the Rise," February 7, 2005, http://www.news.bbc.co.uk/1/hi/ world/4242703.stm.

53. BBC News, "New Taleban Clashes in Nigeria," 7 January 2004, http://news.bbc.co.uk/1/hi/world/africa/3376979.stm.

54. The Gulf of Guinea Commission was proposed by Nigeria to ensure peaceful exploration and exploitation of the resources in the region. Specifically, Article IV of the Gulf of Guinea Commission Treaty mandates it to promote peace and security within the region through a conflict management mechanism that emphasizes dialogue and the use of arbitration to resolve disputes.

55. Richard Williamson, U.S Alternate Representative to the UN, "Conflict Resolution and Lessons from Sierra Leone," statement at the UN Security Council Workshop on West Africa, New York, July 18, 2002, http://www.un.int/usa/02_101.htm.

56. Borger, "US to Lock Africa," 6.

57. Carafano and Gardiner," U.S. Military Assistance for Africa," 6.

20

Radical Islam in the Sahel

Implications for U.S. Policy and Regional Stability

Stephen A. Harmon

Introduction

In recent years there have been increasing reports of an upsurge in radical Islam, or political Islam, among Muslims in the West African Sahel. Evidence for this upsurge includes inroads by Algerian Islamist rebels, an influx of foreign Islamist preachers, and an expansion of indigenous Islamist communities. Four nations in particular, Mauritania, Mali, Niger, and Chad, are widely regarded as vulnerable to the influence of Muslim extremists because they abut the seemingly lawless Sahara, an unpatrolled expanse rife with trafficking and contraband. As a result, the United States currently ranks the Sahel as the number two front for Africa in the War on Terror.[1] In response, various U.S. agencies have focused significant attention and resources on the region. The U.S. Agency for International Development (USAID) recently increased development aid for the Sahel, believing that poverty makes Muslims there susceptible to foreign extremists.[2] The Bush administration's Millennium Challenge Account, which provides supplemental development aid to nations that "respect human rights, and adhere to the rule of law" also targets certain Sahelian countries.[3] In addition, the State Department established a little-publicized program in 2002 called the Pan Sahel Initiative (PSI) for the purpose of providing training and support to Sahelian states to help them interdict Islamist terrorist activity.

This chapter will examine the emergence of radical Islam in the West African Sahel and Sahara and the U.S. response to it, as well as the threats to stability that it may pose in the region. Using a thematic, synchronic approach, I shall argue that there has indeed been an upsurge of radical Islam in the Sahel. However, while this upsurge has dramatically affected U.S. policy, for example, leading to the establishment of the PSI, the movement is not yet serious enough to be considered the primary threat to regional stability. Rather, the primary threats to stability continue to be, as always, chronic poverty and its resulting economic dislocations, along with ethnic rivalries and a tradition of autocratic regimes.

Other terms used for radical Islam include "political Islam" or "Islamism." Mohammed Ayoob defines Islamism as "Islam as a political ideology rather than a religious or theological construct." He uses the terms "political Islam" and "Islamism" interchangeably.[4] Important Islamist movements within Sunni Islam include "Wahhabism" and "Salafism."[5] Wahhabism is a strain of fundamentalist Islam that derives from the Wahhabi movement of mid-eighteenth-century Arabia, founded by the reformist Sunni cleric Muhammad ibn Abd al-Wahhab. Ibn Abd al-Wahhab demanded rigorous purification on the model of the Rashidun age, the age of the Prophet and his companions, and sought purely Islamic remedies to contemporary problems. He wanted to purge Islam of all modern accretions and return to reliance only on the original texts of the faith, the Qur'an and the *hadith*, the collected sayings of the Prophet.[6] Wahhabism, historically tied to the Saudi monarchy, implies rejection of everything after the Rashidun period, including the four established schools of jurisprudence and the Sufi brotherhoods.

"Salafism" refers to a strain of Islamic fundamentalism that, like Wahhabism, relies only on the Qur'an and the *hadith*.[7] Influenced by the teachings of the Egyptian Muslim Brothers, Salafis are characterized by their willingness to attack established Islam as unbelief. Scholars and analysts frequently make a distinction between *Salafiyya 'ilimiyya*, or scholarly Salafis and *Salafiyya jihadiyya*, or fighting Salafis.[8] It is the jihadist or fighting Salafis that engage in terrorist attacks, while the scholarly Salafis are more concerned with building model Islamist communities and imposing their rigorous interpretation of Quranic law. However, jihadists are often recruited from scholarly Salafi communities.[9] Salafism, sometimes called "neo-Wahhabism," is frequently used as a cover term for Saudi-funded Wahhabism as it expands internationally, since Wahhabism is generally regarded by non-Saudis as parochial and complacent.[10] Salafism is also preferred by global jihadists like Osama bin Laden, who, though schooled in Wahhabism, denounces the Saudi rulers as hypocritical tyrants and vassals of the United States. Both Wahhabism and Salafism are firmly entrenched in Arabia and Egypt, but they are relative innovations in West Africa, long a stronghold of mainstream Sunni Islam, Malikite law, and the Sufi brotherhoods.[11]

The Emergence of Radical Islam in the Sahara and Sahel

In the past few years, according to many journalists, diplomats, and non-governmental organization (NGO) spokesmen, radical strains of Islam have emerged or expanded in the Sahelian states. Some strains are taught and disseminated by local Muslim leaders, while some strains are introduced by outsiders. Journalist Paul Marshall notes that Senegal, The Gambia, Niger, Mauritania, and even "historically democratic Mali" are experiencing a rise in Islamist unrest, including in some cases calls for an Islamic state.[12] Nicolas Colombant argues that "hard-line Islam" is on the rise in Mali after more than ten years of democracy. He says that Muslim activists, primarily local, have become the government's main critics, noting that imams of some Friday mosques criticize the government's failure to help the poor.[13] In addition, foreign Muslims are also active in the Sahel. Officials in Burkina Faso report that "bearded ones," foreign Salafist preachers, are showing up in remote areas preaching radical Islam, adding that they are well funded and vocal.[14] Admiral Hamlin B. Tallent, director of operations for the U.S. European Command (EUCOM), which has responsibility for West Africa, reports that U.S. personnel have been approached by local Muslim leaders in Sahelian countries complaining of the growing presence of the "long beards," foreign Islamic extremists advocating jihad.[15] Correspondent Lisa Anderson also comments on the presence of foreign extremists, noting the proliferation of Saudi-funded mosques. She says that sixteen Wahhabi mosques have been built in the past three years in Timbuktu alone, a city of 35,000. She also mentions the Pakistani Salafist organization called Jama'at al-Tabligh, founded by Muhammad Ilyas in 1926,[16] and also known as Da'wa al-Tabligh. Its missionaries are aggressively seeking converts in West Africa. Anderson quotes former U.S. Ambassador to Mali Vicki Huddleston, who frequently expressed concern about the Tablighi and the Wahhabi groups, as well as Salafis from Algeria, all of whom are trying to establish a presence in the Sahel.[17]

We may not be ready to state categorically that there is a rise in domestic Islamic radicalism in the Sahel; however, there is clear evidence that foreign extremists are measurably and continuously establishing a presence there. The four Sahelian states—Mauritania, Mali, Niger, and Chad—are considered vulnerable to penetration by foreign extremists because they all border one or more of their radical neighbors, Algeria, Libya, and Sudan.[18] Indeed, an Algerian rebel movement called the Salafist Group for Call and Combat, known by its French acronym GSPC, has been in recent years the most active foreign Muslim extremist organization operating in the Sahelian states. The GSPC was organized in 1998 as a splinter faction of the Algerian Armed Islamic Group (GIA).[19] It reportedly split from the GIA over the latter's policy of targeting innocent civilians in its decade-long campaign to establish an Islamic state in Algeria.[20] While sharing the ultimate goal, the GSPC rejects attacks on innocent civilians, preferring instead to target Algerian government and security forces. The GSPC was founded by Hassan Hattab, whom Algeria claimed was linked to al-Qaeda.[21] Believed to number around 3,000 fighters in 2003, the GSPC became Algeria's largest and most effective rebel movement.[22] The GSPC figure who gained the most notoriety in the Sahelian states was Amari Saïfi, known by his nom de guerre, Abderrezak al-Para. Al-Para is believed to have made contact with al-Qaeda ideologue Dr. Ayman al-Zawahiri, indicating his willingness to serve as an operative in the Sahara.[23] His mission was, reportedly, to establish himself in the Algeria-Mali border area in order to federate under the al-Qaeda banner all the armed groups opposed to the current regimes in the Sahelian countries.[24]

The Malian Region of Kidal, which borders Algeria, was a center of the 1990–96 antigovernment Tuareg rebellion. It has long been suspected of being a haven for Islamic extremists and proselytizers. Kidal's border with Algeria is porous because of the lack of a military presence, as Mali's border patrols were withdrawn in 1996 as part of the peace accords that ended the Tuareg rebellion.[25] Another GSPC associate, Mokhtar Belmokhtar, a veteran of the anti-Soviet jihad in Afghanistan with links to al-Qaeda, has been known to operate in the Kidal area. Alternating between leading Algerian rebel attacks and pursuing his contraband business interests, Mokhtar Belmokhtar has been described as a smuggling kingpin of the region.[26] U.S. State Department officials have likewise become aware of the operations of foreign Islamist preachers in Kidal, as well as in other parts of the Sahara.[27] Notable among these are the Tablighi missionaries, who have a strong presence in Mali and other Sahelian countries. First established in Bamako as early as 1992 by way of Malian émigrés in France, Jama'at al-Tabligh's focus has been on Kidal since 1997. The organization has made converts in many countries including the UK and the United States, and some of these converts have been successfully recruited by al-Qaeda to engage in terrorist training and/or attacks. Notable among these are the "Shoe Bomber," Richard Reid of London, the alleged "Dirty Bomber," José Padilla of Chicago, Buffalo's "Lackawanna six," and "California Taliban" John Walker Lindh.[28]

Implications for U.S. Policy in the Region

The United States has taken seriously the reported al-Qaeda connection with both foreign Islamist preachers and the Algerian GSPC, as demonstrated by the State Department's formation of the Pan Sahel Initiative (PSI) in November 2002. Earlier U.S. West Africa initiatives, dating back to 1996, generally focused on peacemaking activities. These initiatives included the Africa Crisis Response Force (ACRF), founded in 1996, the African Crisis Response Initiative (ACRI), founded in 1997, and Operation Focus Relief (ORF), established in 2000, which was the first of the West Africa initiatives to go beyond mere peacekeeping, deploying combat troops to Sierra Leone.[29] The Pan Sahel Initiative was initially funded at $7.75 million, more than half of which was channeled to defense and security forces in Mali. The purpose of the PSI was to train government troops in Mauritania, Mali, Chad, and Niger to resist terrorist activity in the Sahara.[30] According to the State Department's official Web site, the PSI is intended to assist the four Sahelian countries in

> detecting and responding to suspicious movement of people and goods across and within their borders through training, equipment and cooperation. Its goals support two US national security interests in Africa: waging the war on terrorism and enhancing regional peace and security.[31]

The border area between Algeria, Mali, Niger, and Libya has been characterized as a zone of permanent insecurity featuring contraband traffic in drugs, cigarettes, arms, and labor migrants.[32] Largely unpatrolled, the region is considered virgin territory for lawlessness and thus a likely spot for terrorist infiltration. The impetus for the creation of the PSI was, among other factors, the presence in North Africa of the Yemeni terrorist Emad Abdulhamid Ahmed Alwan, a known al-Qaeda operative and Zawahiri associate. Alwan was killed by Algerian security forces in September 2002 in Batna Province.[33]

What triggered the PSI's deployment, however, was the highly publicized seizure of thirty-two European tourists, mostly Germans, as hostages in six separate incidents in February and March 2003 by GSPC units led by Abderrezak al-Para.[34] The taking of European hostages by the GSPC, an apparent breach of its policy against attacking civilian targets, confirmed the fears of the U.S. State Department that al-Qaeda-sponsored terrorists were operating in northern Africa. Some of the hostages were freed by Algerian security forces after a gun battle in southern Algeria on May 13, 2003. The kidnappers took the rest of the hostages across the Malian border and held them until August 18, when a ransom of five million euros was reportedly paid by the German government for their release.[35] Rumors soon began to circulate that the GSPC was using the ransom money to buy arms and recruit fighters in northern Mali, an area still awash with weapons and disaffected former rebels left over from the Tuareg rebellion of the 1990s. With growing alarm, American and Algerian intelligence monitored al-Para in the Kidal region in early 2004 as he was purchasing weapons. This "shopping spree" led to a dramatic four-country chase that resulted in a major defeat for the GSPC.[36]

The events that culminated in the border-hopping pursuit began when a U.S. spy satellite spotted a convoy crossing into Mali from Algeria in December 2003, and the United States notified the Malian government.[37] Subsequent reports that al-Para had been buying arms and recruiting in Kidal spurred the Malian government to action. After a visit to Germany in December 2003, President Amadou Toumani Touré vowed to track down al-Para. He was motivated by two factors: German pressure and fears that the GSPC might rally the ethnic Arab minority of northern Mali to rebel again, as it had done, along with the Berber-speaking Tuaregs, in the 1990s.[38] Together, Malian and Algerian army leaders drew up a plan to trap al-Para in a pincer movement. The Algerians feared that al-Para, then second in command of the GSPC, would use the purchased arms to carry on his group's fight to establish an Islamist government in Algeria, while the Malians worried about his recruitment activities.[39] Al-Para was allegedly heading back to Algeria with arms and recruits acquired in Mali when Malian forces intercepted him. The Malian government announced in January 2004 that GSPC units had been chased out of Mali to Niger.[40] Algeria reported that its security forces destroyed an armed unit of GSPC fighters near the southern town of Tamanrasset in February 2004, recovering many weapons. Meanwhile, al-Para and his fighters were pursued from Mali to Niger to northern Chad by the security forces of the three governments. This pursuit culminated in a two-day battle on March 8 and 9 near the northwest Chadian town of Zouar, some fifty kilometers from the Niger border. Forty-three GSPC fighters, including Malians and Nigériens as well as Algerians, were killed. Forces from both Chad and Niger participated in the action and seized a substantial quantity of weapons.[41] U.S. Special Forces operating out of EUCOM supported the Chadians with logistics and resupply and, according to some reports, in combat as well.[42]

The successful destruction of such a large group of GSPC fighters was considered a big victory by the Chadian and Nigérien forces and a major vindication for the PSI. It was after this action that the training of military forces in the four Sahelian countries, as called for in the initiative, began in earnest.[43] U.S. personnel, including marines and members of the Special Forces, began training Malian and Mauritanian troops in counterinsurgency and border security in late March 2004.[44] In April the defense chiefs of nine West and North African countries met at EUCOM headquarters in Stuttgart to discuss plans for following up on the victory over the GSPC insurgents. It was the first time that many of them had met face to face.[45] The second part of the training phase of the PSI, the training of Nigérien and Chadian defense forces, was completed by November 2004. In all, U.S. forces trained some 1,200 troops from the four Sahelian countries in tracking, patrolling, arms and contraband interdiction, and basic combat techniques under the $7.5 million program.[46]

The elusive Abderrezak al-Para and some of his lieutenants escaped the clash with the Chadian forces but were captured shortly thereafter, still in Chad, by fighters of a non-Islamist rebel group called the Chadian Movement for Democracy and Justice (MDJT).[47] Over the next few months, while al-Para was in the custody of the MDJT, negotiations took place regarding offers to hand the GSPC leader over to, variously, the Americans, the Germans, and the Algerians. The negotiations were complicated by the obfuscations of Chad's President Idriss Déby, who objected to the idea of a Chadian rebel group dealing directly with a foreign power.[48] In September 2004, a television crew from the France 2 network interviewed al-Para, still in MDJT custody. The broadcast, which also aired in Algeria, gave the Algerian public their first glimpse of the notorious kidnapper. Smiling through the interview, the GSPC leader said that he and his men had come to the Tibesti region of northern Chad hoping to find support and respite among the desert tribes. He affirmed that his group's ultimate objective was to wage a jihad to replace the current Algerian regime with an Islamist one.[49] Al-Para was finally extradited to Algeria in October. The diplomatic deadlock was broken by the good offices of Libya, who took custody of al-Para from the MDJT and then handed him over to the Algerians.[50]

The United States regarded al-Para's capture, along with the destruction of the GSPC force with him, as a product of the cooperation made possible by the PSI.[51] The operation had resulted from the coordination of the armed forces, security services, intelligence, logistics support, and diplomatic efforts of six countries, Algeria, Mali, Niger, Chad, Libya, and the United States. The affair proved that international cooperation could lead to successful antiterrorist action. It also confirmed that international terrorists were indeed using the Sahara as a staging and recruitment zone. As a result, plans were made by State Department officials as early as June 2004 to transform the PSI into a new, larger, more comprehensive initiative called the Trans-Sahara Counter-Terrorism Initiative (TSCTI).[52] The TSCTI, whose Congressional funding is pending, is to include the discreet deployment of U.S. Special Forces and a commitment to spend $120–32 million in 2005 and $350–400 million over the next five years on follow-up training for the four Sahelian countries.[53] Despite the GSPC debacle in Chad, the United States believes that the Sahara could still become a terrorist haven. Concern over continued illicit arms and human traffic in the Sahel/Sahara area and doubts that a few hundred trained troops in each of the four countries would be adequate to stabilize the immense region convinced the United States to develop the TSCTI. The United States intends to expand the program to include Senegal, Algeria, Morocco, Tunisia, and possibly Nigeria. The TSCTI, if funded, will work in concert with African military and civilian law enforcement agencies to facilitate the location and elimination of terrorists and their sanctuaries and strengthen the agencies' ability to police large expanses of remote terrain.[54] It will also arrange for development assistance and public diplomacy campaigns as part of an overall CT (counterterrorism) strategy, with some 40 percent of the projected funds being distributed through USAID.[55]

Implications for Stability in the Four Sahelian Countries

It is clear that there has been an upsurge of radical Islam in Sahelian West Africa. Some of it has taken the form of foreign Islamist preachers spreading Wahhabist or Salafist ideologies among local Muslim populations. Some of it involves local preachers and scholars taking a more radical Islamist line and supporting Islamist politics. And some of it is in the form of terrorist organizations linked to international networks working toward the goal of global jihad. Islamist movements known to be operating in the Sahel include the GSPC, the Wahhabiyya. and the Tablighis. While the GSPC is clearly *Salafiyya jihadiyya*, the other groups, in their West African manifestations, are largely *Salafiyya 'ilimiyya*. What is less clear is the degree to which this upsurge of political Islam or Islamism represents a genuine threat to the stability of the region. The security situation varies greatly among the four Sahelian states. Niger and Mali are considered relatively stable: both countries have solid, ongoing democratization processes. Mali has earned good marks from international watchdog organizations for freedom of expression and the press, while Niger has achieved a remarkable degree of religious freedom. Antigovernment sentiment has been much stronger in Chad and Mauritania. The Chadian government is coming under criticism chiefly on account of the rampant corruption associated with the current regime. Mauritania's government, prior to the August 2005 coup d'état, was widely resented for clinging to power and refusing political openings to opposition parties. While it is clear that threats to stability are present, as evidenced by the Mauritanian coup, the degree to which these threats may be attributed to radical Islamists is less clear. It is also clear that the Sahara, especially the Algeria-Mali frontier area, is an open zone that supports many kinds of traffic, including traffic in arms, stolen vehicles, and drugs, and illegal human migration. Islamists of various stripes are heavily involved in this traffic.[56] It is believed that the GSPC, for example, has many bases and arms caches scattered across the Sahara and that it maintains ties with rebel groups in Mali, Niger, and Chad.[57] While the GSPC is certainly Islamist and clearly advances its own Islamist agenda, the rebel groups that it is trying to influence, though usually Muslim, are not necessarily Islamist.

Chad

A case in point is the Chadian Movement for Democracy and Justice (MDJT), an antigovernment rebel group based in the Tibesti region of northwestern Chad. The MDJT was founded in 1998 by President Déby's former defense minister, Youssouf Togoimi. Its stated goal is the overthrow of the Déby government for its failure to implement significant democratic reform.[58] The movement is now led by Hassan Abdellah Merdegue, since

Togoimi was killed by a landmine in 2002. As noted above, it was MDJT fighters that captured the GSPC leader Abderrezak al-Para and his lieutenants. The circumstances of al-Para's capture remain unclear, but one account, offered by Merdegue, holds that al-Para, in flight from his comrades' rout at the hands of Chadian forces, offered no resistance when he encountered MDJT forces. Merdegue says that some of al-Para's men even threw down their arms, thinking the Chadian rebels would be friendly to them.[59] Instead, the Chadians took them prisoner. When it detained al-Para and subsequently handed him over to the Algerians for trial, MDJT showed the world that it was not rallying to the al-Qaeda banner.[60] The Chadian rebels strongly emphasized in the course of the September 2004 France 2 television interview that they are not an Islamist organization. They claimed that they were allowing French journalists to interview their prisoner to show that they are fighting for democracy and justice, not, they insisted, to support Salafism.[61]

Most Chadian Muslims practice Sunni Islam and adhere to the Malikite school of law. While Islam has a long history in northern Chad, neither the traditional Sufi brotherhoods nor the modern waves of fundamentalism have had a great impact on it. The Tijaniyya and Sanusiyya brotherhoods are both present in Chad, but they have not historically played a large role in the expansion of Islam or in religious and political organization, as they have in the other Sahelian states.[62] There has been, however, an increase in the influence of domestic Islamists in Chad in the past two decades, and they have been active in the political realm. Chadian journalist Michaël Didama, who is critical of political Islam, says that Islamist fighters supported Déby's guerrillas against the forces of former President Hissène Habré when the latter was toppled in 1990, bringing Déby to power. Didama adds that the imam of the Central Mosque in the capital N'Djamena interfered in the 2001 presidential election on Déby's behalf. Since then, he says, "Muslim extremists proudly wear their beards in the highest echelons of the Chad government."[63] Thus it appears that in the case of Chad, the Islamists are supporting the current government, while the main antigovernment rebel groups are non-Salafist.

Unlike the other three Sahelian states, which are all predominantly Muslim, Chad is only about 50 percent Muslim, with large Christian and traditional communities in the southern part of the country. As such, Chad's demographic situation, with an Arabophone, Islamic north and a black African, Christian, and traditional south, more closely resembles that of its eastern neighbor Sudan than those of its Sahelian neighbors to the west. The ethnic tensions in Chad run between the Arabized and Muslim northerners and the Christian and traditional southerners, as opposed to Mali, for example, where the tensions historically run between the Arab and Berber Muslim desert dwellers and the black African, but Muslim, southerners. The Déby government is largely from the northern Zaghawa ethnic group. Déby himself is from the Sudan border area, which is now hosting vast numbers of Sudanese refugees from the Darfur crisis.[64] Déby's faction aligns itself with the Arabophone, Muslim northern culture against the Francophone, non-Muslim culture of the south. Rebel groups of both the north and south have challenged the government over its corruption and failure to reform. These groups include the southern-based Movement for Democracy and Development (MDD) and the northern-based MDJT.[65] While both groups are challenging the Déby government, neither is doing so on Islamist grounds. Therefore, while there may be considerable instability in Chad, we cannot attribute much of it to radical Islam.

Niger

The case of Niger is more complex. Officially Niger is a secular republic, despite a population that is more than 80 percent Muslim. The law tolerates Muslims of all varieties. The official position is stated succinctly by a Nigérien government spokesman, Minister of Institutional Relations Mohammed Ben Omar: "Le Niger est un pays à 95% musulman, mais c'est une République laïque. Il n'y a pas d'islamisme radical ou militant au Niger. Nous avons un islam tolérant. Il n'y a aucun risque de ce côté-là."[66] Islamism in Niger, militant or otherwise, derives mainly from the south, in neighboring Nigeria.[67] Olivier Meunier describes three types of Islamic movements in Niger, the "traditionalists," the "rationalists," and the "reformists." The traditionalists are linked to the old Sufi brotherhoods, including the Qadiriyya and the Tijaniyya. They have roots in the great nineteenth-century West African jihad movements of Usman dan Fodio and al-Hajj Umar Tall. The rationalists often include French-educated elites. Like the traditionalists, they adhere to Malikite law, but they see Islam as a personal religion, not a social movement. They do not support the Salafist and literalist aspects of the third group, the reformists. The reformists are Salafis who adhere to a literal interpretation of the Qur'an and the *hadith* and seek to purify Nigérien Islam. They reject the secular state and secular education as well as the four schools of Islamic law and the Sufi brotherhoods.[68]

Robert Charlick identifies the Izala movement, or Yan Izala, which he says is inspired by Wahhabism, as the most important of the reformist groups.[69] Its followers tend to live in insular communities, setting up their own schools, mosques, and businesses and prescribing a restrictive, cloistered, nurturing role for women.[70] Yan Izala is clearly Salafist, with its strict interpretation of scripture and its hostility toward modernization, Westernization, and secularism. Like other West African Salafist movements, it rejects Malikite law, Sufism, and saint veneration as examples of Islamic accretions of the post-Rashidun age.[71] It is based on local communities led by local preachers and is only foreign inspired in that it derives from neighboring

Nigeria. While the Izala movement is heavily involved in politics in Nigeria, where it began in 1978 as an Islamic political movement intended to counter the power of the Sufi brotherhoods, in Niger it maintains a relatively low political profile.[72] Its rejection of the secular state, along with its tendency to cling to its own educational system and its traditional application of Islamic law, makes it contrary to certain democratic principles, such as popular sovereignty and freedom of belief.[73] Yet Izala is far from dominant in Niger, and it shares the Islamic stage with the traditionalists and the rationalists. As such, it cannot be considered the main threat to stability in Niger. Nor can it be regarded as a rebel group; rather the movement works within the state system, building a community that matches its Islamist outlook on society, thus fitting the *Salafiyya 'ilimiyya* or scholarly Salafi pattern.

In any case, Izala is rooted in the Hausa ethnic group of the southern part of the country. The north is dominated by Tuareg pastoralists who practice the more traditional Sunni Islam and Malikite law. The Nigérien Tuaregs rebelled against their government in the 1990s at the same time as the Tuaregs of Mali did. But these rebellions were nationalist and ethnic based, rather that Islamist in nature. The northern area is still regarded as unstable, say Nigérien officials, and susceptible to "banditism," especially the part that adjoins northern Mali. Foreign Islamist preachers, notably Tablighi missionaries based in Mali, are trying to establish themselves in the north, but the government is moving to expel them. Government troops escort many of the detained missionaries to the Malian border.[74] As discussed below, Tablighi missionaries in Mali are making converts among former Tuareg rebel leaders, and it is likely that they are trying to do the same in northern Niger. Nigérien government policy regarding freedom of religion is clear: Muslims of all stripes are welcome and tolerated and allowed to preach and build mosques, as long as they do not cross the line that government policy has drawn between religion and politics. Those preachers who do attempt to influence political affairs are either detained or expelled.[75]

It remains to be seen to what degree Niger's recent episode of famine will affect the country's democratization movement and culture of religious freedom. Beginning in late 2004, the combination of an early end to the rainy season and an onslaught of locusts resulted in locally severe food shortages that put millions at risk of starvation. The situation was exacerbated by denials on the part of the government of Mamadou Tandja that a problem existed and a slow response by the international community. By spring 2005, children were dying.[76] The hardest-hit areas were the Tahoua and Maradi districts, both strongholds of the Izala movement. There is some evidence that Yan Izala may benefit from the dislocation caused by the drought. Meunier says that the Izala movement gained many adepts among Nigérien peasants who were victimized by droughts of the 1970s and 1980s and subsequently driven to the towns and cities where Izala communities are located.[77]

Mauritania

In Mauritania, yet another picture emerges. Unlike the other three Sahelian states, Mauritania identifies itself as an Arab country, the majority of its population speaking the Hassaniyya dialect of Arabic. The country has been known since independence in 1960 as the Islamic Republic of Mauritania, and its Islamic identity is closely tied to the old Sufi orders, the Qadiriyya and the Tijaniyya.[78] In this respect, Mauritanian Islam shares some features with the Islam of the "traditionalists" of Niger and the non-Islamist Muslims of Mali. Islamism began to emerge in Mauritania in the 1970s when Wahhabi ideas, such as denunciation of the Sufi brotherhoods and rejection of Western influence, including Marxism, first appeared among the Tajakant group of the southern province of Assaba. Also in the 1970s, students returning from Tunis and Cairo, influenced by the Egyptian Muslim Brothers, brought Islamist ideas back to Mauritania, where they took root in religious schools in the capital, Nouakchott, and in southwestern Trarza province. Jemaa Islamiyya, Mauritania's first Islamist organization, was founded in Nouakchott in 1974, based on the ideology of the Muslim Brothers.[79] Other domestic Islamists, loosely termed Salafists/Wahhabis, preach against foreign (Western) influence and post-Rashidun Islamic accretions like the brotherhoods and saint veneration, both of which are common features of traditional Mauritanian Islam. There are also foreign Islamists present, with the Jama'at al-Tabligh being the most entrenched, primarily in the north of the country. The Tablighi preachers first appeared in Mauritania in 1990, characterized by their highly structured organization, including the diffusion of sermons on cassette tapes.[80] The Islamist movements are now concentrated in the urban areas, where they appeal to Haratine cultivators who have been driven to towns by droughts and young graduates of the religious schools who cannot find jobs because they do not speak French. Such groups, frustrated and poor, are susceptible to the propaganda of the Islamist movements that denounce the entrenched Islam of the brotherhoods and reject foreign influences.[81]

Despite Mauritania's relative ethnic and linguistic homogeneity, it is, nonetheless, regarded as the least stable of the four Sahelian countries.[82] There were four coup attempts in the years 2003 to 2005, the last of which, in August 2005, was successful. The three failed attempts were linked to "Islamists" by the government of former President Ma'aouya Ould Sid' Ahmed Taya. Ould Taya had seized power in a coup of his own in 1984, and until recently his Democratic and Socialist Republican Party (PDRS) dominated the country's politics, though opposition parties held some seats in the legislature.[83] Originally Ould Taya expressed pro-Ba'athist sentiments and sided with Iraq in the first Gulf War. At that time the country had a small, Iraqi-supported Ba'ath Party. In recent years, however, Ould Taya had adopted a pro-Western stance and had been cracking down on both Ba'athists and Islamists.[84] In 1999, Mauritania became only the third Arab country to recognize Israel, a move that angered both the domestic Islamists and the Ba'athists. The first failed coup, in June 2003, came in the wake of a government crackdown on allegedly Islamist opposition elements in the army and the educational system.[85] This coup attempt was one of the factors that prompted the U.S. State Department to establish the PSI.[86] The tank unit that comprised the bulk of the opposition forces had been trained in Iraq, and its tanks were paid for by funding from Saddam Hussein.[87] Indeed, the antigovernment forces appear to have been as much pro-Iraq as pro-Islamist.[88]

President Taya's regime was threatened by further coup attempts in August and September 2004 that were also blamed on "Islamists" in the army. Mauritanian Defense Minister Baba Ould Sidi claimed that these plots were hatched by "the very same people" who staged the coup attempt in June 2003.[89] Another government source, Interior Minister Mohamed Gali Ould Cherif Ahmed, even claimed that the new plotters had been supported by Libya and Burkina Faso.[90] But human rights organizations have questioned the degree to which the Mauritanian opposition was really linked to Islamists, noting that the ensuing crackdown seemed to be directed at opposition groups in general, including Islamist groups, rather than specifically at Islamists. Analysts close to the opposition pointed out that the government's response to the 2004 coup attempts bore the hallmarks of an ethnic-based army purge, noting that the thirty soldiers, including fifteen officers, arrested were from the same ethnic group as the 120 soldiers arrested in the aftermath of the previous year's failed coup.[91] All this caused many to speculate that the Mauritanian regime of the time was trying to profit from the climate of the War on Terror by associating antigovernment forces with Islamists. In this manner, the speculation goes, the Taya government curried favor with the United States, while at the same time legitimizing its denial of democratic initiatives.[92]

The fourth, and ultimately successful, coup attempt occurred on August 3, 2005. A longtime Taya associate, Col. Ely Ould Mohammed Vall, led the coup that brought to power a seventeen-man junta called the Council for Justice and Democracy. Vall, who had participated in the 1984 coup that brought his predecessor to power, promised democratic elections in two years.[93] The new ruling junta has also expressed to U.S. officials its interest in continuing military-to-military relations, which would presumably include the TSCTI.[94] Seen by some observers as a "palace revolution" or an "internal army affair," the coup was reportedly popular with the public and resulted in some street celebrations.[95] The African Union, which at first condemned the coup, sent a delegation to investigate one week later. The delegation reported that the coup was immensely popular at home because of widespread antagonism toward former President Ould Taya as a result of the country's stagnant economy, Taya's foot-dragging on democratic reform, and his seemingly shameless catering to the United States and even Israel.[96] The 2005 coup, therefore, like the earlier attempts, seems to have had relatively little to do with Islamist unrest, though Ould Taya's halfhearted crackdowns on alleged Islamists in the army may have been one of the factors leading to the army's growing resentment of the regime.

Mali

Mali is the country that has made the most progress among the four Sahelian states in creating enduring democratic institutions. Nonetheless it is regarded by U.S. diplomats as the most vulnerable to Islamist activity. Diplomats cite three possible vectors of Islamist unrest in Mali: (1) the GSPC presence in the north; (2) recent increases in Tablighi missionary activity; and (3) the existence of networks for smuggling both illegal workers and contraband. All three of these vectors seem to intersect in the volatile Kidal region.[97] The role of the Tablighi missionaries is particularly troubling to the Malian authorities because of the missionaries' concentration on elements of the former leadership of the Tuareg rebellion. Tuareg notables who have joined the Jama'at al-Tabligh include the mayor of Kidal, the traditional ruler of Kidal, and the former head of the Tuareg rebellion himself, who is now considered the spiritual leader of all of Mali's Tablighis. Also potentially disquieting is the fact that the Hotel Hendrina Kahn in Timbuktu is owned by Dr. Abdul Qadeer Khan, the rogue Pakistani nuclear scientist. Dr. Khan and members of his Pakistani nuclear team have visited the hotel. It is not clear whether Khan's visits to the region were linked to neighboring Niger's uranium deposits or to Khan's known support for the Pakistani Jama'at al-Tabligh.[98] Adding to this worrisome situation is the strong Wahhabi presence in Timbuktu, mentioned above. The Wahhabiyya arrived in West Africa in the 1930s, as Wahhabi beliefs were spread by African students who had studied at al-Azhar University in Cairo.[99] Though the movement generally conforms to the scholarly Salafi pattern, clashes between Wahhabis and mainstream Malian Muslims did break out in the capital, Bamako, in the 1950s.[100] The Wahhabi presence in northern Mali, especially Timbuktu, is of more recent date, and is actively supported by Saudi funding. Given this odd mix of domestic and foreign Islamism, it is not surprising that Mali, despite its stability and developing democracy, should be of particular concern to U.S. antiterrorism specialists, and that more than half of the PSI funds were earmarked for that country.

Yet Mali has a tradition of tolerant Islam and cooperation among ethnic groups.[101] Malians see their democracy as an outgrowth of local traditions, such as the economic complementarity among the various ethnic groups and the consensus democracy that has long been practiced traditionally on the local level, if not nationally.[102] Malian authorities downplay the threat of contagion from Islamists, domestic or foreign.[103] Both religious and political figures urge tolerance within Islam and neutrality in politics on the part of the Muslim leadership. During the May 2004 regional elections, Abderahman ben Esayouti, imam of the principal mosque in Timbuktu, declared his neutrality in the vote, saying that Muslim leaders must remain impartial in politics. Malian President Touré, for his part, claimed recently that "What we have here is an Islam that is very ancient, tolerant and enlightened. We see nothing in our religion that would prevent us from being democratic." During the 2002 presidential election campaign, after a small collective of Islamic associations endorsed a candidate, Issiaka Traoré, president of the Malian Association for the Unity and Progress of Islam (AMUPI), the leading umbrella group of mainstream Muslim associations, officially declared his group's neutrality in the election. He rejected the collective's call for support for a specific candidate or party, saying, "We asked each voter to vote for the candidate of his choice."[104]

Most Malian Muslims are Sunni and practice Malikite law, although the Wahhabis are more rigid in their outlook.[105] Nonetheless, even some Wahhabi leaders stress the importance of Mali's secularity. Mahmoud Dicko, imam of the principal Wahhabi mosque at Bamako, said recently that "It is in everyone's interest for Mali to remain secular."[106] It is true that certain foreign imams and preachers take a more radical and less tolerant stance than do most local Muslim leaders. Northern Mali, from Timbuktu to Kidal, has many "bearded" proselytizers, often from the Jama'at al-Tabligh. In the months following September 11, 2001, Malian authorities arrested a dozen "Pakistani" preachers, some of whom were detained and/or expelled for holding false papers.[107] But according to the U.S. State Department, these foreign preachers attract few local followers, outside of the north, because "their fundamentalist views clash with the country's traditional approach to Islam."[108] The spirit of religious tolerance endorsed by most Malian imams and religious leaders, as well as most political leaders, seems to be accepted by the majority of the people.

The Economic Dimension of Stability in the Sahelian Countries

While there is no doubt that radical Islam, whether domestic or imported, poses a threat to the stability of the Sahelian region, the endemic poverty of the region poses a far greater threat to that stability. I shall not attempt a thorough economic analysis here. Rather I shall highlight some examples to illustrate the fact that poverty is clearly a greater threat to stability and security in the four countries than terrorism or Islamic radicalism (see table 20.1). Popular frustration has mounted for years in the region over such economic factors as deplorable standards of living, the inability of govern-ments to deliver basic services, and the skewed global economic regime, derisively termed "neoliberalism," especially the provision of agricultural subsidies in the developed countries.

As shown in the table 20.1, the four Sahelian countries are among the world's poorest. The per capita GDP (purchasing power parity) ranges from a high of $1,900 in Mauritania to a low of only $830 in Niger. The popula-tion living below the poverty line ranges from a low of 50 percent in Mauritania to a high of 80 percent in Chad. In Chad, Mali, and Niger, 80 percent or more of the population are engaged in subsistence agricultural production and are only marginally connected to the cash economy. In addi-tion, all four countries are heavily dependent on foreign aid. While some bright spots are appearing on the horizon, such as the steady GNP growth in Mali since the prodemocracy coup of 1991, the opening of oil exports from Chad, and the expected oil exports from Mauritania, other problems loom.[109] Recent economic threats to the Sahelian region include the famine in Niger, and the damage to Mali's economy caused by political crises in neighboring Côte d'Ivoire.[110]

Particularly threatening to the well-being of the region's peoples is the chronic inability of governments to provide basic services. In the urban areas, the services most often found wanting include electricity, telephone services, clean water, transportation, health care, and education. Just to give an example, the number of telephone lines in use in the region ranges from a high of 45,000 in Mali to a low of only 9,700 in Chad, or less than one line per 1,000 people, though in both these countries roughly equal numbers of cell phones are in use. In the rural areas the services that are unavailable or inadequate are even more basic: clean water, health centers, stores, wood-lots, and transport. Only about half of Nigériens have access to safe drinking water, while in Mauritania even fewer have such access, only some 37 per-cent.[111] Regarding transport, a simple example illustrates the problem: Mali, which has more than sixteen million head of livestock, for want of a few more roads and a fleet of refrigerator trucks, exports no fresh meat.[112]

Especially frustrating to the peoples of the region is the fact that their dis-mal economic situation is exacerbated by unfair agricultural subsidies in the developed countries. The very nations who boast of their aid programs in the region and who insist on economic responsibility and transparency from the Sahelian countries regularly subsidize their own agricultural producers in ways that cause significant economic harm in these same countries. Robert Guest provides a concise critique of the economic damage caused to African countries by subsidies in the developed world. He notes that farm subsidies in the rich countries, mostly benefiting wealthy and corporate farmers, are running at about $1 billion a day, a sum roughly equivalent to the entire GDP of sub-Saharan Africa. African farmers are virtually helpless in such a skewed economic environment.[113] Among the greatest offenders in terms of commodity subsidies are the United States and the European Union (EU). Mvemba Dizolele argues that cotton subsidies to farmers in the developed world and the poverty that they engender pose the greatest single threat to stability in the region. The U.S. subsidy on domestic cotton production amounts to 89.5 cents for every $1 earned, while the EU subsidizes cotton farmers in Spain and Greece at almost as high a rate.[114] Mali and Chad are among four West African nations that brought suit against U.S. cotton subsidies in the World Trade Organization in 2003. Mali's President Touré was quoted as saying that Malian cotton farmers would see a 30 percent increase in their incomes were it not for the U.S. subsidies. If this is true, this amount would be greater than the total annual amount of U.S. aid to Mali.[115] Even more outrageous are cattle subsidies amounting to nearly $7.00 in Japan and $2.20 in the EU per cow per day.[116] Giving the lie to Western lip service on "free trade," these massive subsidies keep the world price of cotton and beef low, severely hurting Third-World producers. West African cotton farmers and cattle herders simply cannot compete with such a stacked deck.

Despite the fears of Islamic radicalism leading to regional instability, it is clear that chronic and endemic poverty is the greater threat. Of the three most recent coups d'état in the region, Mali in 1991, Niger in 1999, and Mauritania in 2005, none was caused or even greatly influenced by radical Islam. On the contrary, all were influenced to one degree or another by frustration over chronic poverty and the slow pace of economic development and progress toward democratic reform. It is equally clear, however, that poverty, including slow economic growth, the inability of governments to provide services, and the results of the hypocritical global economic regime, can and does prepare fertile ground for Islamic radicalism. Radical Muslim preachers and activists, both foreign and domestic, who appear to offer an alternative to the endemic poverty, the regional governments' corruption and mismanagement, and the cycle of Western aid and exploitation, can easily gain the ears of young Muslim men. Whether these are Nigérien pastoralists driven into the towns by drought and being drawn into the Izala movement, Malian Tuaregs who, angered by their government's legacy of neglect, are recruited by Tablighli preachers, or Mauritanian urban youth who cannot find jobs and are appealed to by Salafist imams, the link between poverty and the growth of radical Islamist movements is not in doubt.[117] Since poverty is clearly a greater threat to stability in the Sahelian region than radical Islam, and poverty is also one of the factors facilitating the spread of radical Islam, it would seem that the wiser approach on the part of the United States and other Western countries would be to do more to alleviate poverty rather than to pour military aid into the region to assist the hunt for terrorists. Reducing or eliminating agricultural subsidies would be a good start.

Conclusion

Radical Islam clearly has a presence in Sahelian and Saharan West Africa, and the influence of both foreign and domestic Islamists is growing. Foreign Islamists include Pakistani Tablighis, Saudi Wahhabis, and Algerian Salafis. Local Islamists include the Wahhabi community of Mali, the members of the Izala movement of southern Niger, disaffected Salafist communities in Mauritania, and scattered imams calling for Islamic reform. Some observers feel that the threat of radical Islam is serious and increasing, citing the endemic poverty of the region and the lavish funding in Saudi petrodollars as causal factors.[118] Others are more circumspect, noting that Muslims in West Africa have accepted Saudi funds for the support of mosques and Quranic schools for years. And while Saudi-trained preachers often come attached to these funds, their presence is not a recent phenomenon. Spokesmen for Saharan indigenes sometimes question the degree to which the Sahara is fertile ground for the growth of Islamism, noting the strong support for secular government among Saharan peoples in Mali and Chad.[119] Other observers comment on the tolerant versions of Islam found in Mali and Niger.[120] Still others suggest that the real threats to stability in the West African Sahelian countries are not Islamic but economic. Such economic factors include poor standards of living, poor access to public services, and the swamping of farming countries with subsidized agricultural products from the West.[121] It is true that such economic dislocations and the endemic poverty and disparity in wealth that they engender may create a climate in which Islamist ideologies can thrive. However, the long view of postcolonial West African history reveals that poverty is the root cause of instability, while Islamism, authoritarianism, and ethnic rivalry are among its symptoms.

Certainly, the United States feels that the threat of radical Islam in the Sahelian states is serious, as shown by the establishment of the PSI and the planning for its successor, the TSCTI. Yet questions persist, especially in Mauritania and Chad, as to whether insurgent groups are really Islamist or just hostile to the government. After all, the GSPC, the real reason behind the PSI, had but a limited presence in Mauritania and Chad. Its presence was stronger in Mali, but the chief concern on the part of the Malians was that it might rally the Arab ethnic minority of the far north to rebel.[122] The Chadians have fought pitched battles with GSPC units, but the real rebel threat of northern Chad is the MDJT, which has declared itself to be secular, not Islamist. In Algeria, certainly, the Salafist threat is real, as renewed GSPC attacks, believed to have been led by Mokhtar Belmokhtar, against Algerian army convoys and bases in early 2005 demonstrate.[123] Yet some question the links between the GSPC and al-Qaeda. Journalist El-Kadi Ihsane suggests that Algeria exaggerated the extent of Hassan Hattab's and Abderrezak

Table 20.1 Sahelian Countries: Demographic and Development Statistics

Country	Chad	Mali	Mauritania	Niger
Population in millions	9.25	11.63	2.91	11.05
% Muslims	51	90	100	80
Per capita GDP (ppp)*	$1,100	$860	$1,900	$830
% in subsistence production	80	80	50	90
% below poverty line	80	64	50	63
% with access to safe water	54	66	37	61
Infant deaths/1,000 live births	96	119	78	124
Telephone lines in use	9,700	45,000	26,000	20,000

* ppp: Purchasing Power Parity (GDP in U.S. dollars adjusted for buying power of local currency)
Sources: United States Central Intelligence Agency, *World Factbook Online*, 2003, https://www.cia.gov/library/publications/the-world-factbook/.

al-Para's links to al-Qaeda in order to get more support from the United States for its campaign against the GSPC.[124] Rights activists for indigenous Saharan peoples have similarly questioned the motives of the PSI countries, noting that these governments had a history of oppressing desert peoples long before the recent rise in Islamist sentiments among them.[125] Likewise, critics of the deposed Mauritanian regime claim that President Ould Taya was "crying Islamism" to garner Western political support.[126]

It seems, therefore, that the level of threat posed by radical, transnational Islamism to stability in Sahelian West Africa is still limited. The reasons why radical Islam has not caught on in the Sahelian countries as it has in North Africa, for example, vary from country to country, They include the much-touted tradition of tolerant Islam in Mali, the cleavage within Nigérien Islam among traditionalists, rationalists, and reformists, and the secular nature of the Chadian rebel groups. Other reasons seem to hold true across the region, for example, the importance of the state and the unique characteristics of the majority Muslim nations. Another regional factor is that the ethos of West African Islamism still generally eschews wanton destruction of life and property.[127] The real threats to security in the Sahara and Sahel seem to be the same as always, poverty, ethnic rivalry, and entrenched authoritarianism. While these threats can be exacerbated and exploited by Islamists, both foreign and domestic, most of them have nothing necessarily to do with radical Islam.

Notes

1. International Crisis Group (ICG), "Islamist Terrorism in the Sahel: Fact or Fiction," *Africa Report* no. 92 (March 31, 2005), 30. The Horn is considered the number one front in Africa.

2. Christine Holzbaur, "Les inquiétants émirs du Sahel," *L'Express*, November 28, 2002, 2.

3. Sandro Magister, "Worldwide Islam Has an Oasis of Democracy: Mali," *L'espresso* (Italy), July 17, 2004, 2; ICG, "Islamist Terrorism," 29. The Millennium Challenge Account (MCA) is a fund created by the Bush administration to provide support for poor countries that demonstrate good standards of government by establishing democratic institutions and opening their economies. The MCA is based on the premise that poverty and repression breed Islamism.

4. Mohammed Ayoob, "Political Islam: Image and Reality," *World Policy Journal* 21, no. 3 (Fall 2004): 1-14; here: 1. William Miles defines political Islam as "organized activity . . . that strives to bring politics into line with Islamic precepts." William F. S. Miles, "Islamism in West Africa: Introduction," *African Studies Review* 47, no. 2 (September 2004): 55–59; here: 58. Graham Fuller, who also uses the terms political Islam and Islamism synonymously, defines an Islamist as "one who believes that Islam . . . has something important to say about how politics and society should be ordered in the contemporary Muslim World and who seeks to implement this idea in some fashion." Graham Fuller, *The Future of Political Islam* (New York: Palgrave-Macmillan, 2003), xi.

5. There are Islamist movements within Shi'ite Islam too, for example, the Islamic Revolution in Iran and Hezbolla in Lebanon. Sunni Islam, however, predominates in North and West Africa. Dan Darling, "ICG Report on the Sahel Region," Winds of Change.NET, April 11, 2005, 4, http://www.windsofchange.net/ archives/006649. php.

6. Lois A. Aroian and Richard P. Mitchell, *The Modern Middle East and North Africa* (New York: Macmillan, 1984), 75; Roger Scruton, "The Political Problem of Islam," *Intercollegiate Review* (Fall 2002): 3–15: here: 8. Abd al-Wahhab wanted to purge Islam of modern accretions and return to reliance only on the Qur'an and *hadith*. An early exponent of this type of Islamic fundamentalist movement was the thirteenth-century scholar Taqi al-Din ibn Taymiyya, who preached a return to the essentials of the faith in the wake of the disastrous Mongol invasions. Ibn Taymiyya's writings serve as basic texts for Wahhabi scholars (Gilles Kepel, *Jihad: The Trail of Political Islam* [Cambridge, MA: Harvard University Press, 2002], 220). Ayoob distinguishes between Wahhabism, as practiced by old-line Saudi sheikhs, and "neo-Wahhabism," which he says is influenced by the writings of the radical Egyptian philosopher and educator Sayyid Qutb (d. 1966) and other leaders of the Egyptian Muslim Brotherhood (*al-Ikhwan*). This fusion of Saudi Wahhabism with the radical, politicized teachings of Qutb and the Muslim Brothers led to the explosively militant variety of political Islam preached by terrorist networks like al-Qaeda that call for global jihad (Fuller, *The Future of Political Islam*, 48, 52; Ayoob, "Political Islam," 4) (see note 8).

7. Fuller, *The Future of Political Islam*, 30. Salafism refers to the *Salaf*, the "forerunners" or "founding fathers" of Islam, the leaders of the original Muslim community, or *umma*, of the Rashidun age. The *Salafiyya* originated outside Arabia in reaction to European

colonialism, which did not so seriously affect the Saudi kingdom. Also influenced by the writings of ibn Taymiyya, Salafists tend to interpret the sacred texts, the Quran and *hadith*, in their most literal sense. Salafist movements thus share two features with the writings of Sayyid Qutb: the anticolonial spirit and the willingness to condemn mainstream Islam as unbelief, neither of which are core principles of Wahhabism.

8. GlobalSecurity.Org, "Salafi Islam," n.d., 2, www.globalsecurity.org/military/intro/islam-salafi.htm; ICG, "Islamist Terrorism," 5. The Egyptian Muslim Brotherhood was founded in the late 1920s by Hassan al-Banna. It was grounded in anticolonialism and hostility to Western influence, concepts that had scarcely penetrated the interior of the Saudi kingdom (Gilles Kepel, *The War for Muslim Minds: Islam and the West* [New York: Belknap Press, 2004], 36). Sayyid Qutb became the Brotherhood's chief theoretician and one of the most influential voices in the entire Islamist movement. His views have been of profound importance in developing the modern radical vision of Islam (Paul Berman, "The Philosopher of Islamic Terror," *New York Times Magazine*, March 23, 2003, 24–67).

9. ICG, "Islamist Terrorism," 8–9.

10. Stephen Schwartz, *The Two Faces of Islam: Saudi Fundamentalism and Its Role in Terrorism* (New York: Anchor, 2002), 138–40 (see note 6).

11. Gilles Kepel calls Salafists the "true fundamentalists of Islam," because they combine fundamental literalism with a commitment to jihad with America as their chief target (Kepel, *Jihad*, 220). See "Saudi Reckoning: Bombing, Crackdown Show New Resolve," *The Estimate* 15, no. 21 (November 14, 2003): 1. Malikite law, developed by Iman Malik bin Annas (d. 796), is one of the four schools of Islamic law established in post-Rashidun times. The other schools are Hanbali, Hanafi, and Shafi'i, each named after its founder. Most North and West African Muslims practice Sunni Islam and follow the Malikite school of law. These traditions stem from the teachings of Imam Sahnun of Qayrawan (d. 854), which were subsequently disseminated throughout the region by the Almoravid movement, the Kunta shaykhs of the Sahara, and the West African scholars of the Saghanougou clan.

12. Paul Marshall, "Radical Islam's Move on Africa," *Washington Post*, October 16, 2003, 1.

13. Nicolas Colombant, "Mali's Muslims Steer Back to Spiritual Roots," *Christian Science Monitor*, February 26, 2002, 1, www.csmonitor.com/2002/0226/p08s02-woaf.html.

14. Craig Smith, "US Training African Forces to Uproot Terrorists," *New York Times*, May 11, 2004, 2., http://query.nytimes.com/gst/fullpage.html?res=9901E7DA133CF932A25756COA9629C8B63.

15. Bruce Greenberg and Daniel Cain, "U.S.-Africa Partnerships Key to Waging War on Terrorism," U.S. Department of State, International Information Programs, March 14, 2005, 1, http://usinfo.state.gov/is/Archive/2005/Mar/15-505791.html.

16. Darling, "ICG Report," 8. The Jama'at al-Tabligh is the world's largest Islamic missionary organization with more than 3,000,000 members worldwide.

17. Lisa Anderson, "Democracy, Islam Share a Home in Mali," *Chicago Tribune*, December 5, 2004, 2, 6.

18. Of these countries, only Sudan is openly Islamist; the governments of Algeria and Libya are secular nationalist in ideology. But Libya has harbored terrorist groups, some of which have been Islamist, while Algeria has Islamist rebel groups active in its territory.

19. The Armed Islamic Group (GIA) was the main insurgent movement responsible for Algeria's civil war of the 1990s. The GIA was a militant, extremist group that had been formed in 1994 as an armed wing of the Islamic Salvation Front (FIS). The FIS, an Islamist political party legalized in 1989 by the government, won parliamentary elections in 1991, leading to a nullification of these election results in January 1992 by the ruling National Liberation Front (NLF). The FIS, denied its election victory, became determined to establish its Islamist agenda by military means. The GIA, due to its reputation for massacring civilians, emerged as the most radical of the armed factions that grew out of the FIS (Keppel, *Jihad*, 254–56). The bloody conflict is believed to have cost over 100,000 lives, mostly civilian, in less than a decade ("Five Killed as Militants Attack Algerian Troops," *Daily Times* [Pakistan], February 13, 2005, 2).

20. ICG, "Islamist Terrorism," 7.

21. "Five Killed," 1. Algerian security forces reported that Hassan Hattab made one phone call to Osama bin Laden prior to the 9/11 attacks. According to some reports, Hattab was killed in an internal GSPC struggle in 2003.

22. Anthony Keats, "The Salafist Group for Call and Combat (GSPC)," CDI Center for Defense Information, January 14, 2003, 1, http://www.cdi.org/terrorism/gspc.cfm; MIPT Terrorism Knowledge Base, Salafist Group for Preaching and Combat, http://www.globaldefensegroup.com/terrorist-networks/salafist-group-for-call-and-combat-gspc.html?Itemid=35; Jonathan Schanzer, "Countering Algerian Terror: Increased U.S. Involvement?" Washington Institute PolicyWatch/ PeaceWatch, October 28, 2003, 1. Schanzer says the GSPC broke with the GIA in 1998.

23. Fayçal Oukaci, "Abderrezak El Para chez les rebelles tchadiens du Tibesti: 'Changer le monde par le djihad,'" September 13, 2004, 2, www.sahariens.info/spip_sahara/article.php3?id_article=528. Al-Para's real name is Amari Saïfi. He formerly served in the elite Algerian army parachutist unit known as the "Paras," hence the nickname al-Para.

24. Hassane Zerrouky, "Abderrazak El Para libéré par les rebelles tchadiens," *Le Matin* (Algeria), June 3, 2001, 1.

25. Holzbaur, "Les inquiétants émirs du Sahel," 1–3; ICG, "Islamist Terrorism," 19.

26. ICG, "Islamist Terrorism," 19.

27. U.S. Department of State, *Annual Report on International Religious Freedom for 2002: Mali* (Washington, DC: Bureau of Democracy, Human Rights, and Labor, September 2002), 2, http://www.state.gov/g/drl/rls/irf/2002/13844.htm. Nicholas Colombant, who feels more strongly than most other analysts that there is a trend toward radical Islam in the Sahel, argues that this trend is due to continuing poverty and the inability of the region's governments to address it. He mentions that some regional hard-line groups have accepted funds from Saudi donors to support their Islamist agenda (Colombant, "Mali's Muslims," 2).

28. ICG, "Islamist Terrorism," 8–9.

29. Ibid., 27, 30. PSI funding allocations varied by country, with Mauritania and Chad each receiving $500,000, while Niger received $1.7 million, and Mali received $3.5 million, over half of the total.

30. Christine Holzbaur, "La chasse aux salafistes du désert," *L'Express*, February 6, 2004, 1.

31. U.S. Department of State, Pan Sahel Initiative, Office of Counterterrorism, Washington, DC, November 7, 2002, http://www.state.gov/s/ct/rls/other/14987.htm.

32. Farid Belgacem, "Le Niger déclare la guerre au GSPC," *Liberté* (Algeria), January 15, 2005, 1. The cigarettes pass in containers through the Mauritanian town of Zerouate to Kidal. From there they go by smaller trucks to Algeria and thence to Europe, entering untaxed through Italy (ICG, "Islamist Terrorism," 18).

33. ICG, "Islamist Terrorism," 7. Ahmed Alwan is believed to have been involved in the attack on the USS *Cole* in a Yemeni port in 2000.

34. Smith, "US Training," 1–2; "European Hostages Released in Mali," August 19, 2003, 1, http://www.cnn.com/2003/WORLD/africa/08/18/algeria.tourists/. An additional factor in the State Department's decision to form the PSI was the 2003 coup attempt in Mauritania, allegedly perpetrated by "Islamists" within the armed forces.

35. Schanzer, "Countering Algerian Terror," 1. Berlin denied paying any ransom, though the figure of 5 million euros was cited in press reports from many nations. Journalist Damien Mcelroy implies that it was really Mali that paid the ransom to the GSPC in exchange for German promises of additional aid funding (Damien Mcelroy, "US Extends the War on Islamic Terror to the Sahara Desert," NEWS Telegraph, June 6, 2004, 2, http://www.telegraph.co.uk/news/main.jhtml?xml=/news/2004/06/06/wsaha06.xml&sSheet=/news/2004/06/06/ixworld.html).

36. Smith, "US Training," 2.

37. Associated Press, "Green Berets Train in Africa," Military.com, March 22, 2004, http://www.military.com/NewsContent/0,13319,FL_africa_032204,00.html.

38. Nick Tattersall, "US Fears Victory of Militants in Sahara Region," *Arab News*, March 19, 2004, 1; B. Mournir, "Bamako se décide à pourchasser le GSPC," *Le Quotidien d'Oran*, December 29, 2003, 1. Ethnic Arabs of Northern Mali constitute a minority within the larger Tuareg (Berber) ethnic group that dominates Mali's three northern regions, Timbuktu, Gao, and Kidal. These ethnic Arabs, also known as Baribaich, joined with the Tuaregs in their rebellion of the 1990s. This rebellion began in the waning months of the regime of Mali's longtime dictator, Moussa Traoré, and continued during the period of democratic transition and into the first term of Mali's first democratically elected president, Alpha Konaré ("Malian Civil War: 1990–1996," OnWar.com. 2000, www.onwar.com/aced/data/mike/mali1 990.htm).

39. Mournir, "Bamako," 1; Smith, "US Training," 2, 3; S. E. Belabès, "Quel sort pour le GSPC?" *El Watan* (Algeria), January 4, 2005, 1.

40. Tattersall, "US Fears Victory," 2; Associated Press, "Green Berets," 1.

41. Smith, "US Training," 2; Edward Harris, "U.S. Green Berets Train Mali Troops" Boston.com News, http://www.boston.com/news/world/africa/articles/2004/03/17/us_green_berets_train_mali_troops/; Mournir, "Bamako," 1; Anderson, "Democracy," 6.

42. Phillip Ulmer, "EUCOM Delivers Aid to Chadian Forces," EUCOM Release, March 14, 2004, http://www.globalsecurity.org/military/library/news/2004/03/mil-040315-eucom01.htm; "Chad Says 43 Militants Killed in Fighting" USA Today, March 12, 2004, 2; Smith, "US Training," 2; ICG, "Islamist Terrorism," 1.

43. Smith, "US Training," 2; John Donnelly, "US-Trained Forces Scour Sahara for Terror links," *Boston Globe*, December 12, 2004, 2.

44. Harris, "U.S. Green Berets," 2.

45. Smith, "US Training," 2.

46. Anderson, "Democracy," 7.

47. Ibid., 6; Oukaci, "Abderrezak El Para," 2; IPACC, "US Military and Oil," 3.

48. Zerrouky, "Abderrazak El Para," 1; Mcelroy, "US Extends the War," 2.

49. Oukaci, "Abderrezak El Para," 1. Al-Para also confirmed that he was born in Geulma in Eastern Algeria of a French mother who is still living in Algeria near Constantine.

50. A. Benchabane, "Abderrezak El Para chez le procureur," *El Watan* (Algeria), January 5, 2005), 1; Belabès, "Quel sort," 1. Algerian journalist Salima Tlemçani confirms this scenario, adding that U.S. authorities, who considered al-Para a major catch, had preferred that he be handed over to the Algerians rather than to the Germans, presumably because they felt that the Algerians would be in a position to "interrogate" him more aggressively (Salima Tlemçani, "Le GSPC annonce la disparition de ses chefs," *El Watan*, July 19, 2004, 1).

51. Holzbaur, "La chasse aux salafistes du désert," 1.

52. Donnelly, "US-Trained Forces," 2. ICG, "Islamist Terrorism," 30.

53. Mcelroy, "US Extends the War," 1, ICG, "Islamist Terrorism," 2.

54. Andrew Koch, "US to Bolster Counter Terrorism Assistance to Africa," *Jane's Defence Weekly*, October 1, 2004, 1. Greenberg and Cain, "U.S.-Africa Partnerships," 1.

55. ICG, "Islamist Terrorism," 30.

56. Holzbaur, "Les inquiétants émirs du Sahel," 1. Mokhtar Belmokhtar was trafficking in arms in the Sahara before his association with the GSPC began, and he continues to do so.

57. Oukaci, Fayçal, "Le Gspc Voulait libérer le 'Para,'" *L'Expression* (Algeria), July 5, 2004, 1, http://www.algeria-watch.de/fr/article/mil/groupes_armes/gspc_el_para.htm. Recent reports indicate that the GSPC has reconfirmed its affiliate status with al-Qaeda and changed its name to al-Qaeda in the Islamic Maghreb, supposedly on the orders of Osama bin Laden himself, and that it is concentrating its activities in Algeria and Tunisia (Craig S. Smith, "North Africa Feared as Staging Ground for Terror," *New York Times*, February 20, 2007, http://www.iht.com/articles/2007/02/20/africa/web-0220tunisia.php).

58. MPIT Terrorism Knowledge Base, "Chadian Army 'Kills' Dozens of Rebels" BBC News, October 15, 2002, http://news.bbc.co.uk/2/low/africa/2330737.stm.

59. Oukaci, "Abderrezak El Para," 2.

60. Zerrouky, "Abderrazak El Para," 1.

61. Oukaci, "Abderrezak El Para," 2.

62. "Islam in Chad," n.d., 1, http://encyclopedia.laborlawtalk.com/Islam_in_Chad.

63. Michaël N. Didama, "Apocalypse in Manhattan: A New Day Dawns," *Le Temps* (Chad), September 19, 2001, 1–2.

64. ICG, "Islamist Terrorism," 22.

65. MIPT Terrorism Knowledge Base, "Terrorist Group Profile," 1.

66. David Cadasse, "Il n'y a pas de famine au Niger, mais une crise alimentaire," Afrik.com, Wednesday, October 5, 2005, 3, http://www.afrik.com/article8844.html. Estimates for the percentage of Niger's population that is Muslim typically range from 80 percent to 95 percent.

67. ICG, "Islamist Terrorism," 21.

68. O. Meunier, *Les voies de l'islam au Niger dans le Katsina indépendant du XIXe au XXe siècle* (Paris: Museum de l'histoire naturelle, 1998), 141–43.

69. Robert B Charlick, "Islamism in West Africa: Niger," *African Studies Review* 47, no. 2 (September 2004): 97–107; here: 98–99.

70. ICG, "Islamist Terrorism," 22. In some Izala communities, the women do no agricultural work because they are not permitted to leave the household without a male relative as an escort.

71. Meunier, *Les voies de l'islam au Niger*, 118–19, 154; Charlick, "Islamism," 102, 103.

72. Ian Linden, "Christianity, Islam and Poverty Reduction in Africa," abstract of thesis, School of Oriental and African Studies (SOAS), London, 2004, 1, http://www.st-edmunds.cam.ac.uk/vhi/fis/cipra.pdf; Meunier, *Les voies de l'islam au Niger*, 117.

73. Peter David, "In the Name of Islam," *Economist*, September 11, 2003, 2, www.economist.com/displayStory.cfm?Story.

74. Holzbaur, "Les inquiétants émirs du Sahel," 2; ICG, "Islamist Terrorism," 9.

75. ICG, "Islamist Terrorism," 21, 34.

76. "Niger: Background to Famine," *AfricaFocus Bulletin*, July 22, 2005, 1, 2; "Niger Leader Denies Hunger Claims," BBC News, August 9, 2005, 1, http://news.bbc.co.uk/2/hi/africa/4133374.stm.

77. Dennis Cordell, review of Olivier Meunier, *Les voies de l'islam au Niger dans le Katsina indépendant du XIXe au XXe siècle* (Paris: Museum de l'histoire naturelle, 1998), in *Anthropologie et Sociétés: Économie politique féministe* 25, no. 1, 2001: 160–62; here: 161.

78. "The Coup Attempt in Mauritania," *The Estimate* 15, no. 12 (June 13, 2003): 3.

79. International Crisis Group (ICG), "L'Islamisme en Afrique du Nord IV: Contestation islamiste en Mauritanie: Menace ou bouc émissaire?" *Middle East/North Africa Report*, no. 41 (May 11, 2005): 15.

80. ICG. "L'Islamisme," i, 16.

81. Ibid., 14–16.

82. Mauritanian society consists of two principal groups, the Bidanes (white Moors) and the Haratines (black Moors). Both speak the Hassaniyya dialect of Arabic, but the Haratines are of lower status, being regarded as descendants of slave cultivators. Beyond this, the Bidan are divided among Hassani (warrior) Zawiyya (clerical), and Lahma (client) classes, along with various artisan castes as well. Historically, groups of Wolof, Fulani, and Sonninke lived in southern Mauritania near the Senegal River and along the border with Mali (Darling, "ICG Report," 12).

83. "Coup Attempt," 4. Mauritania's strong presidential system, along with suspect election practices, helps maintain the PDRS in power, making Mauritania effectively a single-party state.

84. Brian Smith, "Failed Coup Attempt in Mauritania," World Socialist Web Site, WSWS.org, June 17, 2003, 1, www.wsww.org/articles/203/jun2003/maur-j17.shtml.

85. Ibid.

86. Miles, "Islamism in West Africa," 57–58.

87. Ibid., 5.

88. Holger Osterrieder, "After the Coup: Mauritania Needs EU Internationalism, Not US War on Terror," Oxford Council on Global Governance [OCGG] Security

Recommendation no. 4, August 2005, 2, http://www.oxfordgovernance.org/
fileadmin/Publications/SR004.pdf; "Coup Attempt," 4–6. Other perceived pro-U.S.
actions taken by President Ould Taya included changing the weekend from
Friday/Saturday, preferred by most Muslims, to Saturday/Sunday and closing the
mosques when public prayer is not being conducted.

89. "Claims of New Coup Attempt in Mauritania," August 11, 2004, 1, AfrolNews,
www.afrol.com/articles/13683.

90. "Another Coup Attempt Thwarted in Mauritania," September 29, 2004, 1,
Middle East On Line, http://www.middle-east-online.com/english/mauritania/
?id=11414.

91. Ibid., 1.

92. ICG, "Islamist Terrorism," 2, 16, 41; International Crisis Group, "L'Islamisme," i.

93. "Mauritania's New Military Leader," BBC News, August 8, 2005, 1,
http://news.bbc.co.uk/1/hi/world/africa/4746387.stm; Osterreider, "After the
Coup," 5. Mauritania held legislative elections in November 2007 and presidential
elections in March 2007. The presidential poll was won by Sidi Ould Cheikh
Abdellahi, who was supported by El-Mithaq ("Convention"), a block of seventeen
political parties, many of which are linked to the former regime and the ruling military officers ("Mauritania: BBC Q&A on Mauritania 2007 Elections," BBC News,
March 9, 2007, http://news.bbc.co.uk/go/pr/gr/-/1/hi/world/Africa/6435477.
stm; "New President Is Elected in Mauritania," United Press International (UPI),
March 26, 2007, http://www.upi.com/NewsTrack/Top_News/2007/03/26/new_
president_elected_in_mauritania/4413.

94. Herman J. Cohen, "U.S. Relations with Post-Coup Mauritania," *Asian Tribune*,
October 11, 2005, 1.

95. Osterreider, "After the Coup," 1; "Mauritania's New Military Leader, 1.

96. Cohen, "U.S. Relations," 1.

97. ICG, "Islamist Terrorism," 2, 16.

98. Ibid., 17–18. The hotel, named after Khan's Dutch wife, is rumored to have
been built partly with al-Qaeda money. Saudi visitors are said to be frequent guests
there.

99. Ibid., 6.

100. See Lansine Kaba, *The Wahhabiyya: Islamic Reform and Politics in French West
Africa, 1945–1960* (Evanston, IL: Northwestern University Press, 1974). An apparently isolated but tragic incident occurred in Yerere in Western Mali in August 2003,
when a group of Wahhabis building a mosque were attacked by local residents prac-
ticing a more traditional strand of Islam. The attack resulted in at least ten deaths
and several injuries ("Many Die in Mali Sectarian Violence," August 27, 2003, 1, BBC
News, http://news.bbc.co.uk/1/hi/world/Africa/3185635.stm).

101. Magister, "Worldwide Islam," 2.

102. Yaroslav Trofimov, "Islamic Democracy? Mali Finds a Way to Make It Work,"
Wall Street Journal, June 22, 2004, 2, http://www.freerepublic.com/focus/f-
news/1158084/posts.

103. Holzbaur, "Les inquiétants émirs du Sahel," 1.

104. Agence France Presse (AFP), "Les religieux s'invitent dans la campagne élec-
toral," April 26, 2002, 1, www.africatime,com/mali/nouvelle.asp?no_nouvelle=
15727&no_categorie.

105. Wahhabis follow Hanbali law, normally considered more rigid than Malikite law, which prevails in most of West Africa ("Saudi Reckoning," 2).

106. Magister, "Worldwide Islam," 1–3.

107. Holzbaur, "Les inquiétants émirs du Sahel," 2; ICG, "Islamist Terrorism," 9.

108. U.S. Department of State, *Annual Report 2002*, 2.

109. United States Central Intelligence Agency, *World Factbook Online*, 2003, https://www.cia.gov/library/publications/the-world-factbook/; Osterreider, "After the Coup," 3.

110. Adebayo Olukoshi, *West Africa's Political Economy in the Next Millennium: Retrospect and Prospect*, CODESRIA Monograph Series, 2/2001 (Dakar, Senegal: CODESRIA, 2001), 14; Central Intelligence Agency (CIA), *World Factbook—Mali*, 2005, http://www.cia.gov/library/publications/the-world-factbook/geos/ml.html; USAID, *Budget*, Mali, 2003, http://www.usaid.gov/policy/budget/cbj2006/afr/ml.html.

111. CIA, *World Factbook*, 2003, https://www.cia.gov/library/publications/the-world-factbook/geos/ml.html.

112. Mvemba Phezo Dizolele, "'Eye on Africa': Mali's Democracy," United Press International (UPI), December 20, 2004, 2, http://www.howardwfrench.com/archives/2005/03/02/eye_on_africa_malis_democracy/.

113. Robert Guest, *The Shackled Continent: Power Corruption, and African Lives* (Washington, DC: Smithsonian Books, 2004), 165.

114. Dizolele, "Eye on Africa," 2.

115. "Subsidy Struggle," September 9, 2003, 1–5; here: 1, 3, Online NewsHour, http://www.pbs.org/newshour/bb/international/july-dec03/farmers_9-09.html.

116. Jonathan Watts, "Cash Cows," *Guardian*, September 8, 2003, 1, http://www.guardian.co.uk/wto/article/0,2763,1038080,00.html. The cattle subsidies add insult to injury, as most Africans live on less than $1.00 per day.

117. Columbant, "Mali's Muslims," 2; Holzbaur, "Les inquiétants émirs du Sahel," 3.

118. Columbant, "Mali's Muslims," 2.

119. IPACC, "US Military and Oil," 2; Associated Press, "Green Berets," 2. Chadian ambassador to the U.S. Ahmat Soubiane recently said, "the Chadian people have learned through experience that Islamic and non-Islamic believers must co-exist—an idea that is crystallized in the popular consensus in support of a secular government."

120. Magister, "Worldwide Islam," 2; Caddasse, "Il n'y a pas de famine au Niger," 3.

121. Donnelly, "US-Trained Forces," 2.

122. See note 38.

123. Mohamed Abdoun, "Signé Mokhtar Belmokhtar," *L'Expression*, January 5, 2005, 1; "Five Killed," 1. The GSPC attacks killed dozens of Algerian troops in January and February 2005. These are considered the worst attacks since the beginning of Algeria's civil war in 1992.

124. El-Kadi Ihsane, "La thèse de l'affiliation du GSPC à Al-Qaïda purturbée," *Le Quotidien d'Oran*, May 18, 2003, 1. Ihsane notes the differences in tactics between the GSPC and al-Qaeda, pointing out that the GSPC generally refrains from attacks on civilian targets (ICG, "Islamist Terrorism," 34).

125. IPACC, "US Military and Oil," 5.

126. ICG, "L'Islamisme," i.

127. Miles, "Islamism in West Africa," 58.

21

Undoing Oil's Curse?

An Examination of the
Chad-Cameroon Pipeline Project

Ken Vincent

Introduction

The 3.7 billion dollar Chad-Cameroon Petroleum Development and Pipeline Project represents the largest single foreign investment in African history. A consortium of energy companies led by ExxonMobil has developed oil fields in the Doba Region of southern Chad and built a 700-mile pipeline that runs through Cameroon to a loading station in the Gulf of Guinea. Chad possesses oil reserves of more than 900 million barrels. Over the course of the project, government revenues in Chad are expected to grow by 45 to 50 percent.[1] Oil began to flow on October 10, 2003, and reached peak production of 225,000 barrels per day in 2004.[2] This project necessitated substantial improvements in Chad's institutional and physical infrastructure. Chad's history of conflict prevented oil development activities prior to the 1990s. As a result of this timing, Chad entered the petroleum world in an era of heightened awareness about multinational corporate activity.[3]

The World Bank Group is acting as a risk manager for the consortium and as a facilitator for the Chadian government. The World Bank Group is financing the Chadian holding in the pipeline project and assisting the Chadian government with managing the revenues and the project's environmental impact. This role entails auditing oil revenues, helping the Chadian government build capacity, and monitoring all aspects of the project.[4] The Energy Information Administration of the United States has called the bank, which is placing strictures on the Chadian government and the consortium, the "lynchpin of the project."[5] The bank's role and the international scrutiny received by the project impacted the project's execution.

Some observers declared this project a new model for oil development.[6] The Chad project could also become another failure, given Chad's violent past and early signs that the project is not making ideal progress.

Compared to Chad, this project will cause minimal changes in Cameroon. While Chad's GDP and government budget will receive a monumental windfall, the overall increase in Cameroon's GDP as a result of this project is expected to be around 2 percent.[7] However, 85 percent of the physical pipeline lies in Cameroon—making community impact management in Cameroon a massive undertaking for the consortium.[8]

This chapter will examine the positive aspects of the project that differentiate it from past African oil development attempts and will also briefly examine the level of need in Chad. It will then explore Chad's many problems and the ways in which the project's shortcomings could cause it to fail. Finally, the cases of Nigeria and Angola are examined, highlighting the differences between these pronounced hydrocarbon development failures and Chad.

A New Paradigm

Development practitioners and scholars have long sought a way to make petroleum resources work for the citizens of petro-states. This project constitutes a major step in the efforts to achieve this dream. Especially in Africa, oil development has historically consisted of corrupt marriages between unscrupulous oil companies and repressive, unresponsive governments. In the past, reliance on oil rents caused institutional decay in governments and the benefits of oil revenues rarely translated into human development in petroleum-producing countries.[9] The architects of the project seek to depart from this sad history. The roles played by the energy consortium and the Chadian government are balanced by the presence of the World Bank Group. Additionally, Chad's otherwise intractable poverty makes it difficult to argue against a project that should create new prosperity of this magnitude.

Changes in Corporate Behavior

The World Bank now possesses something that has eluded sovereign governments for decades: leverage over a multinational oil corporation. ExxonMobil, the operator of the project, is contractually bound by the guidelines set forth by the bank's environmental management plan.[10] This agreement represents an unprecedented degree of accountability for a major multinational in Africa. ExxonMobil's environmental assessment of the project specifically refers to the World Bank Group's guidelines and documents compliance with them.[11] Critics of the project call the bank's involvement "corporate welfare," which is truly inappropriate.[12] The bank provided less than 5 percent of the costs, and the consortium's interest in the bank arose from a desire to manage risks, not a desire to raise capital. Never before has a major multinational corporation had to adhere to this level of outside regulation in Africa.

Multiple layers of monitoring keep the consortium in check. The External Compliance Monitoring Group (ECMG), which was commissioned by the lenders in the project, focuses both on the capacity-building projects and on adherence to the environmental management plan. This group conducts fieldwork in Chad and Cameroon to see that all parties meet their legal obligations. Its members' reports, which include responses to their concerns, are made public.[13] The International Advisory Group (IAG) is addressing the issues of capacity building, resource and revenue management, governance, the environment, social impact, and community development. The group consists of impartial experts. They are to work with all interested parties on the ground in Chad and Cameroon and report directly to the World Bank's president and board of directors.[14] The two major groups, along with other monitoring institutions, provide scrutiny unmatched by any previous foreign investment project in Africa.

Tom Walters, ExxonMobil's vice president for development in Africa, called the level of consultation in this project "unprecedented in Africa and perhaps in the world."[15] The consortium has conducted thousands of consultation meetings, which have reached tens of thousands of Chadian and Cameroonian people, since 1993.[16] Many of the unique traits of the project resulted from requests made by the people in the oil-producing communities. The consortium rerouted the pipeline's path in Cameroon based on local feedback, which minimized the amount of resettlement necessary to make way for the project. The consortium members also took local feedback into consideration when they chose the offshore location of the loading terminal at the end of the pipeline in Kribi, Cameroon. The pipeline also travels underground, in contrast to other African onshore projects that used above-ground pipelines to cut costs.[17] Above-ground pipelines are more harmful to the local environment and more vulnerable to sabotage. The citizens of Chad's Doba Region and the forests of Cameroon affected the behavior of the world's largest corporation. Many observers of business practices in Africa would have previously called this kind of change impossible.

The consortium undertook special projects to mitigate the impact of the pipeline in Cameroon. In response to concerns about the project's environmental impact, the consortium financed an environmental foundation in Cameroon, which has partnered with the World Wildlife Fund to create two major national parks. The consortium also worked to insure that the project did not damage relations between Bakola Pygmies and their Bantu neighbors living along the pipeline. The educational, agricultural, and health-related needs of the Bakola Pygmies will be addressed under this plan.[18]

Nongovernmental organizations (NGOs) and the international community contributed substantially to the adoption of these measures. In a letter to World Bank Group President James Wolfensohn in 1998, eighty-six NGOs in twenty-eight countries called for the suspension of the bank's involvement in the project. They cited concerns about consultation in the local communities, about transparency on the part of the bank and the consortium, and about the environmental impact of the project.[19] NGOs in Chad and the West continue to voice concerns about the project.[20] Because of the checks on the consortium embedded in the structure of this project, ExxonMobil has worked with NGOs more than any oil company ever has before. The project evolved in response to NGO vigilance. The consortium also works with Chadian NGOs in the production area. These groups consulted with the local population and dispensed compensation and social services to people in the affected areas.[21] While the relationship between NGOs and energy companies can be adversarial, the role of advocacy groups in this project demonstrates that NGOs now command some influence over international economic activity.[22]

ExxonMobil, the operator of the project and the largest investor in the consortium, maintains a better reputation for ethical behavior than many other energy majors. The business ethics of Shell and Elf, who withdrew from the consortium, are often questioned. J. Robinson West, chairman of the Petroleum Finance Company, stated in no uncertain terms that Elf has had a history of doing things "under the table."[23] Shell's dealings in Nigeria have called their ability to operate ethically in African countries into question. ExxonMobil, an American company, must adhere to the Foreign Corrupt Practices Act (FCPA) of 1977, which prohibits Americans and American corporations from unethical practices abroad, including taking or paying bribes of any kind.[24] The corruptor/corrupted relationship that often arises between multinationals and unscrupulous governments is less likely to evolve in this case. All oil companies exist to make money, but the behavior of individual companies varies.

Many critics cite ExxonMobil's past international behavior as reason to doubt the likelihood of their ethical execution of this project. Their participation in the El Cerrejon Norte coal mine in northern Colombia caused considerable international controversy. This major project led to the displacement of indigenous peoples, and ExxonMobil recently divested from it.[25] Critics with an environmental agenda would point to the 1989 Exxon Valdez oil spill, which devastated the coast of Prince William Sound, Alaska.[26] While pessimists might argue that past problems mean that the consortium will necessarily operate carelessly and unethically in this venture, it could also be argued that these past problems resulted in ExxonMobil learning lessons. These disasters contributed to the heightened level of international awareness that caused the innovative aspects of the project under discussion to be put in place.

Changes in Petroleum Development Management

Financially speaking, the project's impact on Cameroon will be smaller than its impact on Chad. While the money that Cameroon receives in transit fees and taxes will be a benefit, along with infrastructural improvements, Cameroon will not receive nearly the windfall that Chad will. Cameroon is no stranger to the pitfalls of oil rent dependency—like many West African nations, Cameroon began exporting oil in the 1970s. Many institutionalized problems, such as rent seeking and corruption, appear in Cameroon—although on a smaller scale than among other West African oil producers.[27] Cameroon's production has decreased in recent years, but it still constitutes a sizable portion of the country's GDP.[28] Because the economic impact on Cameroon is smaller and because public institutions are more developed in Cameroon, the novel revenue management mechanisms being put in place in Chad were not replicated in Cameroon.

The World Bank holds a tremendous amount of leverage over the Chadian government. Chad agreed to give up a degree of sovereignty here because it truly needed the bank's help to execute this important project.[29] This leverage over Chad will help make Chadian oil an instrument of broader development.[30] The World Bank has already demonstrated its ability to influence the Chadian government. In April 2000, the Chadian government spent a portion of a signing bonus from the consortium on military expenditures. Although this bonus was outside the terms of the agreement, Chad's action went against the spirit of the project. The IMF and the World Bank declared that, until corrective steps were taken, they could not propose debt relief for Chad. The government quickly addressed the problem.[31] During the 2001 presidential election in Chad, President Idriss Déby jailed some of his political opponents. Wolfensohn called Déby, which led to the prisoners' expeditious release.[32] These examples illustrate that the Chadian government does not enjoy the carte blanche that most African petro-states enjoy. Hopefully, World Bank's leverage will cause the Chadian government to actually work toward employing oil revenues to benefit the Chadian people.

The Parliament of the Republic of Chad has passed a law to ensure that the revenue from this project is properly managed.[33] This law dictates that direct income accrued from the extraction of oil be kept in an offshore escrow account, which can be monitored by other actors in the consortium. Moreover, 90 percent of direct revenues are to be spent on priority sectors such as health, education, infrastructure, and rural development, and 10 percent of the funds are to be put in savings accounts for the benefit of future generations.[34] The law also establishes the Oil Revenues Control and Monitoring Board, which is to scrutinize spending. This board's unique membership includes representatives of civil society and the legislative branch of government. Approval for expenditures should be more than a rubber stamp matter because of the board's highly publicized role in the project. The law, which governs direct revenue from the fields currently in production, constitutes more of a framework for regulating the use of petroleum revenues than any African country has ever implemented. This should make graft and corrupt spending tremendously difficult.

The World Bank supports Chad's efforts in two ways. First, the International Development Association (IDA) capacity-building projects to increase the Chadian government's revenue management abilities are intended to help the government enforce this law. This places the bank at the center of efforts to make the project work for the people of Chad. The bank is attempting to facilitate government spending in accordance with revenue management law. This constitutes a long-term challenge, considering the institutional void in Chad.[35] Secondly, the bank scrutinizes and audits Chadian government spending.[36] Although the bank must publicly retain its role as an unbiased consultant in countries' economic management, reports suggest that the bank has been extraordinarily vigilant in pushing for proper revenue management.[37] Throughout the execution of this project, the bank has placed its reputation on the line and undertaken many risks, so it has a substantial interest in making the project work. Moreover, the government of Chad cannot resist the bank's demands to the degree that wealthier, more secure governments can. Overall, the structure of the project places the Chadian government in a restricted position, which should prevent bad policy decisions. This structure should also prepare Chad for fluctuations in international oil markets.

Chad's Economic Need

Discourse on this project cannot ignore Chad's drastic level of need. Chad's gross national income per capita is $240 per year, half of the average for sub-Saharan Africa, making Chad one of the poorest nations on earth.[38] Only 3 percent of Chad's land is arable, which prevents widespread agricultural development.[39] Chad's landlocked location has thus far prevented linkage to the global economy. Cotton farming in the south and herding in the north constitute the main sectors of Chad's non-oil economy.[40] Chad has endured the pitfalls of cash-crop development during its postcolonial history. CotonChad, the national cotton company, has attempted to add value to Chadian cotton by producing textiles, but substantive industrialization remains elusive.[41] Chad must import most value-added goods. Herding in the north will not broadly develop the nation's economy because droughts can render this industry helpless.[42] Chad's human development indicators tell the same story. Chad's under-five mortality rate is 200/1,000, and its national illiteracy rate is 52 percent.[43] Insufficient resources render public health services and education quite poor.[44] Revenue from this project could address these needs. Comparable alternative avenues of growth do not exist for Chad.

Dependence on foreign aid also characterizes the Chadian economy. France acted as Chad's primary donor following independence, providing military supplies and monetary advances. Foreign aid to Chad has varied over the years based on the country's strategic importance. Aid has been the primary source of government money for most of the country's history.[45] This phenomenon has placed the interests of Chad's donors ahead of the interests of the Chadian people. Because of its dependence on cash-crop agriculture, Chad must also import food.[46] Revenues from the project should counteract these problems in two ways. First, because cotton and cattle will no longer be needed to provide the government with revenue, Chad can focus concerted attention on food agriculture. Secondly, Chad can reduce its dependence on foreign aid. A steady source of income that is not subject to the geopolitical interests of external actors should facilitate much more stable economic development.

In a capital-intensive industry such as petroleum extraction, employment should be viewed as a secondary benefit rather than a primary benefit. This project does not exist to create jobs and linkages. The revenues that the state will gain constitute the main benefit. However, the local economy in the petroleum-producing area will benefit to some extent. The consortium has attempted to facilitate some local economic development. Thousands of people obtained jobs on a temporary basis during the construction phase of the project. Some people will keep their jobs permanently. Additionally, the consortium facilitated millions of dollars in spending in local businesses.[47] In 2001, the International Finance Corporation (IFC) launched an initiative designed to facilitate local business development; this includes skills enhancement, training programs, and a micro-lending program.[48] Some dissatisfaction arose in Chad about the amount of local business development created by the project.[49] All of the project's guidelines to protect the Chadian environment and people must be followed by all contractors. These regulations present a barrier to entry for many Chadian contractors, but overall they reduce adverse effects. Looking at the potential economic benefits in total, any cost-benefit-analysis would suggest pursuing the project.

The Case against the Project

Doubt whether this project will change Chad's future stems from the country's troubled history and current growing pains. The trends that cause Chad to need this project so badly are also evident in a lack of government capacity. Chad has never become united as a nation, and the government of President Idriss Déby causes many questions to arise about the project's feasibility. NGOs hounded the bank and the consortium throughout the planning stages of the project. They now argue that the project is not proceeding as planned and that the innovations will prove insufficient to bring the benefits of oil development to the Chadian people.

A Country Flawed by Design

Anarchy has dominated most of Chad's independent history. The main societal trends in Chad since 1960 include military coups, rebellions, external intervention, civil war, chaos, lack of personal security, state terror, general terror, warlordism, human rights abuses, and dictatorship.[50] In 1989, Robert Buijtenhuijs, a prominent scholar of Chad, wrote about Chad's apparent recovery under the rule of Hissène Habré.[51] Habré managed to maintain power with help from the U.S. government, which was concerned with establishing a buffer between Gadhafi's Libya and the rest of Africa.[52] Habré's brutal regime, which lasted from 1982 to 1990, killed tens of thousands of people. Chadian and international human rights NGOs are now attempting to bring Habré to justice for extensive human rights abuses.[53] While Habré's rule represented one of the darkest periods in Chadian history, Buijtenhuijs was correct to assert that holding Chad together necessitated rule with an iron fist. A space was open for such a dictator because Chad is an extraordinarily difficult country to govern.

Chad's most fundamental problem is the divide between the north and the south. Arab and Berber northerners practice Islam. Black African residents of the south practice Christianity. French colonial officers exacerbated this ethnic divide to their advantage. Finding the north far more difficult to conquer than the south, France left northern sultans considerable autonomy and used them to administer the northern part of the colony. Northerners refused to educate their children in the French system. The south, on the other hand, endured the typical French colonial experience: conscription, head taxation, forced labor, famine, violent repression, and monocrop agriculture.[54] Northerners herd animals, while southerners farm. This difference causes economic and cultural friction between the two groups.[55] French colonialism left southerners more educated and more capable of holding positions in the civil service. Throughout Chad's independent history, the south has enjoyed relatively more prosperity than the north.[56] All these factors combine to create substantial animosity between the different sections of Chad, animosity that has often erupted into civil war. The project could exacerbate this divide, because the ruling government hails from the north, while the oil lies in the south.

The years of war and insecurity in Chad have caused the delegitimization of the Chadian state. This "divorce between state and society" has called into question the relationship between the N'djamena government and the Chadian people.[57] Often, civil society has assumed the responsibility of providing social services. Professional and village-level groups have attempted to manage infrastructural activity and to provide advocacy for people.

The Chadian government has yet to fulfill even its most basic responsibilities under the social contract.

The influence of outside actors has further delegitimized the Chadian government since independence. The interests of France, the United States, and Libya have together done more to shape Chad's history than Chadians themselves.[58] Some suggest the primary difference between colonialism and this postcolonial dependence in Chad is that leaders have more leeway to choose their external patrons.[59] The project under discussion could be viewed as a continuation of Chad's historic dependence on external actors, but now the external actors in Chad are focused on what will benefit the Chadian people. Still, the government must play a leading role in the execution of the project, and it might not be up to the challenge.

Democratization in Chad followed more than three decades of intense disorder and decay. As in most budding African democracies, democratization proved to be a difficult process. Chad's Sovereign National Conference (CNS) in 1993 sought to establish the framework for multiparty democracy in Chad, taking ethnic and sectional divisions into account. Chadians hailed this development as a true transition from war and dictatorship but became disappointed at the postponement of elections and the continuing violations of civil liberties and human rights. President Déby's decision to "democratize" stemmed from his personal lack of charisma, will, and the capacity for brutality that Habré had used to maintain power.[60] Vote rigging and fraud marred the presidential elections in 1996 and 2001, in which Déby and his party emerged victorious. Recent developments in Chad, such as the abolition of the Senate and the removal of presidential term limits, reflect a trajectory of consolidation of power. Dissatisfaction with this trend materialized in the form of an attempt on Déby's life in 2004.[61]

Human rights abuses in Chad continue. While the Déby government is not the worst to have controlled Chad, its record remains poor. The U.S. Department of State reported extrajudicial killings, political disappearances, arbitrary imprisonment, torture, and the violation of all categories of civil liberties.[62] Amnesty International correctly asserts that the Déby government probably feels more comfortable with committing abuses because the Habré government, which was much worse, has yet to be brought to justice.[63] The government maintains a façade of concern for human rights. The Déby regime established a Human Rights League designed to make the government more aware of civil society's concerns in this area. According to Human Rights Watch, this government agency has been a failure and has simply lowered Chadians' faith in the N'djamena government's regard for their personal security.[64] Although the Doba oil-producing region does not equate to Nigeria's Ogoniland, human rights violations have occurred in relation to the project under discussion. Southerners who spoke out against the project were intimidated and illegally detained.[65] The most grievous violation in the oil-producing region occurred in March 1998, when Chadian security forces massacred more than one hundred unarmed civilians.[66] Such abuses could destabilize the project.

In Africa, oil booms have tended to destabilize governments.[67] Introducing a new, destabilizing factor does not bode well for a historically unstable nation. The Chadian government is central to the project's success, so it must improve upon its disastrous history to give oil development a chance to make a difference. President Déby must realize that continuing the long-established trends of violence and bad governance in Chad will only compromise the project that defines his power base and his legacy. Failure to change will result in Chad becoming another violent petro-state that never reaches its potential. While it is too early for a full appraisal of the project, some signs suggest that it is not proceeding as planned.

Recent Criticisms of the Project

The capacity-building projects in Chad, parts of the oil project that address revenue management and the regulation of oil development, are not proceeding as planned. Some critics argue that there is so little institutional capacity in Chad that bank initiatives might not be sufficient. Thus far, the capacity-building projects intended to bolster Chad's ability to manage oil revenues and regulate the oil project have not accomplished enough. Reports consistently point to the capacity-building projects as inadequate. Now that funding for these projects is exhausted, their role as the main support of the Chadian government's involvement is in jeopardy.[68] All along, capacity-building projects have not proceeded as quickly as the development of the pipeline. Now that production has peaked and revenues are flowing to the government, the degree to which these projects have prepared the government for the boom will be tested.

The monitoring institutions in place do not possess direct leverage over the actors involved. The IAG reports to the bank rather than the consortium that is actually carrying out the project.[69] The IAG's mandate does not specify how the bank is to receive its recommendations and how they are to be carried out.[70] The ECMG has documented the progress of problems it has addressed.[71] However, the ECMG focuses most of its efforts on technical matters, which are not the primary problem with the project. Also, because the ECMG comes from a private consulting firm, conflicts of interest could arise. Neither the IAG nor the ECMG possesses the power to sanction . These monitoring institutions' success will be measured in terms of how far they impact the project's execution.

The consultation process, which is an improvement in comparison with past African petroleum development projects, was carried out in part with armed military officers present.[72] This casts some doubt on the legitimacy of the feedback. It remains to be seen whether the consultation process can be judged a success. Also, the compensation of residents forced to move because of the project remains a contentious issue. Although all those who were forced to move during the course of construction were compensated for their possessions, this compensation gave way to a new problem. Many Chadians were ill prepared for windfalls that accounted for more than their annual income. Many people squandered their entire payment, winding up destitute in a matter of weeks.[73]

The Oil Revenues Control and Monitoring Board could prove ineffective in tackling corruption.[74] Many of the members come from the government, including President Déby's brother-in-law. While the government does not control the group, it certainly maintains an active voice in its operations. The control board does not possess an independent source of funding, which significantly hampers its ability to function.[75] A loophole also exists in the text of the law, which differentiates between direct and indirect revenues from the project. Indirect revenue, such as taxes and fees, does not fall under the jurisdiction of this board and does not have to be spent on the priority sectors. Catholic Relief Service released a report in February 2005 detailing problems with the Chadian government's revenue management to that date. Not only do holes exist in the movement of money itself, but the entire process of resource distribution within the guidelines of the law is vulnerable to corruption.[76] The consortium will be exploring other potential development projects in Chad, outside of the original production region.[77] Revenues from these new projects fall outside the initial agreement.

The project has negatively impacted the local economy in some ways. The construction of the project temporarily employed as many as 10,000 people and pumped substantial amounts of money into the producing area.[78] This surge of employment and spending was only temporary, however. The end of the construction phase caused a "bust" of sorts. Prices in the local economy are now elevated because of the consortium's presence, which detracts from the purchasing power of local residents. Residents of the oil-producing region are not satisfied with the impact of the project.[79] All actors involved should remember that social dissatisfaction in communities where multinationals operate can lead to disaster.

Contrasts with Past Oil Failures

An examination of previous African oil disasters sheds light on Chad's relatively good starting position. A look at cases of Angola and Nigeria shows that the project under review was designed to avoid previous pitfalls. These cases underscore the importance of placing controls on the government at an early stage. Surprisingly, some features of Chadian geopolitics make it less susceptible to the problems seen in these other nations. Also, the nature of the institutionalized Nigerian elite class and the nature of the civil war in Angola are unique and will not be repeated.

Nigeria

Like Chad, Nigeria is a political space with culturally inappropriate colonial borders. Differences in religion, ethnicity, language, and region prevent Nigeria from being a united nation. Colonialism affected Nigeria differently than Chad. The British method of "indirect rule," which entailed the use of co-opted locals to control the population, established a large elite class in Nigeria.[80] Nigeria also developed much more of a colonial economy than Chad, because of its coastal position and abundance of good farmland. Nigeria's elite class was firmly entrenched when oil began to flow. Moreover, the Nigerian government had no checks on its behavior when petroleum revenues began to accrue. With no restrictions, the Nigerian state apparatus and government spending exploded.[81] The Nigerian state has acted for the sole purpose of benefiting itself and redistributing rents.[82] Chad's government has never developed to the point at which the elite could become this entrenched, making the prospect of reform in Chad more hopeful.

Corruption in Nigeria is legendary. The government squandered billions of dollars and Nigeria remains one of the poorest nations in the world in per capita terms.[83] No matter what criticisms of the revenue management plan may be raised, the Chadian government will inarguably receive much more scrutiny than the Nigerian government did during the early stages of its oil development. By the time the international community identified combating corruption as a policy imperative, the Nigerian government had created a system of rent collection and developed a power base that made its position tragically sustainable. The Chadian government will not be able to accomplish this, given the initial constraints of the project.

The Nigerian government spent what money it did not steal very unwisely. Like many nations that experienced a surge in rents, Nigeria ignored other sectors of its economy, especially agriculture.[84] Agriculture in Nigeria, with appropriate policies, could have provided a decent life for a majority of Nigerians. Now, even with fertile land and no need to employ cash-crop agriculture to produce export revenue, Nigeria still must import food.[85] Recovery in the non-oil sectors will prove tremendously difficult in Nigeria. The Chadian government and the World Bank addressed this problem in the revenue management plan, which specifically provides for agricultural and rural development. Nigeria developed a taste for massive, capital-intensive, prestige projects that have yielded minimal material benefits for Nigerians.[86] Often, fluctuations in the international oil market have forced Nigeria to abandon these projects before they are completed.

Revenue management in Chad does not allow for these kinds of wasteful expenditures.

Fluctuations in international oil markets often forced Nigeria to borrow money, using future oil revenues as collateral, to maintain government expenditures. The debt-ridden Nigerian government had to call on the International Monetary Fund in 1983.[87] As the government attempted various fiscal reforms, the elite class of Nigeria found alternative methods of amassing wealth from political rents under the international financial institutions' reforms, methods such as petroleum smuggling, narcotics trafficking, and pocketing privatization profits.[88] Austerity reforms were initiated after the rent-collecting class had firmly established itself. A crucial difference between Nigeria and Chad is that structural adjustment was already in place in Chad as oil began to flow. The international financial institutions (IFIs) have leverage over the Chadian government, which was never the case during the early phases of Nigerian development. This is the first time that an African nation will experience a resource boom of this relative magnitude while under IFI scrutiny.

Protest and repression has characterized the Nigerian oil-producing communities for decades. The actions of General Sani Abacha's dictatorship with regard to Ogoniland, a Nigerian oil-producing community, epitomize the worst potentialities of hydrocarbon development. Protest initially stirred in Nigerian oil-producing communities because citizens adversely impacted by oil development did not receive just compensation from the government.[89] Abacha publicly executed Ken Saro-Wiwa and eight other Ogoni activists to establish his control over oil development issues.[90] Shell, the major multinational corporation operating onshore in Nigeria, facilitated these events by importing arms for Nigerian security forces and openly threatening protestors with violence.[91] All of these events heightened awareness of multinational corporate behavior in the developing world. Because of this attention, oil multinationals cannot afford to blunder in the way Shell did in Nigeria. Specific consideration given to the oil-producing communities in Chad, the extensive consultation and compensation process, the involvement of the World Bank, and the attention given to NGOs all stem partially from a desire not to repeat what happened in Ogoniland. Some revenue from the project is also being specifically dedicated to the producing area.[92] Nigeria's tragedies have become the world's lessons.

Angola

Conflict in Angola began with the struggle for independence from Portugal during the 1960s and 1970s. After independence, the People's Movement for the Liberation of Angola (MPLA), which was backed by the Soviet Union, ended up at war with the National Union for the Total

Independence of Angola (UNITA), which was backed by the United States. This war lasted for almost thirty years.[93] As in the Chadian civil war, Cold War agendas played a massive role in facilitating conflict in Angola. The two conflicts differ in two regards, however. First, no domestic player in Chad has emerged like Jonas Savimbi, the UNITA leader who undoubtedly prolonged the conflict in Angola. While the historical and cultural divisions in Angola and the actions of external powers both exacerbated Angola's war, Savimbi represented the main obstacle to peace during the later years of the conflict.[94] The conflict in Angola ended shortly after Savimbi died, further demonstrating that he was a particularly influential enemy of peace.[95] Secondly, UNITA benefited from its control of diamond mines, which gave it an independent source of government oil revenues with which to wage war.[96] Chad has no resources outside of the Doba oil. The nightmare of two warring factions utilizing different resource bases is not a possibility in Chad. It remains quite unlikely that Chad's future will mirror Angola's past.

To fuel the conflict, Angola spent the lion's share of its oil revenues on the military at the expense of all other sectors. The standards of human development and infrastructure deteriorated almost beyond repair. All other sectors of the Angolan economy were decimated. Farming, fishing, and mining are all stagnant or nonexistent.[97] Chad's revenue management plan will prevent the Chadian government from ignoring agriculture and spending on a wasteful military machine. Revenues began to flow to the Chadian government during a time of peace, which will limit the potential for this kind of behavior. While the signing bonus incident reflected a desire on the government's part to spend on national security, military spending in Chad will never reach the levels that it did in Angola.

Like Nigeria, Angola had to turn to the international financial institutions when the national economy was already in crisis. Two of the mistakes made in Angola will be avoided in the Chad project. First, Angola refused to go to the IFIs for years and survived on loans on bad terms, using their oil as leverage. In Chad, this will not occur, because IFI directives are part of the oil development itself. Second, Angola has made numerous extrabudgetary financial transactions.[98] Chad will benefit from the annual audit the program provides for and the intense scrutiny these audits are receiving. Oil allowed the government of Angola to mismanage its economy for years, without any check on its wasteful spending. Because Chad started the oil development process from a weaker position, it will have less room to maneuver in terms of financial management.

The location of Angola's oil also constitutes a significant difference between Angola and Chad. All of Angola's major producing blocks are located offshore.[99] This circumstance greatly reduces the risk of sabotage and destabilization based on human conditions in the country. Energy interests in Angola can completely isolate themselves from the country's citizens without concern for the impact of instability on production. The isolation of production from internal stability is further evidenced by Angola's continued production during its civil war. This kind of unresponsiveness in Chad will be impossible. The consortium's great care in addressing the needs of the local community indicates that stability in Chad, especially in the oil-producing region, is paramount to the success of the project. Unlike Angola, Chad will not be able to ignore the condition of its people and continue to enjoy petroleum profits.

Conclusion

The Chad-Cameroon Petroleum Development and Pipeline Project represents a unique triangular partnership between a commercial entity, a sovereign government, and an international institution. The World Bank, needed by both the Chadian government and the oil consortium, developed a robust strategy to translate the financial benefits of the project into material benefits for the Chadian people. To achieve this goal, all the actors in the project made unprecedented efforts to insure transparent revenue management and minimize the adverse effects of the project. This project clearly constitutes the best attempt at oil-driven development ever undertaken in an African country. Moreover, the risks of this project make more sense when Chad's alternatives are considered. Nothing else can give this beleaguered nation hope for an improved future.

The project cannot yet be called a success. The success of the project depends largely on the ability of the Chadian government to hold up its end of the bargain. Its capacity to do so is limited at best. Chad's inherited geographic problems and societal divides, which have contributed to war and poverty in the past, might prove insurmountable obstacles to the success of the project. The issues that have arisen since oil begun to flow could either be initial growing pains or signs of imminent failure. It remains too early to judge.

Reflection on the cases of Nigeria and Angola gives cause for optimism. In both cases, the continuing streams of oil money irreparably impacted the structures of economic and geopolitical governance. These countries involved external actors only after substantial crises had occurred. Nothing ever forced these countries to operate with their citizens' interests in mind. The oil project under consideration here represents Chad's only chance. The World Bank realized that nothing else could lift Chad out of poverty and took a chance on this project, bearing in mind the problems that had led to past failures. Obviously, problems will occur in the execution of this project. Many people will never be satisfied with the actions of the consortium. Revenue will take time to translate into material benefits for Chadians, if this happens at all. However, the key arguments in favor of pursuing this project are relative rather than absolute. The improvements made, relative to past attempts at oil development, make this project historically significant. The degree to which this project represents the best option for Chad makes its completion essential.

Notes

1. World Bank Group, "Project Overview," *The Chad-Cameroon Petroleum Development and Pipeline Project,* October 22, 2004, http://www.worldbank.org/afr/ccproj/questions/index.htm (accessed February 27, 2005).

2. Esso, "Quarterly Reports," *The Chad-Cameroon Development and Pipeline Project,* January 2005, http://www.essochad.com/Chad/Library/Reports/Chad_Quarterly Reports.asp (accessed February 27, 2005).

3. Jane I. Guyer, "Briefing: The Chad-Cameroon Petroleum and Pipeline Development Project," *African Affairs* 101 (2002): 109–11.

4. World Bank Group, "Project Overview."

5. Nicolas Cook of the Congressional Research to House International Relations Committee, Subcommittee on Africa, memorandum, September 1, 2001, Congressional Research Service, *Chad-Cameroon Oil Project: Overview and Views of Critics* (Washington, DC: Congressional Research Service, 2001), 4.

6. House Committee on International Relations, *The Chad-Cameroon Pipeline: A New Model for Natural Resource Development,* 107th Congress, 2nd session, April 18, 2002, 6.

7. Esso, "Quarterly Reports."

8. Esso, "Environmental Assessment Executive Summary: An Update," *The Chad-Cameroon Development and Pipeline Project,* 2002, http://www2.exxonmobil.com/Chad/Library/Documentation/Chad_DO_Exec.asp (accessed February 27, 2005).

9. Terry Lynn Karl, "The Perils of the Petro-State: Reflections on the Paradox of Plenty," *Journal of International Affairs* 53, no. 1 (Fall 1999): 31–48.

10. World Bank Group, "Project Overview."

11. Esso, "Environmental Assessment Executive Summary: An Update."

12. Korinna Horta, "Fueling Strife in Chad and Cameroon: The Exxon-Shell-Elf-World Bank Plans for Central Africa," *Multinational Monitor* 18, no. 5 (May 1997): 13.

13. D'Appolonia S.p.A. External Compliance Monitoring Group, "Tenth Site Visit: April–May 2004," *The Chad/Cameroon Petroleum Development and Pipeline Project—Project Monitoring,* February 9, 2005, http://www.worldbank.org/afr/ccproj/project/pro_monitor.htm#ecmg (accessed February 28, 2005).

14. International Advisory Group, "Terms of Reference," *International Advisory Group (IAG) for the Chad-Cameroon Petroleum Development and Pipeline Project,* July 30, 2001, http://www.gic-iag.org/doc/iag_tor_en.pdf (accessed February 27, 2005).

15. House Committee on International Relations, *The Chad-Cameroon Pipeline,* 6.

16. Esso, "Quarterly Reports."

17. Esso, "Environmental Assessment Executive Summary: An Update."

18. Esso, "Environmental Assessment Executive Summary: An Update," and "Quarterly Reports."

19. Korinna Horta, "Open Letter to Mr. James D. Wolfensohn, President of the World Bank, from 86 NGO's in 28 Countries concerning the Chad-Cameroon Oil

and Pipeline Project," Africa Action Home Page, August 1, 1998, http://www.africapolicy.org/docs98/wb9807.htm (accessed February 27, 2005).

20. Delphine Djiraibe. "Chad Oil: Why Develop It?" *Review of African Political Economy* 29, no. 91 (March 2002): 170–73.

21. Esso, "Environmental Assessment Executive Summary: An Update."

22. Jerry Useem, "ExxonMobil's African Adventure," *Fortune* 145, no. 8 (April 15, 2002): 102–14.

23. House Committee on International Relations, *Africa's Energy Potential: Hearing before the Subcommittee on Africa*, 106th Congress, 1st session, March 16, 2000, 23.

24. Kempe Ronald Hope Sr., "Corruption and Development in Africa," in *Corruption and Development in Africa*, ed. Kempe Ronald Hope Sr. and Bornwell C. Chikulo (New York: St. Martin's Press, 2000), 34.

25. Ralph Surette, "The Dirty Story of Where We Get Our Coal," Mines and Communities Website, March 26, 2005, http://www.minesandcommunities.org/Action/press586.htm (accessed October 30, 2005).

26. Robert Gramling and William R. Freudenburg, "The *Exxon Valdez* Oil Spill in the Context of U.S. Petroleum Politics," in *The Exxon Valdez Disaster: Readings on a Modern Social Problem*, ed. J Stephen Picou, Duane A. Gill, and Maurie J. Cohen (Dubuque, IA: Kendall/Hunt, 1997), 71–87.

27. Douglas A. Yates, *The Rentier State in Africa* (Trenton, NJ: Africa World Press, 1996), 221–35.

28. U.S. Energy Information Administration, "Chad and Cameroon," *Country Analysis Briefs*, December 2004, http://www.eia.doe.gov/emeu/cabs/chad_cameroon.html#oil (accessed October 30, 2005).

29. House Committee on International Relations, *The Chad-Cameroon Pipeline*, 10–12.

30. World Bank Group, "IBRD/IDA Project Information Document," *The Chad-Cameroon Petroleum Development and Pipeline Project—Project Documents*, June 23, 1999, http://www.worldbank.org/afr/ccproj/project/td44305.pdf (accessed September 25, 2001), 7.

31. World Bank Group, "Note on the Use of Petroleum Bonus," *The Chad-Cameroon Petroleum Development and Pipeline Project—Project Documents*, June 2001, http://www.worldbank.org/afr/ccproj/project/bonus.pdf (accessed September 25, 2001), 1–2.

32. Useem, "ExxonMobil's African Adventure," 102–14.

33. Ambassador Donald Norland, "Innovations of the Chad-Cameroon Pipeline Project: Thinking Outside the Box," *Mediterranean Quarterly* 14, no. 2 (Spring 2003): 53–55.

34. Parliament of the Republic of Chad, *[Law Concerning] Oil Revenues Management*, Act No. 001/PR/99 (translation) (accessed January 11, 1999).

35. Guyer, "Briefing," 112–15.

36. World Bank Group, "Project Overview."

37. Norland, "Innovations of the Chad-Cameroon Pipeline Project," 53–55.

38. World Bank, "Chad at a Glance," World Development Indicators Database, October 15, 2004, http://www.worldbank.org/data/countrydata/aag/tcd_aag.pdf (accessed February 27, 2005).

39. Central Intelligence Agency (CIA), "Chad," *World Factbook*, February 10, 2005, http://www.cia.gov/cia/publications/factbook/index.html (accessed February 27, 2005).

40. Jean-Paul Azam and Christian Morrison, *The Sahel*, vol. 1, *Conflict and Growth in Africa* (Paris: Organization for Economic Cooperation and Development, 1999), 134–37.

41. Mario J. Azevedo and Emmanuel U. Nnadozie, *Chad: A Nation in Search of Its Future* (Boulder, CO: Westview Press, 1998), 70.

42. Ibid., 8.

43. World Bank, "Chad Data Profile," World Development Indicators Database, August 2004, http://devdata.worldbank.org/external/CPProfile.asp?CCODE=TCD&PTYPE=CP (accessed February 27, 2005).

44. Azevedo and Nnadozie, *Chad*, 103–7.

45. Ibid., 83–88.

46. Azam and Morrison, *The Sahel*, 137.

47. Esso, "Quarterly Reports."

48. International Finance Corporation, "New Initiative in Chad and Cameroon Will Increase Oil Pipeline's Benefits to Local Enterprises," IFC Press Release, June 26, 2001, http://wbln0018.worldbank.org/IFCExt/pressroom/ifcpressroom.nsf/383e2473d662e46485256a5b00788174/2da53dc030db1ae385256a4f005c0758?OpenDocument (accessed February 25, 2005).

49. Useem, "ExxonMobil's African Adventure," 102–14.

50. Robert Buijtenhuijs, "Chad: The Narrow Escape of an African State, 1965–1987," in *Contemporary West African States*, ed. Donal B. Cruise O'Brien, John Dunn, and Richard Rathbone (Cambridge: Cambridge University Press, 1989), 49–52.

51. Ibid., 53–54.

52. Norland, "Innovations of the Chad/Cameroon Pipeline Project," 48–49.

53. Amnesty International, "Chad: The Habré Legacy," Amnesty International Online, October 16, 2001, http://web.amnesty.org/library/Index/ENGAFR20004 2001?open&of=ENG-TCD (accessed October 27, 2005).

54. Azevedo and Nnadozie, *Chad*, 19–32.

55. Robert Buijtenhuijs, "The Chadian Tubu: Contemporary Nomads Who Conquered a State," *Africa* 71, no. 1 (Winter 2001): 155–56.

56. Azam and Morrison, *The Sahel*, 142–44.

57. William F. S. Miles, "Tragic Tradeoffs: Democracy and Security in Chad," *Journal of Modern African Studies* 33, no. 1 (March 1995): 64.

58. William F. S. Miles, "Decolonization and Disintegration: The Disestablishment of the State in Chad," *Journal of Asian and African Studies* 30, no. 1 (June 1995): 49.

59. Sam C. Nolutshungu, *Limits of Anarchy: Intervention and State Formation in Chad* (Charlottesville: University Press of Virginia, 1996), 317.

60. Miles, "Decolonization and Disintegration: The Disestablishment of the State in Chad," 47.

61. U.S. Department of State, Bureau of Democracy, Human Rights, and Labor, "Chad," *Country Reports on Human Rights Practices 2004*, 28 February 2005, http://www.state.gov/g/drl/rls/hrrpt/2004/41595.htm (accessed February 28, 2005).

62. Ibid.

63. Amnesty International, "Chad: The Habré Legacy," 32–38.

64. Human Rights Watch, "Chad," *Protectors or Pretenders? Government Human Rights Commissions in Africa*, 2001, http://www.hrw.org/reports/2001/africa/chad/chad.html (accessed July 18, 2001).

65. Amnesty International, "Chad," *Amnesty International Report 2001*, January 10, 2001, <http://web.amnesty.org/web/ar2001.nsf/0/4836d4e65b44f04380256a48004ab741/$FILE/chad.pdf> (accessed February 28, 2005).

66. Horta, "Open Letter to Mr. James D. Wolfensohn."

67. Jacqueline Coolidge and Susan Rose-Ackerman, "Kleptocracy and Reform in African Regimes: Theory and Examples," in *Corruption and Development in Africa*, ed. Kempe Ronald Hope Sr. and Bornwell C. Chikulo (New York: St. Martin's Press, 2000), 70.

68. International Advisory Group, "Report of Visit to Chad and Cameroon: May 17–June 5 2005," *International Advisory Group (IAG) for the Chad-Cameroon Petroleum Development and Pipeline Project*, July 9, 2004, http://www.gic-iag.org/doc/IAG_Report_7th_visit_Chad-Cameroon.pdf (accessed February 28, 2005).

69. Korinna Horta, "Open Letter to the President of the World Bank Concerning the International Advisory Group," Africa Action Home Page, 3 March 2001, http://www.africapolicy.org/docs01/pipe0103.htm (accessed July 18, 2001).

70. International Advisory Group, "Terms of Reference."

71. D'Appolonia S.P.A. External Compliance Monitoring Group, "Tenth Site Visit."

72. World Bank Group, "Questions and Answers."

73. Useem, "ExxonMobil's African Adventure," 102–14.

74. Parliament of the Republic of Chad, *Oil Revenues Management.*

75. Catholic Relief Services, "Chad's Oil; Miracle or Mirage," *In Focus*, February 18, 2005, http://www.catholicrelief.org/get_involved/advocacy/policy_and_strategic_issues/oil_report.cfm (accessed February 28, 2005).

76. Ibid.

77. Esso, "Quarterly Reports."

78. Ibid.

79. Catholic Relief Services, "Chad's Oil."

80. William D. Graf, *The Nigerian State: Political Economy, State Class and the Political System in the Post-Colonial Era* (London: J. Currey, 1988), 7–9.

81. Ibid., 224–27.

82. Richard Joseph, "Democratization under Military Rule and Repression in Nigeria," in *Dilemmas of Democracy in Nigeria*, ed. Crawford Young and Paul A. Beckett (Rochester, NY: University of Rochester Press, 1997), 139–40.

83. Stephen P. Riley, "Western Policies and African Realities: The New Anti-Corruption Agenda," in *Corruption and Development in Africa*, ed. Kempe Ronald Hope Sr. and Bornwell C. Chikulo (New York: St. Martin's Press, 2000), 148–49.

84. Peter Lewis, "Politics and the Economy: A Downward Spiral," in *Dilemmas of Democracy in Nigeria*, ed. Crawford Young and Paul A. Beckett (Rochester, NY: University of Rochester Press, 1997), 305.

85. House Committee on International Relations, *Africa's Energy Potential*, 23.

86. Graf, *The Nigerian State*, 222–24.

87. Lewis, "Politics and the Economy," 305.

88. Ibid., 306–11.

89. Human Rights Watch, *The Price of Oil: Corporate Responsibility and Human Rights Violations in Nigeria's Oil Producing Communities* (New York: Human Rights Watch, 1999), 49–52.

90. Wole Soyinka, *The Open Sore of a Continent* (New York: Oxford University Press, 1996), 145–53.

91. Human Rights Watch, *The Price of Oil*, 161, 174–77.

92. Parliament of the Republic of Chad, *Oil Revenues Management*.

93. William Minter, "Angola after Savimbi," *The Nation* 274, no. 16 (April 29, 2002): 23–24.

94. Tony Hodges, *Angola from Afro-Stalinism to Petro-Diamond Capitalism* (Bloomington: Indiana University Press, 2001), 18–19.

95. House Committee on International Relations, *Angola: Prospects for Durable Peace and Economic Reconstruction: Hearing before the Subcommittee on Africa*, 107th Congress, 2nd session, June 13, 2002, 1–5.

96. Hodges, *Angola*, 147–51.

97. Ibid., 92–95.

98. Ibid., 112–14.

99. Corporate Council on Africa, *Angola: A Country Profile for US Businesses* (Washington, DC: Corporate Council on Africa, February 2002), 27–31.

22

U.S. Foreign Policy Agenda, 2005–9

Why West Africa Barely Features

Christopher Ruane

Introduction

This chapter examines the positioning of West Africa within the contemporary discourse of U.S. foreign policy. As part of its post–September 11, 2001, disposition, the Bush administration has largely defined itself through its foreign policy. This foreign policy evokes and affirms key elements of the Bush governmental doctrine. These elements are national security, the ideological value of (selective) democratization, moral certitude, and the enduring iconography of the gun-slinging Texan wildcatter challenging all comers on his own terms.

A great deal of the criticism of the first Bush administration was criticism of its foreign policy in general, and the Iraq War and occupation in particular. Critics argued that the political goodwill created by the 2001 terrorist attacks had been squandered on military adventurism that had at best a tangential connection to any Islamic fundamentalist threat. This criticism resonated in West Africa as elsewhere. But for a variety of reasons, the Iraq War has not mobilized the same popular expression of dissatisfaction in most of Africa as it did in Europe and parts of the Middle East.

This chapter considers what this foreign policy means for West Africa. It is argued that as a locus of foreign policy concern to the United States, West Africa is primarily conceptualized in three ways. It is seen as a resource supplier, a potential terrorist base, and an area in which grave abuses of basic rights are widespread. Of these, the first two are the dominant themes in formal foreign policy discourse. They have the ability to become the source of external shocks to the United States. The accusation of widespread basic rights abuses in West Africa is generally less important in formal discourse other than as a short-term, opportunistic policy tool. However, it is more important in the wider U.S. civil society discourse. But the external shock here is in reverse: human rights protection in West Africa can be dependent upon the policy of the United States or other countries. But the human rights discourse in West Africa has little real impact in the United States.

Conceptualization of West Africa in U.S. Foreign Policy Discourse

Rothchild characterizes large parts of postwar U.S. African policy as consisting of "minimal engagement."[1] Even in more active eras, such as the final stages of the Cold War, Rothchild's analysis reflects a policy rooted firmly in a Soviet-centric approach: Africa was of interest largely inasmuch as it was an ideological battleground in the Cold War.

The multifarious competing demands on foreign policy mean that foreign policy machines tend to conceptualize countries in oversimplified ways. A regime can muster only limited political capital and operational capacity. The complex web of international relations is therefore often reduced to a small number of priorities, which are then portrayed in a fairly inflexible manner. This list of priorities is then largely adhered to unless a compelling reason appears for a change, in the form of an external shock such as a war, an act of aggression, or a catastrophe. In line with this analysis, this chapter suggests that the United States tends to conceptualize West Africa in foreign policy terms in three ways.

First, in economic terms, the United States sees Africa as a resource supplier, most crucially of oil. A clear, consistent example of this is the enduring close relationship between the United States and Nigeria. Nigeria is the main regional oil producer and a significant producer of a fairly uncommon form of sweet crude. The United States and Nigeria enjoy a joint security relationship that is in large part traceable to the growing U.S. reliance on Nigerian oil. The U.S. side of this relationship involves support for the Nigerian government and armed forces, and this has been demonstrated by the use of a U.S. aircraft carrier to patrol the West African coast. The Nigerian side of the relationship is a straightforward exertion of influence. Nigeria prides itself on its importance as a supplier to the United States and the financial benefits that it derives from that relationship. At the same time, Nigeria promotes itself regionally as the economic and political hegemonic power.

Second, the United States conceptualizes West Africa as a place that hosts possible terrorists.[2] This conceptualization reflects a number of elements. The foremost of these are supposed links to Islamic terrorists, possibly including the al-Qaeda network. For the most part, these concerns have been based on rumor rather than hard fact. For example, mostly circumstantial evidence has linked ethnically Lebanese diamond traders in Sierra Leone to al-Qaeda.[3] There have also been some better-grounded concerns regarding specific regional threats, such as the Salafist Group for Call and Combat (GSPC) in Algeria and nearby countries. However, this increased focus on the region as a possible base for terrorists has led to a heightened interest in and some transparency of nonterrorist criminal activity in West Africa. Examples of such activity include drug trafficking, oil bunkering off Nigeria, and the sort of crime against foreigners epitomized by the infamous "419s." Such serious organized crime does not directly threaten U.S. interests in the region. But it is still of some interest to Washington and accordingly merits a watching brief. This is often reflected in the changing priorities being given to local alliances on the ground.

The present chapter suggests that post–9/11 policy worldwide has been "terror-centric." Rhetorically at least, regional involvement in Africa and elsewhere has hinged on a polarizing analysis that classifies countries by their commitment to and relevance in the global War on Terror. A secondary polarizing analysis has been democratization. For the first time since the Cold War ended, the United States has hit upon a fundamental ideological clash that allows a sharp distinction to be drawn between allies and everybody else: the acceptance of the democratic ideal. But the U.S. attachment to democracy remains a tactical one. Just as the United States remains happy to ally itself closely to undemocratic regimes such as the House of Saud, it also seems largely unconcerned by the absence or even decline of effective democracy in many West African states. This is why West African policy has been focused on terror-centricity rather than the democratic element of current policy priorities.

Third, West Africa forms part of the American concern overall with Africa as a locus of human rights abuses and social problems. Both the United States and Western Europe continue to display an uncomfortably mixed message when it comes to dealing with African governance. Rhetorically, they emphasize the importance of African solutions to African problems. Western countries thereby largely externalize responsibility for regional security or human rights issues. Concurrently, they take a dim view of much African governance. The United States and many European chancelleries often demonstrate a barely concealed suspicion that Africa is a primitive place where modern policy discourse has limited utility. This may be seen in a comparison of U.S. attitudes toward the spread of democracy in the Middle East with those towards the nondevelopment or even retreat of democracy in some African countries. The human rights discourse is in any case often subsumed under perceived U.S. security interests, as illustrated by the continued democracy assistance supplied to hard-line regimes.[4] This ambiguous position results in what can seem like a reflexive, incoherent set of tactical policies. It leads to overoptimistic expectations, producing local confusion among Africans as to what foreign involvement can be expected in any given situation. It also creates a form of policy doublethink, whereby human rights abuses are cited in some cases as a justification for action, while in other situations the sheer scale of Africa's many human rights catastrophes is used as a justification for nonintervention. Nonetheless, this policy doublethink is slowly gathering momentum. This doublethink is slowly coming under criticism from the Congressional black caucus and black activists across the United States.

The Relationship between the Conceptualization of West Africa and the Wider U.S. Foreign Policy Agenda

To understand the place West Africa occupies within the U.S. foreign policy approach, it is first necessary to understand that approach. At the present time, the War on Terror and U.S. foreign policy seem to be intertwined to an extent that raises the question of what there is of U.S. foreign policy that remains beyond the global War on Terror.[5] To understand this, let us first examine the War on Terror itself.

The strategic goals of the so-called global War on Terror were summarized in 2004 by President Bush as follows:[6]

- dismantling, disrupting, and destroying terrorists and their organizations;
- denying terrorists places of sanctuary or support;
- denying terrorists chemical, biological, and nuclear weapons; and
- working for freedom and reform in the broader Middle East.

These then are the stated aims. We may contrast them to what seem to be the actual aims. This is subject to the caveat that the War on Terror is a rhetorical construct under the guise of which we see a number of activities that may or may not be appropriate within the defined objectives of the global War on Terror. Far and away the most important and indeed highest impact of the stated aims is the last one, working for freedom and reform what is elastically termed the "broader" Middle East. This in fact appears to be a selective aim— reform in Saudi Arabia, for example, seems to be much further down the U.S. list than reform in Syria or even Iran. Denying terrorists chemical, biological, radiological, and nuclear (CBRN) weapons is only part of the aim, which might more accurately be characterized as denying CBRN capability to all actors (at both the nonstate and the state level) who currently lack such a capacity and do not meet the American conception of an ally. Reinforcing the hegemonic American position as the world's only military superpower has a political potency at a time when its autonomy and majesty are threatened by emergent military powers such as China and a world legal order keen to assert its authority and on a collision course with Washington over issues ranging from U.S. Middle East policy to international criminal jurisdiction.

What remains of foreign policy beyond the global war on terror? At the security level, it is difficult to discern much that has not now been swept up. Some alliances continue independently of the global War on Terror with states whose commitment to the war is at best ambivalent, for example,

South Korea. But for the most part, the global War on Terror dominates the short-term foreign policy outlook of the present administration and arguably of the whole government and military machine.

If we play the crude foreign policy game of condensing these wide-ranging aims into just a few words, we might say that U.S. foreign policy as it stands is about selectively opening, enabling, and protecting markets, forcibly imposing an agenda of democratization upon certain foreign nondemocratic states that otherwise threaten the United States, and staking out a lead position in an emerging global cultural war. It is unclear that West Africa is of much appeal to policymakers on any of these grounds. In terms of the American–West African market, there is no clear U.S. incentive to change the current situation. West Africa offers a very limited export opportunity for the United States. With respect to African exports to the United States, there are probably no interests so compelling that they command any form of meaningful military interest on the part of the United States. The one possible exception is oil, and to date even this has attracted only limited military aid to Nigeria in the form of occasional training or marine operations in the Gulf of Guinea by the U.S. Navy. In respect to intervention in foreign states, the United States clearly has no appetite for such action in West Africa. Even a relatively straightforward military operation in a friendly environment has been ruled to be greater than U.S. interest merits. A key recent example was American unwillingness to deploy troops as Monrovia fell in August 2003, other than to protect and evacuate its nationals.

In terms of the cultural conflict, there is little in West Africa with which the United States seeks to conflict. But this is the one area in which U.S. foreign policy does increasingly seem to find a reason to exert its control over West Africa. The United States remains a strongly Christian nation and, especially under the present administration, this is on some levels a strong component of its foreign policy in Africa. As has been seen elsewhere in the continent, most notably Sudan, the United States is keen tacitly to protect the interests of what domestic evangelical Christians perceive to be persecuted Christian groups (although in fact the characterization of the Sudan People's Liberation Army (SPLA) as primarily Christian is an oversimplification that underplays the importance of animism in southern Sudan). In West Africa, there is increasing strife between the Christian south and the Islamic north in a number of countries. To date this has played out primarily in the form of power or resource-based struggles that have not taken on a religious character. But in due course we may expect that some of the Christian groups in West Africa will form more powerful advocacy alliances with American Christians. Some pointers to this are already provided by the rapid growth in U.S.-style Pentecostalism in West Africa. This would likely increase the relevance of U.S. policy and influence in West Africa for the U.S. administration in the domestic context.

West Africa and Islamic Fundamentalist Terrorism

West Africa is gradually emerging as an area of considerable concern to the United States in respect to its connections to Islamic fundamentalist terrorism. There are a number of reasons for this. This chapter will argue that there are "pull" reasons, which attract U.S. interest in their own right. There are also "push" reasons, whereby domestic U.S. policy helps to dictate the level of foreign policy interest in this area. First, on the "pull" side of the equation, there is a sizable Islamic population in West Africa, parts of which understandably feel that non-Islamic elements in their national governments have treated them unfairly. Côte d'Ivoire provides a compelling example, where the largely Muslim north has been politically and financially marginalized by the Christian-dominated south. Because of the nature of the map of West Africa, in which the religious split follows a roughly horizontal line but country borders are mostly vertical, the same problem recurs from Nigeria to Sierra Leone. In these countries, the more prosperous coastal south is Christian controlled, while the interior Muslim populations are economically worse off. This economic unevenness is exacerbated by the tendency for the political elite in these countries to come from within the southern Christian population.

Second, in some ways this Islamic population is ripe for radicalization. Scholars and policymakers disagree as to what the determinants of Islamic radicalization are. Too often a straightforward connection between poverty and radicalization is claimed in a way that is misleading. This does not mean that there is not an increased incidence of terrorist involvement, especially at the operational level, among those who are poor or uneducated. But there is no automatic connection. There is some evidence of radicalization by both Christian and Muslim charitable organizations in West Africa. An Islamic example is the extensive provision of mosques and social infrastructure by Middle Eastern Islamic charitable organizations, some of which are known elsewhere to act as conduits for terrorist funding. Much of this activity is directly traceable to groups in Saudi Arabia that are known supporters of fundamentalist terrorism. In addition, there is more localized evidence of the emergence of a radical Islamic terrorist operational infrastructure. The most obvious example of this to date is the successive local insurgencies of the self-styled "Taliban" (Al Sunna wal Jamma) in Yobe State, Nigeria.

Third there are the operational advantages that are available in West Africa. The geography is well suited to groups seeking to avoid capture. This was shown by the fact that at least some elements of the GSPC were able to sweep across the desert from Algeria to Chad even while under U.S. military surveillance. There is also the perceived closeness to the Middle East, although this obscures the significant cultural and theological differences between Middle Eastern states such as Yemen and the Islamic peoples in West Africa. Finally, there are funding and arms flows in West Africa. For example, it is often claimed that ethnic Lebanese control of the diamond trade in Ivory Coast has allowed fundamentalist organizations to fund themselves through the trading of so-called conflict diamonds. The existence of what are effectively failed states may also be conducive to terrorist operations, although Menkhaus disputes this.[7] He argues that terrorist networks appear to function best where states are governed badly, rather than not at all. Even accepting this analysis, though, the point remains relevant, simply shifting from Liberia and arguably Sierra Leone to other states such as Côte d'Ivoire.

These concerns all have some legitimacy, although none of them is especially compelling in its own right. Operating with fixed resources and far greater immediate security challenges, most notably in the Middle East, it is also understandable that the United States has thus far seen Africa as a low priority in its War on Terror.

What would it take to change this? It is apparent that West Africa has already started to assume a higher importance than previously. This may be seen in the Trans-Sahara Counter-Terrorism Initiative and the deployment of U.S. military forces in the Gulf of Guinea. But such initiatives have echoes of what Walt characterized in the Clinton era as "hegemony on the cheap."[8] The position of West Africa is dependent on what happens elsewhere. There is a perceived centrality of the Middle East to U.S. homeland security, the ongoing U.S. dependence on Middle Eastern oil, and the entrenchment of radical Islam in parts of the Middle East. It therefore seems very unlikely that the U.S. foreign policy outlook will shift markedly from the Middle East to West Africa while the global War on Terror is in progress.

What of the "push" side reasons? It has been suggested above that there is a likelihood of closer links between Christian communities in West Africa and the evangelical Christian movement in the United States. Given this, there is an opportunity for the Christian element in the U.S. administration to characterize Islamic radicalism as an attack on Christendom. To date, the rhetoric employed in the War on Terror has largely avoided this. Indeed, the administration has been at pains to stress that the War on Terror is not an attack on Islam. However, the War on Terror looks very much like an attack on organizations that spring from and find support in Islamic nations. Many millions of citizens in those countries perceive the War on Terror as little more than a rough proxy for a war on Islam. It should therefore be unsurprising if the United States takes the opportunity to attack Islamic fundamentalism with vigor, since arguably this is a defensive measure against what is perceived to be an Islamic attack on Christian values.

Marginal Elements of Foreign Policy

Where a region is not a key locus of foreign policy attention, marginal local benefits from more generally implemented foreign policy can take on increased significance. This likely amounts to an exertion of what Nye terms soft power, even if it is not presented or necessarily even intended in this way.[9] In this sense, the Bush administration's action-led agenda on Africa has quietly delivered significant benefits to the region as a whole, including West Africa. Fifteen billion dollars of foreign aid over five years (including $10 billion of new money) was earmarked in 2003 for fighting AIDS, mostly in Africa. A portion of this money was taken from other foreign aid medical initiatives and the money has also been slow to materialize in practice, as the international outcry over the Iraq invasion has subsided. Information about the deployment of funds is vague, especially at a low level, but to date deployment is significantly behind the rate that is necessary to spread the full expenditure fairly evenly across the life of the program. The inclusion of some faith-based approaches to AIDS prevention has also been a point of contention among critics. However, such earmarked expenditures are only a portion of the total, and in some cases arguably match local education and abstinence policies already promoted in recipient countries. Despite the criticisms, this promise of aid represents a significant policy shift, signaling that the AIDS issue is seen by Washington as a crucial one that is worthy of considerable financial support. This aid in itself will only make a dent in the problem, but it is still a significant step forward. Moreover, other donors seem to have been influenced by the need to show at least some parity with the United States. For example, European Union AIDS funding rose sharply after Bush's announcement.

The Bush administration has also followed the Clinton administration in opening up American markets to more African imports, albeit in a limited and selective fashion. This has been seen primarily in the extension of the liberalizing African Growth and Opportunities Act. This act, originally signed in 2000 and then renewed until 2015, offers a far more liberal U.S. market to most sub-Saharan countries than before. It has recently been supplemented by the Millennium Challenge Account.

Conclusion

The implications of this analysis are both descriptive and prescriptive. Descriptively, a thesis is presented that purports to explain the relative unimportance of West Africa in U.S. foreign policy discourse. Prescriptively, understanding and acting upon this thesis could catalyze a reprioritization of West Africa within U.S. foreign policy discourse. Despite the growth in U.S. foreign policy interest in West Africa, it remains a low-interest and low-priority area. Nothing in the analysis suggests that this is likely to change significantly in the next several years.

West Africa could force its way more powerfully onto the agenda for the years up to 2009 in two ways. The first would be to position itself more clearly within the purview of Washington's terror-centric policy. This seems highly unlikely. Despite some fundamentalist terrorist activity there, there is little evidence that West Africa harbors a systemic terrorist threat to U.S. interests. Second, individual nations could seek to become beacons of democratization in a way that would encourage the United States to groom them as model nations. Given the recent democratic turbulence in the region, this seems very unlikely. If anything, the next few years are likely to bring more of the same in West Africa: ethnic conflict, economic hardship, and significant violence met by Washington with little more than a distant grimace.

Notes

The author of this chapter thanks Martin Kimani and Abdul K. Bangura for their helpful comments on an earlier version of the chapter, presented as a paper at the International Conference on the United States and West Africa, organized by the Africa Program, University of Texas at Arlington, April 2005. The author acknowledges the generosity of the University of Texas at Arlington in assisting him to attend this conference.

1. Donald Rothchild, "The U.S. Foreign Policy Trajectory on Africa," *SAIS Review* 21, no. 1 (Winter–Spring 2001): 179–211; here: 180.

2. Christopher Ruane, *U.S. Foreign Policy and International Terrorism: U.S. Strategy in West Africa post-9/11* (paper presented at the African and African-American Education, Research and Training Institute's 11th annual conference, Springfield College, Springfield, MA, June 2004).

3. Lansana Gberie, *War and Peace in Sierra Leone: Diamonds, Corruption and the Lebanese Connection* (Ottawa: Partnership Africa Canada, 2002); Lansana Gberie, *West Africa: Rocks in a Hard Place* (Ottawa: Partnership Africa Canada, 2003); and Douglas Farah, *Blood from Stones: The Secret Financial Network of Terror* (New York: Broadway Books, 2004).

4. Rothchild, "The U.S. Foreign Policy Trajectory."

5. In this chapter, the terms "War on Terror" and "Global War on Terror" are used interchangeably. While the UK discourse prefers the former, the White House prefers the latter. It remains unclear whether the U.S. discourse will develop the use of different idioms to reflect the domestic and international elements of the (broadly defined) War on Terror.

6. Speech by President George W. Bush at the United States Air Force Academy Graduation Ceremony, June 2, 2004, http://www.whitehouse.gov/news/releases/2004/06/20040602.html.

7. Ken Menkhaus, *Somalia: State Collapse and the Threat of Terrorism*, Adelphi Papers 364 (London: International Institute of Strategic Studies, 2004), 71–75.

8. Stephen M. Walt, "Two Cheers for Clinton's Foreign Policy," *Foreign Affairs* 79, no. 2 (March–April 2000): 63–79; here: 79.

9. Joseph S. Nye Jr., "The Misleading Metaphor of Decline," *Atlantic Monthly*, March 1990, 86–94.

Contributors

ABDUL KARIM BANGURA is professor of political science and research methodology at Howard University. He holds a PhD in political science, a PhD in development economics, a PhD in linguistics, and a PhD in computer science. He is the author and/or editor of fifty-seven books and more than 400 scholarly essays. He is fluent in about a dozen African languages and six European languages, and is now studying to strengthen his proficiency in Arabic and Hebrew. He also is the recipient of numerous scholarly and other awards.

KAREN B. BELL has taught U.S. history and African American history at Savannah State University in Savannah, Georgia, as an assistant professor of history. She is an archivist of U.S. State Department records at the U.S. National Archives and Records Administration in College Park, Maryland, and a PhD candidate at Howard University in Washington, DC. Specializing in nineteenth-century African American history and the African diaspora, Bell has made presentations on U.S.-African cultural relations during the Cold War at the London School of Economics and Political Science Cold War Studies Centre and the University of Texas at Arlington. She has written and published papers on the transatlantic slave trade, the African American experience during Reconstruction, and the southern frontier. She is the recipient of the American Association of University Women Dissertation Fellowship, 2006–7; the William Bacon Stevens Award, Georgia Historical Society, 2002; and a National Endowment for the Humanities Summer Institute Fellowship at the W. E. B. DuBois Institute, Harvard University, 1999. She has also studied at the Regional Oral History Office Advanced Oral History Summer Institute, University of California, Berkeley, 2004; and has traveled and studied in Dakar, Senegal.

PETER A. DUMBUYA is associate professor of history at Fort Valley State University in Georgia. He received his PhD in history from the University of Akron and his JD from Jones School of Law. He is the author of *Tanganyika under International Mandate, 1919–1945*, and is currently completing a manuscript on the civil war in Sierra Leone.

KWAME ESSIEN is a PhD student in the Department of History at the University of Texas at Austin. He focuses on African and African diaspora history and works on two areas: African American returnee communities in Ghana and "Tabom" people, and the descendants of Afro-Brazilians in Ghana. Essien received his MA in African studies at the University of Illinois at Urbana-Champaign, his BA in history at the University of North Carolina at Greensboro, and a diploma from Accra Polytechnic, Ghana. Essien contributed to Don C. Ohadike, *Sacred Drums of Liberation: Religions and Music of Resistance in Africa and the Diaspora* (Trenton, NJ: Africa World Press, 2007).

ANDREW I. E. EWOH is an MPA Director and Professor of Public Administration at Kennesaw State University, Kennesaw, Georgia. He was previously a Professor of Political Science and Coordinator of the Political Science Program in the College of Arts and Sciences at Prairie View A&M University, Texas. His areas of research include public policy, governance, human resource management, privatization, comparative public administration, and government-business relations. His articles have appeared in *Review of Policy Research, Review of Public Personnel Administration, International Review of Public Administration, Journal of Public Management & Social Policy, Public Works Management & Policy*, and numerous scholarly journals. He has contributed to several book chapters. Dr. Ewoh is the Editor-in-Chief of the *African Social Science Review* and Case Study Editor for the *Journal of Public Management & Social Policy.*

TOYIN FALOLA is the Frances Higginbotham Nalle Centennial Professor in History at the University of Texas at Austin as well as a University Distinguished Teaching Professor. A Fellow of the Historical Society of Nigeria and a Fellow of the Nigerian Academy of Letters, Falola is author and editor of more than 60 books. He is coeditor of the *Journal of African Economic History*, series editor of Rochester Studies in African History and the Diaspora, the series editor of Culture and Customs of Africa published by Greenwood Press. Dr. Falola has received various awards and honors, including the Udogu Award for Excellent Teaching, Prolific Scholarship and Humanitarian Service in Africa and Its Diaspora, and the Jean Halloway Award for Teaching Excellence. He has been presented with three Festschriften, various lifetime awards, and an honorary doctorate.

OSMAN GBLA is currently head of the Department of Political Science and dean of the Faculty of Social Sciences and Law, Fourah Bay College, University of Sierra Leone. He is also the founder of the Centre for Development and Security Analysis, Sierra Leone. His areas of research interest are conflict and postconflict peacebuilding, regional security,

security sector reform, and governance, with a specific focus on West Africa. He has published extensively in these areas of research.

JOHN WESS GRANT is an assistant professor of Africana studies at the University of Arizona. He completed his PhD at Michigan State University, where he specialized in African diaspora history and served as a King-Parks-Chavez Fellow. Dr. Grant is currently working on a manuscript examining the various ties that bound together the experiences of blacks living in the American South and Liberia during the nineteenth century.

HAROLD R. HARRIS is an Afro-Caribbean who grew up in Antigua and is now residing in Texas. He graduated from the Leeward Islands Teachers' Training College in 1966 as a specialist in the teaching of geometry. He earned a BA degree at Brock University in 1971, then took a 30-year break from academia to focus on his family. Since 2001, he has earned an MA in history from the University of Texas at Arlington and is currently an ABD, engaged in researching and writing his PhD dissertation. He has been a presenter at several conferences and symposia, and has won several academic awards.

STEPHEN A. HARMON is an assistant professor of history at Pittsburg State University in Pittsburg, Kansas. He earned his PhD in history at UCLA in 1988. He received an NDEA Title IV grant to study Bambara, 1980–83, as well as two Fulbright Research Fellowships to conduct field research in Senegal and Mali, 1983–84 and 1990–91. He was co-writer and director of a Department of Education Title VI grant to internationalize the curriculum at his institution, 1999–2002. He has published recently on democratization in Mali and on Islamic radicalism in North and West Africa. He has completed a year or more of formal study of seven languages, and has lived and worked on five different continents.

OLAWALE ISMAIL is at the Department of Peace Studies, University of Bradford. Prior to this, he had graduate training in international relations at Cambridge University (2001), and he received his bachelor's degree at the Department of International Relations, Obafemi Awolowo University, Ile-Ife, Nigeria (First Class Hons., 1999). Olawale Ismail has three years of work experience in research and policy-related institutions, including the Stockholm International Peace Research Institute (SIPRI); the New York–based Social Science Research Council (SSRC); and the Nigeria-based Centre for Development and Conflict Management Studies (CEDCOMS). He is also currently a research associate involved with the project on Youth Vulnerability and Exclusion in Africa with the Conflict, Security and Development Group, International Policy Institute, King's College, London. His research interests and expertise include Disarmament, Demobilization, and Reintegration (DDR) and postwar reconstruction, security sector reform, youth and child soldiers, political violence and terrorism, conflict and security analysis, and military expenditure. He has a number of recent and forthcoming publications to his credit.

ALUSINE JALLOH is an associate professor of history and founding director of the Africa Program at the University of Texas at Arlington. His publications include *Black Business and Economic Power* (coeditor with Toyin Falola; Rochester, NY: University of Rochester Press, 2002), *African Entrepreneurship: Muslim Fula Merchants in Sierra Leone* (Athens: Ohio University Press, 1999), *Islam and Trade in Sierra Leone* (coeditor with David E. Skinner; Trenton, NJ: Africa World Press, 1997), and *The Africa Diaspora* (coeditor with Stephen E. Maizlish; College Station: Texas A&M University Press, 1996).

FRED L. JOHNSON III is an associate professor of history at Hope College in Holland, Michigan. A former communications-electronics officer in the U.S. Marine Corps and corporate trainer for Aircraft Braking Systems in Akron, Ohio, he earned his master's and doctorate degrees at Kent State University. His specialty areas are nineteenth-century U.S. history (the Civil War), the twentieth-century United States, the U.S. military, and Africa. He is currently completing the research for his latest project, entitled "America's Blind Spot: U.S. Foreign Policy in Africa, 1945 to Present."

STEPHEN KANDEH is an assistant professor of sociology at the University of Science and Arts of Oklahoma. A resources sociologist, Dr. Kandeh's research is in the areas of natural resources, economic development, and law in society.

IBRAHIM KARGBO is an associate professor of history at Coppin State University, Baltimore, Maryland. He teaches courses in African history, Latin American history, U.S. foreign policy, U.S. history, world history, and African American history. He holds a PhD in African history from Howard University in Washington, DC. While at Howard University, his other areas of study were Latin America and the Caribbean, Europe, and the United States. He is the author of numerous published articles and has presented scholarly papers at conferences in China, Japan, Hong Kong, South Korea, Dubai, Grenada, Canada, and the United States. He has traveled extensively in Africa, Europe, Asia, the Middle East, South America, and the Caribbean. He is a member of several professional organizations: the African Studies Association, the Association for the Study of African American Life and History, and the Baltimore Council on Foreign Affairs. He has received a number of fellowships and awards: a Fulbright-Hays Fellowship to conduct research in Ghana and Senegal; a Smithsonian Fellowship at the Museum of American History; the Sierra Leonean of the Year Community Award; a summer fellowship at the U.S. Department of Defense Army Materiel Command

(Office of the Historian); and a U.S. Department of Education Title VI grant to globalize the curriculum. He is currently completing two manuscripts, one on U.S. commercial interests in Sierra Leone and the other on crime and punishment in colonial Sierra Leone.

BAYO LAWAL is a professor of history and strategic studies at the University of Lagos where he received his PhD in history in 1981. He is the head of the History Department, University of Lagos, and a member of the Nigerian Academy of Letters, and an international contributing editor to the *Journal of American History*. He was a Fulbright Fellow at the University of Wisconsin–Madison in 1990, and a Rockefeller Visiting Research Fellow at the University of Western Cape, Bellville, South Africa, in 1994. He is an external examiner for five Nigerian universities and has conducted research in Africa, Europe, and North America on British colonialism, American history, African American history, and the African diaspora. The courses he teaches at present include culture and tourism, economic history, and gender history. He has to his credit fifty articles and chapters published in journals and books in Africa and the United States. He coedited *Fundamentals of Economic History* (Lagos, 2003), and is working on *The Financial Relations between Nigeria and the British Cameroons, 1916–1960*. He is the current editor in chief of an international journal, the *Lagos Historical Review*.

AYODEJI OLUKOJU is professor of history and dean of the Faculty of Arts, University of Lagos, Nigeria. His latest publications include *Culture and Customs of Liberia* (Greenwood, 2006), and *The "Liverpool" of West Africa: The Dynamics and Impact of Maritime Trade in Lagos, 1900–1950* (Africa World Press, 2004). He has held various visiting research fellowships including those of the Japan Foundation, the British Academy, and the Deutscher Akademischer Austauschdienst (DAAD). Olukoju is a member of the editorial boards of *African Economic History* (Madison,WI) and *Afrika-Zamani: Journal of the Association of African Historians* (Dakar, Senegal).

ADEBAYO OYEBADE is professor of history at Tennessee State University, Nashville, where he teaches African history courses. He obtained his PhD in history from Temple University, Philadelphia. He has published many book chapters and journal articles as well as books. He is the author of *Culture and Customs of Angola* (Greenwood, 2006); editor of *The Foundations of Nigeria: Essays in Honor of Toyin Falola* (Africa World Press, 2003) and *The Transformation of Nigeria: Essays in Honor of Toyin Falola* (Africa World Press, 2002); and coeditor of *Africa after the Cold War: The Changing Perspectives on Security* (Africa World Press, 1998). He is presently completing a book on West Africa in U.S. strategic planning during World War II. Dr. Oyebade is on the editorial board of the *Journal of History and Diplomatic Studies*, and he has been a recipient of Ford Foundation, Fulbright, and other scholarly fellowships.

CHRISTOPHER RUANE specializes in Africa-related foreign policy and regime stability, focusing on West Africa. He has recently finished writing a book on contemporary slavery in the region. His current research focuses on the politics of aid and development. He is based in London, England.

ANITA SPRING (PhD, Cornell University) is professor of anthropology and African studies at the University of Florida. She has carried out research in Botswana, Cameroon, Eritrea, Ethiopia, Ghana, Kenya, Malawi, Senegal, South Africa, Swaziland, Uganda, and Zambia. She is the author of "Empowering Women in the African Entrepreneurial Landscape: Micro Entrepreneurs to Business Globalists in the Informal and Formal Sectors," in *Power, Gender and Social Change in Africa and the Diaspora* (2007); "The New Generation of African Entrepreneurs: Changing the Environment for Business Development and Economic Growth," in *Entrepreneurship and Regional Development* (with B. McDade, 2005); "Gender and the Range of Entrepreneurial Strategies: The Typical and the New African Woman Entrepreneur," in *Black Business and Economic Power* (2002); *Women Farmers and Commercial Ventures: Increasing Food Security in Developing Countries* (2000); *African Entrepreneurship: Theory and Reality* (with B. McDade, 1998); *The Tree against Hunger: Enset-Based Agricultural Systems in Ethiopia* (with S. Brandt et al., 1997); and *Agricultural Development and Gender Issues in Malawi* (1995).

IBRAHIM SUNDIATA is Samuel and Augusta Spector Professor of History and Professor of African and Afro-American History at Brandeis University. He received his BA from Ohio Wesleyan University and his PhD from Northwestern University. His fieldwork was carried out in Liberia and Equatorial Guinea. Professor Sundiata is the author of *Black Scandal: America and the Liberian Labor Crisis, 1929–1936* (1980); *Equatorial Guinea, Colonialism, State Terror, and the Search for Stability* (1990); *From Slaving to Neoslavery: The Bight of Biafra and Fernando Po in the Era of Abolition, 1827–1930* (1990); and *Brothers and Strangers: Black Slavery, Black Zion, 1914–1940* (2003). Dr. Sundiata is a member of the Council on Foreign Relations.

HAKEEM IBIKUNLE TIJANI, PhD, is an associate professor of history at Morgan State University, Baltimore, Maryland. He is a coauthor of *Culture and Customs of Ethiopia*, to be published by Greenwood Press. He has also published *Britain, Leftist Nationalists and the Transfer of Power in Nigeria, 1945–1965* (New York: Routledge, 2005); and *Nigeria's Urban History: Past and Present* (Oxford: University Press of America, 2006). In addition, he is the assistant director of the African Studies Program/Center for Latin American and the Caribbean Studies at Morgan State University.

KEN VINCENT is a research associate at the Institute for Science, Technology, and Public Policy at Texas A&M University. He completed a bachelor of arts degree in foreign affairs at the University of Virginia and a master of international affairs degree, with a concentration in international economics, at the George Bush School of Government and Public Service at Texas A&M. He has worked for the U.S. House of Representatives International Relations Committee, the International Republican Institute, the World Trade Division of the Greater Houston Partnership, and Strategic Forecasting. His research interests include the Chinese economy, African oil-producing states, global climate change, and energy.

AMANDA WARNOCK is a PhD candidate in the History Department at the University of Texas at Austin. She is the author of two chapters in *The Atlantic World, 1450–2000*, edited by Toyin Falola and Kevin Roberts (Indiana University Press, 2008). She is also the coeditor, along with Toyin Falola, of *The Encyclopedia of the Middle Passage* (Greenwood Press, 2007). Her primary field is Latin America, with a focus on the African diaspora in the Caribbean. Her dissertation looks at trans-local linkages in the making of the Cuban economy during the late eighteenth and early nineteenth centuries.

Index

Page numbers in italics refer to figures.

Rochester Studies in African History and the Diaspora

Toyin Falola, Senior Editor
The Frances Higginbotham Nalle Centennial Professor in History
University of Texas at Austin
(ISSN: 1092–5228)

Over the last several decades, historians have conducted extensive research into contact between the United States and West African during the era of the transatlantic trade. Yet we still understand relatively little about more recent relations between the two nations. This multidisciplinary volume presents the most comprehensive analysis of the U.S.–West African relationship to date, filling a significant gap in the literature by examining the social, cultural, political, and economic bonds that have, in recent years, drawn these two world regions into increasingly closer contact.

Beginning with examinations of factors that linked the nations during European colonial rule of Africa, and spanning to discussions of U.S. foreign policy with regard to West Africa from the Cold War through the end of the twentieth century and beyond, these essays constitute the first volume devoted to interrogating the complex relationship—both historic and contemporary—between the United States and West Africa.

Contributors: Karen B. Bell, Peter A. Dumbuya, Andrew I. E. Ewoh, Toyin Falola, Osman Gbla, John Wess Grant, Stephen A. Harmon, Olawale Ismail, Alusine Jalloh, Fred L. Johnson III, Stephen Kandeh, Ibrahim Kargbo, Bayo Lawal, Ayodeji Olukoju, Adebayo Oyebade, Christopher Ruane, Anita Spring, Ibrahim Sundiata, Hakeem Ibikunle Tijani, Ken Vincent, and Amanda Warnock.

Alusine Jalloh is associate professor of history and founding director of The Africa Program at the University of Texas at Arlington. Toyin Falola is the Frances Higginbotham Nalle Centennial Professor in History at the University of Texas at Austin.